Handbook of Father Involvement

With contributions from various disciplines, this new edition reviews the latest research and theories on fatherhood. All of the chapters are either extensively revised or entirely new. Biological, evolutionary, demographic, developmental, cultural, sociological, economic, and legal perspectives of father involvement are described along with policy and program implications. Now with a greater international perspective, this edition considers family demographic shifts in the U.S. and Europe.

This extensively revised edition features: an expanded section on biological and evolutionary perspectives that reviews fathering in animals and the hormonal underpinnings of fathering behaviors; new sections on economic and legal issues and another that covers father-child relationships and the father's role in children's development; separate chapters on Black, Latino, and Asian American fathers; new research on cohabitation, gender roles, and intergenerational parenting; the latest demographics and programs influencing father involvement; and cutting-edge topics on methodology and measurement.

All chapters now follow a common structure to enhance readability and interdisciplinary connections. Each chapter features: Historical Overview and Theoretical Perspectives; Research Questions; Research Methods and Measurement; Empirical Findings; Bridges to other Disciplines; Policy Implications; and Future Directions. In addition, each chapter highlights universal and cultural processes to illuminate the ways that theories and methods are guided by multidisciplinary lenses.

Intended for advanced students, practitioners, policymakers, and researchers interested in fatherhood and family processes from a variety of disciplines including psychology, family studies, economics, sociology, and social work, and anyone interested in child and family policy.

Handbook of Father Involvement

Multidisciplinary Perspectives

Second Edition

Edited by
Natasha J. Cabrera
University of Maryland

Catherine S. Tamis-LeMonda
New York University

Routledge
Taylor & Francis Group

NEW YORK AND LONDON

First published 2013
by Routledge
711 Third Avenue, New York, NY 10017

Simultaneously published in the UK
by Routledge
27 Church Road, Hove, East Sussex BN3 2FA, UK

First issued in paperback 2014

Routledge is an imprint of the Taylor & Francis Group, an informa business

Library of Congress Cataloging in Publication Data
A catalog record for this book has been requested

ISBN 13: 978-0-415-87867-8 (hbk)
ISBN 13: 978-1-138-84983-9 (pbk)

Typeset in New Caledonia and Futura
by EvS Communication Networx, Inc.

Contents

About the Editors

Natasha J. Cabrera is Associate Professor in Human Development at the University of Maryland. Dr. Cabrera arrived at the University of Maryland with several years of experience as an SRCD Executive Fellow and Expert in Child Development with the Demographic and Behavioral Sciences Branch (DBSB) of the National Institute of Child Health and Human Development (NICHD). Dr. Cabrera's research, funded by National Institute of Child Development and the Ford Foundation, focuses on: father involvement and children's development; children's developmental trajectories in low income and minority families; ethnic and cultural differences in fathering and mothering behaviors; family processes in a social and cultural context and children's social development; and the mechanisms that link early experience to children's school readiness and children's social development. She has published in peer-reviewed journals on policy, methodology, theory and the implications of father involvement on child development and she co-edited other volumes including *Latina/o Child Psychology and Mental Health* (2011) and *From Welfare to Child Care* (2006).

Catherine S. Tamis-LeMonda is Professor of Developmental Psychology at New York University's Steinhardt School of Culture, Education, and Human Development and Director of the Center for Research on Culture, Development and Education at NYU, where she engages in research on the language, cognitive, social, and emotional development of infants and children from culturally diverse backgrounds across the first years of life. Her focus on early developmental processes highlights the social and cultural contexts of early development, especially the ways in which mothers' and fathers' beliefs and practices shape children's developmental trajectories in different populations within the U.S. and internationally. Tamis-LeMonda's research has been funded by the National Science Foundation, National Institute of Child Development, National Institute of Mental Health, Administration for Children, Youth and Families, the Ford Foundation, and the Robinhood Foundation. She has approximately 100 publications in peer-reviewed journals and books, and has co-edited other volumes including *Child Psychology: A Handbook of Contemporary Issues, 2nd Edition* (2006) and *The Development of Social Cognition and Communication* (2005).

Contributors

Daniela Aldoney
University of Maryland

Amy G. Applegate
Indiana University Maurer School of Law

Karen L. Bales
University of California, Davis and California National Primate Research Center

Lisa Baumwell
New York University

Andrew Behnke
North Carolina State University

David Bishai
Johns Hopkins University

Erika London Bocknek
University of Michigan Health System

Robert H. Bradley
Arizona State University

Sanford L. Braver
Arizona State University

Susan L. Brown
Bowling Green State University

Natasha J. Cabrera
University of Maryland

Tzu-Fen Chang
Michigan State University

Scott Coltrane
University of Oregon

Carolyn Pape Cowan
University of California, Berkeley

Phillip A. Cowan
University of California, Berkeley

Sally Curtin
University of Maryland

Andrea Doucet
Brock University

David J. Eggebeen
The Pennsylvania State University

Ira M. Ellman
Arizona State University

Jay Fagan
Temple University

Hiram E. Fitzgerald
Michigan State University

Alice Goisis
The London School of Economics and Political Science

Frances Goldscheider
University of Maryland

Alan J. Hawkins
Brigham Young University

Sandra L. Hofferth
University of Maryland

Erin Kramer Holmes
Brigham Young University

Amy Holtzworth-Munroe
Indiana University-Bloomington

Ziarat Hossain
University of New Mexico College of Education

Katie Hrapczynski
University of Maryland

James Hull
University of Delaware

Erum Ikramullah
Child Trends

Michael R. Jarcho
University of California, Davis and California
National Primate Research Center

Renske Keizer
Erasmus University Rotterdam

Chris Knoester
The Ohio State University

Michael E. Lamb
University of Cambridge

Melinda S. Leidy
University of California, Riverside

Charlie Lewis
University of Lancaster

Jennifer Manlove
Child Trends

Wendy D. Manning
Bowling Green State University

Brandon McDaniel
The Pennsylvania State University

Rob Palkovitz
University of Delaware

Ross D. Parke
University of California, Riverside

Kristen Peterson
Child Trends

Joseph H. Pleck
University of Illinois at Urbana-Champaign

Desiree Baolian Qin
Michigan State University

Helen H. Raikes
University of Nebraska-Lincoln

Lori A. Roggman
Utah State University

Jaipaul L. Roopnarine
Syracuse University

Kevin Roy
University of Maryland

Thomas J. Schofield
University of California, Riverside

Katherine Schwartz
Indiana University-Bloomington

Mindy E. Scott
Child Trends

Wendy Sigle-Rushton
The London School of Economics and Political
Science

Jocelyn Smith
University of Maryland

Matthew M. Stevenson
Arizona State University

Anne E. Storey
Memorial University of Newfoundland

Catherine S. Tamis-LeMonda
New York University

Ashley M. Votruba
Arizona State University

Carolyn J. Walsh
Memorial University of Newfoundland

David Waynforth
University of East Anglia

Preface

Father involvement is a multidimensional, continually evolving concept—both at the level of scholarship and at the level of cultural awareness. The first edition of the *Handbook of Father Involvement*, published in 2002, presented the field with scholarship spanning a variety of disciplines. This second edition continues the tradition of presenting cutting-edge, multidisciplinary research, and extends and builds on the first edition in three significant ways.

First, it presents new research findings and theoretical advances on fathers, families, child development, programs and policies based on what has been learned over the past decade. Many former contributors are represented in this edition, but they have reworked their chapters to showcase contemporary findings within a common chapter structure (described below). Additionally, we have invited a new cadre of scholars, resulting in extension of topic coverage across the different sections of the handbook. For example, the chapters under Demographic Perspectives report on new trends in family structure and multi-partner fertility in the United States as well as a chapter on fathers and fatherhood in the European Union. This international perspective offers a comparative framework for considering the ways in which demographic shifts in family formation and composition in the United States relate to those of other Western democracies. Similarly, the section on Cultural Perspectives includes chapters on Black, Latino, and Asian American fathers, and the section on Sociological Perspectives includes chapters on cohabitation and parenting, gender roles and fathering, fathers' kin and intergenerational parenting, and fatherhood implications for men.

Second, this edition adds three new sections—Biological Processes and Evolutionary Perspectives, Economic and Legal Perspectives, and Child Development and Family Processes—resulting in more comprehensive disciplinary coverage. The Biological and Evolutionary section expands on the original Evolutionary section by adding topics on the biological basis of mammalian paternal behaviors and fathering in nonhuman primates. Animal models and innovative research on the hormonal underpinnings and genetics of fathering provide mechanistic accounts of the processes that feed into fathering behaviors within and across species. The new section on Economic and Legal Perspectives addresses topics on the economics of fatherhood; marriage, divorce, child custody; and fathers and family dispute resolution. The new section on Child Development and Family Processes covers topics on father-child relationships; father's role in children's language, cognitive, and social development; and, father risk, family context, and coparenting.

Finally, all chapters in the second edition of the *Handbook* contain a common structure that enhances readability and connection among disciplinary perspectives. Chapters are organized according to the following headings: (1) Historical Overview and Theoretical Perspectives; (2) Research Questions/Foci; (3) Methods and Measurement; (4) Empirical Findings; (5) Bridges to other Disciplines; (6) Policy Implications; and (7) Future Directions. Moreover, all contributors highlight both universal and culture-specific processes and mechanisms of fathering. This parallel structure makes transparent the ways that theories, questions, methods, and findings are guided by disciplinary lenses, but also underscores possibilities for collaboration among the multiple perspectives represented in the Handbook.

This second edition of the *Handbook of Father Involvement* will be a valuable resource to students, practitioners, policy makers, and scholars across a range of disciplines including psychology, family studies, economics, sociology, and social work. We hope that this collection of writings is a springboard for new thinking about the processes by which fathers, families, programs and policies shape child development. This new thinking entails major changes to current scientific infrastructures and practices around dissemination and outreach. Most centrally, it requires the training of a new generation of scholars who are able to think and collaborate creatively both within and across disciplines. A deeper understanding of the limitations and strengths of theories, questions, and methods across disciplines will generate new knowledge, rather than merely producing more of the same. It is only at this interdisciplinary juncture that innovative research questions are worth asking. We hope that the second edition of our handbook will inspire the next generation of studies on fatherhood for years to come. We are confident that you will enjoy reading this collection of chapters as much as we enjoyed working with world-renowned experts to bring this pioneering book to fruition.

Acknowledgments

We would like to thank the comments we received from the reviewers. Their comments were instrumental in helping us determine the final contents of the book. The reviewers were V. Jeffrey Evans, NICHD & NIH, Anna Sarkadi, Uppsala University, Sweden, William Fabricius, Arizona State University, Mark Fine, University of Missouri, Columbia, Michael Connor, Alliant International University, and one anonymous reviewer.

Catherine S. Tamis-LeMonda acknowledges funding from the National Science Foundation, grant #021859, and NSF IRADS, grant #0721383.

Natasha J. Cabrera
Catherine S. Tamis-LeMonda

Acknowledgments

I am indebted to many people who over the years have given me support and encouragement in various ways. First, I'm thankful for having had a sabbatical that freed up my time from teaching to devote to this Handbook. Second, many thanks are due to the authors of this Handbook; they produced wonderful scholarship with minimal intervention from us. Third, I'm always thankful for my family, my brothers and mother whose blind faith in me is always a source of encouragement. Third, many thanks to my wonderful friend and co-editor, Cathie, who is the best colleague a person could ever have. And, last, my eternal gratitude to my children, Keanu and Dakota, who make me so incredibly happy and proud, and my husband, Jeff, who's an exemplary husband and an inspirational father. He is loving and completed devoted to his children and family.

Natasha J. Cabrera

First and foremost, I want to thank my husband Richard James LeMonda and father Anthony Francis Tamis for epitomizing what it means to be involved and loving fathers. Although a generation apart, both taught their children the importance of dignity, a strong work ethic, and compassion. Richard, thank you for putting up with me in my continued attempts at juggling the messy worlds of academia and motherhood. Second, I am grateful to Natasha for sharing with me so many exciting endeavors (and cappuccinos) in our joint study of fathering and child development; you will always be an inspiration and dear friend. Third, I thank the fathers, mothers, and children who have participated in our studies. The time you have dedicated to research has shaped the field in countless ways. Finally, I acknowledge support from the National Science Foundation to NYU's Center for Research on Culture, Development and Education (NSF BCS grant #021859 and NSF IRADS grant #0721383), and my colleagues and students at the Center.

Catherine S. Tamis-LeMonda

SECTION I

Biological Processes and Evolutionary Perspectives

Chapter 1

Biological Basis of Mammalian Paternal Behavior

Anne E. Storey and Carolyn J. Walsh

Memorial University of Newfoundland

Historical Background and Theoretical Perspectives

We must consider two perspectives in order to understand the biological basis of human paternal behavior: one involving ultimate and one involving proximate causation (Tinbergen, 1963). The major focus of this chapter is on the proximate factors that affect the individual during his lifetime. These individual factors include how social experiences and environmental cues interact with hormonal and neural mechanisms to affect the development and maintenance of paternal behavior. The chapter begins with ultimate causation, that is, why or how behavior evolves, so as to set the context for the species differences in the underlying developmental and neuroendocrine mechanisms.

Evolution of Mammalian Paternal Care

Paternal care occurs in less than 10% of mammalian species (Kleiman & Malcolm, 1981), whereas maternal care is important in all mammalian species. Male and female mammals maximize reproductive success in different ways: males can increase their reproductive success by caring for offspring and/or by mating with other females. In contrast, the specialized reproductive anatomy and physiology of pregnancy and lactation means that female mammals can rarely increase their reproductive success by increased mating effort (initiating a new pregnancy) if the cost is to invest less in their current dependent offspring.

Paternal care and monogamous mating systems have evolved separately and independently in a number of mammalian lineages (supported by recent genetic analyses, Fink, Excoffier, Heckel, & Orians, 2006). The most plausible hypothesis is that paternal care (actually, biparental care involving both parents) is selected for by difficult environmental conditions. Paternal care has evolved in humans with multiple benefits for offspring and in other primate lineages where young are too heavy for females to carry. It has evolved in wild canids (wolves and foxes) where fathers, and sometimes other group members, help provision the young. Interestingly, paternal care has been lost in domestic dogs (*Canis lupus familiaris*), presumably due to mothers being able raise pups under the relaxed ecological conditions of domestication (cf. Pal, 2005).

Finally, paternal care has evolved in several rodent lineages where a second adult in the nest can provide warmth to altricial (helpless) young. Evidence that environmental harshness selects for biparental care comes from a comparison of different populations of African striped mice (*Rhabdomys pumilio*; Schradin & Pillay, 2005) and two congeneric species of dwarf hamsters (*Phodopus* spp.; Wynne-Edwards, 1995), where in both cases, males provide more care under the harshest conditions. Different populations of striped mice vary in hormone profiles in relation to amount of care provided (Schradin, Scantlebury, Pillay, & Konig, 2009). Thus, ecological factors and male physiology interact to affect the amount of care males provide.

Males should only care for young if care increases their reproductive success more than investing in additional mating effort. Paternal care increases survival of young in several species (Wynne-Edwards & Lisk, 1989; Gubernick, Wright, & Brown, 1993), including humans (Hurtado & Hill, 1992). In species where paternal care is variable, young receiving paternal care have higher growth rates (Alvergne, Faurie, & Raymond, 2009; Schradin & Pillay, 2005; Storey & Snow, 1987), better protection (Buchan, Alberts, Silk, & Altmann, 2003), and they develop more successful behavioral coping styles (Jia, Tai, An, Zhang, & Broders, 2009).

Males should be selected to recognize and differentially invest in their own offspring. In some cases familiarity influences recognition and paternal investment decisions: male mice recognize their adult offspring if they have had physical (not just olfactory contact) with them (Mak & Weiss, 2010). Male savannah baboons (*Papio cynocephalus*) differentially intervene in conflicts on behalf of the juvenile offspring whose mothers they have previously associated with (Buchan et al., 2003). Alternatively, recognition may occur through phenotype matching: Sengelese men differentially invest in offspring with facial and odor similarities to themselves (Alvergne et al., 2009). Further, compared to women in some studies, men showed a greater preference for morphed pictures of infants resembling themselves over control pictures and they show a different pattern of brain response from women during picture exposure (Platek et al., 2004). Other studies report no sex difference; these results may differ due to perceived paternal confidence, with resemblance being more important when perceived paternal confidence is low (Welling, Burriss, & Puts, 2011). These studies suggest that men have an interest in and capability for phenotype matching that allows them to recognize and preferentially invest in closely related young.

History of Research on Parental Care

Research on the biological basis of human paternal care owes much to two historical antecedents: studies of maternal behavior in mammals and of paternal behavior in birds. The rapid onset of mammalian maternal behavior following parturition has been causally linked to elevations in the levels of several hormones (review in Numan & Insel, 2003). These hormones interact with neurotransmitter systems, primarily dopamine, to change how new mothers perceive the attractiveness and rewarding properties of contact with young (Magnusson & Fleming, 1995). Research that extends this animal research to human mothers gives us confidence that findings on paternal behavior in mammals might also inform research on human fathers (e.g., Fleming & Gonzalez, 2009).

Maternal care is the ancestral pattern of parental care in mammals, as indicated by the common specialized reproductive anatomy and physiology, with paternal care having subsequent multiple origins in a small number of species. In contrast, for birds, either male-only or biparental care is ancestral (van Rhijn, 1990). Avian fathers can contribute more care since they can incubate embryos in stationary externally-laid eggs and directly provision young (i.e., no requirement for food to be converted to mother's milk). Biparental care has allowed birds to breed in habitats too rigorous for care to be provided by only one parent (e.g., Antarctic penguins); similarly, the human geographical range is much larger than any of our great ape relatives with uniparental care.

Male birds have high testosterone levels during the early courtship phase of breeding followed by a decline during incubation and chick-rearing (Feder, Storey, Goodwin, Reboulleau, & Silver, 1977). Testosterone mediates the tradeoff between mating and parental behavior in birds: males feed their chicks less often when their testosterone levels are experimentally increased (Hegner & Wingfield, 1987). Despite this usual negative relationship between testosterone and paternal care, ecological pressures can produce a dissociation between ancestral hormone patterns and typical male behaviors, as in polyandrous birds (Rissman & Wingfield, 1984) and when male mating opportunities coincide with critical (not just helpful) paternal care (Lynn, 2008).

Relative to maternal behavior, the biological basis of mammalian paternal behavior has been much less well studied. Because paternal behavior is less common and more variable than maternal care, it was difficult to imagine that it had a biological basis. Further, in rats, a species in which males are not typically parental, males can act paternally without showing any hormonal changes (Samuels & Bridges, 1983). Views began to change when research on naturally paternal species showed hormonal results similar to those in mothers. Levels of prolactin, a hormone involved in milk production and parental behavior, were higher in male marmosets sampled while carrying infants compared to males not engaged in infant contact (Dixson & George, 1982). Furthermore, California mouse fathers had higher prolactin levels than non-fathers (Gubernick & Nelson, 1989). These and subsequent studies suggested a biological basis for paternal behavior in naturally paternal species that might also exist in human fathers.

Current Research Questions

1. *Origins and development of individual variation in paternal behavior.*   Even in paternal species, mammalian paternal behavior is characterized by within and between population variability, produced by genetic and epigenetic (environmentally–induced changes in gene expression) factors. We will describe how social contact during development and adulthood contact and contextual factors (recency of contact with young, presence of mother) influence paternal behavior-hormone interactions.

2. *Role of specific hormones.*   Different hormones have been implicated in paternal behavior in different species. This variation could reflect (a) complexity of multi-hormone determinants involved in different aspects of paternal care, as in mammalian maternal care; (b) focus on different hormones in different species, making direct comparisons difficult; and/or (c) actual species differences in mechanisms, reflecting multiple evolutionary origins of mammalian paternal care.

3. *Neurobiology of paternal behavior.*   This section will focus on sex differences in the neurobiology of parental care.

Research Measurement and Methodology

Hormone levels are traditionally analyzed using radioimmonassays (RIA) and, more recently, via enzyme (e.g., ELISA) assays of blood serum or saliva. Hormone levels are compared, preferably in the same individuals, at different reproductive stages (e.g., before vs. after birth), or as individuals acquire different amounts of parental experience. Behaviors recorded in animal studies include contact time, licking and grooming, and carrying young or retrieving them to the nest. Behaviors in human studies include contact time, type of hold, gaze time, mutual regard, affectionate contact, vocalizations, and play dynamics. Questionnaires can be used to ask about subjective responses or about aspects of non-test experience.

A frequent experimental design in human research involves examining the effects of short-term parent-child interactions on hormonal responses. In these tests, participants provide a baseline blood/saliva sample before and after the individual interacts with young. These interactions have included taped baby cries and birth videos for expectant fathers, as well as 30-minute contact periods of fathers with their babies (Storey, Walsh, Quinton, & Wynne-Edwards, 2000).

The effects of hormones on the brain and behavior are studied by introducing exogenous hormones, hormone blockers, or drugs that interfere with neurohormones and other neuro-transmitters, and by examining neural tissue for specific brain areas and neurons that differ, for example, in number of hormone receptors, with immuno-histochemical techniques. In human studies, brain responses to infant stimuli can be studied through fMRI techniques. Both correlational and experimental designs are used.

The comparative method, comparing the behavior and physiology of closely related species that differ in how much paternal care males provide, helps us to understand the evolution and mechanisms of paternal behavior. Comparative research has been most intensive in voles of the genus *Microtus*, which include the highly-paternal prairie vole (*M. ochrogaster*), the sometimes-paternal meadow vole (*M. pennsylvanicus*), and the non-paternal montane vole (*M. montanus*). Comparative studies have also focused a highly paternal Djungarian dwarf hamster (*P. campbelli*), possibly the most paternal of all mammals studied, where males assist in the delivery of young, and its less paternal congener, the Siberian dwarf hamster (*P. sungorus*).

Empirical Findings

Origin and Development of Individual Variation in Paternal Care

Mammalian paternal behavior is characterized by considerable variation at individual (Gubernick, Schneider, & Jeannotte, 1994; Storey & Joyce, 1995), seasonal (Parker & Lee, 2001) and population levels (Roberts, Williams, Wang, & Carter, 1998; Schradin & Pillay, 2005). Human paternal care is also highly variable (Barry & Paxson, 1971; Belsky, Steinberg, & Draper, 1991). Moderate to high levels of father-infant contact occur in 40% of world societies (Barry & Paxson, 1971), with the extent of paternal care being related to the strength of emotional bonds between parents (Whiting & Whiting, 1975; Belsky et al., 1991). This variability allows individuals to respond optimally to both mating and parental opportunities.

Genetic factors.   Variation in monogamous and paternal tendencies may reflect differences in genes associated with the neuropeptide arginine-vassopresin (AVP), resulting in different patterns of brain AVP receptors. These genetic differences may explain variation both between and within vole species (Hammock & Young, 2005; Parker, Kinney, Phillips, & Lee, 2001). For example, prairie voles with long *avpr1a* microsatellites lick and groom pups more and show greater partner preferences than prairie voles with short *avpr1a* microsatellites (Hammock & Young, 2005). Further, insertion of AVP receptor gene into non-monogamous species increases their partner preferences (Lim et al., 2004). Fink et al. (2006) conclude that "our results demonstrate that the presence of STRs (single tandem repeats) upstream of the *avpr1a* gene is not directly linked to the mating system or basic social organization of these mammals" (p. 10959). They note that while two non-monogamous species do not have this gene conformation, several other non-monogamous microtines do have the gene. Thus, paternal care may develop when the gene is present *and* when environmental conditions select for the evolution of paternal care. Comparative research might support this idea: rodent genera with any paternal/ monogamous species should have the gene whereas genera with no paternal species should not.

Are these rodent findings applicable to primates, including humans? In a sample of men in 5-year relationships, men with two copies of a specific AVP gene scored lower on the Partner Bonding scale than men with no copies and were more likely to have a marital crisis or to not be married than men with zero or one copy (Walum et al., 2008). Rosso, Keller, Kaessmann, and Hammond (2008) argue that there is no clear relationship between AVP gene patterns and primate mating systems (but see the argument about this point in the previous paragraph). The location and repeat motif of the great ape (chimp and human) AVP genes are different than for voles (Fink et al., 2006), so these genes may be analogous (i.e., same function) in rodents and primates, but not homologous (i.e., same evolutionary origin). This lack of homology fits with idea of multiple evolutionary origins of mammalian paternal care and suggests some convergent evolution of function.

Epigenetic factors.   There is increasing evidence that an individual's phenotype is influenced not only by transmission of genetic code from parents, but also by environmentally-induced nongenomic information that can be transmitted through changes in the parental germline (Curley & Mashoodh, 2010), and/or changes in an individual's gene expression (Champagne, 2010; Meaney, 2010). These so-called epigenetic modifications involve alterations to DNA structure and chromatin, but not to the DNA sequence itself, primarily through the processes of DNA methylation and/or histone acetylation, that influence which genes get transcribed (mechanisms reviewed in Weaver et al., 2007). Briefly put, epigenetic changes make some of an individual's genes either more or less likely to be expressed, often resulting in significant phenotypic differences.

Perhaps the best understood example of how early social experiences can induce epigenetic changes that influence an individual's subsequent behavior, stress reactivity, and cognition is offered by Michael Meaney (2010). Some mother rats naturally show high levels of pup licking and grooming (LG) behaviors, while others show low LG. The amount of LG that a female displays can be manipulated through "handling" pups, a procedure which removes them briefly from the mother and which, upon their return, stimulates increases in the mother's LG behavior (Levine, 1994). Offspring that experience high levels of maternal LG show similar high levels of maternal behaviors towards their own pups, are less fearful, and have a more modest neuroedocrine response to stressors compared to offspring raised by low LG mothers (e.g., Caldji et al., 1998; Weaver et al., 2004). Cross-fostering of pups from low LG birth mothers to high LG foster mothers and vice versa demonstrates that the transmission of this effect is not genetic, but epigenetic (e.g., Weaver et al., 2004). Epigenetic influences on maternal care per se appear to involve changes in estrogen receptor alpha (ERα) gene expression in the medial preoptic area (MPO) of the hypothalamus, with daughters of high LG mothers expressing increased levels, rendering them more sensitive to estrogen (Champagne et al., 2006). Other phenotypic changes, such as those involving stress reactivity and emotionality, are mediated by changes in gene expression for glucocorticoid (GC) receptors in brain regions such as the hippocampus, with offspring that received high LG expressing more GC receptors, and showing a dampened response to stressors (e.g., Liu et al., 1997). These data on individual differences have been interpreted in two ways: as either reflecting psychopathology or, alternatively, variation in environmental harshness. In the latter interpretation, mothers whose time/energy budgets are constrained rear pups that are prepared to deal with similar harsh circumstances when they become adults.

Currently, whether paternal care in biparental animals has similar epigenetic influences on offspring is unclear; there are no data on proximate epigenetic mechanisms, although the quality of paternal behavior influences offspring phenotype. Cross-fostered California mice that were, as pups, picked up less often by males retrieve their own pups less frequently (Bester-Meredith & Marler, 2003). In this study, overall levels of paternal behavior were positively correlated with cells in the bed nucleus of the stria terminalis (BNST), a region important for social behaviors, that were immunoreactive for arginine-vasopressin, suggesting a possible nongenomic mechanism through which paternal care could be transmitted across generations. Interestingly, in marmosets, fathers show increases in the abundance of vasopressin receptors in the prefrontal cortex compared to non-fathers (Kozorovitskiy, Hughes, Lee, & Gould, 2006). In biparental Manadarin voles (*M. mandarinus*), when pups raised in the absence of fathers were tested as adults, they showed increased anxiety in open field tests, and decreased social behaviors in social interaction tests, compared to pups raised with both parents, suggesting that paternal care buffers stress responsiveness (Jia et al., 2009). Again, however, the mechanism through which this effect occurs is unknown.

Recent work on the biparental African striped mouse has shown that males' early experiences of paternal care influences the paternal behavior they demonstrate towards their own offspring (Rymer & Pillay, 2011). Contrary to findings for *Peromyscus* mice (Bester-Meredith & Marler, 2003) and voles (McGuire, 1988), male striped mice raised in the absence of fathers increased the amount of paternal behavior (specifically, huddling) towards their pups; an effect likely mediated by the significant increase in huddling and grooming time that mothers raising pups alone demonstrated, relative to mothers with males present. Thus, females compensated for a lack of paternal care by increasing maternal care, which, in turn, influenced sons' paternal behaviors through unknown mechanisms (Rymer & Pillay, 2011). Such compensation for the absence of fathers may not be typical in biparental mammals (Helmeke et al., 2009; Jia et al., 2009).

Given these findings and others which indicate paternal care influences offspring development (e.g., McGuire, 1988), it is tempting to predict we will soon discover epigenetic mechanisms underlying paternal care that are similar to those for maternal care. Furthermore, there is evidence that paternal absence during rearing influences the neural circuitry of offspring that typically receive biparental care. Biparental degus (*Octodon degus*), raised in the absence of fathers, demonstrate both altered synaptic connectivity in the anterior cingulate cortex, a brain region important for cognitive and emotional processing (Ovtscharoff, Helmeke, & Braun, 2006), and suppressed development of circuits in the orbitofrontal cortex, an area implicated in social behavior (Helmeke et al., 2009). Understanding whether paternal and maternal behaviors influence offspring via the same or different neurobiological and epigenetic pathways will further inform us about the role of paternal care in the small number of mammalian species in which it has evolved.

Role of social cues in the development of parental responsiveness.   Hormonal changes and the presence of young are necessary for the rapid initiation of maternal behavior at parturition in rats, and as lactation progresses, the pups becomes more important in maintaining maternal responsiveness (Rosenblatt, Siegel, & Mayer, 1979). Virgin female rats start to act maternally after several days of exposure to rat pups, suggesting that the main role of hormones near birth is to speed up the process so new mothers respond to pups immediately after their birth. New rat mothers assume an arch-back posture to allow pups to nurse (Stern, 1996) and sensory cues from pups become attractive and rewarding to the new mothers (Magnusson & Fleming, 1995).

Although maternal deprivation can diminish later maternal responsiveness, mammalian mothers generally require less social experience to behave parentally than mammalian fathers. For example, female meadow voles require no post-weaning social experience to act maternally with their first litters. In contrast, parentally-naïve male meadow voles differ in their responses to pups, ranging from being infanticidal, ignoring pups or huddling with them, but after siring pups and living with the pregnant female (Storey & Joyce, 1995) or after vasopressin administration (Parker & Lee, 2001), males were no longer infanticidal and many spent significant amounts of time in the nest with pups.

Male meadow voles became paternal in response to exposure to their mates' pups (Storey & Walsh, 1994). Males removed from their mates just before their pups were born did not become paternal, whereas males with olfactory but not physical contact with their mate and pups became less aggressive but did not act paternally when tested with an unrelated pup. Males in olfactory contact with an unfamiliar parturient female and her pups showed no behavioral change. Paternal behavior was also enhanced when males were reared with both parents (Storey & Joyce, 1995) or when they were cross-fostered and reared by pairs of the more paternal prairie vole (McGuire, 1988).

Female meadow voles control male access to pups and thereby affect whether males have the experience to develop paternal responsiveness (Storey, Bradbury, & Joyce, 1994). Female meadow voles from an American population did not allow any males to enter the nest and interact with pups (Oliveras & Novak, 1986). In contrast, female meadow voles from more northern Canadian populations allowed the sires of their litters into the nest with pups, but kept out unfamiliar males. Thus, variability in how paternal parentally-naïve male meadow voles are and whether females allow them into the nest have resulted in the evolution of a system with maximum flexibility, such that individuals can maximize reproductive success in different ways depending on environmental conditions (Storey, Delahunty, McKay, Walsh, & Wilhelm, 2006). This flexibility may be important in species with population and seasonal differences in paternal behavior, such as meadow voles where females and pups may cohabit with males during the colder parts of the breeding season (Madison, Fitzgerald, & McShea, 1984), but live away from males when it is warmer.

In contrast to meadow voles and most other paternal mammals, males of two very highly paternal rodent species do not need particular social interactions as adults in order to provide care for young (Djungarian hamsters, Jones & Wynne-Edwards, 2001; prairie voles, Roberts et al., 1998). It appears that the critical neuroendocrine events in these two species occur just after birth (Cushing & Wynne-Edwards, 2006), not in adulthood. Further, unlike other paternal mammals (e.g., Roberts, Jenkins, Lawler, Wegner, & Newman, 2001), reduction of prolactin levels does not interfere with paternal behavior in male Djungarian hamsters (Brooks, Vella, & Wynne-Edwards, 2005). Taken together, these findings suggest that when paternal care is critical (vs. not just important) for pup survival (as documented in Wynne-Edwards & Lisk, 1989), the underlying neuroendocrine mechanisms may evolve to lose socially-induced flexibility and become fixed earlier in development.

We know little about the development of paternal responsiveness in men. Belsky et al. (1991) suggest that different early experiences in father-present and father-absent homes play a role in determining whether boys grow up to be paternally responsive and capable of committed relationships. Expectant fathers with more than two younger siblings showed greater prolactin increases after exposure to infant cues than did men with fewer than two younger siblings (Delahunty, McKay, Noseworthy, & Storey, 2007), suggesting that early exposure to children may make men more responsive to infant cues.

Pregnant rats tested with pups become maternal faster than virgin females (Rosenblatt et al., 1979), suggesting that changes in responsiveness occur even prior to the birth. In contrast, males differ in how much their behavior and physiology changes in preparation for the arrival of young. Although living with the pregnant mate primes later paternal behavior, male meadow voles do not become more paternal until after pups are born (Storey & Joyce, 1995). In contrast, males of the more paternal California mouse show behavioral changes prior to the birth but neural changes are only detected postnatally (de Jong, Chauke, Harris, & Saltzman, 2009). Among primates, male tamarins and marmosets gain weight before their offspring are born, presumably in preparation for subsequent extensive infant carrying (Ziegler, Prudom, Schultz-Darken, Kurian, & Snowdon, 2006). Males of paternal primate species also show hormonal changes prior to the birth (Storey et al., 2000; Ziegler, Washabaugh, & Snowdon, 2004).

Couvade or male pregnancy symptoms suggest that men experience psychological and physical changes during their partners' pregnancies. Couvade symptoms occur in many cultures (Elwood & Mason, 1994) and can include weight and appetite changes, nausea, and mood shifts. Couvade was viewed as a psychosomatic response; however, these symptoms might function as 'a ritualized expression of biological changes' that prepare men for fatherhood (Elwood & Mason, 1994). Individual variability in men's couvade experiences is linked to their hormone status: men with two or more symptoms had higher prolactin levels and, after exposure to infant stimuli, their testosterone levels dropped more than in men with fewer symptoms (Storey et al., 2000). As with mothers, fathers show increasing attachment to their infants during their partners' pregnancies (Hjelmstedt, Widström, & Collins, 2007).

Role of Specific Hormones

Each section will start with a summary of mammalian maternal behavior, followed by a section on animal studies and concluding with the relevant information on human paternal behavior.

Prolactin.   Mammalian maternal behavior is disrupted if prolactin levels are reduced before (Bridges & Ronsheim, 1990) or just after birth (McCarthy, Curran, & Siegel, 1994; Walsh, Ralph, & Storey, 2009). When virgin female rats are exposed to young in the sensitization process, the individuals that become maternal have higher prolactin levels than those that do not (Marinari & Moltz, 1978).

Elevated prolactin levels may be involved in several aspects of paternal care: in the transition to fatherhood (Ziegler et al., 2004) as for mothers, in short-term responses to infants (Roberts et al., 2001) that may stimulate dopamine and contribute to the rewarding nature of acting parentally, and by affecting decisions to return to or stay with young (Carlson, Russell, et al., 2006). Finally, prolactin is involved in the development of paternal recognition in mice since prolactin suppression blocked the critical olfactory bulb neurogenesis that promoted this recognition (Mak & Weiss, 2010).

Prolactin suppression does not always disrupt paternal behavior, despite the studies discussed previously. Male dwarf hamsters (Brooks et al., 2005) and common marmosets (Almond, Brown, & Keverne, 2006) did not decrease paternal behavior when their prolactin levels were suppressed. Prolactin may be less important for enhancing paternal behavior in these highly paternal species than in less paternal species, a theme we will return to later. Prolactin suppression also may not have affected paternal behavior in some studies because tests were conducted in small enclosures, and the close proximity of young pups may have compensated for the effects of prolactin suppression. In support of this possibility, prolactin suppression increased the time between nest visits in female meadow voles housed in large enough enclosures such that females had to move away from pups to feed, but there was no change for females housed in small cages where they were constantly exposed to cues from nearby pups (Walsh et al., 2009). Further, when prolactin was suppressed in paternally-experienced marmosets there were no effects in the family cage but prolactin-suppressed males were less responsive to infants that had to be retrieved from a distance (Ziegler, Prudom, Zahed, Parlow, & Wegner, 2009). Prolactin may stimulate parents to return to or retrieve offspring, but it may play less of a role in maintaining parental behavior when young are in constant close proximity.

Previous paternal experience also affects prolactin levels. Prolactin was elevated for longer during infant development in experienced males of the primate species where paternal care was most prevalent and persistent (Schradin, Reeder, Mendoza, & Anzenberger, 2003). These results suggest that how experience affects prolactin levels depends on species differences in how important paternal care is to the survival and well-being of offspring, a suggestion that could be tested with field manipulations (Schradin, 2008). In humans, paternal experience changes how males respond hormonally to infant cues (Fleming, Corter, Stallings, & Steiner, 2002; Delahunty et al., 2007). We measured prolactin reactivity, that is, how much prolactin levels increased in response to infant stimuli, as they would, for example, when a mother nurses her baby. Expectant first-time mothers exposed to infant stimuli showed an increase in prolactin before the birth of their first babies. In contrast, men tested before the birth of their first baby showed no increase, and the same men tested just after the birth showed a prolactin decrease after holding their babies (Delahunty et al., 2007). The same men showed a significant prolactin increase when tested after holding their two-month old babies, but when tested after interacting with their 20-months old toddlers, their prolactin levels decreased (Storey, Noseworthy, Delahunty, Halfyard, McKay, 2011). These men did show a prolactin increase right after the birth their second babies (Delahunty et al., 2007), but again these increases were not maintained. It appears that men can develop greater prolactin reactivity with intense infant contact but these changes are not permanent within the span of the first two births.

Men's prolactin reactivity after 30 minutes of child contact was greater when men had not recently held their babies (Delahunty et al., 2007) or spent time with their toddlers (Storey et al., 2011). These findings suggest that changes in patterns of infant contact after the arrival of the second child may have also played a role in the prolactin increases after the second births (Delahunty et al., 2007). Thus, the increase in prolactin reactivity attributed to paternal experience in men may actually be due, in part, to differences between the patterns of fathers' contact with their first- and second-born babies. Second-time fathers may be more involved with caring for the older child while the mother cares for the new baby. This difference would result in second-time fathers having longer intervals between contact bouts with the new baby than first-time fathers, and thus, higher prolactin reactivity. This greater prolactin reactivity after longer separation periods mirrors findings in the maternal behavior literature: researchers augment suckling-induced prolactin reactivity in rats by separating mothers from their pups for several hours prior to testing (e.g., Grosvenor, Whitworth, & Mena, 1981).

Steroid hormones.   The gonadal steroids, primarily estrogen and progesterone in females, and testosterone in males are much involved in parental behavior. High estrogen levels near parturition stimulate the development of central nervous system receptors for the peptide hormones such as oxytocin (Pedersen, 1997) and prolactin (Bridges, 1996). New mothers with an increasing estradiol/progesterone ratio showed stronger attachment to their new babies and felt better than new mothers with a decreasing estradiol/progesterone ratio (Fleming, Ruble, Krieger, & Wong, 1997).

In keeping with the general finding that testosterone diminishes paternal behavior, testosterone levels in males of several biparental species decrease after young are born (e.g., Brown, Murdock, Murphy, & Moger, 1995) or after interacting with young (Prudhom et al., 2008; Storey et al., 2011). In contrast, testosterone enhances paternal care in some species by conversion to estrogen (Trainor & Marler, 2002). Castration does not substantially diminish paternal behavior in males of the most paternal rodent species (e.g., Lonstein & De Vries, 1999).

Human fathers have lower levels of testosterone than non-fathers in many (Gray, Kathlenberg, Barrett, Lipson, & Ellison, 2002; Storey et al., 2000) but not all studies (Gray & Campbell, 2009), and lower testosterone levels are associated with greater paternal responsiveness (Alvergne et al., 2009). After hearing taped infant cries, expectant fathers who reported feeling concern experienced a greater drop in testosterone than less responsive men (Storey et al., 2000). Interaction quality affects whether testosterone decreases after fathers interact with their toddlers: those men with a high paternal responsiveness score after being away from their children all day had a greater drop in testosterone than men whose responsiveness was not affected by the amount of recent child contact. Interestingly, whether men experienced this drop in testosterone depended on the mother's involvement: men were more likely to experience a testosterone decrease if their partners were less actively involved in the test interaction (Storey et al., 2011).

Vasopressin.   The response of paternally-naïve meadow voles to central administration of the arginine vasopressin (AVP) depended on their initial reaction to pups (Parker & Lee, 2001). Aggressive males no longer harmed pups after AVP administration, while non-responsive males spent more time with pups. The behavior of already-paternal males was not changed, suggesting that vasopressin-mediated induction of paternal responsiveness is most important for the least paternal males in a population.

Oxytocin.   Estrogen-primed oxytocin receptors in the brain play a central role in mammalian maternal behavior. Female rats with more oxytocin receptors in the brain areas associated with maternal behavior showed more licking and grooming of their offspring than females with fewer receptors. Further, oxytocin mediated the increase in dopamine signal during a licking bout, an important component of central organization of maternal behavior (Shahrokh, Zhang, Diorio, Gratton, & Meaney, 2010).

Paternal behavior in prairie voles is affected by both perinatal and adult administration of oxytocin. One-day old male prairie voles injected peripherally with oxytocin became more paternal adults than control males; males given oxytocin antagonists were less paternal (Carter, 2003). Carter (2003) notes that we should understand these early hormonal effects in animal models as human neonates are often exposed to high oxytocin levels if their mother's labor was induced and this exposure may affect their subsequent parental responsiveness. Adult prairie voles show diminished paternal responsiveness after a centrally-administered combination of oxytocin and vasopressin antagonists (Bales, Kim, Lewis-Reese, & Carter, 2004). Taken together, these results suggest that paternal behavior in prairie voles is more easily modified early in development whereas in their less paternal relative, the meadow vole, parental experience in adulthood increases oxytocin receptor binding compared to parentally-naïve voles (Parker et al., 2001).

Human fathers and mothers have comparable oxytocin levels during the first few months after their babies are born. Mothers' oxytocin levels were related to their levels of affectionate interaction with their babies, whereas fathers' oxytocin levels were related to affect synchrony (Gordon, Zagoory-Sharon, Leckman, & Feldman, 2010a) and stimulatory play (Gordon, Zagoory-Sharon, Leckman, & Feldman, 2010b). More stimulating fathers and more affectionate mothers had greater increases in oxytocin levels after child interactions than less responsive parents (Feldman, Gordon, Schneiderman, Weisman, & Zagoory-Sharon, 2010).

Glucocorticoids. Higher levels of glucocorticoids (primarily cortisol in primates and corticosterone in rodents and birds) are associated with both heightened and diminished parental responsiveness. Further, higher cortisol/corticosterone levels have been linked to increased foraging related to both increased provisioning of young and increased self-maintenance, with decreased parental provisioning. These conflicting findings highlight why glucocorticoids are called both 'stress' and 'anti-stress' hormones, the latter term used to suggest that these hormones mobilize the organism to respond to challenges and thus overcome stressful conditions (Wingfield & Sapolsky, 2003).

Postpartum women with high cortisol levels are subject to fatigue, depression and diminished affectionate interactions with babies and these high levels may result from early life adversity (Fleming & Gonzalez, 2009). These observations support the general view of cortisol (and other glucocorticoids) as 'stress' hormones. In contrast, mothers with higher levels of cortisol were more responsive to their newborns than women with lower cortisol (Fleming, Steiner, & Corter, 1997). These results suggest that elevated cortisol helps new mothers focus on the challenge of responding to a new baby.

Cortisol is also involved in both positive and negative aspects of paternal functioning. Highly paternal male marmosets had lower cortisol than less paternal individuals (Nunes, Fite, Patera, & French, 2001). In contrast, male meerkats (*Suricata suricatta*) with elevated cortisol levels fed pups more often than males with lower levels (Carlson, Manser, et al., 2006). In humans, cortisol levels increase from early to late pregnancy in both mothers and fathers and then decline in the postpartum period (Storey et al., 2000). We asked expectant fathers to report on their emotional responses to infant stimuli (taped cries and birth video). Men reporting 'concern' in response to the cries had higher cortisol levels in the perinatal period (Storey, Delahunty, &

McKay, 2007), results consistent with those of new mothers (Fleming, Steiner, & Corter, 1997). Men who reported an increase in meal preparation, confirmed by the mother, had higher cortisol than men reporting no change in their domestic work. Alternatively, men whose partners reported that parenting was more difficult than expected had higher cortisol levels than other men (Storey et al., 2007). Taken together, these results highlight the complexities in the relationship between cortisol and parental behavior. Elevations in cortisol, which may result from behavioral interactions, can mobilize the organism to deal with the challenge of being an effective parent. Elevations in cortisol with no effective behavioral solution, however, may result in less effective parental responses and distress. Whether these elevations exceed a threshold that moves the organism into the pathological range depends on developmental and recent challenges that the organism has experienced (Romero, Dickens, & Cyr, 2009).

Neurobiology of Parental Behavior

The neurobiology of primate fathering behavior is elucidated by Bales and Jarcho in this volume. Here we discuss the similarities between mammalian maternal and paternal neural pathways, and the ontogeny of steroid brain receptors in relation to differences in the natural occurrence of rodent paternal behavior in some rodents. While the neural basis of maternal care has been well established, particularly in rodents (e.g., Numan & Insel, 2003), the degree of overlap in the proximate mechanisms underlying maternal and paternal care remains unclear (e.g., Young, Gobrogge, Liu, & Wang, 2011). Animal models suggest that in some species, such as the biparental California mice, there is considerable similarity; new fathers show selective activation of the hypothalamic medial preoptic nucleus (MPO) in response to distal pup cues, as well as BNST activation, implicating these regions in the onset of paternal behavior (de Jong et al., 2009). These brain regions are also implicated in mediating paternal care in *Microtus* voles; following pup exposure, Fos-immunoreactivity in MPO and BNST, as well as in the medial amygdala and accessory olfactory bulb, increases in biparental male prairie voles, but not in non-paternal meadow voles (Wang & Insel, 1996). These neural regions, and their afferent and efferent pathways, regulate the expression of maternal behavior (Numan & Insel, 2003).

In voles and dwarf hamsters, however, there appears to be species-specific differences in the neurohormonal mechanisms underlying paternal and maternal care (e.g., Wynne-Edwards & Timonin, 2007; cf. Schradin, 2007). Such species-specific differences are not unexpected, given the considerable variation in social organization, mating systems, and affiliative behavior across the murid rodents, and they likely reflect the degree to which paternal care is critical in a given species.

Distribution patterns of ERα in voles and hamsters demonstrate the intricate relationship between brain and species-specific behaviors (reviewed in Cushing & Kramer, 2005). In these species, ERα distribution in the medial amygdala and BNST correlate with social organization, such that males, but not females, of the monogamous and highly paternal species (e.g., Djungarian hamsters and prairie voles) exhibit lower ERα-immunoreactivity than the less paternal species. In addition, within species, ERα-immunoreactivity in these brain regions is lower in more social populations compared to less social ones (Cushing et al., 2004; Cushing & Wynne-Edwards, 2006). In the biparental species only, ERα-immunoreactivity is sexually dimorphic, with males showing lower receptor levels than females, particularly early in life (e.g., 8–21 days of age; Yamamoto, Carter, & Cushing, 2006).

Sexually dimorphic patterns of ERα may explain the presence of female-like behaviors in males, such as caring for young (Cushing et al., 2004). Since males have higher steroid hormone and aromatase (an enzyme that converts testosterone to estrogen) activity during early development, males receive relatively more exposure to estrogen than do females, during the time period which sex-specific behaviors are organized. If males and females have the same numbers of ERα, males will be relatively more affected by estrogen, leading to the masculinization of behavior. If, however, males have fewer ERα compared to females, they will be less exposed to the masculinizing effects of estrogen, leading to more feminized behaviors, such as direct care of young.

Changes in levels of steroid hormones (testosterone, estrogen) and neuropeptides (oxytocin, vasopressin) are involved in activating paternal care. These hormones likely set the parameters for how much paternal behavior males will express, via their influence on brain organization during early development. For example, male prairie voles injected with steroids during the second postnatal week showed reduced juvenile alloparental care (Kramer, Perry, Golbin, & Cushing, 2009). Similarly, aromatase inhibition at weaning caused male Djungarian male hamsters to show less paternal care than those exposed to the inhibition later (Timonin & Wynne-Edwards, 2008).

The degree to which paternal care is critical for pup survival in the murid rodents and the neural mechanisms through which this care is established have likely co-evolved. In species with critical paternal care, the neural underpinnings of paternal responsiveness may be extremely robust and largely impermeable to environmental inputs. Establishing this "neural machinery" early in development, for example, with patterns of low ERα in particular brain regions, would be one way to ensure the robustness of the paternal response. In such biparental rodents, juvenile males display alloparental care of pups, indicating that activation of the system during adulthood by mating and/or mate presence is not required for the behavior to be displayed (e.g., Vella, Evans, Ng, & Wynne-Edwards, 2005). The presence of such a pathway in voles and hamsters does not preclude other neurobiological routes to paternal care in other biparental rodents, such as *Peromyscus*, which may have evolved mechanisms like those that underlie maternal behavior (i.e., activation of brain regions such as the MPO in the presence of appropriate reproductive experience and cues, see Gubernick et al., 1994; de Jong et al., 2009). However, when paternal care is facultative or optional, the neural basis underlying male responsiveness to young should be more flexible and responsive to environmental inputs, such as seasonal changes that impact offspring survival or the amount of paternal care that fathers themselves received, particularly if this is related to ecological factors such as habitat (Roberts et al., 1998; Rymer & Pillay, 2011).

Little is known about the neural basis for human paternal care but recent fMRI studies indicate that fathers show a different pattern of cortical activation after hearing infant cries than do non-fathers (Seifritz et al., 2003), which suggests that neural changes occur during the transition to fatherhood in humans as in other species.

Integration and Conclusions

Both hormones and social priming appear to be more important in less paternal species or individuals than for more paternal ones. For example, male meadow voles that were the least paternal became more responsive to pups following vasopressin injections, while behavior of the most paternal males was unaffected (Parker & Lee, 2001). Prolactin is more closely tied to paternal behavior in the less paternal species than in the extremely paternal Djungarian dwarf hamster. Further, in the highly paternal species, critical neuroendocrine events occur early in development, leaving organisms both more paternal and less flexible in their responses to varied mating and parental opportunities. Finally, there is a higher proportion of spontaneously paternally- inexperienced males in species where paternal care is more prevalent (comparison of 70% in prairie voles vs. 20% in meadow voles; Carter, 2003; Storey & Joyce, 1995, respectively).

Are hormonal mechanisms the same for all paternal species, or for males and females? As far as we know, the answer depends on the hormone in question and/or the particular species. It appears that hormones involved in other social behaviors, such as oxytocin and cortisol, may be similar in their parental roles in both sexes. Hormones that are less involved with pro-social behavior, like testosterone and estrogen, may have evolved their links to parental behavior separately in males and females. An exception to the previous statement is the case of the California mouse where the neuroendocrinology of steroid hormones is similar for males and females. There may different hormonal mechanisms associated with the separate evolutionary origins of paternal care in different taxa. For example, even among rodents, the vasopressin story in voles seems distinct from the testosterone/estrogen story for California mice. Even when the role of vasopressin is similar in unrelated taxa (e.g., rodents and primates) there is evidence that these receptors do not result from homologous genes.

Bridges to Other Disciplines

The multi-species approach presented here may be useful to disciplines such as Developmental Psychology where the focus is also on proximate factors, that is, how developmental precursors and environmental cues affect an individual's behavior. Our focus on the evolution of paternal behavior may provide a broader context for considering why so much individual variation in paternal behavior is maintained in our species. In turn, we can benefit from more detailed human investigations in other disciplines that remind us of the complexities of human family interactions.

Policy Implications

On the continuum of mammalian paternal behavior, humans are not as paternal as dwarf hamsters where males assist with the births and females without mates will reabsorb their pregnancies (Wynne-Edwards & Lisk, 1989). In terms of within-species behavioral variability (population and seasonal), we are probably closer to voles, possibly intermediate between prairie and meadow voles. If this is the case, then increasing paternal responsiveness may require more early socialization with emphasis on nurturance and more exposure in adulthood to cues from mates and infants that will enhance the development of paternal responsiveness. Research on the cross-generation transfer of the quality of parental contact suggests that if we can provide circumstances where children receive more nurturance from one or both parents, these children will become better parents when they grow up.

Future Directions

In order to move forward in this field, we need more studies on paternal behavior in natural or semi-natural conditions so that we can assess both how paternal care is integrated into the time budgets of both parents and how hormones affect the patterns of infant contact interspersed with parents' foraging and other activities. Such studies would also provide more information on the extent to which mothers encourage or discourage fathers from becoming more paternal and how females thereby affect the hormonal and behavioral development of fathers.

Acknowledgements

AES and CJW gratefully acknowledge research funding from their NSERC Discovery Grants.

References

Almond, R., Brown, G., & Keverne, E. (2006). Suppression of prolactin does not reduce infant care by parentally experienced male common marmosets (*Callithrix jacchus*). *Hormones and Behavior, 49*, 673–680.

Alvergne, A., Faurie, C., & Raymond, M. (2009). Father–offspring resemblance predicts paternal investment in humans. *Animal Behaviour, 78*, 61–69.

Bales, K. L., Kim, A. J., Lewis-Reese, A. D., & Carter, C. S. (2004). Both oxytocin and vasopressin may influence alloparental behavior in male prairie voles. *Hormones and Behavior, 45*, 354–361.

Barry, H., & Paxson, L. M. (1971). Infancy and early childhood: Cross cultural codes 2. *Ethnology, 10*, 466–508.

Belsky, J., Steinberg, L., & Draper, P. (1991). Childhood experience, interpersonal development, and reproductive strategy: An evolutionary theory of socialization. *Child Development, 62*, 647–670.

Bester-Meredith, J. K., & Marler, C. A. (2003). Vasopressin and the transmission of paternal behavior across generations in mated, cross-fostered *Peromyscus* mice. *Behavioral Neuroscience, 117*, 455–463.

Bridges, R. S. (1996). Biochemical basis of parental behavior in the rat. *Advances in the Study of Behavior, 25*, 6807–6815.

Bridges, R. S., & Ronsheim, P. M. (1990). Prolactin (PRL) regulation of maternal behavior in rats: Bromocriptine treatment delays and PRL promotes the rapid onset of behavior. *Endocrinology, 126*, 837–848.

Brooks, P. L., Vella, E. T., & Wynne-Edwards, K. E. (2005). Dopamine agonist treatment before and after the birth reduces prolactin concentration but does not impair paternal responsiveness in Djungarian hamsters, *Phodopus campbelli. Hormones and Behavior, 47*, 358–366.

Brown, R. E., Murdoch, T., Murphy, P. R., & Moger, W. H. (1995). Hormonal responses of male gerbils to stimuli from their mate and pups. *Hormones and Behavior, 29*, 474–491.

Buchan, J. C., Alberts, S. C., Silk, J. B., & Altmann, J. (2003). True paternal care in a multi-male primate society. *Nature, 425*, 179–81.

Caldji, C., Tannenbaum, B., Sharma, S., Frances, D. D., Plotsky, P. M., & Meaney, M. J. (1998). Maternal care during infancy regulates the development of neural systems mediating the expression of behavioral fearfulness in adulthood in the rat. *Proceedings of the National Academy of Sciences, USA, 95*, 5335–5340.

Carlson, A. A., Manser, M. B., Young, A. J., Russell, A. F., Jordan, N. R., McNeilly, A. S., & Clutton-Brock, T. (2006). Cortisol levels are positively associated with pup-feeding rates in male meerkats. *Proceedings of the Royal Society of London, Series B, Biological Science, 275*, 571–577.

Carlson, A. A., Russell, A. F., Young, A. J., Jordan, N. R., McNeilly, A. S., Parlow, A. F., & Clutton-Brock, T. (2006). Elevated prolactin levels immediately precede decisions to babysit by male meerkat helpers. *Hormones and Behavior, 50*, 94–100.

Carter, C. S. (2003). Developmental consequences of oxytocin. *Physiology and Behavior, 79*, 383–397.

Champagne, F. A. (2010). Epigenetic influence of social experiences across the lifespan. *Developmental Psychobiology, 52*, 299–311.

Champagne, F. A., Weaver, I. C., Diorio, J., Dymov, S., Szyf, M., & Meaney, M. J. (2006). Maternal care associated with methylation of the estrogen receptor-alpha1b promoter and estrogen receptor-alpha expression in the medial preoptic area of female offspring. *Endocrinology, 147*, 2909–2915.

Curley, J. P., & Mashoodh, R. (2010). Parent-of-origin and trans-generational germline influences on behavioral development: The interacting roles of mothers, fathers, and grandparents. *Developmental Psychobiology, 52*, 312–330.

Cushing, B. S., & Kramer, K. M. (2005). Mechanisms underlying epigenetic effects of early social experience: The role of neuropeptides and steroids. *Neuroscience and Biobehavioral Reviews, 29*, 1089–1105.

Cushing, B. S., Razzoli, M., Murphy, A. Z., Epperson, P. M., Le, W-W., & Hoffman, G. E. (2004). Intraspecific variation in estrogen receptor alpha and the expression of male sociosexual behavior in two populations of prairie voles. *Brain Research, 1016*, 247–254.

Cushing, B. S., & Wynne-Edwards, K. E. (2006). Estrogen receptor-α distribution in male rodents is associated with social organization. *Journal of Comparative Neurology, 494*, 595–605.

de Jong, T. R., Chauke, M., Harris, B. N., & Saltzman, W. (2009). From here to paternity: Neural correlates of the onset of paternal behavior in California mice (*Peromyscus californicus*). *Hormones and Behavior, 56*, 220–231.

Delahunty, K. M., McKay, D. W., Noseworthy, D. E., & Storey, A. E. (2007). Prolactin responses to infant cues in men and women: Effects of parental experience and recent infant contact. *Hormones and Behavior, 51*, 213–220.

Dixson, A. D., & George, L. (1982). Prolactin and parental behavior in a male New World primate. *Nature, 299*, 551–553.

Elwood, R., & Mason, C. (1994). The couvade and the onset of paternal care: A biological perspective. *Ethology and Sociobiology, 15*, 145–156.

Feder, H. H., Storey, A., Goodwin, D., Reboulleau, C., & Silver, R. (1977). Testosterone and 5α-dihydrotestosterone levels in peripheral plasma of male and female ring doves (*Streptopelia risoria*) during the reproductive cycle. *Biology of Reproduction, 16*, 666–677.

Feldman, R., Gordon, I., Schneiderman, I., Weisman, O., & Zagoory-Sharon, O. (2010). Natural variations in maternal and paternal care are associated with systematic changes in oxytocin following parent-infant contact. *Psychneuroendocrinology, 35*, 1133–1141.

Fink, S., Excoffier, L., Heckel, G., & Orians, G. H. (2006). Mammalian monogamy is not controlled by a single gene. *Proceedings of the National Academy of Sciences, USA, 103*, 10956–10960.

Fleming, A. S., Corter, C., Stallings, J., & Steiner, M. (2002). Testosterone and prolactin are associated with emotional responses to infant cries in new fathers. *Hormones and Behavior, 42*, 399–413.

Fleming, A. S., & Gonzalez, A. (2009). Neurobiology of human maternal care. In Ellison, P. T. & Gray, P. B. (Eds.), *Endocrinology of social relationships* (pp. 294–318). Cambridge, MA: Harvard University Press.

Fleming, A. S., Ruble, D., Krieger, H., & Wong, P. Y. (1997). Hormonal and experiential correlates of maternal responsiveness during pregnancy and the puerperium in human mothers. *Hormones and Behavior, 31*, 145-158.

Fleming, A. S., Steiner, M., & Corter, C. (1997). Cortisol, hedonics, and maternal responsiveness in human mothers. *Hormones and Behavior, 32*, 85–98.

Gordon, I., Zagoory-Sharon, O., Leckman, J. F., & Feldman, R. (2010a). Prolactin, oxytocin, and the development of paternal behavior across the first six months of fatherhood. *Hormones and Behavior, 58*, 513–518.

Gordon, I., Zagoory-Sharon, O., Leckman, J. F., & Feldman, R. (2010b). Oxytocin and the development of parenting in humans. *Biological Psychiatry, 68*, 377–382.

Gray, P. B., & Campbell, B. C. (2009). Human male testosterone, pair bonding and fatherhood. In P. T. Ellison & P. B. Gray (Eds.), *Endocrinology of social relationships* (pp. 270–293). Cambridge, MA: Harvard University Press.

Gray, P. B., Kathlenberg, S. M., Barrett, E. S., Lipson, S. F., & Ellison, P. T. (2002). Marriage and father-hood are associated with lower testosterone in males. *Evolution and Human Behavior, 23,* 193–201.

Grosvenor, C. E., Whitworth, N. S., & Mena, F. (1981). Evidence that the depletion and release phases of prolactin secretion in the lactating rat have different activation thresholds in response to exterocep-tive stimulation from rat pups. *Endocrinology, 108,* 820–824.

Gubernick, D. K., & Nelson, R. J. (1989). Prolactin and paternal behavior in the biparental California mouse, *Peromyscus californicus. Hormones and Behavior, 23,* 203–210.

Gubernick, D. J., Schneider, K. A., & Jeannotte, L. A. (1994). Individual differences in the mechanisms underlying the onset and maintenance of paternal behavior and the inhibition of infanticide in the monogamous biparental California mouse, *Peromyscus californicus. Behavioral Ecology and Sociobiology, 34,* 225–231.

Gubernick, D. J., Wright, S. L., & Brown, R. E. (1993). The significance of father's presence for offspring survival in the monogamous California mouse, *Peromyscus californicus. Animal Behaviour, 46,* 539–546.

Hammock, E. A. D., & Young, L. J. (2005). Microsatellite instability generates diversity in brain and sociobehavioral traits. *Science, 308,* 1630–1634.

Hegner, R. E., & Wingfield, J. C. (1987). Effects of experimental manipulation of testosterone levels on parental investment and breeding success in male House Sparrows. *The Auk, 104,* 462–469.

Helmeke, C., Seidel, K., Poeggel, G., Bredy, T. W., Abraham, A., & Braun, K. (2009). Paternal depriva-tion during infancy results in dendrite- and time-specific changes of dendritic development and spine formation in the orbitofronttal cortex of the biparental rodent *Octodon degus. Neuroscience, 163,* 790–798.

Hjelmstedt, A., Widström, A., & Collins, A. (2007). Prenatal attachment in Swedish IVF fathers and controls. *Journal of Reproductive and Infant Psychology, 25,* 296–307.

Hurtado, A. M., & Hill, K. R. (1992). Paternal effects of offspring survivorship among Ache and Hiwi hunter-gatherers: Implications for modeling pair-bond stability. In B.S. Hewlett (Ed.), *Father-child relations: Cultural and biosocial contexts* (pp. 153–176). New York: Aldine de Gruyter.

Jia, R., Tai, F., An, S., Zhang, X., & Broders, H. (2009). Effects of neonatal paternal deprivation or early deprivation on anxiety and social behaviours of the adults in manderin voles. *Behavioural Processes, 82,* 271–278.

Jones, J. S., & Wynne-Edwards, K. E. (2001). Paternal behaviour in biparental hamsters, *Phodopus campbelli,* does not require contact with the pregnant female. *Animal Behaviour, 62,* 453–464.

Kleiman, D. G., & Malcolm, J. R. (1981). The evolution of male parental investment in mammals. *Quar-terly Review of Biology, 52,* 39–68.

Kozorovitskiy, Y., Hughes, M., Lee, K., & Gould, E. (2006). Fatherhood affects dendritic spines and vasopressin V1a receptors in the primate prefrontal cortex. *Nature Neuroscience, 9,* 1094–1095.

Kramer, K. K., Perry, A. N., Golbin, D., & Cushing, B. S. (2009). Sex steroids are necessary in the second postnatal week for the expression of male alloparental behavior in prairie voles (*Microtus ochra-gaster). Behavioral Neuroscience, 123,* 958–963.

Levine, S. (1994). The ontogeny of the hypothalamic-pituitary-adrenal axis: The influence of maternal factors. *Annals of the New York Academy of Sciences, 746,* 275–288.

Lim, M. M., Wang, Z., Olazábal, D. E., Ren, X., Terwilliger, E. F., & Young, L. J. (2004). Enhanced partner preference in a promiscuous species by manipulatin the expression of a single gene. *Nature, 429,* 754–757.

Liu, D., Diorio, J., Tannenbaum, B., Caldji, C., Francis, D., Freedman, A., et al. (1997). Maternal care, hippocampal glucocorticoid receptors, and hypothalamic-pituitary-adrenal responses to stress. *Sci-ence, 277,* 1659–1662.

Lonstein, J. S., & De Vries, G. (1999). Sex differences in the parental behaviour of adult virgin prairie voles: Independence from gonadal hormones and vasopressin. *Journal of Neuroendocrinology, 11,* 441–449.

Lynn, S. E. (2008). Behavioral insensitivity to testosterone: Why and how does testosterone alter paternal and aggressive behavior in some avian species but not others? *General and Comparative Endocrinology, 157,* 233–240.

Madison, D. M., Fitzgerald, R. W., & McShea, W. J. (1984). Dynamics of social nesting in overwintering meadow voles, *Microtus pennsylvanicus*: Possible consequences for population cycling. *Behavioral Ecology and Sociobiology, 15,* 9–17.

Magnusson, J. E., & Fleming, A. S. (1995). Rat pups are reinforcing to the maternal rat: Role of sensory cues. *Psychobiology, 23,* 69–75.

Mak, G. K., & Weiss, S. (2010). Paternal recognition of adult offspring mediated by newly generated CNS neurons. *Nature Neuroscience, 13,* 753–758.

Marinari, K. T., & Moltz, H. (1978). Serum prolactin levels and vaginal cyclicity in concaveated and lactating female rats. *Physiology & Behavior, 21,* 525–528.

McCarthy, M. M., Curran, G. H., & Siegel, H. I. (1994). Evidence for the involvement of prolactin in the maternal behaviour of the hamster. *Physiology & Behavior, 55,* 181–184.

McGuire, B. (1988). Effects of cross-fostering on parental behavior in the meadow vole (*Microtus pennsylvanicus*). *Journal of Mammalogy, 69,* 332–341.

Meaney, M. J. (2010). Epigenetics and the biological definition of gene x environment interactions. *Child Development, 81,* 41–79.

Numan, M., & Insel, T. R. (2003). *The neurobiology of parental behavior.* New York: Springer.

Nunes, S., Fite, J. E., Patera, K. J., & French, J. A. (2001). Interactions among paternal behavior, steroid hormones and parental experience in male marmosets. *Hormones and Behavior, 39,* 70–82.

Oliveras, D., & Novak, M. (1986). A comparison of paternal behaviour in the meadow vole (*Microtus pennsylvanicus*), the pine vole (*M. pinetorum*) and the prairie vole (*M. ochrogaster*). *Animal Behaviour, 34,* 519–526.

Ovtscharoff, W., Helmeke, C., & Braun, K. (2006). Lack of paternal care affects synaptic development in the anterior cingulate cortex. *Brain Research, 1116,* 58–63.

Pal, S. K. (2005). Parental care in free-ranging dogs, *Canis familiaris. Applied Animal Behaviour Science, 90,* 31–47.

Parker, K. J., Kinney, L. F., Phillips, K. M., & Lee, T. M. (2001). Paternal behavior is associated with central neurohormone receptor binding patterns in meadow voles (*Microtus pennsylvanicus*). *Behavioral Neuroscience, 115,* 1341–1348.

Parker, K. J., & Lee, T. M. (2001). Central vasopressin administration regulates the onset of paternal behavior in *Microtus pennsylvanicus. Hormones and Behavior, 39,* 285–294.

Pedersen, C. A. (1997). Oxytocin control of maternal behavior: Regulation by sex steroids and offspring stimuli. In C. S. Carter, I. I. Lederhendler, & B. Kirkpatrick (Eds.), *The integrative neurobiology of affiliation* (pp. 126–145). New York: New York Academy of Sciences.

Platek, S. M., Raines, D. M., Gallup, G. G., Mohamed, F. B., Thomson, J. W., Myers, T. E., et al. (2004). Reactions to children's faces: Males are more affected by resemblance than females are, and so are their brains. *Evolution and Human Behavior, 25,* 394–405.

Prudom, S. L., Broz, C. A., Schultz-Darken, N., Ferris, C. T., Snowdon, C., & Ziegler, T. E. (2008). Exposure to infant scent lowers serum testosterone in father common marmosets (*Callithrix jacchus*). *Biology Letters, 4,* 603–605.

Rissman, E. F., & Wingfield, J. C. (1984). Hormonal correlates of polyandry in the spotted sandpiper, *Actitis macularia. General and Comparative Endocrinology, 56,* 401–405.

Roberts, R. L., Jenkins, K. T., Lawler, T., Jr., Wegner, F. H., & Newman, J. D. (2001). Bromocriptine administration lowers serum prolactin and disrupts parental responsiveness in common marmosets (*Callithrix j. jacchus*). *Hormones and Behavior, 39,* 106–112.

Roberts, R. L., Williams, J. R., Wang, A. K., & Carter, C. S. (1998). Cooperative breeding and monogamy in prairie voles: Influence of the sire and geographic variation. *Animal Behaviour, 55,* 1131–1140.

Romero, M., Dickens, M. J., & Cyr, N. E. (2009). The reactive scope model — A new model integrating homeostasis, allostasis, and stress. *Hormones and Behavior, 55,* 375–389.

Rosenblatt, J. S., Siegel, H. I., & Mayer, A. D. (1979). Progress in the study of maternal behavior in the rat: Hormonal, nonhormonal, sensory, and developmental aspects. *Advances in the Study of Behavior, 10,* 225–311.

Rosso, L., Keller, L., Kaessmann, H., & Hammond, R. L. (2008). Mating system and *avpr1a* promoter variation in primates. *Biology Letters, 4,* 375–378.

Rymer, T. L., & Pillay, N. (2011). The influence of the early rearing environment on the development of paternal care in African striped mice. *Ethology, 117,* 284–293.

Samuels, M. H., & Bridges, R. S. (1983). Plasma prolactin concentration in parental male and female rats: Effects of exposure to rat young. *Endocrinology, 113,* 1647–1654.

Schradin, C. (2007). Comments to K. E. Wynne-Edwards and M. E. Timonin 2007. Paternal care in rodents: Weakening support of hormonal regulation of the transition to behavioral fatherhood in rodent animal models of biparental care, Horm & Behav 52: 114–121. *Hormones and Behavior, 52,* 557–559.

Schradin, C. (2008). Differences in prolactin levels between three alternative male reproductive tactics in striped mice (*Rhabdomys pumilio*). *Proceedings of the Royal Society of London, Series B, Biological Science, 275,* 1047–1052.

Schradin, C., & Pillay, N. (2005). The influence of the father on offspring development in the striped mouse. *Behavioral Ecology, 16,* 450–455.

Schradin, C., Reeder, D. M., Mendoza, S. P., & Anzenberger, G. (2003). Prolactin and paternal care: Comparison of three species of monogamous new world monkeys (*Callicebus cupreus, Callithrix jacchus,* and *Callimico goeldii*). *Journal of Comparative Psychology, 117,* 166–175.

Schradin, C., Scantlebury, M., Pillay, N., & Konig, B. (2009). Testosterone levels in dominant sociable males are lower than in solitary roamers: Physiological differences between three male reproductive tactics in a sociably flexible mammal. *The American Naturalist, 173,* 376–388.

Seifritz, E., Esposito, F., Neuhoff, J. G., Luthi, A., Mustovic, H., Dammann G., et al. (2003). Differential sex-independent amygdala response to infant crying and laughing in parents versus nonparents. *Biological Psychiatry, 54,* 1367–1375.

Shahrokh, D. K., Zhang, T. Y., Diorio, J., Gratton, A., & Meaney, M. J. (2010). Oxytocin-dopamine interactions mediate variations in maternal behavior in the rat. *Endocrinology, 151,* 2276–2286.

Stern, J. M. (1996). Somatosensation and maternal care in Norway rats. *Advances in the Study of Behavior, 25,* 243–294.

Storey, A. E., Bradbury, C. G., & Joyce, T. L. (1994). Nest attendance in male meadow voles: The role of the female in regulating male interactions with pups. *Animal Behaviour, 47,* 1037–1046.

Storey, A. E., Delahunty, K. M., & McKay, D. W. (2007, June). Are elevated cortisol levels associated with enhanced or reduced parental responsiveness? Poster presented at the Parental Brain Conference, Boston.

Storey, A. E., Delahunty, K. M., McKay, D. M., Walsh, C. J., & Wilhelm, S. I. (2006). Social and hormonal bases for individual differences in the parental behaviour of bird and mammals. *Canadian Journal of Experimental Psychology, 60,* 237–245.

Storey, A. E., & Joyce, T. L. (1995). Pup contact promotes paternal responsiveness in male meadow voles. *Animal Behaviour, 49,* 1–10.

Storey, A. E., Noseworthy, D. E., Delahunty, K. M., Halfyard, S. J., & McKay, D. W. (2011). The effects of social context on the hormonal and behavioural responsiveness of human fathers. *Hormones and Behavior, 60,* 353–361.

Storey, A. E., & Snow, D. T. (1987). Male identity and enclosure size affect paternal attendance of meadow voles, *Microtus pennsylvanicus. Animal Behaviour, 35,* 411–419.

Storey, A. E., & Walsh, C. J. (1994). The role of physical contact from females and pups in the development of paternal responsiveness in meadow voles. *Behaviour, 131,* 139–151.

Storey, A. E., Walsh, C. J., Quinton, R., & Wynne-Edwards, K. E. (2000). Hormonal correlates of paternal responsiveness in new and expectant fathers. *Evolution and Human Behavior, 21,* 79–95.

Timonin, M. E., & Wynne-Edwards, K. E. (2008). Aromatase inhibition during adolescence reduces adult sexual and paternal behaviour in the biparental dwarf hamster *Phodopus campbelli*. *Hormones and Behaviour, 54,* 748–757.

Tinbergen, N. (1963). On aims and methods of ethology. *Zeitschrift für Tierpsychology, 20,* 410–433.

Trainor, B. C., & Marler, C. A. (2002). Testosterone promotes paternal behaviour in a monogamous mammal via conversion to oestrogen. *Proceedings of the Royal Society of London, Series B, 269,* 823–829.

van Rhijn, J. G. (1990). Unidirectionality in the phylogeny of social organization, with special reference to birds. *Behaviour, 115,* 153–174.

Vella, E. T., Evans, C. D., Ng, M. W. S., & Wynne-Edwards, K. E. (2005). Ontogeny of the transition from killer to caregiver in dwarf hamsters (*Phodopus campbelli*) with biparental care. *Developmental Psychobiology, 46,* 75–85.

Walsh, C., Ralph, T., & Storey, A. (2009). Enclosure size and hormonal state affect timing of nest return in female meadow voles (*Microtus pennsylvanicus*). *Journal of Comparative Psychology, 123,* 115–124.

Walum, H., Westberg, L., Henningsson, S., Neiderhiser, J. M., Reiss, D., Igl, W., et al. (2008). Genetic variation in the vasopressin receptor 1a gene (*AVPR1A*) associates with pair-bonding behavior in humans. *Proceedings of the National Academy of Sciences, USA, 105,* 14153–14156.

Wang, Z., & Insel, T. R. (1996). Parental behavior in voles. *Advances in the Study of Behavior, 25,* 361–384.

Weaver, I. C. G., Cervoni, N., Champagne, F. A., D'Allesio, A. C., Sharma, S., Seckl, J. R., et al. (2004). Epigenetic programming by maternal behavior. *Nature Neuroscience, 7,* 847–854.

Weaver, I. C. G., DiAlessio, A. C., Brown, S. E., Hellstrom, I. C., Dymov, S., Diorio, J., et al. (2007). The transcription factor NGFI-A mediates epigenetic programming: Altering epigenetic marking through immediate early genes. *Journal of Neuroscience, 27,* 1756–1768.

Welling, L. L. M., Burriss, R. P., & Puts, D. A. (2011). Mate retention behavior modulates men's preferences for self-resemblance in infant faces. *Evolution and Human Behavior, 32,* 118–126.

Whiting, J. W., & Whiting, B. B. (1975). Aloofness and intimacy of husband and wives: A cross-cultural study. *Ethos, 3,* 183–207.

Wingfield, J. C., & Sapolsky, R. M. (2003). Reproduction and resistance to stress: When and how. *Journal of Neuroendocrinology, 15,* 711–724.

Wynne-Edwards, K. (1995). Biparental care in Djungarian but not Siberian dwarf hamsters (*Phodopus*). *Animal Behaviour, 50,* 1571–1585.

Wynne-Edwards, K. E., & Lisk, R. D. (1989). Differential effects of paternal presence on pup survival in two species of dwarf hamster (*Phodopus sungorus* and *Phodopus campbelli*). *Physiology & Behavior, 45,* 465–469.

Wynne-Edwards, K. E., & Timonin, M. E. (2007). Parental care in rodents: Weakening support for hormonal regulation of transition to behavioral fatherhood in rodent animal models of biparental care. *Hormones and Behavior, 52,* 114–121.

Yamamoto, Y., Carter, C. S., & Cushing, B. S. (2006). Neonatal manipulation of oxytocin affects expression of estrogen receptor alpha. *Neuroscience, 137,* 157–164.

Young, K. A., Gobrogge, K. L., Liu, Y., & Wang, Z. (2011). The neurobiology of pair bonding: Insights from a socially monogamous rodent. *Frontiers in Neuroendocrinology, 32,* 53–69.

Ziegler, T. E., Prudom, S. L., Schultz-Darken, N. J., Kurian, A. V., & Snowdon, C. T. (2006). Pregnancy weight gain: Marmoset and tamarin dads show it too. *Biology Letters, 2,* 181–183.

Ziegler, T. E., Prudom, S. L., Zahed, S. R., Parlow, A. F., & Wegner, F. (2009). Prolactin's mediative role in male parenting in parentally experienced marmosets (*Callithrix jacchus*). *Hormones and Behavior, 56,* 436–443.

Ziegler, T. E., Washabaugh, K. F., & Snowdon, C. T. (2004). Responsiveness of expectant male cotton-top tamarins, *Sanguinus oedipus,* to mate's pregnancy. *Hormones and Behavior, 45,* 84–92.

Chapter 2

Evolutionary Perspectives on Father Involvement

David Waynforth

University of East Anglia

Theoretical Perspectives and Historical Overview

The crux of evolutionary approaches to variation in paternal involvement is quite straightforward: evolutionary theorists attempt to understand and predict variation in paternal involvement based on the premise that men will provide a level of paternal involvement which maximizes their reproductive success. Any genetically influenced paternal trait which does not maximize genetic contribution to future generations will occur less and less frequently with the passing of generations. Because in our evolutionary past paternal behavior is likely to have had a significant impact on men's reproductive success through influencing child survival and viability, human paternal behavior is almost certain to have a strong evolutionary underpinning. However, in practice, demonstrating evolutionary influences on paternal involvement is quite complex and fraught with difficulties. One problem is that the environments in which humans evolved, and in which paternal behaviors were shaped by natural and sexual selection, are not necessarily similar to present day conditions due to the rapid changes to human societies and environments that occurred with the development of modern technology and medicine. Thus, studying the reproductive consequences of paternal behavior in present-day humans may not provide the evolutionary insights that researchers hope to achieve, and important questions, such as quantifying typical benefits of paternal care for children's survival and viability, become difficult to answer. Without answers, it is impossible to say with any degree of certainty what paternal involvement patterns are reproductively optimal, and therefore what our fundamental paternal genetic adaptations will consist of: evolution will have produced a pattern of typical paternal care based on its reproductive costs and benefits in past generations. A partial solution to this problem has been to collect data on father involvement and its outcomes in living hunter-gatherers and in the shrinking number of other societies which remain at the subsistence level today. This approach has, not surprisingly, been adopted and applied by evolutionary anthropologists in the past three decades, while evolutionary psychologists have generally focused on attempting to discover evolved cognitive mechanisms rather than measuring reproductive outcomes (e.g., see Cosmides & Tooby, 1995).

Current Research Questions

In this chapter I focus on the following areas of current research: first, the questions of why paternal care evolved in the human lineage, and what kinds of paternal behavior were likely to have been selected for by evolution in early humans. The chapter continues with related issues of anthropological evidence for what types or aspects of childcare an average human male provides, and the impact of this care on the survival and success of children. The next sections address evolutionary theoretical perspectives on the effects on children's development of father-absent rearing due to divorce, issues surrounding fathering and biological paternity, and variation among individual men in evolutionarily optimal levels of paternal care. Research in these areas span the range of theoretical approaches briefly discussed above, and thus should provide the novice reader in evolution and human behavior with a balanced introduction to how evolutionary theory has been applied to help understand patterns of father involvement.

Research Measurement and Methodology

Research methodology in evolutionary anthropology and psychology relies on the ability to make accurate theoretical predictions about what Darwinian natural selection will favor. This first step can be achieved in some cases by verbal logical argument, and by mathematical modeling. Because basic principles of evolution should apply across species, the principles can be tested with animals using case-control study designs with random assignment into experimental groups. Randomized case-control studies are often not possible or ethical to perform with human participants, and evolutionary theorists have utilized a very wide variety of potential data sources to test Darwinian hypotheses. Choice of methodology often reflects the disciplinary background of the researcher, with father-involvement researchers most commonly applying methods utilized in experimental psychology, as well as quantitative anthropological and demographic methods. The research highlighted in this chapter has employed some particularly inventive methodology. For example, evolutionary theory postulates that paternal effort should primarily be directed at biological offspring (with some exceptions). To get at this without genetic testing, researchers have focused on creating proxies for genetic similarity between a child and its putative father, such as by using forced-choice experiments to assess father-child similarity in body scent.

Empirical Findings

Why Did Paternal Care Evolve in the Human Lineage?

Paternal involvement in child-rearing is uncommon in mammals, including in our closest living relatives, apes and other primates (with some notable exceptions in New World monkeys). Mathematical modeling techniques have been applied to understand the maintenance of paternal care as an evolutionarily stable behavior. John Maynard Smith constructed a game theoretical model of parental care in which effects on parental fertility and offspring mortality by each sex of parent (and both combined) were modeled to find out under what conditions each parental strategy could be invaded by an alternative strategy (an evolutionary stable strategy or ESS model) (Maynard Smith, 1977). His model is quite straightforward in its implications: men should contribute to parenting their offspring when offspring survival is higher under biparental care than with maternal care only. At the same time, females should not desert their offspring leaving them to be cared for by males when their fertility is higher when males are present to help care for offspring. These conditions together should result in the evolution of parental care by both the father and mother. More recent theoretical arguments have focused on exactly what aspects of male parental involvement began to influence infant survival in the human lineage. Lee Gettler (2010) argued that male carrying of infants, the primary paternal role in some primate species, initially spurred the evolution of paternal involvement in the human lineage. An alternative argument is that when compared with great apes, one param- eter that stands out as unusual in humans is that we have much shorter inter-birth intervals than chimpanzees, who on average have inter-birth intervals of over five years (see Gettler, 2010), while hunter-gatherer women have inter-birth intervals of close to three years (see Table 8.2 in Hill and Hurtado, 1996). A number of evolutionary theorists have suggested that male food-provisioning to females was a key underlying factor, giving ancestral human females an energy-balance advantage which allowed short inter-birth intervals when men were present to help care for children (e.g., Hamilton, 1984; Lancaster & Lancaster, 1983; Lovejoy, 1981). This argument states that it is not male influence on infant survival that results in increased reproductive success, but instead male provisioning to females that results in increased female fertility when the father is present.

As Gettler's (2010) research implies, evolutionary theorists often tend to consider resource- based paternal involvement separately from direct childcare, such as holding or carrying infants. Although determining whether direct childcare or male provisioning to women and children was more important is a difficult task, two relevant questions can be addressed with data on living humans: (a) How much direct paternal care do men typically perform?, and (b) What are the effects of paternal care (provisioning and direct childcare) on infant survival in subsistence-level societies?

The amount of time that men in modern industrialized nations can devote to direct child- care is for many confined by set work hours which usually take up all day for five days per week. In living hunter-gatherers and other subsistence-level societies, men's work activities may often be time-consuming, but there can be more flexibility and opportunity to spend time caring for children. Anthropologists have measured men's time allocation to childcare using scan sampling techniques. Because anthropologists usually live in the community that they are studying and people's activities are more easily observed than in industrialized societies, randomly timed visual scans of who is caring for each infant and child in a community can be collated to produce an estimate of how much time men spend performing direct parental care. Time allocation studies in hunter-gatherers reveal a great deal of variability between groups in paternal holding and monitoring of infants and children. At one end of the spectrum, Hewlett (1991) found that in the Central African Republic, Aka infants spent 22% of their time in their father's arms. At the low end of the spectrum, in some other African hunter-gatherer groups, infants spend less than 2% of their time being held by the father (see Gettler, 2010). The average for hunter-gatherers and other subsistence level societies is probably close to 5% (e.g., Waynforth, 2011).

The bulk of male investment in children comes as resource-based investment, such as food provisioning and housing, although this does not mean that the small amount of direct pater- nal care provided to infants is unimportant, as it may strengthen father-child bonds and ensure continued resource-based male care.

From an evolutionary perspective, a key question about paternal care is its effect on child survival: if lack of paternal involvement or father absence had a large impact on child mortal- ity in our evolutionary past, then we would expect that genetically influenced desire to be an involved father will be strong. The most comprehensive recent review of effects of different classes of biological kin on child mortality across human societies was carried out by Rebecca Sear and Ruth Mace. Their (2008) review showed that there is a wide range of variation of effects of fathers on child survival across societies. For example, in South American Ache hunter-gatherers, the death of the father increases the probability that his child will die in childhood by around three times (Hill & Hurtado, 1996), and parental divorce also has a large impact on subsequent child mortality. However, Sear and Mace's (2008) review shows that the father's death only significantly affects child mortality in around half of the hunter-gatherer and subsistence-level societies for which relevant mortality data exist. On average across subsistence-level human populations, having maternal or paternal grandparents alive has a greater impact on child survival than having the father alive during a child's infancy and childhood. These data call into question the necessity of fathers for child survival in many cases, but there could be other disadvantages of being raised father-absent that will affect a child's future reproductive success, and in turn create evolutionary selection pressure for father involvement. Second, as Sear and Mace (2008) argue, differences in local conditions affect the direct importance of fathers for child survival, with some conditions, such as strong ties with maternal kin and grandparents, making fathers appear to be unimportant for child survival. It may therefore be erroneous to conclude from these data that paternal care is unimportant in human evolutionary history.

Lifetime reproductive success may be affected by a number of potential outcomes of father absence or lack of paternal involvement. One influence on lifetime reproductive success is age at first reproduction: a later start on reproduction will typically result in a shorter reproductive lifespan unless there are advantages to growing larger before beginning to reproduce. For example, Ache hunter-gatherer women show higher lifetime fertility at larger adult body weights (Hill & Hurtado, 1996). Results of studies in subsistence-level societies on the effect of father absence on offspring age at first reproduction have shown mixed results: in some groups father absence due to divorce delays offspring age at first reproduction (Waynforth, 2001; Waynforth, Hurtado, & Hill, 1998), but in many others father absence due to divorce has the opposite effect, appearing to accelerate reproductive maturity and age at first birth. Father absence due to death and due to divorce both reduce financial and direct childcare-based paternal investment, but evolutionary developmental psychologists have theorized that divorce constitutes a special condition under which developmental trajectories of children of divorced parents are altered by other evolutionary processes independently of resource and childcare effects. This developmental theory of father absence is the focus of the next section in the chapter.

Evolution and Father Absence

A very influential theory of evolution and paternal involvement is Draper and Harpending's (1982) hypothesis that reproductive success is maximized in different ecological contexts by the development of sexual strategies that are appropriate for the context. Specifically, in environments where marriages or pair-bonds are not lasting, children develop trajectories in which men focus on mating competition rather than preparing to be devoted fathers, and women reach reproductive maturity at a young age, typically becoming mothers while young and not in a stable marriage. In 1991, Belsky, Steinberg, and Draper published a more detailed theoretical paper in *Child Development*, outlining two types of reproductive trajectories which correspond to stable and unstable ecological and marital contexts. In their model, marital instability, lack of resources, harsh and inconsistent parental care result in offspring outcomes which include insecure attachment styles and early maturity and reproduction. These behaviors were hypothesized to be reproductively advantageous in unstable environments because devoting time and effort to forming and maintaining a stable mating relationship will not have benefits in a fundamentally unstable environment in which resources are not always available. In a more stable ecological context, later reproduction with stable marriage is hypothesized to be favored by natural selection.

Between them, Draper and Harpending's (1982) and Belsky et al.'s (1991) two seminal papers have been cited over 700 times in the Web of Science® at the time of this writing, making their theory one of the most highly cited in the field of evolutionary psychology. This is in part due to continued development of the theory by other authors, and numerous empirical studies which confirm the predicted links between father absent rearing and girls' menarche and early reproduction. These studies include analyses carried out on large and/or longitudinal datasets: for example Ellis, McFadyen-Ketchum, Dodge, Pettit, and Bates (1999) found that number of measures of father involvement, including the father's presence and his involvement in child-rearing predicted later age at menarche. Nettle, Coall, and Dickins (2010) used a large longitudinal British sample to investigate the relationship between paternal involvement and women's age at first birth, and found that low paternal involvement doubled the risk of early reproduction.

Belsky et al.'s (1991) theory of divergent reproductive strategies paralleled developments in evolutionary life-history theory clarifying why early reproduction is favored in unstable environments. A number of experimental studies have shown that reproductive parameters are altered in animals when they are exposed to predation. For example, Stibor (1992) exposed Daphnia (a freshwater invertebrate) to chemicals associated with the presence of predators. With these chemicals present without their associated predation risk, Daphnia matured and reproduced at an earlier age than a control group not exposed to predator chemicals. This maximizes reproductive success because a later start to reproduction increases the risk of never reproducing due to dying while still a juvenile. Optimal age at first reproduction is therefore dependent on mortality rates in a given environment. However, early maturity is only selected for in higher mortality conditions up to the point where disadvantages of early reproduction, such as resultant small adult body size, are not so great that they cancel out the mortality risk-reduction advantages.

Chisholm (1999a,b; Chisholm, Quinlivan, Petersen, & Coall, 2005) began to integrate Belsky's et al's (1991) hypothesis with the life-history theoretical perspective. Chisholm's research in U.S. and Australian samples has shown that women who perceive that they live in a risky or uncertain environment are more likely to have an earlier age at menarche, first sex, and first birth. In Chisholm's life-history-based model, father absence during childhood is considered as one of a number of indicators that the environment is unstable, and is not itself the root cause of variation in age at maturity, with the root cause being variation in mortality risk. However, if environmental uncertainty includes food scarcity, reproductive maturity may not be reached at a very early age regardless of mortality risk (see Waynforth, 2001; Waynforth et al., 1998).

Stepparenting and Paternity

Stepparents have almost unerringly been vilified in works of fiction. While it is plausible that this is a culturally-based literary tradition, Canadian psychologists Margo Wilson and Martin Daly (e.g., Daly & Wilson, 1988; Wilson, Daly, & Weghorst, 1980) argued that the more likely cause is related to the proposition that humans evolved to maximize inclusive fitness: parenting another individual's child is wasted effort from a genetic viewpoint, and humans are likely to have evolved to limit their parental investment in unrelated children, in some circumstances to the point of serious neglect, abuse, or child homicide. Daly and Wilson studied police records to assess relative risk of child neglect, abuse, and homicide in U.S. and Canadian samples. Their (1988) data analyses showed in some samples a hundred-fold difference in the risk of abuse and of murder in homes with a step-parent present. The risk was particularly high for very young children. It should be noted that it is not necessarily the step-parent who perpetrates abuse, as a woman with an infant and a new partner who is not the father may decide to terminate investment in her current child.

While Daly and Wilson's work highlighted the risks to children of marital dissolution followed by remarriage, the flip side is that it is also possible that stepfathers will be devoted parents to the unrelated children in their household because this paternal care can act to support and cement the relationship between a mother and her new partner. In evolutionary terms, this behavior is parenting as male mating effort directed at the mother rather than for genetic benefits accrued through influencing the survival and success of related offspring. Kermyt Anderson analyzed data on paternal investment in the four possible father types: fathers who live with their biological children; fathers who do not live with their biological children due to separation from the mother; stepfathers living with children who are not their biological children; and stepfathers who are no longer living with their stepchildren due to separation from the mother of their stepchildren (Anderson, Kaplan, Lam, & Lancaster, 1999). It might be expected under kin selection theory that men will maintain more investment on average in their biologically related children after divorce than in a new partner's existing children. Anderson's et al.'s data collected on paternal involvement and spending showed that although men invest the most in their genetic children who live with them, they show significant investment in their step-children, and that this is best interpreted as mating effort with the new partner.

Stepfathers by definition are aware that they are parenting unrelated children, but the potential for female sexual infidelity means that a father will usually not be totally certain of biological paternity of his partner's children. Anderson (2006) compiled data from populations around the world on non-paternity rates determined using genetic testing. The majority of populations sampled were in Western industrialized nations, and the overall rate of nonpaternity (i.e., men rearing children that they believe are their own but are not) was quite low at around 2%. Data on hunter-gatherers and other small scale societies often show or suggest higher non-paternity rates, up to about 30% (e.g., see Hrdy, 2009). Some South American groups have cultural practices which take non-paternity risk into account and provide social roles for men who have had sex with a woman in the period broadly around the time of conception. This practice is known as secondary fatherhood, and secondary fathers typically provide less paternal investment than primary fathers (see Hill & Hurtado, 1996), but they do provide some childcare. In Ache hunter-gatherers in Paraguay, having one or more secondary fathers can benefit child survival because paternal investment is provided by two or more men: child survival is highest in the Ache for children with one secondary father in addition to a living primary father (Hill & Hurtado, 1996).

Because biological paternity is so important to men's reproductive success in that parenting children who are not genetic descendants is wasted effort from an evolutionary point of view (except in the case of stepfathering to gain sexual access to a woman with existing children), the ability to recognize biological children using various cues is a likely candidate for a human male evolved trait. Alvergne, Faurie, and Raymond (2009) studied levels of paternal involvement of Senegalese men in relation to visual and olfactory similarity between fathers and children. In the visual similarity experiments the researchers presented to raters facial photographs of a child with three adult male faces on the same page, one of which was of the (assumed) biological father. They collated these data to establish the degree of visual resemblance of the father to his child. Men who looked similar to their children provided more paternal investment, and similar results were found when Alvergne et al. analyzed the degree of similarity in smell between fathers and children. If visual and olfactory signals genuinely correlate closely with shared genes, then these cues allow men to direct paternal care at their genetic descendants.

Paternal Time Allocation

Behavioral biologists applying evolution to animal behavior have pursued the question of whether animals are able to allocate their food foraging time optimally, for example by switching from a depleting resource patch and traveling to a new patch at precisely the time that maximizes caloric gain. The ability to make optimal foraging decisions is likely to ultimately affect reproductive success through better nutrition or energy balance. Optimal time allocation should theoretically also be important for other time allocation decisions, including paternal care. For example, for a man providing direct childcare to his child, the opportunity costs of not pursuing alternate activities will increase the longer he spends caring for the child. At the same time, the benefits of caring for a child are likely to decrease with time as the child's needs are met, for example through feeding, cleaning or interacting with the child.

Frank Marlowe (1999) studied men's time allocation trade-off between mating and parenting in Hadza hunter-gatherers in Tanzania. He found that the more single women present in the hunter-gatherer camp, the less time men spent playing with their own young children. Men were also less likely to maintain physical proximity to their children or nurture them when more single or fertile women were in camp. This pattern is consistent with men shifting their time allocation towards mating effort and away from direct paternal care when it is evolutionarily optimal to do so, and is conceptually identical to switching foraging patches to a more productive area when the caloric returns to foraging decrease in the current patch to below what can be achieved in another location.

Mating effort will have higher returns for some men than it does for others. There are a number of potential reasons why, but often the difference is likely to be related to physical attractiveness. Lower mating success as a function of time spent seeking mating opportunities will affect the optimal amounts of time spent in each different activity such that, in general, men who are less attractive to women should spend less time seeking mating opportunities than more attractive men unless no mating access can be achieved at all (Waynforth, 1999, 2011). Waynforth (1999) studied Belizean Mayan men's time allocation to mating versus family (including fathering and spending time with relatives), and found that men who were rated as more facially attractive spent more of their leisure time seeking sexual access, and less time with family. Apicella and Marlowe (2007) reported similar results using men's self-perceived attractiveness as a predictor of mating effort.

Although some evolutionary psychologists have avoided arguments and research which might suggest that humans are general-purpose evolutionary fitness maximizers who are able to optimally allocate time among a wide range of activities (see arguments by Cosmides & Tooby, 1995; Tooby & Cosmides, 1989), the cognitive underpinnings of the ability to behave optimally in a wide range of circumstances may not require a level cognition that is biologically unrealistic. From a cognitive perspective, the ability to optimally allocate time among activities may require that reward systems in the brain are activated when a potentially high returns activity is being performed, such as foraging in a new and unexploited patch, or flirting with single women when there are eligible women in a hunter-gatherer camp. Also required is the ability to recognize diminishing benefits to an activity, and to be able to weigh the benefits of pursuing an alternate activity. These would need to map onto an evolved bias or propensity to want to engage in particular types of activity, such as hunting, or flirting, or childcare, more than less evolutionarily fitness-enhancing activities.

Bridges to Other Disciplines

One of the ways that evolutionary psychology and anthropology have progressed in the past is through incorporation of concepts from other disciplines. For example, evolutionary psychology has rapidly been incorporating life-history theory in biology. An example of this is the application of life-history theory to divergent reproductive strategies that result from being raised father absent, discussed above. One of the next major areas of attention is likely to be the field of epigenetics. In this section I will demonstrate its applicability to the question of effects of father absence, as understanding epigenetics may help researchers gain a more detailed picture of the potential mechanisms underlying divergent reproductive strategies.

The hormonal basis of some paternal behavior is beginning to be understood, for example testosterone levels appear to vary according to whether men are with a long-term sex partner, or are fathers: lower testosterone levels should bias men's behavior away from mating effort and are more consistent with parenting behavior, and in accord with this, lower testosterone levels tend to be found in married men and fathers (e.g., Burnham et al., 2003; Gray, Parkin, & Samms-Vaughn, 2007). In addition to hormonal and other physiological mechanisms involved in variation in paternal care, if it is evolved through evolutionary processes there must additionally be underlying genetic and epigenetic processes that create variation in reproductive strategies and male parenting.

Although the Genome Project has identified all of the genes present in human DNA, the genetic basis of human behavioral traits is largely unknown: a complete knowledge would require discovering the function of the more than 20,000 genes in the human genome, including how traits are influenced by multiple genes. In addition, genes are often expressed differently depending on environment encountered by the organism, resulting in different phenotypes being produced from a single genotype. Epigenetics is the field specializing in how the genotype can produce different phenotypes (expressions of the genotype) through exposure to environment, and it thus offers the underlying basis for understanding how father absence can result in differing ages at menarche and reproductive trajectories.

Belsky and colleagues (1991) described two distinct pathways which include father presence or absence and their associated reproductive trajectories. If the adaptation to father absence and risky environment genuinely has two options, in epigenetics it is called a polyphenism. Where there is a continuous range of possible phenotypes, the phenotypic plasticity is called a reaction norm (e.g., Stearns, de Jong, & Newman, 1991). The relationship between risky environment and reproductive development is presumably a reaction norm in humans.

Many polyphenisms are permanent once the developmental trajectory has begun: for example in Daphnia, mentioned earlier, reproduction begins earlier in the presence of predation, and these Daphnia additionally develop into a distinct physical morph that helps lower predation risk (see Adler & Harvell, 1990). This change is irreversible, but this is not the case for all polyphenisms. In ermine and other mammals that live in Arctic or sub-Arctic regions, an epigenetic switch sensitive to the angle of sunlight determines when the brown summer coat is shed and is replaced by a white winter coat, and vice versa in the spring. This epigenetic process is entirely reversible dependent on sunlight (Feder, 1990, in Gilbert & Epel, 2009). Menarche is an irreversible process, but many aspects of reproductive strategy, such as having short unstable marital relationships when the environment is unstable could potentially be reversible polyphenisms or reaction norms.

Genetic processes occur through gene mutation and natural or sexual selection subsequently favoring advantageous mutations. Epigenetics concerns which genetic traits are expressed, when they are expressed in the phenotype, and how strongly they are expressed. A key role in gene expression is played by the process of DNA methylation. Methylation prevents expression of genes in the gene transcription process, and has been demonstrated to be involved in behavioral differences which result from differences in parental care in rats. In a set of experiments (Weaver et al., 2004; 2007) studied methylation at the site for *Egr1* transcription factor in infant rats, which is not methylated at birth, but is methylated within about one day of birth. Infants of mothers who were licked intensively by their mother lost methylation at the site within a week of birth, whereas those not licked intensively after birth retained methylation. Retention of methylation at the site is associated the development of fewer glucocorticoid receptors, thus lack of maternal care (less licking) results in the development of different stress responses such that those who have received less care cope with stress less effectively.

Weaver et al.'s research (2004, 2007) has demonstrated how differences in parental care or environment can result in different development, and subsequently affect the adult phenotype. But how having fewer glucocorticoid receptors could be an evolutionarily adaptive response to harsh rearing environment is less clear. It is possible that what was observed was a phenotypic correlation: poor environmental conditions and/or a lower quality genotype resulted in less maternal care (in the form of licking), and as a consequence retention of methylation that would ordinarily have been lost in better conditions. Thus, what was observed in the experiments was the development of a disadvantageous trait (fewer glucocorticoid receptors). Father absence in Belsky et al.'s (1991) model of divergent reproductive strategies could similarly just result in the development of disadvantageous traits (early menarche, inability to maintain stable sexual relationships, etc.) that are not any more adaptive in harsh or unstable environments than the other pathway of later menarche and ability to form stable relationships. While early menarche in unstable conditions might result from a reaction norm or polyphenism similar to that observed in Daphnia and other species, we do not know whether having the early maturing phenotype offsets mortality risk sufficiently to offset some known disadvantages of early maturity, including smaller body size due to a shorter period of growth (which is usually disadvantageous to lifetime fertility; see earlier section and Hill & Hurtado, 1996).

Remarkably, epigenetic influence has been shown to be passed to the next generation through the both maternal and paternal lines. For example, methylation can be encouraged using diets rich in methyl donors, for example a folate-rich diet. When pregnant mice are fed methyl donors during pregnancy, the resulting pattern of methylation can be passed on directly to offspring, i.e., the state of the epigenetic switch is inherited (see Jirtle & Skinner, 2007). In this case metabolism and subsequent obesity are affected. This raises the possibility that father absent rearing conditions in humans could set off a response which persists for generations via epigenetic processes. On the other hand, human generation times are much longer than rat or mouse generation times, and one would perhaps expect there to be evolutionary selection pressure on producing adaptation to current breeding conditions rather than having our reproductive strategy set by an irreversible epigenetic switch during childhood: humans are a long-lived species who may experience significant changes in environment in a lifetime.

In summary, epigenetics may help to address a number of questions about offspring phenotypes that result from father absence and unstable environment including what kind of epigenetic process or switch is involved, whether it is partially reversible, what specific processes are involved at the molecular level (e.g., at which sites methylation is affected) and whether the phenotype can be inherited. On a broader scale, understanding human evolution and behavior at the molecular level represents a level of analysis which has only just begun to be explored, and alongside improving our understanding of physiological mechanisms such as hormonal precursors of behavior, the next few decades may produce far more comprehensive explanations for variation in human behavior.

Policy Implications

Like most social science disciplines, evolutionary anthropology and psychology are not primarily oriented towards producing social change or influencing public policy; they offer theoretical understanding of the origin and purpose of observed behavior and physiology. Despite this, there are a steadily growing number of applications to law, policy, health, and happiness, no doubt partly driven by pressure or requirements from funders of academic research and from governments for work carried out in universities to have obvious social and economic benefits. For the topic of father involvement, it is probably fair to make the assumption that marital relationship stability and father-present child rearing are the policy goals, and that public policy should be directed towards creating an environment in which these occur for the greatest number of individuals. In this section I will apply some current thinking in evolution to public policy pertinent to the goal of encouraging father involvement.

Paternal Leave From Work

As I write this chapter, the British government is considering extending paid paternal leave, and some European nations already have generous paternal leave policies in place. Anthropological research on men's time allocation suggests that fathers are not a particularly important category of childcare provider: in many societies female relatives such as grandmothers provide more childcare than fathers. Moreover, optimality approaches suggest that men may experience significant opportunity costs to pursuit of other activities (such as work) if they spend too much time providing direct care to infants. This implies that generous paternal leave policies may be wasted effort that will have low uptake if men are not biologically oriented towards infant care and do not maximize evolutionary fitness through high levels of time allocation to direct childcare. On the other hand, extended family networks have very often been broken in modern economies; a high proportion of individuals do not have grandmothers nearby to help contribute to the care of infants and children. Day-care facilities may alleviate this problem somewhat, but often must be paid for by families, and cannot offer the one-to-one care that grandmothers and other relatives could provide. Hewlett's (1991) work on Aka hunter-gatherer fathers suggests that fathers contribute more care to their infants when they do not have large or conveniently located extended family networks, and thus there is evidence that fathers willingly provide infant care when conditions favor it.

Second, optimality models of men's time allocation between mating and parenting effort show that men should vary in their propensity to provide direct childcare because the fitness returns to activities vary among individuals (Apicella & Marlowe, 2007; Waynforth, 1999). Paternal leave would allow men to freely allocate their time among activities, and, for some, would fulfill their desire to provide substantial levels of direct childcare, and as such would allow men to meet their evolutionarily-driven time allocation desires. But if the income lost due to paternal leave is too great, then uptake of optional paternal leave schemes will be low, as it will in essence be a removal of fathers from another evolutionarily relevant key part of their parental role of providing resources. Reducing the opportunity costs of lost income should go a long way towards encouraging men to take paternity leave, and there is recent evidence from changes to Norwegian paternity leave policy which suggests that this is the case (Rege & Solli, 2010).

Workplace Equality

Paternal care is likely to be influenced by a wide variety of government policies in addition to those specifically formulated to encourage paternal involvement. Policies aimed at equality in the workplace are one such area. Hunter-gatherers and other subsistence economies have division of labor which creates interdependency of the sexes. The advent of workplace equality in modern industrialized nations eliminates division of labor and interdependency of the sexes, and allows women the ability to raise offspring without the financial contribution of a husband. There are other societies in which mothers do not necessarily require paternal financial help, and Sear and Mace's (2008) cross-cultural review of kin effects on child survival shows that fathers do not influence child survival in around half of subsistence-level societies.

If paternal help is not required for child survival in part due to implementation of policies requiring workplace equality (on top of other evolutionarily novel reasons, such as effects of modern medicine on child survival), then why do so many men fulfill their paternal care duties? An important part of the answer may be related to the fundamental trade-off between quantity and quality of offspring produced. This trade-off was first noted by the biologist David Lack (1947), who discovered that in birds, intermediate clutch sizes usually maximize parental reproductive success: providing more care and resources for a smaller number of offspring than the physiological maximum number that can be produced results in offspring that are more likely to survive and reproduce (also see Stearns, 1992).

Building on the concept of optimal clutch size, Kaplan (1996) proposed that humans respond to the benefits of parental care in their particular environment. His argument is that the shape of the relationship between parental investment and offspring outcomes (offspring income in his model) differs depending on context. In most hunter-gatherer societies there is a diminishing relationship between parental time invested in caring for children and children's survival and success: at some point a child has been adequately nurtured such that additional care will not improve their chances of survival or affect their ability to hunt or gather successfully. Kaplan argued that in modern industrialized economies with advancing technology, the benefits to children of each unit of parental investment do not decline, and parents respond to this by heavily investing in a few children. This requires being able to perceive that placing a large amount of parental investment in a few offspring is the optimal strategy in our particular environment, for example by being able to see that nurturing a child closely then working to get them into the best possible schools, etc., produces the most viable and successful offspring.

Put into the context of father involvement, in modern economies the mother requires paternal involvement to maximize the chances of offspring success in a competitive labor market. Hence, we do not see declining paternal involvement with increasing maternal financial independence. We perhaps might only see a decline in paternal involvement if all children received and exploited the same educational opportunities regardless of social class and other social factors. In this case there would be no benefit of paternal investment to future offspring income.

In summary, evolutionary arguments are clearly relevant to public policy issues in father involvement, but using evolutionary theories to predict how men will respond to changes in public policy is a difficult task that requires thinking about a much wider range of policies than simply those directly connected to father involvement. For example, as discussed above, workplace equality should theoretically affect paternal involvement in combination with other variables related to parenting, including equality in educational opportunities.

Future Directions

I introduced this chapter with the statement that paternal involvement in humans consists of an evolved set of behaviors, and as such, evolutionary approaches can help us to understand and predict paternal behavior at individual and group or societal levels. Evolved behaviors are often thought of outside of biology as genetically predetermined and unchangeable. However, as I have discussed here, within the field of human evolutionary science, many researchers have focused on how environment influences behavior via the evolution of reaction norms or polyphenisms. In addition, physiological mechanisms which appear to help to regulate paternal care have begun to be explored in studies using human participants, such as work suggesting that the down-regulation of testosterone in fathers helps support paternal involvement in part by reducing motivation for continued mating effort in fathers (Burnham et al., 2003; Gray et al., 2007). With increased understanding of evolved physiological mechanisms, underlying paternal care, and the nascent understanding of epigenetic processes that underlie how variability in environment can produce different adaptive behavioral and morphological responses, evolutionary approaches offer an increasingly sophisticated and useful framework for understanding the roles of fathers.

References

Adler, F., & Harvell, C. (1990). Inducible defences, phenotypic variability, and biotic environments. *Trends in Ecology and Evolution, 5,* 407–410.

Alvergne, A., Faurie, C., & Raymond, M. (2009) Father-offspring resemblance predicts paternal investment in humans. *Animal Behaviour, 78,* 61–69.

Anderson, K. G. (2006). How well does paternity confidence match actual paternity? Evidence from worldwide nonpaternity rates. *Current Anthropology, 48,* 511–518.

Anderson, K. G., Kaplan, H., Lam, D., & Lancaster, J. (1999). Paternal care by genetic fathers and stepfathers II: reports from Xhosa school children. *Evolution and Human Behavior, 20,* 433–451.

Apicella C., & Marlowe F. (2007). Men's reproductive investment decisions: Mating, parenting, and self-perceived mate value. *Human Nature 18,* 22–34.

Belsky, J., Steinberg, L., & Draper, P. (1991). Childhood experience, interpersonal development, and reproductive strategy: An evolutionary theory of socialization. *Child Development, 62,* 647–670.

Burnham, T., Chapman, J., Gray, P., MacIntyre, M., Lipson, S., & Ellison, P. (2003). Men in committed, romantic relationships have lower testosterone. *Hormones and Behavior, 4,* 119–122.

Chisholm, J. (1999a). Attachment and time preference: relations between early stress and sexual behavior in a sample of American university women. *Human Nature, 10,* 51–83.

Chisholm, J. (1999b). *Death, hope and sex: Steps to an evolutionary ecology of mind and morality.* Cambridge, UK: Cambridge University Press.

Chisholm, J., Quinlivan, J., Petersen, R., & Coall, D. (2005). Early stress predicts age at menarche and first birth, adult attachment and expected lifespan. *Human Nature,16,* 233–265.

Cosmides, L., & Tooby, J. (1995). From function to structure: the role of evolutionary biology and computational theories in cognitive neuroscience. In M. Gazzaniga (Ed.), *The cognitive neurosciences* (pp. 1199–1210). Cambridge MA: MIT Press.

Daly, M., & Wilson M. (1988). *Homicide.* Hawthorne, NY: Aldine de Gruyter.

Draper, P., & Harpending, H. (1982). Father absence and reproductive strategy: an evolutionary perspective. *Journal of Anthropological Research, 38,* 255–279.

Ellis, B. J., McFadyen-Ketchum, S., Dodge, K., Pettit, G., & Bates, J. (1999). Quality of early family relationships and individual differences in the timing of pubertal maturation in girls: a longitudinal test of an evolutionary model. *Journal of Personality and Social Psychology, 77,* 387–401.

Gettler, L. T. (2010). Direct male care and hominin evolution: Why male-child interaction is more than a nice social idea. *American Anthropologist, 112,* 7–21.

Gilbert, S., & Epel, D. (2009). *Ecological developmental biology: Integrating epigenetics, medicine and evolution.* Sunderland MA: Sinauer Associates.

Gray, P., Parkin, J., & Samms-Vaughn, M. (2007). Hormonal correlates of human paternal interactions: a hospital-based investigation in urban Jamaica. *Hormones and Behavior, 52,* 499–507.

Hamilton, W. J. (1984). Significance of paternal investment by primates to the evolution of male-female associations. In D. M. Taub (Ed.), *Primate paternalism* (pp. 309–335). New York: Van Nostrand Reinhold.

Hewlett, B. S. (1991). *Intimate fathers: The nature and context of Aka Pygmy paternal infant care.* Ann Arbor: University of Michigan Press.

Hill, K. R., & Hurtado, A. M. (1996). *Ache life history: The ecology and demography of a foraging people.* New York: Aldine de Gruyter.

Hrdy, S. (2009). *Mothers and others: The evolutionary origins of mutual understanding.* Cambridge: Harvard University Press.

Jirtle, R., & Skinner, M. (2007). Environmental epigenomics and disease susceptibility. *Nature Reviews Genetics, 8,* 253–264.

Kaplan, H. (1996). A theory of fertility and parental investment in traditional and modern human societies. *Yearbook of Physical Anthropology, 39,* 91–135.

Lack, D. (1947). The significance of clutch size. *Ibis, 89,* 302–352.

Lancaster, J. B., & Lancaster, C. S. (1983). Parental Investment: The hominid adaptation. In D. J. Ortner (Ed.), *How humans adapt: A biocultural odyssey* (pp. 33–66). Washington, DC: Smithsonian Institution Press.

Lovejoy, C. O. (1981). The origin of man. *Science, 211,* 341–350.

Marlowe, F. (1999). Male care and mating effort among Hadza foragers. *Behavioral Ecology and Sociobiology, 46,* 57–64.

Maynard Smith, J. (1977). Parental investment: a prospective analysis. *Animal Behaviour, 25,* 1–9.

Nettle, D., Coall, D., & Dickins, T. (2010). Birthweight and paternal involvement predict early reproduction in British women: evidence from the National Child Development Study. *American Journal of Human Biology, 22,* 172–179.

Rege, M., & Solli, I. F. (2010). The impact of paternity leave on father long-term involvement. CESifo Working Paper Series No. 3130. Retrieved from SSRN, http://ssrn.com/abstract=1649344

Sear, R., & Mace, R. (2008). Who keeps children alive? A review of the effects of kin on child survival. *Evolution and Human Behavior, 29,* 1–18.

Stearns, S. (1992). *The evolution of life histories.* Oxford, UK: Oxford University Press.

Stearns, S., de Jong, G., & Newman, R. (1991). The effects of phenotypic plasticity on genetic correlations. *Trends in Ecology and Evolution, 6,* 122–126.

Stibor, H. (1992). Predator induced life-history shifts in a freshwater cladoceran. *Oecologia, 92,* 162–165.

Tooby, J., & Cosmides, L. (1989). Evolutionary psychologists need to distinguish between the evolutionary process, ancestral selection pressures, and psychological mechanisms. *Behavioral and Brain Sciences, 12,* 724–725.

Waynforth, D. (1999). Differences in time use for mating and nepotistic effort as a function of male attractiveness in rural Belize. *Evolution and Human Behavior, 20,* 19–28.

Waynforth, D. (2001). Mate-choice trade-offs and women's preference for physically attractive men. *Human Nature 12,* 207–220.

Waynforth, D. (2011). Mate choice and sexual selection. In V. Swami (Ed.), *Evolutionary psychology: A critical introduction* (pp. 107–126). Chichester UK: BPS Blackwell.

Waynforth, D., Hurtado, M., & Hill, K. (1998). Environmentally contingent reproductive strategies in Mayan and Ache Males. *Evolution and Human Behavior, 19,* 369–385.

Wilson, M., Daly, M., & Weghorst, S. (1980). Household composition and the risk of child abuse and neglect. *Journal of Biosocial Science, 12,* 333–340.

Weaver, I., D'Alessio, A., Brown, S., Hellstrom, I., Dymov, S., & Sharma, S. (2007). The transcription factor nerve growth factor-inducible protein A mediates epigenetic programming: altering epigenetic marks by immediate-early genes. *Journal of Neuroscience, 27,* 1756–1768.

Weaver, I., Cervoni, N., Champagne, F., D'Alessio, A., Sharma, S., & Seckl, J. R. (2004). Epigenetic programming by maternal behaviour. *Nature Neuroscience, 7,* 847–854.

Chapter 3

Fathering in Non-Human Primates

Karen L. Bales and Michael R. Jarcho

University of California, Davis and California National Primate Research Center

Human males display large amounts of variation in the quantity and quality of their contributions to infant care. Variation in these contributions is known to influence biological (Ellis, 2004; Ellis, Figueredo, Brumbach, & Schlomer, 2009; Tither & Ellis, 2010) and social Paschall, Ringwalt, & Flewelling, 2003; Pfiffner, McBurnett, & Rathouz, 2001) development in offspring (also see Parke, this volume). An obvious place to examine the social and biological bases of this variation is in non-human primates, our closest evolutionary relatives.

Historical Overview and Theoretical Perspectives

Monogamy and the Evolution of Biparental Care

From a taxonomic perspective, the occurrence of male parenting behavior in non-human primates is closely associated, but not completely confounded, with the occurrence of social monogamy. Social monogamy in primates is characterized by group structure consisting of a mated male and female, sometimes with associated offspring (Fuentes, 1999; Kleiman, 1977). Although the male of the pair usually fathers a large proportion of the female's offspring, mating exclusivity is not essential for this definition, and extra-pair copulations can occur. In addition to fathering, traits which may be found in monogamous species include alloparenting (in which older offspring care for younger offspring), delayed maturation or even suppression of young, and low sexual dimorphism (Kleiman, 1977); however, not all of these traits are found in all species considered monogamous. Sociobiological theory predicts that paternal behavior will evolve where parental certainty is high (Wilson, 1975). In certain species (e.g., hamadryas baboons) the mechanism driving this parental certainty is the fact that a single dominant male monopolizes the mating. This social structure, however, is clearly not monogamous. Another mechanism by which monogamy can evolve is in situations where females are unable to raise infants alone, but in which the habitat does not support the cohabitation of multiple females on the same territory (Kleiman, 1977). In this case, paternal care is obligate for the survival of his offspring (Westneat & Sherman, 1993). New World monkey species exhibiting paternal care

37

tend to have a very high offspring-maternal weight ratio, supporting this hypothesis (Kleiman, 1985). This increased offspring size is hypothesized to create a larger burden for a single parent which results in obligate biparental care.

In non-human primates, social monogamy primarily occurs in the New World monkeys, including owl monkeys (*Aotus spp.*), titi monkeys (*Callicebus spp.*), and saki monkeys (*Pithecia spp.*). These species contrast in the level to which males are involved in infant care, with owl and titi monkeys displaying high levels of care and saki males not displaying infant care. In contrast, New World marmoset and tamarins (family Callitrichidae), which display high levels of male care, exhibit flexible social systems which can be characterized as monogamy, polygyny (multiple females mating with a single male), or polyandry (multiple males mating with a single female) both within and across species (Albuquerque, Sousa, Santos, & Ziegler, 2001; Baker, Bales, & Dietz, 2002; Baker, Dietz, & Kleiman, 1993; Dietz & Baker, 1993; Goldizen, 1987, 1989; Goldizen, Mendelson, Van Vlaardingen, & Terborgh, 1996). No Old World monkeys display significant levels of fathering behavior, while the only apes to do so are the siamangs (*Symphalangus syndactylus*), which may display social monogamy or polyandry (Lappan, 2008; Palombit, 1995).

Summary of Non-human Primate Taxa in Which Fathering Occurs

Titi monkeys.   Titi monkeys are small, arboreal New World monkeys that have been extensively studied as to their pair-bond relationships (Cubiciotti & Mason, 1975; Mason, 1966, 1974; Mendoza & Mason, 1997). Titi monkey fathers (Figure 3.1) are the primary infant-carriers, in most pairs carrying infants up to 90% of the time (Mendoza & Mason, 1986). As such, infants develop an emotional attachment to their father rather than their mother (Hoffman, Mendoza, Hennessy, & Mason, 1995), including an exaggerated stress response during separation from their father. Males, on the other hand, display their primary attachment to their pair-mate, and do not experience a rise in stress hormones if their infant is removed from the group (Mendoza, 1991; Mendoza & Mason, 1997).

Titi monkey fathers respond to distress calls from their infants (Mason & Mendoza, 1998) and are tolerant of infant contact, usually carrying the infant transversely across their necks. However, titi monkeys of any sex or age class do not appear to be attracted to infants (Mendoza & Mason, 1986; Welker, Jantschke, & Klaiber-Schuh, 1998) and become hyper-responsive to stressful stimuli when there are small infants in the group (Reeder, 2001). Many mothers are only motivated to retrieve infants from the father in order to nurse them (and thus relieve pressure from full mammaries). During early development, titi monkey infants must learn to navigate relatively independently between their father and mother; however, this navigation is facilitated by the large proportion of time that the adult pair-mates spend in contact with each other (Mendoza & Mason, 1986).

When titi infants begin to eat solid food, both parents share food with their offspring. There is no display of active food-sharing as has been demonstrated in some tamarin species (Addessi, Chiarotti, Visalberghi, & Anzenberger, 2007; Joyce & Snowdon, 2007; Ruiz-Miranda et al., 1999); however, infants take food both from their parents' hands and through direct mouth-to-mouth contact, often without any resistance. Males also groom infants and juveniles; a report on one family of wild *Callicebus torquatus* found that the parents spent equal amounts of time grooming the two juveniles, and the juveniles received more grooming than they gave to the

FIGURE 3.1 A titi monkey father carries an infant (approximately 3 months old). Photo: Kathy West/California National Primate Research Center (used with permission).

parents (Kinzey & Wright, 1982). Most reports suggest that older offspring do not contribute significant amounts to infant care in titi monkeys, at least not on a regular basis (Mendoza & Mason, 1986); however, observations in an extant colony found large amounts of variability in this measure (Bales, Dietz, Baker, Mason, & Mendoza, 2007).

Owl monkeys.   Owl monkeys closely resemble titi monkeys in many aspects of their social system, including maintenance of a common territory and the presence of older offspring in the group (Wright, 1994). Owl monkey fathers are also the primary carriers of their offspring, and the most attractive member of the group to other family members (Welker et al., 1998), although there are several significant differences in behavior between owl monkeys and titi monkeys. While titi monkey fathers often carry their infants from the first day of life, owl monkey fathers typically do not begin carrying until week three (Welker et al., 1998; Welker & Schafer-Witt, 1987). In addition, while titi monkey fathers carry infants transversely across the neck, owl monkey fathers usually carry infants ventrally in a way such that they are covered by the thigh. When carried on the back, the infants are carried longitudinally (Welker & Schafer-Witt, 1987).

Owl monkey siblings only rarely carry infants (Welker & Schafer-Witt, 1987). However, an infant owl monkey was reared without a father in a captive group (Jantschke, Welker, & Klaiber-Schuh, 1998). While the mother's carrying did not decrease, the lack of the male was primarily made up by the increased involvement of an older female sibling. However, the infant was completely independent of carriers much earlier than normal (three months), probably due to lower tolerance of the sibling carrier when compared to the father. Infant care by older siblings was also observed during the replacement of an adult male in a wild owl monkey group

(Fernandez-Duque, Juarez, & Di Fiore, 2008). After the new male was established in the group, he began to care for the infant as well; however, the infant disappeared at four months of age and was presumed dead, perhaps suggesting that its care was sub-optimal.

Another difference observed between owl monkeys and titi monkeys, in a colony which raised both species for decades, was that titi monkeys were more tolerant of their offspring and displayed aggressive behavior towards them much more rarely (Welker et al., 1998).

Owl monkeys also display food sharing both in captivity (Wolovich, Feged, Evans, & Green, 2006) and in the wild (Wolovich, Perea-Rodriguez, & Fernandez-Duque, 2008). In both captive and wild monkeys, the father is the primary sharer with offspring (Wolovich et al., 2008; Wolovich et al., 2006). In captive owl monkeys (Wolovich et al., 2006), at least some of the transfers from males to offspring are initiated by the male rather than the offspring.

Marmosets and tamarins.   Marmosets and tamarins (family Callitrichidae) are small-bodied, arboreal Central and South American monkeys which produce twins approximately 80% of births in the wild (Bales, O'Herron, Baker, & Dietz, 2001; Savage et al., 1997) and even larger litter sizes in captivity (Jaquish, Gage, & Tardif, 1991; Jaquish, Cheverud, & Tardif, 1996; Tardif & Jaquish, 1997; Tardif, Layne, & Smucny, 2002). Because they experience a fertile post-partum estrus (Hearn, 1983), females can give birth to two litters per year, and are therefore sometimes lactating and pregnant simultaneously. This is presumably a rather large energy expenditure, and requires help from other family members to maintain the high reproductive rate.

Males contribute to infant care both by carrying infants and by sharing food (Epple, 1975; Ruiz-Miranda et al., 1999; Tardif, 1994; Tardif, Carson, & Gangaware, 1990). In the wild, males contribute more care to infants which are more closely related, such as full siblings or those for which they have higher paternity certainty (Baker, 1991). The number of adult males predicts infant survivorship in wild golden lion tamarins, particularly in newly formed groups (Bales, Dietz, Baker, Miller, & Tardif, 2000). Alloparenting is very common in marmosets and tamarins (Tardif, 1997), and breeding males often reduce their contribution to infant care when helpers are available (Bales et al., 2000). In wild golden lion tamarins, breeding males which have more helpers also have longer reproductive tenures (the same is not true for females who have more helpers) (Bales et al., 2000).

Significant variations do exist between callitrichid species in the details of infant care behaviors; these are reviewed in detail elsewhere (Tardif, 1994; Tardif et al., 2002; Tardif & Garber, 1994; Tardif, Harrison, & Simek, 1987; Welker & Schafer-Witt, 1987). Perhaps one of the most interesting comparison species is *Callimico goeldii*, common name Goeldi's monkey. While closely related to the marmosets and tamarins, Goeldi's monkeys give birth only to one offspring per litter instead of twins. The father starts carrying the infant much later when compared to marmoset and tamarin species (Schradin & Anzenberger, 2001; Schradin & Anzenberger, 2003; Porter & Garber, 2009).

Siamangs and gibbons.   Siamangs and gibbons are the only apes which demonstrate a monogamous social system (Fuentes, 1999), although it can also be polyandrous in some cases (Lappan, 2008). Despite the characterization of gibbons as monogamous, they have not been reported to display significant amounts of male care (Lappan, 2008). In contrast, male siamangs often carry infants (Chivers, 1974; Dielenthis, Zaiss, & Geissman, 1991; Lappan, 2008), particularly older infants in the second year of life (Chivers, 1974; Lappan, 2008, 2009). Juvenile males also sleep with the adult male after the birth of a new infant in the group (Dielenthis et al., 1991; Lappan, 2008), while the mother and infant sleep together in a different place. Infants in monogamous groups received more care by adult males than infants in polyandrous groups, even when carrying by both males was summed (Lappan, 2008). Male care in polyandrous groups did not appear to be positively correlated with the male's affiliative relationship with the mother (Lappan, 2008). Care by males did reduce the carrying by the mother (Lappan, 2008), and mothers providing more care had longer interbirth intervals, suggesting that male care may increase successful female reproduction. Care by juveniles is not common but was noted in a zoo in which twins were born (Dielenthis et al., 1991), where a juvenile male was sometimes noted to carry one of the twins.

Summary

Monogamy in primates is hypothesized to be an evolutionary solution to the problem of increasing infant to mother weight ratios, as exemplified by many New World callitrichid species. Indeed, several of the species that have the highest infant to mother weight ratios are the same species that engage in some degree of paternal care and exhibit a monogamous social system. Monogamy has been observed in titi monkeys (*Callicebus*), owl monkeys (*Aotus*), marmosets and tamarins (Family: Callitrichidae), and siamangs (*Symphalangus*). In most of these species, paternal care is common, and is usually expressed through paternal carrying of infants and food sharing. However, monogamy is not always the social system employed by all of these species, and even in those cases in which monogamy is employed, it is not always accompanied by paternal care.

Current Research Questions

Factors Affecting Expression of Fathering in Non-human Primates

How and why do we see variation in components of male parenting across species? Why do we see individual variation in components of male parenting within species? It is important to distinguish all of the factors which can impact the demonstration of male care. These include attraction to infants, motivation to interact with infants, tolerance of infants, and actual demonstration of male parenting behavior such as carrying or sharing food. These factors can vary between species with male care and within species according to other factors such as the age or prior experience of a male, either as a parent or as an alloparent.

Hormonal Bases of Fathering in Non-human Primates

What are the hormonal mechanisms for male parenting? Do male primate care-givers suppress testosterone during periods of care? If so, how do they suppress testosterone while (in some species) simultaneously mating with their pair-mate during her postpartum estrus? One of the most active areas of research on male care is the search for hormonal mechanisms. Testosterone, due to its well-known association with aggression, is usually hypothesized to be negatively associated with male care (Gray & Campbell, 2009; Wingfield, Hegner, Duffy Jr., & Ball, 1990). Hormones associated with female parenting, such as prolactin, estrogen, and oxytocin, have also been hypothesized to be positively associated with male care.

Neurobiological Bases of Fathering in Non-human Primates

What areas of the brain are involved in male parenting? Are these the same as the areas involved in female parenting? What neurotransmitters and receptor systems facilitate male care? While hormonal samples are relatively easy to obtain in saliva, blood, urine, or feces (see section 3b), the neurobiological study of male care is much more difficult to perform in non-invasive, non-terminal studies. Terminal studies of male parenting are relatively rare in non-human primates. The advent of imaging technologies such as positron emission tomography (PET) and functional magnetic resonance imaging (fMRI) have opened up this area of study.

Contributions of Fathers in Non-monogamous Species

What are the species and proximate circumstances in which this occurs? Although this chapter has focused on males of monogamous species that provide what (in some cases) may be care which is required for infant survival, males of other species may occasionally exhibit infant care.

Research Measures and Methodology

In studying paternal behavior, the starting point is observation and analysis of those behaviors performed by the father that are believed to be critical to the survival of his offspring. The exact behaviors that are performed may vary significantly depending on the species; as described earlier, infant care in male primates consists primarily of carrying and food-sharing with infants. In the following sections, we discuss the methodology of conducting observational research and both traditional and more recent methods of investigating the mechanisms driving behavior.

Behavioral Data Collection

Many considerations may affect behavioral data collection including whether data are from a captive colony or wild primates, what type of sampling is being done (focal, ad libitum, scan, etc.), and reliability of observers.

Captive vs. field.   Researchers with captive colonies have extensive control over environmental factors including the temperature of their colony, the number of hours of light and dark each day, the timing of feeding, etc. They also have the convenience of always knowing where the subjects are located, and with daily health checks, they are immediately notified of any new births in the colony. All of these factors make observing any behavior, including paternal behaviors, more predictable and convenient. However, several behaviors exhibited in the wild are seemingly absent when animals are housed in captivity. For example, most primate species are highly social animals in their natural environments and maintain relationships with dozens of other conspecifics (Altmann, 1965). However, many nonhuman primate housing facilities have animals housed individually or in small groups (Schapiro, 2000). In many cases, this housing situation might limit the social behavior that a given animal encounters from other individuals and engages in itself. In addition, the physical dimensions might limit the types of behaviors that an individual can engage in. Therefore, capturing the full spectrum of a species' behavioral repertoire often requires observation in the species' natural environment.

Behavioral sampling. There are several possible behavioral sampling methods, each of which is ideal for addressing a certain type of research question. The type of behavioral sampling employed by a researcher should be chosen in order to optimize the ability of the observational data to address the research question. Potential sampling methods include *ad libitum* sampling, focal animal sampling, all occurrences sampling, one-zero sampling, and instantaneous or scan sampling (Altmann, 1974).

Inter-observer reliability. Most current behavioral research is conducted in a collaborative fashion, with multiple observers and multiple people scoring different behaviors of interest. Given this, some attention must be paid to consistency between observers. Inter-observer (a.k.a. inter-rater) reliability quantifies accuracy between observers. When working with discrete variables, inter-observer reliability can be calculated simply by dividing the number of observations that are agreed upon between observers by the total number of observations (Gwet, 2008).

Hormonal Data Collection

Peripheral and central hormones provide potential mechanisms affecting paternal behaviors. While central neurotransmitters are more directly tied to behavior, sampling these substances requires more invasive techniques and may not be possible in certain circumstances. Peripheral hormone concentrations can be measured through analysis of urine, fecal, or blood samples, but the relevance of these measures depends on the hormone being sampled. The benefits and consequences of the type of samples collected, and several other variables concerning hormonal sampling will be discussed further in the following sections.

Sample type. Different sample types can be useful in answering different questions, and can be more or less feasible to collect depending on several other factors. For example, as mentioned above, central measurements of neurotransmitter concentrations may not be feasible if a researcher is observing animals in their natural environments. Cerebrospinal fluid (CSF) may be used to measure neurotransmitters and/or their metabolites, but obtaining CSF is possible only after immobilizing the animal. It is an invasive technique and requires anesthesia. So while central concentrations are the most direct link to behavior, they are not always feasible.

Another measure is through the plasma component of peripheral blood. Many of the hormones that are thought to play critical roles in behavior are produced peripherally and have centrally located receptors. For example, anxiety-like traits are often correlated with glucocorticoids produced by the adrenal glands, which have receptors in the central nervous system (Capitanio, Mendoza, & Bentson, 2004). Feeding behaviors are influenced by insulin produced by the pancreas (Rodin, Wack, Ferrannini, & DeFronzo, 1985). Reproductive behaviors are influenced by concentrations of the steroid hormones testosterone (produced in the testes) (Crews, Traina, Wetzel, & Muller, 1978) and estrogen (produced in the ovaries) (Brawer, Naftolin, Martin, & Sonneschein, 1978). Blood samples represent internal conditions over a very short time period (i.e. seconds to minutes). Obtaining blood samples is a common technique for sampling hormone concentrations in both laboratory and wild studies of nonhuman primates (Coe, Mendoza, Smotherman, & Levine, 1978; Hennessy, Mendoza, & Kaplan, 1982; Sapolsky, 1985; Sapolsky & Krey, 1988). In order to reduce the stress of plasma sampling, some nonhuman primate subjects have been trained to present an arm for obtaining a blood sample (Phillippi-Falkenstein & Clarke, 1992; Reinhardt, 1991).

Many hormones are excreted in the body's waste. Importantly, the concentrations that are excreted are typically correlated to the concentrations of the active hormones in the blood. The benefit of sampling urine or feces is that they are the least invasive methods of obtaining hormonal information. For this reason, these methods are commonly used in field studies (Lynch, Ziegler, & Strier, 2002; Weingrill, Gray, Barrett, & Henzi, 2004). In addition, labs conducting long-term hormonal monitoring on many animals (Altmann, Gesquiere, Galbany, Onyango, & Alberts, 2010) often use one of these sampling methods because they allow a single researcher to collect samples from multiple animals in a relatively short time. Hormone concentrations from urine or fecal samples are summed over a relatively long time period (i.e., hours). For example, the hormone concentration in a morning urine sample represents the internal hormone state over the course of the previous night (Munro et al., 1991). For this reason, the types of questions that can be answered with urine samples are different than those that can be answered with blood samples.

A more recently developed method of obtaining estimates of hormone concentrations is through hair samples. Because hair grows at a fairly slow rate, the hormones estimated from hair samples represent concentrations averaged over the entire length that the hair was present on the animal's body. One method that has been employed in order to narrow the temporal window represented in a given hair sample is shaving the area to be sampled ahead of time, then allowing a certain amount of time (weeks to months) to pass before collecting the hair that has grown in the shaved area (Davenport, Tiefenbacher, Lutz, Novak, & Meyer, 2006).

Imaging

With the advent of non-invasive imaging, it has become much easier to study brain activity in both humans and in non-human primates. However, until now it has been little used to address the question of fathering in non-human primates, but more so actually in humans (Seifritz et al., 2003; Swain, 2008; Swain, Lorberbaum, Kose, & Strathearn, 2007). Most important is the choice of the proper imaging technology. While functional MRI provides superior temporal resolution, position emission tomography (PET) has the advantage of being able to image many different radio-tracers, as well as allowing the subject animal to be unconscious in the scanner (Bandettini, 2009; Otte & Halsband, 2006). The brain activity measured during the scan, however, reflects the uptake period for the radioactive ligand, during which the animal was unrestrained and freely behaving. This can remove the confounding effects of stress on brain metabolism.

Summary of Research Measures and Methodology

Several methods for studying monogamy and paternal behavior exist. Selection of a certain methodology by investigators should be done carefully in order to avoid using a method that is flawed, outdated, or inappropriate. The research measures should be selected so that they can appropriately answer the specific research question(s) being posed by the investigator. Once a methodology is selected, it is critical that the investigator becomes familiar with the inherent limitations of their methods in order to avoid making inaccurate conclusions.

Empirical Findings

Factors Affecting Expression of Fathering in Non-human Primates

As discussed previously, species may vary in how attractive infants are to males, males' levels of responsiveness, and the full expression of male parental care (Pryce, 1996). For instance, male titi monkeys are only tolerant of, not attracted to infants (Mendoza & Mason, 1986), but carry infants extensively due to the intolerance of females. In contrast, male common marmosets (Zahed, Prudom, Snowdon, & Ziegler, 2007) are strongly attracted to infant cries and motivated to carry infants, whether the cry is coming from their own infant, a strange infant, or an iPod playing infant recordings.

Even within species in which paternal care is the norm, there is still substantial variation in male parenting, and there may be several factors that affect the likelihood that an individual will exhibit paternal care. Experience, either with his own infants or as an alloparent may contribute significantly to whether a male will exhibit paternal behaviors towards his offspring (Ziegler, 2009). Male common marmosets that had experience with their own infants responded with lower latencies to infant stimuli, whether familiar or unfamiliar (Zahed et al., 2007). In titi monkeys, infants born to parents with previous experience with their own infants had significantly higher survival; within experienced parents, it did not matter if they were wild-born or laboratory-born or how many previous litters they had raised (Reeder, 2001).

The effects of experience are often modulated hormonally (see the next section). While juvenile experience with siblings and adult experience as a father may explain some of the individual variation in behavior, it is notable that alloparenting itself is extremely variable both between and within species. In studies of marmosets and tamarins, sex differences in alloparenting are inconsistent, suggesting other sources of individual variation (Bales et al., 2000). It is possible that paternal style will turn out to be highly influenced by the style of fathering received as an infant, as has been shown for mothering in various species (Francis, Diorio, Liu, & Meaney, 1999) and for fathering in monogamous prairie voles, *Microtus ochrogaster* (Stone & Bales, 2010), and California mice, *Peromyscus californicus* (Bester-Meredith & Marler, 2003).

Hormonal Basis of Fathering in Non-human Primates

Prolactin (PRL) is a peptide hormone that in females is critical for milk production during lactation (Freeman, Kanyicksa, Lerant, & Nagy, 2000) and is involved in the onset and maintenance of maternal behavioral care of infants (Wynne-Edwards & Timonin, 2007). In males, PRL has been implicated in paternal behavior in taxa that are characterized by biparental care including rodents, non-human primates, and humans (Schradin, Reeder, Mendoza, & Anzenberger, 2003; Wynne-Edwards, 2001; Ziegler & Snowdon, 1997a), however the data linking PRL with paternal behavior remain somewhat equivocal. Essentially, species vary as to whether males experience rises in PRL around the birth of infants, and whether they experience acute rises when carrying infants.

Reduced testosterone has been associated with paternal care in two nonhuman primate species: cotton-top tamarins (*Saguinus oedipus*; Ziegler, Wegner, & Snowdon, 1996) and black tufted-ear marmosets (*Callithrix kuhlii*; Nunes, Fite, Patera, & French, 2001). In the marmosets, high-carrying effort males showed not only reduced testosterone, but also reduced estradiol and reduced cortisol in comparison to non-father males of the same age and with similar numbers of previous litters. This suggests that something about the presence of new offspring is responsible for the reduced testosterone. In black-tufted-ear marmosets, the number of previous litters that a male had cared for (either as a sibling or as a father) significantly predicted his urinary testosterone concentrations (Nunes, Fite, & French, 2000). Perhaps most interesting is that experienced marmoset fathers show a reduction in testosterone when exposed to the scent of their own infant (Prudom et al., 2008).

Cortisol in some primate males also appears to respond to the birth of their own offspring. However, the direction of the response is not consistent. For example, cotton-top tamarin males with female partners at mid-gestation show increased cortisol concentrations (Almond, Ziegler, & Snowdon, 2008). However, Ziegler and colleagues (1996) showed that in the same species postpartum cortisol levels are lower in experienced males than they were in first-time fathers. In another biparental primate, the black tufted-ear marmoset fathers that were categorized as displaying "high carrying" effort had significantly lower cortisol than "low carrying" fathers during the first two weeks postpartum (Nunes et al., 2001).

Neurobiological Bases of Fathering in Non-human Primates

The neurobiology of male parenting has primarily been studied in monogamous rodents such as the prairie vole and the California mouse, and the neuropeptide arginine vasopressin has been implicated in both rodent species (Bester-Meredith & Marler, 2003; Wang, Liu, Young, & Insel, 2000; Wang, Young, De Vries, & Insel, 1998). However, one of the few primate studies to examine neural changes associated with paternal behavior (Kozorovitskiy, Hughes, Lee, & Gould, 2006) showed that male marmoset fathers had higher vasopressin V1a receptor binding in the prefrontal cortex compared to pair-bonded non-fathers. There were no changes in vasopressin V1b, oxytocin, or prolactin receptors. Within fathers, the receptor binding was negatively correlated with the age of the father's youngest offspring, suggesting continued plasticity across the lifespan.

One window into the neurobiology of paternal behavior may be through the neurobiology of pair-bond formation. (For recent review, please see Fernandez-Duque, Valeggia, & Mendoza, 2009). Male titi monkeys that were in long-term pair-bonds showed differences in glucose uptake in many brain areas when compared with males living alone (Bales, Mason, Catana, Cherry, & Mendoza, 2007). The lone males in that study were subsequently paired, and PET scans showed changes in neural activity in the direction of males in long-term relationships.

Contributions of Fathers in Non-monogamous Primate Species

Many studies in polygynous species have used molecular genetic analysis to determine paternity (Altmann et al., 1996; Di Fiore & Fleischer, 2005; Gagneux, Boesch, & Woodruff, 1999; Keane, Dittus, & Melnick, 1997). Genetic evidence has then been used to suggest that some males in polygynous species intervene and defend their own offspring from infanticidal males. Importantly, offspring defense of infanticidal males does not appear to be universal, in that only genetically related infants are defended by a given male (Borries, Launhardt, Epplen, Epplen, & Winkler, 1999; Buchan, Alberts, Silk, & Altmann, 2003; Charpentier, Van Horn, Altmann, & Alberts, 2004). Although these interventions were shown to improve the survival of offspring, the nature of this form of "care" is qualitatively different from that observed in monogamous species, in which infant carrying, infant retrieval, and food sharing are common.

Summary of Empirical Findings

Experiential and neurobiological factors are known to affect paternal care in nonhuman primates. In many species, whether the male has previously engaged in paternal behavior, either of his own offspring or of younger siblings, affects his future participation in paternal care. First time fathers behave differently than experienced fathers. Those individuals that were in their natal group when their younger siblings were born, and engaged in or observed parental care by their parents are more likely to behave appropriately when they become parents. Changes in prolactin, testosterone, and cortisol are all observed in male nonhuman primates around the time of parturition. Neurobiological changes in V1a receptor density in relationship to paternal care have also been observed in common marmosets.

Bridges to Other Disciplines

Research on non-human primate fathering is helpful in understanding the evolution of fathering and the circumstances under which it is displayed. For human fathering, it highlights the importance of considering differences in the motivation vs. the expression of fathering; the role of parenting experience; and also the role of alloparenting experience (exposure to babies as a child or teenager). Programs such as the Roots of Empathy (http://www.rootsofempathy. org) have even used interactions with infants as a treatment to increase pro-social behavior in schools.

In addition, the experimental control and higher level of invasiveness available in studies of non-human primates (as opposed to humans) allow examination of physiological and neurobiological mechanisms which would be difficult in humans. Many of the less invasive physiological techniques described here are now being applied to humans, particularly consideration of the role of testosterone in fathering (Gray, 2003; Gray & Campbell, 2009; Gray, Parkin, & Samms-Vaughan, 2007). Testosterone in human fathers appears to drop after the transition to fatherhood, similar to non-human primate fathers.

Policy Implications

Findings on fathering in non-human primates suggest that the role of positive experiences with infants (both own and others') should be weighted heavily in programs to promote good fathering. Although it has been little studied to date, information on the consequences of "bad" fathering could be used to suggest treatment options for affected children. In addition, findings in non-human primates could help identify males that are at risk of poor fathering and suggest mechanisms for treatment. Finally, understanding the relationship between the mechanisms for pair-bonding and parenting may have relevance to understanding the relationships between these factors in humans.

Future Directions

Additional topics of interest in the physiology and neurobiology of male parental care are reviewed elsewhere (Bales, Maninger, & Hinde, 2011). In particular, in both human and non-human primates, the neurobiology of male parenting is vastly under-studied. With use of new imaging technologies, these studies are now possible. Furthermore, the energetics of fatherhood (the changes in caloric demand and metabolism that are associated with the carrying of infants and other paternal behaviors), which have been studied some in non-human primates, are almost completely unstudied in human males.

Acknowledgments

The authors would like to thank Julie Van Westerhuyzen and Kathy West for contributions to the chapter, as well as our funding sources: NIH 053555, NIH RR00169, and the Good Nature Institute.

References

Addessi, E., Chiarotti, F., Visalberghi, E., & Anzenberger, G. (2007). Response to novel food and the role of social influences in common marmosets (*Callithrix jacchus*) and Goeldi's monkeys (*Callimico goeldii*). *American Journal of Primatology, 69,* 1210–1222.

Albuquerque, A. C. S. R., Sousa, M. B. C., Santos, H. M., & Ziegler, T. E. (2001). Behavioral and hormonal analysis of social relationships between oldest females in a wild monogamous group of common marmosets (*Callithrix jacchus*). *International Journal of Primatology, 22,* 631–645.

Almond, R. E. A., Ziegler, T. E., & Snowdon, C. T. (2008). Changes in prolactin and glucocorticoid levels in cotton-top tamarin fathers during their mate's pregnancy: The effects of infants and paternal experience. *American Journal of Primatology, 70,* 560–565.

Altmann, S. A. (1965). Sociobiology of rhesus monkeys. II: Stochastics of social communication. *Journal of Theoretical Biology, 8,* 490–522.

Altmann, J. (1974). Observational study of behavior. *Behaviour, 49,* 227–266.

Altmann, J., Alberts, S. C., Haines, S. A., Dubach, J., Muruthi, P., Coote, T., et al. (1996). Behavior predicts genetic structure in a wild primate group. *Proceedings of the National Academy of Sciences, 93,* 5797–5801.

Altmann, J., Gesquiere, L. R., Galbany, J., Onyango, P. O., & Alberts, S. C. (2010). Life history context of reproductive aging in a wild primate model. *Annals of the New York Academy of Sciences, 1204,* 127–138.

Baker, A. J. (1991). *Evolution of the social system of the golden lion tamarin (Leontopithecus rosalia): mating system, group dynamics, and cooperative breeding.* University of Maryland, College Park.

Baker, A. J., Dietz, J. M., & Kleiman, D. G. (1993). Behavioural evidence for monopolization of paternity in multi-male groups of golden lion tamarins. *Animal Behaviour, 46,* 1091–1101.

Baker, A. J., Bales, K. L., & Dietz, J. M. (2002). Mating system and group dynamics in lion tamarins. In D. G. Kleiman & A. B. Rylands (Eds.), *Lion Tamarins: Biology and Conservation* (pp. 188–212). Washington, D.C.: Smithsonian Institution Press.

Bales, K., Dietz, J., Baker, A., Miller, K., & Tardif, S. D. (2000). Effects of allocare-givers on fitness of infants and parents in callitrichid primates. *Folia Primatologica, 71,* 27–38.

Bales, K .L., Dietz, J. M., Baker, A. J., Mason, W. A., & Mendoza, S. P. (2007). Perspectives on cooperative breeding from golden lion tamarins and coppery titi monkeys. *American Journal of Primatology, 69*(S1): 128.

Bales, K. L., Maninger, N., & Hinde, K. (2011). New directions in the neurobiology and physiology of paternal care. In O. Gillath, G. Adams, & A. D. Kunkel (Eds.), *New directions in relationship research: Integrating across disciplines and theoretical approaches* (pp. 91–111). Washington, DC: American Psychological Association.

Bales, K. L., Mason, W. A., Catana, C., Cherry, S. R., & Mendoza, S. P. (2007). Neural correlates of pair-bonding in a monogamous primate. *Brain Research, 1184,* 245–253.

Bales, K., O'Herron, M., Baker, A. J., & Dietz, J. M. (2001). Sources of variability in numbers of live births in wild golden lion tamarins (*Leontopithecus rosalia*). *American Journal of Primatology, 54,* 211–221.

Bandettini, P. A. (2009). What's new in neuroimaging methods? *Annals of the New York Academy of Sciences, 1156,* 260–293.

Bester-Meredith, J. K., & Marler, C. A. (2003). Vasopressin and the transmission of paternal behavior across generations in mated, cross-fostered Peromyscus mice. *Behavioral Neuroscience, 117,* 455–463.

Borries, C., Launhardt, K., Epplen, C., Epplen, J. T., & Winkler, P. (1999). Males as infant protectors in Hanuman langurs (*Presbytis entellus*) living in multimale groups-defense pattern, paternity and sexual behaviour. *Behavioral Ecology and Sociobiology, 46,* 350–356.

Brawer, J. E., Naftolin, F., Martin, J., & Sonneschein, C. (1978). Effects of a single injection of estradiol valerate on the hypothalamic arcuate nucleus and on reproductive function in the female rat. *Endocrinology, 103,* 501–512.

Buchan, J. C., Alberts, S. C., Silk, J. B., & Altmann, J. (2003). True paternal care in a multi-male primate society. *Nature, 425,* 179-181.

Capitanio, J. P., Mendoza, S. P., & Bentson, K. L. (2004). Personality characteristics and basal cortisol concentrations in adult male rhesus macaques (*Macaca mulatta*). *Psychoneuroendocrinology, 29,* 1300–1308.

Charpentier, M. J. E., Van Horn, R. C., Altmann, J., & Alberts, S. C. (2004). Paternal effects of offspring fitness in a multimale primate society. *Proceedings of the Royal Society of London Series B-Biological Sciences, 105,* 1988–1992.

Chivers, D. J. (1974). The siamang in Malaya: A field study of a primate in a tropical rain forest. *Contributions to Primatology, 4,* 1-335.

Coe, C. L., Mendoza, S. P., Smotherman, W. P., & Levine, S. (1978). Mother-infant attachment in the squirrel monkey. *Behavioral Biology, 22,* 256–263.

Crews, D., Traina, V., Wetzel, F. T., & Muller, C. (1978). Hormonal control of male reproductive behavior in the lizard, *Anolis carolensis*: Role of testosterone, dihydrotestosterone, and estradiol. *Endocrinology, 103,* 1814–1821.

Cubiciotti, D. D. I., & Mason, W. A. (1975). Comparative studies of social behavior in *Callicebus* and *Saimiri*: Male-female emotional attachments. *Behavioral Biology, 16,* 185–197.

Davenport, M. D., Tiefenbacher, S., Lutz, C. K., Novak, M. A., & Meyer, J. S. (2006). Analysis of endogenous cortisol concentrations in the hair of rhesus macaques. *General and Comparative Endocrinology, 147,* 255–261.

Di Fiore, A., & Fleischer, R. C. (2005). Social behavior, reproductive strategies, and population genetic structure of *Lagothrix poepigii*. *International Journal of Primatology, 26,* 1137–1173.

Dielenthis, T. F., Zaiss, E., & Geissman, T. (1991). Infant care in a family of siamangs (*Hylobates syndactylus*) with twin offspring at Berlin Zoo. *Zoo Biology, 10,* 309–317.

Dietz, J. M., & Baker, A. J. (1993). Polygyny and female reproductive success in golden lion tamarins, *Leontopithecus rosalia*. *Animal Behaviour, 46,* 1067–1078.

Dixson, A. F., & Fleming, D. (1981). Parental behaviour and infant development in owl monkeys (*Aotus trivirgatus griseimembra*). *Journal of Zoology, 194,* 25–39.

Ellis, B. J. (2004). Time of pubertal maturation in girls: An integrated life history approach. *Psychological Bulletin, 130,* 920–958.

Ellis, B. J., Figueredo, A. J., Brumbach, B. H., & Schlomer, G. L. (2009). Fundamental dimensions of environmental risk: The impact of harsh versus unpredictable environments on the evolution and development of life history strategies. *Human Nature, 20,* 204–268.

Epple, G. (1975). Parental behavior in Saguinus fuscicollis ssp. (*Callitrichidae*). *Folia Primatologica, 24,* 221–238.

Fernandez-Duque, E., Juarez, C. P., & Di Fiore, A. (2008). Adult male replacement and subsequent infant care by male and siblings in socially monogamous owl monkeys (*Aotus azarai*). *Primates., 49,* 81–84.

Fernandez-Duque, E., Valeggia, C. R., & Mendoza, S. P. (2009). The biology of paternal care in human and non-human primates. *Annual Review of Anthropology, 38,* 115–130.

Francis, D., Diorio, J., Liu, D., & Meaney, M. J. (1999). Nongenomic transmission across generations of maternal behavior and stress responses in the rat. *Science, 286,* 1155–1158.

Freeman, M. E., Kanyicksa, B., Lerant, A., & Nagy, G. (2000). Prolactin: structure, function, and regulation of secretion. *Physiological Reviews, 80,* 1523–1631.

Fuentes, A. (1999). Re-evaluating primate monogamy. *American Anthropologist, 100,* 890–907.

Gagneux, P., Boesch, C., & Woodruff, D. S. (1999). Female reproductive strategies, paternity, and community structure in wild West African chimpanzees. *Animal Behaviour, 57,* 19–32.

Goldizen, A. W. (1987). Facultative polyandry and the role of infant-carrying in wild saddle-back tamarins (*Saguinus fuscicollis*). *Behavioral Ecology and Sociobiology, 20,* 99–109.

Goldizen, A. W. (1989). Social relationships in a cooperatively polyandrous group of tamarins (*Saguinus fuscicollis*). *Behavioral Ecology and Sociobiology, 24,* 79–89.

Goldizen, A. W., Mendelson, J., Van Vlaardingen, M., & Terborgh, J. (1996). Saddle-back tamarin (*Saguinus fuscicollis*) reproductive strategies: evidence from a thirteen-year study of a marked population. *American Journal of Primatology, 38,* 57–83.

Gray, P. B. (2003). Marriage, parenting, and testosterone variation among Kenyan Swahili men. *American Journal of Physical Anthropology, 122,* 279–286.

Gray, P. B., & Campbell, B. C. (2009). Human male testosterone, pair-bonding, and fatherhood. In P. T. Ellison & P. B. Gray (Eds.), *Endocrinology of social relationships* (pp. 270–293). Cambridge, MA: Harvard University Press.

Gray, P. B., Parkin, J. C., & Samms-Vaughan, M. E. (2007). Hormonal correlates of human paternal interactions: A hospital-based investigation in urban Jamaica. *Hormones and Behavior, 52,* 499–507.

Gwet, K. L. (2008). Computing inter-rater reliability and its variance in the presence of high agreement. *British Journal of Mathematics and Statistical Psychology, 61,* 29–48.

Hearn, J. P. (1983). The common marmoset (*Callithrix jacchus*). In *Reproduction in new world primates: New models in medical science* (pp. 181–215). Boston: MTP Press Limited.

Hennessy, M. B., Mendoza, S. P., & Kaplan, J. N. (1982). Behavior and plasma cortisol following brief peer separation in juvenile squirrel monkeys. *American Journal of Primatology, 3,* 143–151.

Hoffman, K. A., Mendoza, S. P., Hennessy, M. B., & Mason, W. A. (1995). Responses of infant titi monkeys, *Callicebus moloch*, to removal of one or both parents: Evidence for paternal attachment. *Developmental Psychobiology, 28,* 399–407.

Jantschke, B., Welker, C., & Klaiber-Schuh, A. (1998). Rearing without paternal help in the Bolivian owl monkey *Aotus azarae boliviensis*: A case study. *Folia Primatologica, 69,* 115–120.

Jaquish, C. E., Cheverud, J. M., & Tardif, S. D. (1996). Genetic and environmental impacts on litter size and early infant survival in three species of Callitrichids. *Journal of Heredity, 87,* 74–77.

Jaquish, C. E., Gage, T. B., & Tardif, S. D. (1991). Reproductive Factors Affecting Survivorship in Captive *Callitrichidae*. *American Journal of Physical Anthropology, 84,* 291–305.

Joyce, S. M., & Snowdon, C. T. (2007). Developmental changes in food transfers in cotton-top tamarins (*Saguinus oedipus*). *American Journal of Primatology, 69,* 955–965.

Keane, B., Dittus, W. P. J., & Melnick, D. J. (1997). Paternity assessment in wild groups of toque macaques *Macaca sinica* at Polonnaruwa, Sri Lanka using molecular markers. *Molecular Ecology, 6,* 267–282.

Kinzey, W. G., & Wright, P. C. (1982). Grooming behavior in the titi monkey (*Callicebus torquatus*). *American Journal of Primatology, 3,* 267–275.

Kleiman, D. G. (1977). Monogamy in mammals. *Quarterly Review of Biology, 52,* 39–69.

Kleiman, D. G. (1985). Paternal care in New World primates. *American Zoologist, 25,* 857–859.

Kozorovitskiy, Y., Hughes, M., Lee, K., & Gould, E. (2006). Fatherhood affects dendritic spines and vasopressin V1a receptors in the primate prefrontal cortex. *Nature Neuroscience, 9,* 1094–1095.

Lappan, S. (2008). Male care of infants in a siamang (*Symphalangus syndactylus*) population including socially monogamous and polyandrous groups. *Behavioral Ecology and Sociobiology, 62,* 1307–1317.

Lappan, S. (2009). The effects of lactation and infant care on adult energy budgets in wild siamangs (*Symphalangus syndactylus*). *American Journal of Physical Anthropology, 140,* 290–301.

Lynch, J. W., Ziegler, T. E., & Strier, K. B. (2002). Individual and seasonal variation in fecal testosterone and cortisol levels of wild male tufted capuchin monkeys, *Cebus apella nigritus. Hormones and Behavior, 41,* 275–287.

Mason, W. A. (1966). Social organization of the South American monkey, *Callicebus moloch*: a preliminary report. *Tulane Studies in Zoology, 13,* 23–28.

Mason, W. A. (1974). Comparative studies of *Callicebus* and *Saimiri*: Behaviour of male-female pairs. *Folia Primatologica, 22,* 1–8.

Mason, W. A., & Mendoza, S. P. (1998). Response to infant titi monkeys in distress: effects of parental experience. *American Journal of Primatology, 45,* 194.

Mendoza, S. P. (1991). Behavioural and physiological indices of social relationships: Comparative studies of New World monkeys. In H. O. Box (Ed.), *Primate responses to environmental change* (pp. 311–335). London: Chapman and Hall.

Mendoza, S. P., & Mason, W. A. (1986). Parental division of labour and differentiation of attachments in a monogamous primate (*Callicebus cupreus*). *Animal Behaviour, 34,* 1336–1347.

Mendoza, S. P., & Mason, W. A. (1997). Attachment relationships in New World primates. *Annals of the New York Academy of Sciences, 807,* 203–209.

Munro, C. J., Stabenfeldt, G. H., Cragun, J. R., Addiego, L. A., Overstreet, J. W., & Lasley, B. L. (1991). Relationship of serum estradiol and progesterone concentrations to the excretion profiles of their major urinary metabolites as measured by enzyme immunoassay and radioimmunoassay. *Clinical Chemistry, 37,* 838–844.

Nunes, S., Fite, J. E., & French, J. A. (2000). Variation in steroid hormones associated with infant care behaviour and experience in male marmosets (*Callithrix kuhli*). *Animal Behaviour, 60,* 857–865.

Nunes, S., Fite, J. E., Patera, K. J., & French, J. A. (2001). Interactions among paternal behavior, steroid hormones, and parental experience in male marmosets (*Callithrix kuhlii*). *Hormones and Behavior, 39,* 70–82.

Otte, A., & Halsband, U. (2006). Brain imaging tools in neuroscience. *Journal of Physiology, 99,* 281–292.

Palombit, R. A. (1995). Longitudinal patterns of reproduction in wild female siamang (*Hylobates syndactylus*) and white-handed gibbons (*Hylobates lar*). *International Journal of Primatology, 16,* 739–760.

Paschall, M. J., Ringwalt, C. L., & Flewelling, R. L. (2003). Effects of parenting, father absence, and affiliation with delinquent peers on delinquent behavior among African-American male adolescents. *Adolescence, 38,* 15–34.

Pfiffner, L. J., McBurnett, K., & Rathouz, P. J. (2001). Father absence and familial antisocial characteristics. *Journal of Abnormal Child Psychology, 29,* 357–367.

Phillippi-Falkenstein, K., & Clarke, M. R. (1992). Procedure for training corral-living rhesus monkeys for fecal and blood sample collection. *Laboratory Animal Science, 42,* 83–85.

Porter, L. M., & Garber, P. A. (2009). Social behavior of callimicos: mating strategies and infant care. In S. M. Ford, L. M. Porter, & L. C. Davis (Eds.), *Smallest anthropoids: The marmoset/callimico radiation* (pp. 87–101). New York: Springer.

Prudom, S. L., Broz, C. A., Schultz-Darken, N., Ferris, C. T., Snowdon, C. T., & Ziegler, T. E. (2008). Exposure to infant scent lowers serum testosterone in father common marmosets (*Callithrix jacchus*). *Biology Letters, 4,* 603–605.

Pryce, C. R. (1996). Socialization, hormones, and the regulation of maternal behavior in non-human primates. In J. S.Rosenblatt & C. T. Snowdon (Eds.), *Parental care: Evolution, mechanisms, and adaptive significance* (pp. 643–689). San Diego, CA: Academic Press.

Reeder, D. M. (2001). *The biology of parenting in the monogamous titi monkey (Callicebus moloch).* University of California, Davis.

Reinhardt, V. (1991). Training adult rhesus monkeys to actively cooperate duirng in-homecage venipuncture. *Animal Technology, 42,* 11–17.

Rodin, J., Wack, J., Ferrannini, E., & DeFronzo, R. A. (1985). Effects of insulin and glucose on feeding behavior. *Metabolism, 34,* 826–831.

Ruiz-Miranda, C., Kleiman, D. G., Dietz, J. M., Moraes, E., Gravitol, A. D., Baker, A. J., et al. (1999). Food transfers in wild and reintroduced golden lion tamarins. *American Journal of Primatology, 48,* 305–320.

Sanchez, S., Pelaez, F., Gil-Burmann, C., & Kaumanns, W. (1999). Costs of infant-carrying in the cotton-top tamarin *(Saguinus oedipus)*. *American Journal of Primatology, 48,* 99–111.

Sapolsky, R. M. (1985). Stress-induced suppression of testicular function in the wild baboon: Role of glucocorticoids. *Endocrinology, 116,* 2273–2278.

Sapolsky, R. M., & Krey, L. (1988). Stress-induced suppression of LH concentrations in wild baboons: role of opiates. *Endocrinology, 66,* 722–727.

Savage, A., Shideler, S. E., Soto, L. H., Causado, J., Giraldo, L. H., Lasley, B. L., et al. (1997). Reproductive events of wild cotton-top tamarins *(Saguinus oedipus)* in Colombia. *American Journal of Primatology, 43,* 329–337.

Schapiro, S. J. (2000). A few new developments in primate housing and husbandry. *Scandinavian Journal of Laboratory Animal Science, 27,* 103–110.

Schradin, C., & Anzenberger, G. (2001). Infant carrying in family groups of goeldi's monkeys *(Callimico goeldii)*. *American Journal of Primatology, 53,* 57–67.

Schradin, C., & Anzenberger, G. (2003). Mothers, not fathers, determine the delayed onset of male carrying in Goeldi's monkey *(Callimico goeldii)*. *Journal of Human Evolution, 45,* 389–399.

Schradin, C., Reeder, D. M., Mendoza, S. P., & Anzenberger, G. (2003). Prolactin and paternal care: comparison of three species of monogamous New World monkeys *(Callicebus cupreus, Callithrix jacchus,* and *Callimico goeldii)*. *Journal of Comparative Psychology, 117,* 166–175.

Seifritz, E., Esposito, F., Neuhoff, J. G., Luthi, A., Mustovic, H., Dammann, G., et al. (2003). Differential sex-independent amygdala response to infant crying and laughing in parents versus nonparents. *Biological Psychiatry, 54,* 1367–1375.

Stone, A. I., & Bales, K. L. (2010). Intergenerational transmission of the behavioral consequences of early experience in prairie voles. *Behavioural Processes, 84,* 732–738.

Swain, J. E. (2008). Baby stimuli and the parent brain: Functional neuroimaging of the neural substrates of parent-infant attachment. *Psychiatry, 5,* 28–36.

Swain, J. E., Lorberbaum, J. P., Kose, S., & Strathearn, L. (2007). Brain basis of early parent-infant interactions: Psychology, physiology, and *in vivo* functional neuroimaging studies. *Journal of Child Psychology and Psychiatry, 48,* 262–287.

Tardif, S. D. (1994). Relative energetic cost of infant care in small-bodied neotropical primates and its relation to infant-care patterns. *American Journal of Primatology, 34,* 133–143.

Tardif, S. D. (1997). The bioenergetics of parental behavior and the evolution of alloparental care in marmosets and tamarins. In N. G. Solomon & J. A. French (Eds.), *Cooperative breeding in mammals* (pp. 11–33). New York: Cambridge University Press.

Tardif, S. D., Carson, R. L., & Gangaware, B. L. (1990). Infant-care behavior of mothers and fathers in a communal-care primate, the cotton-top tamarin *(Saguinus-Oedipus)*. *American Journal of Primatology, 22,* 73–85.

Tardif, S. D., & Garber, P. A. (1994). Social and reproductive patterns in neotropical primates — relation to ecology, body-size, and infant care. *American Journal of Primatology, 34,* 111–114.

Tardif, S. D., Harrison, M. L., & Simek, M. A. (1987). Infant care in marmosets and tamarins. *International Journal of Primatology, 8,* 436.

Tardif, S. D., & Jaquish, C. E. (1997). Number of ovulations in the marmoset monkey (Callithrix jacchus): Relation to body weight, age and repeatability. *American Journal of Primatology, 42,* 323–329.

Tardif, S. D., Layne, D. G., & Smucny, D. A. (2002). Can marmoset mothers count to three? Effect of litter size on mother-infant interactions. *Ethology, 108,* 825–836.

Tither, J. M., & Ellis, B. J. (2010). Impact of fathers on daughters' age at menarche: A genetically and environmentally controlled sibling study. *Developmental Psychology, 44,* 1409–1420.

Wang, Z. X., Liu, Y., Young, L. J., & Insel, T. R. (2000). Hypothalamic vasopressin gene expression increases in both males and females postpartum in a biparental rodent. *Journal of Neuroendocrinology, 12,* 111–120.

Wang, Z. X., Young, L. J., De Vries, G. J., & Insel, T. R. (1998). Voles and vasopressin: A review of molecular, cellular, and behavioral studies of pair bonding and paternal behaviors. *Progress in Brain Research, 119,* 483–499.

Weingrill, T., Gray, D. A., Barrett, L., & Henzi, S. P. (2004). Fecal cortisol levels in free-ranging female chacma baboons: Relationship to dominance, reproductive state and environmental factors. *Hormones and Behavior, 45,* 259–269.

Welker, C., Jantschke, B., & Klaiber-Schuh, A. (1998). Behavioural data on the titi monkey *Callicebus cupreus* and the owl monkey *Aotus azarae boliviensis*: A contribution to the discussion on the correct systematic classification of these species. *Primate Eye, 51,* 29–42.

Welker, C. & Schafer-Witt, C. (1987). On the carrying behaviour of basic South American primates. *Human Evolution, 2,* 459–473.

Westneat, D. F., & Sherman, P. W. (1993). Parentage and the evolution of parental behavior. *Behavioral Ecology, 4,* 66–77.

Wilson, E. O. (1975). *Sociobiology: The new synthesis.* Cambridge, MA: Harvard University Press.

Wingfield, J. C., Hegner, R. E., Duffy Jr., A. M., & Ball, G. F. (1990). The 'challenge hypothesis': Theoretical implications for patterns of testosterone secretion, mating systems, and breeding strategies. *American Naturalist, 136,* 829–846.

Wolovich, C. K., Feged, A., Evans, S., & Green, S. M. (2006). Social patterns of food sharing in monogamous owl monkeys. *American Journal of Primatology, 68,* 663–674.

Wolovich, C. K., Perea-Rodriguez, J. P., & Fernandez-Duque, E. (2008). Food transfers to young and mates in wild owl monkeys (*Aotus azarai*). *American Journal of Primatology, 70,* 211–221.

Wright, P. C. (1994). The behavior and ecology of the owl monkey. In J. Baer, R. E. Weller, & I. Kakoma (Eds.), *Aotus: The owl monkey* (pp. 97–112). New York: Academic Press.

Wynne-Edwards, K. E. (2001). Hormonal changes in mammalian fathers. *Hormones and Behavior, 40,* 139–145.

Wynne-Edwards, K. E., & Timonin, M. E. (2007). Paternal care in rodents: weakening support for hormonal regulation of the transition to behavioral fatherhood in rodent animal models of biparental care. *Hormones and Behavior, 52,* 114–121.

Zahed, S. R., Prudom, S. L., Snowdon, C. T., & Ziegler, T. E. (2007). Male parenting and response to infant stimuli in the common marmoset (*Callithrix jacchus*). *American Journal of Primatology, 70,* 84–92.

Ziegler, T. E. (2009). Variation in male parenting and physiology in the common marmoset. *American Journal of Human Biology, 21,* 739–744.

Ziegler, T. E., Prudom, S. L., Schultz-Darken, N. J., Kurian, A. V., & Snowdon, C. T. (2006). Pregnancy weight gain: Marmoset and tamarin dads show it too. *Biology Letters, 2,* 181–183.

Ziegler, T. E., & Snowdon, C. T. (1997a). Role of prolactin in paternal care in a monogamous new world primate, *Saguinus oedipus. Integrative Neurobiology of Affiliation, 807,* 599–601.

Ziegler, T. E., & Snowdon, C. T. (1997b). Role of prolactin in paternal care in a monogamous New World primate, *Saguinus oedipus. Annals of the New York Academy of Sciences, 807,* 599-601.

Ziegler, T. E., Wegner, F. H., & Snowdon, C. T. (1996). Hormonal responses to parental and nonparental conditions in male cotton-top tamarins, *Saguinus oedipus*, a New World primate. *Hormones and Behavior, 30,* 287–297.

SECTION II

Demographic Perspectives

Chapter 4

Family Structure and Men's Motivation for Parenthood in the United States[1]

Sandra L. Hofferth

University of Maryland

Joseph H. Pleck

University of Illinois at Urbana-Champaign

Frances Goldscheider, Sally Curtin, and Katie Hrapczynski

University of Maryland

Between the 1980s and the 1990s, men who lived with children increased their involvement with them (Sandberg & Hofferth, 2001; Sayer, Bianchi, & Robinson, 2004). However, we do not know whether their involvement has continued to increase; furthermore, there is likely to be substantial variability in such involvement across families, given that the structure of families has become increasingly complex. In addition to families with two married, biological parents, children living with men in today's families include those with two unmarried biological parents, married or cohabiting stepfathers, single fathers, and fathers living with another potential caregiver. Because they are present on a daily basis, men in these other father family types may play a critical role in their children's lives; therefore, more needs to be known about men's involvement with their residential children in the context of different family types.

The present chapter builds on previous research on men's involvement with coresidential children. First, it examines trends in family structure over the past decade, with a focus on the family types of coresidential fathers (father family structure): married, cohabiting, or single biological fathers as well as married or cohabiting stepfathers. Second, it describes the motivations of men both for fatherhood and for involvement with children and barriers to that involvement. Third, it examines levels and types of involvement of fathers with residential children and predictors of such involvement, focusing on how father family types, father attitudes, and other factors affect levels, types, and changes in father involvement.

Brief Historical Overview and Theoretical Perspectives

Between 1996 and 2008, the living arrangements of children under 18 changed (Table 4.1, top panel). First, the proportion living with two married biological parents declined 2%, from 62.4% to 61.3%, and the proportion living with two biological cohabiting parents increased more than 50%, from 1.8% to 2.8%, although the absolute level is still low. Second, the proportion of children living with one biological parent and one (married) stepparent declined 13%, from 6.7% in 1996 to 5.8% in 2008. Most of this decline was offset by increased cohabitation among single parents, paralleling the retreat from marriage for biological parent couples. If we include as stepfamilies the categories "mother and partner" and "father and partner," each

Table 4.1   Relationship of U.S. Children under 18 to Their Parents

2008	All Race	White	Black	Hispanic
Two bio parents	**64.0%**	**71.3%**	**32.5%**	**64.6%**
Married parents	61.3%	69.3%	30.0%	59.5%
Unmarried parents	2.8%	2.0%	2.4%	5.0%
One bio, one stepparent	**5.8%**	**6.5%**	**4.9%**	**5.1%**
Single bio mother	**22.8%**	**15.5%**	**51.2%**	**24.1%**
Mother only	20.5%	13.2%	48.8%	21.8%
Mother and partner	2.3%	2.3%	2.3%	2.3%
Single bio father	**3.5%**	**4.1%**	**3.4%**	**2.4%**
Father only	2.8%	3.4%	2.8%	1.7%
Father and partner	0.7%	0.7%	0.6%	0.7%
No bio parent	**3.8%**	**2.6%**	**8.1%**	**3.9%**
Total	**100.0%**	**100.0%**	**100.0%**	**100.0%**

Source: 2008 SIPP data.

1996	All Races	White	Black	Hispanic
Two bio parents	**64.2%**	**71.5%**	**31.7%**	**62.9%**
Married parents	62.4%	70.1%	29.9%	58.7%
Unmarried parents	1.8%	1.4%	1.8%	4.2%
One bio, one stepparent	**6.7%**	**7.5%**	**5.2%**	**5.2%**
Single bio mother	**22.7%**	**15.5%**	**52.5%**	**25.7%**
Mother only	20.6%	13.4%	50.2%	23.3%
Mother and partner	2.1%	2.1%	2.3%	2.4%
Single bio father	**2.5%**	**2.8%**	**2.0%**	**1.7%**
Father only	2.1%	2.4%	1.7%	1.3%
Father and partner	0.4%	0.4%	0.3%	0.4%
No bio parent	**3.9%**	**2.7%**	**8.5%**	**4.4%**
Total	**100.0%**	**100.0%**	**100.0%**	**100.0%**

Source: 1996 SIPP data, reported in America's Children: Key National Indicators of Well-being, 2000.
Note: "Bio" means "biological." Children of adoptive parents are included with those of biological parents.

of which increased, the decline was only 4%, from 9.2% in 1996 to 8.8% in 2008. Although a biological parent's cohabiting partner is less likely to consider him or herself a stepparent than is a married partner (Teachman, 2008), many do.

Third, there was a 40% increase in the proportion of children living with a single biological father, from 2.5% in 1996 to 3.5% in 2008. Increases occurred among both children living only with a father and those living with a father and his partner. Breaking the long-term trend towards increased single motherhood (Moffitt & Rendall, 1995), the proportion living with a single biological mother stayed the same, as did the proportion living with no biological parent.

Racial and ethnic differences in children's living arrangements remain large. Although 71% of White children and almost two-thirds of Hispanic children lived with two biological parents in 2008, only one-third of African American children did so. Furthermore, although 16% of White children and about one-quarter of Hispanic children lived with a single biological mother, half of African American children did so. In spite of these overall differences in family structure, however, the trends between 1996 and 2008 were similar for all three racial and ethnic groups, with increased proportions of children living with unmarried biological parents or one biological parent and a cohabiting partner. Increases in the proportion of children living with a single biological father occurred in all three groups, with the increase largest for Black children, 70%, compared with 36% for White children and 41% for Hispanic children.

We have observed that children who live with their biological fathers are increasingly likely not to have their parents married or even to have their mothers living with them at all. Other children are living with stepfathers. Might changes in children's family experiences growing up have contributed to changes in fathering over time? The experience of family instability over time is linked with fathering trajectories. Men who experienced an unstable childhood family have been found to transition to biological parenthood early, particularly to nonresidential fatherhood and, among residential fathers, to cohabiting fatherhood rather than married fatherhood (Hofferth & Goldscheider, 2010). Differences in parenting processes across family types partially explained this association; men who had little say in family rules transitioned to fatherhood early. Of these fathers, those who had warm relations with parents were likely to live with their children; those who did not have warm relations were less likely to live with their children. Further, men who experienced a disrupted family structure in childhood were both more willing to become stepfathers (Goldscheider & Kaufman, 2006), and more likely to do so (Goldscheider, Kaufman, & Sassler, 2009). Men who were already fathers, particularly single fathers, were also more likely to enter a union that made them stepfathers (Goldscheider & Sassler, 2006). Entry into single fatherhood is also influenced by childhood family structure. Having experienced four or more parental transitions as a child was associated with a male being likely to become a single father (Hofferth & Goldscheider, 2010).

Studying Father Involvement

Does father involvement differ for children living with the father only, the father and another caregiver, or a married or unmarried stepfather compared with living with two biological parents (married or unmarried)? How does fathering motivation vary across these family types?

Motivation for Father Involvement

The present section describes a biological-evolutionary perspective for why biological parenthood, together with type of partner relationship, should influence men's involvement with children, and then describes a broader psychosocial perspective on fathers' motivation for involvement that may lead to an association between father family type and involvement.

Biological-evolutionary motivations. Our understanding of men's motivations for involvement with children is rooted in evolutionary theory, which focuses on the quantity of children and biological relationship of children (Waynforth, this volume), as well as the costs-and-benefits-of-children theory (Fawcett, 1983). In both approaches, men are more motivated for involvement with biological children and, in contemporary societies, motivated to rear "high quality" children (Willis, 1973) who will become independent adults, raise grandchildren, and be financially and emotionally supportive as parents age. A higher degree of parental investment, including transfers requiring production (food, money) and direct caregiving (time), increases the ability of the next generation to reproduce and become successful adults (Waynforth, this volume).

The important contribution of evolutionary theory is to note that men benefit more from investing in children who are genetically related because selective investment maximizes their reproductive success and reduces conflict; in fact, research has shown lower involvement of married stepfathers or partners of the mother compared with biological fathers (e.g., Hofferth & Anderson, 2003). Even so, stepfathers become involved with their stepchildren. Men spend about 9.2 hours per week engaged with stepchildren (compared with 15.6 with biological children) (Hofferth & Anderson, 2003). Many of men's perceived motivations for fatherhood can be achieved with stepchildren. One motivation for involvement is likely to be that of relationship investment. Children's mothers benefit from their investments in their children, and would benefit further if the stepparents invested as well. By investing in their spouses' children from a prior union, men improve the quality of their current union and, perhaps, the prospect of further childbearing (Hofferth & Anderson, 2003). Thus, securing the relationship to a partner may motivate increased fathering behavior. Men's involvement with their residential stepchildren may also depend on their commitment to biological children living elsewhere (Hofferth & Anderson, 2003) and on maternal gatekeeping, which is greater for stepfathers than for biological fathers (Allen, Baucom, Bernett, Epstein, & Rankin-Esquer, 2010).

Single fathers without a partner should be more involved than married biological fathers because the former are sole parents. Although single fathers who live with a partner who is not the child's mother may be slightly less motivated to be involved than single fathers who do not have a partner, they should be more involved than married biological fathers because their partner is not the child's mother; her motivation for caregiving will, presumably, be lower.

Psychosocial motivations. In addition to biological and couple relationship, Lamb, Pleck, Charnov, and Levine (1985) suggested that men's attitudes about fathering are foremost among the immediate psychosocial determinants of paternal involvement. Such motivation may be especially important for fathers compared to mothers because it is less normative for fathers to be involved than mothers in the day to day care of children (Maurer, Pleck, & Rane, 2001). Fathers' behavior may be motivated in large part by their beliefs about what fathers should do, assessed by "the extent to which a parent believes the father's role is important in child development" (Palkovitz, 1984, p. 1056). Prior research on the association between fathering attitudes and actual involvement is limited in that it does not control for relevant potentially confounding variables, it uses small convenience samples, it reports only cross-sectional relationships, and/or it does not take into account whether the father is a biological father or a stepfather. In addition, few prior studies have investigated the predictors of fathering attitudes (see, for example, Rane, 1999).

Selection. Finally, it is important to consider potential bias in studies of fathering caused by men selecting into different family types according to their preferences and attitudes. If so, father family types may be less important than father attitudes and other factors in predicting involvement. We utilize analytic methods that eliminate the effects of both observed family variables such as race/ethnicity and unobserved variables such as poor mental health.

Conceptualizing Father Involvement

Although the wording in the evolutionary-biological literature refers to investments in children and benefits from this investment, most of the fatherhood literature refers more broadly to father "involvement." Lamb and his colleagues (1985) introduced the construct of father involvement as encompassing three components: (a) engagement, (b) accessibility, and (c) responsibility. Subsequent investigations predominantly assessed father engagement, often treating it as synonymous with involvement. Although Lamb et al. (1985) defined engagement as fathers' direct interaction with children during all time spent with them, researchers have operationalized engagement time more specifically as positive engagement activities (e.g., bathing the child, playing games, reading). Most studies of positive engagement activities focus on three common types of activities of fathers with children: caregiving, play, and teaching (Yeung, Sandberg, Davis-Kean, & Hofferth, 2001). In addition, researchers often incorporate measures of the quality of father-child interactions or relationship (e.g., warmth-responsiveness and control) in definitions of father engagement. Pleck (2010) has argued that this usage should be made explicit, and has proposed a revised conceptualization of engagement that includes three core components: (a) positive engagement activities, (b) warmth-responsiveness, and (c) control.

Current Research Questions

This chapter addresses four important questions in the father involvement literature. First, has coresidential father involvement increased over the past decade? Second, how important is the structure of the family (whether there are two biological parents, one biological and one nonbiological parent, or a single father) to father involvement? Third, do fathering attitudes (reflecting motivation) explain variation in father involvement and, when added to the full model, attenuate the relationship between father family structure and father involvement? Finally, using family and individual fixed effects models, does family structure or variation in fathering attitudes across time account for differences in father involvement once heterogeneity across families or children is controlled?

Research Measurement and Methodology

Data

One of the core assumptions of demography is that the data used represent a known population of individuals, families, or whatever unit is to be described. Statistical methods are used to draw the sample and to obtain the appropriate weights so that the sample is representative. The strengths of such data include large samples capable of being subdivided to represent rare subgroups and high quality data collection, coding, and documentation. However, because such surveys cover a range of topics, weaknesses in the depth of coverage of specific topics often exist. Issues in analyzing secondary data are summarized in Hofferth (2005).

Accordingly, the data for the present study were drawn from the 1997 Child Development Supplement (CDS) to the Panel Study of Income Dynamics (PSID). The PSID is a 40-year longitudinal survey of a representative sample of U.S. men, women, children, and the families in which they reside. With funding from the National Institute of Child Health and Human Development (NICHD), data were collected in 1997 on up to two randomly selected children aged 0–12 of PSID respondents, both from the primary caregivers and from the children themselves. Interviews were completed with 2,380 households containing 3,563 children under age 13. The response rate was 88%. A second wave of data was collected between fall 2002 and spring 2003. We refer to this wave by its end date of 2003. Of 3,271 eligible participants in Wave II, 2,907 (89%) participated. Post-stratification weights based upon the Current Population Survey make the data nationally representative and adjust for nonresponse.

Study Sample

In this chapter we focus on a sample of 2,233 children ages 6 to 12 years either in 1997 or in 2003 who were reported by the primary caregiver to be living with a father or a father-figure. This sample consists of two cross-sectional samples of similar-age children at two points in time; it does not follow individual children as they age. Sample sizes permitted distinguishing among children who lived with two biological parents, a biological mother and a partner who is a nonbiological father married or cohabiting with the mother (stepfather), or a single biological father, either with or without another caregiver (most of whom are the partner of the father). Children living with a single mother were excluded, as well as those living with no biological parents, because our focus was on residential fathers. In this sample, almost all of the children living with two biological parents were living with two married parents; there were not sufficient cases to separate children living with two biological cohabiting parents. Previous U.S. research has found few significant differences between married and cohabiting father involvement with biological children in large-scale studies (Hofferth & Anderson, 2003).

Our main analytic sample included cases in which fathers reported on their involvement, either as a primary or secondary caregiver. In two-parent families, the mother was nearly always primary and the father secondary; men in unmarried mother-partner families were less likely to be reported as a caregiver and were, therefore, less likely to be interviewed. Response rates were considerably lower for secondary caregivers (60%); therefore, the amount of missing information was greater for fathers than for mothers. After deleting cases missing on independent and dependent variables, the sample size for our main analytic sample was 1,119.

We also created a validation sample in which data about father engagement were available from time diaries completed by mothers and children, with a higher response rate (83%) than the secondary caregiver module. The sample size with time diaries was 1,981; after deleting data missing on key dependent and independent variables, the sample size was 1,748.

Finally, we created a longitudinal sample consisting of 809 cases with children participating in the CDS in 1997 and 2003, residing in two-parent families in both years, and for whom father reports were available. After selecting cases in which the key variables were present in 1997 and 2003, the longitudinal sample included 523 cases. This sample is used for following individual children and their fathers over time.

Because of the large amount of missing data on fathers, we conducted a missing data analysis to compare characteristics of fathers who provided data in the main analytic sample and those who did not. Stepfathers were less likely to provide information than biological fathers living with the child's mother, whereas single fathers with or without a partner were more likely to provide this information. This is not surprising; single fathers were more likely than stepfathers to be primary caregivers; the latter had a much higher response rates than secondary caregivers. Father education and family income were also higher in families in which fathers participated than in families in which the father did not report about their interactions with their children. Finally, minority fathers were less likely to participate than were White fathers. We included controls for these variables in all analyses. However, as another check on bias, we replicated portions of the analyses of father engagement using the larger validation sample of 1,748 cases to see whether the results were affected by potential sample selection and report findings when appropriate.

Measures of Parental Involvement and Parenting

Consistent with the Pleck formulation, the PSID-CDS collected multiple measures of parental involvement, including engagement, warmth, control, and discussion of rules. Many of the items were from standard scales used in studies of parenting and fathering; however, there were two innovations for a large-scale nationally representative survey.

First, the PSID-CDS obtained child-specific information on parenting for up to two children under age 13. Second, in addition to standard survey questions of fathers about their involvement with children, detailed 24-hour time diaries were provided by children and primary caregivers. Time diary data have higher internal consistency and reduced social desirability bias compared to standard single-item questions asked in most surveys (Hofferth, Davis-Kean, Davis, & Finkelstein, 1999; Juster & Stafford, 1985). Research suggests a high degree of agreement between mothers' and fathers' reports of father involvement (Wical & Doherty, 2005).

Number of engagement activities with the father.   The CDS asked each father directly about 13 different activities in which he may have engaged with his child in the past month (scored as 1 for yes and 0 for no). These included washing or folding clothes, doing dishes, cleaning house, preparing food, looking at books or reading stories, talking about the family, working on homework, building or repairing something, playing computer or video games, playing a board game, card game or puzzle, and playing sports or outdoor activities. The total score has a reliability (Cronbach's alpha) of 0.78.

Time children spend engaged with their father.   The CDS collected one weekday and one weekend day diary for each child age 0–12 in the family. The time diary followed the child's flow of activities over a 24-hour period beginning at midnight of the randomly assigned designated day. Questions identified the primary activity that was going on at that time, when it began and ended, and whether any other activity was taking place. An additional question —"Who was doing the activity with child?"—provided a report of the interaction of others with the child while that activity was taking place (Juster & Stafford, 1985). Codes were provided for fathers and stepfathers of the child. For the present analysis, three specific types of activities were examined: caregiving, play, and teaching—and the specific diary codes assigned to each of these activities were the same as used in previous research (Yeung et al., 2001). Times in all spells in which the residential father or stepfather was reported as engaged in a caregiving activity with a child, for example, were summed for weekdays and weekends for each child.

Weekly time was computed by multiplying weekday time by 5 and weekend day time by 2. We focus on the total number of weekly hours spent, with "0" for *none*.

Parental warmth.   The warmth of the relationship between child and father was measured by 6 items asking how often in the past month the father hugged each child, expressed his love, spent time with, joked or played with, talked with, and told his child he appreciated what his child did (Hofferth et al., 1999). The 5 response categories range from (1) not in the past month to (5) every day, with a mean above 4. The scores were summed and averaged over the 6 items to create a scale with a reliability coefficient of 0.77.

Paternal control and discussion of rules.   To assess paternal control of the child's behavior, fathers were asked how often they set limits on the amount of time children can watch television in a day, limit the types of programs they watch, permit TV watching during the evening meal, set limits on how late children can stay up at night, set limits on snacks, control which children they spend time with, control how time is spent after school, set a time when the children do homework. The items were reverse coded so that a high score represents more control: 1 = *never* and 5 = *very often*. We created dummy variables for each item by coding never, seldom and sometimes to 0 and often and very often to 1. The sum indicates the number of behaviors which the parents control, with a reliability of .80. Fathers were also asked whether they discussed these rules with their children, recoded 1 = *never* and 5 = *very often*. This item was kept as a separate indicator of monitoring.

Fathering attitudes.   To assess fathers' attitudes towards involvement with children we used questions on fathering drawn from the "Being a Father" scale (Pleck, 1997) and from the "Role of the Father" questionnaire (Palkovitz, 1984), tapping the belief that the father role is important in child development. The 7 items include: "a father should be as heavily involved in the care of his child as the mother," and "in general, fathers and mothers are equally good at meeting their children's needs." The responses ranged from 1 = *strongly disagree* to 4 = *strongly agree*. Factor analysis using principal components analysis identified a one-factor solution. After recoding so that a high score indicated a positive attitude towards fathering and substituting mean values for individual missing items, the total score on the 7 items was obtained by summing and averaging across items. The scale reliability was 0.70.

Control Variables

Prior research has identified numerous factors associated with father involvement that should be controlled (Hofferth, 2003; Hofferth & Anderson, 2003). Characteristics of fathers that may affect their ability and motivation to become involved include age, general health status (1 = *poor* to 5 = *excellent*), depression (a 6-item scale of depressive symptoms from the Comprehensive International Diagnosis Inventory (CIDI) (Hofferth et al., 1999)), education (years of schooling), and weekly employment hours (coded as continuous hours or as dummy variables for categories).

Gender, age, and general health status of the child (1 = *poor* to 5 = *excellent*) are related to father involvement. Fathers' involvement declines as children get older and fathers tend to be more involved with boys than girls (Mammen, 2011). Children's health may limit the ability of fathers to engage with their children. Finally, family characteristics include family income and race/ethnicity. Previous research has shown greater involvement of fathers in minority families (operationalized by fathers' race-ethnicity) on some dimensions, such as caregiving and monitoring (Hofferth, 2003). Income affects the resources fathers have available to utilize in engaging with their children.

Analytic Strategy

Using a sample of children living with a father or father-figure, we first show mean levels of father involvement and fathering attitudes in 1997 and 2003. This addresses the simple association between father family structure, fathering attitudes, and father involvement across time. In order to test the association between fathering attitudes and father involvement in a multivariate context, we regressed father attitudes on year, father family type, and the control variables. To test the full effects of father family types and the potential mediation of fathering attitudes, we then regressed the father-reported involvement measures (engagement, warmth, control, and whether the father discusses rules) on year, father family types, fathering attitudes and control variables introduced in blocks. Specifically, in Model 1 we include family structure and the year in which the data were collected (2003 vs. 1997), to test change over time. In Model 2 we add fathering attitudes, to examine mediation. In the Model 3 we add controls for father, child, and family characteristics to reduce selection effects. We then repeat these analyses and models for the measures of father involvement calculated from the time diaries: weekly time spent in caregiving, playing, and teaching. Effect size was calculated by dividing the unstandardized coefficient by the standard error of the dependent variable.

Finally, we turn to fixed effects analyses that adjust for unobserved heterogeneity. We first use family fixed effects to test whether differences in father engagement across families are due to heterogeneity across families in other factors related to family structure or are due to family structure. We are able to make this comparison because children's relationships with parents vary across children in the same family. We then use the longitudinal two-parent sample to create individual fixed effects models examining changes in father-reported involvement as a function of changes in father attitudes and employment and child health over the period. In this model we test whether changes in father attitudes and other characteristics are associated with concomitant changes in father involvement. Because it compares individuals to themselves over time, this analysis tests whether the effects of attitudes shown in the earlier analyses were correlational or potentially causal. Variables that do not change over time are not included in the model and employment variables are coded as continuous rather than categorical.

Empirical Findings

Distribution of Background Characteristics by Father Family Types

Table 4.2 shows the means and proportions of variables weighted to represent all American children. About half the data came from 1997 and half from 2003 (top panel). Similar to Table 4.1, 9 out of 10 children living with their fathers lived with two biological parents; 4% lived with a biological and a nonbiological parent, 2% lived with a biological father and another caregiver (90% of whom are partners), and 2% lived with a single father.

A few father characteristics differed across family types. For example, single fathers living with another caregiver were more likely to work 60 or more hours per week than fathers in

Table 4.2 Means and Standard Deviations of Independent and Dependent Variables Used in Regressions, by Father Family Type

	Total		Two biological Parents		Bio mother, stepfather			Bio father, other caregiver			Bio father, no other caregiver		
	Mean	SD	Mean	SD	Mean	SD	sig[a]	Mean	SD	sig[a]	Mean	SD	sig[a]
Independent variables													
Year and type of family													
Year is 2003	0.50	0.48	0.49	0.49	0.54	0.42		0.67	0.42		0.41	0.45	
Father family type													
Bio mother/bio father	0.92	0.27	—	—	—	—		—	—		—	—	
Bio mother/stepfather	0.04	0.20	—	—	—	—		—	—		—	—	
Bio father/other caregiver	0.02	0.13	—	—	—	—		—	—		—	—	
Single father	0.02	0.14	—	—	—	—		—	—		—	—	
Father characteristics													
Health status	3.91	0.90	3.92	0.91	3.89	0.74		3.58	0.88		3.79	0.85	
Depression scale	1.57	0.54	1.57	0.55	1.66	0.48		1.56	0.47		1.47	0.33	
Education	13.31	2.88	13.34	2.95	12.73	2.50		12.75	1.50		13.79	1.89	
Does not work	0.09	0.27	0.08	0.27	0.13	0.28		0.11	0.28		0.22	0.38	
Works 1–34 hrs/wk	0.05	0.20	0.05	0.21	0.05	0.18		0.04	0.17		0.00	0.06	
Works 35–49 hrs/wk	0.52	0.48	0.52	0.49	0.53	0.42		0.46	0.44		0.70	0.42	
Works 50–59 hrs/wk	0.21	0.39	0.22	0.41	0.12	0.27		0.11	0.28		0.07	0.23	
Works 60+ hrs/wk	0.13	0.33	0.13	0.33	0.19	0.33		0.28	0.40	°	0.00	0.00	
Age	39.98	6.14	40.15	6.03	36.91	6.03	°°°	36.05	5.05	°°	42.11	8.56	
Child and family characteristics													
Male	0.49	0.48	0.48	0.49	0.46	0.42		0.74	0.39	°	0.46	0.45	
Age 9–12 (vs. 6–8)	0.58	0.48	0.57	0.49	0.61	0.41		0.52	0.45		0.78	0.37	

Health status	4.50	0.70	4.51	0.71	4.37	0.58		4.23	0.86		4.54	0.53
Family income	76.02	69.79	77.49	71.79	67.67	54.94		65.77	43.55		40.14	30.36
White	0.77	0.41	0.77	0.41	0.73	0.37		0.85	0.32		0.91	0.26
Black	0.06	0.22	0.05	0.22	0.15	0.30	°°	0.05	0.19		0.09	0.26
Hispanic	0.11	0.31	0.12	0.32	0.07	0.21		0.06	0.21		0.00	0.00
Asian	0.03	0.16	0.03	0.16	0.03	0.15		0.00	0.00		0.00	0.00
Other race	0.49	0.48	0.48	0.49	0.46	0.42		0.74	0.39		0.46	0.45
Father attitudes	3.26	0.35	3.26	0.35	3.16	0.33		3.31	0.3		3.49	0.33 °°
Dependent variables												
Father behavior												
Father engagement	8.93	2.62	8.96	2.63	7.59	2.56	***	9.3	2.17		10.03	2.14
Father warmth	3.81	0.77	3.84	0.75	3.33	0.86	°°°	3.52	0.77		3.86	0.75
Father control	4.93	2.14	4.9	2.19	5.4	1.6		5.38	1.9		4.85	1.7
Father discusses rules	3.81	1.01	3.81	1.02	3.95	0.82	°°°	3.77	1.05		3.75	0.74
N (Father report sample)	1,119		998		66			26			29	
Weekly time in hours and minutes												
Father engaged in caregiving	3:55	3:19	3:55	3:22	3:05	2:28	°	5:40	3:46 °		4:25	2:38
Father engaged in play/ companionship	5:00	5:45	5:04	5:54	3:11	3:05	°°	5:13	5:54		6:23	5:40
Father engaged in teaching/ achievement	1:05	2:21	1:04	2:22	0:19	0:48	°°°	1:30	2:59		3:02	3:28 °°°
N (Validation sample)	1,748		1551		124			33			40	

ᵃ Significance level of t-test comparing category with two biological parent families

°°° p <. 001 °° p < .01, °p < .05, 2-tailed test

two-biological-parent families (Table 4.2, second panel). Stepfathers and single fathers living with another caregiver were about 4 years younger (36 compared with age 40) than men in two-biological-parent families.

Of child and family characteristics, children living with their fathers and another caregiver were more likely to be male than those in two biological parent families (Table 4.2, third panel). There were no significant age differences. Additionally, a higher proportion of children living with a stepfather were Black than were children in two-biological-parent families.

Bivariate Association of Father Family Types with Fathering Attitudes and Involvement

Men in single father, no other caregiver families, had more positive fathering attitudes than men in two-biological-parent families (Table 4.2, fourth panel), and stepfathers' attitudes were marginally less positive than those of men in two-biological-parent families ($p < .10$).

Compared with biological fathers in two-biological-parent families, stepfathers reported themselves to be significantly less engaged with and less warm towards their children (Table 4.2, fifth panel) and spent less time with children in all three categories (sixth panel). Single fathers living with another caregiver spent significantly more time in caregiving, and fathers living alone spent more time in educational activities than those in two-biological-parent families.

Fathering Attitudes

Moving to a multivariate framework, we first examined the associations of year and family structure with fathering attitudes (Table 4.3). The results show that fathering attitudes became more positive over time, with a higher average in 2003 compared with 1997 (Model 1), a result that became significant at <.05 with the introduction of control variables (Model 2). Family structure was linked to attitudes. Single fathers not living with another caregiver reported significantly more positive attitudes about fathering than fathers in two-biological-parent families, a result that became more highly significant with the addition of control variables (b = .24, effect size = .69). Of background factors, the variable most significantly related to attitudes was paternal education; fathers with more education reported more positive attitudes. In addition, those who worked part time reported more positive attitudes than those who worked full-time or who did not work at all. No other child and family characteristics were significantly linked with father attitudes.

Father Involvement, as Reported by Fathers in 1997 and 2003

In order to test change in involvement over time, we regressed each of the four types of self-reported father involvement on the year of data collection and father family type in Model 1, adding father attitudes and then controls in the second and third models (Table 4.4). The results showed that both father *warmth* and father *discusses the rules* were significantly lower in 2003, but *control* was higher in 2003 than in 1997. The coefficient for year was not significant for father engagement. These associations were not altered by the inclusion of the child's initial age category or other controls in Model 3.

Table 4.3 Factors Predicting Father Attitudes, by Type of Family and Father and Child Characteristics, 1997 and 2003

	Father attitudes	
	Model 1	Model 2
Constant	3.23°°°	3.02°°°
Year and type of Family		
Year is 2003	0.05+	0.06°
Bio mother/bio father	ref	ref
Bio mother/stepfather	–0.10	–0.08
Bio father/other caregiver	0.05	0.07
Single father	0.23°	0.24°°
Father characteristics		
Health status		0.02
Depression scale		–0.05+
Education		0.02°°°
Does not work		0.00
Works 1–34 hrs/wk		0.15°
Works 35–49 hrs/wk		ref
Works 50–59 hrs/wk		0.02
Works 60+ hrs/wk		–0.06
Age		0.00
Child and family characteristics		
Male		0.00
Age 9–12 (vs 6–8)		–0.02
Health status		0.01
Family income		–0.15
White		ref
Black		–0.02
Hispanic		0.06
Asian		–0.08
Other race		0.09+
R-squared	0.02	.07

N = 1,119
°°° p <. 001 °° p < .01, °p < .05, + p < .10, 2-tailed test

Father family structure, also included in the first model, was linked to father engagement and warmth. Stepfathers were significantly less engaged (b = –1.36, effect size = .52) and less warm (b = –.50, effect size = .65) than biological fathers in two-biological-parent families. Single fathers engaged with their children more (b = 1.05, effect size = .57), but the result was only significant at the .10 level, and was not significant once father attitudes were added.

Table 4.4 Factors Predicting Self-Reported Fathering Behavior, 1997 and 2003

	Father engagement			Father warmth			Father control			Father discusses rules		
	Model 1	Model 2	Model 3	Model 1	Model 2	Model 3	Model 1	Model 2	Model 3	Model 1	Model 2	Model 3
Constant	9.08***	4.79***	5.70***	3.90***	1.79***	2.58***	4.55***	0.23	0.55	3.89***	1.90***	2.32***
Year and type of family												
Year is 2003	−0.23	−0.29	−0.26	−0.14*	−0.17**	−0.15*	0.70***	0.64***	0.68***	−0.16*	−0.19*	−0.18*
Bio mother/ bio father	ref	ref	ref	ref	ref	ref	ref	ref	ref	ref	ref	ref
Bio mother/ stepfather	−1.36**	−1.23*	−1.27*	−0.50**	−0.43**	−0.40*	0.47	0.60+	0.55+	0.15	0.21	0.17
Bio father/ other caregiver	0.38	0.31	0.35	−0.29	−0.32	−0.34	0.36	0.29	0.37	−0.01	−0.04	−0.04
Single father	1.05+	0.74	0.86	0.01	−0.14	−0.08	0.01	−0.31	−0.34	−0.07	−0.21	−0.22
Father attitudes		1.33***	1.07***		0.65***	0.59***		1.34***	1.06***		0.62***	0.58***
Father characteristics												
Health status			−0.06			−0.02			0.03			−0.01
Depression scale			−0.23			−0.19*			−0.49**			−0.19*
Education			0.10+			0.00			0.10**			0.00
Does not work			0.05			−0.10			0.38			0.21

Works 1–34 hrs/wk	0.79	0.08	0.37	0.20
Works 35–49 hrs/wk	ref	ref	ref	ref
Works 50–59 hrs/wk	0.13	−0.09	−0.29	−0.10
Works 60+ hrs/wk	−0.47	−0.12	−0.34	−0.09
Age	−0.04°	−0.01	−0.02	0.00
Child and family characteristics				
Male	0.06	0.02	−0.04	0.02
Age 9–12 (vs 6–8)	−0.34+	−0.21***	−0.39**	−0.16°
Health status	0.25+	0.04	0.14	0.03
Family income	−0.29	0.76°	1.09	1.05+
White	ref	ref	ref	ref
Black	0.45	−0.24+	0.93**	0.43**
Hispanic	0.50	−0.10	0.13	−0.09
Asian	0.14	0.05	−0.10	0.32+
Other race	−1.17	−0.18	−0.19	−0.38°
	0.02	0.03	0.03	0.01
	0.05	0.12	0.08	0.05
R-squared	0.09	0.17	0.14	0.10

N= 1,119

*** p<.001 ** p<.01, ° p<.05, + p<.10, 2-tailed test

Stepfathers reported marginally more control (b = .55, effect size = .25) than biological fathers, but this was only significant at the .10 level in Model 3. There were no significant father family type differences in whether the father discussed the rules with his child.

Positive father attitudes, added in Model 2, were associated with significantly higher levels of all four indicators of father involvement: father engagement (b = 1.33, effect size = .51) warmth (b = .65, effect size =.84), control (b = 1.34, effect size = .63), and discussion of rules (b = .62, effect size = .61), all large effects. The association of single father family type with father attitudes was significant, and the association of single father family type with father engagement was also significant before adding in father attitudes; therefore, we tested for a mediating effect of attitudes in the association between single father and father engagement. Including father attitudes attenuated 30% of the effect of single father family type on engagement. According to the Sobel test, the mediating effect was statistically significant (t = 2.89, p = .004).

Of other father characteristics, there were no significant effects of father health or work hours on involvement. Greater father depression was associated with less warmth, less control, and less rule discussion. Greater father education was associated with more warmth and control, but not engagement. Older fathers reported significantly less engagement than younger fathers.

Of child characteristics, we see that fathers were consistently less involved with older (9–12) compared with younger (6–8) children, with negative associations with all four types of father involvement. There were two significant associations between race and father behaviors. Consistent with previous studies, Black children's fathers reported more control and more discussion of rules with their children than White children's fathers; Hispanic and Asian fathers did not differ from White fathers in level of involvement.

Father Time Spent Caregiving, Playing, and Teaching

Table 4.5 shows the time the father engaged in caregiving, play, and teaching based on time diary information regressed on survey year, father family structure, father attitudes, and control variables. Some of the conclusions drawn using father involvement measured using time diary data differ from those using father self-reported involvement (Table 4.4), although the sample used was the same. Consistent with the results for self-reported activity engagement, the actual time spent engaged by fathers in caregiving, play, and teaching did not differ significantly between 1997 and 2003 after controls were introduced.

The negative association between being a stepfather and diary time spent playing (b = –1.60, effect size = .28) and teaching the child (b = –.69, effect size = .30) before adding controls is consistent with the results for self-reported engagement. The inclusion of control variables reduced the association with teaching by 23%, though it remained significant. However, adding controls reversed the association between being a stepfather and playing with the child, such that controlling for background factors, stepfathers spent more time playing with stepchildren than did biological fathers in two-parent families. A similar reversal of direction occurred for caregiving, although the result was not significant. The reversal of direction suggests that selection effects may be operating; men who are likely to be better fathers may be the ones marrying women who already have children, even though they might disproportionately have other characteristics normally linked with less involvement. Analysis of missing data showed that fathers were more likely to participate in father interviews in 2003 than they

Table 4.5 Factors Predicting Fathering Time from Diaries, 1997 and 2003

	Weekly time father engaged in caregiving		Weekly time father engaged in play		Weekly time father engaged in teaching	
	Model 1	Model 2	Model 1	Model 2	Model 1	Model 2
Constant	3.73°°°	1.92	5.12°°°	3.25+	0.89°°°	−1.73
Year and type of family						
Year is 2003	0.50+	0.30	0.36	0.48	0.34°	0.27
Bio mom/bio father	ref	ref	ref	ref	ref	ref
Bio mother/ stepfather	−0.85	0.50	−1.60°	0.65°	−0.69°°°	−0.53°°
Bio father/other caregiver	2.32°	1.08°	1.11	1.57	0.50	0.55
Single father	0.18	0.68	1.94	1.55	2.06+	1.88+
Father attitudes		0.43		0.63		0.41+
Father characteristics						
Health status		0.19		0.26		−0.10
Depression scale		0.38		0.42		−0.18
Education		0.06°°		0.10		0.13°°°
Does not work		0.56		1.04		0.29
Works 1–34 hrs/wk		0.51		1.09		−0.22
Works 35–49 hrs/wk		ref		ref		ref
Works 50–59 hrs/wk		0.30°		0.60		−0.18
Works 60+ hrs/wk		0.55		0.71		−0.34
Age		0.02		0.04		−0.01
Child and family characteristics						
-Male		0.25		0.44		0.20
Age 9–12 (vs. 6–8)		0.25°		0.41		−0.12
Health status		0.21		0.28		0.16
Family income		2.19		2.62+		0.23
White		ref		ref		ref
Black		0.47		0.79+		−0.15
Hispanic		0.77°		0.84		0.61
Asian		0.52°°		1.76		0.42
Other race		0.67		1.07		−0.50°
R-squared	0.02	0.06	0.01	0.03	0.03	0.07

N = 1,119
°°° p < .001 °° p < .01, °p < .05, + p < .10, 2-tailed test

were in 1997; this may be because of the types of positive attitudinal changes we document or increased sample selectivity.

Examining custodial-father families, the results suggest that a custodial biological father living with another caregiver who is not a biological parent spent significantly more time engaged in caregiving than a biological father living with the child's other parent (b = 2.32, effect size = .70). This effect was cut in half but remained statistically significant when controls were added. Custodial biological fathers living by themselves also spent marginally (p < .10) more time engaged in teaching (b = 2.06, effect size = .88).

The effects of fathering attitudes on time spent in fathering activities differed from their effects on self-reported engagement behavior. Whereas attitudes were strongly associated with self-reported engagement, in the time diary data the only category of father time with which attitudes were associated was teaching activities, marginally significant at p < .10 (b = .41, effect size = .18). We tested the mediating effect of attitudes in the association between single father family type and teaching activities. There was a 9% reduction in the effect of single custodial father when attitudes were included, and this was marginally significant (t = 1.80, p < .07).

Greater father education was associated with more time spent caregiving and teaching but not playing. Fathers' work hours had much more impact on time diary reports of father involvement than on fathers' self-reported involvement (where no relationship appeared). For the time diary measures, fathers' work hours were associated with the amount of time the father cared for the child, but not in the direction one would expect. Fathers working 50–59 hours per week spent significantly more time providing care than those working 35–49 hours per week, the reference category. Also, in contrast to self-reported involvement, time diary measures show fathers to be engaged in *more* caregiving with older than younger children. As with self-reported fathering behaviors, no gender differences in involvement were significant, but there were race/ethnic differences. Hispanic and Asian fathers engaged in more caregiving than White fathers; Black fathers engaged in marginally more play with their children.

In order to confirm that the smaller sample was not biased by missing father reports, we ran exactly the same model appearing in Table 4.5 but without father attitudes and father depression for the sample of 1,119 used in the previous analyses and for the larger sample of 1,748. The coefficients were almost identical (not shown) but the significance levels were appropriately stronger in the larger sample. In particular, the coefficient for the influence of the custodial single father without another caregiver on time spent teaching was statistically significant at p < .05 (b = 1.94, effect size = .83). The conclusions drawn from analyses of the two samples were the same. Although this parallel analysis is not conclusive, it assures us that our conclusions are not biased by missing father self-reported involvement for many children.

Family Fixed Effects Model of Father Engagement Time: Within-Family Comparisons

To test whether differences in father engagement across father family type are due to heterogeneity across family type, we conducted family fixed effects analyses on father involvement measured by time diaries, and used the full "validation" sample. Father attitudes and father depression were not included in this analysis in order to maximize sample size.

Once we examined differences within families, some previously identified family structure associations disappeared (Table 4.6). The primary example is that stepfathers spent about the

Table 4.6 Family Fixed Effects Models of Self-Reported Father Involvement within Families, Children 6–12 in 1997 and 2003

	Weekly time father engaged in:		
	caregiving	play	teaching
Constant	3.23°	7.13°°	0.93
Year and type of family			
Year is 2003	−0.27	−0.23	−0.05
Bio mother/bio father			
Bio mother/stepfather	−0.10	−1.53	−0.19
Bio father/other caregiver	3.49+	4.51	2.64+
Single father	−0.73	−0.82	3.06°°
Father characteristics			
Health status	0.17	−0.36	−0.15
Work hours	0.01	−0.06°	−0.01
Child and family characteristics			
Age	−0.03	0.24°	0.04
Health status	−0.04	−0.01	0.14
Family income	3.19	−2.47	0.23
R^2 within	0.01	0.03	0.02

N = 1,748
°°° $p < .001$ °° $p < .01$, ° $p < .05$, + $p < .10$, 2-tailed test

same amount of time with stepchildren as did biological fathers (living with the child's biological mother) with biological children; the coefficient for play was negative and about the same size as in the previous analyses (b = −1.53, effect size = .27), but was not statistically significant. This supports previous research suggesting that the processes leading men to become stepfathers may also be linked to their involvement with children; men's involvement with biological children and stepchildren *in the same household* did not differ.

In contrast to the decline in the difference between biological father (living with child's mother) and stepfather involvement after adjusting for fixed effects, single fathers' involvement with children remained strong. The association between living with a biological father and another caregiver and father involvement was large and positive for all three activities—caregiving (3.49, effect size = 1.05), playing (b = 4.51, effect size = .78), and teaching (b = 2.64, effect size = 1.13)—although it was only marginally significant for caregiving and teaching and not significant for playing. The increased time spent teaching by single fathers without a partner remained large and significant (b = 3.06, effect size = 1.31). Year was no longer associated with father involvement, which indicated that there was no change in father involvement over time.

Unlike the OLS regressions but as expected, greater paternal work hours were associated with less time spent playing with children. Within families, fathers appeared to spend more time engaged in play with older than younger children.

Within-Individual Fixed Effects Model of Father Involvement over Time

Using the longitudinal sample, we also tested whether changes in our independent variables (father attitudes, and child, father, and mother characteristics) were associated with changes in father involvement over time for individual child-father pairs. To this end, we ran a model in which each 1997 variable was subtracted from the same variable in 2003 (Table 4.7). Father family structure was excluded because change in family type was rare in the longitudinal sample due to the selection of children in a two-parent family at both waves. Our particular interest in the role of father attitudes required that we use the smaller sample in which father reports were available. The results suggested that in families in which father attitudes became more positive, father warmth (b = .26, effect size = .34) and control of their children (b = .92, effect size = .43) increased.

In this analysis, fathers became less involved in activities as their children became older. Fathers with more schooling showed a decline in warmth and control over time as children got older. This finding might be related to the increased time spent studying or attending classes and increased time spent with peers. Changes in maternal or paternal work hours were not associated with changes in father involvement. Fathers who reported increased depressive symptoms demonstrated a decline in warmth over time. Finally, as children became healthier, father control increased.

In summary, analyses comparing involvement within families showed that stepfathers and biological fathers living with the biological mother were equally involved with their children at

Table 4.7 Individual Fixed Effects Models, Change in Self-Reported Father Involvement, 1997 to 2003

Change in Independent Variable	Change in Father Activities	Change in Father Warmth	Change in Father Control
Constant	13.96°°	0.00	0.48
Fathering attitudes	0.02	0.26°°	0.92°
Child characteristics			
Child age	-2.33°	–0.13	–0.11
Child health	0.27	0.05	0.47°°
Family income	0.00	0.00	0.00
Father and mother characteristics			
Father education	0.69	–0.19°°	–0.78°°
Father hours worked	0.00	0.00	–0.01
Mother hours worked	-0.01	0.00	–0.01
Father physical health	0.03	-0.05	0.19
Father depression	0.03	–0.16°	–0.03
R^2 within	0.02	0.05	0.06
N	523	520	452

+ p < .10 ° p < 0.05 °°p < .01 °°°p < .001

least up through age 12. What was important was the absence of the biological mother; single fathers were the most involved with their children. Analyses comparing cohorts of children over time found that both father attitudes and father involvement increased between 1997 and 2003. Their more positive fathering attitudes partially explained the association between single father family type and engagement in activities with children. Finally, both positive fathering attitudes and father monitoring and teaching increased between 1997 and 2003.

Bridges to Other Disciplines

This chapter is uniquely interdisciplinary. It examines the interconnections between father family structure—a demographic concept—and men's involvement with residential children—a family and developmental construct—over time. It investigates time trends in father involvement, and the role of changes in family structure in these trends. It also examines how father motivation for involvement with children—a psychological construct—affects father involvement, as well as explains the influence of family type on father involvement.

The analyses suggest that father involvement changed between 1997 and 2003, but these changes vary by the dimension of involvement and by who is reporting it. In self-reports, fathers' control increased, warmth and discussing rules decreased, and engagement activities remained stable. In diary reports from mothers with children, fathers' caregiving and teaching increased, and play did not change. These findings combined suggest that fathers have increased in the more instrumental aspects of parenting (control, caregiving, teaching), but have not changed or have even decreased in the more expressive aspects (engagement activities, warmth, play), with rule discussion being the exception to the pattern.

The results show that the biological relationship is not consistently predictive of father involvement. For example, although in our initial analyses stepfathers were less warm and less engaged in activities, play, and teaching than biological fathers living with the child's mother (but exhibited higher control), these results did not hold up after controlling for unobserved differences between these families using family fixed effects models. These models examined how differences in relationships of fathers to children within families were linked to differences in time the father spent with the child, controlling for all fixed unobserved characteristics, such as father temperament, that may have affected father involvement. The results supported our expectation that single fathers would be the most involved with children but did not support our hypothesis that stepfathers would be less involved. Involvement of stepfathers and fathers in two-biological-parent couples did not differ once potential selectivity in who becomes a father is taken into account. However, the presence or absence of a partner was critical. In all analyses, single fathers were most involved, measured by actual time spent—in teaching, in particular—a consistent finding regardless of analytic method.

This chapter is the first to show that fathering attitudes mediate the effect of family structure on father involvement with children, using not only self-report of fathering behavior but also the objective time diary data reported by primary caregiver and child. After father attitudes are added to a model with just the family structure and year variables, the effects of family structure decline.

This research also finds that fathering attitudes directly affect father involvement with his children. However, *who* reports on father involvement matters in the association between father involvement attitudes and behavioral involvement, just as it did in the analysis of change over time. Although attitudes were associated with several types of father involvement when father self-report of involvement was used, father attitudes toward involvement with children were associated only with teaching engagement when the engagement information came from time diaries. On the one hand, previous analyses of father involvement may have overestimated their linkage by having the same individual report on both attitude and involvement. On the other hand, time diaries reported by the mother may also not accurately reflect the level of father involvement because mothers may not know what fathers are doing when they are not present.

To test whether there is a true causal association between attitudes and behavior, we used an individual fixed effects model that examines change in attitudes and behavior between 1997 and 2003. This analysis examined how changes in father-reported attitudes were linked to changes in fathers' self-reports of engagement activities, warmth, and control, taking into account all fixed unobserved characteristics that may have affected both attitudes and involvement. These individual fixed effects analyses suggest that attitudes may have a causal and not just a correlational association with father-reported involvement; in two-parent families, changes in father attitudes were associated with increased warmth and control over time. These findings only examined fathers' self-reported involvement. Research needs to be conducted examining diary measures of engagement over time as well.

Future Directions

One of the major limitations of the study is that the data were drawn from surveys conducted in 1997 and 2003. Although there are other large nationally representative surveys that have collected contemporary data on fathering, they have neither time diary data nor data on fathering attitudes. The 2008 Census data used to describe family structure do not include measures of father involvement or father attitudes. Levels of father involvement may have continued to increase after 2003, especially because the recession that began in December 2007 may have led some fathers to spend more time with their children (Hofferth & Goldscheider, 2010). However, the recession is unlikely to have changed the association between family structure and fathering or between attitudes and fathering.

A second limitation is that the study did not include nonresidential fathers. Because nonresident fathers' nonresponse on the self-report questionnaire was very high, we were unable to include nonresidential father involvement in this study. We know that nonresidential fathers spend less time engaged with their children than residential biological fathers because they do not live with them. However, there is substantial variability in father involvement that may be related to their attitudes towards fathering and their current family structure and living arrangements. This topic would merit some attention in the future.

A third limitation is that, in spite of the large size of the overall sample, less-common marital status categories could not be examined. Single-father families would be a worthwhile focus of research, particularly in examining patterns of caregiving, how partners influence father involvement with biological children, and how parenting roles vary across these new types of households. Additionally, it would have been helpful to have examined how attitudes interact with other factors promoting father involvement (e.g., support from the co-parent, other social support, and absence of institutional barriers) specified in Lamb et al.'s (1985) four-factor model of the sources of father involvement. Further, some (but not all) of our measures of father involvement were based on father reports, which may have shared method variance with the fathering attitudes measure. Finally, we did not control for father involvement prior to age 6 or measure whether the child has a parent living in another household. Both may affect custodial parent involvement.

Policy Implications

This chapter has reported evidence that some aspects of father involvement—control and teaching—increased, whereas others—warmth, discussion of rules decreased over the 1997–2003 period. We conclude that at least some measures of father involvement have continued to increase across time in spite of changes in father family type. For policy makers who wish to improve the well-being of children, an exclusive focus on biological fathers is certainly not justified. Stepfathers did not differ from biological fathers in degree of involvement when family involvement was compared within households. Fathering attitudes had a very strong influence on father involvement. Motivating men to be more involved with children may be an objective to explore further; the results suggest that positive mental health, part-time work hours, and greater education are associated with greater motivation for involvement. Family structure was less critical than initially believed except for one group: single fathers without another caregiver. The latter have the most positive fathering attitudes. They are effectively the sole parent; as such, they have accepted the responsibility to care for their children. Much more needs to be known about how father attitudes about fathering, interactions with partners, and the availability of other potential caregivers influence men's involvement with residential children. Single fathers were clearly the most involved of all father family structures. Supports could usefully be provided to single fathers to ensure that they know how to parent their children and have the resources to do so.

Note

1 This project was supported in part by funding from the Eunice Kennedy Shriver National Institute of Child Health and Human Development through grant number P01 HD-045610 to Cornell University with a subcontract to the University of Maryland. Part of the work reported here was also supported by the USDA National Institute of Food and Agriculture, Hatch Project ILLU 45 0366 to Joseph H. Pleck.

References

Allen, E. S., Baucom, D., Bernett, C., Epstein, N., & Rankin-Esquer, L. (2010). Decision-making power, autonomy, and communication in remarried spouses compared with first-married spouses. *Family Relations, 50*, 326–334.

Fawcett, J. (1983). Perceptions of the value of children: Satisfactions and costs. In R. Bulatao & R. Lee (Eds.), *Determinants of fertility in developing countries, Vol.1: Supply and demand for children* (pp. 429–457). New York: Academic Press.

Goldscheider, F., & Sassler, S. (2006). Creating stepfamilies: Integrating children into the study of union formation. *Journal of Marriage and the Family, 68*, 275–291, erratum # 3.

Goldscheider, F., & Kaufman, G. (2006). Willingness to stepparent: Attitudes towards partners who already have children. *Journal of Family Issues, 27*, 1415–1436.

Goldscheider, F., Kaufman, G., & Sassler, S. (2009). Navigating the "New" marriage market: How attitudes towards partner characteristics shape union formation. *Journal of Family Issues, 30*, 719–737.

Hofferth, S. L. (2003). Race/ethnic differences in father involvement in two-parent families: Culture, context, or economy. *Journal of Family Issues, 24*, 185–216.

Hofferth, S. L. (2005). Secondary data analysis in family research. *Journal of Marriage and Family, 67*, 891–907.

Hofferth, S. L., & Anderson, K. (2003). Are all dads equal? Biology vs. marriage as basis for paternal investment. *Journal of Marriage and Family, 65*, 213–232.

Hofferth, S., Davis-Kean, P., Davis, J., & Finkelstein, J. (1999). *1997 user guide: The Child Development Supplement to the Panel Study of Income Dynamics*. Ann Arbor, MI: Institute for Social Research.

Hofferth, S. L., & Goldscheider, F. (2010). Family structure and the transition to parenthood. *Demography, 47,* 415–437.

Juster, F., & Stafford, F. P. (1985). *Time, goods, and well-being.* Ann Arbor, MI: Institute for Social Research.

Lamb, M. E., Pleck, J. H., Charnov, E. L., & Levine, J. A. (1985). Paternal behavior in humans. *American Zoologist, 25,* 883–894.

Mammen, K. (2011). Fathers' time investments in children: Do sons get more? *Journal of Population Economics, 24,* 839–871.

Maurer, T. W., Pleck, J. H., & Rane, T. R. (2001). Parental identity and reflected appraisals: Measurement and gender dynamics. *Journal of Marriage and the Family, 63,* 309–321.

Moffitt, R., & Rendall, M. (1995). Cohort trends in the lifetime distribution of female family headship in the United States, 1968 to 1985. *Demography, 32,* 407–424.

Palkovitz, R. (1984). Parental attitudes and father's interactions with their 5-month-old infants. *Developmental Psychology, 20,* 1054–1060.

Pleck, J. (1997, February 10). *Being a father scale.* Retrieved from items and reliability for the Fathering Attitudes Scale. Unpublished manuscript.

Pleck, J. H. (2010). Paternal involvement: Revised conceptualization and theoretical linkages with child outcomes. In M. E. Lamb (Ed.), *The role of the father in child development, 5th edition* (pp. 67–107). New York: Wiley.

Rane, T. R. (1999, May). Father involvement and identity: A theoretical examination. *Dissertation abstracts International,* 4293.

Sandberg, J. F., & Hofferth, S. L. (2001). Changes in parental time with children. *Demography, 38,* 423–436.

Sayer, L. C., Bianchi, S. M., & Robinson, J. P. (2004). Are parents investing less in children? Trends in mothers' and fathers' time with children. *American Journal of Sociology, 110,* 1–43.

Teachman, J. (2008). Complex life course patterns and the risk of divorce in second marriages. *Journal of Marriage and Family, 70,* 294–305.

Wical, K., & Doherty, W. (2005). How reliable are fathers' reports of involvement with their children? A methological report. *Fathering: A Journal of Research, Theory, and Practice, 32,* 81–93.

Willis, R. J. (1973). A new approach to the economic theory of fertility behavior. *Journal of Political Economy, 81*(2, Part II), S14–S64.

Yeung, W. J., Sandberg, J., Davis-Kean, P. E., & Hofferth, S. L. (2001). Children's time with fathers in intact families. *Journal of Marriage and Family, 63,* 136–154.

Chapter 5

Fathers and Fatherhood in the European Union

Wendy Sigle-Rushton and Alice Goisis

The London School of Economics and Political Science

Renske Keizer

Erasmus University Rotterdam

Brief Historical Overview and Theoretical Perspectives

Over the past two decades, issues related to fathers and fatherhood have attracted the attention of policy makers and researchers in both the United States and Europe, but in somewhat different ways. Public concerns about early and unmarried parenthood, increasing numbers of fathers living apart from their children, and the role of (biological) fathers in family life have been key issues in the United States (Eggebeen, 2002; Marsiglio, Amato, Day, & Lamb, 2000; Pleck, 2004). On the other side of the Atlantic, new social and political challenges such as global economic competitiveness, low fertility, and the long-term financial sustainability of social programs raised questions about gendered policy logics concerning paid work and child care. Directly and indirectly, fathers were incorporated into European Union (EU) debates about how best to promote equal opportunities, to increase female labor market participation, and to improve child outcomes. Most notably, strong incentives to encourage greater father involvement, at least when their children are young, have been embraced as both legitimate and achievable policy goals. In what follows, we draw on theoretical perspectives of gendered welfare regimes to trace how shifting policy logics concerning work and care have incorporated new understandings and expectations of the role of fathers in Europe.

The Male Breadwinner as Basis for European Welfare Regimes

The decades following the Second World War were, in most western European countries (the countries that comprised the EU prior to the fifth enlargement which began in 2004), characterized by rapid economic growth and welfare state expansion. At that time, the male breadwinner was the ideal (if not always the norm, especially in working-class families), and good fathering was implicitly equated with being steadily employed and a good economic provider (Gillis, 2000). Against this backdrop, new and generous welfare state policies were developed which presumed, reinforced, and rewarded a gendered division of labor in which men took responsibility for earning an income and women took responsibility for unpaid work and child care. Indeed, prior to the 1970s, all western European welfare states more or less subscribed to a strong "male breadwinning" ideology (Lewis, 1992). The welfare models that were built around this ideology relied, in most European countries, on the assumption of a generous supply of well-paid jobs, a growing working age population (to fund generous benefits for both workers and their dependent wives and children), and legally recognized and stable (if not permanent) marriages.

Sustainability of Male Breadwinner Welfare Systems Challenged

From the 1970s, economic and social changes resulted in new risks, some of which directly challenged the underlying policy logics of strong male breadwinner welfare regimes. Existing policy approaches were not well equipped to deal with the challenges of a post-industrial economy with its insecure employment and downward pressure on wages (Fraser, 1994). Alongside these economic changes, the form and function of the European family changed as well. Although there was (and still is, especially when we consider the larger set of countries that now make up the EU) substantial variation in trends and rates, marriage was increasingly delayed, cohabitation gained in popularity, and divorce rates increased in all countries of Europe. Fertility fell to replacement or below replacement levels, and population ageing emerged as a key policy concern (Sigle-Rushton & Kenney, 2004).

In the absence of full (male) employment and a growing working age population, questions were raised about how the funding for large and generous welfare state programs could be sustained in the absence of a growing population. One strategy was to increase the percentage of the working age population who are engaged in paid work and contributing tax revenue (Esping-Andersen, 1999). At the EU level, women and mothers were identified as target groups for employment activation (Commission of the European Communities, 2004, 2005). Because poor male employment prospects and high rates of relationship breakdown make large families and a rigid gendered division of labor risky, particularly for women who have specialized in unpaid work and care in the private sphere (Oppenheimer, 1997; Sigle-Rushton, 2010), greater female labor force participation also offered a solution to some of the new risks that individuals were confronting as a consequence of social and family change. Although embracing this strategy required a rather dramatic ideological shift for some (particularly Continental European) countries, increased female employment resonated with a Scandinavian-inspired (Duncan, 2002) but somewhat instrumental approach to the promotion of gender equality (Lewis, 2006; Lombardo & Meier, 2008).

Policy Debates: Bringing Men Into the Private Sphere

In a context where policy makers increasingly needed women to assume the roles of both worker and mother, and where a traditional gendered division of labor made meeting the demands of work and motherhood difficult, it is not surprising that men and fathers were drawn into policy debates. Because the time constraints of unpaid work increase with the transition to parenthood and because women might not want (additional) children if combining work and care is too difficult, EU documents evidenced a new and increasing preoccupation with men and fathers and their role in the private sphere. A strategy of shifting support from the male breadwinning family model to the dual earner/dual career family model emerged, at least for a short time, as a policy goal at the EU level. Although some have argued that the original aspiration of redistributing unpaid work and care responsibilities to men has been watered down or even abandoned (see, for example Lewis, 2006 and Stratigaki, 2004), female employment and low fertility remain key policy concerns. Moreover, recent shifts towards the "social investment" function of social policy have led to an intensified focus on children and youth (Jenson, 2008). This agenda dovetails with concerns in the United States about how different types and varying extents of father involvement shape men's (Eggebeen & Knoester, 2001) and especially children's (Carlson, 2006; Hawkins, Amato, & King, 2007) life outcomes. Thus, although the emphasis and motivation has changed over the course of years, fatherhood is and will likely remain on the European policy agenda. This agenda requires a solid and comparable evidence base, both to inform policy design and to aid in the evaluation of new policies. The state of the current evidence base is the primary focus of our chapter. Our main aim is to identify gaps in knowledge on fathers and fatherhood in the countries of the European Union, and consider how these limitations affect evidence-based policy.

Outline of the Chapter

In the sections that follow, we provide information about what existing data sources are able to tell us about the demography and practices of European fathers. Because the quality and availability of data differs across the countries of the EU, knowledge about fathers is far more detailed and complete in some European countries and regions than in others. While idiosyncratic data sources make valuable contributions to knowledge, they cannot be used to construct a portrait of and draw meaningful conclusions about fatherhood and the lives and fathers at the EU-level. For this reason, we turn our attention to three harmonized micro-data sources that are available for the countries of the EU, and, with reference to the measurement and conceptualization of fathers and fatherhood, we discuss their strengths and limitations. Based on our evaluations of these data sources, we suggest that existing survey designs, which have allowed *good enough* statistics and analyses of motherhood, are unable to capture the nuances and complexities of fathers' family and parenting experiences. We then discuss whether the evidence provided by the existing literature and current data sources are adequate to inform the design of, and sufficient to evaluate social policies related to fathers and fatherhood at the EU level. Despite the valuable work carried out by Eurostat to harmonize data and statistical information, we argue that data limitations lead to important gaps in knowledge that are likely to have negative repercussions. Here we suggest ways that European data sources could be made more amenable to a descriptive and analytical study of the lives and life chances of European fathers. The remaining sections outline the broader academic relevance of our main arguments by mapping some of the most obvious bridges to other social science disciplines and review the implications of our findings. Our primary conclusion is that more information on fathers' union and fertility histories would go a long way towards improving our knowledge of European fatherhood and facilitating the development of evidence based policy both at the EU- and the Member State-level.

Current Research Focus

Taking the increased policy interest in fathers at the EU level as our point of departure, we describe the status of current information about the characteristics, circumstances, and practices of European fathers, with the overarching goal of assessing whether sufficient data exist to effectively inform the development and evaluation of policies that concern these men and/or target their behaviors. Given that the value of evidence-based policy is well-recognized and that substantial resources are invested in collecting and producing good harmonized economic and social indicators at the EU-level, it is important to know whether and with what effect data on the characteristics and circumstances of fathers is under-developed and limited.

To this end, we critically assess three of the most important EU-level micro data sources. First, we provide an overview of how concepts of fathers and fatherhood are defined and what aspects of fatherhood are prioritized in the development of survey instruments. Next, we analyze some of the practical implications of these data limitations with reference to two broad social policy areas in which fathers have figured prominently: work-family reconciliation and social exclusion and poverty.

Although a focus on EU-level policy and concomitantly EU countries, necessarily excludes a number of important European countries, we feel this level of analysis is appropriate for a number of reasons. First, the European Union has grown in both size and political strength over the past two decades. Since its origins in the late 1960s, it has grown from a community of 6 countries to a union of 27 Member States. The second reason relates to the EU's role in influencing public policy. Initially conceived as an economic union supporting freedom of trade and movement, it has always had a good deal of regulatory power over economic policy and competition issues to facilitate market integration. In other policy domains, the principle of subsidiarity—that policy issues should be addressed as locally as practicable—has meant that the EU's ability to intervene in other policy domains has been relatively restricted. Nonetheless, EU policy has, over time, moved beyond a narrow interpretation of economic policy and, by harnessing social issues to economic concerns, extended its range of influence to non-economic interventions (Walby, 2004). Importantly, both hard and soft law measures have been developed that directly relate to the circumstances and behaviors of fathers ("soft" law policy instruments are flexible and non-binding rather than "hard" law approaches which are characterized by some form of compulsion and carry penalties for non-compliance (see Marginson & Sisson, 2006, for a discussion)). For different reasons, both types of legal interventions require an evidence base of high quality, comparable indicators and data. Given its size, policy competencies, and institutional mechanisms, the EU provides a particularly relevant and rich legislative context in which to explore how fathers and fatherhood have been conceptualized across policies and data sources. This will allow us to identify some of the most important, policy-relevant gaps in knowledge about fathers in Europe.

Research Measurement and Methodology

The increased focus on and reinterpretation of European fatherhood, along with debates about the role that policy can play in effecting change, emerged at a time when, with the exception of Denmark and Britain, there was no real evidence base to guide and inform policy on male fertility and fatherhood (Clarke, Cooksey, & Verropoulo, 1998). Scholarly work on European fathers has proliferated over the last decade, but the development of knowledge has been geographically and substantively uneven. Because the quality and availability of secondary survey and administrative data sources differs across the countries of the EU, knowledge is far more advanced in some countries than in others. Those studies on fathers and father-hood which have adopted a comparative approach have done so only on few countries and have predominantly looked at narrowly defined policy issues while leaving unanswered other important questions concerning European fathers. For example, register data in Scandinavian countries have allowed researchers to examine a range of issues which have to do with male fertility and fatherhood. Recent examples include an assessment of men's propensity to take up parental leave in Sweden (A. Duvander & Johansson, 2010) and an examination of multiple partner fertility in Norway (Lappegård, Rønsen, & Skrede, 2009). Because the same kinds of administrative data are collected across different Scandinavian countries, within Nordic-region comparisons are possible allowing for some cross-national comparison. As valuable as these country-level or intra-regional analyses can be, we still know very little about the social, demographic and economic characteristics of fathers from these sorts of analyses. Despite very complete data on fathers, most single or intra-regional studies of fertility pay more attention to the experiences of women than of men (see, for example, Duvander, Lappegård, & Andersson, 2010). This means register data have the potential to contribute to the development of a cross-nationally comparative descriptive portrait of fatherhood for a subset of EU countries in the Nordic region, but not, of course, for the EU as a whole.

Although a cross-national comparative description of European fathers has not been pro-duced using country-level data sources, there is a cross-national comparative literature that investigates the extent to which differences in family policies across Europe are related to cross national differences in the incentives for fathers to make use of paternity and parental leave entitlements (Fatherhood Institute, 2010; O'Brien, 2004, 2009; O'Brien & Moss, 2010) or for increased father involvement (Smith & Williams, 2007). Even these more comprehensive and comparative policy studies tend to devote more attention to some parts of the European Union than others. Knowledge about the policies of Eastern European countries, and to a lesser extent Southern European countries, remains sparse (but see Robila, 2010). Although there is clearly some untapped potential in existing data sources, when knowledge about fathers is required at the EU-level, the use of country-specific data sources or research findings will almost certainly mean limitations in terms of scope and/or geographic coverage. This under-scores the need for developing and maintaining high quality, harmonized data sources at the EU-level.

Harmonized Data Sources

Given the large number of European countries and the varying availability and design of coun-try-specific data sources, researchers wanting to construct a comprehensive cross-national por-trait of European fathers or to evaluate policies that target fathers will almost certainly have to rely on harmonized data sources. For countries (and candidate countries) of the European Union (EU) and the EFTA, Eurostat has played an important role in providing researchers with harmonized secondary survey data (Burkhauser & Lillard, 2005). Although Eurostat is involved in both ex ante (at the point of survey design) and ex post (after the data are collected) harmonization efforts, it does not organize data collection centrally. National statistical offices or ministries must respond to requests for information from the Commission or Directorates, and Eurostat is charged with collecting, consolidating, and disseminating this information at the European level. As part of this process, Eurostat works to ensure comparability of data across countries, but, its ability to produce comparable data and statistics depends on the quality of data collected by the Member States.

Strengths of the three data sources. For researchers who are interested in European fatherhood, the three most important harmonized data sources that Eurostat is currently responsible for harmonizing are the Harmonized European Time Use data (HETUS), the Survey of Income and Living Conditions (EU-SILC) (and its predecessor, the European Community Household Panel Survey (ECHP)), and the European Labour Force Survey (EU-LFS). Each data source has its own particular strengths. The HETUS data, which is available for 14 EU countries as well as Norway, provides detailed information on how men and women allocate their time. The data, mostly collected at the turn of the century, are collected using time diaries and in most cases individuals are asked to provide time use information for both one week day and one weekend day. Although the HETUS data are highly comparable, the harmonization guidelines, first issued in 2000 (Eurostat, 2000) and most recently updated in 2008 (Eurostat, 2009), did not stipulate that time use information be collected from all individuals living in the same household. Nonetheless, all countries have made an effort to collect diary information from respondents and their partners (most also ask older children to fill in diaries), which makes an intra-household analysis of time use possible. Although this particular strength of the European time use data has been somewhat underutilized and most studies continue to use individuals as the unit of analysis, measures of time allocation using matched couples (see, for example, Craig & Mullan, 2010) or members of the same household are possible. The data have recently been incorporated into the larger Multinational Time Use Study making it possible to compare a larger number of countries (see for example, Gauthier, Smeeding, & Furstenberg, 2004) and to examine change over time in the time use patterns of mothers and fathers in same country (see, for example, Dribe & Stanfors, 2009 for Sweden and Sullivan, Coltrane, Mcannally, & Altintas, 2009) for a cross-country comparison of change over time). However, MTUS efforts to harmonize data from a larger number of surveys comes at the cost of even more limited information on the presence and age of children in European households relative to the HETUS (Sullivan et al., 2009).

The EU-SILC data aim to collect detailed comparative measures of income and deprivation. The data cover all Member States plus Norway and Iceland and comprise both a cross-sectional and a longitudinal component. The longitudinal component is a key strength of these data because it allows researchers to follow households over time. Transitions and their consequences can be well measured, at least within the four years the households are followed. Measures of income and deprivation are particularly detailed and carefully measured. In some ways, the EU-SILC is less ambitious than its predecessor, the European Community Household Panel (ECHP) Survey, which began with a sample of about 65,000 households and 130,000 individuals in 1994 with annual follow-ups until 2001 when the survey was discontinued. The ECHP followed the same households for a longer period of time and collected a wider range and breadth of information than the EU-SILC. For example, it contains information on time spent caring for children, and so provides some information on parental time investments in child care (Smith, 2004; Smith & Williams, 2007). However, the ex-ante harmonization process ran into a range of problems such as attrition and a failure to incorporate country-level expertise (Burkhauser & Lillard, 2005). Moreover the ECHP was discontinued before the 2004 accession and so lacks information on the new Member States. The EU-LFS follows a random sample of respondents aged 15 and older in all EU, three candidate, and three EFTA (Iceland, Norway, and Switzerland) countries for five calendar quarters. Although data have been collected for much longer, EU-LFS micro-data is available extending back to 1983. It provides an excellent source of information for describing employment status, work choices, aspirations and constraints over five calendar quarters. A primary advantage of the EU-LFS is its large sample size which allows researchers to examine small population sub-groups, such as ethnic minorities or immigrants (the 2010 quarterly data contain approximately 1,500,000 observations in total), and it also has an excellent response rate. Respondents who are currently unemployed or working part-time hours are asked to provide reasons for that choice. Options include caring commitments and lack of adequate child care. For those who are currently employed, there is also information on satisfaction with working hours. This information, when combined with information on household structure, can shed light on the work-life balance strategies parents choose as well as unmet demand for better work-life balance or working hours (Thévenon, 2008).

Limitations of the three data sources.   Despite a range of strengths and complementarities, the three data sources (and the discontinued ECHP) also share important limitations, not least for the study of European fathers. In some sense, this is to be expected given the central role that Eurostat has assumed in the development and harmonization of the three. For example, the EU-LFS has influenced the design and approach to the EU-SILC. In none of the three data sources are fertility histories or family formation histories collected. At most, we know a respondent's marital and cohabitation status at the time (s)he was first interviewed. We know whether (s)he was ever married, but we do not know when changes occurred. For several northern European countries, information on household composition is not collected in their national labor force survey and so this is missing for those countries in the harmonized EU-LFS. The lack of fertility histories means that mothers and fathers are only identified when they are observed living with their children. Because children tend to live with their mothers throughout childhood, researchers have developed techniques that allow them to infer fertility histories by using information on co-resident children (Cho, Retherford, & Choe, 1986). This method has been used successfully when mothers are the unit of analysis. Usually, the age range is restricted to women below either age 40 or 45 in order to avoid misclassifying respondents whose children have already left home. Although there is some potential for measurement error, the own child method has allowed researchers to examine the fertility of women in the absence of detailed fertility histories. However, this sort of method cannot be meaningfully applied to men because many will have children who are not residing with them at the time of interview. We do not know if men have children living in another household, and, as a consequence, cannot use the data to calculate even rough estimates of men's fertility histories or family size. In addition, there is insufficient information in any of the data sources to distinguish biological from social/stepfather relationships. The panel element of EU-SILC and the EU-LFS allows researchers to observe births that take place over the course of the panel (4 years in the EU-SILC but only over the course of five calendar quarters in the EU-LFS), but for children born before their families entered the study, information on relationships between adults and children is limited and inadequate. In the EU-SILC there is no household grid, although information is collected so that the presence of (married or cohabiting) partners, parents, or children living in the same household as the respondent can be identified. Unfortunately, these data do not clearly distinguish biological parents from stepparents (Iacovou & Skew, 2010). In the EU-LFS or the HETUS data, there are variables that record the relationship between each household member and the household reference person (EU-LFS) or all other household members (HETUS). In both surveys, the "child" code refers both to biological children of the respondent or of the respondent's cohabiting partner/spouse. Similarly to the EU-SILC, there are additional variables that contain the sequence number of the father and mother, but the distinction between biological and social parents is not clearly made (Eurostat, 2000, 2009, 2010).

Because men are more likely to assume a step-parent role and women most often remain the custodial parent, the inability to distinguish social and biological parents has far more important implications for the description and analysis of fatherhood than of motherhood. Without union histories to identify the start of a relationship, it is difficult to make inferences about biological paternity. Moreover, because the guidelines of the HETUS only require that information be collected about whether activities were carried out with or in the presence of "other household members" or an unspecified "other person that you know," information on the time non-resident fathers spend with their children is not well captured in these data. The ECHP data contained some additional information on the presence of step, fostered, or adopted children in the family which researchers have used (Koslowski, 2011), but the exact relationship between the father and each child is not well recorded. In a context where family structures have become increasingly unstable and complex and where the roles and responsibilities of biological and social parents are likely to differ, this is a substantial limitation.

Empirical Findings

In the previous section we provided information on the strengths and limitations of three harmonized data sources which contain information about families and which are likely to provide the best aggregate and cross-national comparative information on fathers and fatherhood in the EU. Most importantly, current guidelines are not sufficiently attentive to distinctions between biological and social parenthood. As a consequence, researchers who wish to use any of these harmonized data sources to document and analyze the demography of fatherhood in Europe have to be content with measures of fatherhood that are rather crudely specified and poorly measured. In this section, we discuss the practical implications of this and some other limitations of the three data sources. To do this, we explore the issues through the lens of two broad areas where a strong evidence base could usefully inform the development, design, and evaluation of EU policy. We first consider the area of work life reconciliation. The Parental Leave Directive, a hard law measure first introduced in the mid-1990s, resulted in a number of provisions and a good deal of cross-national policy variation across EU countries, particularly in their attempts to create incentives for greater father involvement. We identify gaps between what information is needed to evaluate effectively the success and impact of different policy specifications and what information is currently available at the EU-level. Next, we consider the implications of limitations in the harmonized data sources for the development of measures to combat poverty and social inclusion which take into account the circumstances of fathers or the role they play in addressing child poverty and promoting child well-being.

Work-family Reconciliation: Parental Leave Policy and the Redistribution of Care

Parental leave has a long history on the EU social policy agenda and has figured prominently in debates surrounding gender equality and work-family reconciliation. A (hard law) Directive on Parental Leave was first proposed by the EU-Commission in 1983, but despite widespread support, its adoption was thwarted, in part, by strong opposition from the UK Government. Parental leave is also mentioned in the 1989 Community Charter of the Fundamental Social Rights of Workers (Commission of the European Communities, 1990), which states that "measures should ... be developed enabling men and women to reconcile their occupational and family obligations.". Progress in obtaining a binding agreement at the EU-level was slow, although the agenda was taken forward with independent and often creative innovations by several Member States. For example, policies with strong incentives for men to take parental leave—in the form of "use it or lose it", non-transferable entitlements—were implemented by several Scandinavian countries in the 1990s. Individual entitlements with high levels of wage replacement were believed to offer the greatest incentive for men to take more (or any) parental leave and to redistribute some of the costs and benefits of caring for children from women to men (Bruning & Plantenga, 1999). Although not going as far as many Scandinavian countries, the 1996 Parental Leave Directive (96/34/EC) stipulated individual entitlements of three months job-protected leave be available to each parent to care for a child up until age 8. Many details concerning the design and implementation, for example whether the leave was paid or whether it could be taken part-time, were left to the discretion of Member States, however (Council of the European Union, 1996). The result is a good deal of variation in the design and generosity of parental leave policies in the EU and EFTA, particularly in the strength of the incentives they provide for fathers to take leave (Moss, 2010).

To assess whether developments and innovations in parental leave have had their intended consequences, one of which is the redistribution of child care work from women to men (O'Brien, 2009), we need to examine the extent to which men take leave (including the share of leave days) as well as any changes in behavior that might be attributed to increased leave taking. Unfortunately, except for a few recent studies, there is little empirical evidence on the extent to which taking parental leave increases father involvement either in the shorter- or longer-term. Studies by Haas and Hwang (2008) and Rege and Solli (2010), draw on Swedish and Norwegian data, respectively, and show that the introduction of individual, non-transferable entitlements is positively associated with father involvement. This is an important result as it suggests that paternity and parental leave policies could have implications for child well-being (Rege & Solli, 2010). Nonetheless, the analyses are confined to the Nordic region, which raises issues of generalizability to other institutional contexts. As a consequence, there is only weak evidence available to guide policymakers who are interested designing leave policies which foster greater father involvement.

Cross-national comparisons of leave taking amongst men are far more common than studies that examine the consequences of leave taking. For example, research shows that in those countries where there is no remuneration for men, they are less likely to take parental leave (Plantenga & Remery, 2005). While it is useful to establish which designs increase fathers' propensity to make use of parental leave arrangements, if leave taking is a means to achieve better child outcomes, increased fertility or some other policy target, many important questions remain unanswered. Several of these questions remain unanswered because existing data sources are inadequate to address them. There are surprisingly few studies, either single country or cross-national, that document how parents who are on leave—mothers or fathers—spend their time, much less whether early experiences of one-to-one care by fathers, incentivized by innovations in parental leave policies, translates into greater involvement in subsequent years. Similarly, there is limited information on whether a more equal distribution of the leave entitlement results in a redistribution of responsibilities so that the other partner spends less time caring. In other words, does a father's care substitute for the mother's time or simply increase the total amount of care provided? To answer these kinds of questions, we require information on current and retrospective use of parental leave, preferably with samples both before and after a policy innovation was implemented, as well as good quality information on current time use patterns, for both resident and non-resident parents. Unfortunately, existing micro-data for EU countries does not contain this level of detail. Researchers can assess whether the time use of fathers across countries with different parental leave policies differs. This kind of study design is possible using data drawn from the ECHP (Smith & Williams, 2007) or by making use of MTUS/HETUS data (Craig & Mullan, 2010; Sullivan et al., 2009). The development by Sullivan and colleagues (2009) of a new database, which links institutional-level macro-policy indicators to existing time use studies, will facilitate and greatly enhance research of this kind. However, this kind of research design produces tentative results, because it is difficult to disentangle cause and effect (Craig & Mullan, 2010; Sigle-Rushton, 2009). The design and implementation of parental leave policies, which involve a degree of discretion from the Member States, is endogenous to the institutional context and social norms of each country. Countries with generous and inclusive leave policies may have them because the population preferred shared care and governments responded to those preferences (Pfau-Effinger, 2004) or because policy changes resulted in a change of attitudes and behavior (Himmelweit & Sigala, 2004). Policies, preferences, and behavior are mutually constitutive at any level and make causal interpretations suspect, but data which allow a closer links between policy parameters and individual behavior both before and after policy changes, would be a move in the right direction. There are also issues of omitted variable bias to consider. If countries with higher fertility also have more generous parental leave, it could be that fathers spend more time on child care in countries with generous parental leave because the average number of children per adult is larger in those countries. If countries with generous parental leave are also countries where dissolution rates are higher, it is important to control not just for the presence of children in the household but for non-resident children who may nonetheless visit with and be cared for by their biological father. Retrospective questions on men's fertility and partnership histories and on the use of parental leave in the HETUS would add substantially to knowledge about the extent and nature of father involvement across the diversity of countries that comprise the EU and would provide a stronger evidence base for policy makers. Moreover, it would allow researchers to construct better measures of the "demand" for child care and in that way better control for confounding factors that might bias estimated relationships between parental leave and desired outcomes—either father involvement or child well-being. This kind of information would have been particularly useful when amendments to the Parental Leave Directive were recently debated and approved (2010/18/EU). These changes, which will increase the minimum amount of parental leave that EU countries have to offer from six to eight months, but, at the same time, make it possible for countries to allow all but one month (rather than the three previously required) to be transferable between parents, will likely increase the share of leave taken by women in those countries which choose to weaken incentives for shared leave. The impact of the change on parents and children can only be speculated, and unless new information becomes available, the effects of the policy amendment cannot be effectively evaluated.

Poverty and Social Exclusion

Social policies to combat poverty and social exclusion, although regulated through soft rather than hard law measures, and with a less marked historical tradition than policies related to work-life reconciliation, have been identified by the EU policy agenda as key areas for action.

The new EU Youth Strategy (2010–2018) (Commission of the European Communities, 2009) has defined social inclusion as one of the "fields of action," and the European Commission and the Member States have made combating child poverty a priority under the Open Method of Coordination (OMC) on Social Protection and Social Inclusion. Since 2000, the European Union has used the OMC as a way of guiding national strategy development on issues related to social policies. As part of the process, Member States are called upon to produce periodic national action plans detailing the way in which OMC priorities are or will be addressed at the national level. The aim is to identify and share the best practice of high performers and to inspire innovation and reform where performance could be improved. Both the inherently comparative nature of the OMC and its reliance on harmonized indicators to monitor progress, underscore the importance of high quality and comparable data. Although the European Platform against Poverty and Social Exclusion identifies the promotion of "evidence based social innovation" (European Commission, 2010, p. 5) as an area for action and although this is a policy area for fathers and fatherhood, the empirical evidence base remains under-developed.

A good deal of attention has been devoted to the measurement of poverty and social exclusion in the EU-SILC data, but there are several policy areas involving fathers where more complete data could add to knowledge and inform policy dialogue and development. The Recommendation on Child Poverty, planned for 2012 (European Commission, 2010), provides an obvious example. Poverty rates differ substantially across countries, but children living with lone mothers are, on average, more likely to be poor than children living in two-parent families in the same country (Rainwater & Smeeding, 2004). This explains, at least in part, why lone mothers or one-parent families more generally, are frequently identified by the European Commission and in many European countries' National Action Plans as vulnerable to poverty and social exclusion. Since the design of child support policies differs substantially across EU and EFTA countries (Skinner, Bradshaw, & Davidson, 2007), the evaluation of best practice in child support policy and its contribution to the economic well-being of children requires information on the role that child maintenance plays in the income packages of one-parent or, to a lesser extent, stepfamilies. Although the EU-SILC collects information on the payment and receipt of child maintenance, the lack of information on non-resident fathers and their children makes it impossible to measure how many men are non-resident fathers and are paying, or indeed not paying, regular maintenance. Moreover, because in reconstituted families it is not clear whether the children in the household are living with both biological parents or whether they are living with a stepfather, the amount of maintenance per eligible child cannot be (well) measured either. In this area of policy as well, fertility and union histories are needed to put the income data to good use (i.e., by enabling data users to identify "biological" relationships as opposed to "social" relationships) and to provide good cross-national comparative information on the design of effective child maintenance policies that work to reduce child poverty.

Another plan to support social inclusion under the EU Youth Strategy (2010–2018) (Commission of the European Communities, 2009) is the "promotion of specific support for young families." Although teenage and young parenthood is not a source of general anxiety, the need for support is motivated more by the recognition that early parenthood may curtail investments in education. In a context where the 2000 Lisbon Strategy aims to make the EU "the most competitive knowledge-based economy in the world," young families may be less able to compete in a post-industrial labor market. Conversely, prolonged investments in education may contribute to even lower fertility, a competing EU policy concern. Designing policies that encourage investments in education while at the same time helping families to have the number of children they want, requires a better understanding of obstacles to family formation and how they change at different points in the transition to adulthood. However, most of the European research on the consequences of the timing of first birth has focused on women. There is very little evidence on the effects of early parenthood on men. This is a particularly salient issue in the enlarged EU where in some countries the entry to parenthood, at least among mothers, has not been delayed to the same extent across socio-economic groups, raising further questions about the economic capabilities of young parents (McLanahan, 2004). More detailed information on the fertility and union histories of both women and men in the EU-SILC would add substantially to knowledge about the longer term risks and challenges facing young parents and their children.

Bridges to Other Disciplines

In this chapter we have drawn on the theoretical perspectives of social policy and used examples from social policy to illustrate the pressing need for new or improved data on the characteristics and behaviors of European fathers. However, many academics have argued that social policy is more precisely defined as a subject area than a discipline because it draws on a wide range of social science disciplines, including for example, demography, sociology, economics, and psychology, to advance knowledge in the area of policy (Blakemore & Griggs, 2007). To the extent that this is true, our use of a social policy perspective to motivate and evaluate the state of knowledge on the demography of fatherhood in Europe implicitly incorporates the interests and concerns of a wide range of disciplines. In this sense, other disciplines are already well integrated in our perspective and approach.

Nonetheless, it is clear that the benefits of more detailed, comparable, and high quality data on fatherhood, would serve the interests in researchers working on more broadly defined issues related to fatherhood. As Goldscheider and Kaufman (1996) argue, many of the practical justifications demographers gave for neglecting men's fertility (for example, that women are more likely to be home and available for interview) are no longer very convincing or valid. They discuss several important blind spots that they attribute to a (nearly) exclusive focus on women in studies of fertility, many of which resonate with the issues we discuss in this chapter. Sociologists, economists, and psychologists who are interested in studying the relationship between family structure and child well-being would put forward equally convincing arguments about the limitations of data that do not clearly distinguish biological fatherhood from social fatherhood. Sociologists and psychologists who are interested in assessing the importance of family ties that connect individuals across households (see, for example, Smock & Rose Greenland, 2010) would similarly take issue with survey designs that pay so little attention to non-resident fathers.

Summary

In recent years, European policy makers have increasingly seen fathers as both workers and carers. Although the "rise and fall" of the male breadwinner is something of an overstatement, it is clear that the male breadwinner (perhaps to a lesser extent than the female carer) no longer reflects preferences or reality in much of Europe. And the potential benefits of policies that support the dual earner/dual career family model—including higher fertility, greater economic security for families, a higher tax base for social security, and improved child well-being—have not escaped the attention of EU policy makers. As our analyses in the previous sections have demonstrated, existing EU data sources will not provide the solid evidence base that is needed to reform existing policies and to develop new policy instruments that reflect both social change and new policy priorities. A good deal of effort has gone into the conceptualization, measurement, and harmonization of employment and income indicators. However, support for the dual earner/dual carer family means more than moving women into the work place. It also means a more equal distribution of unpaid work and care, particularly in families with children where demands for unpaid work and care are high and often unevenly distributed. With high rates of union dissolution, it means that parenting responsibilities, which include both earning and caring, will often be allocated to social fathers as well as extend across household boundaries. The current evidence base is inadequate to support the development and evaluation of policies that address these latter issues. There is a clear need for better and more detailed information on the circumstances, needs and practices of European fathers and which is representative of the wide diversity of Member States which are now (and will in the future be) part of the EU.

Future Directions

Social and demographic change will always create new data demands. Two decades ago, survey data started to change in ways that made it easier to document the prevalence of cohabiting unions and to examine the characteristics and circumstances of individuals who chose to cohabit (at least temporarily) rather than marry. As fathers are expected to contribute more to the care of their children, and as policy makers seek to reinforce this behavior, we need data that allow us to measure and understand the extent and consequences of behavioral change. Because fathers, after separating from the mother of their children, still tend to live away from their biological children, this means we need more information on men's non-resident children and more retrospective information on men's previous partnerships. Family life is increasingly complex, and home life increasingly involves multiple locations. Attempts to collect new data of this kind will be expensive. In addition, survey designs will need to be developed with great care, not least because research suggests that men often fail to provide complete fertility histories (Rendall, Clarke, Peters, Ranjit, & Verropoulou, 1999). However, there is a growing body of evidence on best practice, largely from U.S. studies, that could be used to guide any new efforts at data collection (Joyner et al., 2012). And there are cross-national comparative projects which have sought to collect male fertility histories, such as the Generations and Gender Study, from which additional lessons could be drawn. Although a risky endeavor, we have to consider the risks that accompany the status quo. Data that fails to capture the complexity of modern family life will be partial and limited, and its ability to inform policy and practice will be severely compromised.

References

Blakemore, K., & Griggs, E. (2007). *Social policy: An introduction*. Buckingham, UK: Open University Press.

Bruning, G., & Plantenga, J. (1999). Parental leave and equal opportunities in eight European countries. *Journal of European Social Policy, 9*(3), 195–209.

Burkhauser, R. V., & Lillard, D. R. (2005). *The contribution and potential of data harmonization for cross-national comparative research*. Discussion Papers of DIW.number 486. Berlin: Deutsches Institut für Wirtschaftsforschung (German Institute for Economic Research).

Carlson, M. J. (2006). Family structure, father involvement, and adolescent behavioral outcomes. *Journal of Marriage and Family, 68*(1), 137–154.

Cho, L.-J., Retherford, R. D., & Choe, M. K. (1986). *The own-children method of fertility estimation.* Honolulu, HI: East-West Center.

Clarke, L., Cooksey, E. C., & Verropoulo, G. (1998). Fathers and absent fathers: socio demographic similarities in Britain and the United States. *Demography, 35*(2), 217–228.

Commission of the European Communities. (1990). *Charter of the Fundamental Social Rights of Workers.* Luxembourg: Office of Official Publications of the European Communities.

Commission of the European Communities. (2004). *Report of the High Level Group on the Future of Social Policy in an Enlarged European Union.* Luxembourg: Office of Official Publications of the European Communities.

Commission of the European Communities. (2005, March 16). *Green paper confronting demographic change: A new solidarity between the generations.* Document 94 final. Brussels: Author.

Commission of the European Communities. (2009, April 4). *An EU strategy for youth- investing and empowering. A renewed open method of coordination to address youth challenges and opportunities.* Document 200 final. Brussels: Author.

Council of the European Union. (1996, June 19). Directive 96/34/EC of 3 June 1996 on 'The framework agreement on parental leave concluded by UNICE, CEEP, and the ETUC. *Official Journal of the European Communities,145,* 0004–0009.

Craig, L., & Mullan, K. (2010). Parenthood, gender and work-family time in the United States, Australia, Italy, France, and Denmark. *Journal of Marriage and Family, 72,* 1344–1361.

Dribe, M., & Stanfors, M. (2009). Does parenthood strengthen a traditional household division of labor? Evidence From Sweden. *Journal of Marriage and Family, 71*(1), 33–45.

Duncan, S. (2002). Policy discourses on in the EU. *Social Policy and Society, 1*(4), 305–314.

Duvander, A., & Johansson, M. (2010). *What are the effects of reforms promoting fathers' parental leave use?* Stickholm, Sweden: Stockholm University Linnaeus Center on Social Policy and Family Dynamics in Europe.

Duvander, A. Z., Lappegård, T., & Andersson, G. (2010). Family policy and fertility: fathers' and mothers' use of parental leave and continued childbearing in Norway and Sweden. *Journal of European Social Policy, 20*(1), 45–57.

Eggebeen , D. J. (2002). The changing course of fatherhood. *Journal of Family Issues, 23*(4), 486–506.

Eggebeen, D. J., & Knoester, C. (2001). Does fatherhood matter for men? *Journal of Marriage and Family, 63*(2), 381–393.

Esping-Andersen, G. (1999). *Social foundations of post industrial economies.* Oxford, UK: Oxford University Press.

European Commission. (2010, December 16). *The European Platform against Poverty and Social Exclusion: A European framework for social and territorial cohesion.* Document 758 final Brussels: Author.

Eurostat. (2000). *Guidelines on harmonized European time use survey.* Luxembourg: Eurostat.

Eurostat. (2009). *Harmonised European time use surveys, 2008 guidelines.* Luxembourg: Office for Official Publications of the European Communities.

Eurostat. (2010). *EU labour force survey database user guide.* Luxembourg: Eurostat.

Fatherhood Institute. (2010). *The fatherhood report 2010–11: The fairness in families index.* London: The Fatherhood Institute.

Fraser, N. (1994). After the family wage: Gender equity and the welfare state. *Political Theory, 22*(4), 591–618.

Gauthier, A. H., Smeeding, T. M., & Furstenberg, F. F. J. (2004). Are parents investing less time in children? Trends in selected industrialized countries. *Population and Development Review, 30*(4), 647–671.

Gillis, J. R. (2000). Marginalization of fatherhood in Western countries. *Childhood, 7*(2), 225–238.

Goldscheider, F., & Kaufman, G. (1996). Fertility and commitment: Bringing men back in. *Population and Development Review, 22* (Supplement), 87–99.

Haas, L., & Hwang, C. P. (2008). The impact of taking parental leave on fathers' participation in childcare and relationships with children: Lessons from Sweden. *Community, Work & Family, 11*(1), 85–104.

Hawkins, D. N., Amato, P. R., & King, V. (2007). Nonresident father involvement and adolescent well-being: Father effects or child effects? *American Sociological Review, 72*(6), 990–1010.

Himmelweit, S., & Sigala, M. (2004). Choice and the relationship between identities and behaviour for mothers with pre-school children: Some implications for policy from a UK study. *Journal of Social Policy, 33*(3), 455–478.

Iacovou, M., & Skew, A. (2010). *Household structure in the EU*. Eurostat methodologies and working papers. Luxembourg: Publications Office of the European Union.

Jenson, J. (2008). Writing women out, folding gender in: The European Union 'modernises' social policy. *Social Politics: International Studies in Gender, State & Society, 15*(2), 131–153.

Joyner, K., Peters, H. E., Hynes, K., Sikora, A., Rubenstein, J., & Rendall, M. S. (2012). The quality of male fertility data in major U.S. surveys. *Demography, 49*(1), 101–124.

Koslowski, A. S. (2011). Working fathers in Europe: Earning and caring. *European Sociological Review, 27*(2), 230–245.

Lappegård, T., Rønsen, M., & Skrede, K. (2009, September). *Socioeconomic differentials in multi-partner fertility among fathers*. Paper presented at the XXVI IUSSP International Population Conference, Marrakesh, Morocco.

Lewis, J. (1992). Gender and the development of European welfare regimes. *Journal of European Social Policy 2*(3), 159–173.

Lewis, J. (2006). Work/family reconciliation, equal opportunities and social policies: The interpretation of policy trajectories at the EU level and the meaning of gender equality. *Journal of European Public Policy, 13*(3), 420–437.

Lombardo, E., & Meier, P. (2008). Framing gender equality in the European Union political discourse. *Social Politics: International Studies in Gender, State & Society, 15*(1), 101–129.

McLanahan, S. (2004). Diverging destinies: How children are faring under the second demographic transition. *Demography, 41*(4), 607–627.

Marginson, P., & Sisson, K. (2006). *European integration and industrial relations – Multi-level governance in the making*. London: Palgrave Macmillan.

Marsiglio, W., Amato, P., Day, R. D., & Lamb, M. E. (2000). Scholarship on fatherhood in the 1990s and beyond. *Journal of Marriage and Family, 62*(4), 1173–1191.

Moss, P. (2010). International review of leave policies and related research. Employment relations research series no. 115. London: Department for Business, Innovation and Skills. Retrieved from http://www.leavenetwork.org/archive_2005_2009/annual_reviews/

O'Brien, M. (2004). Social science and public policy perspectives on fatherhood in the European Union. In M. E. Lamb (Ed.), *The role of the father in child development* (pp. 121–145). New York: Wiley.

O'Brien, M. (2009). Fathers, parental leave policies, and infant quality of life: International perspectives and policy impact. *The Annals of the American Academy of Political and Social Science, 624*(1), 190–213.

O'Brien, M., & Moss, P. (2010). Fathers, work and family policies in Europe. In M. E. Lamb (Ed.), *The role of the father in child development* (pp. 551–577). New York: Wiley.

Oppenheimer, V. K. (1997). Women's employment and the gain to marriage: The specialization and trading model. *Annual Review of Sociology, 23*, 431–453.

Pfau-Effinger, B. (2004). Socio-historical paths of the male breadwinner model: An explanation of cross national differences. *British Journal of Sociology, 55*(3), 377–399.

Plantenga, J., & Remery, C. (2005). *Reconciliation of work and private life: A comparative review of thirty European countries*. European Commission, Luxembourg: Office for Official Publications of the European Communities.

Pleck, J. H. (2004). Paternal involvement: levels, sources, and consequences. In M. E. Lamb (Ed.), *The role of the father in child development* (pp. 66–103). New York: Wiley.

Rainwater, L., & Smeeding, T. M. (2004). Single-parent poverty, inequality, and the welfare state. In D. P. Moynihan, T. M. Smeeding, & L. Rainwater (Eds.), *The future of the family* (pp. 96–115). New York: Russell Sage Foundation.

Rege, M., & Solli, I. F. (2010). *The impact of paternity leave on long-term father involvement.* CESIFO Working paper. Paper series 3130. Munich: CESIFO.

Rendall, M. S., Clarke, L., Peters, E., Ranjit, N., & Verropoulou, G. (1999). Incomplete Reporting of men's fertility in the United States and Britain: A research note. *Demography, 36*(1), 135–144.

Robila, M. (2010). Family policies in Eastern Europe: A focus on parental leave. *Journal of Child and Family Studies,* 1–10.

Sigle-Rushton, W. (2009). Comparative methods in research on gender and welfare states. *21st Century Society, 4*(2), 137–148.

Sigle-Rushton, W. (2010). Men's unpaid work and divorce: Reassessing specialization and trade. *Feminist Economics, 16*(2), 1–26.

Sigle-Rushton, W., & Kenney, C. (2004). Public policy and families. In M. Richards, J. Scott, & J. Treas (Eds.), *Companion to the sociology of families* (pp. 457–477). New York: Blackwell.

Skinner, C., Bradshaw, J., & Davidson, J. (2007). *Child support policy: An international perspective.* Department of Work and Pensions Report Vol 405. Leeds, UK: Corporate Document Services.

Smith, A. J. (2004). *Who cares? European fathers and the time they spend looking after children.* Sociology Working Papers: 2004–2005. Oxford: University of Oxford.

Smith, A. J., & Williams, D. R. (2007). Father-friendly legislation and paternal time across western Europe. *Journal of Comparative Policy Analysis, 9*(2), 175–192.

Smock, P. J., & Rose Greenland, F. (2010). Diversity in pathways to parenthood: Patterns, implications, and emerging research directions. *Journal of Marriage and Family, 72,* 576–593.

Stratigaki, M. (2004). The cooptation of gender concepts in EU policies: The case of "reconciliation of work and family." *Social Politics: International Studies in Gender, State & Society, 11*(1), 30–56.

Sullivan, O., Coltrane, S., Mcannally, L., & Altintas, E. (2009). Father-friendly policies and time-use data in a cross-national context: Potential and prospects for future research. *The ANNALS of the American Academy of Political and Social Science, 624*(1), 234–254.

Thévenon, O. (2008). *Labour force participation of women with children: Disparities and developments in Europe since the 1990s.* EconomiX Working Papers 2008-1, University of Paris West - Nanterre la Défense, EconomiX.

Walby, S. (2004). The European Union and gender equality: Emergent varieties of gender regime. *Social Politics: International Studies in Gender, State & Society, 11*(1), 4–29.

Chapter 6

Multiple Partner Fertility among Unmarried Nonresident Fathers[1]

Mindy E. Scott, Kristen Peterson, Erum Ikramullah, and Jennifer Manlove

Child Trends

In the United States, high rates of divorce and increases in nonmarital fertility have led to increasing rates of nonresident fatherhood and multiple partner fertility (MPF)—or the process of having biological children with more than one partner—which have negative consequences for men, families, and children. These demographic trends, as well as a growing awareness of the importance of father involvement in the lives of their children, have resulted in the need for a better understanding of nonresident father involvement and how it may be associated with men's MPF. In this chapter, we first provide an overview of recent demographic trends in men and women's relationship and fertility formation that have contributed to MPF. We next describe the theoretical perspectives that provide a framework for examining nonresident father involvement. Within this framework, we provide a brief review of the current research questions and empirical findings related to nonresident father involvement and MPF, while also introducing new research questions that have yet to be addressed. Specifically, a number of studies have examined whether and how MPF and the presence of new biological (and sometimes step) children affects men's involvement with prior children (Carlson & Furstenberg, 2007; Manning & Smock, 1999, 2000; Mincy & Huang, 2002); however, research on how involvement with prior children influences their subsequent fertility behaviors, including MPF, is limited.

To address these research gaps, we present new estimates of MPF and factors associated with men's transition to MPF using data from the National Longitudinal Survey of Youth, 1997 Cohort (NLSY97). These analyses provide us with information about how unmarried nonresident first-time fathers are involved with their children, and extend previous research by examining the association between men's involvement with and commitment to prior children and the transition to MPF among a recent cohort of young fathers. We conclude this chapter by discussing the results from our analyses with a focus on bridges to other disciplines, policy implications, and future directions for research.

Brief Historical Overview and Theoretical Perspectives

Historical Overview

In recent decades, couples have begun marrying later and divorcing more frequently, and cohabitation has increased dramatically (Cherlin, 2009; Moynihan, Smeeding, & Rainwater, 2004; Wu & Wolfe, 2001). Rates of cohabitation have increased across all populations, with nationally representative data indicating that in 2002, nearly half (49%) of men had ever cohabited (Martinez, Chandra, Abma, Jones, & Mosher, 2006). These trends have been observed across all groups, but certain disadvantaged populations including racial/ethnic minorities and low-income populations have experienced greater declines in marriage and increases in cohabitation than others (Goldstein & Kenney, 2001; Martin, 2006). There is also evidence that cohabitation has different meanings within different racial and ethnic cultures, with research showing that Hispanics and Blacks frequently view cohabitation as a substitute for marriage (Landale & Oropesa, 2007; Musick, 2007), whereas Whites typically view it as a precursor to marriage (Musick, 2007).

Given the overall trends in marriage, divorce, and cohabitation, children have increasingly been born to young adult couples outside of marriage. In 1950, only 4% of children were born to unmarried parents; by 2009, 41% of all children were born outside of marriage (Hamilton, Martin, & Ventura, 2010; Ventura, 2009), and 63% of children were born to women younger than 30 (Hamilton et al., 2010). Although some of these nonmarital births are to teenagers (21% in 2009) an increasingly large number are to men and women in their 20s who are delaying marriage, but not delaying childbearing (Cherlin, 2010; Martinez et al., 2006), and many of these nonmarital births occur within cohabitation (Kennedy & Bumpass, 2008). Moreover, there are substantial racial and ethnic differences in union status at birth. Research shows that 76% of births to White mothers occur within marriage whereas just 21% of births to Black mothers do. And Black women are also much more likely to experience a birth outside of any union (50%) compared with native-born Hispanic (23%) and White women (9%) (Manlove, Ryan, Wildsmith, & Franzetta, 2010).

The trends in delayed marriage, steady rates of divorce, and increases in cohabitation and nonmarital childbearing have contributed to a rise in marital and non-marital MPF. Data from the National Longitudinal Study of Adolescent Health (Add Health) indicate that 3% of women aged 19–25 experience MPF (Guzzo & Furstenberg, 2007b), and National Survey of Family Growth (NSFG) data indicate that among all men, nearly 8% report MPF (Guzzo & Furstenberg, 2007a; Manlove, Logan, Ikramullah, & Holcombe, 2008). Among fathers, this number jumps to 17%, 29% of whom have had all their births outside of marriage (Guzzo & Furstenberg, 2007a; Manlove et al., 2008). These rates are higher among unmarried parents, with one study using data from the Fragile Families and Child Well-being Study (Fragile Families) reporting that among all children born to unmarried parents, 59% had at least one parent who had a child by another partner (Carlson & Furstenberg, 2006).

Although national estimates suggest that multiple partner fertility occurs only among a fairly small group of men, these estimates are higher among *fathers*, particularly minority fathers and fathers who are more disadvantaged (Smeeding, Garfinkel, & Mincy, 2011). Namely, MPF is more common among Black men and women (Carlson & Furstenberg, 2006; Manlove et al., 2008; Mincy, 2001), those with lower education levels (Carlson & Furstenberg, 2006), and those who experienced their first birth outside of marriage (Carlson & Furstenberg, 2006; Guzzo & Furstenberg, 2007a,b; Manlove et al., 2008). Nearly a third (32%) of

Black fathers had experienced MPF compared with 17% of Hispanic fathers and 14% of White fathers (Guzzo & Furstenberg, 2007a). Black fathers are also substantially more likely than White and Hispanic fathers to have all of these births occur outside of a marital union (Manlove et al., 2008). A better understanding of the correlates and consequences of MPF for these more disadvantaged groups of parents and children is important for informing program and policy efforts to help these families.

Changing trends in nonmarital childbearing have led to increases in single parent households. High stable rates of divorce also contribute to the number of single-parent households, although the trajectories of father involvement and subsequent relationship formation and fertility may be very different for men who never lived with their children versus those that were married and residential at some point in their children's lives. These changes have led to a corresponding focus on the associations between children living apart from their fathers and child well-being, and the importance of nonresident fathers' continued involvement.

Despite many barriers to nonresident father involvement, a large proportion of unmarried fathers report at the time of the birth that they hope to play an active, involved role in their children's lives, yet actual levels of involvement after the birth appear to be relatively low and decline over time (McLanahan et al., 2003; Tach, Mincy, & Edin, 2010). However, nonresident fathers' continued presence in the lives of their children is positively associated with child well-being, among both never-married and divorced fathers (Amato & Gilbreth, 1999; Lamb, 2010; Marsiglio, Amato, Day, & Lamb, 2000). Although nonresident fathers may be most at risk of experiencing subsequent MPF due to weaker ties to their partners and children, we expect that commitment to prior children may influence men's decisions and behaviors related to MPF.

Theoretical Perspectives

A number of theoretical mechanisms contribute to our understanding of nonresident fathers' commitment and involvement with their children, and how this commitment may influence their subsequent relationship and fertility decisions and behaviors. Given our focus on the role of fathers' obligations and commitment to children as potential motivators for MPF, we incorporate three main perspectives in our approach: competing obligations (Furstenberg & Cherlin, 1991), resource dilution (Blake, 1981; Downey, 2001), and paternal identity theory (Marsiglio, 1998; Pleck, 1997). However, we recognize that there are a number of other factors underlying men's decisions to have children, and a number of other perspectives that could be considered—many of which are discussed in other chapters of this volume (see, for example, Bishai, this volume; Hofferth, Pleck, Goldscheider, Curtin, & Hrapczynski, this volume; Waynforth, this volume).

The competing obligations and resource dilution perspectives examine the availability and distribution of men's social and financial resources across families and children. Much of the application of these frameworks has been in studies of how the presence of *subsequent* children (with the same or a different partner) influences men's involvement with and financial support of *prior* children. These studies suggest that paternal resources are diminished with multiple children, especially when these children reside with different families, because additional children dilute the total quantity of time, attention, and material goods and possessions any one child receives. The competing obligations perspective also posits that men tend to concentrate their attention and resources in their current households, often at the cost of resources they are able to provide to their nonresident children (Carlson & Furstenberg, 2007; Guzzo, 2010; Manning & Smock, 1999, 2000).

The notion of competing obligations also provides a useful framework for considering how a man's greater investment with his first child may influence his decision to have additional children (with new partners). Based on this perspective, we expect that men who are more highly committed to their first-born child may be less willing to have additional children in order to preserve resources. Thus, when all other factors are equal, men with greater involvement with a first child may be less likely to transition to MPF. However, an alternative hypothesis for how a nonresident father's commitment to his first child may influence his motivation to have additional children is supported by our third perspective—the role of paternal identity.

Paternal identity theory posits that the main predictor of a father's commitment to children is his parenting role identity (Ihinger-Tallman, Pasley, & Buehler, 1993). That is, his commitment is contingent upon the salience of the father role to his sense of self, the satisfaction that father role enactment provides, and the perceived assessment of his performance in the father role by significant others (Fox & Bruce, 2001). This theory distinguishes between a man's commitment to his father identity versus his commitment to specific children (Ihinger-Tallman et al., 1993). Based on this distinction, if a father has a strong commitment to enhancing his identity as a father, he may be motivated to have a greater number of children to strengthen his role as a father. Given the tenuous nature of many nonresident father-child relationships, particularly in the event that the parents no longer have a romantic relationship, unmarried nonresident first-time fathers have a high likelihood of repartnering. It is possible that men who place a high value on father involvement and who identify strongly with the father role may be more motivated to repartner and have additional children, despite (or at the same time) maintaining high levels of involvement with their first child.

Current Research Questions

Although studies have examined how MPF influences men's involvement with their first child, only limited research focuses on how men's commitment to and involvement with their first child influences subsequent relationship and union formation and fertility. Studies of MPF using qualitative data as well as NSFG, Add Health, and Fragile Families data have examined the prevalence of MPF for men and women, and have identified a number of correlates of MPF (Carlson & Furstenberg, 2006; Guzzo & Furstenberg, 2007a,b; Manlove et al., 2008). These studies have been mainly descriptive and focus on individual characteristics and characteristics of the first union and the mother-father relationship. Some emerging research also focuses on the implications of MPF for mothers, fathers, couples and children (Bronte-Tinkew, Horowitz, & Scott, 2009; Carlson & Furstenberg, 2007; Monte, 2011; Turney & Carlson, 2011), and on the policy implications of MPF and increasing family complexity (Anderson, 2011; Meyer, Cancian, & Cook, 2005; Mincy & Huang, 2002). However, prior research on MPF has not examined fathers' relationships with their children as a predictor of the *transition* to MPF. A key goal for this chapter, then, is to introduce new data from the NLSY97 to provide preliminary findings on patterns of nonresident father involvement among young, unmarried, nonresident first-time fathers and whether this involvement is associated with men's transition to MPF.

We focus on a number of different domains of father involvement. Examining multiple domains of involvement enables us to examine which types of involvement are most salient for nonresident fathers, and whether certain types of involvement encourage MPF, while others discourage this transition. Many of these domains are derived from Lamb, Pleck, Charnov, and Levine's (1985) conceptualization of father involvement as three distinct constructs: accessibility, responsibility, and engagement/interaction, but we move beyond these domains to examine additional types of father involvement that are unique to nonresident fathers, such as prenatal involvement and involvement around the time of the first child's birth.

Our general hypothesis, based on the competing obligations and resource dilution perspectives, is that a man's involvement with his first child may decrease his motivation to have additional children who will compete for his resources. In contrast, based on identity theory, a highly involved man who is particularly committed to the father role may desire additional children.

Research Measurement and Methodology

In addition to a number of qualitative studies that focus on the processes surrounding disadvantaged men and women's complex family formation, and on unmarried or nonresident fathers' commitment and obligations to children (see, for example, England & Edin, 2007; Waller, 2002), three large-scale national datasets have been used most often to study these issues. These datasets, all mentioned earlier in this chapter, include the Add Health (Harris et al., 2003), the NSFG, and the Fragile Families study (McLanahan et al., 2003), and each provides complementary strengths and weaknesses.

The NLYS97 study provides an opportunity to develop and test additional research questions related to MPF that cannot be answered using these datasets. This study, sponsored and directed by the Bureau of Labor Statistics, U.S. Department of Labor, is a nationally-representative sample of 8,984 youth aged 12 to 16 in 1997. Youth were initially interviewed in 1997, and we included annual follow-up data through 2008. These data provide information on respondents' fertility histories, monthly union status, family background factors, and demographic characteristics. Fertility history data are collected and compiled into child rosters which consist of an identifier for each child and for the child's other (non-respondent) parent, and the child's birth month and year, gender, and residence status in each round. These data allow us to measure the timing (e.g., year of birth, parity) and circumstances (e.g., partner status, residence status at birth) for each child's birth. Additionally, data are collected on father involvement and fathering activities, with specific questions for nonresident fathers (e.g., questions about paternity establishment, child support and visitation). Thus, these data uniquely allow us to study how prenatal involvement and involvement around the time of a first child's birth are associated with the likelihood that nonresident fathers transition to MPF.

For our analyses, we analyzed data from Rounds 1–12 of the NLSY97 (1997–2008). The NLSY97 sample includes 1,596 men who became parents between Rounds 2 and 11. We restricted our analyses to 534 men who were unmarried and nonresident (based on information on residence status from the child roster) at the time of their first biological child's birth or at the round the birth was first reported, and at risk for subsequent MPF.

Measures

Dependent variable. The dependent variable of interest was the occurrence and timing of first multiple partner fertility (MPF). This was measured using the other parent identifiers. If a respondent was assigned more than one other parent id number and had two or more children, they were coded as having experienced MPF. In order to capture the timing of MPF, we first placed each of the father's children into the round, or survey year that corresponded to their year and month of birth (i.e. Round 2 = 1998, Round 3 = 1999, etc.). Next, we looked at the other parent id number of each child in order, and thus were able to determine whether a subsequent birth occurred with a new partner. For each survey year in which fathers were at risk of MPF, we coded them as a 0 if they did not transition to a birth with a new partner and 1 if they did, to be used in event history models.

Independent variables. In keeping with our framework of multiple dimensions of nonresident father involvement, we identified measures of paternity establishment, custody arrangement, father accessibility, responsibility, engagement, and prenatal involvement all measured starting for births reported in Round 4 (2000). All measures were taken in the round that the father first reported the birth, so that father involvement is measured shortly after the birth of the child (usually within one to two years).

Paternity establishment and custody arrangement. We measured whether or not the father established paternity for his first child in some way, including through a blood-test, a signature on the birth certificate, a court ruling, or through other legal paperwork or court proceedings. We also measured type of custody agreement with a three-category variable: no custody agreement, informal custody agreement, and formal custody agreement.

Father accessibility. We included a dichotomous measure of whether or not the father saw his child in the past month.

Father responsibility. In addition to examining fathers' custody arrangements, we created a three-category measure of type of child support agreement: no agreement, formal court-ordered support agreement, and formal non-court-ordered support agreement. We also measured the amount of the child support award, coding it into three categories: low, medium, and high. Low was coded as less than one standard deviation below the sample mean and high was coded as greater than one standard deviation above the mean. All variables with categories of low, medium, or high were created using this approach. Those without a formal child support agreement were included in the low category.

Father's prenatal involvement. We examined four dichotomous measures of prenatal involvement based on retrospective questions asked in the round the father first reported the birth: whether the father bought things for the child before birth, whether he was at the hospital at the time of the birth, whether he went to a prenatal doctor's appointment with the mother, and whether he felt the baby move before the birth. An index of prenatal involvement was created by summing across the four items, and the index was then divided into categories of low, medium, and high. Measures of prenatal involvement were only asked through Round 10, thus preventing us from examining the prenatal involvement of respondents who became fathers after Round 10.

Father engagement. We examined four frequency measures of men's engagement in various activities including singing/talking to, bathing, playing with, and reading to the child. Values for these variables ranged from 0 (not at all) to 5 (more than once a day). Fathers who had not seen their children in the past month were included in the 0 category. We recoded each of these measures into low, medium, and high categories and we also combined all of the measures to create a father engagement scale, with categories of low, medium, and high.

Overall father involvement. To measure overall father involvement across each of the separate dimensions, we combined measures of paternity establishment, custody arrangement, father responsibility, the prenatal index and the engagement scale to create one index of overall father involvement. For this index, we coded prenatal involvement, father engagement, and type of custody agreement into dummy variables coded as "1" for any prenatal involvement, any father engagement, and any formal or informal custody agreement. We then summed these values, along with the dummy variables for paternity establishment and formal child support agreement to create the index of overall father involvement that ranged from 0 (low) to 5 (high).

We also created a categorical measure of overall father involvement: low involvement (not establishing paternity, not having a custody agreement, not having a formal child support agreement, low levels of prenatal involvement, and low levels of engagement), high involvement (established paternity, having a custody agreement, having a formal child support agreement, high levels of prenatal involvement, and high levels of engagement), and medium involvement. There were skip pattern errors for measures of father engagement in Round 8, and questions were not measured in Round 9, thus we did not include data for these rounds.

Controls. We controlled for several individual, family background, relationship context, and child characteristics in our multivariate models to account for additional factors that may influence nonresident father involvement and multiple partner fertility. These measures include father's race/ethnicity, childhood family structure, parent education, age at first birth, and child gender; time-varying measures of whether the respondent was currently employed or enrolled in school, the number of births that each respondent had with the mother of their first child, age of the child's mother, and a continuous measure of years of educational attainment.

Methods

We used the sample of 534 unmarried, nonresident first-time fathers in the NLSY97 to examine factors associated with MPF. We first compared this sample to all first-time fathers in the NLSY97. Next, we ran cross-tabulations and chi-square analyses to assess bivariate associations between measures of father involvement and MPF. We also created a person-year file containing multiple observations for each father—one observation for each year in which he was at risk for transitioning to MPF. We used this file (N = 5127) to run preliminary multivariate discrete-time event history models. All analyses were weighted and run in Stata.

Empirical Findings

In addition to presenting results from our own analyses in this chapter, we also reviewed current research findings on the ways in which nonresident fathers are involved with their children and how this involvement may influence the relationship and fertility processes that lead to MPF so as to better understand how nonresident father involvement may influence men's subsequent relationships and fertility. We present the findings from prior research first, and then discuss how our findings confirm and build upon this work.

Paternity establishment and custody arrangement.   Establishing legal paternity is linked to paternal visitation (Argys & Peters, 2001; Mincy, Garfinkel, & Nepomnyaschy, 2005; Nepomnyaschy, 2007) and prior research suggests that unmarried men who established paternity are more likely to have seen their children one year and three years after the births, compared with those who had not established paternity (Guzzo, 2009a). Never-married, nonresident fathers are much less likely to establish paternity than married or coresident fathers (Argys & Peters, 2001). Further, unmarried fathers (particularly those who have not established paternity) do not typically have the same legal custody and visitation rights as married fathers at the time of their children's births (Insabella, Williams, & Pruett, 2003). Men who lack a legal connection to their children through either a formal paternity or custody agreement may feel less connected to their children, and may be more likely to transition to MPF.

Father accessibility.   For nonresident fathers, contact or visitation is a critical first step in meaningful father involvement, yet 2002 NSFG data showed that only four percent of men with one nonresidential child (aged 0–18) reported visiting their children every day, and 25% reported not seeing their children at all in the past month (Guzzo, 2009b). Some research suggests that nonresident fathers visit their children more frequently when children are younger (Carlson, McLanahan, & Brooks-Gunn, 2008), but this may be due more to the increased likelihood of fathers' continued romantic involvement with the mother only a few years after their children's birth (Cabrera et al., 2004; Lerman & Sorensen, 2000). Research also suggests that there are racial/ethnic differences in levels of nonresident father accessibility and engagement (King, Harris, & Heard, 2004); with nonresident Black fathers demonstrating higher levels of involvement than White or Hispanic nonresident fathers (Cabrera, Ryan, Mitchell, Shannon, & Tamis-LeMonda, 2008). Further, studies suggest that fathers' subsequent childbearing has implications for reduced contact with previous children (Manning, Stewart, & Smock, 2003); although we do not know whether the opposite is true (i.e., whether involvement with prior children influences men's subsequent fertility).

Father responsibility.   Financial contributions to nonresident children suggest greater levels of paternal involvement. Indeed, child support payments have been linked directly and indirectly to greater levels of other types of father involvement (Hofferth, Forry, & Peters, 2010) and fathers who provide some sort of child support are more likely to visit their nonresident children (Guzzo, 2009a; Huang, 2003; Mincy et al., 2005; Nepomnyaschy, 2007), although the causal direction of this association needs to be considered (Nepomnyaschy, 2007). Payment of child support and visitation may have reciprocal effects, or may both be caused by other factors such as prenatal involvement which influence men's commitment to children after they are born.

Although not examined in this study due to data limitations, nonresident fathers' in-kind support to children should also be considered. Focusing solely on formal child support arrangements may under-represent some father's responsibility to children. Low-income, never married, nonresident fathers who are unable to contribute formally may provide other resources and support such as paying for medicine or doctors, or buying clothing, toys or presents, reflecting their greater commitment to children (Cabrera et al., 2008).

Fathers' subsequent fertility also has financial implications. Fathers provide less economic support to nonresident children when they have new coresident biological children (Carlson & Furstenberg, 2007; Manning & Smock, 2000). In families with formal child support arrangements, the collection of child support becomes more difficult when fathers have children by another partner (Meyer, Cancian, & Cook, 2005). Men's financial commitments to previous children may also signal to new partners that these men will be less able to provide financially for subsequent children. However, if we consider the perspective that increased child support payments may make men more attractive to new partners—assuming that child support payments reflect men's investment in the paternal role and, potentially, a greater amount of financial resources—we would hypothesize that men who pay child support may be more likely to transition to MPF than men who pay little or no child support.

Father engagement.   Men's accessibility allows nonresident fathers to connect with their children, but the type and quality of fathers' interaction with their children also matter. Fathers with MPF are required to invest their time and resources across multiple households (Hamer, 1998), thus reducing engagement with children (Bronte-Tinkew et al., 2009), perhaps especially first-born children. Fathers may "swap" families, reducing time spent with former children when they form new relationships and families (Furstenberg, Nord, Peterson, & Zill, 1983; Manning & Smock, 1999, 2000). The current study examined whether engagement with prior children influences the transition to MPF. The empirical evidence for this association is limited, with one previous study finding that father engagement among men who were in a relationship with the mother of their child (either married, cohabiting, or dating) was not associated with a transition to MPF (Scott et al., 2010).

Fathers' prenatal involvement.   Fathers who were involved in the decision-making and planning of a pregnancy (Marsiglio, 1998) and who experienced positive attitudes toward a pregnancy (Peitz, Fthenakis, & Kalicki, 2001) were more likely to be involved in child care tasks after the birth of their child compared with men who were not as involved or who viewed the pregnancy less favorably. Prior research also suggests that unmarried men who were actively involved during the pregnancy through doctor's visits, purchasing supplies for the child, etc. were more likely to be involved in a range of activities with their children, as well as their partners, following the birth of their child (Cabrera, Fagan, & Farrie, 2008; Cabrera, Shannon, West, & Brooks-Gunn, 2006; Tach et al., 2010).

Furthermore, a study of low-income families found that for Black fathers, prenatal involvement was a stronger predictor of the timing of when they left the household than their nonresidential status at birth (this was the reverse for Whites and Hispanics). This study also found that a greater percentage of fathers who were prenatally engaged remained involved in their children's lives through age 5 compared with fathers who were not involved prenatally (Shannon, Cabrera, Tamis-LeMonda, & Lamb, 2009). As another example, prenatal involvement may also stabilize unmarried fathers' relationships with the mothers of their children (Cabrera, Fagan, & Farrie, 2008), thus reducing relationship dissolution and subsequent fertility.

The Current Study

Building on these findings, we analyzed data from the NLSY97 to examine the associations between unmarried, nonresident father involvement and transitions to MPF.

Table 6.1 provides a brief demographic portrait of all first-time fathers in the NLSY97, as well as for a subset of unmarried, nonresidential first-time fathers. On average, first-time fathers in the NLSY97 tended to be young (about 22 years old) and unmarried, with 31% of

Table 6:1 Characteristics of all First-time Fathers and Unmarried, Nonresident Fathers in the NLSY97

	First-time fathers in the NLSY97	Unmarried, nonresident first-time fathers in the NLSY97
Age at first birth	21.55	19.88
Union status at first birth		
Married	30.9%	—
Cohabiting	30.6%	14.0%
Outside a union	38.5%	86.0%
Had any subsequent birth	40.4%	47.6%
Had a subsequent birth with a new partner	13.7%	29.1%
Lived with first child	69.4%	—
N=	1596	534

fathers in a cohabiting union at the time of their child's birth and 39% of fathers having their first child outside of marriage or cohabitation. Four in 10 first-time fathers went on to have subsequent children during the study period, and 14% had additional children with a new partner. More than two-thirds of first-time fathers (69%) resided with their children at the time of the birth. Our sample of first-time, unmarried, nonresident fathers was younger (about 20 years old) and mostly in non-cohabiting unions (86%). Although none of the fathers were living with their children, some could have been living with a partner at the time of the birth, most likely not the mother of their children. Nearly half of these men (48%) went on to have additional children and 29% experienced MPF.

Table 6.2 shows background characteristics and levels of father involvement among our sample. The majority (78%) of unmarried nonresident fathers had established paternity, and about one-third had a custody agreement (11% with a formal agreement and 21% with an informal agreement). Twenty-two percent did not have any contact with their children in the past month. In terms of father responsibility, more than half (56%) had a formal child support agreement in place, including 35% of fathers with a court-ordered agreement. The average amount of child support paid was $160 per month.

Levels of prenatal involvement were fairly high across measures. Most of these unmarried, nonresident fathers bought things for their child (84%), felt the child move before they were born (82%), were at the hospital when the child was born (75%), and went to a prenatal appointment with the child's mother (70%). On average, they participated in 3.1 out of the 4 prenatal involvement activities.

Turning to levels of father engagement (on a scale of 0–5) among our analytic sample: fathers were most frequently involved in singing/talking to their child (2.73), closely followed by playing with their child (2.57). Frequencies of bathing and reading to their child were lower (1.86 and 1.44, respectively). On average, father engagement activities occurred at the level of 2.20 (a little more than a few times per month). Finally, levels of overall father involvement, which combined measures across all domains of involvement, averaged 3.26 on a scale of 0–5, with fathers engaging in about 3 out of the 5 types of involvement, on average. Four percent of

Table 6.2 Levels of Father Involvement, Characteristics of the Union, Birth, and First Child's Parent, and Individual and Family Background Characteristics among Unmarried Nonresident First-time Fathers, NLSY97, N = 534

	Nonresident Fathers		Nonresident Fathers
Experienced multiple partner fertility	29.1%	**Individual characteristics**	
		Race/ethnicity	
Paternity established	78.4%	White/other	41.0%
Type of custody agreement		Black	45.2%
Formal	10.7%	Hispanic	13.9%
Informal	21.2%	Education	11.14
None	68.1%	R is employed or enrolled	69.6%
Father accessibility		**Family background**	
No contact with child in past month	22.1%	R lived with two biological/adoptive parents	31.7%
Father responsibility		Parent education	
Type of child support agreement		Less than high school	23.0%
Formal, court-order child support	35.0%	High school/GED	41.1%
Formal, other child support agreement	21.3%	Some college or more	36.0%
No formal child support agreement	43.7%	**Characteristics of the union and birth**	
Child support amount (dollars per month)	160.33	Number of births with first other parent	1.29
Father's prenatal involvement		Age at first birth	19.88
Buy things for child before born	83.6%	Child's age	—
At hospital when child born	74.8%	Child is male	51.4%
Go to a doctor's appointment with mother	70.1%	**Characteristics of 1st child's parent**	
Feel child move before born	81.8%	Other parent's age	18.98
Index of prenatal involvement (0-4)	3.14		
Father engagement			
Frequency of singing/talking to child (0–5)	2.73		
Frequency of bathing child (0–5)	1.86		
Frequency of reading to child (0–5)	1.44		
Frequency of playing with child (0–5)	2.57		
Father engagement scale (0–5)	2.20		
Overall father involvement			
Index of involvement (0–5)	3.26		
Involvement level			
Low	3.8%		
Medium	88.8%		
High	7.4%		

fathers had low levels of overall involvement, 89% had medium levels, and 7% had high levels of overall father involvement. These findings support previous results, mainly from the Fragile Families study, that found that unmarried fathers tend to be highly involved prior to the birth, and plan to remain involved after the birth (McLanahan et al., 2003; Tach et al., 2010).

Table 6.3 presents bivariate associations between the dimensions of father involvement and subsequent MPF for the total analytic sample of unmarried, nonresident fathers. Only two measures of father responsibility (type of child support agreement and amount of support) were associated with MPF. Specifically, MPF was more likely to occur among fathers with a formal, court-ordered support agreement (49%) than among fathers with other formal support agreements (29%) or no support agreement (34%). In addition, fathers with higher amounts of child support payments were most likely to experience MPF; 43% among fathers who pay high amounts, compared with 38% and 27% of fathers with middle and low levels of child support payment amounts.

We tested preliminary event history models to examine the multivariate associations between father responsibility and the transition to MPF (results not shown). Results generally match the bivariate findings. We found, net of all controls, that fathers with formal, court-ordered child support agreements are more than twice as likely to experience MPF, compared with fathers with no formal support agreement (OR = 2.17). We tested models with all father involvement measures at the same time and separately by domain, but no other measures were significant.

The finding that a formal child support agreement increases men's likelihood of transiting to MPF supports one study that found that having a legal child support agreement was associated with greater odds of transitioning to MPF among urban fathers (Scott et al., 2010) but contradicts the finding that child support payments lower the probability of a subsequent birth (Anderson, 2011). However, Anderson did find that men who pay child support were more likely to remarry. The author suggests that child support payment signals a commitment to the fathering role, which may make men more attractive to future marriage partners. Men with a formal child support agreement may have greater resources than other nonresident fathers, which makes them more likely to have to pay child support, but also makes them more attractive to new partners.

Other research examining links between MPF and child support suggests that fathers provide less economic support for nonresident children when they have new coresident biological children (Carlson & Furstenberg, 2007; Manning & Smock, 2000), but these studies approach these issues from a resource perspective, rather than a paternal identity perspective, and focus on men who have already formed subsequent families. Additional research is needed to explain how child support obligations prospectively influence men's motivations for subsequent fertility.

Similar to Anderson's (2011) argument, our results related to father responsibility support a pro-father identity model that suggests that more involved fathers may be motivated to have additional children. Parents who were never married have the lowest rates of child support agreements (Grall, 2009). Taken in conjunction with our results, and with the assumption that these men are more committed to the father role, this suggests that never-married, nonresident fathers who are able to pay child support and have a court-ordered agreement may be a unique population. Future research should focus on the context of multiple partner births in order to assess how child support payments are associated with subsequent residential versus nonresidential births.

Table 6.3 Bivariate Associations between Measures of Father Involvement and Multiple Partner Fertility, NLSY97, N = 145

	Experienced MPF		Experienced MPF
Paternity established		Index of prenatal involvement	
Yes	28.9%	Low	28.5%
No	27.9%	Medium	31.0%
Type of custody agreement		High	26.9%
Formal	27.3%	**Father engagement**	
Informal	29.3%	Frequency of singing/talking to child	
None	33.5%	Low	31.3%
Father accessibility		Medium	31.4%
Contact		High	22.2%
Saw child in past month	24.8%	Frequency of bathing child	
Did not see child in past month	35.0%	Low	32.6%
Father responsibility		Medium	19.0%
Type of child support agreement	°°°	High	34.5%
Formal, court-ordered support	48.5%	Frequency of reading to child	
Formal, other child support agreement	29.4%	Low	29.8%
No formal child support agreement	21.7%	Medium	30.4%
Child support amount	+	High	29.1%
Low	27.0%	Frequency of playing with child	
Medium	38.0%	Low	27.8%
High	42.5%	Medium	33.4%
Father's prenatal involvement		High	25.2%
Buy things for child before born		Father Engagement Scale	
Yes	27.8%	Low	33.0%
No	30.3%	Medium	27.6%
At hospital when child born		High	29.9%
Yes	25.2%	**Overall father involvement**	
No	26.6%	Low	26.8%
Go to a doctor's appointment with mother		Medium	28.7%
Yes	27.6%	High	44.3%
No	32.3%		
Feel child move before born			
Yes	27.9%		
No	30.0%		

°°°p<.001; +p<.10

Bridges to Other Disciplines

This chapter focused on nonresident fathers' commitment to first-born children as the main factor influencing whether or not they transition to MPF. However, we recognize that men's motivations for repartnering and childbearing are varied, and that many other factors may influence MPF. For example, it is important to consider issues such as whether or not first and subsequent births were intended, the role of the mother-father relationship, mothers' own subsequent relationship and fertility behaviors, as well as men's motivations for entering into new sexual relationships following the birth of a child.

Other disciplines and theoretical perspectives can enhance our knowledge of these various factors and can inform our understanding about how men's economic resources and paternal identity influence their family formation behaviors. The economic perspectives presented by Bishai (this volume) help to explain why men with greater resources may be more likely to experience MPF. However, some economic and evolutionary perspectives suggest that the most disadvantaged men will be the least motivated to experience MPF given their lack of resources to support high-quality children. Other frameworks such as psychosocial or biological theories are also useful for understanding factors beyond economic resources such as attitudes about sex, relationships, or parenting that may increase or decrease men's likelihood of experiencing MPF (Hofferth et al., this volume). Integrating these frameworks with one that emphasizes non-economic motivations for childbearing (such as a strong paternal identity) is key. Focusing more on the processes through which men form relationships and how their behaviors influence child well-being may also require anthropological or developmental perspectives. Also, limited data on child well-being in many datasets suggests the need for developmental psychologists to contribute to better measurement.

Policy Implications

Much of the policy debate around MPF focuses on child support policies, child support enforcement and marriage promotion policies. Our findings suggest that policy makers should consider who is most likely to pay child support, and which characteristics influence their likelihood of MPF. It may be that although men with stricter child support orders are more likely to be involved with their nonresident children, they are also more likely to transition quickly to a new relationship and have additional children, which may result ultimately in lower involvement with nonresident children.

In terms of marriage promotion policies, in the early 2000s, the federal government began implementing these policies to direct funding to promote marriage among the poor (Coontz & Folbre, 2010), although it remains to be seen if these policies are effective. To the extent that MPF is lower among parents who were married or cohabiting at the time of the birth, marriage and relationship promotion programs may serve as a deterrent to MPF. However, the research evidence showing declines in nonresident father involvement once new partnerships and children have been established (see Carlson & Furstenberg, 2007; Manning & Smock, 1999, 2000) would suggest that although marriage promotion policies may benefit children born into the new relationship, previous children may complicate these programs (Coontz & Folbre, 2010).

A greater understanding of the increasing complexity of families and men's commitment to both nonresident and coresident children will inform policies that aim to strengthen the stability of parental relationships, but also encourage and support men's continued involvement with previous children. Because so many young first-time fathers go on to have additional children and many do so in a new relationship, continuing demographic trends toward delays in marriage and increases in nonmarital fertility may lead to further increases in MPF (Guzzo & Furstenberg, 2007a), especially across a series of nonmarital relationships (Manlove et al., 2008). Based on these trends, additional program and policy approaches that increase the likelihood that first births were intended and occur within a stable union are also needed.

Future Directions

The results presented here provide preliminary information about the fertility behaviors and patterns of father involvement among unmarried, nonresident first-time fathers in the NLSY97—a nationally representative sample of a recent cohort of adolescents who have been followed until age 23 to 27, with additional follow-ups planned. Fathers in our analytic sample were all first time fathers and approximately half (51%) were teens at the time of their first birth. We found that a substantial proportion (almost one-third) of the fathers in our sample experienced MPF and any subsequent fertility observed for this group of men occurred fairly soon after the birth of their first child. As additional rounds of data are collected, we may see an even greater number of men experiencing MPF, which will improve our ability to model the transition to MPF and assess a number of different factors, including nonresident father involvement that may influence this transition.

Many of the fathers in our sample are likely to have another birth with a new partner, despite their commitment to and involvement with their first child, and we only examined father involvement at one point in time. Future analyses should examine trajectories of involvement over time and should consider examining other domains of nonresident father involvement. Pleck's (2010) revised conceptualization of father involvement as described in Hofferth et al., (this volume) may be a starting point for developing these domains, although the unique circumstances of men who don't live with their children need to be considered.

Some of the limitations of the current study reflect the general limitations of any large-scale quantitative dataset. In general, the motivations for and process of MPF are not well understood and are difficult to measure. These data can be used to answer particular questions about the timing and circumstances of fertility for large samples of parents, but are more limited in their ability to assess the underlying motivations for these behaviors. Future research should also support qualitative studies that can shed light on many of these issues.

Additional suggestions for future research reflect many of the issues discussed in this chapter. Future research on MPF should be interdisciplinary, and should consider a range of factors that motivate men's behaviors including their involvement with both nonresident and resident children (Guzzo, 2006, 2010), the role of the mother-father relationship, the role of mothers' subsequent fertility (Tach et al., 2010), and pregnancy intendedness. Considering the multiple ways in which men's commitments to their paternal identity and to specific children influences involvement and fertility is also important. Men that are the most committed to raising specific (prior) children may be less likely to have additional children, but men who identify more strongly with the father role, rather than specific children, may be motivated to have more children as a way to strengthen their identity.

Future research should also consider the consequences of MPF for children. To date, only a limited number of studies have examined the impact of MPF on child well-being (see, for example, Bronte-Tinkew et al., 2009). The competing obligations and resource dilution perspectives can be used to explain how children from families with MPF may be at greater risk of adverse outcomes due to resource constraints and more limited economic support for all children (Bronte-Tinkew et al., 2009; Carlson & Furstenberg, 2007; Furstenberg, 1995; Manning & Smock, 2000), as well as the competing demands that parents may have when children live across different households (Meyer, Cancian, & Cook, 2005). Furthermore, MPF disproportionately occurs in low-income and minority subgroups (Carlson & Furstenberg, 2006; Guzzo & Furstenberg, 2007a, 2007b; Manlove et al., 2008), which may further contribute to the negative implications of being raised in economically disadvantaged households. The future development of both qualitative and quantitative data on the processes and mechanisms through which men's MPF affects the well-being of both previous and subsequent children will improve policy and program efforts aimed at increasing father involvement and family stability and at reducing multiple partner fertility, with the ultimate goal of improving outcomes for children.

Note

1. Research made possible with the generous support of the National Institute of Child Health and Human Development (NICHD) through Grant # 1PO1-HD045610-01A1 and Grant # 1R03HD061633-01A1.

References

Amato, P. R., & Gilbreth, J. G. (1999). Nonresident fathers and children's well-being: A meta-analysis. *Journal of Marriage and the Family, 61*(3), 557–573.

Anderson, K. G. (2011). Does paying child support reduce men's subsequent marriage and fertility? *Evolution and Human Behavior, 32*(2), 90–96.

Argys, L., & Peters, H. E. (2001). Interactions between unmarried fathers and their children: the role of paternity establishment and child-support policies. *American Economic Review Papers and Proceedings, 91*(2), 125–129.

Blake, J. (1981). Family size and the quality of children. *Demography, 18*(4), 421–442.

Bronte-Tinkew, J., Horowitz, A., & Scott, M. E. (2009). Fathering with multiple partners: Links to children's wellbeing in early childhood. *Journal of Marriage and Family, 71*, 608–631.

Cabrera, N., Fagan, J., & Farrie, D. (2008). Explaining the long reach of fathers' prenatal involvement on later paternal engagement. *Journal of Marriage and Family, 70*(5), 1094–1107.

Cabrera, N., Ryan, R., Mitchell, S. J., Shannon, J. D., & Tamis-LeMonda, C. S. (2008). Low-income biological father involvement with their toddlers: Variation by fathers' race and ethnicity. *Journal of Family Psychology, 22*(4), 643–647.

Cabrera, N., Ryan, R. M., Shannon, J. D., Brooks-Gunn, J., Vogel, C., Raikes, H., et al. (2004). Low-income fathers' involvement in their toddlers' lives: Biological fathers from the Early Head Start Research and Evaluation Study. *Fathering, 2*(1), 5–30.

Cabrera, N. J., Shannon, J. D., West, J., & Brooks-Gunn, J. (2006). Parental interactions with Latino infants: Variation by country of origin and English proficiency. *Child Development, 77*(5), 1190–1207.

Carlson, M., & Furstenberg, F. (2007). The consequences of multi-partnered fertility for parental involvement and relationships. *Center for Research on Child Wellbeing, Working Paper #2006-28-FF*. Princeton, NJ: Princeton University.

Carlson, M., McLanahan, S., & Brooks-Gunn, J. (2008). Coparenting and nonresident fathers' involvement with young children after a nonmarital birth. *Demography, 45*(2), 461–488.

Carlson, M. J., & Furstenberg, F. (2006). The prevalence and correlates of multipartnered fertility among urban U.S. parents. *Journal of Marriage and Family, 68*(3), 718–732.

Cherlin, A. (2009). *The marriage-go-round: The state of marriage and the family in America today.* New York: Alfred A. Knopf.

Cherlin, A. (2010). Demographic trends in the United States: A review of research in the 2000s. *Journal of Marriage and Family, 72*(3), 403–419.

Coontz, S., & Folbre, N. (2010). Briefing paper: Marriage, poverty, and public policy. In B. J. Risman (Ed.), *Families as they really are* (pp. 185–193). New York: W.W. Norton & Company.

Downey, D. B. (2001). Number of siblings and intellectual development: The resource dilution explanation. *American Psychologist, 56*(6/7), 497–504.

England, P., & Edin, K. (2007). Unmarried couples with children: Hoping for love and the white picket fence. In P. England & K. Edin (Eds.), *Unmarried couples with children* (pp. 3–21). New York: Russell Sage Foundation.

Fox, G. L. & Bruce, C. (2001). Conditional fatherhood: Identity theory and parental investment theory as alternative sources of explanation of fathering. *Journal of Marriage and Family, 63*(2), 394–403.

Furstenberg, F. F. (1995). Fathering in the inner city: Paternal participation and public policy. In W. Marsiglio (Ed.), *Fatherhood: Contemporary theory, research, and social policy* (pp. 41–56). Thousand Oaks, CA: Sage.

Furstenberg, F. F., & Cherlin, A. J. (1991). *Divided families: What happens to children when parents part.* Cambridge, MA: Harvard University Press.

Furstenberg, F. F., Nord, C. W., Peterson, J. L., & Zill, N. (1983). The life course of divorce: Marital disruption and parental contact. *American Sociological Review, 48,* 656–668.

Goldstein, J. R., & Kenney, C. T. (2001). Marriage delayed or marriage foregone? New cohort forecasts on first marriages for U.S. women. *American Sociological Review, 66,* 506–519.

Grall, T. S. (2009). *Custodial mothers and fathers and their child support: 2007.* Current Population Reports. Washington, DC: United States Census Bureau.

Guzzo, K. (2006, October 19–20). *Competing obligations, child support, and men's visitation with nonresident children.* Paper presented at the National Center for Health Statistics National Survey of Family Growth Research Conference, Bethesda, MD.

Guzzo, K. (2009a). Maternal relationships and nonresidential father visitation of children born outside of marriage. *Journal of Marriage and Family, 71*(3), 632–649.

Guzzo, K. (2009b). Men's visitation with nonresidential children: Do characteristics of coresidential and nonresidential children matter? *Journal of Family Issues, 30*(7), 921–944.

Guzzo, K. (2010, April). *Complicated families and men's involvement with coresidential children.* Paper presented at the 2010 Population Association of America Annual Meeting, Dallas, TX.

Guzzo, K., & Furstenberg, F. F. (2007a). Multipartnered fertility among American men. *Demography, 44*(3), 583–601.

Guzzo, K., & Furstenberg, F. F. (2007b). Multipartnered fertility among young women with a nonmarital first birth: Prevalence and risk factors. *Perspectives on Sexual and Reproductive Health, 39*(1), 29–38.

Hamer, J. F. (1998). What African-American noncustodial fathers say inhibits and enhances their involvement with children. *Western Journal of Black Studies, 22*(2), 117–127.

Hamilton, B. E., Martin, J. A., & Ventura, S. J. (2010). *Births: Preliminary data for 2009.* National Vital Statistics Reports, 59(3). Hyattsville, MD: National Center for Health Statistics.

Harris, K. M., Florey, F., Tabor, J., Bearman, P. S., Jones, J., & Udry, J. R. (2003). *The National Longitudinal Study of Adolescent Health: Research design.* Retrieved August 30, 2004, from http://www.cpc.unc.edu/projects/addhealth/design

Hofferth, S., Forry, N., & Peters, E. (2010). Child support, father-child contact, and preteens' involvement with nonresident fathers: Racial/ethnic differences. *Journal of Family and Economic Issues, 31,* 14–32.

Huang, C. (2003). Child support enforcement, joint legal custody, and parental involvement. *Social Service Review, 77,* 255–278.

Ihinger-Tallman, M., Pasley, K., & Buehler, C. (1993). Developing a middle-range theory of father involvement postdivorce. *Journal of Family Issues, 14*, 550–571.

Insabella, G. M., Williams, T., & Pruett, M. K. (2003). Individual and coparenting differences between divorcing and unmarried fathers: Implications for family court services. *Family Court Review, 41*(3), 290–306.

Kennedy, S., & Bumpass, L. (2008). Cohabitation and children's living arrangements: New estimates from the United States. *Demographic Research, 19*(47), 1663–1692.

King, V., Harris, K. M., & Heard, H. E. (2004). Racial and ethnic diversity in nonresident father involvement. *Journal of Marriage and Family, 66*, 1–21.

Lamb, M. E. (2010). *The role of the father in child development, 5th edition*. Hoboken, NJ: Wiley.

Lamb, M. E., Pleck, J. H., Charnov, E. L., & Levine, J. A. (1985). Paternal behavior in humans. *American Zoologist, 25*, 883–894.

Landale, N. S., & Oropesa, R. S. (2007). Hispanic families: Stability and change. *Annual Review of Sociology, 33*, 381–405.

Lerman, R., & Sorensen, E. (2000). Father involvement with their nonmarital children: Patterns, determinants, and effects on their earnings. *Marriage & Family Review, 29*(2–3), 137–158.

Manlove, J., Logan, C., Ikramullah, E., & Holcombe, E. (2008). Factors associated with multiple partner fertility among fathers. *Journal of Marriage and Family, 70*(2), 536–548.

Manlove, J., Ryan, S., Wildsmith, E., & Franzetta, K. (2010). The relationship context of nonmarital childbearing in the U.S. *Demographic Research, 23*(22), 615–654.

Manning, W. D., & Smock, P. J. (1999). New families and nonresident father-child visitation. *Social Forces, 78*(1), 87–116.

Manning, W. D., & Smock, P. J. (2000). Swapping families: Serial parenting and economic support for children. *Journal of Marriage and Family, 62*(1), 111–122.

Manning, W. D., Stewart, S. D., & Smock, P. J. (2003). The complexity of fathers' parenting responsibilities and involvement with nonresident children. *Journal of Family Issues, 24*(5), 645–667.

Marsiglio, W. (1998). *Procreative man*. New York: New York University Press.

Marsiglio, W., Amato, P. R., Day, R., & Lamb, M. (2000). Scholarship on fatherhood in the 1990s and beyond. *Journal of Marriage & the Family, 62*(4), 1173–1191.

Martin, S. P. (2006). Trends in marital dissolution by women's education in the United States. *Demographic Research, 15*, 537–560.

Martinez, G., Chandra, A., Abma, J., Jones, J., & Mosher, W. D. (2006). Fertility, contraception, and fatherhood: Data on men and women from Cycle 6 of the 2002 National Survey of Family Growth. *Vital and Health Statistics, 23*(26), 1–156.

McLanahan, S., Garfinkel, I., Reichman, N., Teitler, J., Carlson, M., & Norland Audigier, C. (2003). *The fragile families and child wellbeing study: Baseline national report*. Princeton, N.J.: CRCW.

Meyer, D. R., Cancian, M., & Cook, S. T. (2005). Multiple-partner fertility: Incidence and implication's for child support policy. *Social Service Review, 79*(4), 577–601.

Mincy, R., Garfinkel, I., & Nepomnyaschy, L. (2005). In-hospital paternity establishment and father involvement in fragile families. *Journal of Marriage and Family, 67*, 611–626.

Mincy, R., & Huang, C.-C. (2002). *The "M" Word: The rise and fall of interracial coalitions of fathers and welfare reform*. Center for Research on Child Wellbeing, Working Paper #02-07-FF. Princeton, NJ: Princeton University.

Mincy, R. B. (2001, November). *Who should marry whom?: Multiple partner fertility among new parents*. Paper presented at the Association for Public Policy Analysis and Management Research Conference, Washington, DC.

Monte, L. M. (2011). Multiple partner maternity versus multiple partner paternity: What matters for family trajectories. *Marriage & Family Review, 47*(2), 90–124.

Moynihan, D. P., Smeeding, T. M., & Rainwater, L. (Eds.). (2004). *The future of the family* New York: Russell Sage Foundation.

Musick, K. (2007). Cohabitation, nonmarital childbearing, and the marriage process. *Demographic Research, 16*(9), 249–286.

Nepomnyaschy, L. (2007). Child support and father-child contact: Testing reciprocal pathways. *Demography, 44*(1), 93–112.

Peitz, G., Fthenakis, W. E., & Kalicki, B. (2001, April). *Determinants of paternal involvement during the child's third year of life: child-care tasks versus pleasure activities.* Paper presented at the 2001 SRCD Biennial Meeting, Minneapolis, MN.

Pleck, J. (2010). Paternal involvement: Revised conceptualization and theoretical linkages with child outcomes. In M. E. Lamb (Ed.), *The role of the father in child development* (5th ed., pp. 67–107). Hoboken, NJ: Wiley.

Pleck, J. H. (1997). Paternal involvement: Levels, sources, and consequences. In M. E. Lamb (Ed.), *The role of the father in child development* (3rd ed., pp. 66–103). New York: Wiley.

Scott, M. E., Bronte-Tinkew, J., Logan, C., Franzetta, K., Manlove, J., & Steward, N. R. (2010). Subsequent fertility among urban fathers: The influence of relationship context. *Fathering: A Journal of Theory, Research, and Practice about Men as Fathers, 8*(2), 244–267.

Shannon, J. D., Cabrera, N. J., Tamis-LeMonda, C. S., & Lamb, M. E. (2009). Who stays and who leaves? Father accessibility across children's first 5 years. *Parenting: Science and Practice, 9*(1-2), 78–100.

Smeeding, T. M., Garfinkel, I., & Mincy, R. (2011). Young disadvantaged men: Fathers, families, poverty, and policy. *The Annals of the American Academy of Political and Social Science, 635*, 6–21.

Tach, L., Mincy, R., & Edin, K. (2010). Parenting as a "package deal": Relationships, fertility, and nonresident father involvement among unmarried parents. *Demography, 47*(1), 181–204.

Turney, K., & Carlson, M. (2011). Multipartnered fertility and depression among fragile families. *Journal of Marriage and Family, 73*(3), 570–587.

Ventura, S. J. (2009). *Changing patterns of nonmarital childbearing in the United States. National Center for Health Statistics* (data brief no. 18). Hyattsville, MD: National Center for Health Statistics.

Waller, M. (2002). *My baby's father: Unmarried parents and parental responsibility.* Ithaca, NY: Cornell University Press.

Wu, L. L., & Wolfe, B. (2001). *Out of wedlock: Causes and consequences of nonmarital fertility.* New York: Russell Sage Foundation.

SECTION III

Child Development and Family Processes

Chapter 7

Father-Child Relationships

Michael E. Lamb

University of Cambridge

Charlie Lewis

University of Lancaster

Introduction and Brief Historical Overview

Although societal images of fathers and fatherhood have been evident throughout recorded history, father-child relationships only became the focus of researchers in the early 1970s. Their initial efforts were responsive to four existing themes—psychoanalytically inspired clinical case studies and reports, several decades of research on the effects of 'father absence' on children's (especially boys') adjustment, Talcott Parsons' sociological theory in which male and female roles in the family were at center stage, and the rising power of social learning theory, with its emphasis on the role of social experience in shaping behavior—but their interests have broadened and deepened in the succeeding decades. Psychologists have played a prominent role in reshaping perceptions of the fathers' roles but their work has been enriched by contributions from neighboring disciplines, especially sociology, demography, and history. Our goal in this chapter is to summarize our contemporary understanding of father-child relationships, emphasizing the processes through which they develop, their status within a network of significant relationships and experiences, and the impact they appear to have on children's development. Although fathers in contemporary society may relate to children in a variety of contexts, our discussion emphasizes the place of fathers in 'traditional contexts' as the biological fathers who live with the children and their mothers; other chapters in this volume pay closer attention to the other important ways in which father-child relationships are often transacted. Our discussion is organized longitudinally, beginning with the stirring of fatherly feelings during pregnancy, and continuing with discussion of father-child relationships as children develop from infants, into toddlers, preschoolers, school-age children, adolescents, and ultimately, adults. We then discuss recent research placing father-child relationships in the context of a network of family relationships. The relevant literature is now vast, but in the interests of space, citations are few. Interested readers can refer to more detailed reviews recently published by the authors (Lamb & Lewis, 2010, 2011).

Current Research Questions

Largely animated by attachment theory, research on the development of father-child relationships has been organized around a tightly interconnected series of questions about the
emergence of paternal emotional engagement and responsiveness, the impact this has on the
formation of infant-father attachment, and the resultant impact of father-child relationships
of varying quality on subsequent development and adjustment. These questions are explored
more fully in the sections that follow.

Empirical Findings

The Origins of Father-Child Relationships

Like pregnant women, men in developed countries begin to anticipate their future role as
parents prenatally, with many reporting feelings of attachment which appear to help prepare
men psychologically for postnatal adjustment to parenthood (Hjelmstedt & Collins, 2008).
Although men adapt to fatherhood in diverse ways, the majority are elated (and begin to experience feelings of connectedness that persist over time, even though fatherhood does not affect
their lives as profoundly as it does the lives of new mothers.

New fathers interact tenderly with their newborns (just like new mothers), with psychological and behavioral characteristics synergistically related to hormonal changes (increasing
levels of prolactin and cortisol and decreased levels of testosterone and estradiol) around parturition (Storey, Walsh, Quinton, & Wynne-Edwards, 2000), although the female hormone
estrogen appears to make younger women more sensitive to infantile cuteness than either men
or menopausal women (Sprengelmeyer et al., 2009).

Men quickly learn about the uniqueness of their own newborn children, although they are
often less perceptive than mothers, who tend to have more opportunities to hone their skills.
Perhaps as a result, some new mothers soothe their newborns more effectively than new fathers,
although young infants and fathers both attend closely and respond sensitively to their partners' emotional expressions. Other researchers have reported that new mothers and fathers are
equivalently responsive to newborns and young infants and that they both adjust their singing
and speech patterns—speaking more slowly and at high pitch, using shorter phrases, imitat-
ing, and repeating themselves more when talking to infants rather than adults. Gleason (1975)
and Rowe, Coker, and Pan (2004) have suggested that, because fathers use more imperatives,
attention-getting utterances, and utter more complex sentences than mothers when talking
to their children, they contribute in unique, though still poorly understood, ways to linguistic
development, perhaps forcing children to learn more complex linguistic conventions.

Of course, fathers vary with respect to their eagerness to become involved in their infants'
care. Experiences (including parenting classes and opportunities), circumstances (e.g., premature birth), personality, and self-perceptions and the child's gender can all be influential.
Whatever factors influence fathers' tendencies to be more or less involved in interactions with
their children, there appears to be substantial stability, at least during infancy and toddlerhood. According to Lamb, Chuang, and Hwang (2004), the amount of time that Swedish
fathers spent interacting with their children declined as the children grew older, although
the amount of time that they were accessible (both awake and in the home) increased as the
children moved from infancy into childhood and adolescence. Stability over a 15-year period
was quite low, however.

Probably because mothers tend to spend more time than fathers caring for their infants, discrepancies between their levels of sensitivity tend to emerge over time, with fathers becoming less sensitively responsive and more intrusive, although preferential responsiveness to sons has also been observed. Greater involvement, as one might expect, is also associated with greater sensitivity, which in turn is associated with the magnitude of the hormonal changes experienced by new fathers (Storey et al., 2000). Individual differences in paternal sensitivity appear quite stable over time reflecting the impact of a variety of factors shaping paternal sensitivity. Researchers have shown that men who recall loving and secure relationships with their parents are more sensitive, attentive, and involved than fathers who recall poor relationships, although some men are motivated by a desire to be "better" than their own fathers or mothers.

Paternal responsiveness is a crucial factor, because infants form attachments to those who respond to their signals and needs, and whatever the factors shaping their behavior, most fathers are sufficiently responsive to their infants that attachments should form provided that a sufficient amount of father-infant interaction takes place. Attachment formation represents one of the first steps in social and emotional development. According to Bowlby's (1969) attachment theory, infants come to focus their bids for attention on a small number of familiar individuals over the first few months of life. When adults respond promptly and appropriately to infant signals, infants come to perceive them as predictable or reliable and secure infant-parent attachments result, whereas insecure attachments may develop when adults do not respond sensitively (Thompson, 2006).

Although Bowlby (like other students of socialization) emphasized the formation of relationships with mothers only, early researchers using a variety of methods, including maternal reports, observations in laboratory experiments, and observations in the naturalistic home environment showed conclusively that most babies formed attachments to both of their parents during the first two years of life. Further, close observations of young infants and parents at home showed that babies formed attachments to both parents at the same time in the middle of the first year of life (Lamb, 1977a, 1977b).

According to attachment theory (Bowlby, 1969), preferences among attachment figures may not be evident when infants do not need comfort or protection from attachment figures, but when infants are distressed, they should focus increasingly on the most preferred attachment figure available. During the first year of life, infants organize their attachment behavior similarly around whichever parent is present but when both parents are present, distressed 12- and 18-month-olds turn to their mothers preferentially whereas 8- and 21-month-olds show no comparable preferences (see review by Lamb & Lewis, 2010). Especially between 10 and 20 months of age, therefore, mothers appear to be more reliable sources of comfort and security, even though fathers are more desirable partners for playful interaction, especially with sons. Notwithstanding these preferences, infants clearly view both parents as potential sources of information in ambiguous settings, and they are equally responsive to information from either.

Somewhat unexpectedly, however, Lamb, Frodi, Hwang, and Frodi (1983) found that Swedish 8- and 16-month-olds showed clear preferences for their mothers, regardless of the fathers' relative involvement in child care, perhaps because these Swedish fathers were not especially active as playmates; Lamb et al. (1983) speculated that playfulness may enhance the salience of fathers, and that in the absence of such cues infants develop clear-cut preferences for their primary caretakers.

Attachment theorists have long emphasized the significance of the quality rather than the strength of relationships (Ainsworth, 1969) and so, having established that most infants formed attachments to their fathers, researchers switched focus to the security of these relationships.

Regardless of cultural context, just under two-thirds of the attachments to both mothers and fathers are rated secure (e.g., Ahnert, Pinquart, & Lamb, 2006). Although some contrary findings have been reported, the security of infant-father attachment (Van IJzendoorn & DeWolff, 1997), like the security of infant-mother attachment (DeWolff & van IJzendoorn, 1997), appears to be determined by variations in parental sensitivity, with secure relationships developing when parents have been more sensitively responsive and affectionate. Those variations in sensitivity may reflect enduring differences in personality, perceptions of the individuals' early experiences, and adverse effects of ongoing or recent stress, as attachment theory would predict. Perhaps because the relevant paternal characteristics are quite stable, the quality of child-father attachment is also stable over time. In addition, fathers' participation in play/leisure activities is associated with the security of the toddler-mother attachments.

The security of children's attachments to both of their parents appears to affect children's adjustment, although there has been much less research on the effects of child-father than of child-mother attachment, and there is some evidence that infant-mother attachments have greater and more consistent predictive power than infant-father attachments, especially in more traditional families, but the two relationships appear to have independent and non-overlapping effects. Especially in less traditional family contexts, furthermore, the effects of father-child attachment quality and paternal sensitivity can be substantial, affecting social skills, behavior problems, and motivation. Paternal involvement and stimulation can also affect motivation and cognitive performance perhaps because more involved fathers are more sensitive and have better relationships with their children than uninvolved fathers. Grossmann et al. (2002) reported that teenagers' sense of self-worth is predicted by the quality of their play with their fathers some 13 years earlier. Further, Boyce et al. (2006) showed that lower father involvement in infancy coupled with abnormal autonomic, adrenocortical, and behavioral reactivity at 7 years of age together predicted mental health problems at 9 years of age. Children who had also experienced maternal depression in infancy had the most pronounced problems.

Relationships in Childhood

The transition from infancy to early childhood brings dramatic changes in the roles of parents because physical, mental, and language development make new behavioral capacities possible and facilitate the comprehension of more complex parental communication (Maccoby, 1984) while also bringing progressive reductions in the amounts of child care performed by parents. Baumrind (e.g., 1975) distinguished four patterns of parenting, which they labeled authoritarian, authoritative, permissive, and nonconformist. According to Baumrind, authoritarian parents value obedience and recommend forceful imposition of the parents' will, permissive parents believe that they should be nonintrusive but available as resources, while nonconformist parents, although opposed to authority, are "less passive and exert more control than permissive parents" (Baumrind, 1975, p. 14). Between the extremes represented by authoritarian and permissive parents fall authoritative parents, who encourage independence, attempt to shape their preschoolers' behavior using rational explanation, and are sensitive to and facilitate their children's changing sense of self. Studying the parents of 305 Australian preschoolers, Russell and his colleagues (1998) found that mothers were more likely to identify with authoritative parenting, whereas fathers were more likely to describe themselves as either authoritarian or permissive; both were more authoritarian when dealing with sons. Well-educated American parents, however, agreed by a slim margin that fathers tended to be stricter and less patient than mothers of preschoolers (Bretherton et al., 2005), but it is still not clear how authoritative parents shape their children's development. And regardless of parenting style or influence, it is important to note that most children view themselves as close to their fathers, even when they do not live together; children do not as commonly feel close to their stepfathers (Dunn, 2008).

The parenting styles described by Baumrind (1975) appear to involve some of the same features of effective parenting that are emphasized by attachment theorists, especially warmth, commitment, and sensitivity to the children's individual and developmental needs. Several researchers have shown that differences among fathers on these dimensions are associated with later differences in children's performance. For example, Martin, Ryan, and Brooks-Gunn (2007) found that supportiveness by both mothers and fathers at age 2 independently predicted the children's language and arithmetic scores just before school entry at the age of 5. Similarly, Belsky et al. (2008) found that, although both parents' support for children's (especially boys) independent thinking was related to 6- to 8-year-olds' reading and arithmetic, fathers' support for autonomy was related particularly to changes between grades 1 and 3. The amounts of parental conversation and parental limit setting affect achievement, with no clear differences between mothers and fathers, while a recent study of low-income American families found that paternal book reading to children predicted children's cognitive outcome but not language development (Duursma, Pan, & Raikes, 2008). Similarly, Flouri and Buchanan (2004) reported that British children with more involved fathers had higher IQs at 7 years of age, Nettle (2008) reported a link between early paternal involvement and IQ at 11 years, Lewis, Newson, and Newson (1982) found that the reported involvement of British fathers in two-parent households at ages 7 and 11 predicted the children's performance in national examinations at age 16, as well as the absence of criminal records by age 21, and Bhanot and Jovanovic (2009) found that American fathers' perceptions of their children's ability was associated with the children's perceptions of both task value and ability. Paternal involvement in childhood also predicts social interaction styles, adjustment to spousal relationships, and self-reported parenting skills in adulthood.

Of course, maternal and paternal influences often have overlapping effects, and they may be supplemented by family- and community-level effects. Recognizing this, McBride, Schoppe-Sullivan, and Ho (2005) attempted to distinguish paternal influence on education from the effects of wider familial and neighborhood influences. They found that paternal involvement in schooling predicted variations in the children's performance even after maternal (and other) contributions were taken into account. Across the preschool years, at least, fathers who are supportive appear to promote language and cognitive development (Cabrera, Shannon, & Tamis-LeMonda, 2007).

In a large British cohort study, maternally reported father involvement at age 7 predicted the children's self-reported closeness to fathers at 16 and lower levels of police contact as reported by the child's mothers and teachers (Flouri & Buchanan, 2002a). When fathers and sons were separated by paternal imprisonment during the first 10 years of the boys' lives, however, the sons had more internalizing problems in adulthood (Murray & Farrington, 2008). Koestner, Franz, and Weinberger (1990) reported significant associations between paternal involvement at age 5 and the children's feelings when they were in their early 30s—some 26 years later. Similarly, Franz, McClelland, Weinberger, and Peterson (1994) re-interviewed children initially studied by Sears, Maccoby, and Levin (1957) and reported that "over a period of 36 years, the children of warm, affectionate fathers, and boys with warm mothers and less stressful childhood years were more likely to be well adjusted adults who, at age 41, were mentally healthy, coping adequately, and psychosocially mature" (p. 141). Results such as these suggest that, in the long term, patterns of father-child closeness might be crucial predictors of later psychosocial adjustment. Other forms of childhood adversity can also have long-term effects, leading to lower paternal warmth and poorer attachments to subsequent children.

These large scale survey studies relied predominantly on maternal reports of early paternal involvement and warmth, however, and we must be cautious inferring paternal influences from these data, because marital closeness is a strong predictor of psychological well-being as well. It could be that maternal reports of high paternal involvement reflect something else, like family harmony or the mother's own psychological well-being, and this would explain why levels of paternal involvement are sometimes unrelated to contemporaneous indices of adjustment.

Parke and his colleagues (2004) have argued that fathers and mothers affect the development of peer relationships differently. Specifically, physically playful, affectionate, and socially engaging father-son interaction predicts later popularity, just as mothers' verbal stimulation predicts popularity. Parke and his colleagues suggested that father-child interactions teach children to read their partners' emotional expressions and that these skills are later displayed in interactions with peers. Similarly, fathers who are more sensitive to their 5-year-olds' emotional states have more socially competent children 3 years later (Gottman, Katz, & Hooven, 1997). Rah and Parke (2008) suggested that paternal involvement influences school-aged children's understanding of peer relationships, which in turn affects their peer acceptance. Rubin et al. (2004) reported that maternal and paternal support was independently related to perceived self-competence and peer-reported behavior problems among American 10-year-olds.

McElwain, Halberstadt, and Volling (2007) suggested that mothers and fathers play complementary roles that are not gender specific whereas La Bounty, Wellman, Olson, Lagattuta, and Liu (2008) found that mothers' emotional expressiveness was related to the children's grasp of emotions, while fathers' "causal explanatory" language was related to the child's concurrent (3.5 years) and later (5 years) "theory of mind" competence. This recent result adds to the plethora of studies showing connections between children's social understanding and the nature and complexity of social relationships (Carpendale & Lewis, 2006).

Little attention has been paid to the security or quality of *child*-parent relationships, and the hierarchy among them, with child-mother relationships more significant, although closeness, affection, and attachment were emphasized by both the mothers and fathers interviewed by Bretherton et al. (2005), who agreed that most children were closer to their mothers, with many equally close to both parents. As in infancy, the security of child-father attachment affects children's adjustment, particularly their relationships with other children. Diener, Isabella, Behunin, and Wong (2008) reported that 6-, 8-, and 10-year-old American girls reported more secure attachments to mothers than to fathers, whereas the reverse was true of their male counterparts. Similarly, Booth-LaForce et al. (2006) found that 10-year-olds reported more secure attachments to their mothers than to their fathers. Secure attachments were associated with superior academic competence, and the strength of the association increased with age. Children who reported secure attachments to both parents felt more competent than those who felt securely attached to only one parent. Similarly, Lieberman, Doyle, and Markiewicz (1999) reported that the security of attachments to both parents were associated with various indices of positive friendship qualities among 9- to 14-year-olds.

Of course, fathers' negative characteristics affect children, too. For example, Cummings, Schermerhorn, Keller, and Davies (2008) found that paternal and maternal depressive symptoms when the children were 5 exerted independent influences on the children's subsequent attachment representations and externalizing symptoms, while in a much earlier study, Lewis, Newson, and Newson (1982) reported that harsh paternal discipline was correlated with later behavior problems. However, recent longitudinal research suggests that such relationships may not be simple. For example, Capaldi, Pears, Kerr, and Owen (2008) found that maternal adjustment problems and disciplinary strategies predicted the father's disciplinary strategies, even when controlling for factors like the father's own adjustment problems. This suggests a network of family relationships and influences in which maternal contributions are more important. Similar findings have been obtained in studies concerned with the origins of behavior problems in preadolescents (Underwood, Beron, Gentsch, Galperin, & Risser, 2008) and young adolescents (Fanti, Henrich, Brookmeyer, & Kuperminc, 2008). Foster, Reese-Weber, and Kahn (2007) reported that men who displayed more negative behavior had sons who were more disruptive and aggressive at school, while Tither and Ellis (2008) reported an unusually complex network of social and biological influences on girls' physiological development. Phares, Rojas, Thurston, and Hankinson (2010) have reviewed a wealth of evidence documenting the effects of dysfunctional paternal behavior and father-child relationships on children's psychopathology, clinical symptomatology, and behavior problems. As these authors further showed, the efficacy of clinical intervention often depends on the extent to which fathers engage constructively in the process.

Overall, paternal involvement is typically advantageous for children. A systematic review of 24 longitudinal studies involving 22,300 children reported that 21 of 22 studies revealed positive and only one negative effects of paternal involvement on children's cognitive and personality development (Sarkadi, Kristiansson, Oberklaid, & Bremberg, 2008), with most effects still significant after other influences (e.g., socioeconomic status) were taken into account.

Father-Adolescent Relationships

Because the two parents' behaviors, attributions, and attitudes are complexly interrelated, it is often hard to identify patterns of paternal influence, but paternal influences on children's behavior and adjustment appear to continue as adolescence begins, with some intriguing suggestions that maternal influences become less important than they were in infancy and childhood. Using longitudinal data from the U.K. National Child Development Study, as mentioned earlier, Flouri (2005; Flouri & Buchanan 2002a, 2002b) showed links between parental reports of paternal involvement at the age of 7 and lower levels of later police contact as reported by the mothers and teachers (Flouri & Buchanan, 2002a). Similarly, father and adolescent reports of their closeness at age 16 were correlated with measures of the children's depression and marital satisfaction at age 33 (Flouri & Buchanan, 2002b). The teenagers' reported closeness to their mothers at age 16 predicted marital satisfaction 17 years later, but not the children's satisfaction with life. These findings should be interpreted cautiously, of course, because the quality of father- (or mother-) child relationships may simply be a marker of the quality of all relationships in the families. Other studies show that some fathers have positive influences on their children's academic performance and achievement, particularly in sports, while maternal and paternal depression have additive effects on adolescents' adjustment. In the longer term, Burns and Dunlop (1998) reported that adults' feelings about their relationships and peer interactions were positively correlated with their experiences of parental care in the adolescent years while earlier paternal involvement predicted adult children's later feelings of satisfaction in spousal relationships and self-reported parenting skills. By contrast, fathers' restrictiveness and expressions of hostility (like measures of maternal hostility) toward their 16-year-olds predicted the degree of hostility and low ego resiliency reported in the children by close friends at age 25 (Allen, Hauser, O'Connor, & Bell, 2002).

Several researchers have described the relationships between fathers and their adolescent children, noting that the biological changes associated with puberty along with educational transitions and the refocusing of peer relationships foster change and promote distance and conflict between parents and increasingly assertive children. The effects of these biological changes in adolescence are mediated by the family's social circumstances, so teenagers' passage through these transitions is influenced by both whether or not the father is resident and the closeness of adolescent-father relationships.

Adolescents believe that their mothers know them better than their fathers do, and feel closer to them, and although they care about both parents, daughters are more likely than sons to differ with parents regarding the degree of closeness. The vast majority of adolescents continue to rely on their parents for advice, support, and emotional intimacy, however, suggesting that parent-adolescent relationships are marked by increasing interdependence and mutuality rather than by detachment and conflict. Flouri (2005) has also shown that paternal "effects" may be mediated by the children's gender and family social backgrounds. For example, fathers' participation is related to daughters', but not sons', educational achievements in adult life, appears to protect sons from delinquency, and protects sons in impoverished families from homelessness in adulthood.

Mothers continue to engage in more frequent interactions with adolescent offspring (especially interactions involving caretaking and routine family tasks) than fathers do, with most father-child interactions involving play, recreation, and goal-oriented actions and tasks. However, mothers and fathers are equivalently involved in activities related to their children's and adolescents' scholastic and extracurricular performance and achievement, and both parents frequently behave nurturantly (Russell & Russell, 1987). Mothers tend to engage in more shared activities with daughters, and fathers with sons, however, perhaps reducing paternal influences on daughters.

Interesting insights into paternal influences have been identified by researchers focused on adolescents in diverse cultural settings, including those created by migration (Antonucci, 2006). East Asian adolescent girls living in the United States were less likely than boys to be influenced by their parents' values (Koh, Shao, & Wang, 2009), perhaps because East Asian parents find it a challenge to socialize daughters rebelling against traditional values. Parental conflict in immigrant families may also affect boys and girls differently; in its presence, adolescent Hmong girls drank more, while males performed better at college and smoked less (Lee, Jung, Su, Tran, & Bahrassa, 2009). Koh et al. (2009) reported that East Asian immigrant mothers affected their adolescents' relationship identity, whereas fathers affected their adolescents' identity in the achievement domain.

Characteristics of Mother- and Father-Child Interaction

Fathers and mothers often appear to engage in different types of interactions with their children from early in infancy. Borke, Lamm, Eickhorst, and Keller (2007) suggested that fathers tend to engage in a more "distal" style of interaction, whereas mothers are more proximal (i.e., they used bodily contact). Other researchers have emphasized that fathers are consistently more likely than mothers to stimulate and play with their infants, but less likely to engage in caretaking, and to specialize in physically stimulating and unpredictable play, although rough physical play becomes less prominent as children grow older (see Lamb & Lewis, 2010, for a review). Because physically stimulating play elicits more positive responses from infants, young children who have more traditional fathers often prefer to play with their fathers when they have the choice, and because they associate their fathers with play, may prefer to be held by them as well. Secular increases in the extent to which men are involved in child care almost certainly mean that these "differences" between maternal and paternal styles—which have never been as large as some commentators suggest—are decreasing, however. Furthermore, there are many cultures in which special paternal playfulness is not found and sharply defined differences between maternal and paternal roles are being softened by secular changes, with men increasingly involved in the types of activities—feeding, cleaning, nurturing, soothing— and behaviors that were previously seen as the exclusive province of women and mothers. Nevertheless paternal playfulness may still be influential, to the extent that it allows children and fathers to discover the pleasures of meaningful relationships and it increases the affective salience of relatively small amounts of time in mutual interaction (e.g., Lamb et al., 1983), both factors that foster the formation of infant-father attachments.

Social learning theorists have long assumed that the different interactional styles of mothers and fathers must somehow help boys and girls acquire gender appropriate behavioral repertoires. Consistent differences between parents have been hard to identify, however. For example, Lytton and Romney's (1991) meta-analysis of 172 studies involving over 27,000 children revealed only one consistent difference between mothers and fathers—a significant, but small, tendency for fathers to encourage the use of sex-typed toys more than mothers did. Unfortunately, researchers typically observe mothers and fathers in the same context. Different settings typically impose different constraints on parents, and most researchers do not sample contexts in such a way that different parental styles might be expressed.

Interestingly, children as young as preschoolers clearly differentiate between the stereotyped roles of mothers and fathers in a variety of cultures, and there have been some accounts of interesting differences in the ways in which mothers and fathers relate to their adolescent sons and daughters (Collins & Russell, 1991) with mothers engaging in more frequent interaction with children in middle childhood and adolescence (especially interactions involving caretaking and routine family tasks) than fathers do and that most father-child interactions during this developmental period involve play, recreation, and goal-oriented actions and tasks. However, mothers and fathers are equivalently involved in activities related to their children's and adolescents' scholastic and extracurricular performance and achievement and both parents frequently engage in nurturant caretaking in middle childhood.

Father-Child Relationships in Family Contexts

Of course, relationships between children and their fathers must be viewed in the context of the complex web of relationships that children experience, especially within the family, and this has become a dominant theme in contemporary research (McHale, 2007). Over the past 30 years, researchers have shown that fathers not only influence children by interacting with them, but also affect maternal behavior, just as mothers influence paternal behavior and involvement and children influence their parents. Thus, for example, Davis, Schoppe-Sullivan, Mangelsdorf, and Brown (2009) found that the infant's temperament influenced the quality of parenting, particularly those aspects shared between the two parents, over the first year of life.

In particular, the quality of marital relationships appears to be a key marker of the way that parents interact with their children from an early age. Fathers are consistently more involved in interaction with their infants when both they and their partners have supportive attitudes regarding paternal involvement. Gable, Crnic, and Belsky (1994) reported robust associations among marital quality, the quality of parent-child relationships, and child outcomes in a study of American 2-year-olds. In the year after the birth of the first child, Grych and Clark (1999) reported that marital quality predicted the amount of appropriate stimulation that fathers gave their 4- and 12-month-olds, while Lundy (2002) reported that marital dissatisfaction adversely affected paternal synchrony and thus the security of infant-father attachment. Likewise, Goldberg and Easterbrooks (1984) found that high marital quality was associated with both more sensitive maternal and paternal behavior as well as higher levels of functioning on the part of the toddlers. Japanese mothers of securely attached infants reported greater levels of spousal support than did the mothers of insecurely attached infants (Durrett, Otaki, & Richards, 1984).

Harmony between the parents thus seems to be a key predictor of father-child relationships. This pattern seems to hold even when the father's own psychological makeup is taken into account. After controlling for individual differences in the fathers' psychological adjustment, for example, Cox, Owen, Lewis, and Henderson (1989) reported that American men in close, confiding marriages had more positive attitudes toward their 3-month-old infants and toward their roles as parents than did fathers in less successful marriages, whereas mothers in close, confiding marriages were warmer and more sensitive. Meanwhile, Heinicke and Guthrie (1992) reported that couples who were well adapted to one another provided better care than parents whose spousal adaptation was poor or declining. Interestingly, Belsky, Gilstrap, and Rovine (1984) and Lamb and Elster (1985) both reported that American fathers' interactions with their infants were influenced by the ongoing quality of interaction with their partners much more profoundly than mothers' behavior was. This may be because paternal behavior and engagement are somewhat discretionary or at the behest of mothers, whereas maternal behavior is driven by clearer conventions and role definitions. In any event, marital conflict consistently has harmful effects on socio-emotional development and child adjustment (Cummings, Merrilees, & George, 2010; Kelly, 2000; Lamb, 2012), presumably because it adversely affects the parents' interactions with their children. However, the quality of the relationship between parents does not always predict children's development (Belsky, Jaffee, Sligo, Woodward, & Silva, 2005).

Overall, the same factors predict the quality and intensity of paternal relationships throughout infancy, childhood, and adolescence. Pike, Coldwell, and Dunn (2005) found that a range of factors predicted paternal involvement in middle childhood; the warmth of men's relationships with their children was greater when they had good relationships with the children's mothers, when the homes were "well organized," and when the families regularly engaged in activities together, and the same is true when fathers and mothers do not live together (Flouri, 2005).

The psychological adjustment of either parent also affects other relationships and family dynamics. For example, Bronte-Tinkew, Scott, Horowitz, and Lilja (2009) found that having a mistimed or unwanted pregnancy predicted higher levels of paternal depression as well as lower marital quality and supportiveness, as well as greater marital conflict. Maternal dysphoria is often associated with deficient mothering (Murray & Cooper, 1999) and paternal sensitivity (Broom, 1994).

Of course, both maternal and paternal depression have direct and indirect long-term consequences, too: When fathers were depressed 8 weeks after the delivery, their children, particularly their sons, were more likely to have conduct problems or hyperactivity almost 3 years later, even when later paternal and maternal depression were taken into account (Ramchandani et al., 2005). This effect was independent of maternal depression but related to the father's history of depression before the birth (Ramchandani et al., 2008), although it is likely that the long-term correlation is a marker of chronicity rather than of the effects of postpartum depression per se. In the late preschool period, major depression in men was associated with an eight-fold increase in the likelihood of behavior problems and a 36-fold increase in the likelihood of difficulties with peers (Dave, Sherr, Senior, & Nazareth, 2008).

The association between spousal and parent-child relationships has to be understood within the context of a network of factors outside the home. For example, parental employment patterns influence the amount of paternal and paternal care and the closeness of father-child relationships. Work demands affect levels of paternal involvement with less supportive work environments associated with lower sensitivity and engagement (Goodman, Crouter, Lanza, & Cox, 2008). Higher levels of father involvement in child care are related to the hours and status of maternal employment (Gregg & Washbrook, 2003; Sidle Fuligni & Brooks-Gunn, 2004), but increased involvement by men is not always correlated with increased harmony between the involved partners.

Research Methods and Approaches

As the above review makes clear, a number of different strategies have been employed to obtain information on father-child relationships and their impact. Especially where infants are concerned, careful observations in both naturalistic and structured settings have been popular since the 1970s, although researchers have often made use of interviews, especially with parents, to better understand their beliefs and motivations. Standardized questionnaires are widely used to assess both outcomes (e.g., children's adjustment or behavior problems) and key influences (e.g., marital quality) that are harder to assess by observation, while surveys, especially in the context of the longitudinal British cohort studies, have been the method of choice for assessing predictive association over time.

Implications for Other Disciplines

As we make clear above, research on fatherhood and father-child relationships has been a multi-disciplinary affair, with developmental psychologists taking the lead, but with guidance from the family sociologists who have drawn thoughtfully from large scale surveys following representative samples of children or families over time. Collaborations between the disciplines, especially in the context of these studies, have in turn informed the design of later large scale studies, including new cohort studies in both the United States (the National Child Development Study) and the UK (the Millenium Cohort Study). Large-scale surveys have also been the forum for interactions with family economists interested in the intersection between family dynamics, labor market participation, and well-being, as we have noted in the above summary.

Implications for Policy and Practice

Interest in fatherhood has undoubtedly been driven over the last few decades by recognition that fathers play diverse roles in their children's lives. Ensuring that fathers contribute economically to their children's care whether or not they live with them or their mothers has been a central concern, not only of policy makers devising child support and welfare policies, but also of judges and court professionals striving to keep men actively and positively involved (emotionally, psychologically, and financially) following the dissolution of adult partnerships. But fathers also affect children, for good and for ill, in other ways, and so there has been pressure on the medical sector to make it possible for them to be constructively involved in child-birth and preventative health, on the educational sector to foster active paternal involvement in their children's learning, and on mental health professionals to recognize that their interventions will be more effective when fathers' roles in the genesis of problems and in their treatment are taken fully and frankly into account.

Conclusions and Future Directions

Although most research on father-child relationships has focused on early development, documenting the strength and importance of the relationships formed early in the children's lives, it has also become clear that relationships and their effects on childhood functioning have to be understood in the context of children's other relationships and cultural experiences. Multi-level, multi-dimensional, and longitudinal research has shown that father-child relationships have significant impact on later psychosocial development. Whereas early researchers sought to assess the strength of direct effects of early experiences (e.g., infant-father attachment security or paternal behavioral sensitivity) on later behavior and adjustment, more recent analyses have recognized that men's behavior, and the quality of the relationships they establish with their children, are parts of complex and dynamic networks of relationships, with the quality of relationships between the adults, for example, affecting the way both behave in interaction with their children. The power of these associations, and the demonstrable impact of such ephemeral constructs as family harmony, underscores the futility of trying to assess the unique impact of individual factors (paternal sensitivity) and set the parameters for future efforts to understand, in social context, the role and importance of father-child relationships.

References

Ainsworth, M.D.S. (1969). Object relations, dependency, and attachment: A theoretical review of the infant-mother relationship. *Child Development, 40,* 969–1025.

Ahnert, L., Pinquart, M., & Lamb, M. E. (2006). Security of children's relationships with nonparental care providers: a meta-analysis. *Child Development, 77,* 664–679.

Allen, J. P., Hauser, S. T., O'Connor, T. G., & Bell, K. L. (2002) Prediction of peer-rated adult hostility from autonomy struggles in adolescent–family interactions. *Development and Psychopathology, 14,* 123–137.

Antonucci, T. C. (Ed.). (2006). *Immigration, adaptability, and well-being across the life-span.* Mahwah, NJ: Erlbaum.

Baumrind, D. (1975). *Early socialization and the discipline controversy.* Morristown, NJ: General Learning Press.

Belsky, J., Booth-LaForce, C., Bradley, R., Brownell, C. A., Burchinal, M., Campbell, S. B., et al. (2008). Mothers' and fathers' support for child autonomy and early school achievement. *Developmental Psychology, 44,* 895–907.

Belsky, J., Gilstrap, B., & Rovine, M. (1984). The Pennsylvania Infant and Family Development Project, I: Stability and change in mother–infant and father–infant interaction in a family setting at one, three, and nine months. *Child Development, 55,* 692–705.

Belsky, J., Jaffee, S. R., Sligo, J., Woodward, L., & Silva, P. A. (2005). Intergenerational transmission of warm-sensitive-stimulating parenting: A prospective study of mothers and fathers of 3-year-olds. *Child Development, 76,* 384–396.

Bhanot, R. T. & Jovanovic, J. (2009). The links between parental behaviors and boys' and girls' science achievement beliefs. *Applied Developmental Science, 13,* 42–59.

Booth-LaForce, C., Oh, W., Kim, A. H., Rubin, K. H., Rose-Krasnor, L., & Burgess, K. (2006). Attachment, self-worth, and peer-group functioning in middle childhood. *Attachment & Human Development, 8,* 309–325.

Borke, J., Lamm, B., Eickhorst, A., & Keller, H. (2007). Father–infant interaction, paternal ideas about early child care, and their consequences for the development of children's self-recognition. *Journal of Genetic Psychology, 168,* 365–379.

Bowlby, J. (1969). *Attachment and loss: Vol. 1. Attachment.* New York: Basic Books.

Boyce, W. T., Essex, M. J., Alkon, A., Goldsmith, H. H., Kraemer, H. C., & Kupfer, D. J. (2006). Early father involvement moderates biobehavioral susceptibility to mental health problems in middle childhood. *Journal of the American Academy of Child and Adolescent Psychiatry, 45,* 1510–1520.

Bretherton, I., Lambert, J. D., & Golby, B. (2005). Involved fathers of preschool children as seen by themselves and their wives: Accounts of attachment, socialisation, and companionship. *Attachment and Human Development, 7,* 229-251.

Broom, B. L. (1994). Impact of marital quality and psychological well-being on parental sensitivity. *Nursing Research, 43,* 138–143.

Bronte-Tinkew, J., Scott, M. E., Horowitz, A., & Lilja, E. (2009). Pregnancy intentions during the transition to parenthood and links to coparenting for first-time fathers of infants. *Parenting: Science and Practice, 9,* 1–35.

Burns, A., & Dunlop, R. (1998). Parental divorce, parent–child relations and early adult relationships: A longitudinal study. *Personal Relationships, 5,* 393–407.

Cabrera, N. J., Shannon, J. D., & Tamis-LeMonda, C. (2007). Fathers' influence on their children's cognitive and emotional development: From toddlers to pre-K. *Applied Developmental Science, 11,* 208–213.

Capaldi, D. M., Pears, K., C., Kerr, D. C. R., & Owen, L. D. (2008). Intergenerational and partner influences on fathers' negative discipline. *Journal of Abnormal Child Psychology, 36,* 347–358.

Carpendale, J. I. M., & Lewis, C. (2006). *How children develop social understanding.* Oxford, UL: Blackwell.

Collins, W. A., & Russell, G. (1991). Mother–child and father–child relationships in middle childhood and adolescence: A developmental analysis. *Developmental Review, 11,* 99–136.

Cox, M. J., Owen, M. T., Lewis, J. M., & Henderson, U. K. (1989). Marriage adult adjustment, and early parenting. *Child Development, 60,* 1015–1024.

Cummings, E. M., Merrilees, C. E., & George, M. W. (2010). Fathers, marriages, and families: Revisiting and updating the framework for fathering in family context. In M. E. Lamb (Ed.), *The role of the father in child development* (5th ed., pp. 154–176). Chichester, UK: Wiley.

Cummings, E. M., Schermerhorn, A. C., Keller, P. S., & Davies, P. T. (2008). Parental depressive symptoms, children's representations of family relationships, and child adjustment. *Social Development, 17,* 278–305.

Dave, S., Sherr, L., Senior, R., & Nazareth, I. (2008). Associations between paternal depression and behaviour problems in children of 4–6 years, *European Child & Adolescent Psychiatry, 17,* 306–315.

Davis, E. F., Schoppe-Sullivan, S. J., Mangelsdorf, S. C., & Brown, G. L. (2009). The role of infant temperament in stability and change in coparenting across the first year of life. *Parenting: Science and Practice, 9,* 143–159.

DeWolff, M. S., & Van IJzendoorn, M. H. (1997). Sensitivity and attachment: A meta-analysis on parental antecedents of infant attachment. *Child Development, 68,* 571–591.

Diener, M. L., Isabella, R. A., Behunin, M. G., & Wong, M. S. (2008). Attachment to mothers and fathers during middle childhood: Associations with child gender, grade, and competence. *Social Development, 17,* 84–101.

Dunn, J. (2008). *Family relationships, children's perspectives.* London: One Plus One.

Durrett, M. E., Otaki, M., & Richards, P. (1984). Attachment and the mothers' perception of support from the father. *International Journal of Behavioral Development, 7,* 167–176.

Duursma, E., Pan, B. A., & Raikes, H. (2008). Predictors and outcomes of low-income fathers' reading with their toddlers. *Early Childhood Research Quarterly, 23,* 351–365.

Fanti, K. A., Henrich, C. C., Brookmeyer, K. A., & Kuperminc, G. P. (2008). Toward a transactional model of parent-adolescent relationship quality and adolescent psychological adjustment. *Journal of Early Adolescence, 28,* 252–276.

Flouri, E. (2005). *Fathering and child outcomes.* Chichester, UK: Wiley.

Flouri, E., & Buchanan, A. (2002a). Father involvement in childhood and trouble with the police in adolescence: Findings from the 1958 British cohort. *Journal of Interpersonal Violence, 17,* 689–701.

Flouri, E., & Buchanan, A. (2002b). What predicts good relationships with parents in adolescence and partners in adult life: Findings from the 1958 British birth cohort. *Journal of Family Psychology, 16,* 186–198.

Flouri, E., & Buchanan, A. (2004). Early fathers' and mothers' involvement and child's later educational outcomes. *British Journal of Educational Psychology, 74,* 141–153.

Foster, P. A., Reese-Weber, M., & Kahn, J. H. (2007). Fathers' parenting hassles and coping: Associations with emotional expressiveness and their sons' socioemotional competence. *Infant and Child Development, 16,* 277–293.

Franz, C. E., McClelland, D. C., Weinberger, J., & Peterson, C. (1994). Parenting antecedents of adult adjustment: A longitudinal study. In C. Perris, W. A. Arrindell, & M. Eisemann (Eds.), *Parenting and psychopathology* (pp. 127–144). New York: Wiley.

Gable, S., Crnic, K., & Belsky, J. (1994). Family processes and child and adolescent development. *Family Relations, 43,* 380–386.

Gleason, J. B. (1975). Fathers and other strangers: Men's speech to young children. In D. P. Dato (Ed.), *Language and linguistics* (pp. 289–297). Washington, DC: Georgetown University Press.

Goldberg, W. A., & Easterbrooks, M. A. (1984). The role of marital quality in toddler development. *Developmental Psychology, 20,* 504–514.

Goodman, W. B., Crouter, A. C., Lanza, S. T., & Cox, M. J. (2008). Paternal work characteristics and father-infant interactions in low-income rural families. *Journal of Marriage and the Family, 70,* 640–653.

Gottman, A. E., Katz, L., & Hooven, C. (1997). *Meta-emotion.* Mahwah, NJ: Erlbaum.

Gregg, P., & Washbrook, E. (2003). *The effects of early maternal employment on child development in the UK.* CMPO Working Paper Series No 03/070. University of Bristol, UK: Department of Economics. Retrieved from http://www.bris.ac.uk/cmpo/workingpapers/wp70.pdf

Grossmann, K., Grossmann, K. E., Fremmer-Bombik, E., Kindler, H., Scheuerer-Englisch, H., & Zimmermann, P. (2002). The uniqueness of the child–father attachment relationship: Fathers' sensitive and challenging play as a pivotal variable in a 16-year long study. *Social Development, 11,* 307–331.

Grych, J. H., & Clark, R. (1999). Maternal employment and development of the father–infant relationship in the first year. *Developmental Psychology, 35,* 893–903.

Heinicke, C. M., & Guthrie, D. (1992). Stability and change in husband–wife adaptation and the development of the positive parent–child relationship. *Infant Behavior and Development, 15,* 109–127.

Hjelmstedt, A., & Collins, A. (2008). Psychological functioning and predictions of relationships in IVF fathers and controls. *Scandinavian Journal of Caring Science, 22,* 72–78.

Kelly, J. B. (2000). Children's adjustment in conflicted marriage and divorce: A decade review of research. *Journal of the America Academy of Child and Adolescent Psychiatry, 39,* 963–973.

Koestner, R., Franz, C., & Weinberger, J. (1990). The family origins of empathic concern: A 26-year longitudinal study. *Journal of Personality and Social Psychology, 58,* 709–717.

Koh, J. B. K., Shao, Y., & Wang, Q. (2009). Father, mother and me: Parental value orientations and child self-identity in Asian American immigrants. *Sex Roles, 60,* 600–610.

La Bounty, J., Wellman, H. M., Olson, S., Lagattuta, K., & Liu, D. (2008). Mothers' and fathers' use of internal state talk with their young children. *Social Development, 17,* 757–775.

Lamb, M. E. (1977a). The development of mother–infant and father–infant attachments in the second year of life. *Developmental Psychology, 13,* 637–648.

Lamb, M. E. (1977b). Father–infant and mother–infant interaction in the first year of life. *Child Development, 48,* 167–181.

Lamb, M. E. (2012). Critical analysis of research on parenting plans and children's well-being. In K. Kuehnle & L. Drozd (Eds.), Parenting plan evaluations: Applied research for the family court (pp. 214–243). New York: Oxford University Press.

Lamb, M. E., Chuang, S. S., & Hwang, C. P. (2004). Internal reliability, temporal stability, and correlates of individual differences in paternal involvement: A 14-year longitudinal study in Sweden. In R. D. Day & M. E. Lamb (Eds.), *Conceptualizing and measuring father involvement* (pp. 129–148). Mahwah, NJ: Erlbaum.

Lamb, M. E., & Elster, A. B. (1985). Adolescent mother–infant–father relationships. *Developmental Psychology, 21,* 768–773.

Lamb, M. E., Frodi, A. M., Frodi, M., & Hwang, C. P. (1982). Characteristics of maternal and paternal behavior in traditional and nontraditional Swedish families. *International Journal of Behavioral Development, 5,* 131–141.

Lamb, M. E., Frodi, M., Hwang, C. P., & Frodi, A. M. (1983). Effects of paternal involvement on infant preferences for mothers and fathers. *Child Development, 54,* 450–458.

Lamb, M. E., & Lewis, C. (2010). The development and significance of father–child relationships in two-parent families. In M. E. Lamb (Ed.), *The role of the father in child development* (5th ed., pp. 94–153). Chichester, UK: Wiley.

Lamb, M. E. & Lewis, C. (2011). Parent-child relationships. In M. H. Bornstein & M. E. Lamb (Eds.), *Developmental science* (6th ed.). New York: Psychology Press.

Lee, R. M., Jung, K. R., Su, J. C., Tran, A. G. T. T., & Bahrassa, N. F. (2009). The family life and adjustment of Hmong American sons and daughters. *Sex Roles, 60,* 549–558.

Lewis, C., Newson, L. J., & Newson, E. (1982). Father participation through childhood. In N. Beail & J. McGuire (Eds.), *Fathers: Psychological perspectives* (pp. 174–193). London: Junction.

Lieberman, M. A., Doyle, A. B., & Markiewicz, D. (1999). Developmental patterns in security of attachment to mother and father in late childhood and early adolescence: Associations with peer relations. *Child Development, 70,* 202–213.

Lundy, B. L. (2002). Paternal socio-psychological factors and infant attachment: The mediating role of synchrony in father–infant interactions. *Infant Behavior and Development, 25,* 221–236.

Lytton, H., & Romney, D. M. (1991) Parents' differential socialization of boys and girls: A meta-analysis. *Psychological Bulletin, 109,* 267–296.

Maccoby, E. (1984). Middle childhood in the context of the family. In W. A. Collins (Ed.), *Development during middle childhood: The years from six to twelve* (pp. 184–239). Washington, DC: National Academy of Sciences Press.

Martin, A., Ryan, R. M., & Brooks-Gunn, J. (2007). The joint influence of mother and father parenting on child cognitive outcomes at age 5. *Early Childhood Research Quarterly, 22,* 423–439.

McBride, B. A., Schoppe-Sullivan, S. J., & Ho, M. H. (2005). The mediating role of fathers' school involvement on student achievement. *Journal of Applied Developmental Psychology, 26,* 201–216.

McElwain, N. L., Halberstadt, A. G., & Volling, B. L. (2007). Mother- and father-reported reactions to children's negative emotions: Relations to young children's emotional understanding and friendship quality. *Child Development, 78,* 1407–1425.

McHale, J. P. (2007). When infants grow up in multiperson relationship systems. *Infant Mental Health Journal, 28,* 370–392.

Murray, L., & Cooper, P. (Eds.). (1999). *Post-partum depression and child development.* New York: Guilford.

Murray, J., & Farrington, D. P. (2008). Paternal imprisonment: Long-lasting effects on boys. *Department and Psychopathology, 20,* 273–290.

Nettle, D. (2008). Why do some dads get more involved than others? Evidence from a large British cohort. *Evolution and Human Behaviour, 29,* 416–423.

Parke, R. D., Dennis, J., Flyn, M. L., Morris, K. L., Killian, C., McDowell, D. J., & Wild, M. (2004). Fathering and children's peer relationships. In M. E. Lamb (Ed.), *The role of the father in child development* (4th ed., pp. 307–340). Hoboken, NJ: Wiley.

Phares, V., Rojas, A., Thurston, I. B., & Hankinson, J. C. (2010). Including fathers in clinical interventions for children and adolescents. In M. E. Lamb (Ed.), *The role of the father in child development* (5th ed., pp. 459–485). New York: Wiley.

Pike, A., Coldwell, J., & Dunn, J. (2005). Sibling relationships in early/middle childhood: Children's perspectives and links with individual adjustment. *Journal of Family Psychology, 19,* 523–532.

Rah, Y., & Parke, R. D. (2008). Pathways between parent–child interactions and peer acceptance: The role of children's social information processing. *Social Development, 17,* 341–357.

Ramchandani, P., Stein, A., Evans, J., O'Connor, T. G. & the ALSPAC Study Team. (2005). Paternal depression in the postnatal period and child development: A prospective population study. *Lancet, 365,* 3201–3205.

Ramchandani, P. G., Stein, A., O'Connor, T. G., Heron, J., Murray, L., Evans, J. (2008). Depression in men in the postnatal period and later child psychopathology: A population cohort study. *Journal of the American Academy of Child and Adolescent Psychiatry, 47,* 390–398.

Rowe, M. L., Coker, D., & Pan, B. A. (2004). A comparison of fathers' and mothers' talk to toddlers in low-income families. *Social Development, 13,* 278–291.

Rubin, K., Dwyer, K. M., Booth-Laforce, C., Kim, A. H., Burgess, K. B., & Rose-Krasnor, L. (2004). Attachment, friendship, and psychosocial functioning in early adolescence. *Journal of Early Adolescence, 24,* 326–356.

Russell, A., Aloa, V., Feder, T., Glover, A., Miller, H., & Palmer, G. (1998). Sex-based differences in parenting styles in a sample with preschool children. *Australian Journal of Psychology, 50,* 89–99.

Russell, G., & Russell, A. (1987). Mother–child and father–child relationships in middle childhood. *Child Development, 58,* 1573–1585.

Sarkadi, A., Kristiansson, R., Oberklaid, F., & Bremberg, S. (2008). Fathers' involvement and children's developmental outcomes: A systematic review of longitudinal studies. *Acta Pediatrica, 97,* 153–158.

Sears, R. R., Maccoby, E. E., & Levin, H. (1957). *Patterns of childrearing.* Evanston, IL: Row, Peterson.

Sidle Fuligni, A., & Brooks-Gunn, J. (2004). Measuring mother and father shared caregiving: An analysis using the panel study of income dynamics–child development supplement. In R. D. Day & M. E. Lamb (Eds.), *Re-conceptualizing and measuring father involvement* (pp. 341–357). Mahwah, NJ: Erlbaum.

Sprengelmeyer, R., Perrett, D. I., Fagan, E. C., Coinwell, R. E., Lobmaier, J. S., Sprengelmeyer, A., et al. (2009). The cutest little baby face: A hormonal link to sensitivity to cuteness in infant faces. *Psychological Science, 20,* 149–154.

Storey, A. E., Walsh, C. J., Quinton, R. L., & Wynne-Edwards, R. E. (2000). Hormonal correlates of paternal responsiveness in new and expectant fathers. *Evolution and Human Behavior, 21,* 79–95.

Thompson, R. A. (2006). The development of the person: Social understanding, relationships, conscience, self. In N. Eisenberg, W. Damon, & R. M. Lerner (Eds.), *Handbook of child psychology social, emotional and personality development* (Vol. 3, 6th ed., pp. 24–98). Hoboken NJ: Wiley.

Tither, J. M., & Ellis, B. J. (2008). Impact of fathers on daughters' age at menarche: A genetically and environmentally controlled sibling study. *Developmental Psychology, 44,* 1409–1420.

Underwood, M. K., Beron, K. J., Gentsch, J. K., Galperin, M. B., & Risser, S. D. (2008). Family correlates of children's social and physical aggression with peers: Negative interparental conflict strategies and parenting styles. *International Journal of Behavioral Development, 32,* 549–562.

Van IJzendoorn, M. H., & DeWolff, M. S. (1997). In search of the absent father—meta-analyses of infant–father attachment: A rejoinder to our discussants. *Child Development, 68,* 604–609.

Chapter 8

Fathers' Role in Children's Language Development

Catherine S. Tamis-LeMonda and Lisa Baumwell

New York University

Natasha J. Cabrera

University of Maryland

Historical Overview and Theoretical Perspectives

Sociocultural theories of language development emphasize the importance of children's interactions with primary caregivers in the emergence of early language. This perspective is reflected in Vygotsky's (1979) "Zone of Proximal Development," in which children are guided by more knowledgeable others; Luria's (1979) description of parents as 'external agents' or primary teachers in children's language development; and Bruner's (1981) conceptualization of the "Language Assistance System." These theorists share a common focus on describing how parents and others "scaffold" children's language development by accommodating their own language and communicative behaviors to meet the changing needs of their developing children. The process of scaffolding is elegantly illustrated in Catherine Snow's (1972) case study observations of mother-child interactions, in which mothers astutely adapted the pragmatic and grammatical complexity of their language in response to their children's language skills.

However, the majority of research on parents' role in children's language development is based on observations of mother-child interactions (e.g., Bloom, 1998; Bruner, 2002; Hoff & Naigles, 2002; Hollich, Hirsh-Pasek, & Golinkoff, 2000; Huttenlocher, Haight, Bryk, Selzer, & Lyons, 1991; Nelson, 1996; Tamis-LeMonda, Bornstein, & Baumwell, 2001; Tamis-LeMonda, Bornstein, Kahana-Kalman, Baumwell, & Cyphers, 1998). For the most part, fathers have not been included in such research, leaving a dearth of knowledge regarding their role in children's early language development. Although there has been a gradual movement towards including fathers in language research over the past two decades, this oversight is partly rooted in historically narrow characterizations of fathers as "breadwinners" and/or "rough-and-tumble playmates" (see Shannon, Tamis-LeMonda, London, & Cabrera, 2002 for critique), as well as in a dominant research focus on associations between father "absence" or "presence" and children's behavior problems, delinquency, and school drop out (e.g., Yeung, Duncan, & Hill, 2000). Moreover, mothers are generally more available to researchers than fathers; are expected to be more familiar with their children and to be children's principal communicative partners; and, are thought to influence their children's language development more so than fathers (Huttenlocher, Vasilyeva, Waterfall, Vevea, & Hedges, 2007; Lovas, 2011).

Nonetheless, there exist several practical and theoretical reasons for broadening the scope of language development studies to include fathers. First, trends over the past several decades have resulted in rising numbers of mothers joining the labor market; changes to the distribution of household labor; and, major shifts in family structure (see too Hofferth et al. and Palkovitz et al., this volume). As a result, many fathers are actively involved in the daily lives of their young children, whether by choice or necessity (see Cabrera, Hofferth, & Chae, 2011). This trend is high even in populations facing the social-demographic risks of poverty and father non-residency. For example, findings from the Early Head Start studies (Cabrera et al., 2004; Vogel, Boller, Faerber, Shannon, & Tamis-LeMonda, 2003) reveal that between 70% and 85% of low-income fathers regularly participate in their children's lives in the routines of feeding, changing, diapering, and play. Accordingly, it can be assumed that as fathers engage in these daily activities, they provide their children with meaningful language experiences that build on and/or complement the interactions children have with their mothers.

Second, it is particularly important to understand fathers' role in the language development of children living in low-income households. Children from low-income backgrounds score below average on standardized measures of language and cognition during the preschool years and on entry to school (Gershoff, 2003), and these delays can have long-lasting effects on school performance. Early disparities in the language skills of low-income versus middle-income children can be traced to differences in their early language experiences (Hoff, 2006). Children in middle-income professional families hear more words than children in working class families who hear more words than children in poorer families (Hart & Risley, 1995). However, these overall averages mask the substantial heterogeneity that characterizes both the language environments and language skills of children from low-income backgrounds. To the extent that fathers are main contributors to these variations, children who exhibit delays in language may be those whose fathers are absent from their lives or provide fewer opportunities for language-rich interactions. Research on the influence of fathers on children's language development also has implications for programs and policies that seek to promote positive parent-child interactions in efforts to support children's learning and school achievement.

Finally, efforts to advance a deeper theoretical understanding of children's early language development in social context rests on documenting the full range of language "inputs" to the system (including mothers', fathers', and other adults' lexicons, syntax, pragmatics, and so forth) in relation to the full range of emerging language "products," including growth in children's receptive and productive vocabularies, syntactic and pragmatic skills. Including fathers in language research moves investigators a step closer to understanding the major "inputs" in children's language environments.

Current Research Questions

In light of sociocultural theories that emphasize the practical and social significance of understanding children's language development in social context, we present four research questions to frame this chapter and guide future studies on fathers' role in children's early language development. We focus on fathers' influences during the first years of life, as this is a time when children's language skills undergo rapid change and caregivers are primary partners in communicative interactions.

The first question concerns indirect and direct pathways of father influence. *What are the pathways through which fathers might influence the language development of their children?* For example, do fathers affect children's language by affecting mothers' language? And/or do fathers directly affect children's language development through the provision of household resources, language, and other behaviors they display during interactions with their children? Studies of mothers' influence on children's language development largely target their direct role in children's language growth; however, in households where fathers are expected to be family providers first and foremost, fathers' influence might also be indirect.

Second, at a group level, to what extent *do mothers and fathers display similarities and/or differences* in the language they direct towards their young children? For example, do fathers (on average) talk more or less to their children than mothers when placed in similar situations? Is fathers' language more or less grammatically complex than mothers' language? Do fathers use language for different purposes than do mothers? Sociocultural theories of language development emphasize the ways that mothers scaffold children's language, for example by sensitively attuning to children's interests, providing contingent language, and modifying language to match the skills of children. However, little is known as to whether fathers' language is also characterized by these supportive modifications.

Third, to what extent *are individual fathers and mothers matched in the language they direct to children*? That is, do associations exist between specific measures of language used by fathers and mothers in the same family (e.g., more father word "types" being associated with more mother word "types")? Or instead might there be compensatory processes at play such that fathers speak more to children when mothers are less involved, and vice-versa? Attention to connections between mother and father language in individual families provides a comprehensive picture of the sociocultural context of children's language development.

Finally, if fathers' language directly influences children's language development, *which aspects of fathers' language relate to which aspects of children's language development*? And, if specific aspects of fathers' language are associated with specific aspects of children's language, do associations maintain above mothers' language to children?

Research Measurement and Methodology

A variety of methods and measures can be used to address the above questions, and we review those used in the assessment of both children's and parents' language. Common techniques of data collection include parent report and interviews, direct assessments, and naturalistic (typically videorecorded) observations.

Parent report is generally used to assess the size of young children's receptive and productive vocabularies as key measures of early language skill. The MacArthur Communicative Development Inventory (CDI; Fenson et al., 1994) is one such inventory that demonstrates good concurrent and predictive validity (Duursma, Pan, & Raikes, 2008; Reese & Read, 2000). Parents report on their infants' and toddlers' receptive and/or productive language, depending on age and children's vocabulary sizes can be compared to standardized samples of children's language. However, parent report does not permit assessment of parents' own language with children, and parents from different backgrounds may vary in their abilities to accurately gauge their children's language skills,

Direct assessments also provide valuable data on children's language and/or cognitive skills, the latter being highly correlated with language development. Virtually all cognitive tasks require children to effectively understand and respond to various commands (e.g., "Can you put the circle in the hole?"). Assessments of language-specific skill often fall into two main categories: receptive language and expressive language. For example, the Peabody Picture Vocabulary Test-Revised (PPVT; Dunn & Dunn, 1997) is an untimed standardized measure of receptive language in which children are presented with a series of four pictures and are asked to point to the one that corresponds to the examiner's spoken word(s). The PPVT has the advantage of offering a normative basis for interpreting scores of individual children or groups of children but has the disadvantage of forcing children to interact with unfamiliar adults in communicative activities that are outside children's naturally occurring contexts. It is widely used as a quick estimate of verbal ability (Duursma et al., 2008) for children across the socioeconomic spectrum (Pan, Rowe, Spier, & Tamis-LeMonda, 2004). Similarly, the Expressive One Word Picture Vocabulary Test (EOWPVT; Brownell, 2000) assesses children's productive language skills by asking children to name pictures to which an examiner points. Of course, these measures also provide challenges, as children's reactions to testing and examiner can influence their responses.

Some researchers rely on standardized cognitive batteries, such as the Bayley Scales of Infant Development (BSID-II; Bayley, 1993), which yields an overall score of children's cognitive status, but also permits evaluation of a subset of language-specific items (e.g., Pan et al., 2004; Roggman, Boyce, Cook, Christiansen, & Jones, 2004). The Mental Development Index (MDI) consists of items that tap into such cognitive spheres as language, problem solving, and memory. Given its reliance on children's language for performance, and strong associations to a variety of language measures (Pan et al., 2004), it has been considered a proxy for language competency in young children (Tamis-LeMonda, Cristofaro, Rodriguez, & Bornstein, 2006).

Direct assessments of parents' language or literacy skills are also sometimes used in research on the parent predictors of children's language skills as parents who themselves are more literate or verbal might in turn provide more language opportunities to their children. However, most researchers study proxies of those skills, such as years of education or self reported language proficiency, rather than relying on direct testing of parents.

Naturalistic observations (videorecording of parent-child interactions), in contrast to reports and direct assessments, are especially valuable in studies of children's early language development in a social context (Pan et al., 2004), as they permit the coding of multiple measures of language in *both* child and parent, and yield information on the sequencing and timing of individuals' verbal and non-verbal communicative behaviors. From videorecords, researchers often transcribe parent and child utterances and then analyze the transcripts with publicly available software such as the Systematic Analysis of Language Transcripts (SALT; Miller & Chapman, 1993) and Computerized Language ANalysis (CLAN; MacWhinney, 2000) within the Child Language Data Exchange System (CHILDES) (e.g., see Pan et al., 2004; Pancsofar & Vernon-Feagans, 2006; Rowe, Coker, & Pan, 2004; Tamis-LeMonda, Baumwell, & Cristofaro, in press). This software generates data on various measures of language, including word types, word tokens, and Mean Length of Utterance (MLU). Word types reflect the number of different root words in the transcript and are considered a measure of lexical diversity (Brown, 1973; Hoff, 2003b; Huttenlocher et al., 2007; Pancsofar, Vernon-Feagans, Odom, & Roe, 2008). Word tokens indicate the sheer number of words spoken by parents and children and is regarded as a measure of volubility (Pan et al., 2004). MLU, a standard indicator of grammatical complexity, assesses the average number of morphemes per utterance (e.g., Pancsofar & Vernon-Feagans, 2006; Rowe et al., 2004). A drawback, however, is the time and cost required to transcribe interactions and prepare transcripts for CHILDES, which limits both the length of the speech sample and the number of families who can be studied (Pan et al., 2004).

Videotaped observations also enable researchers to code additional behaviors, such as joint attention, gestures, affect, and so forth, also found to support children's language development. For example, in our work, we code pragmatic functions in fathers' and mothers' language.

These include how often they label or describe objects or events; elicit verbal information through questions ("What's that?"); and, direct children's attention ("Look!") or actions ("Put it there"), and so forth, using a taxonomy adapted from extant coding systems of parents' language (e.g., Barnes, Gutfruend, Satterly, & Wells, 1983; Tamis-LeMonda et al., 2001) and children's language (e.g., Bates, Bretherton, & Snyder, 1988; Tamis-LeMonda & Bornstein, 1994). Pragmatic functions move beyond word counts to assess the variety of ways parents use language to communicate with their young. Data can be assessed in terms of how often a parent uses particular language functions. Coding of language functions also yields a composite score of "communicative diversity," reflecting the number of *different* utterances used by parent (or child). For example, if a child used language to label objects ("Spider"), to ask questions ("What?"), and to express possession ("Mine"), the child would receive a communicative diversity score of 3. Mothers' communicative diversity predicts children's language outcomes across different socioeconomic groups (Hampson & Nelson, 1993; Hoff, 2003b; Tamis-LeMonda & Bornstein, 1994, 2002; Tamis-LeMonda et al., 2006), but it has only recently been applied to fathers' language (Tamis-LeMonda et al., 2012).

Finally, videorecorded observations permit researchers to code qualitative aspects of parents' interactions with children, including sensitivity, intrusiveness, positive regard, negative regard, among others, typically rated on likert scales (e.g., 1 = not at all sensitive; 7 = always sensitive). Some researchers assess parents' verbal *responsiveness* at a more micro-genetic level, by evaluating the *timing* of parents' behaviors (e.g., questions, statements) relative to children's vocal and exploratory behaviors (e.g., does a parent label the object "ball" within two seconds of the infant touching the ball) (e.g., Bornstein, Tamis-LeMonda, Hahn, & Haynes, 2008; Tamis-LeMonda et al., 2001, 2006, 2012).

Empirical Findings

In this section, we revisit the four questions that frame this chapter on fathers' role in children's language development. Specifically, we address the pathways through which fathers might influence children's language development; compare fathers' language to that of mothers; ask whether associations exist between the language of mothers and fathers of the same children; and, examine specific associations between aspects of fathers' language and children's language.

Pathways of Influence

In terms of pathways of influence, fathers may indirectly affect children through their effects on the mother-child relationship, provisioning of resources that promote learning and language, and directly through their interactions with children (Tamis-LeMonda, Niwa, Kahana-Kalman, & Yoshikawa, 2008).

Fathers who have more positive relationships with the mothers of their children, employed fathers, and those more able to provide financially, may positively influence children's development *through effects on mothers' interactions* with children. For example, in a sample of 290 low-income families, fathers and mothers were separately videotaped at play with their children when children were 2 and 3 years of age, and measures of their sensitivity, positive affect, and cognitive stimulation (indexing "supportive parenting") were assessed. Fathers' income and education predicted mothers' supportive engagements during play with children; these associations were maintained after covarying fathers' supportive engagements with children.

Additionally, fathers' supportiveness predicted mothers' supportiveness over time. In turn, mothers' supportiveness predicted children's scores on the Peabody Picture Vocabulary Test, 3rd ed. (PPVT-III; Dunn & Dunn, 1997) and Mental scale of the BSID-II (Bayley, 1993) (Tamis-LeMonda, Shannon, Cabrera, & Lamb, 2004).

Fathers might also influence their children's language by *providing resources* to the family (Coleman, 1990). Material resources enable families to have better housing in safer neighborhoods as well as nutritious food, which in turn predict desirable childhood outcomes, including language skills (Cabrera & Peters, 2000). Fathers with more education are able to provide more resources and learning opportunities to their children than fathers with less education. In turn, children who have access to material resources such as books and good schools have opportunities to engage and learn from "learned others" (Vygotsky, 1979). During the infant and toddler years, availability of books is a core feature of the literacy environment and is associated with shared bookreading and children's receptive and productive vocabularies (Raikes et al., 2006; Rodriguez et al., 2009; Rodriguez & Tamis-LeMonda, 2011). A meta-analysis indicates that the time parents (albeit mostly mothers) spend reading books to their preschoolers predicts children's language growth, emergent literacy, and reading skills (Bus, van Ijzendoorn, & Pelligrini, 1995). In one study, the frequency of bookreading to 2- and 3-year-olds predicted 3-year Bayley MDI scores; for fathers with high school education, shared bookreading predicted the receptive language of 36-month old children (Duursma et al., 2008). Thus, fathers who provide resources to their children are also more likely to engage in positive interactions with their children, such as reading, which in turn might mediate links to children's outcomes.

Additionally, fathers *directly* affect children's language development through their interactions with children, as will be elaborated in the balance of this chapter. We next take a more targeted approach to reviewing what is known about the characteristics of fathers' language to children as well as the influence of fathers' language on children's early language development.

Comparing Fathers' Language with Mothers' Language

The comparison of fathers' and mothers' language addresses questions regarding whether fathers and mothers scaffold children's language development and learning in similar and/ or unique ways. For example, if fathers talk to children in different ways than do mothers (e.g., more questions of clarification, e.g., "What did you say?"), their interactions may promote specific language skills in children (e.g., reframing utterances to be clear to the listener). The limited research on the comparability of mothers' and fathers' language interactions with young children has yielded mixed results. In many ways, mothers and fathers are similar in their language to children (e.g., Bellinger & Gleason, 1982). During free play, the number of mothers' and fathers' didadic interactions (i.e., those in which parents describe, label and teach children about objects and activities in the environment) are equivalent (Bornstein, Vibbert, Tal, & O'Donnell, 1992). Both mothers and fathers use more explicit than implicit directives (Golinkoff & Ames, 1979) and they do not differ on the length of their utterances (e.g., Hladik & Edwards, 1984; Pancsofar & Vernon-Feagans, 2006; Rowe et al., 2004), repetitions, or expansions of children's vocalizations (Gleason, 1975). Both mothers and fathers adjust their speech to young children by using simplified language and shorter utterances (Golinkoff & Ames, 1979).

Similarities are also seen in the *topics* that mothers and fathers talk about with their children during shared personal narratives. In one study, we compared the language of fathers and mothers during shared personal narratives with their preschoolers (Cristofaro &

Tamis-LeMonda, 2008). A group of 37 low-income Latino mothers and fathers were asked to talk about a special experience with their preschoolers. Both father-child narratives and mother-child narratives contained themes that communicated the importance of family (e.g., discussion of a special birthday party with grandma), gender roles (e.g., discussion of being brave or afraid at an amusement park), and educational achievements (e.g., discussion of getting a good grade or doing well at school). In this research, children's gender seemed to matter more for what parents spoke about than parents' gender. Specifically, fathers and mothers of boys alike generally emphasized actions, emotional strength, and bravery in their shared conversations with children. In contrast, parents of girls typically emphasized family-related experiences, social activities, companionship, and sometimes fear. Thus, through the language used during personal narratives with children, fathers and mothers trasmit cultural and social messages to children.

Nonetheless, in other ways, mothers and fathers *differ* in the quantity and quality of their language to children, although findings are also mixed. Mothers produce more talk and display more frequent and longer conversational turns with children than do fathers (Davidson & Snow, 1996; Ely, Berko Gleason, MacGibbon, & Zaretsky, 2001; Golinkoff & Ames, 1979; Hladik & Edwards, 1984), although equivalent amounts of mother and father talk have also been documented (Tamis-LeMonda et al., in press). In middle-class families, mothers make more references to both written and spoken language than fathers during dinner time conversations with their young children (Ely et al., 2001). Middle-class mothers also display more emotion language to their children than fathers (LaBounty, Wellman, Olson, Lagattuta, & Liu, 2008).

In contrast, fathers' speech to children has been characterized as more demanding and challenging. For example, fathers' speech to children includes more directives, requests for clarification, open-ended questions (i.e., "wh questions"), references to past events, imperatives, and contentless utterances compared to mothers (e.g., Bellinger & Gleason, 1982; Gleason & Greif, 1983; Leaper, Anderson, & Sanders, 1998; McLaughlin, White, McDevitt, & Raskin, 1983; Tomasello, Conti-Ramsden, & Ewert, 1990). The use of "wh questions" is especially demanding to young children who must respond non-imitatively and verbally (Rowe et al., 2004). Similarly, requests for clarification ("What?") impose the expectation that the child will repeat and/or modify what has just been said. Fathers are also less attuned to children's language skills and are less likely than mothers to continue children's topic in conversations, follow their children's attentional focus, and acknowledge their children's contributions ("Yes, that's nice!") (see Abkarian et al., 2003, for a review). Thus, if fathers' speech to children is similar to the "untuned" speech of people outside the family, fathers offer children opportunities to make communicative adjustments that will enable children to more effectively share meaning in language interactions with others (Abkarian et al., 2003). As such, fathers may serve as a 'bridge' to the outside world (Gleason, 1975; Rowe et al., 2004).

However, the bridge hypothesis was first postulated in the 1970's when the roles of mothers and fathers were more constrained. With changing economic conditions and family structure—including increased sharing of childcare duties within families—some researchers have reexamined the bridge hypothesis to test its current applicability to ethnically diverse low-income families (e.g., Rowe et al., 2004).

In one such investigation, we found that the speech that low-income mothers and fathers directed to their 2-year-olds was similar in terms of the number of total utterances, word types, MLU, and communicative diversity. However, when we looked at the pragmatic functions of parents' language to children, differences emerged, lending some support to the bridge hypothesis. As compared to mothers, fathers used more action directives, affirmations, and were more likely to ask their children to repeat or clarify their utterances (Tamis-LeMonda et. al., in press). It is feasible that because fathers may be less familiar with their young children's language, they demand more from them conversationally (e.g., Gleason, 1975; Rowe et al., 2004). Mothers were more likely than fathers to repeat their children's utterances, which accords with the speculation that mothers are attuned to their children's speech, and therefore more likely than fathers to "understand" what their children are saying. Nonetheless, in the context of these few differences, mothers' and fathers' speech was more similar than different, suggesting the changing role of fathers in children's language.

In the same study, we also compared children's talk with their mothers to their talk with fathers. If fathers are core communicative partners for children and if fathers impose unique communicative demands on children, then children might be expected to talk with their fathers as much as they do with their mothers or to perhaps use different language functions with each parent. In support of this hypothesis, children's language with fathers did not differ from their language with mothers in terms of total number of utterances and MLU. However, children expressed more word types and referred to locations (e.g., "in here") more often with their fathers than mothers; but described objects (e.g., "big book") more frequently with their mothers than fathers. Children's expression of more word types with their fathers than mothers might be explained by the greater pragmatic demands of fathers' language (Rowe et al., 2004; Tamis-LeMonda et al., in press). Similarly, "descriptors" (spoken with mothers) are less sophisticated semantically than are expressions of object locations (spoken with fathers), indicating that fathers may support child expressions that are unique from those expressed with mothers. Others find that toddlers talked more and expressed more diverse speech (e.g., word types) when conversing with their fathers than with their mothers. Fathers specifically asked more wh-questions, and children, in turn, produced more verbal responses (Rowe et al., 2004). Together, findings indicate that children talk differently with different people and in different situations (e.g., Bornstein, Haynes, Painter, & Genevro, 2000; Rowe et al., 2004).

Associations between Fathers' and Mothers' Language in the Same Households

To what extent is the language that fathers and mothers of the same household direct to their children associated? If fathers' language use with children relates to mothers' language use at an individual level, it would mean that some children hear a lot of language from *both* fathers and mothers, thereby placing them at a language advantage relative to children who experience impoverished language from both parents or those who live in housesholds with just one parent.

To date, the little research that exists in this area suggests modest to strong associations between fathers' and mothers' language to children. Children from low-income backgrounds who are more likely than middle class children to live with parents who have low levels of education or to live with one parent, are also more likely to experience low levels of talk from *both* mothers and fathers, which places them at risk for difficulties in language development and future readiness for school. In one study of father and mother supportiveness in the Early Head Start Research and Evaluation Project (Martin, Ryan, & Brooks-Gunn, 2007), 5-year-olds with two supportive parents scored highest on language whereas those with two unsupportive parents scored lowest. Homogamy between mothers' and fathers' sensitivity to young children has been documented (Belsky & Fearon, 2004). We also documented moderate to strong associations between fathers' and mothers' supportiveness based on parents' play with their 2- and 3-year-olds (Tamis-LeMonda et al., 2004).

Similarly, when we examined associations between the word types, MLU, and communicative diversity of fathers and mothers at play with their 2-year-olds, associations were large in magnitude. Thus, the combined contributions of mothers' and fathers' language was additive—presenting an advantage to children who heard more lexically and pragmatically stimulating language from both parents, but compromising the language development of children who did not (Tamis-LeMonda et al., in press).

What might explain the strong associations documented between the language and behaviors of fathers and mothers? One possibility is that people select mates of similar age, race, and education (Blackwell & Lichter, 2000; Jepsen & Jepsen, 2002), although selection practices vary by ethnicity (Hutchinson, 1999). If parents pair up on the basis of education, for example, they would be likely to exhibit similar language skills and language use with children. Alternatively, it is also possible that parents who cohabitate grow in the similarity of their language over time, which would then be seen in associations between the language of fathers and mothers. This latter explanation received preliminary support in one study where we found that the association between fathers' and mothers' lexical diversity (i.e., word types to children) was stastically stronger in fathers and mothers who lived together than in those who lived apart (Tamis-LeMonda et al., 2012). Of course, couples who separated or otherwise chose not to reside together may have been those who were dissimilar at the start.

The strong associations between the language of individual fathers and mothers might also be the result of child effects on parents, as highlighted in transactional models of development (Sameroff, 2009). Children who are more advanced in their own language might elicit richer language from both their mothers and fathers. To the extent that both mothers and fathers are responsive to their children's growing language skills, parents of children who are more advanced in their productive language might express more diverse communicative functions, more word types, and longer utterances with their children than parents of less advanced children.

Notably, however, even if children's language skills predict parents' language use, it does not discount the importance of parental influences on children's language. For example, during brief 10–15 min play observations, children expressed 45 word types on average, whereas parents expressed 150 word types. Thus, consistent with Vygotsky's theoretical views, children are likely to continually benefit from the more advanced level of their parents' language, even if their own language skills affect their parents' language use. Moreover, a transactional model implies escalating risks for children who lag in their language development. If both fathers and mothers respond to their less communicative children with less language, the cycle of delay will persist; these children will continue to hear fewer words than their more linguistically advanced peers.

Prediction from Fathers' Language to Children's Language

A final, but perhaps most central, question we address concerns direct influences between fathers' language and children's language. Which aspects of fathers' language predict which aspects of children's language? We focus on aspects of fathers' parenting found to relate to children's language and cognitive development: supportiveness/sensitivity towards children, language diversity (both at the level of words and utterances), and engagement in learning activities such as bookreading.

Maternal and paternal supportive/sensitive interactions are often contrasted with interactions that are "intrusive" or unrelated to children's own initiatives. For example, a father would be interacting sensitively with his child if his child picked up a block and he responded "That's a block. Let's build." In various studies, parenting sensitivity is also comprised of indicators of positive affect or positive regard. Parenting sensitivity predicts children's cognitive and language development across income and ethnic groups because parents who are sensitive to children's cues ease the task of referent-mapping and provide children with opportunities to engage, ask question, and explore, all of which support emerging skills (Cabrera, Shannon, West, & Brooks-Gunn, 2006; Rodriguez et al., 2009; Shannon et al., 2002; Tamis-LeMonda et al., 2004; Tamis-LeMonda & Baumwell, 2011).

In our work, in a sample of 290 low-income families participating in the Early Head Start National Evaluation study, fathers' supportiveness during play (a composite of sensitivity, positive regard, and cognitive stimulation) uniquely predicted 24-month and 36-month MDI scores and PPVT scores, above fathers' education, income, and mothers' supportiveness, within and across time (Tamis-LeMonda et al., 2004). In another study of 65 inner-city fathers observed at play with their 24-month-olds, fathers' responsive-didactic interactions with their infants predicted children's MDI performance scores even after controlling for children's own behaviors during interactions. Moreover, fathers high on a responsive-didactic score (based on summing various indicators of sensitivity) were nearly 5 times more likely to have children within the normal range on the MDI than were low-scoring fathers (Shannon et al., 2002).

The above studies are based mainly on global ratings of fathers' sensitivity or supportiveness during interactions with their children. In studies based on transriptions of fathers' language to children, the diversity of fathers' language to children relates to children's early language development. For example, in one longitudinal study of middle-income families, fathers' and mothers' language conversations during triadic play with their young children were transcribed (Pancsofar & Vernon-Feagans, 2006). Specifically, fathers' number of different root words at 24 months predicted children's expressive language development at 36 months whereas mothers' language did not predict. The authors suggest a possible ceiling effect for middle-class mothers in their sample, with fathers' word types being more variable than mothers' word types.

These authors extended their investigation of the effects of father language on children's language to the study of low-income fathers and young children (Pancsofar, Vernon-Feagans, & The Family Life Project Investigators, 2010). Specifically, they assessed the communicative competence of over 500 children during the first 3 years of life in a sample of rural, low-income families. Fathers were observed interacting with their 6-month-olds during bookreading. Fathers' vocabulary (word types) predicted children's language at 15- and 36-months of age even after demographics, child characteristics, maternal education, and maternal language were controlled. Interestingly, associations between mothers' vocabulary and children's vocabulary were not significant, again suggesting that fathers' language during picture bookreading may have unique consequences for children's early language development.

In our work, we also assessed the unique contributions of multiple measures of fathers' and mothers' language to a composite score of children's language skill (i.e., a factor score of children's word types, MLU, and communicative diversity during interactions with parents). The inclusive model represented a very conservative approach to parent-child language, as six measures of language (i.e., mother and father word types, MLU, communicative diversity) were assessed for their unique contributions above one another and after controlling for a number of demographic variables (Tamis-LeMonda et al., in press). Fathers' communicative diversity and mothers' MLU were each unique contributors to children's language development, suggesting that fathers and mothers influence children's language development above the influences of one another. Differences in the nature of father-child versus mother-child associations may be due to different patterns of covariation among measures of fathers' and mothers' language. For example, fathers' communicative diversity was not associated with longer utterances (MLU). For mothers, however, individuals with longer MLU also used more word types. Perhaps because fathers on average spend less time with their children than mothers, certain aspects of fathers' language might be especially salient to children.

Finally, fathers' contributions to children's language and cognitive development are long lasting. We have recently shown that fathers' interactions in learning/literacy activities (e.g., bookreading, storytelling, singing songs) with their children during the first years of life (i.e., 2 years, 3 years, PreKindergarten) predict children's math and reading outcomes in early adolescence (fifth grade) after controlling for earlier and later father residency (McFadden, Tamis-LeMonda, & Cabrera, 2012). Moreover, although fathers of boys do not differ from fathers of girls in their sensitivity/supportiveness or specific language features (e.g., word types, communicative diversity), fathers of girls are more likely to engage their children in learning/literacy activities early in development than are fathers of boys (Leavell Smith, Tamis-LeMonda, Ruble, Zosuls, & Cabrera, 2012). Gender differences in fathers' literacy activities may forecast gender differences in children's reading and school performance.

Together, the studies reviewed indicate that the quality of fathers' interactions, as measured by global ratings of sensitivity and support, engagement of children in learning/literacy activities, as well as more specific features of fathers' language, notably diversity of word types and pragmatic functions, consistently predict measures of children's language and cognition. Children benefit from interacting with fathers who are sensitively attuned to their cues, who frequently engage in activities such as bookreading, who use relatively large vocabularies, and who use language to express a range of communicative functions, including expanding on what children say, referring to objects and events, eliciting actions, directing attention, prompting play, and so forth (Tamis-LeMonda et al., 2012). Notably, these father-child associations maintain after covarying mothers' behaviors (rated either globally or more specifically), and the magnitude of father influences are equal to and sometimes larger than those seen for mothers.

Bridges to Others Disciplines

The study of fathers' influence on children's language development is relevant to scholars in disciplines spanning education, economics, sociology, and cultural psychology/anthropology. We have shown that fathers promote emerging language and cognitive skills in children in ways that are both similar and unique to that of mothers; therefore, fathers' interactions with children are likely foundational to children's school readiness and later academic achievement. Educators who seek to foster family involvement in early learning and schooling should reach out to fathers as well as mothers.

Traditionallly, economists have largely emphasized the financial investments that men make in their children, or the ways that mothers and fathers come to "specialize" in work within and outside the home. However, as family forms and functions change, so must theories regarding fathers' contributions to children. As noted by Bishai (this volume), economists know surprisingly little about the differential influences of father's time with children from mother's time with children, even though such questions are central to the field. The current findings on fathers' contributions to children's language challenge the assumption that mothers' time is privileged, and also suggest that sharp separation of family roles may not be in children's best interest if children experience fewer opportunities to interact directly with their fathers.

Findings also suggest the importance of collabortion between Developmental Psychologists, Economists, and Sociologists in designing cost-effective yet valid measures of father involvement for national studies. Fathers' direct interactions, evaluated for specific apects of language (e.g., types, communicative diversity) and/or qualitative features of supportiveness, sensitivity, or responsiveness, yield stronger effects on children's development than cruder measures of involvement (e.g., absence/presence; time with child) and financial investments. Yet the cost of studying fathers in large-scale national studies is high, and measures of father language to children require substantial investments of time and money. Solutions that effectively balance study costs with benefits require collaboration across disciplines.

Finally, from a cultural perspective, children are members of families who themselves are embedded in broader, socio-cultural contexts. Parent-child interactions are influenced by the beliefs and values of cultural communities, and by culturally prescribed linguistic conventions that are a part of children's socialization (Ochs & Schieffelin, 1984; Tamis-LeMonda, Baumwell, & Dias, 2011). A fuller picture of children's language experiences and development rests on attention to the cultural ecology of children's worlds—including their interactions with siblings, parents, and grandparents (Iglesias & Fabiano, 2003). Yet, researchers have only begun to examine how cultural views and practices affect fathers' interactions with children.

Policy Implications

Practitioners and policymakers should consider effective ways to promote father involvement in the realm of children's language development. It may be especially important to support programs aimed at low-income families, as low-income children are less likely than middle-class children to hear facilitative language from their parents (e.g., Hoff, 2003a,b; 2006). Moreover, new fathers want to be involved in programs that support fathering, and low-income fathers have been shown to benefit from early intervention. For example, in one Early Head Start site that emphasized father involvement and sensitivity to children's cues during home visits, fathers in the treatment group exhibited more complex play than fathers in a comparison group; in turn, their play interactions contributed to children's language achievement beyond children's earlier language competence (Roggman et al., 2004). Thus, work with fathers should start early and build on the birth experience.

Additionally, programs for fathers should aim to identify everyday family routines in which fathers are participants, as mundane activities such as dressing, play, and mealtime offer children rich opportunities to learn about the world through language interactions with others. For example, mealtimes provide ideal occasions for children to practice language skills with family members (Ely et al., 2001), and many fathers regularly share meals with their children starting in infancy (Tamis-LeMonda, Kahana-Kalman, & Yoshikawa, 2009). Thus, rather than attempting to engage fathers in new and perhaps foreign activities, fathers should be encouraged to take advantage of the times they already share with their children.

Future Directions

Collectively, the research reviewed here expands discourse on father involvement beyond that of playmate, to highlight the significant influence fathers have on children's language development. Nonetheless, research in this area is rare, and the science of early language development in social context will only advance if fathers continue to be included in research. Longitudinal studies are likewise needed on the effects of fathers' interactions over time, as well as the factors that come to shape when and how fathers talk to their young children. Finally, policymakers and practitioners should promote messages that mothers *and* fathers are responsible for providing supportive language and learning environments to young children, and that the benefits of rich communicative interactions begin in early infancy. Parents' interactions with infants quickly crystallize into patterns of engagement that may continue to either strengthen or hinder the development of skills that children need for school and life success.

References

Abkarian, G. G., Dworkin, J. P., & Abkarian, A. K. (2003). Fathers' speech to their children: Perfect pitch or tin ear? *Fathering, 1,* 27–50.

Barnes, S., Gutfreund, M., Satterly, D., & Wells, G. (1983). Characteristics of adult speech which predict children's language development. *Journal of Child Language, 10,* 65–84.

Bates, E., Bretherton, I., & Snyder, L. (1988). *From first words to grammar: Individual differences and dissociable mechanisms.* Cambridge, UK: Cambridge University Press.

Bayley, N. (1993). *The Bayley scales of infant development.* San Antonio, TX: Psychological Corporation.

Bellinger, D. C., & Gleason, J. B. (1982). Sex differences in parental directives to young children. *Sex Roles, 8,* 1123–1139.

Belsky, J., & Fearon, R. M. (2004). Exploring marriage-parenting typologies and their contextual antecedents and developmental sequelae. *Development and Psychopathology, 16,* 501–523.

Blackwell, D. L., & Lichter, D. L. (2000). Mate selection among married and cohabiting couples. *Journal of Family Issues, 21,* 275–302.

Bloom, L. (1998). Language acquisition in its developmental context. In D. Kuhn & R. S. Siegler (Eds.), *Handbook of child psychology: Vol 2. Cognition, perception, and language* (5th ed., pp. 309–370). New York, NY: Wiley.

Bornstein, M. H., Haynes, O. M., Painter, K. M., & Genevro, J. L. (2000). Child language with mother and with stranger at home and in the laboratory: A methodological study. *Journal of Child Language, 27,* 407–420.

Bornstein, M. H., Tamis-LeMonda, C. S., Hahn, C., & Haynes, O. M. (2008). Maternal responsiveness to young children at three ages: Longitudinal analysis of a multidimensional, modular, and specific parenting construct. *Developmental Psychology, 44,* 867–874.

Bornstein, M., Vibbert, M., Tal, J., & O'Donnell, K. (1992). Toddler language and play in the second year: Stability, covariation, and influences of parenting. *First Language, 12,* 323–338.

Brown, R. (1973). *A first language: The early stages.* Cambridge, MA: Harvard University Press.

Brownell, R. (2000). *Expressive One-Word Picture Vocabulary Test Manual.* Novato, CA: Academic Therapy Publications

Bruner, J. (1981). The social context of language acquisition. *Language & Communication, 1,* 155–178.

Bruner, J. (2002). *Making stories: Law, literature, life.* New York, NY: Farrar, Straus, and Giroux.

Bus A. G., van Ijzendoorn, M. H., & Pellerini, A. D. (1995). Joint book-reading makes for success in learning to read: A meta-analysis on intergenerational transmission of literacy. *Review of Educational Research, 65,* 1–21.

Cabrera, N. J., Hofferth, S., & Chae, S. (2011). Patterns and predictors of father-infant engagement across race/ethnic groups. *Early Childhood Research Quarterly, 26,* 365–375.

Cabrera, N., & Peters, E. (2000). Public policies and father involvement. *Marriage and Family Review,* 295–314.

Cabrera, N. J., Shannon, J. D., Vogel, C., Tamis-LeMonda, C., Ryan, R., Brooks-Gunn, J., ... Cohen, R. (2004). Low-income fathers' involvement in their toddlers' lives: Biological fathers from the Early Head Start Research and Evaluation Study. *Fathering: A Journal of Theory, Research, and Practice About Men As Fathers, 2,* 5–30.

Cabrera, N. J., Shannon, J. D., West, J., & Brooks-Gunn, J. (2006). Parental interactions with Latino infants: Variation by country of origin and English proficiency. *Child Development, 77,* 1190–1207.

Coleman, J. (1990). *Foundations of social theory.* Cambridge, MA: Harvard University Press.

Cristofaro, T. N., & Tamis-LeMonda, C. S. (2008). Lessons in mother-child and father-child personal narratives in Latino families. In A. McCabe, A. Bailey, & G. Melzi (Eds.), *Spanish-language narration and literacy* (pp. 54–91). New York, NY: Cambridge University Press.

Davidson, R., & Snow, C. (1996). Five-year-olds' interactions with fathers vs. mothers. *First Language, 16,* 223–242.

Dunn, L., & Dunn, L. (1997). *Peabody Picture Vocabulary Test* (3rd ed.). Circle Pines, MN: American Guidance Service.

Duursma, E., Pan, B. A., & Raikes, H. (2008). Predictors and outcomes of low-income fathers' reading with their toddlers. *Early Childhood Research Quarterly, 23,* 351–365.

Ely, R., Berko Gleason, J., MacGibbon, A., & Zaretsky, E. (2001). Attention to language: Lessons learned at the dinner table. *Social Development, 10,* 355–373.

Fenson, L., Dale, P. S., Reznick, J. S., Bates, E., Thai, D., & Pethick, S. J. (1994). Variability in early communicative development. *Monographs of the Society for Research in Child Development, 59*(5, serial no. 242).

Gershoff, E. (2003). *Living at the edge: Low income and the development of America's kindergarteners.* New York, NY: National Center for Children in Poverty.

Gleason, J. B. (1975). Fathers and other strangers: Men's speech to young children. In D. P. Dato (Ed.), *Developmental psycholinguistics: Theory and applications* (pp. 289–297). Washington, DC: Georgetown University Press.

Gleason, J. B., & Greif, E. B. (1983). Men's speech to young children. In B. Thorne, C. Kramerae, & N. Henley (Eds.), *Language, gender, and society* (2nd ed., pp. 140–150). Rowley, MA: Newbury House.

Golinkoff, R. M., & Ames, G. J. (1979). A comparison of fathers' and mothers' speech with their young children. *Child Development, 50,* 28–32.

Hampson, J., & Nelson, K. (1993). The relation of maternal language to variation in rate and style of language acquisition. *Journal of Child Language, 20,* 199–215.

Hart, B., & Risley, T. (1995). *Meaningful differences in the everyday experiences of young American children.* Baltimore, MD: Paul H. Brookes.

Hladik, E., & Edwards, H. (1984). A comparison of mother-father speech in the naturalistic home environment. *Journal of Psycholinguistic Research, 13,* 321–332.

Hoff, E. (2003a). Causes and consequences of SES-related differences in parent-to-child speech. In M. H. Bornstein & R. H. Bradley (Eds.), *Socioeconomic status, parenting, and child development* (pp. 147–160). Mahwah, NJ: Erlbaum.

Hoff, E. (2003b). The specificity of environmental influence: Socioeconomic status affects early vocabulary development via maternal speech. *Child Development, 74,* 1368–1378.

Hoff, E. (2006). How social contexts support and shape language development. *Developmental Review, 26,* 55–88.

Hoff, E., & Naigles, L. (2002). How children use input to acquire a lexicon. *Child Development, 73,* 418–433.

Hollich, G., J., Hirsh-Pasek, K., & Golinkoff, R. M. (Eds.). (2000). Breaking the language barrier: An emergentist coalition model for the origins of word learning. *Monographs of the Society for Research in Child Development, 65* (3, serial no. 262).

Hutchinson, J. F. (1999). The hip hop generation: African American male-female relationships in a nightclub setting. *Journal of Black Studies, 30,* 62–84.

Huttenlocher, J., Haight, W., Bryk, A., Seltzer, M., & Lyons, T. (1991). Early vocabulary growth: Relation to language input and gender. *Developmental Psychology, 27,* 236–248.

Huttenlocher, J., Vasilyeva, M., Waterfall, H. R., Vevea, J. L., & Hedges, L. V. (2007). The varieties of speech to young children. *Developmental Psychology, 43,* 1062–1083.

Iglesias, A. & Fabiano, L. (2003). Latino bilingual students: The contexts of home and school. In V. I. Kloosterman (Ed.), *Latino students in American schools: Historical and contemporary views* (pp. 79–94). Westport, CT: Praeger.

Jepsen, L. K., & Jepsen, C. A. (2002). An empirical analysis of the matching patterns of same-sex and opposite-sex couples. *Demography, 39,* 435–453.

LaBounty, J., Wellman, H. M., Olson, S., Lagattuta, K., & Liu, D. (2008). Mothers' and fathers' use of internal state talk with their young children. *Social Development, 17,* 757–775.

Leaper, C., Anderson, K. J., & Sanders, P. (1998). Moderators of gender effects on parents' talk to their children: A meta-analysis. *Developmental Psychology, 34,* 3–27.

Leavell Smith, A., Tamis-LeMonda, C. S., Ruble, D. R., Zosuls, K., & Cabrera, N. C. (2012). Black, White and Latino fathers' activities with their sons and daughters across early childhood. *Sex Roles, 66*(1), 53–65.

Lovas, G. S. (2011). Gender and patterns of language development in mother-toddler and father-toddler dyads. *First Language, 31,* 83–108.

Luria, A. R. (1979). *The making of mind: A personal account of Soviet psychology* (M. Cole, Trans.). Cambridge, MA: Harvard University Press.

MacWhinney, B. (2000). *The CHILDES project: Tools for analyzing talk.* Mahwah, NJ: Erlbaum.

Martin, A., Ryan, R. M., & Brooks-Gunn, J. (2007). The joint influence of mother and father parenting on child cognitive outcomes at age 5. *Early Childhood Research Quarterly, 22,* 423–439.

McFadden, K., Tamis-LeMonda, C. S., & Cabrera, N. J. (2012). Quality Matters: Low-Income father engagement in learning activities in early childhood predict children's academic performance in fifth grade. *Family Science, 2*(2), 120–130.

McLaughlin, B., White, D., McDevitt, T., & Raskin, R. (1983). Mothers' and fathers' speech to their young children: Similar or different? *Journal of Child Language, 10,* 245–252.

Miller, J., & Chapman, R. (1993). *SALT: Systematic analysis of language transcripts.* Madison: University of Wisconsin.

Nelson, K. (1996). *Language in cognitive development: Emergence of the mediated mind.* Cambridge, UK: Cambridge University Press.

Ochs, E., & Schieffelin, B. B. (1984). Language acquisition and socialization: Three developmental stories. In R. Shweder & R. LeVine (Eds.), *Culture theory: Essays on mind, self, and emotion* (pp. 276–320). New York, NY: Cambridge University Press.

Pan, B. A., Rowe, M. L., Spier, E., & Tamis-LeMonda, C. S. (2004). Measuring productive vocabulary of toddlers in low-income families: Concurrent and predictive validity of three sources of data. *Journal of Child Language, 31,* 587–608.

Pancsofar, N., & Vernon-Feagans, L. (2006). Mother and father language input to young children: Contributions to later language development. *Journal of Applied Developmental Psychology, 27,* 571–587.

Pancsofar, N., Vernon-Feagans, L., Odom, E., & Roe, J. R. (2008). Family relationships during infancy and later mother and father vocabulary use with young children. *Early Childhood Research Quarterly, 23,* 493–503.

Pancsofar, N., Vernon-Feagans, L., & The Family Life Project Investigators. (2010). Fathers' early contributions to children's language development in families from low-income rural comunities. *Early Childhood Research Quarterly, 25,* 450–463.

Raikes, H., Pan, B. A., Luze, G., Tamis-LeMonda, C. S., Brooks-Gunn, J., Constantine, J., ... Rodriguez, E. T. (2006). Mother-child bookreading in low-income families: Correlates and outcomes during the first three years of life. *Child Development, 77,* 924–953.

Reese, E., & Read, S. (2000). Predictive validity of the New Zealand MacArthur Communicative Development Inventory: Word and sentences. *Journal of Child Language, 27,* 255–266.

Rodriguez, E. T. & Tamis-LeMonda, C. S. (2011). Trajectories of the home learning environment across the first 5 years: Associations with children's vocabulary and literacy skills at prekindergarten. *Child Development, 82,* 1058–1075.

Rodriguez, E. T., Tamis-LeMonda, C. S., Spellmann, M. E., Pan, B. A., Raikes, H., Lugo-Gil, J., ... Luze, G. (2009). The formative role of home literacy experiences across the first three years of life in children from low-income families. *Journal of Applied Developmental Psychology, 30*, 677–694.

Roggman, L. A., Boyce, L. K., Cook, G. A., Christiansen, K., & Jones, D. (2004). Playing with daddy: Social toy play, Early Head Start, and developmental outcomes. *Fathering, Special Issue: Fathers in Early Head Start, 2*, 83–108.

Rowe, M. L., Coker. D., & Pan, B. A. (2004). A comparison of fathers' and mothers' talk to toddlers in low-income families. *Social Development, 13*, 278–291.

Sameroff, A. (Ed.). (2009). *The transactional model of development: How children and contexts shape each other.* Washington, DC: American Psychological Association.

Shannon, J. D., Tamis-LeMonda, C. S., London, K., & Cabrera, N. (2002). Beyond rough and tumble: Low-income fathers' interactions and children's cognitive development as 24 months. *Parenting: Science and Practice, 2*, 77–104.

Snow, C. E. (1972). Mothers' speech to children learning language. *Child Development, 43*, 549–565.

Tamis-LeMonda, C. S., & Baumwell, L. (2011). Parent sensitivity in early development: Conceptualization, methods, measurement, and generalizability. In D. W. Davis & M. C. Logsdon (Eds.), *Maternal sensitivity: A scientific foundations for practice* (pp. 1–15). Hauppauge, NY: Nova Publishers.

Tamis-LeMonda, C. S., Baumwell, L., & Cristofaro, T. N. (2012). Parent-child conversations during free play. *First Language*.

Tamis-LeMonda, C. S., Baumwell, L., & Dias, S. (2011). School readiness in Latino immigrant children in the U. S. In S. Chuang & R. Moreno (Eds.), *Immigrant children: Change, adaptation, and cultural transformation* (pp. 213–237). New York, NY: Lexington Books.

Tamis-LeMonda, C. S., & Bornstein, M. H. (1994). Specificity in mother-toddler language-play relations across the second year. *Developmental Psychology, 30*, 283–292.

Tamis-LeMonda, C. S., & Bornstein, M. H. (2002). Maternal responsiveness and early language acquisition. *Advances in Child Development, 29*, 89–127.

Tamis-LeMonda, C. S., Bornstein, M. H., & Baumwell, L. (2001). Maternal responsiveness and children's achievement of language milestones. *Child Development, 72*, 748–767.

Tamis-LeMonda, C. S., Bornstein, M. H., Kahana-Kalman, R., Baumwell, L., & Cyphers, L. (1998). Predicting variation in the timing of linguistic milestones in the second year: An events-history approach. *Journal of Child Language, 25*, 675–700.

Tamis-LeMonda, C. S., Cristofaro, T. N., Rodriguez, E. T., & Bornstein, M. (2006). Early language development: Social influences in the first years of life. In L. Balter & C. S. Tamis-LeMonda (Eds.), *Child psychology: A handbook of contemporary issues* (Vol. 2, pp. 79–108). London: Psychology Press.

Tamis-LeMonda, C. S., Kahana-Kalman, R., & Yoshikawa, H. (2009). Father involvement in immigrant and ethnically diverse families from the prenatal period to the second year: Prediction and mediating mechanisms. *Sex Roles, 60*(7-8), 496–509.

Tamis-LeMonda, C. S., Niwa, E., Kahana-Kalman, R., & Yoshikawa, H. (2008). Immigrant Fathers and Families at the transition to Parenthood. In S. Chuang & R. Moreno (Eds.), *On new shores: Understanding fathers in North America* (pp. 229–253). New York, NY: Lexington Books.

Tamis-LeMonda, C. S., Shannon, J. D., Cabrera, N. J., & Lamb, M. E. (2004). Fathers and mothers at play with their 2- and 3-year-olds: Contributions to language and cognitive development. *Child Development, 75*, 1806–1820.

Tomasello, M., Conti-Ramsden, G., & Ewert, B. (1990). Young children's conversations with their mothers and fathers: Differences in breakdown and repair. *Journal of Child Language, 17*, 115–130.

Vogel, C. A. Boller, K., Faerber, J., Shannon, J. D., & Tamis-LeMonda, C. S. (2003). *Understanding fathering: The early head start study of fathers of newborns* (No. 8517). Princeton, NJ: Mathematica Policy Research.

Vygotsky, L. S. (1979). Consciousness as a problem in the psychology of behaviour. *Soviet Psychology, 17*, 3–35.

Yeung, W. J., Duncan, G. J., & Hill, M. S. (2000). Putting fathers back in the picture: Parental activities and children's adult outcomes. In H. E. Peters, G. W. Peterson, S. K. Steinmetz, & R. D. Day (Eds.), *Fatherhood: Research, interventions and policies* (pp. 97–113). New York, NY: Hayworth Press.

Chapter 9

Fathers' Contributions to Children's Social Development

Melinda S. Leidy, Thomas J. Schofield, and Ross D. Parke

University of California, Riverside

Brief Historical Overview and Theoretical Perspectives

Families have long been recognized as a major socialization agent for the development of children's social behavior. However, the definition of family has changed to view the family as a social system in which fathers, siblings, and the marital relationship all affect social development. It has also become increasingly important to examine the effects of contextual processes on child social development. These include extended family, adult mentors, and children's peers. The aim of this chapter is to examine the links between fathers and children's social development, especially their relationships with peers. We define social development as the description and explanation of changes in children's social behavior, perceptions, and attitudes across age (Parke & Clarke-Stewart, 2010). Our chapter also focuses primarily on father's contributions to children's social development in middle childhood because, in part, children's opportunities for social interaction with peers and non-family adults intensify during this period as children attend school on a regular basis.

Evidence that fathers matter for children's social development comes initially from studies of father absence. Although these studies have been criticized (Pedersen, 1976), they provide suggestive evidence. Stolz (1954) found that children whose fathers were absent during their infancy due to World War II had poorer peer relationships at 4 to 8 years old. Studies of the sons of Norwegian sailors, who are away for many months at a time, pointed to the same conclusion: the boys whose fathers were often absent were less popular and had less-satisfying peer-group relationships than boys whose fathers were regularly available (Lynn & Sawrey, 1959).

More compelling evidence of the effects of fathers' absence on children's social adjustment comes from the National Longitudinal Study of Youth (Mott, 1994). Children in homes where fathers were absent were at a higher risk for school and peer problems. White boys and girls from father-absent homes were less liked by their age-mates than children from father-present families. The effects are reduced, however, when factors linked with the disruption of the father's departure—such as family income or long-term maternal health—are taken into account. For African American boys or girls, there is little evidence of adverse behavior being associated with a father's absence, perhaps due to the traditional reliance of African American families on extended kin networks for support and the higher contact rates between both children (Mott, 1994) and the child's mother (Cabrera, Ryan, Mitchell, Shannon, & Tamis-LeMonda, 2008) among non-resident African American fathers compared to White fathers.

Recently, the Fragile Families and Child Wellbeing Study found that children whose fathers were incarcerated were more aggressive than their peers (Wakefield, 2008). Similarly, Geller, Garfinkel, Cooper, and Mincy (2009) concluded that children of incarcerated fathers had higher childhood aggression and more attention problems than children whose fathers were absent due to other reasons such as divorce or death. Clearly, the context in which paternal absence occurs is likely to affect child outcomes. Furthermore, research indicates that children in stepfather families displayed higher externalizing behaviors and more negative self-feelings than children with continuously married parents while controlling for socioeconomic status (SES) and mothering (Carlson, 2006; Leidy et al. 2011). These findings suggest that it is not simply the presence of a father figure that affects child outcomes but perhaps other fathering factors, such as father involvement, that mediate the relationship between father absence and child outcomes.

Current Research Questions

To better understand the specific aspects of the father-child relationship that may be important in explaining father's role in social development, we propose three different pathways of father influence on children's social behavior. These three paths include lessons learned in the context of the father-child relationship, fathers' direct advice concerning peer relationships, and fathers' regulation of access to peers and peer-related activities (McDowell & Parke, 2009). We first present the current research pertaining to each of these paths below. While the focus of this chapter is on fathers, mothers play these roles as well, and thus, we will note how fathers and mothers differ in how they influence their children's social relationships. In accordance our theoretical view of the embeddedness of fathers in a family system, we recognize that the effects of fathers are best understood in the context of the mother-father dyad. Current research questions on how the mother-father dyad impacts the father-child relationship and child social competence will be outlined below. Finally, research questions regarding the effects of fathers on children's social relationships in various cultures and subcultures will be discussed.

Quality of the Father-Child Relationship

How does the quality of the father-child relationship affect children's social relationships? We will examine this question using two perspectives, specifically the attachment and father-child interaction perspectives. Furthermore, what child mediators link father-child interaction to child social development? We focus on the three sets of mediating processes, namely affect management skills, cognitive representational processes, and attention-regulation skills.

Fathers as Advisers and Social Guides

Fathers assume various roles in their child's life that affect the child's relative success in social interactions outside the family. How do fathers affect child social relationships through their role as social guides and advisers? Does their role change over development?

Fathers as Monitors and Sources of Social Opportunities

Parents often provide social opportunities for their children, especially younger children. How do these social opportunities impact child social development? What role do fathers play in facilitating children's involvement in extracurricular activities and, in turn, in child social relationships? In addition to providing social activities for their children, parents also monitor their child's whereabouts. How does parental monitoring impact child social development?

Mother-Father Dyad as a Contributor to Children's Peer Relationships

The marital relationship influences how fathers interact with their children, and, in turn, children's social competence. How do marital relationships affect child social competence? We will address this question using direct and indirect effects models of the links between the mother-father relationship and children's social development. While in many cases the mother and father are married, in some cases there is a stable relationship but one in which the parenting partners are not legally married. In most of the work that we review, the marital dyad is involved but the pattern of finding is substantially similar in stable but unmarried parental dyads.

Cultural Considerations in the Father-Child Relationship

As a corrective to the limited prior work examining the influence of father-child relationships on children's social competence in different cultural contexts, current research on this issue will be examined. How do fathers influence child social competence in different cultures and among ethnic groups in our own culture?

Research Measurement and Methodology

The study of fathers' contributions to children's social development has seen several advances in research measurement and methodology. First, researchers have recognized the need to have independent sources of data for fathering and mothering rather than relying on a single source for reports on both parents. The use of a single reporter will inflate the correlation between reports of mothers and fathers, thus making it less likely that both will be significant predictors of developmental outcomes. Second, by including both maternal and paternal measures in models, the unique contribution of fathering after controlling for maternal contributions can be assessed. Third, there has been an increased reliance on multiple sources of information about fathering through the use of a latent-variable approach, which has allowed researchers to consider only the variance that is common across reporters as meaningful. It has also made possible the use of sensitivity analyses where tests are run on each data source separately. Fourth, researchers have recognized the importance of independent sources of data for measures of fathering and children's social development in order to avoid problems of shared method variance. Fifth, advances in modeling techniques permit the testing of interactions between mothers and fathers as well as test for differences between mothering and fathering coefficients, instead of simply assuming they are different. Thus, we have learned some of the ways in which fathers and mothers are similar as well as different. Sixth, assessing multiple dimensions of fathering, such as hostility or acceptance, in addition to measures of quality of involvement (e.g., affect and management) has furthered an understanding of the roles of

fathers in their children's lives. Seventh, being able to test for the nonlinear effects of fathering has revealed that certain fathering dimensions may be especially beneficial or harmful to
child outcomes (Leidy et al., 2011). Eighth, more sophisticated strategies for analyzing longitudinal data about the effects of fathering that explicitly test for change (such as autoregressive
models for rank-order change, growth models, and dual-change models) allows researchers to
make causal inferences as well as to test reciprocal associations between fathering and child
development. Fathering does not simply influence children, but children influence fathers and
fathering behavior as well. Finally, multilevel modeling allows us to examine multiple levels
of analysis (children within a single family; dyads and triads) while the social relations model
(Rasbash, Jenkins, O'Connor, Tackett, & Reiss, 2011) permits a more adequate analysis of the
embeddedness of fathers in the family system. These techniques further an understanding
of the complexity of the father-child relationship and how it relates to the family system and
children's social development.

Empirical Findings

The Quality of the Father-Child Relationship

Researchers have examined how the quality of the father-child relationship impacts children's
relationships with their peers from two perspectives: (a) by examining connections between
infant-father attachment and social development, and (b) by examining associations between
the quality of the father-child interaction, especially in play and children's social outcomes.

Attachment

An impressive amount of research suggests that the quality of the child-mother attachment is
related to children's later social and emotional development in preschool, middle childhood,
and even in adolescence. A secure attachment is likely to lead to better social and emotional
adjustment. Children are better liked by others, have higher self-esteem, and are more socially
skilled (Thompson, 2006). The evidence is mixed as to whether the quality of the infant's or
child's attachment to the father matters. While some early work suggested that the quality of
infant-father attachment is related to children's willingness to engage an adult play partner
(Main & Weston, 1981), recent work by the Grossmanns and colleagues (Grossmann et al.,
2002; Grossman, Grossman, Kindler, & Zimmermann, 2008) argues that father and mother
attachment relationships derive from different sets of early social experiences. While mothers
provide emotional security when the child is distressed, fathers "provide security through sensitive and challenging support as a companion when the child's exploratory system is aroused"
(Grossmann et al., 2002, p. 311). In short, mothers function as distress regulators and fathers
as challenging but reassuring play partners. In support of their argument, Grossmann et al.
(2002) found that fathers' play sensitivity and quality of infant-mother attachment predicted
children's internal working models of attachment at age 10. Furthermore, adolescents whose
fathers were more sensitive in their early play interactions had more secure partnership representations of their current romantic partners (Grossmann et al., 2008). Thus, their results
support the assumption that fathers' play sensitivity rather than the security of their attachment relationship with their infants is a better predictor of the children's long-term attachment
representations (Grossmann et al., 2008).

The influence of father-child attachment on child social competence has been further supported by other studies. In a Belgian longitudinal study, preschool children's positive self-image was better predicted by child-mother attachment representations, whereas anxious/withdrawn behavioral problems were better predicted by child-father attachment representations (Verschueren & Marcoen, 1999). At age 9, the quality of children's attachment representations to their fathers was more influential in children's peer nominations of shy/withdrawn, same-sex peer acceptance, and peer sociometric status (Verschueren & Marcoen, 2005). Thus, these studies confirm that father attachment relationships play a unique role in child social competence.

Father-Child Interaction

In contrast to the attachment tradition, researchers in the cognitive social learning tradition assume that face-to-face interactions between children and fathers may afford children the opportunity to learn social skills that are necessary for successful social relationships with peers (see Parke & Buriel, 2006, for a fuller description). In an early study with 3- and 4-year-old children, MacDonald and Parke (1984) found that fathers who exhibited high levels of physical play with their children and elicited high levels of positive feelings during the play sessions had children who received higher teacher-rated peer popularity ratings in preschool. Boys whose fathers were both highly physical and low in directiveness received the highest popularity ratings, and the boys whose fathers were highly directive received lower popularity scores. Girls whose teachers rated them as popular had physically playful and feeling-eliciting but nondirective fathers. Later studies confirm this general pattern. Popular children have fathers who are able to sustain physical play for longer periods and use less directive or coercive tactics (see McDowell & Parke, 2009; Parke & O'Neil, 2000).

Other researchers report that the style of father-child play is important as well. Hart et al. (1998) found that greater playfulness, patience, and understanding with children, especially among fathers, was associated with less aggressive behavior with peers among both Russian and Western children. Flanders and colleagues (Flanders, Leo, Paquette, Pihl, & Séguin, 2009; Flanders et al., 2010) emphasize the importance of the quality of the father child relationship as an important moderator of the links between physical play and children's later behavior with peers. Specifically rough-and-tumble play was associated with more aggression but only when fathers were less dominant and only when fathers were unable to maintain an authoritative position in the play interactions. The physical play context is important but only when used effectively by the adult play partner to teach the child to regulate his/her actions, which means communicating to the child when he /she has exceeded the partner's comfort zone. Low dominant, possibly permissive or uninvolved, fathers who do not set boundaries may provide opportunities for children to learn that their excessively rough/aggressive behavior is acceptable. In turn, this is reflected in peer-peer interactions. It is not any kind of physical play, but modulated and regulated physical play is positively linked to social outcomes.

Mediating Processes Between Father-Child Interaction and Children's Social Development

What child mediators link father-child interaction to child social development? Several processes have been hypothesized as mediators, including affect management skills such as emotion encoding and decoding, emotion regulatory abilities, cognitive representations, attributions and beliefs, problem-solving skills, and attention-regulation abilities (Parke, McDowell, Kim, & Leidy, 2006). It is assumed that these abilities or beliefs are acquired through parent-child interchanges over the course of development and, in turn, guide the nature of children's behavior with their peers. We focus on three sets of processes: affect management skills, cognitive representational processes, and attention-regulation skills.

Affect management and emotional regulation.   It is not only the quality of emotions that fathers display that matters to children's social development, but also how children and fathers deal with emotional displays. What do children learn during play with their fathers? Being able to read a play partner's emotional signals and send clear emotional cues is critical for successfully maintaining play activities. These skills allow partners to modulate their playful behavior so that neither becomes overly aroused or understimulated, and play continues at an optimal level of excitement for both (Flanders et al., 2010). Children learn to recognize others' emotions, improve their own emotional production skills, and regulate their emotions in the context of parent-child play (Paquette, 2004; Parke et al., 1992). Fathers provide a unique opportunity to teach children about the role of emotions in the context of relationships due to the wide range of intensity of affect that father's display and the unpredictable character of their playful exchanges with their children (Parke, 1995, 1996; Parke & Brott, 1999).

Are fathers accepting and helpful when children become distressed, angry, or sad or are they dismissing and rejecting? Several researchers have found that fathers' comfort and acceptance of their children's emotional distress is linked with more positive peer relationships. Gottman, Katz, and Hooven (1997) found that fathers' acceptance of and assistance with their children's sadness and anger at 5 years of age was related to the children's social competence with their peers 3 years later. Girls were less negative with friends and boys were less aggressive. Fathers who reported emotion- and problem-focused reactions to the expression of negative emotions had children who were described by teachers as less aggressive/disruptive (see Parke & O'Neil, 1997, for further details and the mother's role in this process). In addition, both parental control and affect were related to children's emotional regulation and coping. McDowell and Parke (2005) found that when fathers were more controlling, their fourth-grade children exhibited less emotion regulation. However, more paternal positive affect and less paternal negative affect were associated with more positive coping strategies on the part of their children. Other work has found that child knowledge of and use of display rules, a form of emotional regulation, is linked with higher levels of peer acceptance (McDowell, & Parke, 2000; Parke et al., 2006). In summary, in the context of father-child interaction, children learn not only the communicative value of emotions for modifying others' behavior during social exchanges but also important lessons in emotional regulation as well. These "emotion lessons" in turn, contribute positively to children's social development.

Cognitive representational models.   One of the major problems facing the area of family-peer relations is how children transfer the strategies that they acquire in the family context to their peer relationships. Several theories assume that individuals possess internal mental representations that guide their social behavior. Attachment theorists offer "working models" (Bowlby, 1969), whereas social and cognitive psychologists have suggested scripts or cognitive maps as guides for social action (Bugental & Grusec, 2006). Researchers within the attachment tradition have found support for Bowlby's argument that representations vary as a function of child-parent attachment history (Main, Kaplan, & Cassidy, 1985). For example, children who had been securely attached infants were more likely to represent their family in their drawings in a coherent manner, with a balance between individuality and connection, than children who had been insecurely attached. In turn, securely attached children have better peer relationships (Thompson, 2006).

Research in a social interactional tradition reveals links between parent and child cognitive representations of social relationships (Burks & Parke, 1996). McDowell, Parke, and Spitzer (2002) found that fathers' but not mothers' cognitive models of relationships were linked to children's social competence. Fathers whose strategies for dealing with interpersonal conflict dilemmas were rated high on confrontation and instrumental qualities were associated with lower child social competence. Children of fathers with relational goals were less often nominated as aggressive by peers and rated more liked and less disliked by teachers. Rah and Parke (2008) found that children who had more positive interactions with their fathers in fourth grade had fewer negative goals and strategies for solving interpersonal problems with their fathers in fifth grade. They were less likely to endorse negative goals and strategies in solving social dilemmas with peers, which was related to higher peer acceptance. However, for mothers, this relation was only found among girls. Thus, fathers seem to play a particularly important role in the links between child social information processing and peer relationships.

Attention regulation.   Attentional regulatory processes have also been viewed as an additional mechanism through which familial socialization experiences might influence the development of children's social competence. These processes include the ability to attend to relevant cues, to sustain attention, to refocus attention through such processes as cognitive distraction and cognitive restructuring, and other efforts to purposefully reduce the level of emotional arousal in a situation that is appraised as stressful. Attentional processes organize experience and play a central role in cognitive and social development beginning in early infancy (Rothbart & Bates, 2006). Thus, Wilson (1999) considers attention-regulatory processes as a "shuttle" linking emotion regulation and social cognitive processes because attentional processes organize both cognitions and emotions and, thus, influence relationship competence. Using a national longitudinal study, the NICHD Early Child Care Research Network (2009) found that both mother-child and father-child relationship quality at 54 months predicted children's ability to sustain attention (using an independent lab based measure) as well as ratings of attentional problems in first grade, and, in turn, mediated the links between parenting and higher social skills ratings in first and third grade. Maternal and paternal interactions accounted for unique variance in these outcomes. In summary, the ability to regulate attention is a further important mediating pathway through which paternal behavior may influence children's peer functioning.

Fathers as Advisers and Social Guides

Learning about relationships through interaction with parents can be viewed as an indirect pathway because the goal is often not explicitly to influence children's social relationships with extrafamilial partners such as peers. In contrast, parents influence children's relationships directly in their roles as instructors, educators, or advisers. In these roles, parents explicitly set out to educate their children concerning the appropriate manner of initiating and maintaining social relationships. Research suggests that young children in preschool and early elementary school gain competence with peers when parents supervise and facilitate their experiences, whereas among older children (middle school and beyond), greater parental supervision and guidance of children's peer relationships may function more as a remediatory effort (Parke &

O'Neil, 2000). In a study of parental supervision, Bhavnagri and Parke (1991) found that 2- to 5-year-old children, especially the 2- to 3-year-olds, exhibited more cooperation and turn taking and had longer play bouts when assisted by an adult than when playing without assistance.

As children develop, the forms of management shift from direct involvement or supervision of the ongoing activities of children and their peers to a less-public form of management, involving advice or consultation concerning appropriate ways of handling peer problems. Using a triadic advice-giving session in which mothers, fathers, and their third grader discussed how to handle peer interaction problems, Wang and McDowell (1996) found that parental style of interaction appeared to be a better predictor of children's social competence than the actual solution quality generated in the advice-giving session. Specifically, fathers' controlling style and warmth and mothers' support during the advice-giving task were significant predictors of children's social competence. In a recent longitudinal study, McDowell and Parke (2009) found that the parent advice giving of both mothers and fathers predicted children's social competence, and, in turn, social acceptance 1 year later. Since the model was tested with both mothers and fathers and both were related to child outcomes, this underscores the important role that fathers as well as mothers play in their children's social development. The direction of effects in each of these studies, of course, is difficult to determine. Under some circumstances, parents may be providing advice in response to children's social difficulties (see also Ladd & Golter, 1988; Mize, Pettit, & Brown, 1995). Highly involved parents, for example, may simply be responding to their children's poor social abilities. Nevertheless, the bulk of evidence suggests that direct parental influence in the form of supervision and advice giving can significantly increase the social competence of young children and illustrates the utility of examining direct parent strategies as a way of teaching children about social relationships.

Fathers as Sources and Monitors of Social Opportunities

Both fathers and mothers play an important role in the facilitation of their children's peer relationships by initiating informal contact between their own children and potential play partners, especially among young children (Reich & Vandell, 2011). Ladd and Golter (1988) found that children of parents who arranged peer contacts had a larger range of playmates and more frequent play companions outside of school than children of parents who were less active in initiating peer contacts. When children entered kindergarten, boys, but not girls, with parents who initiated peer contacts were better liked and less rejected by their classmates than boys with non-initiating parents.

Parents also influence their children's social relationships by providing them with the opportunity to participate in more formal afterschool activities such as team sports, Brownies, and Cub Scouts. Participating in these institutions allow children access to a wider range of activities than more informal play situations and can contribute to their social and cognitive development. Although some studies have found that mothers are more involved in the interface between children and social institutions and view these settings as being more important for children's development of social skills than do fathers (Bhavnagri & Parke, 1991), few studies have investigated father's participation in formal afterschool activities with their children. McDowell and Parke (2009) found that both mothers' and fathers' provision of opportunities for their fourth grade child was related to higher levels of positive social competence in fifth grade. However, little is known about the specific nature of father involvement. Since many fathers may serve as coaches of their children's sports team or lead their scout groups, future research should examine the effects of these interactions on their children's social development. Involvement in religious institutions is another way that fathers and mothers can provide their children with opportunities to gain positive experience with peers. Adolescents who were involved in church activities in 8th grade had better peer relationships in 12th grade (Elder & Conger, 2000).

Another way fathers can affect their children's social relationships is through monitoring their social activities, especially as children move into preadolescence and adolescence which marks a relative shift in importance of family and peers as sources of influence on social relationships. Monitoring refers to a range of activities including the supervision of children and choice of social settings, activities, and friends. Poorly monitored children have lower academic skills, lower peer acceptance (Sandstrom & Cole, 1999), higher school truancy and substance abuse rates (Furstenberg, Cook, Eccles, Elder, & Sameroff, 1999), higher rates of delinquent and externalizing behavior (Hair, Moore, Garrett, Ling, & Cleveland, 2008; Xiaoming, Stanton, & Feigelman, 2000), and associate more with deviant peers (Knoester, Haynie, & Stephens, 2006).

It is important to underscore that these three pathways of influence do not operate independently. As McDowell and Parke (2009) found, father-child interaction, paternal advice giving, and provision of opportunities together provided a better prediction of social competence than any of these paternal socialization strategies in isolation.

The Mother-Father Dyad as a Contributor to Children's Social Development

Another way in which fathers influence their children's peer relationships is through their relationships with the mother of their children (Parke et al., 2001). Two perspectives, specifically the direct and indirect effects models, have been offered to explain the possible links between marital relationships and children's social relationships.

According to the direct effect model, exposure to parent-parent conflict may directly alter children's capacity to function effectively in other social contexts (Cummings & Davies, 2010). These direct effects seem to be mediated by two sets of intervening processes: (a) children's perceptions of conflict, and (b) emotional regulation (for a review of these theoretical arguments see Parke et al., 2001). Katz and Gottman (1993) found that couples who exhibited a hostile style of resolving conflict had children who tended to be described by teachers as exhibiting antisocial characteristics. When husbands were angry and emotionally distant while resolving marital conflict, children were described by teachers as anxious and socially withdrawn. Furthermore, O'Neil, Flyr, Wild, and Parke (1999) found that more negative paternal problem-solving strategies were associated with greater peer-rated avoidance and lower teacher-rated acceptance. In another study, Kim, Parke, and O'Neil (1999) found that frequent parental conflict was associated with teacher ratings of shy behavior and sadness, and child self-blame was associated with peer ratings of dislike, verbal and physical aggression, and peer and teacher ratings of externalizing behaviors. In addition, adolescents whose parents fought frequently were less likely to be accepted by their peers, had fewer friends, and expressed negative qualities in their best friendships (Vairami & Vorria, 2007). Research has indicated the differential influences of mother and father marital processes and child outcomes. Cummings, Goeke-Morey, Papp, and Dukewich (2002) found that mothers' reported increased negative emotionality (comprised of anger, sadness, and fear), in children as a response to destructive behavior by their fathers. Furthermore, both fathers' and mothers' reports of fathers' negative emotionality, predicted child anger, sadness, and fear as well as decreased levels of positive emotionality in children. Crockenberg and Langrock (2001) found that fathers' marital aggression predicted boys' and girls' externalizing problems even after controlling for parenting factors.

The indirect effect model proposes that marital relationships alter parent-child relationships, and consequently affect child outcomes (Fauber & Long, 1991). Poor parenting and poor marriages often go together, and some father effects are best understood by recognizing this link between parenting and marriage. Gottman and Katz (1989) found that a poor parenting style, characterized as cold, unresponsive, angry, and low in limit setting and structuring, was linked to higher levels of anger and noncompliance on the part of 5-year-old children when interacting with their parents, which, in turn, led to poor peer outcomes. Children from these homes had lower levels of positive play with peers, more negative peer exchanges, and poorer physical health. Further support for the indirect model comes from a study by Stocker and Youngblade (1999) who found that paternal, but not maternal, hostility served as the mediator between marital conflict and problematic peer relationships. Finally, family systems theory suggests that marital discord not only adversely affects mother-child and father-child relationships but also impairs qualities of the triadic mother-father-child relationships by reducing the effectiveness of how well mothers and fathers work together with their children (for more information on co-parenting, see chapter by Palkovitz, Fagan, & Hull, this volume).

Cultural Considerations in the Father-Child Relationship

The relative impact of parents and peers in different cultures and the nature of the family-peer linkages may differ across and within cultures (Chen & French, 2008). Although relatively few studies have examined this relation, numerous studies have reported that parental and peer correlates of child social competence are similar. Family relationships, such as parent-child conflict, parental warmth, and parental monitoring, and peer approval/disapproval of misconduct were related to child misconduct similarly across European, Chinese American, and Chinese subgroups (Chen, Greenberger, Lester, Dong, & Guo, 1998). In a Chinese sample, Chen and Rubin (1994) found that authoritarian parenting and punitive disciplinary practices were linked with childhood aggression and peer rejection, while parental warmth and authoritative parenting predicted social competence, which then predicted peer acceptance. Recently, Leidy et al. (2011) found that father acceptance, monitoring, consistent discipline, and interactions with his child were associated with positive child adjustment, whereas father rejection was negatively associated with positive child adjustment. These findings were seen in both Mexican American and European American step and intact families while controlling for SES, child gender, marital quality, and mothers' parenting behaviors, suggesting that fathering is associated with child adjustment regardless of family type in both ethnic groups.

It is crucial to extend examination of father-peer relationships and especially the mediating processes to a wider range of cultures. For example, we argued that emotion-regulatory skills are acquired, in part, in the context of father-child physical play and are mediating processes between fathers and social competence. However, evidence from Chinese Malaysia, Taiwan, Thailand, Sweden, and India has suggested that fathers and mothers rarely engage in physical play with their children (Lamb, 1997; Sun & Roopnarine, 1996). These cross-cultural variations alert us to the possibilities that other mediators may be involved for non-Western cultures or that emotion-regulatory and other aspects of emotional competence may be learned in nonphysical play contexts or in interaction with other socialization agents.

In terms of parental management, similarities and differences across cultures are evident as well (Hart et al., 1998). In Russia, China, and the United States, mothers who initiated more peer contacts had children who were more accepted by peers. However, Chinese children were given more autonomy in their initiating activities with peers. Mothers in all cultures were more likely to arrange peer contacts if their children were perceived by teachers as less socially competent. Parental monitoring has similar positive effects on children's misconduct in a variety of cultures, including Denmark (Arnert & Balle-Jensen, 1993), China (Chen et al., 1998), and Australia (Feldman, Rosenthal, Mont-Reynaud, & Leung, 1991). Across a variety of cultures, the relative influence of families and peers on children's social behavior may differ, but the family processes by which these socialization agents achieve their influence are similar.

Bridges to Other Disciplines

The study of fatherhood has become a fully realized interdisciplinary enterprise. In part, this broadening of disciplinary interest is due to the reconceptualization of fathering not solely as an interactive parent-child enterprise but as a fully contextualized inquiry in which fathers are viewed as members of a larger set of social systems. Fathers are part of family systems which, in turn, requires that the mother-father relationship be recognized as well as fathers multiple and distinctive relationships with the full set of siblings in the family (Cummings & Davies, 2010). Fathers are part of biological systems just as mothers are, which has led to the assessment of hormonal related changes in men across the transition to fatherhood (Storey, this volume; Storey, Walsh, Quinton, & Wynne-Edwards, 2000). As sociologists have shown, fathering is influenced by extra-familial contexts such as work, neighborhood, and social class (Coltrane, 2007; Guzzo & Furstenberg, 2007). In turn, fathers' links with the legal and medical establishments has enticed legal and medical scholars to join the effort to understand fathering (Maccoby & Mnookin, 1998; Pruett, 2000). And not all fathers function adequately; some are depressed, others are violent while some are uninvolved. This has led psychiatrists, social workers, clinical psychologists, and educators to become involved in this inquiry as well (Bender et al., 2007; Cowan, Cowan, Pruett, Pruett, & Wong, 2009). Finally historians (Pleck, 2004) have provided a glimpse at fathering in earlier times while demographers (Hernandez, Denton, & Macartney, 2008) are helping us track changes over time and aid in our policy planning for the future. It is fully recognized that the study of fatherhood is too important and too diverse to be left in the hands of a single discipline, and that these multiple disciplines will further our understanding of how fathers impact child social development.

Policy Implications

While there remain many unanswered questions, there is ample evidence that fathers do indeed affect children's relationships with peers. Thus policies should take into account the important role that both mothers and fathers play in children's social competence. In an age of increased school violence, shootings, and gangs, it is especially important to take a family systems perspective in developing and evaluating the effectiveness of interventions aimed at increasing peer competence, decreasing youth violence, and promoting positive youth development in children. Furthermore, ways of involving and engaging fathers in schools and extra-curricular activities may have positive benefits for children's peer relationships. Recognizing the importance of the mother-father relationship, especially the marital relationship, is central to efforts to improve the quality of the father-child relationship. Family systems interventions and community-based resources should encourage father involvement in recognition of the vital role of fathers in children's social development.

Future Directions

While there have been shifts in the extent to which fathers are active caregivers and participants in the lives of their children (Parke & Brott, 1999; Pleck, 2010), less is known about how these shifts, in turn, alter children's social competence. Men are becoming fathers at later ages and many men are re-experiencing fatherhood in middle or old age as a result of divorce and remarriage. The effects of the shift in timing in the onset of first-time or repeated fatherhood on men's interaction patterns with their children, and consequently, on their children's social development, remain unclear.

Another poorly understood issue concerns the cross-cultural generality of the finding in North American and Western European studies that fathers' physical play style has been suggested as a unique way in which fathers influence their children's social adaptation. In light of the cross-cultural evidence that physical play is not a universal feature of the father-child interactive style, this is clearly not the only way in which fathers influence their children's social outcomes. Therefore, a more detailed examination of the alternative pathways through which children learn emotional competence that are important for successful peer relationships is warranted. Moreover, the relative importance of fathers as interactive agents, advisers, or managers of social opportunities is not clearly understood (McDowell & Parke, 2009). It is clear that more effort needs to be devoted to partialing out the relative contributions to different aspects of the fathers' roles as well as differences across mother and father roles. We need to explore the possibility of a typology of fatherhood in which different types of fathers devote various amounts of their socialization effort to each of the three pathways. We do not currently know the effects of different combinations of paternal socialization investment strategies on children's peer outcomes. Different combinations may produce different but equally socially competent children.

Finally, the direction of effects continues to be an unresolved issue. Although it is implicitly assumed that fathers are influencing their children's peer relationships, the correlational and often cross-sectional nature of the majority of studies suggest that the direction of causality may flow from child to parent as well. A transactional model (Sameroff, 2009) in which fathers and children mutually influence each other across time will prove most useful for guiding research in this area. A related issue concerns the question of how the peer system influences fathers and families and vice-versa. Both positive and negative effects need to be better understood.

Although it is common to assume that fathers are essential to the successful socialization of children, recent evidence concerning the impact of gay and lesbian parents on children's development challenges this basic assumption. Recent work suggests that the development of children raised by lesbian parents is well within normal limits (Golombok, 2006; Patterson, 2006). Although research on the effects of being reared by two male parents is even more limited than the work on two female parents, the available data suggest that the gender identities of children of gay fathers are similar to those of children of heterosexual fathers (Patterson, 2006). One important challenge faced by children of gay and lesbian parents, however, is their possible stigmatization by others. An issue that requires concerted attention in this debate is the role of social norms and attitudes toward children growing up in same-gender child-rearing unions. This may have particularly important implications for children's social competence with peers.

Furthermore, if children reared in homes with two parents of the same gender are developing well, it raises the question about the necessity of fathers or mothers in the socialization mix. As Silverstein (2002) suggests, our focus on the gender of the parent may be too narrow a conceptualization of the issue. Instead, it may be helpful to recast the issue to ask whether exposure to male and female parents is the key, or whether it is exposure to the interactive style typically associated with either mothers or fathers that matters. At the same time, it seems premature to conclude that fathers or mothers are replaceable based on this evidence. Studies have relied largely on small samples of highly educated individuals in stable relationships. In addition, two key issues need to be addressed in ongoing work. More needs to be understood about the extent to which role division in lesbian or gay families approximates role division in heterosexual families as well as the degree to which same-gender couples expose their children to opposite-sex role models. Many challenges remain.

References

Arnert, J., & Balle-Jensen, L. (1993). Cultural bases of risk behavior: Danish adolescents. *Child Development, 64*, 1842–1855.

Bender, H. L., Allen, J. P., McElhaney, K. B., Antonishak, J., Moore, C. M., Kelly, H. O., & Davis, S. M. (2007). Use of harsh physical discipline and developmental outcomes in adolescence. *Development and Psychopathology, 19*, 227–242.

Bhavnagri, N., & Parke, R. D. (1991). Parents as direct facilitators of children's peer relationships: Effects of age of child and sex of parent. *Journal of Personal and Social Relationships, 8*, 423–440.

Bowlby, J. (1969). *Attachment and loss.* New York, NY: Basic Books.

Bugental, D. B., & Grusec, J. E. (2006). Socialization theory. In N. Eisenberg (Ed.), *Handbook of child psychology. Volume 3: Social, emotional, and personality development* (pp. 366–428). New York, NY: Wiley.

Burks, V. S., & Parke, R. D. (1996). Parent and child representations of social relationships: Linkages between families and peers. *Merrill-Palmer Quarterly, 42*, 358–378.

Cabrera, N., Ryan, R., Mitchell, S., Shannon, J., & Tamis-Lemonda, C. (2008). Low-income, nonresident father involvement with their toddlers: Variation by fathers' race and ethnicity. *Journal of Family Psychology, 22*, 643–647.

Carlson, M. (2006). Family structure, father involvement, and adolescent behavioral outcomes. *Journal of Marriage and Family, 68*, 137–154.

Chen, C., & French, D. C. (2008). Children's social competence in cultural context. *Annual Review of Psychology, 59*, 591–616.

Chen, C., Greenberger, E., Lester, J., Dong, Q., & Guo, M. (1998). A cross-cultural study of family and peer correlates of adolescent misconduct. *Developmental Psychology, 34*, 770–781.

Chen, X., & Rubin, K. H. (1994). Family conditions, parental acceptance, and social competence and aggression in Chinese children. *Social Development, 3*, 269–290.

Coltrane, S. (2007). What about fathers? *American Prospect*, A20–23.

Cowan, P. A., Cowan, C. P., Pruett, M. K., Pruett, K., & Wong, J. J. (2009). Promoting fathers' engagement with children: Preventive interventions for low-income families. *Journal of Marriage and the Family, 71*, 663–679.

Crockenberg, S., & Langrock, A. (2001). The role of emotion and emotional regulation in children's responses to interparental conflict. In J. H. Grych & F. D. Fincham (Eds.), *Interparental conflict and child development: Theory, research, and application* (pp. 129–156). New York, NY: Cambridge University Press.

Cummings, E. M., & Davies, P. T. (2010). Marital conflict and children: An emotional security perspective. New York, NY: Guilford Press.

Cummings, E. M., Goeke-Morey, M. C., Papp, L. M., & Dukewich, T. L. (2002). Children's responses to mothers' and fathers' emotionality and tactics in marital conflict in the home. *Journal of Family Psychology, 16*, 478–492.

Elder, G., & Conger, R. (2000). *Children of the land*. Chicago: University of Chicago Press.

Fauber, R. L., & Long, N. (1991). Children in context: The role of the family in child psychotherapy. *Journal of Consulting and Clinical Psychology, 59*, 813–820.

Feldman, S., Rosenthal, D. A., Mont-Reynaud, R., & Leung, K. (1991). Ain't misbehavin': Adolescent values and family environments as correlates of misconduct in Australia, Hong Kong and the United States. *Journal of Research on Adolescence, 1*, 109–134.

Flanders, J. L., Leo, V., Paquette, D., Pihl, R. O., & Séguin, J. R. (2009). Rough-and-tumble play and the regulation of aggression: An observational study of father-child play dyads. *Aggressive Behavior, 35*, 285–295.

Flanders, J. L., Simard, M., Paquette, D., Parent, S., Vitaro, F., Pihl, R. O., & Séguin, J. R. (2010). Rough-and-tumble play and the development of physical aggression and emotion regulation: A five-year follow-up study. *Journal of Family Violence, 25*, 357–367.

Furstenberg, C. E., Cook, T. D., Eccles, J., Elder, G. G., & Sameroff, A. (1999). *Managing to make it*. Chicago: University of Chicago Press.

Geller, A., Garfinkel, I., Cooper, C. E., & Mincy, R. B. (2009). Parental incarceration and child wellbeing: Implications for urban families. *Social Science Quarterly, 90*, 1186–1202.

Golombok, S. (2006). New family forms. In K. A. Clarke-Stewart & J. Dunn (Eds.), *Families count: Effects on child and adolescent development* (pp. 273–298). Cambridge, England: Cambridge University Press.

Gottman J. M., & Katz, L. F. (1989). Effects of marital discord on young children's peer interaction and health. *Developmental Psychology, 25*, 373–381.

Gottman, J. M., Katz, L. F., & Hooven, C. (1997). *Meta-emotion: How families communicate emotionally*. Mahwah, NJ: Erlbaum.

Grossmann, K., Grossmann, K. E., Fremmer-Bombik, E., Kindler, H., Scheuerer-Englisch, H., & Zimmerman, P. (2002). The uniqueness of the child-father attachment relationship: Fathers' sensitive and challenging play as a pivotal variable in a 16-year longitudinal study. *Social Development, 11*, 307–331.

Grossmann, K., Grossman, K. E., Kindler, H., & Zimmerman, P. (2008). Attachment and exploration: The influence of mothers and fathers on the development of psychological security from infancy to adulthood. In J. Cassidy & P. R. Shaver (Eds.), *Handbook of attachment: Theory, research, and clinical applications* (2nd ed., pp. 857–879). New York, NY: Guilford Press.

Guzzo, K. B., & Furstenberg, F. F. Jr. (2007). Multipartnered fertility among American men. *Demography, 44*, 583–601.

Hair, E. C., Moore, K. A., Garrett, S. B., Ling, T., & Cleveland, K. (2008). The continued importance of quality parent-adolescent relationships during late adolescence. *Journal of Research on Adolescence, 18*, 187–200.

Hart, C. H., Yang, C., Nelson, D. A., Jin, S., Bazarakaya, N., Nelson, L., & Wu, P. (1998). Peer contact patterns, parenting practices and preschoolers' social competence in China, Russia and the United States. In P. T. Slee & K. Rigby (Eds.), *Children's peer relations* (pp. 3–30). London: Routledge.

Hernandez, D. J., Denton, N. A., & Macartney, S. E. (2008). Immigrant fathers: A demographic portrait. In S. S. Chuang & R. P. Moreno (Eds.), *On new shores: understanding immigrant fathers in North America* (pp. 47–103). Lanham, MD: Lexington Books

Katz, L. F., & Gottman, J. M. (1993). Patterns of marital conflict predict children's internalizing and externalizing behaviors. *Developmental Psychology, 29*, 940–950.

Kim, M., Parke, R. D., & O'Neil, R. (1999, April). *Marital conflict and children's social competence:*

Concurrent and predictive analyses. Poster presented at the annual meeting of the Western Psychological Association, Irvine, CA.

Knoester, C., Haynie, D. L, & Stephens, C. M. (2006). Parenting practices and adolescents' friendship networks. *Journal of Marriage and Family, 68*, 1247–1260.

Ladd, G. W., & Golter, B. S. (1988). Parents' management of preschoolers' peer relations: Is it related to children's social competence? *Developmental Psychology, 24*, 109–117.

Lamb, M. E. (Ed.). (1997). *The role of the father child development* (3rd ed.). New York, NY: Wiley.

Leidy, M. S., Schofield, T. J., Miller, M. A., Parke, R. D., Coltrane, S., Braver, S., … Adams, M. (2011). Quantity and quality of father involvement and adolescent adjustment in European American and Mexican American intact and stepfather families. *Fathering, 9*, 44–68.

Lynn, D. B., & Sawrey, W. L. (1959). The effects of father absence on Norwegian boys and girls. *Journal of Abnormal and Social Psychology, 59*, 258–262.

Maccoby, E. E., & Mnookin, R. H. (1998). *Dividing the child: Social and legal dilemmas of custody.* Cambridge, MA: Harvard University Press.

MacDonald, K., & Parke, R. D. (1984). Bridging the gap: Parent-child play interaction and peer interactive competence. *Child Development, 55*, 1265–1277.

Main, M., Kaplan, N., & Cassidy, J. (1985). Security in infancy, childhood and adulthood: A move to the level of representation. In I. Bretherton & E. Waters (Eds.), *Growing points in attachment theory and research. Monographs of the Society for Research in Child Development, 50*(1-2).

Main, M., & Weston, D. R. (1981). The quality of the toddler's relationship to mother and to father: Related to conflict behavior and the readiness to establish new relationships. *Child Development, 52*, 932–940

McDowell, D. J., & Parke, R. D. (2000). Differential knowledge of display rules for positive and negative emotions: Influences from parents, influences on peers. *Social Development, 9*, 415–432.

McDowell, D. J., & Parke, R. D. (2005). Parental control and affect as predictors of children's display rule use and social competence with peers. *Social Development, 14*, 440–457.

McDowell, D. J., & Parke, R. D. (2009). Parental correlates of children's peer relations: An empirical test of a tripartite model. *Developmental Psychology, 45*, 224–235.

McDowell, D. J., Parke, R. D., & Spitzer, S. (2002). Parent and child cognitive representations of social situations and children's social competence. *Social Development, 11*, 469–486.

Mize, J., Pettit, G., & Brown, E. (1995). Mothers' supervisions of their children's play: Relations with beliefs, perceptions, and knowledge. *Developmental Psychology, 31*, 311–321.

Mott, F. L. (1994). Sons, daughters and fathers' absence: Differentials in father-leaving probabilities and in home environments. *Journal of Family Issues, 15*, 97–128.

NICHD Early Child Care Research Network. (2009). Family-peer linkages: The meditational role of attentional processes. *Social Development, 18*, 875–895.

O'Neil, R., Flyr, M. L., Wild, M. N., & Parke, R. D. (1999, April). *Early adolescents' exposure to marital conflict: Links to relationships with parents and peers.* Paper presented at the biennial meeting of the Society for Research in Child Development, Albuquerque, NM.

Paquette, D. (2004). Theorizing the father-child relationship: Mechanisms and developmental outcomes. *Human Development, 47*, 193–216.

Parke, R. D. (1995). Fathers and families. In M. H. Bornstein (Ed.), *Handbook of parenting: Vol. 3. Status and social conditions of parenting* (pp. 27–63). Mahwah, NJ: Erlbaum.

Parke, R. D. (1996). *Fatherhood.* Cambridge, MA: Harvard University Press.

Parke, R. D., & Brott, A. (1999). *Throwaway Dads.* Boston: Houghton-Mifflin.

Parke, R. D., & Buriel, R. (2006). Socialization in the family: Ecological and ethnic perspectives. In W. Damon & R. M. Lerner (Series Eds.) & N. Eisenberg (Vol. Ed.), *Handbook of child psychology: Vol. 3. Social, emotional, and personality development* (6th ed., pp. 429–504). New York, NY: Wiley.

Parke, R. D., Cassidy, J., Burks, V. M., Carson, J. L., & Boyum, L. (1992). Familial contribution to peer competence among young children: The role of interactive and affective processes. In R. D. Parke

& G. W. Ladd (Eds.), *Family–Peer Relationships: Modes of Linkage* (pp. 107–134). Hillsdale, NJ: Erlbaum.

Parke, R. D., & Clarke-Stewart, K. A. (2010). *Social development*. New York, NY: Wiley.

Parke, R. D., Kim, M., Flyr, M. L., McDowell, D. J., Simpkins, S. D., Killian, C., & Wild, M. (2001). Managing marital conflict: Links with children's peer relationships. In J. Grych & F. Fincham (Eds.), *Child development and interparental conflict* (pp. 291–314). New York, NY: Cambridge University Press.

Parke, R. D., McDowell, D., Kim, M., & Leidy, M. S. (2006). Family-peer relationships: The role of emotional regulatory processes. In D. K. Snyder, J. A. Simpson, & J. N. Hughes (Eds.), *Emotion regulation in families: Pathways to dysfunction and health* (p. 143–162). Washington, DC: American Psychological Association.

Parke, R. D., & O'Neil, R. (1997). The influence of significant others on learning about relationships. In S. Duck (Ed.), *The handbook of personal relationships* (2nd ed., pp. 29–60). New York, NY: Wiley.

Parke, R. D., & O'Neil, R. (2000). The influence of significant others on learning about relationships: From family to friends. In R. Mills & S. Duck (Eds.), *The developmental psychology of personal relationships* (pp. 15–47). London: Wiley.

Patterson, C. J. (2006). Children of lesbian and gay parents. *Current Directions in Psychological Science, 15*, 241–244.

Pedersen, F. A. (1976). Does research on children reared in father-absent families yield information on father influence? *Family Coordinator, 25*, 457–464.

Pleck, E. H. (2004). Two dimensions of fatherhood: A history of the good dad-bad dad complex. In M. E. Lamb (ed.), *The role of the father in child development* (4th ed., pp. 32–57). Hoboken, NJ: Wiley.

Pleck, J. (2010). Paternal involvement: Revised conceptualization and theoretical linkages with child outcomes. In M. E. Lamb (Ed.), *The role of the father in child development* (5th ed., pp. 58–93). Hoboken, NJ: Wiley.

Pruett, K. D. (2000). *Fatherneed: Why father care is as essential as mother care for your child*. New York, NY: Broadway.

Rah, Y., & Parke, R. D. (2008). Pathways between parent-child interactions and peer acceptance: The role of children's social information processing. *Social Development, 17*, 341–357.

Rasbash, J., Jenkins, J., O'Connor, T. G., Tackett, J., & Reiss, D. (2011). A social relations model of observed family negativity and positivity using a genetically informative sample. *Journal of Personality and Social Psychology, 100*, 474–491.

Reich, S. M., & Vandell, D. L. (2011). The interplay between parents and peers as socializing influences in children's development. In P. K. Smith & C. Hart (Eds.), *Wiley-Blackwell handbook of child social development*. New York, NY: Wiley-Blackwell. doi:10.1002/9781444390933.ch14

Rothbart, M. K., & Bates, J. E. (2006). Temperament. In N. Eisenberg, W. Damon, & R. M. Lerner, (Eds.), *Handbook of child psychology: Vol. 3. Social, emotional, and personality development* (6th ed., pp. 99–166). New York, NY: Wiley.

Sameroff, A. (Ed.). (2009). *The transactional model of development: How children and contexts shape each other.* Washington, DC: American Psychological Association.

Sandstrom, M. J., & Cole, J. D. (1999). A developmental perspective on peer rejection: Mechanisms of stability and change. *Child Development, 70*, 955–966.

Silverstein, L. B. (2002). Fathers and families. In J. McHale & W. Grolnick (Eds.), *Retrospect and prospect in the psychological study of families* (pp. 35–64). Mahwah, NJ: Erlbaum.

Stocker, C., & Youngblade, L. (1999). Marital conflict and parental hostility: Links with children's sibling and peer relationships. *Journal of Family Psychology, 13*, 598–609.

Stolz, L. M. (1954). *Father relations of war-born children.* Stanford, CA: Stanford University Press.

Storey A., Walsh C., Quinton, R., & Wynne-Edwards, K. (2000). Hormonal correlates of paternal responsiveness in new and expectant fathers. *Evolutionary Human Behavior, 21*, 79–95.

Sun, L. C., & Roopnarine, J. L. (1996). Mother-infant, father-infant interaction and involvement in child care and household labor among Taiwanese families. *Infant Behavior and Development, 19,* 121–129.

Thompson, R. A. (2006). The development of the person: Social understanding, relationships, self-conscience. In W. Damon (Series Ed.), *Handbook of child psychology, Vol. 3. Social, emotional, and personality development* (6th ed., pp. 24–98). Hoboken, NJ: Wiley.

Vairami, M., & Vorria, P. (2007). Interparental conflict and (pre)adolescents' peer relationships. *Hellenic Journal of Psychology, 4,* 257–280.

Verschueren, K., & Marcoen, A. (1999). Representation of self and socioemotional competence in kindergarteners: Differential and combined effects of attachment to mother and to father. *Child Development, 70,* 183–201.

Verschueren, K., & Marcoen, A. (2005). Perceived security of attachment to mother and father: Developmental differences and relations to self-worth and peer relationships at school. In K. A. Kerns & R. A. Richardson (Eds.), *Attachment in middle childhood* (pp. 212–230). New York, NY: Guilford Press.

Wakefield, S. (2008). *The impact of incarceration for parents and children.* Unpublished doctoral dissertation, University of Minnesota.

Wang, S. J., & McDowell, D. J. (1996). *Parental advice-giving: Relations to child social competence and psychosocial functioning.* Poster session presented at the annual meeting of the Western Psychological Association, San Jose, CA.

Wilson, B. J. (1999). Entry behavior and emotion regulation abilities of developmentally delayed boys. *Developmental Psychology, 35,* 214–223.

Xiaoming, L., Stanton, B., & Feigelman, S. (2000). Impact of perceived parental monitoring on adolescent risk behavior over 4 years. *Journal of Adolescent Health, 1,* 49–56.

Chapter 10

Fathers, Children, and the Risk-Resilience Continuum

Hiram E. Fitzgerald

Michigan State University

Erika London Bocknek

University of Michigan Health System

Reviewing the literature on the father's role in child development, Nash (1965, p 261) concluded that the "relative neglect of the father may have distorted our understanding of the dynamics of development and ... adversely affected the rearing of males." Nash's article was a catalyst for considerable research on father-child interactions during the remainder of the century. And yet, we continue to have insufficient answers to the basic question: What difference do fathers make in child development beyond their genetic contribution?

Despite anecdotal and sometimes passionate testimony, there is no broad consensus on what the answer to this question may be. There is no comprehensive theory of fatherhood or father involvement to guide research on fathers (Cabrera, Fitzgerald, Bradley, & Roggman, 2007). However, there is compelling empirical evidence to support the contention that fathers contribute to child development both directly and indirectly, particularly in the areas of cognitive development, behavior regulation, and mental health symptomatology.

In this chapter, we discuss theoretical and empirical scholarship describing the continuum of risk and resilience as related to fathers and children. We focus in particular on young children given the special importance of the earliest relationships in children's development. Given the large population of children living in poverty, we further focus on two important related risks: alcoholism among fathers and fathers who are absent from their children's lives, differentiating psychological presence when physically absent from psychological absence when physically present.

To illustrate these foci, we consider findings from two major longitudinal studies within a risk-resilience context that illustrate fathers' direct and indirect effects on their children's development. The first study is the Michigan Longitudinal Study (MLS) of families at risk for alcoholism and life course psychopathology (Zucker et al., 2000). The second study is the Early Head Start Father Involvement with Toddlers Study (FITS) (Boller et al., 2006). In the first study, the defining feature of interest is father's alcoholism and antisocial behavior. In the second study, the defining feature is father's low-income and presence or absence.

Historical Overview and Theoretical Perspectives

Historical analyses of family life demonstrate a changing definition of fatherhood in the United States, often dependent upon social and cultural norms of the time period (Lamb, 2010). The American Industrial Revolution required more and more men to be away from home in order to earn a living. Lamb (1987) suggests this trend sharpened the definition of father as bread-winner and mother as nurturer, influenced a normative pattern of father absence, and over-all defined fathers as playmates but not necessarily as significant caregivers. Cross-culturally, normative patterns of father absence have been linked to patterns of work and productivity (Madhavan, Townsend, & Garey, 2008). Other research has emerged in recent years increas-ingly demonstrating that many fathers are engaged in the care and nurturing of their children, influencing important developmental outcomes (e.g., Shannon, Tamis-LeMonda, London, & Cabrera, 2002). Generally, the roles that fathers play in children's lives vary widely, more widely than maternal roles, and are deeply influenced by historical context and cultural codes (Lamb, 2010).

During early childhood in particular, mothers provide bonding behaviors, organized struc-ture and responsiveness to needs, protection, teaching, and discipline, which in turn predict children's security exploration, physiological and affective regulation, vigilance, learning, and self-control, respectively. During early childhood, fathers also play a key role in the devel-opment of regulatory skills through rich interactions with their children, but often in ways that are different from mothers. Fathers are more likely to provide opportunities for children to experience high emotional arousal and regulate those emotions through play and through more active forms of parent-child interaction (Roggman, Boyce, Cook, Christiansen, & Jones, 2004).

In recent years, scholars have cautioned against narrow definitions of fatherhood rather than the whole of fatherhood (Boller et al., 2006). However, the risks related to a lack of father involvement are particularly salient to children living in under-resourced families. Compared to families with more resources, low-income fathers are less likely to be formally identified as their children's father, less likely to be married to their children's mother, and less likely to reside with their children (Tamis-LeMonda & McFadden, 2010). Categorizing children on a risk-resilience continuum is helpful to understanding the ways in which risks may be of greater impact and predictive value to long-term outcomes for some children as compared to others.

The developmental framework illustrated in Figure 10.1 rests on the assumption that from the moment of birth until the moment of death, each individual can be located somewhere on the risk-resilience continuum. Further, throughout the life-course, one's place on the con-tinuum will change as a function of the dynamic interplay of genetic factors, the organization of endophenotypes, and the individual's experiences. Some individuals will spend their life-course on only a small portion of the risk-resilience continuum. For others, movement along the continuum can be abrupt, or gradual. In this chapter we examine data from individuals and families commonly referred to as "at-risk" for some negative life-course outcome.

Nearly all developmental scientists today hold to the view that development is "a hierarchi-cally integrative process in which earlier patterns of adaptation provide a framework for, and are transformed by, later experiences to yield increasingly complex flexibility, and organization"

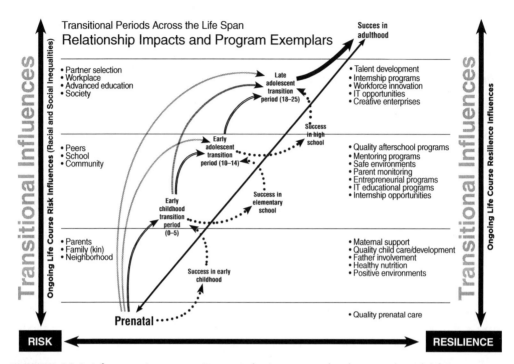

FIGURE 10.1 Infancy to Innovation Framework: A systemic developmental model for assessing child development from the prenatal period through the emergent adulthood years. Fitzgerald, H. E. (2010). Birth to work: A community driven framework for systems change. *The Engaged Scholar, 5,* 20–21. Reprinted with permission.

(Yates, Egeland, & Sroufe, 2003, pp. 246–247). Developmental process increasingly is understood as emergent, epigenetic, systemic, organized, constructive, hierarchically integrated, complex, and sometimes chaotic. Sameroff (1989) defines the organized system of interactions within the family as a network of codes, interacting and regulating behavior at multiple levels. Through family codes and daily interactions, children learn behavior that is acceptable, according to their unique family rules, imparted by their parents' behaviors. Further, children's responsive behaviors impact the development of family codes through their continuing participation in interactions. The idea of family relationships as a context for development is inherent in the structural nature of families and represents an active process of regulation across development

Several conceptual frameworks have been developed within systems frameworks to advance understanding of father effects on child development. Lamb and his colleagues proposed a tripartite model (Lamb, Pleck, Charnov, & Levine, 1987, suggesting that father involvement includes paternal engagement (e.g., interaction with the child such as play or teaching); paternal accessibility (e.g., temporal and proximal indicators); and paternal responsibility (e.g., making arrangements for care). Cabrera, Fitzgerald, et al. (2007) advanced a heuristic model consistent with theories based on developmental systems perspectives, that incorporates mediated and moderated relationships among predictors of father involvement as well as the relationships between father involvement and child outcomes.

Models describing the role that fathers play in their children's lives have become increasingly complex, stressing the ipsative multiplicity of influences on child development, best demonstrated through cascade models of development that include fathering characteristics (e.g., Pemberton et al., 2010). Today, theoretical models related to parental influences on children are most likely to be embedded in biopsychosocial models that recognize the effects of gene-environment interplay and the dynamic relationships between experience and underlying neurobiological organization.

Systems, boundaries, and fathers.   Throughout development, individuals and families interface with adjunctive systems such as work place, social institution, peer group, neighborhood, school, religious institution, and kinship networks. In most instances, adjunctive systems have well defined boundaries and associated rules, regulations, and policies for inclusion, purpose, and access. Although many families have equally well-defined boundaries that set caregiving roles, many families do not. The degree to which family role boundaries are difficult for children to discern, the more difficult it will be for them to develop expectancy structures as internal guides for their behavior.

Boundary ambiguity refers to "a state in which family members are uncertain in their perception about who is in or out of the family and who is performing what roles and tasks within the family system" (Boss & Greenberg, 1984, p. 536). Such roles and tasks, indicators of family boundaries, include the physical and psychological processes relevant to particular family roles. Thus, meaning-making is central to the study of boundary ambiguity. Children's early relationships with significant primary caregivers give them lasting expectations about who they are and what they can expect from others. When a family member dies, there is typically a degree of certainty about loss, at least over the long term. However, there are other ways a family member may leave their family, and in some scenarios, the certainty about "loss" can be ambiguous, at least to a very young child.

Development of boundary ambiguity.   Two types of ambiguous loss have been identified (Boss, 1977): psychological presence with physical absence and physical presence with psychological absence. Psychological presence is defined by surviving family members' maintenance of a lost family member's role without that family member being physically present. Psychological presence may occur in relation to life stressors such as divorce, illness, or military service (Gorman & Fitzgerald, 2007). Psychological presence may be the result of normative life transitions and mark a period of reorganization in a family that is only temporary, particularly when a family defines the stressor as normative and maintains resources to effectively cope (Boss, 1980). In other circumstances, when the meaning the family makes of the stressful life event is negative, incongruent, or lacking coherent meaning, the ambiguity in the family may cause dysfunction. Psychological absence is defined by a family member's physical maintenance of his/her family role while behaving as absent at the level of psychological and emotional processes, often due to depressive symptoms, mental illness, substance abuse, and dementia.

Known outcomes for children as a result of boundary ambiguity.   The research on boundary ambiguity has mostly focused on the risks present for adult members of families. A limited number of studies have presented empirical findings demonstrating the impact of ambiguous loss on children (e.g., Bocknek, Sanderson, & Britner, 2009). These studies demonstrate that family boundary ambiguities negatively impact children's attachment security, adjustment processes, and mental health outcomes (e.g., Bocknek et al., 2009). Inconsistencies between psychological presence and physical presence are associated with children's less optimal functioning in the context of family processes.

Psychological absence is associated with emotional and psychological pathology for the family members who experience the loss (Boss, 1977, 1980; Boss & Greenberg, 1984). As is true for the construct of psychological absence, the literature describing the effects of psychological presence on young children is limited. However, the literature relating to psychological presence often focuses on fathers whose roles have become ambiguous in the system due to family structural changes or due to parental behaviors that make the boundaries between parents and children psychologically ambiguous. We address this issue later when we discuss aspects of mentalization as it pertains to young children's emerging concepts of men, father, and husband.

Resilience is an ongoing process of gathering resources to effectively adapt to stresses and challenges, often evidenced in studies of social competence. Many children who have access to enabling resources learn how to use those resources to achieve positive adaptations despite prior adversity. We focus on how fathers affect their children's life-course transit along the risk-resilience continuum, noting especially the extent to which they directly or indirectly influence children's opportunities to develop resilience and social competence.

Current Research Questions

Within the framework illustrated in Figure 10.1, we examine questions concerning the extent to which father presence and absence affects children's developmental pathways. How do fathers in at-risk families affect children's development? What early life course experiences guide young children to high risk developmental pathways? What aspects of father behavior contribute to risk accumulation predisposing very young children to develop mental health symptoms or mental health problems? How do fathers contribute to resilience structures that enable children to weave their way through, or to avoid, potentially risky situations?

Research Measurement and Methodology

As noted, in this chapter we will use two studies to describe the findings related to fathers and their children in contexts of risk: the Michigan Longitudinal Study (MLS) of families at risk for alcoholism and life course psychopathology (Zucker et al., 2000) and the Early Head Start Father Involvement with Toddlers Study (FITS) (Boller et al., 2006). The MLS is a population based study, whereas the FITS includes a nationally representative sample of low income fathers.

The MLS was designed to identify pathways to alcoholism, to specify the determinants of those pathways, and to generate recommendations for policy and prevention based on scientific knowledge of etiology. The MLS has been following a population based sample of court and community-recruited families since the mid-1980s in order to identify risk and resilience factors related to alcoholism. Families were recruited into the study based on father characteristics (alcoholism diagnosis) and whether or not they had a 3- to 6-year-old son (these children are now 28 to 31 years old). The total sample of 2,467 individuals includes all family members who have remained in the study for 25 years, and includes adults who entered into families following the death or divorce of a parent. Regardless of alcoholic recruitment group, alcoholic families were functioning at poorer levels than non-alcoholic families at the beginning of the study, particularly with respect to family income, social-economic status, and parental education. They also differed in father characteristics: depression, antisocial behavior, and lifetime alcohol use were higher than in controls, and general functioning was lower (Zucker et al., 2000). The social visibility of alcoholism was positively correlated with census tract prevalence rates of poverty, divorce/separation, female head of household, family receipt of public assistance, unemployment, and renter occupied households. Alcoholism with comorbid antisocial behavior is related to earlier onset of alcoholic disorder, with higher levels of other psychopathology, and with a denser family history of alcoholism in the pedigree (Zucker, Ellis, Bingham, Fitzgerald & Sanford, 1996). Thus, alcoholic families were nested in a system of factors that influenced their life course outcomes and which needed to be considered in the etiologic models of alcoholism.

The national evaluation of Early Head Start included 3,001 low-income families; among these families, 727 fathers participated directly in the study when the child was 24 months old, and 698 participated again when their children were 36 months old (60% of the men interviewed were residential biological fathers, 16% were nonresident biological fathers, and 15% were residential social fathers; for complete study details see Boller et al., 2006).

Children whose life course shifts them away from inter-generational risk are generally referred to as resilient in the face of adversity (Luthar, 2003). The MLS probabilistic risk-cumulation conceptual framework posits that aggressive behavior, negative emotions, and alcohol involvement accumulate and become interconnected, exposing children to increasingly higher risks for alcohol use disorders and co-morbid psychopathology (Zucker et al., 1995). From this perspective, risk is organized within the inter-dynamics of individual, familial, and psychosocial environmental variables. The challenge is to find variables that move children at risk onto developmental pathways that either lock them in to hard continuity risk pathways, or provide options for more discontinuous pathways and the full range of risk-resilience outcomes.

Prior to these studies, the body of knowledge on fathers and their children lacked information on the socioemotional development of children and, importantly, relied on maternal reports. Current knowledge on this matter has been well-informed by studies drawn from the MLS and FITS datasets. Both studies adopt a longitudinal perspective and include assessments (self-report as well as observation) with both mothers and fathers and their children.

Empirical Findings

Michigan Longitudinal Study (MLS).   The purpose of the MLS study is to examine the pathways of transmission between parents and children regarding alcoholism and life course psychopathology. Findings from this study demonstrate that children of alcoholics (COAs) are more likely to develop a wide range of behavioral problems, including aggression, antisocial behavior, delinquency, incompetent interpersonal relationships, emotional and personality problems, cognitive deficits, and school failure (Fitzgerald, Puttler, Refior, & Zucker, 2007). Below we describe specific findings related to the risk present in the environments of COAs, the pathways of transmission, and children's outcomes.

Environmental Risk for Children of Alcoholics

It is estimated that nearly 2.5 million children between the ages of birth to 6 years are being reared in families where one or more adults are addicted to alcohol. These children are six times more likely than children not reared in such homes to develop addictive behaviors or some co-morbid psychopathology. Adolescents who began alcohol use by the third grade to fifth grade are 4 times more likely to develop an alcohol use disorder (AUD) than are those who delay use until around age 20. Antisocial alcoholic (AAL) fathers are more likely to have a history of childhood behavior problems, illegal behavior, frequent arrests, chronic lying, relationship disturbances, depression, neuroticism, poor achievement and cognitive functioning, and low socioeconomic status (see Fitzgerald et al., 2007). In addition, findings demonstrate the negative influence of alcoholism on marital interactions, particularly with respect to antisocial alcoholic fathers (Floyd, et al., 2006). Non-antisocial alcoholic (NAALs) fathers have significantly less antisociality than their AAL counterparts. Clearly, children's rearing environments in the MLS at the least range from the middle to the risk side of the continuum depicted in Figure 10.1.

Children reared in risky home environments with high rates of paternal psychopathology and marital conflict, developed risky behaviors that at least within the antisocial alcoholic families, seem to have set them on pathways leading to life course outcomes that resemble those of their fathers. Children in the NAAL families and control families are more resilient and therefore have a broader set of life course options. Importantly, as described, many of the risks present for COAs are already evident as early as preschool.

Pathways of Transmission

The more heritable form of AUD is linked to antisociality, a comorbid characteristic that loads heavily on males and is associated with high impulsivity and distractability. One hypothesis is that children of alcoholics (COAs) inherit a genotypic predisposition to nonspecific biological dysregulation that might be expressed as alcoholism or some other form of psychopathology (hyperactivity, conduct disorder, aggression, depression) depending on the child's developmental history. Fuller et al. (2003) identified two intergenerational pathways of risk, one of which involved transmission of aggression (marital conflict, ASB, parent-child conflict) across two generations, from grandparent to parent. The second pathway, which was unique to men, involved grandfather alcoholism to father alcoholism, which then predicted sons' behavioral problems and aggression. As was the case for aggression and alcoholism, there is evidence for inter-generational transmission of neuropsychological executive function from mother and father to sons and daughters, independent of parental IQ (Jester et al., 2009)

Child outcomes: Preschool through adolescence. In preschool, COAs have higher levels of hyperactivity, more negative mood, more problematic social relationships, greater deficits in cognitive functioning, higher levels of aggressive behavior, and more precocious acquisition of cognitive schemas about alcohol and other drugs than children from control families (Mun, Fitzgerald, Puttler, Zucker, & von Eye, 2001; Zucker et al., 2000). Family conflict and father-son conflict accounted for associations between parental antisocial behavior and child externalizing behavior, whereas child lack of control mediated parental alcoholism effects (Loukas, Fitzgerald, Zucker, & von Eye, 2001). The mediational role of family conflict was consistent across both maternal and paternal models; that is, higher lifetime antisocial behavior of parents during the preschool years predicted child externalizing behavior during the early elementary years (e.g., Wong, Zucker, & Zucker, 1999).

A number of studies demonstrate that highly under-controlled children tend to persist in their lack of control over time. Although externalizing behavior decreases over time, the rate of decline is not the same for all children. Boys show fewer disruptive behavior problems as they grew older, but retain their rank order over a six year period (Loukas, Zucker, Fitzgerald,

& Krull, 2003). Children with high levels of behavior problems and slow or nonexistent rates of decline are at maximum risk for early onset of drinking and other risk behaviors.

The relationship between parental alcohol use and concurrent mental health problems and children's poorer outcomes is mediated by lower parental support provided children in multiple areas. In one longitudinal study, lower emotional support and lower intellectual stimulation by the parents in early childhood predicted child membership in the high problem class of inattention/hyperactivity when the trajectory of aggression was held constant. Conversely, conflict and lack of cohesiveness in the family environment predicted membership in a trajectory of aggressive behavior when the inattention/hyperactivity trajectories were held constant. Aggressive behavior decreased throughout childhood but inattentive/hyperactivity behavior levels were constant over a 10-year period (Jester et al., 2005).

Efforts focus on identifying etiologic factors that can predict early onset drinking. Six to 10-year-old children identified as early first drinkers (EFD) were less involved with conventional after-school activities (Mayzer, Fitzgerald, & Zucker, 2009). As preschoolers, EFD are more likely to have both externalizing (cruel to animals, lie, set fires, destroy things) and internalizing (sad, depressed, worried) behaviors and are often reported to be immature, overweight, nervous, to express "strange ideas," and to have trouble sleeping. At school age, teachers are more likely to attribute behavior problems to EFD children than non-EFD children. During adolescence, EFD's are more likely to be associated with delinquent peers and peers that are negatively involved with the juvenile justice system.

EFD children are more likely to be exhibit problems of delinquency than aggression, particularly when delinquent behaviors show strong continuity from preschool to mid-adolescence. Independent of externalizing behavior, children with slower rates of increase in behavioral control are more likely to use alcohol and other drugs in adolescence (Wong et al., 2006). Children with higher initial levels of resiliency are less likely to begin using alcohol. Beginning in the preschool years, children with the lowest levels of behavior control are the least resilient in adolescence, whereas children with moderately high levels of behavioral control are the most resilient. Children reported to have sleep problems during the preschool period are more likely to use alcohol, marijuana, and other drugs during late childhood and early adolescence. Sleep problems also increase the risk for early onset of occasional or regular cigarette use (Wong, Brower, Fitzgerald, & Zucker, 2004).

Teachers' descriptions of children's behavior are consistent with the AAL, NAAL, and control groupings, even though these groupings are completely unknown to teachers. When asked to forecast child performance in middle school, elementary teachers projected the poorest school performance for AAL children. Teachers also reported that AAL parents showed less interest in their children's school performance than NAAL or control parents (Fitzgerald & Zucker, 2002). Differences in behavioral regulation and social competence match differences in school achievement: sons of AALs do more poorly than do sons of NAALs or controls.

A family risk index was developed to scale parental psychopathology, taking into account both the currency and the severity of parental alcohol use disorder among both parents, as well as the presence or absence of parental antisocial behavior (Zucker, Wong, Puttler, & Fitzgerald, 2003). The child's adaptation index was characterized by a global sociobehavioral psychopathology index. Children were classified into four types: resilient, nonchallenged, vulnerable, and troubled. Nonchallenged children had the lowest level of externalizing behavior problems. From age 3 to age 17, vulnerable children had the highest level of externalizing behavior problems and were significantly different from the least challenged group. Although resilient children did not differ from their nonchallenged peers as preschoolers on externalizing behaviors, they consistently showed a slightly higher level of externalizing behavior as they grew older. Nonchallenged children also had the lowest levels of internalizing behavior problems, followed by resilient children. By early adolescence, the nonchallenged group was significantly lower than all other groups, with the resilient children showing an increase in risk for internalizing behavior to the same level seen in the vulnerable and troubled children by ages 12–14. Thus, by early adolescence, the vulnerable children were at highest risk, the nonchallenged children were at lowest risk, and the resilient children were at intermediary risk, particularly because of the rise in internalizing behavior problems during puberty. Thus, children reared in families characterized by high levels of parental psychopathology (predominately paternal alcoholism and antisocial behavior and maternal depression) are especially at risk for externalizing and internalizing behavior problems at all ages from three to 17.

Early Head Start FITS

The purpose of the FITS study was to examine the impact of fathering relationships on children's outcomes in a low-income sample. Children living in poverty and who therefore already experience multiple risk factors associated with poverty are also more likely to reside in households without their fathers. We explore this particular area of risk within findings of the FITS study and via a boundary ambiguity framework, differentiating physical and psychological absence. First, we briefly summarize the body of knowledge on father absence. Then, we describe findings from the FITS study on fathering and child development.

Father Absence

Research demonstrates that father absence is related to numerous worrisome outcomes for children and, further, that father presence is a protective factor for children living in at-risk circumstances (Martinez, DeGarmo, & Eddy, 2004). There is some evidence that boys at varying ages may be particularly vulnerable when fathers are not present (Feldman, 2003). However, this area of research is less well-studied among very young children. Father differences in involvement based on child gender may reflect the attitudes and behaviors of mothers around fathering role expectations and child gender (Wood & Repetti, 2004). Children may be more likely than previously thought to have varying amounts of contact with their fathers. For example, 80% of 2-year-olds in the Early Head Start Research and Evaluation Project had some degree of access to their biological fathers; by 36 months, 72% of these children had contact with their biological fathers, and researchers report that father presence was generally consistent for these children across toddlerhood (Boller et al., 2006). Cabrera et al. (2004) report that that these fathers were actually engaged with their children. Furthermore, prenatal father involvement is shown to be a strong predictor of later father involvement (Cabrera, Fagan, & Farrie, 2008).

Researchers explain the inconsistencies in the research on father involvement and children's outcomes by suggesting that a complex interplay of factors within the broader family context predicts relationships between fathers and their children; a level of complexity that is perhaps unique to the father-child relationship. Variables describing the structural patterns of the family, particularly those defining the mother's role in the family, predict the level of involvement fathers may have in their relationships with children, including the quality of their relationships with their children's mothers as well as their marital status (Hofferth, Pleck, Stueve, Bianchi, & Sayer, 2002).

There is wide variation in the amount of contact children have with their fathers, with the majority experiencing some contact (Boller et al., 2006). Because the definition of fatherhood varies widely, especially for non-residential fathers, there is a high potential for ambiguities and inconsistencies to occur in this role, particularly early in childhood when the rules and patterns related to family roles in young families may still be evolving. Indeed, children with unstable or transient relationships with their fathers are less likely to demonstrate optimal outcomes, whereas children with stronger relationships with their fathers tend to have more adaptive regulatory competencies.

The FITS study: EHS fathers and child development.   Research demonstrates that "involvement" or even "presence" may be defined in multiple ways. Fathers reported that they believed their special roles as fathers involved helping to guide, discipline, protect and support their children's social and emotional development (Summers et al., 1999). Biological fathers, compared to social father figures or step-fathers, are the most likely to be involved with their children, and residential status plays a role in level of involvement. For example, residential status has been associated with fathers' sensitivity during structured teaching interactions, likely because fathers who interact with their infants on a daily basis are more familiar with their infants' behaviors and therefore respond differently during the teaching tasks than do non-residential fathers (Brophy-Herb, Gibbons, Omar, & Schiffman, 1999). Maternal reports about father involvement suggest that father involvement is most clearly associated with child outcomes among White families, compared to other racioethnic groups (Vogel, Bradley, Raikes, Boller, & Shears, 2006), suggesting that cultural meaning-making processes may mediate father-child interaction effects.

Longitudinal follow-up studies of FITS fathers indicate that their social-emotional growth fostering during preschool years predicted child cognitive functioning at ages 5 and 10. Father interactions with preschool children were positively related to children's receptive vocabulary, problem solving and letter-word identification at age 5, and with receptive vocabulary and math skills at age 10 (McKelvey, Schiffman, & Fitzgerald, 2010). In addition, fathers' human capital mattered for children's language and cognitive skills at 24 months (Tamis-LeMonda, Shannon, Cabrera, & Lamb, 2004) as well as at preschool (Cabrera, Shannon, & Tamis-LeMonda, 2007).

Shannon, Tamis-LaMonda, and Cabrera (2006) identified two types of father engagement during videotaped semi-structured and free play father-infant interactions: Responsive-Didactic and Negative-Overbearing. Fathers who were older, better educated, married, and with higher incomes tended to be classified as the Responsive-Didactic type during interactions with their 8-month-old infants. Father age and his report of the quality of the marital relationship predicted whether he remained in the Responsive-Didactic classification during interactions with his 16-month-old toddler.

Children with high levels of self-regulation and lower levels of aggression tended to have residential or involved nonresidential biological fathers. Cabrera, Shannon, & Tamis-LeMonda (2007) found significant relationships between paternal behaviors (supportiveness and intrusiveness) and children's socioemotional outcomes when children were 2 years old but not when they were 3 years old, suggesting that additional variables mediate the relationships between fathering and children's socioemotional development. Father involvement is also affected by children's health and developmental status (McKelvey, Hart, Barton,

Whiteside-Mansell, & Fitzgerald, 2006). Fathers of children with developmental delays experienced higher distress than fathers of children with no special needs or untoward health conditions. Fathers of children with developmental delays and chronic illnesses reported higher rates of dysfunctional interactions than fathers whose children had developmental delays. Finally, fathers of children with known developmental delays and chronic illness reported higher levels of parenting distress.

Father and neighborhood characteristics also have an impact on the organization of children's self-regulatory behavior and social competence. EHS fathers who reported being exposed to a high rate of antisocial behavior during their own childhoods perceived themselves as having poor parenting skills (Shears, Robinson, & Emde, 2002). In another study, FITS teen and non-teen residential biological and social fathers were compared on their relationships with their very young children (Fitzgerald & McKelvey, 2005). Compared to older fathers, teen fathers used more punitive forms of punishment (especially residential social fathers), were more depressed (especially residential biological teen fathers), and were more likely to have higher levels of parent-child dysfunctional interactions. Teen fathers were more detached during play interactions, and less empathic to their children's developmental needs. Residential teen fathers reported more family conflict, had more unrealistic expectations for their children, and perceived their children to be more aggressive. Conversely, teen fathers were more likely to help with basic caregiving tasks, to engage in more social play, and to be more invested in their children (especially if they were residential biological fathers).

Using measures based on the MLS, Fitzgerald, McKelvey, Schiffman, and Montanez (2006) examined the impact of FITS father's antisocial behavior and the level of family exposure to neighborhood violence on three-year-old children's behavior. Fathers were classified into four groups based on their scores on a measure of antisocial behavior (high vs. low) and their scores on a measure of neighborhood violence exposure (high vs. low). EHS children who were exposed to high levels of marital conflict, father's depression, and antisocial behavior, and low scores on a measure on the quality of the home environment, scored lower on measures of their self-regulatory behavior than those experiencing fewer of these risks. For example, children exposed to high neighborhood violence were 1.9 times more likely to be spanked than those exposed to low levels of neighborhood violence. Children with fathers scoring low in antisocial behavior but who resided in high violence neighborhoods were 3.25 times more likely to be spanked than were children in higher risk groups. Overall, the findings suggested a pattern of child effects strikingly similar to MLS findings for preschool age children with antisocial, alcoholic fathers. In a follow-up study, McKelvey et al. (2010) examined the relationship between maternal and paternal depressive symptoms, their reports of neighborhood crime, and father antisociality at child age 3, on children's behavior at age 10. Risk for neighborhood violence was the most salient predictor of child development at age 10. Residing in high violence neighborhoods at age 3 was related to poorer school achievement. In addition, children at age 10 had higher levels of externalizing behaviors, including rule-breaking and delinquency, characteristics that Mayzer et al. (2009) found to be related to high risk for early first drinking and high risk taking during adolescence.

Bridges to other Disciplines

Children's earliest relationships provide the most significant context for early development. Emde (1989, p. 44) writes, "Affect provides a sense of coherence over time and a continual orientation about what is familiar." But what is "familiar" turns out to be partly the child's construction and partly the result of co-constructions of reality forged by the child in interaction with significant others. According to Nelson and Fivush (2004), "there is now abundant evidence that the ways in which parents, and especially mothers, structure conversations about past events with their preschool children have strong and enduring influences on how children come to construct their own narrative life history" (p. 497). They imply that mothers and daughters spend more time elaborating and co-constructing a shared past than do mothers and sons. If fathers are not in residence, or if father figures are transient during the 2 to 5 age period, what male is available to participate in the co-construction of the child's emergent mental representations and cognitive constructions about self, others, and self-other relationships? These are questions about the emergence of autobiographical memory, self-other differentiation, intersubjectivity, mental representations about relationships, and cognitive schemas about self and other behavior (Zucker, Kincaid, Fitzgerald, & Bingham, 1995). They are fundamentally phenomenological questions about issues related to who I am, who are others, and what is the nature of our relationships. However, today we know that they are also questions about the organization of brain neural networks and hormonal stress regulatory systems, which together play a crucial role in the regulation of behavior, stress, and emergent cognitive functions.

Neurobiology and mental representations. Mental representations of events have been associated with stressful and traumatic experiences in early childhood. It is reasonable to ask whether mental representations of experience mirror the structural and functional organization of the prefrontal cortex and stress regulatory systems. Mounting evidence suggests that they do. Stress responses increase glucosteroid release, which has a negative effect on the hippocampus and medial temporal lobe networks (Markowitsch, Thiel, Kessler, von Stockhausen, & Heiss, 1997) that affect memory and stress regulation. Fonagy, Lynton, & Strathern (2011), study the connections between behavioral indicators of emotion dysregulation, impulsivity, and disturbed interpersonal functioning and the dopaminergic and oxytocinergic regulatory systems with respect to the early origins of borderline personality disorder. Each of these systems influences the regulation of emotional and social behavior. As technology continues its accelerated pace, it soon will be possible to link genetic markers with organizing endophenotypes and layer them onto richly descriptive phenotypes to obtain true biopsychosocial descriptors of life course pathways.

Culture and mental representations. Culture refers to the shared values, customs, history, folklore, and institutions of some specified group of people. When groups live in neighborhoods, intergenerational transmission of culture flows naturally. In today's society, however, most children are reared in communities that have multiple cultures, ethnicities, and racial groups and within-family constructions of others will increasingly be challenged by children's experiences with others. The effects of shifting family codes, family stories, and rituals embedded within changes in the structure of the American family on children's representations remain to be determined. If family representations and individual characteristics are not part of the co-constructions about others, self, and self-other relationships, efforts to build a multicultural society will continue to produce slowly changing outcomes. It is equally clear that fathers must be part of that co-constructive process if they are to have a sustaining part in their children's life course narratives. Mental representations about alcohol use are already encoded into the autobiographical stories of preschool age children, reared in very high risk families (Fitzgerald & Zucker, 2006). These mental representations or expectancies are components of

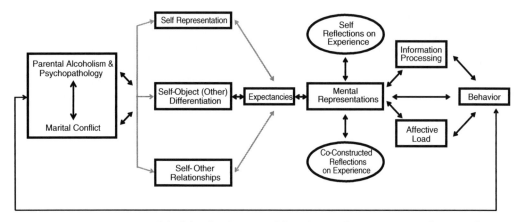

FIGURE 10.2 Heuristic model of the developmental flow from self recognition, self-other differentiation, and the organization of expectancies and mental representations of events during infancy and early childhood. Fitzgerald, H. E. (2010). Origins of alcohol use disorders: Mental representations, relationships, and the risk-resilience continuum. Presented at the biennial meeting of the World Association for Infant Mental Health, Leipzig, German. Reprinted with permission of H. E. Fitzgerald.

cognitive-affective schemas that are bound to children's observations of others. Father presence/absence, representations of fathers communicated by others, and father-mother/father-child relationships, all play a role in structuring children's autobiographical memories and internal representations of others. Autobiographical memory for events develops during the second and third postnatal years, roughly at the same time that children develop "a knowledge structure whose features serve to organize memories of experiences that happened to me" (Howe & Courage, 1997, p. 499). According to Nelson and Fivush (2004), autobiographical memory emerges from "basic memory systems, the acquisition of complex spoken or signed language, narrative comprehension and production, memory talk with parents and others, style of parent talk, temporal understanding, representation of self, person perspectives, and psychological understanding (theory of mind)" (p. 486). Father's physical and psychological presence or absence, and the degree to which he participates in caregiving, should have substantial impacts on the organization of his children's bio-behavioral regulatory capacity and their mental representations of what men, fathers, and husbands do. Figure 10.2 illustrates a model designed to assess the development of mental representations of self, others, and self-other relationships during early childhood, but especially within children who are reared in high risk families and high risk external environments (Fitzgerald, Wong, & Zucker, in press). One critical question concerns the role that fathers play in the organization of the complex systems that lead children to one side or another of the risk-resilient continuum. The studies of two types of high risk fathers/families in this chapter suggest that fathers play a far more critical role than we have yet acknowledged, especially for their sons.

Policy Implications

Figure 10.1 embodies the policy implications applicable to both types of family systems that we have reviewed. We discussed the risks present for children in regard to fathering in two main areas: (a) the risks related to physically present fathers who may demonstrate antisocial and addictive behaviors and (a) the risks related to physically and/or psychologically absent fathers. The major policy implications of both areas of risk is broadly the need for more supportive programming to help men assume the fathering role effectively, via parenting education and accessible mental health and substance abuse treatment. In addition, families without present fathers would benefit from initiatives that help mothers and their parenting partners improve the boundaries related to parenting, thereby increasing clarity related to roles and responsibilities. Programs designed to inform physical and psychologically present fathers about their importance for their children's development, could invoke stronger and more positive father-child relationships. Finally, the findings presented in this chapter underscore the need for high quality early intervention provided to families at risk, given the patterns of risk present in the youngest children and increasing evidence that core aspects of neurobiological and mentalistic structures are rapidly organizing and canalizing life course pathways.

Future Directions

We will continue to explore aspects of the questions raised above in each of the data sets described. The MLS will soon have the capacity to link genotype with the rich phenotypic data set that has cumulated over 25 years, and continues. The FITS data set is publicly available and many studies are forthcoming from the Early Head Start Father's Work Group, among others. We will also be exploring all of the concepts reviewed herein with our research team working with American Indian Early Head Start/Head Start programs in Michigan. We are especially interested in discerning the impact of Historic Trauma on family dynamics and mental representations (Fitzgerald & Farrell, 2012) within American Indian families with very young children.

References

Bocknek, E. L., Sanderson, J., & Britner, P. A. (2009). Ambiguous loss and post-traumatic stress in a sample of school-age children of prisoners. *Journal of Child and Family Studies, 18*(3), 323–333. doi: 10.1007/s10826-008-9233-y

Boller, K., Bradley, R., Cabrera, N., Raikes, H., Pan, B., Shears, J., & Roggman, L. (2006). The Early Head Start father studies: Design, data collection, and summary of father presence in the lives of infants and toddlers. *Parenting: Science and Practice, 6,* 117–143.

Boss, P. (1977). A clarification of the concept of psychological father presence in families experiencing ambiguity of boundary. *Journal of Marriage and the Family, 39,* 141–151. Retrieved from http://www.jstor.org/stable/351070

Boss, P. (1980). The relationship of psychological father presence, wife's personal qualities, wife/family dysfunction in families of missing fathers. *Journal of Marriage and the Family, 42,* 541–549. Retrieved from http://www.jstor.org/stable/351898

Boss, P., & Greenberg, J. (1984). Family boundary ambiguity: A new variable in family stress theory. *Family Process, 23,* 535–546. doi: 10.1111/j.1545-5300.1984.00535.x

Brophy-Herb, H. E., Gibbons, C., Omar, M. A., & Schiffman, R. F. (1999). Low-income fathers and their infants: Interaction during teaching episodes. *Infant Mental Health Journal, 20,* 305–321. doi:10.1002/(SICI)1097-0355(199923)20:3<305::AID-IMHJ7>3.0.CO;2-Z

Cabrera, N. J., Fagan, J., & Farrie, D. (2008). Explaining the long reach of fathers' prenatal involvement on later parental enjoyment. *Journal of Marriage and the Family, 70,* 1094–1107.

Cabrera, N., Fitzgerald, H. E., Bradley, R. H., & Roggman, L. (2007). Modeling the dynamics of paternal influences on children over the life course. *Applied Developmental Science, 11*(4), 185–189.

Retrieved from http://faculty.mwsu.edu/psychology/dave.carlston/Writing%20in%20Psychology/Fathering/3/cabera.pdf

Cabrera, N., Moore, K., Bronte-Tinkew, J., Halle, T., West, J., Brooks-Gunn, J., et al. (2004). The DADS Initiative: Measuring father involvement in large scale surveys. In R. Day & M. Lamb (Eds.), *Conceptualizing and measuring father involvement* (pp. 417–452). Mahwah, NJ: Erlbaum.

Cabrera, N. J., Shannon, J. D., & Tamis-LeMonda, C. (2007). Fathers' influence on their children's cognitive and emotional development: From toddlers to preK. *Applied Developmental Science, 11,* 208–213.

Emde, R. N. (1989). The infant's relationship experience: Developmental and affective aspects. In A. J. Sameroff & R. N. Emde (Eds.), *Relationship disturbances in early childhood* (pp. 33–51). New York, NY: Basic Books.

Feldman, R. (2003). Infant-mother and infant-father synchrony: The coregulation of positive arousal. *Infant Mental Health Journal, 24*(1), 1–23. doi: 10.1002/imhj.10041

Fitzgerald, H. E., & Farrell, P. (2012). Fulfilling the promise: Creating a child development research agenda with Native Communities. *Child Development Perspectives, 6*(1), 75–78.

Fitzgerald, H. E., & McKelvey, L. (2005). Low-income adolescent fathers: Risk for parenthood and risky parenting. *Zero to Three, 25,* 35–41.

Fitzgerald, H., McKelvey, L., Schiffman, R., & Montanez, M. (2006). Exposure of low-income families and their children to neighborhood violence and paternal antisocial behavior. *Parenting: Science & Practice, 6*(2–3), 243–258. Retrieved from EBSCOhost.

Fitzgerald, H. E., Puttler, L. I., Refior, S., & Zucker, R. A. (2007). Family responses to children and alcohol. *Alcoholism Treatment Quarterly: Families and Alcoholism., 25,* 11–25.

Fitzgerald, H. E., Wong, W. W., & Zucker, R. A. (in press). Early origins of alcohol use and abuse: Mental representations, relationships, and the risk-resilience continuum. In N. Suchman, M. Pajulo, & L. C. Mayes (Eds.), *Parenting and substance addiction: Developmental approaches to interventions.* New York: Oxford University Press.

Fitzgerald, H. E., & Zucker, R. A. (2002). Effets a court et a long terme de l'alcoolisme parental sur les enfants (Short and long term effects of parental alcoholism on children). *Devenir, 14,* 169–182.

Fitzgerald, H. E., & Zucker, R. A. (2006). Growing up in an alcoholic family: Pathways of risk aggregation for alcohol use disorders. In K. Freeark & W. Davidson III (Eds.), *The crisis in youth mental health. Vol. 3. Families, children and communities* (pp. 249–271). Westport CT: Praeger.

Floyd, F. J., Cranford, J., Klotz-Daugherty, Zucker, R. A., & Fitzgerald, H. E. (2006). Marital interaction in alcoholic and nonalcoholic couples. *Journal of Abnormal Psychology, 115,* 121–130.

Fonagy, P., Lynton, P., & Strathern, L. (2011). Borderline personality disorder, mentalization, and the neurobiology of attachment. *Infant Mental Health Journal, 32,* 47–69. doi: 10.1002/imhj.20283

Fuller, B. E., Chermack, S. T., Cruise, K. A., Kirsch, E., Fitzgerald, H. E., & Zucker, R. A. (2003). Predictors of childhood aggression across three generations in children of alcoholics: Relationships involving parental alcoholism, individual and spousal aggression, and parenting practices. *Journal of Studies on Alcohol, 64,* 472–483. Retrieved from http://dionysus.psych.wisc.edu/Lit/Articles/FullerB2003a.pdf

Gorman, L. A., & Fitzgerald, H. E. (2007). Ambiguous loss, family stress, and infant attachment during times of war. *Zero to Three, 7,* 20–26. Retrieved from http://www.zerotothree.org/site/PageServer?pagename=est_journal_index_archives

Hofferth, S., Pleck, J., Stueve, J. L., Bianchi, S., & Sayer, L. (2002). The demography of fathers: What fathers do. In C. S. Tamis-LeMonda & N. Cabrera (Eds.), *Handbook of father involvement: Multidisciplinary perspectives* (pp. 63–90). Mahwah, NJ: Erlbaum.

Howe, M. L., & Courage, M. L. (1997). Origins of autobiographical memory. *Developmental Psychology, 35,* 1338–1348.

Jester, J. M., Nigg, J. T., Adams, K., Fitzgerald, H. E., Puttler, L. I., Wong, M. M., & Zucker, R. A. (2005). Inattention/hyperactivity and aggression from early childhood to adolescence: Heterogeneity of trajectories and differential influence of family environment characteristics. *Development and Psychopathology, 17,* 1–27. doi: 10.1017/S0954579405050066

Jester, J. M., Nigg, J. T., Puttler, L. I., Long, J. C., Fitzgerald, H. E., & Zucker, R. A. (2009). Intergenerational transmission of neuropsychological executive function. *Brain and Cognition, 70,* 145–153. doi: 10.1016/j.bandc.2009.01.005

Lamb, M.E. (Ed.). (1987). *The father's role: Cross-cultural perspectives.* Hillsdale, NJ: Erlbaum

Lamb, M. E. (2010). How do fathers influence children's development? Let me count the ways. In M. E. Lamb (Ed.), *The role of the father in child development* (5th ed.; pp. 1–26). Hoboken, NJ: Wiley.

Lamb, M. E., Pleck, J. H., Charnov, E. L., & Levine, J. A. (1987). A biosocial perspective on paternal behavior and involvement. In J. B. Lancaster, J. Altmann, J. Rossi, A. S. Rossi, & L. R. Sherrod (Eds.), *Parenting across the lifespan: Biosocial dimensions* (pp. 11–14). New York, NY: Aldine de Gruyter.

Loukas, A., Fitzgerald, H. E., Zucker, R. A., & von Eye, A. (2001). Parental alcoholism and co-occurring antisocial behavior: Prospective relationships to externalizing behavior problems in their young sons. *Journal of Abnormal Child Psychology, 29,* 91–106. doi: 10.1023/A:1005281011838

Loukas, A., Zucker, R. A., Fitzgerald, H. E., & Krull, J. (2003). Developmental trajectories of disruptive behavior problems among sons of alcoholics: effects of parent psychopathology, family conflict, and child under control. *Journal of Abnormal Psychology, 112,* 119–131 doi: 10.1037/0021-843X.112.1.119

Luthar, S. S. (Ed). (2003). *Resilience and vulnerability. Adaptation in the context of childhood adversities.* The Edinburgh Building; Cambridge UK: Cambridge University Press.

Madhavan, S., Townsend, N. W., & Garey, A. I. (2008). Absent breadwinners: Father-child connections paternal support in rural South Africa. *Journal of South African Studies, 34*(3), 647–663. doi: 10.1080/03057070802259902

Markowitsch, H. J., Thiel, A., Kessler, J., von Stockhausen, H. M., & Heiss, W. D. (1997). Ecphorisig semi-conscious episodic information via the right temporal polar cortex: A PET study. *Neurocase, 3,* 445–449.

Martinez , C. R., DeGarmo, D. S., & Eddy, J. M. (2004). Promoting academic success among Latino youths. *Hispanic Journal of Behavioral Sciences, 26,* 128–151. doi: 10.1177/0739986304264573

Mayzer, R., Fitzgerald, H. E., & Zucker, R. A. (2009). Anticipating early problem drinking risk form antisocial behavior in preschool and thereafter: Testing a hard continuity model. *Journal of the American Academy of Child and Adolescent Psychiatry, 48,* 820–827. doi:10.1097/CHI.0b013e3181aa0383

McKelvey, L., Fitzgerald, H. E., & Schiffman, R. (2010, July). Risk exposure in toddlers of low-income fathers: Links to child functioning at age 10. Poster presented as part of the poster workshop (N. Cabrera & L. Roggman, chairs), "The influence of early father involvement on children's perception of their relationship with their father," at the 11th biennial meeting of the World Association for Infant Mental Health, Leipzig, Germany.

McKelvey, L., Hart, A., Barton, L., Whiteside-Mansell, & Fitzgerald, H. E. (2006, July). Parenting stress in fathers of children with special needs. Poster presented at the biennial meeting of the World Association for Infant Mental Health, Paris.

McKelvey, L., Schiffman, R., & Fitzgerald, H. E. (2010, July). Father behaviors in interaction with toddlers: Impacts on child cognitive outcomes. Poster presented at the 11th biennial meeting of the World Association for Infant Mental Health, Leipzig, Germany.

Mun, E- Y., Fitzgerald, H. E., Puttler, L. I., Zucker, R. A., & von Eye, A. (2001). Temperamental characteristics as predictors of externalizing and internalizing child behavior problems in the contexts of high and low parental psychopathology. *Infant Mental Health Journal, 22,* 393–415. doi: 10.1002/imhj.1008

Nash, J. (1965). The father in contemporary culture and current psychological literature. *Child Development, 36,* 261–297. Retrieved from http://www.jstor.org/pss/1126797

Nelson, K., & Fivush, R. (2004). The emergence of autobiographical memory: A social cultural developmental theory. *Psychological Review, 111,* 486–511. doi: 10.1037/0033-295X.111.2.486

Pemberton, C. K., Neiderhiser, J. M., Leve, L. D., Natsuaki, M. N., Shaw, D. S., Reiss, D., & Ge, X. (2010). Influence of parental depressive symptoms on adopted toddler behaviors: An emerging developmental cascade of genetic and environmental effects. *Development and Psychopathology, 22,* 803–818. doi: 10.1017/S0954579410000477

Roggman, L. A., Boyce, L. K., Cook, J., Christiansen, K., & Jones, D. (2004). Playing with daddy: Social toy play, Early Head Start, and developmental outcomes. *Fathering, 2*(1), 83–108. doi: 10.3149/fth.0201.83

Sameroff, A. J. (1989). Principles of development and psychopathology. In A. J. Sameroff & R. N. Emde (Eds.), *Relationship disturbances in early childhood* (pp. 17–32). New York, NY: Basic Books.

Shannon, J. D., Tamis-LeMonda, C. S., London, K., & Cabrera, N. (2002). Beyond rough and tumble: Low-income fathers' interactions and children's cognitive development at 24 months. *Parenting: Science and Practice, 2,* 77–104. doi: 10.1207/S15327922PAR0202_01

Shannon, J. D., Tamis-Lamonda, C., & Cabrera, N. J. (2006). Fathering in infancy: Mutuality and stability between 8 and 16 months. *Parenting: Science and Practice, 6,* 167–188. Retrieved from EBSCOhost

Shears, J., Robinson, J., & Emde, R. (2002). Fathering relationships and their associations with juvenile delinquency. *Infant Mental Health Journal, 23,* 79–87. doi: 10.1002/imhj.10005

Summers, J. A., Raikes, H., Buttler, J., Spicer, P., Pan, B., Shaw, S., … Johnson, M. K. (1999). Low-income father and mothers' perceptions of the father role: A qualitative study in four EHS communities. *Infant Mental Health Journal, 20,* 291–304. doi: 10.1002/(SICI)1097-0355(199923)20:3<291::AID-IMHJ6>3.0.CO;2-G

Tamis-LeMonda, C. S., & McFadden, K. E. (2010). Low-income fathers: Myths and evidence. In M. E. Lamb (Ed.), *The role of the father in child development* (pp. 296–318). Hoboken, NJ: Wiley.

Tamis-LeMonda, C. S., Shannon, J. D., Cabrera, N. J., & Lamb, M. E. (2004). Fathers and mothers at play with their 2- and 3-year-olds: Contributions to language and cognitive development. *Child Development, 75*(6), 1806–1820. doi: 10.1111/j.1467-8624.2004.00818.x

Vogel, C, A., Bradley, R. H., Raikes, H. H., Boller, K., & Shears, J. K. (2006). Relations between father connectedness and child outcomes. *Parenting: Science and Practice, 6,* 189–209. Retrieved from EBSCOhost

Wong, M. M., Brower, K. J., Fitzgerald, H. E., & Zucker, R. A. (2004). Sleep problems in childhood and early onset of alcohol and other drug use in adolescence. *Alcoholism: Clinical and Experimental Research, 28,* 578–587. doi: 10.1097/01.ALC.0000121651.75952.39

Wong, M. M., Nigg, J. T., Puttler, L. I., Fitzgerald, H. E., Jester, J. M., Glass, J., … Zucker, R. A. (2006). Behavioral control and resiliency in the onset of alcohol and illicit drug use: A prospective study from preschool to adolescence. *Child Development, 77,* 1016–1033. doi: 10.1111/j.1467-8624.2006.00916.x

Wong, M. M., Zucker, R. A., & Zucker, R. A. (1999). Heterogeneity of risk aggregation for alcohol problems between early and middle childhood. *Development and Psychopathology, 11,* 727–744. doi: 10.1017/S0954579499002291

Wood, J. J., & Repetti, R. L. (2004). What gets dad involved? A longitudinal study of change in parental child caregiving involvement. *Journal of Family Psychology, 18*(1), 237–249. doi: 10.1037/0893-3200.18.1.237

Yates, T. M., Egeland, B. L., & Sroufe, A. (2003). Rethinking resilience. In S. S. Luthar (Ed), *Resilience and vulnerability: Adaptation in the context of childhood adversities* (pp. 243–266). Cambridge, UK: Cambridge University Press.

Zucker, R. A., Ellis, D. A., Bingham, C. R., Fitzgerald, H. E., & Sanford, K. P. (1996). Other evidence for at least two alcoholisms, II: Life course variation in antisociality and heterogeneity of alcoholic outcome. *Development and Psychopatholoy, 8,* 831–848. doi: 10.1017/S0954579400007458

Zucker, R. A., Ellis, D. A., & Fitzgerald, H. E. (1994). Developmental evidence for at least two alcoholisms, I: Biopsychosocial variation among pathways into symptomatic difficulty. *Annals of the New York Academy of Science, 708,* 134–146. doi: 10.1111/j.1749-6632.1994.tb24706.x

Zucker, R. A., Fitzgerald, H. E., Refior, S. K., Puttler, L. I., Pallas, D. M., & Ellis, D. A. (2000). The clinical and social ecology of childhood for children of alcoholics: Description of a study and implications for a differentiated social policy. In H. E. Fitzgerald, B. M. Lester, & B. Zuckerman (Eds), *Children of addiction: Research, health, and social policy issues* (pp. 109–141). New York, NY: Garland Press.

Zucker, R. A., Kincaid, S. B., Fitzgerald, H. E., & Bingham, C. R. (1995). Alcohol schema acquisition in preschoolers: Differences between children of alcoholics and children of nonalcoholics. *Alcoholism: Clinical and Experimental Research, 19,* 1011–1017. doi: 10.1111/j.1530-0277.1995.tb00982.x

Zucker, R. A., Wong, M. M., Clark, D. B., Leonard, K. E., Schulenberg, J. E., Cornelius, J. R., … Puttler, L. I. (2006). Predicting risky drinking outcomes longitudinally: What kind of advance notice can we get? *Alcoholism: Clinical and Experimental Research, 30,* 243–252. doi: 10.1111/j.1530-0277.2006.00033.x

Zucker, R. A., Wong, M. M., Puttler, L. I., & Fitzgerald, H. E. (2003). Resilience and vulnerability among sons of alcoholics: Relationship to developmental outcomes between early childhood and adolescence. In S. S. Luthar (Ed.), *Resilience and vulnerability: Adaptation in the context of childhood adversities* (pp. 76–103). New York, NY: Cambridge University Press.

Chapter 11

Fathers in Family Contexts

Lori A. Roggman

Utah State University

Robert H. Bradley

Arizona State University

Helen H. Raikes

University of Nebraska-Lincoln

Understanding how fathers influence children requires a consideration of both the immediate context of the family and the contexts in which the family lives. This chapter considers relevant theoretical perspectives and the research questions, methods, and empirical findings that illuminate our understanding of fathers in family contexts.

Historical Overview and Theoretical Perspectives

The number of article titles in developmental research journals that include "father, fathering, or paternal" has doubled in the last decade. Of these, almost half the article titles also include "mother, mothering, or maternal." Despite this expanding research, our understanding of fathers in families is challenged by ongoing changes in the nature and stability of employment and social expectations of parenting roles. Increases in maternal employment in the 20th century increased the need for fathers to share their children's care with working mothers and other care providers (Bianchi, 2000; Cabrera, Tamis-LeMonda, Bradley, Hofferth, & Lamb, 2000). This is especially true when mothers are employed for more hours than fathers or employed when fathers are unemployed (Bonney, Kelley, & Levant, 1999), as became more common in the 21st century (US Department of Labor, 2011). The rise of the feminist ideal of egalitarian parenting (Rosser & Miller, 2003), together with changing attitudes about marriage and divorce (Clarkberg, Stolzenberg, & Waite, 1995), has created even greater variation in parents' roles.

Theoretical perspectives about fathers and children in families have not been well aligned with these social realities that influence paternal behavior. Early ethological models of social development focused on mother-child attachment, limiting fathers to perform roles as alternative or secondary attachment figures. More recently, theorists have expanded this perspective to propose a more central role for fathers as facilitators of the exploration system, encouraging children to interact with the external world, helping them overcome wariness of novelty, and joining them in playful risk taking (Grossmann et al., 2002; Paquette, 2004). From Paquette's perspective, the father's role complements the mother's role: The father supports the child's outer-directed exploration while the mother responds to the child's inner-felt expressions of distress, a balance that helps a child coordinate systems of attachment and exploration. Although perhaps drawn too dichotomously, this focus on father involvement in the exploration side of attachment nevertheless connects better to a view, emerging in many societies, of children as autonomous actors in a dynamic social-emotional context (Lewis, 1997).

A more contextual view from ecological systems theory (Bronfenbrenner, 1986) places the father within the family microsystem, itself embedded in ever-widening contextual spheres of exosystem and macrosystem, mediated by inter-level mesosystem interactions, and evolving within the chronosystem over time. The mesosystem includes the interface of the family microsystem with fathers' exosystem contexts of work and social organizations outside the family that may or may not support fathering (Ransford, Crouter, & McHale, 2008). A father's role in facilitating his child's entry into community contexts suggests that traditional notions about supporting families with parenting classes or home visits may be too limited, and fathers' work or community contexts such as recreation, church, scouting, or community service programs may offer better opportunities to engage some fathers in supporting children's development in the contexts in which they are already involved. The macrosystem of societal, cultural, political, and historical contexts influences fathers and families through social pressures and public policies regarding employment, marriage, custody, and the establishment of paternity. Powerful messages about fathers' roles have changed in response to rising maternal employment and falling fertility (McLanahan, 2004; US Census Bureau, 2004, 2010) to reflect societal expectations of more direct father involvement with their children (Cabrera et al., 2000).

Social capital theory (Coleman, 1988) advances a more dynamic view of fathers by contrasting financial capital, a father's monetary or material contributions, with social capital, the opportunities a father provides by socializing his child and connecting his child to beneficial social networks. Given the rapidly evolving worlds of work, family, and social networks, considerations of *family* capital more than just father capital may help explain the contributions of father involvement to child development (Berger, Carlson, Bzostek, & Osborne, 2008). Social capital theory (see Bishai, this volume) currently concerns mostly "inputs" from key system components (i.e., father investment in children), but could also address regulatory processes that drive those inputs (i.e., what determines the degree of father investment), how those inputs promote the function of other inputs (e.g., co-parenting), and what affects "uptake" on the child's side (e.g., child age). The uptake of any parental input may depend, for example, on the response to that input by the child, a conscious actor (Lewis, 1997) with his or her own perspective.

More elaborated systems theories offer both complexity and power for describing fathers' roles in families. Family systems theory (Anderson & Sabatelli, 1999) places the father-child subsystem within a larger dynamic family system, in which rules and relationships help determine family roles and interaction patterns. The self-organizing tendencies (e.g., feedback and feedforward loops) of the family system move the family toward a set of self-sustaining structural inter-relationships in response to everyday challenges and opportunities. These processes include adaptive forms of parenting (Richmond & Stocker, 2006); but family system maintenance may also include maladaptive parenting, such as may happen with family conflict (Franck & Buehler, 2007). System and subsystem boundaries established for and by fathers, both within the family and between the family and outside persons, may maintain stability of the family system but can either promote or interfere with children's adaptive functioning (Madden-Derdich, Leonard, & Christopher, 1999).

Developmental systems theory places the father in the midst of a multi-level multi-generational cascading process, in which complex contextual influences are in dynamic transaction with the developing child and fathers are seen as a dynamic influence, simultaneously direct, indirect, interactive, and transactive; embedded in self-organizing adaptive systems changing over time; and interacting with other system components (Capaldi, Pears, Kerr, & Owen, 2008; Fitzgerald, Zucker, & Yang, 1995; Klimes-Dougan et al., 2010; Lerner, Rothbaum, Boulos, & Castellino, 2002; Pemberton et al., 2010). To make sense of this complexity, some father theorists have taken a smaller set of components to explore dynamic processes while avoiding the "everything is related to everything" conundrum of systems level analyses. A focus on understanding fathers in family systems primarily in terms of their influence on children's development is exemplified in the heuristic model described by Cabrera and colleagues, in which family context components include the child's characteristics and the father's biological and social history (Cabrera, Fitzgerald, Bradley, & Roggman, 2007). Nevertheless, many principles of general systems theory (e.g., multi- and equi-finality, reciprocal process, and self-organization) or dynamic systems (chaos) theory may usefully inform research on fathers, particularly regarding fathers in families faced with instability or trauma that elicits reorganization of family rules, behavior, and interaction (Bütz, Chamberlain, & McCown, 1997).

These complex models of father involvement are likely to further evolve as new conceptualizations emerge, but those who work directly with fathers may need more than just theory to understand fathers themselves. Research from a more person-centered approach, both theoretically and methodologically, addresses variations over time within fathers and father-child relationships (e.g., Molenaar & Campbell, 2009) and could reveal the conditions under which what we say about fathers in general is also true for individual fathers.

Current Research Questions

Understanding fathers in family context requires clarifying how father involvement and family context are defined and conceptualized in relation to child outcomes. Questions about fathers' influences on children's development have evolved from simple comparisons of children in father present versus father absent households to complex models of father influences in contexts not only of marriage and divorce, but also employment, culture, and technology. Current research questions, broadly stated, concern how we define father involvement, how we consider family contexts, and how fathers influence children's development in family contexts.

Father involvement is not defined consistently in the research literature, but several studies have used the three-part definition first proposed by Lamb, Pleck, Charnov, and Levine (1985): *engagement*—interacting directly with the child, *availability*—being accessible, and *responsibility*—providing financial support or making decisions about the child. *Father engagement* with children may have both direct effects on children's development and indirect effects through the mother. As father engagement increases, particularly in caregiving, the family system may require more negotiation of co-parenting. *Father availability*, constrained by the mother-father relationship and fathers' work demands, would have relatively more indirect effects, by providing opportunities for more engagement and by allowing a more complex parenting system. *Father responsibility* for children would have primarily indirect effects through fathers' support of mothers and decision-making about children's environments and care. Parenting roles, however, often change with employment, financial resources, additional children, extended family involvement, and child care or school environments. Studying fathers in these non-stable contexts requires more flexible definitions of father involvement and more sophisticated analyses of change. The question remains: how can we define father involvement and its important components in ways that allow for responsiveness to context?

The contexts of father involvement vary widely. Despite changes in marriage and divorce rates and increases in non-marital childbearing and adoption, most American children (67%) live with both their married biological parents (US Census Bureau, 2010). Of the children who live with only one biological parent, 84% live with their mothers, while only 16% live with their fathers (US Census Bureau, 2010). The capacity of divorced fathers to influence their children is often constrained in traditional custody and visitation arrangements, but even nonresident fathers may provide support and facilitate mesosystem connections to other social networks. The mother-father relationship, whether married or not, may have direct effects, mediated effects, and moderator effects on father involvement (Papp, Goeke-Morey, & Cummings, 2004). Thus a question of interest to researchers is how do family structure and father-mother relationship influence father involvement and, in turn, child outcomes?

Another set of research questions focus on the mechanism by which fathers influence children's development within various family contexts. Does family structure or the father-mother relationship moderate the influence of the father on the child by facilitating or hindering the effects of father involvement? One moderator effect of the mother-father relationship is through maternal gatekeeping, in which mothers limit or facilitate father involvement opportunities (Fagan & Barnett, 2003; Freeman, Newland, & Coyl, 2008; McBride et al., 2005; Schoppe-Sullivan, Brown, Cannon, Mangelsdorf, & Sokolowski, 2008). Although most mothers, even single mothers, express supportive beliefs about father involvement (Carlson, McLanahan, & Brooks-Gunn, 2008; Sano, Richards, & Zvonkovic, 2008), and fathers who value involvement with their children are likely to overcome barriers that include maternal gatekeeping (Freeman et al., 2008), variability in mothers' encouragement for father involvement remains an important aspect of the family context for fathering. Maternal gatekeeping may also limit researchers' access to fathers and thereby bias research samples toward more involved fathers.

Lastly, researchers are concerned about how fathers facilitate or hinder extra-familial opportunities for their children. For example, father involvement in the community offers opportunities to enrich children's environments, and father employment may affect residential location and stability, which in turn affect children's school and community opportunities, particularly as children get older. Diversity of father involvement is seen not only across father roles as breadwinners, co-parents, step parents, divorced parents, gay parents, and grandparents, but also across contexts related to residence, culture, and socio-economic status (SES). Considering culture and other extra-familial influences may reveal the supports parents need to promote child development that is optimal for a particular culture.

Research Measurement and Methodology

Despite the upswing in father research in the last decade, father-specific research methodologies are still emerging. Among the challenges father researchers face are including both fathers and mothers in studies of parenting, measuring fathering without over-reliance on maternal measures, and analyzing complex family-level data.

Because parents often share goals, intentions, and experiences with their children (Holmes & Huston, 2010; Pleck & Hofferth, 2008), father researchers have emphasized the need to consider mothering effects when studying the effects of fathering (Cabrera, Shannon, &

Tamis-LeMonda, 2007; Tamis-LeMonda, Shannon, Cabrera, & Lamb, 2004). Guided by theoretical models that emphasize context and methodological considerations of covariation, father
researchers increasingly test models in which the mother's influence is either statistically controlled or examined as a specific mediating or moderating component (e.g., Holmes & Huston,
2010). Thus, published studies on fathers and fathering include mothers and mothering in the
title about five times as often as the reverse. Because fewer fathers than mothers are primary
caregivers or single parents, and more mothers than fathers have been included in research,
we know more about single mothers than single fathers and more about married fathers than
single fathers. Research on single fathers is especially scant. Researchers could expand our
knowledge of fathering by designing parenting studies to include both fathers and mothers
and more effectively recruiting both married and non-married fathers to participate in such
studies.

Typical measures of father involvement are too narrow, static, and dependent on a middle
class Western maternal template. For example, in the Early Head Start Research and Evaluation project, fathers were asked a set of questions about their parenting activities that differed
little from the parenting activities questions asked of mothers (Administration for Children and
Families, 2002). Few measures of fathering have a long history, and there are almost no measurement comparisons to determine which works best. Not surprisingly, maternal measures
have often been used to measure fathers with little adaptation or validity testing (cf, Adamsons
& Buehler, 2007). Such an approach neglects the specific developmental supports for children
that may be offered by father involvement and assumes that what children need from parents
is "universal," an assumption widely criticized in cross-cultural research as reflecting a misunderstanding of the critical distinction between form and function (Bornstein, 1995).

Nothing in the developmental literature has yet suggested that children need something
vastly different from fathers than from mothers—but how they get it could be different.
Thus, recommendations for measuring father involvement suggest both: (a) documenting and
observing multiple aspects of paternal behavior to determine how things come together in the
real world; and (b) using broad qualitative ratings—what Palkovitz (2007) calls the "essence"
of good fathering—rather than more nuanced coding schemes designed to measure maternal
behavior. Systematically coding specifically defined paternal behaviors, while avoiding mother-
based nuanced coding, seems particularly valuable in view of the diversity of fatherhood across
residence and biological relatedness (Sweeney, 2007). The exception is when research supports
the same behavioral indicator of a particular construct or when similar mother and father measures are needed to test the independent influence of fathers on child outcomes.

When data collection from fathers is limited by maternal gatekeeping, some researchers rely
on mother or child reports of fathering that correlate only modestly, at best. Even when fathers
report what they do, quantitative approaches often simply tally all that a father might do in
relation to all that a child or family might need, rather than examining what individual fathers
do in the complex circumstances of family life. By integrating more qualitative approaches,
father researchers can move beyond the "more is better" assumption of linear additive models
and instead use a more dynamic multi-method approach to study father involvement.

Analytic issues in father research concern the unit of analysis and how fathers together with
mothers influence children. The family is the unit of analysis when father and mother influences are tested in the same analytic model. Analysis of mediators and moderators in father
research models tests direct and indirect effects from familial influences to child outcomes.
Father involvement may have effects on children that are mediated by mother interactions
(e.g., Coley & Schindler, 2008; Tamis-LeMonda et al., 2004) or moderated by factors that

buffer or enhance fathers' influences (e.g., Kosterman, Haggerty, Spoth, & Redmond, 2004). Father involvement may also mediate or moderate other influences on child outcomes, such as marital quality or culture (e.g., Papp et al., 2004).

Empirical Findings

Key recent studies of fathers reflect a growing research literature on fathering in family contexts. From the perspective of Bronfenbrenner's ecological systems model, fathers influence children directly and indirectly in embedded contexts of the father-child relationship, the mother-father relationship, parent employment, culture, and technology.

Fathers, Mothers, and Child Development

Studies that include both maternal and paternal influences in the same analytic models show considerable support for unique contributions by fathers, over and above the contributions of mothers, during several developmental periods. Father supportiveness and play sensitivity with young children predicted children's self-regulation and later attachment, respectively, even though the same behaviors by mothers did not (Cabrera et al., 2007; Grossmann et al., 2002). Both mothers' and fathers' mutual responsiveness with toddlers predicted better social behavior when the children were preschool age, but the effects were more direct for fathers (Kochanska, Aksan, Prisco, & Adams, 2008). Parent supportiveness by both mothers and fathers predicted less anxiety in preschoolers, although children's poor self-regulatory capacity increased their vulnerability to fathers' but not mothers' lack of supportiveness (Hastings et al., 2008). Fathers' negative parenting interactions independently predicted young children's aggression and other externalizing behaviors (NICHD Early Child Care Research Network, 2004). Father involvement, independent of mother involvement, influenced cognitive and language development for infants and preschoolers from low-income families (Cabrera et al., 2007; Martin, Ryan, & Brooks-Gunn, 2007; Rowe, Coker, & Pan, 2004; Pancsofar, Vernon-Feagans, & The Family Life Project Investigators, 2010; Ryan, Martin, & Brooks-Gunn, 2006; Shannon, Tamis-LeMonda, London, & Cabrera, 2002; Tamis-LeMonda et al., 2004, in press) and academic achievement for adolescents from middle SES families (Harris, Furstenberg, & Marmer, 1998).

Similar behaviors by mothers and fathers may influence children differently: Compared with father intrusiveness, mother intrusiveness with young children predicted more negative outcomes across a broader age range (Cabrera et al., 2007), and in conversations about internal states, mothers' references to emotion predicted children's emotional understanding, while fathers' explanations of emotions predicted their theory of mind (LaBounty, Wellman, Olson, Lagattuta, & Liu, 2008). Sometimes the same parenting behavior by either parent makes a difference: Supportiveness in play interactions by one parent predicted better child outcomes, even if the other parent was not supportive (Martin et al., 2007; Ryan et al., 2006). Sometimes it is better when parents differ: When only one parent helped a child to cope with negative emotions and the other did not, children understood emotions better and had less intense peer conflicts than when both parents were supportive (McElwain, Halberstadt, & Volling, 2007).

In addition to including both father and mother variables in analyses, father researchers have considered both father and mother in co-parenting or triadic interactions, which appear to offer a different context than dyadic interactions. For example, fathers showed just as much interactional synchrony as mothers in dyadic contexts with young children but were less synchronous in triadic contexts (de Mendonça, Cossette, Strayer, & Gravel, 2011); and both fathers and mothers were more positive in dyadic than triadic interactions with adolescents (Smetana, Abernethy, & Harris, 2000). Fathers' positive dyadic interactions with young children indirectly supported children's self-perceptions by buffering the effects of children's reactive temperaments, while positive triadic interactions directly supported children's self-perceptions (Brown, Mangelsdorf, Neff, Schoppe-Sullivan, & Frosch, 2009). Experiences in one context may influence other contexts: Co-parenting conflict was correlated with couple conflict in infancy (Cabrera, Shannon, & La Taillade, 2009), and supportive triadic co-parenting of 4-year-olds was correlated with more dyadic play and less caregiving by fathers (Jia & Schoppe-Sullivan, 2011).

Fathers may influence children indirectly by decreasing maternal stress and supporting better maternal parenting (Coley & Schindler, 2008). Indirect effects may also come from father's financial and other responsibilities to their children: When nonresident teenage fathers provided more financial and material support, including car seats and toys, children were less likely to have poor cognitive and social development (Mollborn & Lovegrove, 2011). Fathers may also buffer the negative effects of maternal depression (Fletcher, 2009; Mezulis, Hyde, & Clark, 2004) or exacerbate the negative association of mothers' avoidance style of marital conflict on children's social behavior (Marchand & Hock, 2003). Direct and indirect influences of fathers on children's development reveal the complexity of fathers' influences in family context because the context of the family itself varies and changes with transitions in mother-father relationships, parental employment, families' cultures, and technological advances.

Fathers, Mothers, Marriage, Divorce, and Residence

Mother-father relationships affect fathers' roles and influence on children. Rapid social changes in parental relationships point to the need for new paradigms for studying fatherhood in the context of the mother-father relationship. Traditional fatherhood research, however, has lacked paradigms for framing the complexity of fatherhood roles and residency. Falling marriage rates, increasing single parenting, rising diversity of nonresident and resident fatherhood, changing custody laws, and shifting mores leading to acknowledgement that significant numbers of children have gay fathers (or mothers) (Bozett, 1989; US Census Bureau, 2010) have all brought changes to the family context of fathering and ways of thinking about fathers.

Over the past 25 years, the U.S. marriage rate has fallen to its lowest point in history, despite a leveling off in divorce rates, and as a result, more than a quarter of U.S. children under age 21 live with only one of their parents, mostly with custodial mothers, but an increasing number with custodial fathers (US Census Bureau, 2010). Variability in paternal residency and roles has led to large variations in fatherhood configurations that include, but are not limited to, biological fathers (resident and nonresident, married and unmarried), stepfathers, and social fathers, and combinations of father types in a single child's life (Hofferth, Pleck, Stueve, Bianchi, & Sayer 2002). Emerging efforts to involve separating parents in dispute resolution may keep nonresident fathers more involved after divorce or relationship dissolution (see Applegate, Schwartz, & Holtzworth-Munroe, this volume). In the Fragile Families study, unmarried biological fathers' who were more involved during pregnancy were more likely to be involved 3 years later (Cabrera, Fagan, & Farrie, 2008), but involvement of a mother's new partner—a resident non-biological father—was as beneficial for young children's well-being as that of a resident biological father, regardless of how much the child's nonresident biological father remained involved (Bzostek, 2008), and stepfathers were as involved and engaged as biological fathers with school-age children in the NICHD Study of Early Child Care (Adamsons, O'Brien, & Pasley, 2007). Also, two fathers in same-sex marriages or partnerships may mean two residential fathers in the same family—biological or not—who share parenting.

Despite this diversity in fathers' relationships and residence, father research is based primarily on biological fathers residing with biological mothers, often comparing all other fathers to the standard: biological resident fathers. Even much of the literature on gay fathers compares gay fathers to biological resident fathers (or to lesbian mothers) (Bozett, 1989). Yet, variability in who fathers are and where they live suggests equal variability in contextual factors affecting how fathers influence children's development. Research from the Early Head Start Research and Evaluation project has shown stronger influences on children's development by nonresident African-American fathers than by nonresident White or Hispanic fathers (Vogel, Bradley, Raikes, Boller, & Shears, 2006), perhaps because they are more likely, at least compared with White nonresident fathers, to maintain a romantic relationship with the child's mother (Cabrera, Ryan, Mitchell, Shannon, & Tamis-LeMonda, 2008).

Mother-father relationship quality introduces still more variability as mother-father conflict and relationship satisfaction have been associated with father involvement in caregiving (Aldous, Mulligan, & Bjarnason, 1998). And qualitative studies of gay fathers have illustrated a different process whereby fatherhood behaviors require integration with the fathers' identities as gay men (Bozett, 1989). Moreover, the recent trend of more adult children returning home (Goldscheider & Goldscheider, 1994) has given rise to new research on fathering with adult children (Messineo, 2005). A new generation of research is likely to focus on the great diversity of fathering—resident and nonresident fathers, biological and stepfathers, heterosexual and gay fathers—in the context of relationships and cultures across childhood and adulthood.

Fathers, Families, and Work

Changes in the context for fathering arise from the rapid increase in maternal employment, increased unemployment for men more than women, and concomitant changes in the work-family balance and roles within the family (Almeida, Maggs, & Galambos, 1993; Bonney et al., 1999; US Census Bureau, 1990, 2006). For over 20 years, the majority of U.S. children have lived in households where the single custodial parent or both parents are employed (US Census Bureau, 1990). Ample evidence shows that both mother's and father's parenting behaviors changed with increases in maternal employment. For example, the number of hours a mother spent in paid labor consistently predicted fathers' time with their children (Almeida et al., 1993; Bonney et al., 1999), and fathers have provided the non-maternal care for one-fourth of US preschool children whose mothers work (US Census Bureau, 2006).

Fathers' individual work schedules and economic shifts have predicted father involvement in caregiving (Brayfield, 1995; Casper & O'Connell, 1998), but fathers' time in caregiving has also varied by child gender, with fathers in dual-earner households spending more time with sons than daughters (Manlove & Vernon-Feagans, 2002). Moreover, fathers who spent more time alone with their infants, such as by providing caregiving, developed wider repertoires of interaction with their children than fathers who spent less time alone with their infants (Pedersen, Suwalsky, Cain, Zaslow, & Rabinovich, 1987). Generally, mothers have spent more time in caregiving than fathers and, not surprisingly, experienced more role strain in balancing work and family (Lee, Vernon-Feagans, Vazquez, & Kolak, 2003). For both mothers and fathers, however, high work pressure in the absence of support has resulted in more family conflict and less closeness in relationships with their children (Ransford et al., 2008).

Fathers, Families, and Culture

The diverse and changing nature of family contexts challenges father research. Particularly in ethnic minority communities, life can be unpredictable, requiring frequent adjustments in residence, family configuration, and employment (Coley, 2001). In such unstable circumstances, fathers may have ill-defined roles and obligations with their children. For example, low-income Mexican American fathers more often took on roles that ran counter to their cultural heritage when mothers were employed many hours, but this practical adjustment was more often found in recently immigrated men than in more acculturated men (Coltrane, Parke, & Adams, 2004): More acculturated Latino men, particularly from countries other than Mexico, were more likely to be generally engaged with their children (Cabrera, Shannon, West, & Brooks-Gunn, 2006). Changing demands and opportunities for father involvement in families (Cabrera et al., 2007; Summers et al., 1999) may not always play out in predictable ways.

Historically, fathers' roles have been dynamically responsive to environmental conditions. Fathering in US middle SES families, compared with impoverished families and especially compared with families in most developing countries, is less restricted by social norms, more likely to reflect personal preferences and individual family circumstances, and thus much more variable (Belsky & Jaffee, 2006; Berger et al., 2008; Cabrera et al., 2007; Coltrane et al., 2004; Foster & Kalil, 2007; McFadden & Tamis-LeMonda, in press). Fathers' instrumental roles of supporting, protecting, and disciplining children continue to be emphasized over expressive roles in the United States (Finley & Schwartz, 2006), but there is not a unified cultural norm, especially for nonresident fathers (Cabrera et al., 2008). By contrast, parenting roles in poorer countries are highly constrained by economic circumstances and prevailing cultural beliefs, such that fathers tend to act primarily as head of the household and authority figure. That said, parenting roles could change quickly with societal transformation. Chinese mothers and fathers from Beijing, for example, showed wide variation in how they addressed children's responsibilities for homework and schoolwork, informed partly by Confucian principles and partly by rapid cultural changes (Bowes, Chen, San, & Yuan, 2004). In middle-class Kadazan families in Malaysia, who have a strong tradition of caregiving as a female role but are experiencing increased maternal employment, fathers, when compared with mothers, reported spending less time in caregiving but similar amounts of time in play (Hossain, Roopnarine, Ismail, Hashmi, & Sombuling, 2007). Le and colleagues (2008) describe the challenge of disentangling cultural, economic, and social influences on parenting generally, a challenge likely to be greater for fathers given their less well-prescribed role.

Fathers, Families, and Technology

Any consideration of how fathers matter for children must consider the primary function of parenting: preparing children for full participation in adult society, a process that in more highly technological societies requires considerably more education and goes on for a longer period of time. At the same time, advancing technologies have raised both new opportunities and new challenges for parents regarding their children's entertainment, education, monitoring, and personal relationships (Livingstone, 2002). These concerns seem warranted in light of research showing poorer relationships with parents, particularly for sons with fathers, when adolescents in Finland used more entertainment and communication technology (Punamäki, Wallenius, Hölttö, Nygård, & Rimpelä, 2009). Because of these technologies, some of the research on fathering may no longer fully apply to the new realities of daily life, but there is little authoritative new research on how technology can influence fathering and its effects on children. It is not clear how fathers can most effectively engage their children in using learning resources from the internet, help them evaluate the content of online media and advertisements, guide and monitor their use of social media, or use technology to maintain good relationships with their children.

In the past, parents often had reasonably complete knowledge of what it would take to function well as a member of society—not nearly so true today, when children may have stronger technology skills than their parents. Thus, fathers are not always in a good position to provide appropriate support and guidance. As children grow into adolescents and young adults, fathers engage with them in qualitatively different ways, particularly as regards guidance and control, which their offspring are often not inclined to accept. There is some evidence for intergenerational transmission of constructive aspects of fathering (e.g., socio-emotional support) (Kerr, Capaldi, Pears, & Owen, 2009) but less evidence regarding control aspects. In some ways fathers can take advantage of emerging technologies to assist in the process of parenting, but their children's greater familiarity with and value of technology can create difficulties in the father-child relationship and even undermine the parenting process. Fathers may benefit from joining their offspring in using emerging technologies as avenues for stimulating, nurturing, and monitoring their children, but much more research is needed to help optimally guide this effort.

Policy Implications

The available empirical evidence regarding father contributions to child development, over and above mother contributions, suggests encouraging fathers' direct involvement with children when forming social policies related to marriage, the military, and economics. Cabrera and Peters (2000) note the policy challenge of addressing two opposing trends: the increase of father involvement in intact families and the absence of nonresident fathers from their children's lives, which can result in a widening gap in father influence between these groups. Programs and policies can narrow this gap by empowering fathers to be active participants in their children's lives, regardless of residence. Support for father involvement should be implemented in family-level interventions, such as Head Start, early intervention for children with disabilities (IDEA), or youth programs. Parenting education should include fathers, not just mothers, and should recognize father-child interactions that offer unique opportunities for fathers to guide children's development. Early Head Start, for example, reduced spanking and improved interactions by fathers in the program (Administration for Children and Families, 2002). Cabrera and Peters (p. 310) suggest that the expansion of research on fathers' influence on children "has created an urgent impetus to revise social and cultural conceptions of fatherhood. This cultural shift has important consequences for policies and research."

Bridges to Other Disciplines

The diverse activities of parents (Parke, 2004) are under partial control of multiple psychobiological systems that interact in complex ways (Belsky & Jaffee, 2006). Because parenting is regarded as central to human functioning, scholars have used propositions and methodologies from other disciplines to explain paternal parenting. For example, Rogoff (2003), Super and Harkness (2002), Weisner (2002) and others have drawn from cultural anthropology to devise a more comprehensive account of fathering. From a biological evolutionary perspective

(Geary, 2000), fathers invest in the physical and social well-being of their offspring to ensure not only the survival of those offspring but their ascendance in the social order. The notion of fathers' "investment" in terms of economists' market principles and investment strategies suggests propositions on why men allocate time to improving the prospects of their children (Becker, 1981), guides models of fathers' and mothers' provision of resources (see Bishai, this volume), and underlies social capital theory in which families (and by extension, fathers) are seen as potential contributors of social and cultural as well as financial capital to children (Coleman, 1988). From a sociological perspective, fathers contribute to social capital both directly by socializing their children (Pleck, 2007) and indirectly by connecting their children to social networks and community opportunities, especially in adolescence and early adulthood (Amato, 1998). Sociology and social psychology concepts can also inform a broader understanding of fatherhood in relation to changing gender and parenting roles in society (Marsiglio, Hutchinson, & Cohan, 2004). Finally, the idea that men are part of multiple interacting systems means that research on fathering is likely to be informed by general systems theory (GST), which spans multiple disciplines and applies to functioning within any system of actors, objects, and settings (Lerner, Rothbaum, Boulos, & Castellino, 2002).

Future Directions

Understanding fathers' influences on children's development requires a dynamic and contextualized view of fathers within their families. The frame of parenting applied to mothering has been dominated by theories so focused on a rather narrow set of influences in early life that it has prevented a broader lens on parenting and parental influences, including that of fathers. Theoretical advances recognizing the dynamic process of parenting in families call for research designs that do not require static or linear conceptualizations of fathers' influences on children. Empirical findings about fathers in family contexts reveal what fathers bring to the parenting system, not only by being directly involved with their children but also by facilitating, buffering, or exacerbating parenting by mothers and negotiating a balance of work and cultural demands with the practical needs of their partners and children. Our approach to research needs to consider multiple methods, measures, reporters, and levels of context. Our results need to be applied to increasing positive opportunities for many kinds of fathers in a wide range of circumstances to contribute to their children's development.

References

Administration for Children and Families. (2002). *Making a difference in the lives of infants and toddlers and their families: The impacts of Early Head Start*. Washington, DC: US Department of Health and Human Services.

Adamsons, K., & Buehler, C. (2007). Mothering vs fathering vs parenting: Measurement equivalence in parenting measures. *Parenting: Science and Practice, 7*(3), 271–303.

Adamsons, K., O'Brien, M., & Pasley, K. (2007). An ecological approach to father involvement in biological and stepfather families. *Fathering, 5*(2), 129–147.

Aldous, J., Mulligan, G. M., & Bjarnason, T. (1998). Fathering over time: What makes the difference. *Journal of Marriage and the Family, 60,* 809–820.

Almeida, D. M., Maggs, J. L., & Galambos, N. L. (1993). Wives' employment hours and spousal participation in family work. *Journal of Family Psychology, 7,* 233–244.

Amato, P. R. (1998). More than money? Men's contribution to their children's lives. In A. Booth, & A.

C. Crouter (Eds.), *Men in families: When do they get involved? What difference does it make?* (pp. 241–278). Mahwah, NJ: Erlbaum.

Anderson, A., & Sabatelli, R. (1999). *Family interaction: A multigenerational developmental perspective.* Boston: Allyn and Bacon.

Belsky, J., & Jaffee, S. (2006). The multiple determinants of parenting. In D. Cichetti & D. Cohen (Eds.), *Developmental Psychopathology, 2nd Ed., Vol. 3: Risk, disorder and adaptation* (pp. 38–85). New York: Wiley.

Berger, L. M., Carlson, M. J., Bzostek, S. H., & Osborne, C. (2008). Parenting practices of resident fathers: The role of marital and biological ties. *Journal of Marriage and the Family, 70,* 625–639.

Bianchi, S. M. (2000). Maternal employment and time with children: Dramatic change or surprising continuity? *Demography, 37*(4), 401–414.

Bonney, J. F., Kelley, M. L., & Levant, R .F. (1999). A model of fathers' behavioral involvement in dual-earner families. *Journal of Family Psychology, 13,* 401–415.

Bornstein, M. H. (1995). Form and function: Implications for studies of culture and human development. *Culture and Psychology, 1,* 123–137.

Bowes, J. M., Chen, M., San, L., & Yuan, L. (2004). Reasoning and negotiation about child responsibility in urban Chinese families: Reports from mothers, fathers, and children. *International Journal of Behavioral Development, 28*(1), 48–58.

Bozett, F. W. (1989). Gay fathers: A review. *Journal of Homosexuality, 18*(1–2), 137–162.

Brayfield, A. (1995). Juggling jobs and kids: The impact of employment schedules on fathers' caring for children. *Journal of Marriage and the Family, 57,* 321–332.

Bronfenbrenner, U. (1986). Ecology of the family as a context for human development: Research perspectives. *Developmental Psychology, 22,* 723–742.

Brown, G. L., Mangelsdorf, S. C., Neff, C., Schoppe-Sullivan, S. J., & Frosch, C. A. (2009). Young children's self-concepts: Associations with child temperament, mothers' and fathers' parenting, and triadic family interaction. *Merrill-Palmer Quarterly: Journal of Developmental Psychology, 55*(2), 184–216.

Bütz, M. R., Chamberlain, L., & McCown, W. G. (1997). *Strange attractors: Chaos, complexity and the art of family therapy.* New York: Wiley.

Bzostek, S. H. (2008). Social fathers and child well-being. *Journal of Marriage and Family, 70*(4), 950–961.

Cabrera, N., Fagan, J., & Farrie, D. (2008). Explaining the long reach of fathers' prenatal involvement on later paternal engagement. *Journal of Marriage and Family, 70*(5), 1094–1107.

Cabrera, N., Fitzgerald, H., Bradley, R., & Roggman, L. (2007). Modeling the dynamics of paternal influences on children over the life course. *Applied Developmental Science, 11*(4), 185–190.

Cabrera, N. J., & Peters, H. E. (2000). Public policies and father involvement. *Marriage and Family Review, 29-4,* 295–314.

Cabrera, N. J., Ryan, R., Mitchell, S. J., Shannon, J., & Tamis-LeMonda, C. S. (2008). Low-income, non-resident father involvement: Variation by fathers' race and ethnicity. *Journal of Family Psychology, 22,* 643–647.

Cabrera N., Shannon, J., & La Taillade, J. (2009). Predictors of coparenting in Mexican American families and links to parenting and child social emotional development. *Journal of Infant Mental Health, 30*(5), 523–548.

Cabrera, N. J., Shannon, J. D., & Tamis-LeMonda, C. (2007). Fathers' influence on their children's cognitive and emotional development: From toddlers to pre-K. *Applied Developmental Science, 11*(4), 208–213.

Cabrera, N., Shannon, J. D., West, J., & Brooks-Gunn, J. (2006). Parental interactions with Latino infants: Variation by country of origin and English proficiency. *Child Development, 74,* 1190–1207.

Cabrera, N. J., Tamis-LeMonda, C. S., Bradley, R. H., Hofferth, S., & Lamb, M. E. (2000). Fatherhood in the twenty-first century. *Child Development, 71*(1), 127–136.

Capaldi, D., Pears, K., Kerr, D., & Owen, L. (2008). Intergenerational and partner influences on fathers' negative discipline. *Journal of Abnormal Child Psychology, 36,* 347–358.

Carlson, M., McLanahan, S. S., & Brooks-Gunn, J. (2008). Co-parenting and nonresident father involvement with young children after a non-marital birth. *Demography, 45*(2), 461–488.

Casper, L. M., & O'Connell, M. (1998). Work, income, the economy, and married fathers as child care providers. *Demography, 35*(2), 243–250.

Clarkberg, M., Stolzenberg, R. M., & Waite, L. J. (1995). Attitudes, values, and entrance into cohabitational versus marital unions. *Social Forces, 74,* 609–634.

Coley, R. L. (2001). (In)visible men: Emerging research on low-income, unmarried, and minority fathers. *American Psychologist, 56,* 743–753.

Coley, R., & Schindler, H. S. (2008). Biological fathers' contributions to maternal and family functioning. *Parenting: Science and Practice, 8*(4), 294–318.

Coleman, J. S. (1988). Social capital in the creation of human capital. *American Journal of Sociology, 94,* 95–120.

Coltrane, S., Parke, R. D., & Adams, M. (2004). Complexity of father involvement in low-income Mexican-American families. *Family Relations, 53,* 179–189.

de Mendonça, J., Cossette, L., Strayer, F. F., & Gravel, F. (2011). Mother-child and father-child interactional synchrony in dyadic and triadic interactions. *Sex Roles, 64*(1–2), 132–142.

Fagan J., & Barnett M. (2003). The relationship between maternal gatekeeping, paternal competence, mothers' attitudes about the father role, and father involvement. *Journal of Family Issues, 24*(8), 1020–1043.

Finley, G. E., & Schwartz, S. J. (2006). Parsons and Bales revisited: Young adults characterization of the fathering role. *Psychology of Men and Masculinity, 7,* 42–55.

Fitzgerald, H. E., Zucker, R. A., & Yang, H. (1995). Developmental systems theory and alcoholism: Analyzing patterns of variation in high-risk families. *Psychology of Addictive Behaviors, 9*(1), 8–22.

Fletcher, R. (2009). Promoting infant well-being in the context of maternal depression by supporting the father. *Infant Mental Health Journal, 30*(1), 95–102.

Foster, E. M., & Kalil, A. (2007). Living arrangements and children's development in low-income white, black, and Latino families. *Child Development, 78,* 1657–1674.

Franck, K. L, & Buehler, C. (2007). A family process model of marital hostility, parental depressive affect, and adolescent problem behavior: The roles of triangulation and parental warmth. *Journal of Family Psychology, 21,* 614–625.

Freeman, H., Newland, L., & Coyl, D. (2008). Father beliefs as a mediator between contextual barriers and father involvement. *Early Child Development and Care, 178*(7-8), 803–819.

Geary, D. C. (2000). Evolution and the proximate expression of human paternal investment. *Psychological Bulletin, 126,* 33–77.

Goldscheider, F. K., & Goldscheider, C. (1994). Leaving and returning home in the twentieth century. *Population Bulletin, 48*(4), 2–35.

Grossmann, K., Grossmann, K. E., Fremmer-Bombik, E., Kindler, H., Scheuerer-Englisch, H., & Zimmermann, P. (2002). The uniqueness of the child-father attachment relationship: Fathers' sensitive and challenging play as a pivotal variable in a 16-year longitudinal study. *Social Development, 11*(3), 307–331.

Harris, K., Furstenberg, F., & Marmer, J. (1998). Paternal involvement with adolescents in intact families: The influence of fathers over the life course. *Demography, 35*(2), 201–216.

Hastings, P. D., Sullivan, C., McShane, K. E., Coplan, R. J., Utendale, W. T., & Vyncke, J. D. (2008). Parental socialization, vagal regulation, and preschoolers' anxious difficulties: Direct mothers and moderated fathers. *Child Development, 79*(1), 45–64.

Hofferth, S. L., Pleck, J., Stueve, J. F., Bianchi, S., & Sayer, L. (2002). The demography of fathers: What fathers do. In C. Tamis-LeMonda & N. Cabrera (Eds.), *Handbook of father involvement* (pp. 63–90). Mahwah, NJ: Erlbaum.

Holmes, E. K., & Huston, A. C. (2010). Understanding positive father-child interaction: Children's, father's, and mother's contributions. *Fathering, 8*(2), 203–225.

Hossain, Z., Roopnarine, J. L., Ismail, R., Hashmi, S. I., & Sombuling, A. (2007). Fathers' and mothers' reports of involvement in caring for infants in Kadazan families in Sabah, Malaysia. *Fathering, 5*(1), 58–72.

Jia, R., & Schoppe-Sullivan, S. L. (2011). Relations between co-parenting and father involvement in families with preschool-age children. *Developmental Psychology, 47*(1), 106–118.

Kerr, D. C. R., Capaldi, D. M., Pears, K., & Owen, L. (2009). A prospective three generational study of fathers' strong parenting: Influences from family of origin, adolescent adjustment, and offspring temperament. *Developmental Psychology, 45*(5), 1257–1275.

Klimes-Dougan, B., Long, J., Lee, C., Ronsaville, D., Gold, P., & Martinez, P. (2010). Continuity and cascade in offspring of bipolar parents: A longitudinal study of externalizing, internalizing, and thought problems. *Development and Psychopathology, 22*(1), 849–866.

Kochanska, G., Aksan, N., Prisco, T. R., & Adams, E. E. (2008). Mother-child and father-child mutually responsive orientation in the first 2 years and children's outcomes at preschool age: Mechanisms of influence. *Child Development, 79*(1), 30–44.

Kosterman, R., Haggerty, K., Spoth, R., & Redmond, C. (2004). Unique influence of mothers and fathers on their children's antisocial behavior. *Journal of Marriage and Family, 66*(3), 762–778.

LaBounty, J., Wellman, H. M., Olson, S., Lagattuta, K., & Liu, D. (2008). Mothers' and fathers' use of internal state talk with their young children. *Social Development, 17*(4), 757–775.

Lamb, M. E., Pleck, J. H., Charnov, E. L., & Levine, J. A. (1985). Paternal behavior in humans. *American Zoologist, 25*, 883–894.

Le, H-N., Cembalo, R., Chao, R., Hill, N. E., Murray, V. M., & Pinderhughes, E. E. (2008). Excavating culture: Disentangling ethnic differences from cultural influences on parenting. *Applied Developmental Science, 12*, 163–175.

Lee, M., Vernon-Feagans, L., Vazquez, A., & Kolak, A. (2003). The influence of family environment and child temperament on work/family role strain for mothers and fathers. *Infant and Child Development, 12*(5), 421–439.

Lerner, R. M., Rothbaum, F., Boulos, S., & Castellino, D. (2002). Developmental systems perspective on parenting. In M. H. Bornstein (Ed.), *Handbook on parenting, vol. 2* (pp. 315–344). Mahwah, NJ: Erlbaum.

Lewis, M. (1997). *Altering fate.* New York: Guilford.

Livingstone, S. (2002). *Young people and new media.* London: Sage.

Madden-Derdich, D. A., Leonard, S. A., & Christopher, F. S. (1999). Boundary ambiguity and co-parental conflict after divorce: A family systems model of the divorce process. *Journal of Marriage and the Family, 61*, 588–598.

Manlove, E. E., & Vernon-Feagans, L. (2002). Caring for infant daughters and sons in dual-earner households: Maternal reports of father involvement in weekday time and tasks. *Infant and Child Development, 11*(4), 305–320.

Marchand, J. F., & Hock, E. (2003). Mothers' and father's depressive symptoms and conflict-resolution strategies in the marriage and children's externalizing and internalizing behaviors. *Journal of Genetic Psychology, 164*(2), 227–239.

Marsiglio, W., Hutchinson, S, & Cohan, M. (2004). Envisioning fatherhood: A social psychological perspective on young men without kids. *Family Relations, 49*, 133–142.

Martin, A., Ryan, R. M., & Brooks-Gunn, J. (2007). The joint influence of mother and father parenting on child cognitive outcomes at age 5. *Early Childhood Research Quarterly, 22*(1), 423–439.

McBride, B., Brown, G., Bost, K., Shin, N., Vaughn, B., & Korth, B. (2005). Paternal identity, maternal gatekeeping, and father involvement. *Family Relations, 54*(3), 360–372.

McElwain, N. L., Halberstadt, A. G., & Volling, B. L. (2007). Mother- and father-reported reactions to children's negative emotions: Relations to young children's emotional understanding and friendship quality. *Child Development, 78*(5), 1407–1425.

McLanahan, S. (2004). Diverging destinies: How children are faring under the second demographic transition. *Demography, 41* (4), 607–627.

Messineo, M. (2005). Influence of expectations for parental support on intergenerational coresidence behavior. *Journal of Intergenerational Relationships, 3*(3), 47–64.

Mezulis, A. H., Hyde, J., & Clark, R. (2004). Father involvement moderates the effect of maternal depression during a child's infancy on child behavior problems in kindergarten. *Journal of Family Psychology, 18*(4), 575–588.

Molenaar, P. M., & Campbell, C. G. (2009). The new person-specific paradigm in psychology. *Current Directions in Psychological Science, 18*(2), 112–117.

Mollborn, S., & Lovegrove, P. J. (2011). How teenage fathers matter for children: Evidence from the ECLS-B. *Journal of Family Issues, 32*(1), 3–30.

National Institute of Child Health and Human Development Early Child Care Research Network. (2004). Fathers' and mothers' parenting behavior and beliefs as predictors of children's social adjustment in the transition to school. *Journal of Family Psychology, 18,* 628–638.

Palkovitz, R. (2007). Challenges to modeling dynamics in developing and developmental understanding of father-child relationships. *Applied Developmental Science, 11,* 190–195.

Pancsofar, N., Vernon-Feagans, L., & The Family Life Project Investigators. (2010). Fathers' early contributions to children's language development in families from low-income rural communities. *Early Childhood Research Quarterly, 25,* 450–463.

Papp, L. M., Goeke-Morey, M. C., & Cummings, E. (2004). Mothers' and fathers' psychological symptoms and marital functioning: Examination of direct and interactive links with child adjustment. *Journal of Child and Family Studies, 13*(4), 469–482.

Paquette, D. (2004). Theorizing the father–child relationship: Mechanisms and developmental outcomes. *Human Development, 47,* 193–219.

Parke, R. D. (2004). Fathers, families, and the future: A plethora of plausible predictions. *Merrill-Palmer Quarterly, 50,* 456–470.

Pedersen, F. A., Suwalsky, J. T. D., Cain, R. L., Zaslow, M. J., & Rabinovich, B. A. (1987). Paternal care of infants during maternal separations: Associations with father-infant interaction at one year. *Psychiatry, 50,* 193–205.

Pemberton, C. K., Neiderhiser, J. M., Leve, L. D., Natsuaki, M. N., Shaw, D. S., Reiss, D., et al. (2010). Influence of parental depressive symptoms on adopted toddler behaviors: An emerging developmental cascade of genetic and environmental effects. *Development and Psychopathology, 22*(1), 803–818.

Pleck, J. H. (2007). Why could father involvement benefit children? Theoretical perspectives. *Applied Development Science, 11*(4), 196–202.

Pleck, J. H., & Hofferth, S. L. (2008). Mother involvement as an influence on father involvement with early adolescents. *Fathering, 6*(3), 267–286.

Punamäki, R., Wallenius, M., Hölttö, H., Nygård, C., & Rimpelä, A. (2009). The associations between information and communication technology (ICT) and peer and parent relations in early adolescence. *International Journal of Behavioral Development, 33*(6), 556–564.

Ransford, C. R., Crouter, A. C., & McHale, S. M. (2008). Implications of work pressure and supervisor support for fathers', mothers' and adolescents' relationships and well-being in dual-earner families. *Community, Work & Family, 11*(1), 37–60.

Richmond, M. K., & Stocker, C. M. (2006). Associations between family cohesion and adolescent externalizing behavior. *Journal of Family Psychology, 20,* 663–669.

Rogoff, B. (2003). *The cultural nature of human development.* New York: Oxford.

Rosser, S. B., & Miller, P. H. (2003). Viewing developmental psychology through the lenses of feminist theories. *Annuario de Psicologica, 34*(2), 291–303.

Rowe, M. L., Coker, D., & Pan, B. (2004). A comparison of fathers' and mothers' talk to toddlers in low-income families. *Social Development, 13*(2), 278–291.

Ryan, R. M., Martin, A., & Brooks-Gunn, J. (2006). Is one good parent good enough? Patterns of mother and father parenting and child cognitive outcomes at 24 and 36 months. *Parenting: Science and Practice, 6*(2–3), 211–228.

Sano, Y., Richards, L. N., & Zvonkovic, A. M. (2008). Are mothers really "gatekeepers" of children? Rural mothers' perceptions of nonresident fathers' involvement in low-income families. *Journal of Family Issues, 29*(12), 1701–1723.

Schoppe-Sullivan, S. J., Brown, G. L., Cannon, E. A., Mangelsdorf, S. C., & Sokolowski, M. (2008). Maternal gatekeeping, co-parenting quality, and fathering behavior in families with infants. *Journal of Family Psychology, 22*(3), 389–398.

Shannon, J. D., Tamis-LeMonda, C. S., London, K., & Cabrera, N. (2002). Beyond rough and tumble: Low-income fathers' interactions and children's cognitive development at 24 months. *Parenting: Science and Practice, 2*, 77–104.

Smetana, J. G., Abernethy, A., & Harris, A. (2000). Adolescent–parent interactions in middle-class African American families: Longitudinal change and contextual variations. *Journal of Family Psychology, 14*(3), 458–474.

Summers, J. A., Raikes, H., Butler, J., Spicer, P., Pan, B., Shaw, S., et al. (1999). Low-income fathers' and mothers' perceptions of the father role: A qualitative study in four Early Head Start communities. *Infant Mental Health Journal, 20*(3), 1097–0355.

Super, C. M., & Harkness, S. (2002). Culture structures the environment for development. *Human Development, 45*, 270–274.

Sweeney, M. M. (2007). Stepfather families and the emotional well-being of adolescents. *Journal of Health and Social Behavior, 48*, 33–49.

Tamis-LeMonda, C. S., Baumwell, L., & Cristofaro, T. (in press). Parent-child conversations during play. *First Language.*

Tamis-LeMonda, C. S., Shannon, J. D., Cabrera, N. J., & Lamb, M. E. (2004). Fathers and mothers at play with their 2- and 3-year-olds: Contributions to language and cognitive development. *Child Development, 75*(6), 1806–1820.

US Census Bureau. (1990). Who's minding the kids? Child care arrangements: Winter 1986–87. *Current Population Reports, Series P-70, 20.* Washington, DC.

US Census Bureau. (2004). Retrieved from http://www.census.gov/population/www/pop-profile/files/dynamic/Fertility.pdf

US Census Bureau. (2006). Who's minding the kids? Child care arrangements: Summer 2006. Retrieved from http://www.census.gov/population/www/socdemo/child/tables-2006.html

US Census Bureau. (2010). Retrieved from http://www.census.gov/population/www/socdemo/hh-fam/cps2010.html

US Department of Labor. (2011). Women in the labor force, 2010. Retrieved May 1, 2011, from http://www.dol.gov/wb/factsheets/Qf-laborforce-10.htm

Vogel, C. A., Bradley, R. H., Raikes, H. H., Boller, K., & Shears, J. K. (2006). Relation between father connectedness and child outcomes. *Parenting: Science and Practice, 6*, 189–209.

Weisner, T. S. (2002). Ecocultural understandings of children's developmental pathways. *Human Development, 45*, 275–281.

Chapter 12

Coparenting and Children's Well-being

Rob Palkovitz

University of Delaware

Jay Fagan

Temple University

James Hull

University of Delaware

Historical Overview and Theoretical Perspectives

The importance of coparenting as a construct has risen in the context of a rapidly changing landscape in American families and increased awareness among researchers and policy makers concerning the influence that fathers have on children's development. In the last two decades, rapid changes in typical patterns of partnering and re-partnering have led to increased diversity in family form and functioning. Current family trajectories are characterized by changes in cohabitation, marriage and fertility patterns with a concordantly increasing prevalence of serial relationships, multi-partner fertility, step-families, and complex and fluid family structures. Decreases in the proportion of stable nuclear families has brought greater awareness of the importance of building and maintaining positive coparenting relationships across changing family configurations, living arrangements, and time. The rising importance of coparenting is directly related to the increasing likelihood that children are raised in households without the presence of the biological father. Researchers have suggested that healthy coparenting relationships among the parental figures in a child's life may be even more important for these families than for families in residential relationships because of the numerous barriers nonresidential fathers face in establishing an active role in their child's life (Futris & Schoppe-Sullivan, 2007). Fathers in nonresidential relationships, particularly never-married fathers, are more likely to experience poverty, unemployment, lack of education, legal problems, substance abuse, and low psychological well-being (Quinlivan & Condon, 2005). Fathers and their partners may perceive these barriers as costly impediments to staying involved with their children (Futris & Schoppe-Sullivan, 2007). Establishing a supportive coparenting relationship may be one of the few ways in which fathers in nonresidential relationships can offset the negative effects of these barriers and manage to stay positively and actively involved in their child's life.

Research has documented that positive coparenting relationships enhance parent-child relationships above and beyond other aspects of partner relationships (Morrill, Hines, Mahmood & Cordova, 2010). This chapter will review definitions, conceptualizations, and research issues related to the study of coparental relationships as they influence fathers' involvement with children over time, and children's well-being.

Defining of the Construct of Coparenting

Co-parenting can be simply defined as "the ways that parents work together in their roles as parents" (Feinberg, 2003, p. 1499). Bonach (2005) and Ahrons (1981) elaborate the construct by noting that a quality coparenting relationship can be conceived of as an ongoing, interactive, cooperative, and mutually supportive relationship that is primarily focused on raising children, with both parents actively engaged in the lives of their children and childrearing. Coparenting can be contrasted with "parallel parenting" or "individual parenting" where mothers and fathers are viewed to maintain a separate, individual and distinct relationship with the child (e.g., traditional main-effects views of fathers' direct involvement with the child and mothers' direct involvement with the child in the absence of consideration of indirect, mediating, and/ or moderating family systems interactions between parents).

As the prevalence of multi-partner fertility increases, co-parental relationships have become more difficult to conceptualize and assess. This realization goes beyond the limited resources of most studies, but holds significant implications for the daily functioning of contemporary families. Current patterns of partnering and re-partnering often leads to complex family forms where a biological parent and a step parent co-reside and both (directly or indirectly) engage in negotiating coparental relationships with nonresidential biological parents, grandparents, and parental figures who have played significant roles in a focal child's life over time. Thus, emerging understandings of coparenting need to be inclusive when considering how parents work together in their roles as parents, extending beyond a focus on biological parents to inclusion of extended family members.

Coparenting is influenced by multiple contextual variables such as coresidence, relational closeness, communication effectiveness, and a range of individual parent and individual child variables such as gender and relational style. For parents living apart, coparenting may represent the principal—or sole—recurring interaction they have with one another as they attempt to coordinate their parental interests and efforts across households (Margolin, Gordis, & John, 2001). Both quantitative and qualitative investigations of nonresident father-child relationships have documented that they are fragile over time, particularly if the father briefly or never lived with the child (Furstenberg & Harris, 1993).

While researchers tend to agree on the general definition of coparenting (Van Egeren & Hawkins, 2004), there is considerable disagreement about the number of components of this construct as well as the ways that different facets interact with one another. For example, some definitions of coparenting include differences and similarities in childrearing philosophies (Van Egeren, 2004) while others do not (Waller, 2009). Several researchers have referred to broad-based domains of coparenting such as harmonious coparenting, hostile-competitive coparenting, and coparenting discrepancy (Van Egeren, 2004), while others have focused on narrower aspects of coparenting such as the parenting alliance (McBride & Rane, 1998). The following components are present in many definitions of coparenting: coparenting support (Feinberg, 2002; Van Egeren & Hawkins, 2004), maintaining an ongoing communication with one another around the needs of the child (Feinberg, 2002; McBride & Rane, 1998), shared parenting (Feinberg, 2002), and coparenting solidarity (McBride & Rane, 1998; Van Egeren & Hawkins, 2004).

Coparenting support is defined as "strategies and actions that support and extend the partner's efforts to accomplish parenting goals" (Van Egeren & Hawkins, 2004, p. 169). For example, parents may support their partner while playing with the child by answering the telephone so that the parent engaged with the child does not need to interrupt his/her interaction with the child.

Communication between parents about the child or child-related matters may be positive (e.g., encouragement) or disruptive, as when parents undermine each other's parenting behavior or compete with each other in an effort to "outdo" each other in their efforts to work successfully with the child (Schoppe-Sullivan, Mangelsdorf, Brown, & Sokolowski, 2007; Van Egeren & Hawkins, 2004). Westerman and Massoff (2001) suggest that undermining can be either overt (e.g., such as name calling) or covert (e.g., interrupting one's partner). Qualitative studies of young nonresidential fathers reveal high levels of undermining between new parents, particularly when fathers fall behind in financial support of children (Young & Holcomb, 2007).

Shared parenting refers to fathers' and mothers' division of labor in relation to childcare and childrearing (Feinberg, 2002; McHale, 2009). The domains of parenting typically assessed in this area are participation in caregiving tasks, playing with children and supporting their learning/development, assuming responsibility for children's well-being, and providing care to the child while the other parent works, corresponding to Lamb, Pleck, Charnov, and Levine's (1987) engagement and responsibility constructs. Shared labor on behalf of children begins before the birth of the child, as when parents collaboratively obtain furniture and clothing for the newborn, coordinate plans for caring for the child while their partner works or goes to school, take actions to ensure the baby's health during the prenatal period, and learn how to care for an infant.

Coparenting solidarity has also been referred to as supportive alliances between coparenting partners (McHale, 2009). Cohen and Weissman (1984) defined a parenting alliance as the capacity of partners to "acknowledge, respect, and value the parenting roles and tasks of the partner" (p. 35). There has also been agreement in the literature that coparenting is a dyadic process characterized by bidirectional influences (Van Egeren & Hawkins, 2004). McHale (2009) has suggested that couples establish dyadic patterns of support, coordination, opposition, and detachment as early as three months following the baby's birth, and these patterns remain fairly stable over time. Recently, researchers have also argued for understanding coparenting as part of both dyadic and triadic relationships between parents and children (McHale, 2009).

The Rising Importance of the Coparenting Construct

A six-fold increase in the rates of nonmarital childbearing across the last half of the past century (Ventura & Bachrach, 2000) has been associated with large numbers of fathers who coparent but live away from their children (Amato, 2005). Currently, 37% of all births in the United States are to unmarried parents, with higher proportions occurring among racial and ethnic minorities (Martin et al., 2006). Given that nonmarital childbearing has become an increasingly likely life experience for couples, there is a greater need to analyze factors that are related to coparenting in such relationships (Bronte-Tinkew, Horowitz, & Carrano, 2010). While many parents are cohabiting at the time of their child's conception, about half of these parents will be living apart by their child's third birthday (Osborne & McLanahan, 2007). Census data indicate that the proportion of children living in single parent families increased from 15% in

1970 to 32% in 1996, with 57% of Black and 32% of Hispanic children living in single-parent families (U.S. Census, 1996). These trends, along with the growing evidence of the developmentally facilitative benefit of fathers' positive involvement in children's lives (Cabrera, Tamis-LeMonda, Bradley, Hofferth, & Lamb, 2000; Lamb, 2010), have directed researchers' and policy makers' attention to the factors that promote fathers' positive involvement with children after the romantic relationship between parents has ended. For example, Carlson, McLanahan, and Brooks-Gunn (2008) reported that positive coparenting robustly predicted nonresident fathers' engagement with children over time, whereas fathers' involvement is a significant (but comparatively weak) predictor of coparenting. Coparenting may have a stronger influence on parent-child relationships than partner relationship quality because it is more proximally related to parenting (McHale, 2009).

Theoretical Perspectives

Family systems theory is a particularly appropriate approach to understanding coparental relationships (see, e.g., Bronte-Tinkew et al., 2010; Cox, Paley, & Harter, 2001) and their effects on father involvement and child well-being. Family systems theory stresses the notion of interdependence, i.e., that the family is comprised of subsystems that exert influence on one another. This understanding necessitates interdependent considerations of the mother-father, mother-child, father-child, and sibling dyads as they exert direct and indirect influence on one another (with consequences for coparenting). A further foundational premise of family systems theory is the notion that the family has a developmental trajectory as well. This tenet holds the implication that changes in the family over time will be associated with differences in coparental functioning and associated outcomes (Bronte-Tinkew et al., 2010). For example, family development means that coparenting for an infant is related to, yet distinct from, coparental interactions in relation to the same child when he/she is school-aged. Family systems theory can also provide important perspective on changes in coparental relationships as family constellations change over time (e.g., repartnering).

Another important theoretical approach to coparental relationships is afforded by the *parenting stress framework* (Abidin, 1992). This approach conceives that the experiential stress of a parent is the cumulative effect of individual parent characteristics, couple characteristics, child characteristics, and contextual or situational factors that are directly connected to the enactment of parental roles (Bronte-Tinkew et al., 2010). Accumulations of parental stress are posited to be inversely related to functional parenting. Positive coparental relationships may be considered to be a resilience factor or a positive coping mechanism from a parenting stress framework.

Belsky's (1984) *family process model* would suggest that convergent roles and contexts (e.g., work stress, relational disharmony, and parenting stress) are interdependent and that functioning in one realm has spillover (for better or for worse) into other realms of functioning. The implications are that positive coparenting may alleviate experiential pressures in other realms, while conversely, stressful conditions in other realms may challenge positive coparental relationships.

Gender theory would highlight the importance of accounting for differences in coparenting that may manifest in perceptions of internal versus external factors in coupling/decoupling and mother's and father's satisfaction after decoupling. For example, Bonasch, Sales, & Koeske (2005) argue that in comparison to men, on average, women make greater investments in direct childcare and relational components of family relationships. Therefore, women may experience greater feelings of loss, pain, and grief when the partner relationship ends. If this is the case, the higher engagement in negative affective judgment by women after uncoupling has important implications for coparenting because disproportionately high percentages of mothers have physical custody of the children. Similar to Bernard's (1972) classic distinctions between "his and her" marriages, fathers and mothers are likely to have contrasting views of coparental relationships.

Feinberg (2003) has articulated a multi-domain *ecological model of coparenting*. His model summarizes four interacting components of coparenting (joint family management, support/undermining, division of labor, and childrearing agreement) as well as influences on coparental relationships (e.g., environmental support and stress, individual parental characteristics). Sensitizing constructs of family systems theory, parenting stress theory, family process models, and gender theory have informed the emergence of Feinberg's model (2002) and empirical investigations that have resulted.

Current Research Questions

For the purposes of this chapter, we will focus attention on research questions articulating relationships between coparental relationships and issues directly related to father involvement in children's lives. Recent empirical investigations of coparenting and father involvement in childrearing have focused on five primary areas:

1. effects of coparental relationship quality on father involvement in childrearing;
2. effects of coparenting on children's well-being and developmental outcomes;
3. maternal and paternal differences in the perceptions and coparenting experiences;
4. effectiveness of coparenting interventions aimed at improving quality of parental interactions and positive father involvement; and
5. positive coparenting between residentially discordant former partners.

Following a brief focus on measurement and methodology issues, we will review empirical findings as they relate to these five areas of enquiry on coparenting and father involvement.

Research Measurement and Methodology

Conceptualization

While there is generalized agreement about the nature and importance of coparenting in facilitating positive father involvement in children's lives, scholars vary in more nuanced approaches to defining, conceptualizing, operationalizing and analyzing components of coparental relationships in relation to family well-being and outcomes. Any considerations of coparenting effects on father involvement are grounded in varying conceptualizations of father involvement as well as in different levels of application of family systems, parenting stress, and gendered family process approaches to studying human development and family studies. As scholars engage in expanding the empirical base, greater differentiation of constructs and integration of contextual sensitivity will advance conceptual development in regard to coparenting and father involvement in child development. In many of the existing large-scale studies, especially those that are longitudinal, measures of father involvement and coparental relationships consist of a thin set of narrowly measured behavioral data.

Units of Analysis

The dynamic family system, by necessity, forms the unit of analysis in empirical work on coparenting. By definition, coparenting requires the presence of two parents (or parent figures) and at least one child interacting over time. While most research to date has focused on the effects of adult's relationships on coparental quality and associated patterns of father involvement, the field would benefit from employing multiple units of analysis, each in the context of family systems and processes over time. For example, the empirical literature is nearly silent in regard to the effects of coparental quality on maternal engagement with children, coparental influences on adult development in either parent, how sibling alliances influence coparental functioning, and cultural and intercultural variability in coparental relationships. As empirical investigations expand into these areas, theoretical synthesis across levels of analysis will provide a more elaborated understanding of the processes and meanings of various aspects of coparental relationships.

Temporality

Understanding that development takes time poses some unique challenges to empirically validating causal links between specific aspects of coparenting and later family states or traits. The availability of several large-scale longitudinal data sets has recently allowed researchers to conduct studies measuring various aspects of coparental characteristics and later contexts of parenting and child outcome measures. Longitudinal studies are better suited to disentangle the associations between coparenting and parenting with children because the temporal aspect of these variables can be addressed.

Sampling

There are multiple challenges in relation to sampling in coparenting research. How many informants should be tapped for each family unit, and what does a researcher do to reconcile differences in perspective across participants with differing social addresses? Can the perspectives of former spouses or partners be trusted to provide accurate estimates of involvement quality and quantity of others? Do custodial and non-custodial parents view coparenting similarly or differently, and does that vary by sex of parent and sex of child? How does one's experience and perception of engagement change when transitioning from co-residential biological father to non-residential biological father, to non-residential biological father where there is a step father in your former household and there is a new romantic interest in yours (with or without children)? Are there advantages to building samples and subsamples around target children, or is it more important to look at parental characteristics when designing sampling frames? When family constellations evolve and encompass more than two parental figures across different locations, how does one obtain access to participants, treat differences in data reported by different informants, and understand the effects of participants' emotions in estimating relational quality and involvement patterns? How do researchers obtain culturally diverse samples and create adequate subsamples of participants in numbers that allow meaningful analyses? Is there a clear understanding of coparental ideals across diverse ethnicities and family forms? How do researchers categorize participants in families representing more than one value on variables tapping ethnicity, custody status, or residential status?

Linking Coparenting to Child Well-being without Experimental Manipulation

For obvious ethical reasons, it is not possible to conduct true experimental research by randomly assigning families to different levels of coparental quality, family forms, or father involvement. As such, longitudinal studies establishing temporal precedence and covariation among variables have become important windows into probable causal links (Palkovitz, 2009) between coparenting and developmental outcome measures. Despite these notable challenges to quality empirical investigations, researchers have made significant progress in detailing findings related to the five primary areas of enquiry regarding coparenting and father involvement.

Empirical Findings

Effects of Coparental Relationship Quality on Father Involvement

Researchers have inquired whether the association between coparenting and father involvement is influenced by other aspects of the mother-father relationship. Schoppe-Sullivan, Brown, Cannon, Mangelsdorf, and Sokolowski (2008) examined the moderating effects of maternal gatekeeping and encouragement on the association between coparenting quality (defined as parenting alliance) and fathers' relative involvement and parenting competence with infants. The authors found that coparenting quality was significantly associated with fathers' involvement and competence only when mothers engaged in high levels of encouragement of father involvement. This study highlights the complexity of the association between coparenting and father involvement and the idea that coparenting quality and father involvement may be conditional on specific mother-father contexts. In support of this idea, Fagan and Palkovitz (2011) found a longitudinal association between coparenting support and paternal engagement with toddlers among parents in nonresidential-nonromantic relationships but not among parents in co-residential or nonresidential-romantic relationships. The importance of family type was also noted in Feinberg, Kan, and Hetherington's (2007) study of coparenting and adolescent offspring. These authors found that coparenting conflict was more strongly related to father's negativity toward adolescents among stepfathers compared with nondivorced fathers.

Researchers have further examined different aspects of the father-child relationship in relation to coparenting. The father-child attachment relationship has been one such area. Brown, Schoppe-Sullivan, Mangelsdorf, and Neff (2010) have suggested that the coparenting relationship directly shapes the child's internal working model of attachment relationships. That is, support and harmony between parents produces a sense of security in the child's relationship to the father. They have also suggested an indirect association between coparenting and parent-child attachment. Supportive coparenting relationships have a direct effect on parents' sensitivity and responsiveness to the child, which, in turn, correlates with secure child-parent attachment. The findings of their study revealed that supportive coparenting was associated with greater infant-father attachment security but not greater infant-mother attachment security, giving support to the hypothesized central importance of the association between positive coparenting and father-child attachment.

Another area of focus has been fathers' interactions with infants during triadic play. Observations of fathers and mothers playing together with their infants revealed that when mothers engaged in coparenting mutuality with their partners (defined as actively supporting the partner's interaction efforts with the child), fathers were significantly more likely to display positive affect, gaze at the child, and touch the child than fathers whose partners did not show coparenting mutuality (Gordon & Feldman, 2008). Fathers' coparental mutuality was not significantly related to mothers' behaviors toward the child. Additionally, fathers but not mothers who withdraw from coparenting discussions with their partners are also more likely to disengage during triadic play (Elliston, McHale, Talbot, Parmley, & Kuersten-Hogan, 2008). These findings suggest that fathers' triadic play interactions may be more sensitive than mothers' triadic play interactions to partners' coparenting support, again highlighting the nonsymmetrical importance of coparenting in facilitating men's and women's ongoing engagement with children.

Researchers have also examined the relationship between coparenting quality and fathers' caregiving involvement and nurturance. Futris and Schoppe-Sullivan (2007) found that adolescent mothers' perceptions of parenting alliance with their partners were significantly related to young fathers' engagement in nurturing activities with young children. Sobolewski and King (2005) also found a positive association between nonresident fathers' cooperative coparenting with the child's mother and responsive fathering. Interestingly, they found that the association between positive coparenting and responsive fathering resulted from nonresident fathers' increased contact with their children.

Coparenting conflict has been examined in relation to fathers' negativity toward adolescent offspring. In their study of co-residential couples, Feinberg and his associates (2007) found a longitudinal association between coparenting conflict and fathers' negativity toward adolescents. Moreover, coparenting conflict was found to predict more variance in fathers' negativity than did marital quality. This study was significant because it showed that coparenting among parents is also relevant to parenting adolescent offspring as well as the unique contributions of coparenting quality as a factor distinct form marital quality.

To summarize, the growing body of research on coparenting suggests that both the quantity and quality of fathers' involvement with children is associated with the quality of the coparenting relationship. Moreover, fathers' involvement with children appears to be more strongly associated with the quality of the coparenting relationship than is mothers' involvement with children.

Effects of Coparenting on Children's Well-being

Within the context of intergenerational relationships, coparenting has developmental implications for children's well-being. Generally speaking, research on the effects of coparenting on children has shown that children benefit most when coparenting is cooperative and supportive and are negatively affected when coparenting is conflicted (Carlson et al., 2008). These effects have been linked with multiple developmental periods including preschool, kindergarten, and adolescence (Feinberg, 2003). However, a majority of the empirical studies focusing on the effects of coparenting on child outcomes have been limited to early childhood, with little attention given to adolescence or early adulthood (Feinberg et al., 2007). Future research in these developmental eras would be beneficial given the growing number of young adults opting to remain living with their parents well into adulthood.

Fagan, Lee, Palkovitz, and Cabrera (2011) examined the effects of coparental relationships among stable nonresident parents on toddler development. They found that 24-month-old children in stable nonresident families have lower cognitive abilities and less positive social behavior than peers in co-resident families. While nonresidential families report higher levels of interparental conflict than residential families, conflict level did not mediate the associations between stable nonresidence and child outcomes. Children's compromised outcome scores were partly explained by the lower quality of mothers' supportive interactions with their children. These findings demonstrate that coparental relationship qualities may be secondary to parent-child relational characteristics and other contextual factors in influencing child outcomes.

Feinberg (2002) states the effects of parental distress during early developmental periods are reflected in preschool and elementary school. For example, academic performance has been linked to coparenting quality in preschool and school-aged children (McConnell & Kerig, 2002). Children's externalizing behavioral problems (Feinberg, 2003; Katz & Low, 2004) and internalizing problems, like self-blame, have also been linked to the exposure to coparental conflict during childhood (Feinberg, 2002). Children's ability to demonstrate emotional regulation during frustration-tolerance tasks has been correlated with coparenting processes (Katz & Low, 2004), perhaps because coparental conflict undermines parent's ability to both model and assist children in emotional regulation (Feinberg, 2003). Cooperative coparenting has benefits on children's well-being as well. An obvious benefit is a demonstrative social model for the child's future social encounters. Children gain valuable insight and information about relationships and conflict resolution (Katz & Low, 2004).

Maternal and Paternal Differences

Sex and gender interact in multiple ways to influence parents' perceptions of interactions with their children as well as their satisfaction with their partners' contributions to parenting (Palkovitz, 2009). While a rich empirical literature documents gender differences in parental perceptions and satisfactions, parallel detail is currently lacking in the coparenting literature. Ahrons (1981) found that men perceived greater degrees of interaction with ex-partners than women's perception of men's involvement. Differential gender role expectations may explain the discrepant perceptions. Ahrons states that men and women have "different yardsticks by which to measure relationships; thus their expectations differ" (1981, p. 425).

Because men and women may use different yardsticks for measuring their relationships, they are likely to have different expectations of, approaches to, and perceptions of coparenting when their relationships break up. Bonach (2007) reports that the perceived realities of coparenting between mothers and fathers may or may not coincide because of the fundamentally different perceptions each partner maintains to be true. Furstenberg and Harris (1993) have noted that custodial parents disproportionately assume the responsibility of childcare, with women more likely to have physical custody of children. Disproportional involvement leads to low satisfaction with former partners' level of involvement in childrearing tasks. Mothers credit fathers with little decision-making authority (responsibility) and convey that direct substantive conversations about the child rarely, if ever, take place (Furstenberg & Harris, 1993).

Intergenerational gender interactions between parents and children influence coparenting as well. For example, in a study of married parents, Lindsey, Caldera, and Colwell (2005) found that mothers of daughters displayed more intrusive coparenting behavior than mothers of sons; this relationship was not observed for fathers. In a separate study of married couples, fathers were more likely to engage in coparenting when their first child was male (Fish, New, & Van Cleave, 1992).

Effectiveness of Coparenting Interventions

The growing awareness of the effects of coparenting behavior on parenting behavior and child development has led to the implementation of coparenting intervention studies. These studies have examined the effects of coparenting interventions on couples' coparenting and parenting behavior and various child outcomes. One such program is Family Foundations, an eight-session coparenting curriculum delivered to couples before the child's birth in hospital settings (Feinberg, 2002). Findings from a randomized study revealed that fathers experienced less distress in the parent-child relationship and higher levels of coparental support of mothers at a 6-month post-test (Feinberg et al., 2009). One year after the child's birth parents in the coparenting intervention demonstrated significantly higher levels of warmth during partner interactions, fathers demonstrated greater positivity and lower negativity in interactions with children, and children showed higher levels of self-soothing compared with control group families (Feinberg et al., 2009).

Several coparenting intervention studies have targeted low-income families. Cowan, Cowan, Pruett, and Pruett (2007) conducted a randomized study using identical curricula for father-only and couple-only groups to determine the effects on father involvement with children and couple relationships. The curricula focused on dealing constructively with conflicts around couple and coparenting issues as well as coping with depression, family of origin issues, parenting behavior, and seeking extra-familial resources. Cowan et al. found that the couple intervention had a significantly stronger and longer term positive effect on fathers' engagement with children, couple relationship quality, and children's problem behaviors than did the father-only intervention, suggesting that programs which focus on the couple as a coparenting team may be more effective than programs that target fathers alone.

Several researchers have examined coparenting interventions for adolescent and young couples. Adolescent parents often have great difficulty establishing and maintaining positive coparenting partnerships. Romantic and co-residential relationships between adolescent parents frequently end within the first few years following the child's birth, and when this happens young fathers' and mothers' coparenting relationships often cease (Futris & Schoppe-Sullivan, 2007). Fagan (2008) suggested that these findings appear to have significant implications for intervention programs with adolescent parents.

Fagan (2008) conducted a randomized experimental study to test the effects of two interventions—coparenting intervention (experimental group) and childbirth/baby care intervention (comparison group)—on young fathers and adolescent mothers. The results of this study showed that fathers' participation in the five-session coparenting intervention was associated with improvements in coparenting between pretest and post-test as perceived by fathers, compared with fathers in the childbirth intervention and no intervention. At follow-up, Fagan also found that fathers in the coparenting intervention were more engaged with their three-month-olds than fathers in the comparison and control groups.

Coparenting interventions have also been developed for divorcing parents, although to the best of our knowledge they have not been rigorously evaluated for their effectiveness. The basis for coparenting interventions with divorcing couples is that former partners must continue to interact with each other on behalf of their children. Bonach (2007) developed a coparenting intervention that focused on forgiveness between former partners. The goal of this intervention approach is to move beyond hostilities to mutually supportive interactions as coparents.

To summarize, the small number of outcome studies of coparenting interventions seem to show promising results. Coparenting programs not only have positive effects on partners' coparenting relationships, but they also have positive effects on fathers' positive involvement with children. Moreover, coparenting prevention programs seem to have positive effects on middle and lower income families. The few studies that have included assessments of children also seem to show positive effects on children. Fagan (2008) has recommended that future studies should explore coparenting intervention approaches that result in longer-term effects on parents and children. There is also a need for additional studies that examine interventions that are effective with parents in at-risk families.

Positive Coparenting between Residentially Discordant Former Partners

Feinberg (2002) hypothesized that the effects of positive coparenting are generalizable across family structures. Most foundational empirical study has been conducted on intact families. Recently, researchers have begun to focus greater attention on the relationships between positive coparenting, paternal engagement and child well-being in varied family forms. A foundationally important empirical question has to do with the amount or degree of positive coparenting documented between residentially discordant former partners.

A relatively high degree of coparenting among custodial mothers and nonresident fathers of young children has been reported by participants in the Fragile Families and Child Wellbeing data set during the 5 years following a nonmarital birth (Carlson et al., 2008). Perhaps the more important question is whether it can be established that there is a causal relationship between coparenting and nonresident fathers' involvement, or whether the personality and relational styles of men who are able to effectively coordinate parenting with mothers are predisposed to remain involved with their children. Carlson and her colleagues (2008) report notable consistency about the association between coparenting and fathers' involvement using subsamples of families (based on race, incarceration history, having children with a previous partner, pattern of cohabitation, etc.) across the first five years of a target child's life. Consistent with Sobolewski and King (2005), Carlson et al. report few significant differences by subgroup in how coparenting is linked with fathers' involvement. The only strongly significant moderator of the association between coparenting and father involvement is the father's having children by a previous partner. They conclude that there is significant evidence that coparenting promotes *nonresidential* father-child contact when fathers have a child by a previous partner, but that it has a stronger effect when fathers do not have any children by other partners.

Bronte-Tinkew et al. (2010) also used the Fragile Families data set to longitudinally follow a sample of 522 never-married nonresident fathers to examine factors associated with fathers' coparenting 36 months after the birth of their child. Analyses documented that a wide range of contextual factors predicted never-married, nonresident fathers' perceived coparental supportiveness. Specifically, lower levels of coparental supportiveness were reported for fathers who had been incarcerated, had completed high school, had a greater number of children with the child's mother, in couples where the mother had lower educational attainment, the fathers did not maintain an ongoing relationship with the focal child's mother, when fathers had a new romantic partner, and if fathers saw their child more frequently. In contrast, more supportive coparental relationships were perceived among fathers of sons, fathers with higher incomes, and higher educational attainment, fathers who are employed, and fathers who provided informal support. Insabella, Williams, and Pruett (2003) found that never-married fathers reported more conflicted coparenting and lower levels of shared decision-making than divorced fathers.

Because of discrepancies in legal rights, never-married fathers face a greater range of barriers to ongoing engagement as they attempt to stay involved with their children. In never-married former couples, mothers have greater legal latitude to impede visitation, access to children, time spent together, and daily decision-making around parenting issues (Insabella et al., 2003). Consequently, for legal as well as structural and contextual reasons, unmarried, nonresident fathers are distinguished from co-resident and married fathers by lower observed levels of daily involvement with their children (Insabella et al., 2003).

Researchers have recently documented that there is considerable variability in levels of father involvement with children among nonresident fathers (Cabrera et al., 2000). As such, the significance of the coparenting relationship for fathers may also depend on the presence of a romantic relationship between mother and father. Romantic involvement is a critical variable linked to the degree to which nonresident parents are motivated and able to work together as parents. It implies greater emotional closeness than friend or acquaintance relationships, and a greater commitment to dyadic agreement than less close relationships. Reciprocity norms in romantic relationships require consideration of the other's perspectives and feelings to a greater degree than friendships or acquaintance relationships. Parents in romantic relationships may be more motivated to engage in supportive coparenting than parents in non-romantic relationships. However, romantic involvement also implies more frequent proximity between the father and mother and hence the father and child (Fagan, Palkovitz, Roy, & Farrie, 2009). Fathers who are not romantically involved with mothers face greater barriers to ongoing engagement as they attempt to stay involved with their child. In the absence of coparenting support, non-romantically involved fathers may have little chance to stay engaged with the child.

Further decrements in ongoing father involvement are associated with recoupling of either the mother or the father with a new partner, and even greater decrements are documented when subsequent relationships result in the birth of children with later partners (multi-partner fertility). It is well documented that nonresident fathers' involvement with a given child is affected by the presence of children from his other partnerships (Manning, Stewart, & Smock, 2003). Maintenance of positive coparenting relationships that can withstand the extreme stresses of repartnering and parenting with new partners, who may have vested interests in keeping previous partners at a distance (Marsiglio, 2004), represents considerable levels of challenge that must be navigated for a significant proportion of fathers.

A Glimpse into Race, Ethnicity, and Culture

While there is little empirical research that has effectively focused on the role of cultural diversity in understanding patterns of coparenting and father involvement, notable exceptions do exist. Cabrera et al. (2009) found that couple conflict in a sample of Mexican American families was the greatest predictor of coparental conflict, which, in turn, negatively affected mother-infant interaction and father engagement. Moreover, the effects of coparenting conflict on father caregiving varied by fathers' level of acculturation. Specifically, in comparison to less acculturated fathers, more acculturated fathers engaged in more caregiving among conflicted couples. However, coparental conflict was not predictive of infant social development.

Caldera, Fitzpatrick, and Wampler (2002) studied differences in mothers' and fathers' perceptions of coparenting in intact Mexican American Families. They reported on managing parental responsibilities and coparental strategies, concluding that resilience factors facilitate positive trajectories through parenting issues in flux. In a manner parallel to studies of coparenting in other ethnicities, they reported that joint decision-making, support, coordination, compensation, and cooperation provided family strengths for Mexican-American families coping with coparenting issues.

Bridges to Other Disciplines

Theoretical, empirical and applied perspectives, reviewed above, amply demonstrate that coparenting represents fertile ground for the development of new multidisciplinary scholarship and intervention work in multiple arenas. Disciplinary contributions from family studies, community psychology, clinical psychology, sociology, communication and public policy are evident in the theoretical and empirical perspectives reviewed above. Increased cross-disciplinary communication promises fruitful enhancements to theoretical, empirical, and applied consideration of coparental issues in father involvement. Specifically, training and program evaluation in marriage and family therapy and family life education and relationship skill building reciprocally contribute to furthering our understanding of coparenting as it influences father involvement and child well-being. The literature on coparenting also creates some potentially fruitful bridges to interdisciplinary teams involved in creating and evaluating community development and support programs aimed at enhancing partner communication and valuing of positive coparenting, particularly in communities with low marriage rates and high multi-partner fertility. Similarly, coparental components of parent education and support in the context of programs for incarcerated parents represent significant links to practitioners in corrections and rehabilitative services.

Policy Implications

The intention of joint custody following divorce is to provide the opportunity for both parents to remain actively involved in the lives of their children (Bonach, 2005), but it is the quality of parenting exhibited by both parents as well as the cooperative nature of their relationship that is critical (Garrity & Baris, 1994). Research findings from multiple samples and contexts focused on coparenting suggest that more than half of divorced spouses experience continuing anger and conflict with their former partners according to Garrity and Baris. The importance of studying and supporting ongoing positive coparental interaction between former partners is heightened because some form of shared parenting is typically mandated by the courts. Growing awareness of the deleterious effects of post-divorce inter-parental conflict coupled with the trend towards joint custody necessitates broader initiation and implementation of divorce education programs with a focus on the importance of positive coparenting.

Healthy marriage initiatives funded under the Deficit Reduction Act of 2005 (U.S. Public Law 109-171; 120 Stat. 4 [2006]) had an explicit goal to increase the percentage of children who are raised by two parents in a healthy marriage. It has become abundantly clear that programs should address coparenting relationship issues in addition to partner relationship issues. However, further research is also needed to determine the extent to which such programs are effective with participants (Fagan, 2008).

Future Directions

The bulk of prior research on coparenting has centered on two-parent co-residential families or on divorced couples and has used small or non-representative samples of White middle-class families (Arendell, 1996; Van Egeren, 2004). In order to be pertinent to contemporary family constellations, coparenting research needs to intensify focus on factors influencing the functioning of coparental relationships beyond biological coparents. Because of the prevalence of children living in recombined families, it would be particularly beneficial to identify which coparental relationships are most important to support, and whether intervention strategies forged in the context of biological parents are effective in more diverse coparental contexts. Though earlier work has established that fathers' beliefs, values, and behaviors influence family interactions and overall functioning (Arditti & Kelly, 1994), research on coparenting from the perspective of fathers is sparse in the coparenting literature (Insabella et al., 2003). Because of the prevalence of issues associated with poor levels of coparenting, the majority of research findings address the negative aspects of coparenting (Caldera et al., 2002; Katz & Low, 2004; Margolin et al., 2001), while tending to neglect the processes and meanings of positive, health-promoting, well-functioning coparental relationships (McHale, 2009). Perhaps due to the inequalities of physical custody skewed toward mother-child dyads in the absence of co-resident fathers, the empirical literature almost exclusively addresses the effects of coparenting on father involvement as opposed to mother involvement. Family systems, parenting stress, family process and gender theory each dictate the necessity of extending empirical work to consider the effects of coparenting on mother-child relationships and development.

In a manner that closely parallels the conceptualization and operationalization of father involvement (Palkovitz, 1997), empirical investigations of coparenting tend to emphasize behavioral components of parental engagement while overlooking or deemphasizing the affective and cognitive components of coparental relationships and parental engagement. Future investigations may further understanding of the range of coparental experience by creating measures that represent cognitive and affective realms of coparental relationships as they impinge on parental involvement across a broad array of interaction contexts, styles and meanings. The literature would further benefit from exploration of various coparental styles (Bronte-Tinkew et al., 2010).

Intergenerational contributions to coparental modeling (or "transmission") represent yet another area of promising scholarship. Parents both model and rework patterns of family interaction experienced previously in their families of origin (Palkovitz, 2002), emerging from their experiences and observations with an understanding of how family interactions work.

Conclusions

It is not possible to consider coparenting apart from a greater view of father involvement under differing contexts. Thus, the literature on coparenting is subject to all of the challenges of including diverse groups of fathers situated in a broad array of residential, developmental, educational, socio-economic, and competing multiple roles and contexts. While the nature and quality of the coparental relationship exerts considerable influence on the couple's perception of the quality of paternal care, gatekeeping, access, and relational harmony; and while these factors do interact in family systems and contextual manners of influencing behaviors and developmental trajectories, they are, nonetheless, part of a greater system of father involvement. That, after all, is what warrants the inclusion of this chapter in a *Handbook of Father Involvement* and also explains why this chapter is neither among the lead nor concluding chapters.

Just as the concept of father presence and absence evolved into more nuanced constructs around father involvement, kinds of father involvement, styles of father involvement, goodness of fit with child and family characteristics, and ways to measure involvement and its effects on both children and other members of the family system, the construct of coparenting has evolved into more advanced understandings as well. While coparenting has been demonstrated to exert significant influence on father involvement in the context of married residential fathers or stable co-residential couples where men have daily access to their children, the importance of coparenting has ascended in the more challenging contexts of keeping nonresidential fathers (who may have re-partnered and have new children with a new partner) connected with their biological children (living in another household, possibly with a new stepfather or father figure). Coparenting is not as great of a contributor to paternal engagement differences among residential fathers, particularly, well-educated, employed, happily married men who are biological fathers (of sons). On the margins are never married, poorly-educated, unemployed, incarcerated, re-partnered men with multiple partner fertility whose former partners share similar circumstances. In those settings, coparenting makes a world of difference in facilitating positive father engagement with children.

Macro-analytic synthesis and evaluation has documented that several aspects of coparenting are noteworthy in influencing paternal engagement over time and consequently, have the potential to effect child well-being. Designing community-based interventions around these factors holds promise for enhancing father positive involvement in children's lives.

Elsewhere in this volume, great diversity in fathering contexts, levels, styles, and covariates have been documented and elaborated. Family systems, process, gender, and parenting stress perspectives identify different levels of variables and relationships that may cause and moderate father involvement both independent of and in conjunction with coparental characteristics. As coparenting has been documented to influence paternal engagement, it comes into the mix as one of myriad variables with considerable variability across contexts and settings. Gender theory considerations establish that coparenting most likely has different processes, meanings, and expressions for male and female partners engaged in coparenting, and those differences will 1) correlate differently to observed parent-parent interaction patterns 2) play out differently in terms of parental behaviors with children, and 3) engage with child well-being in different ways. Yet, the diversity of contexts, meanings, and processes of coparenting cannot deter us from looking for prevalent patterns of relationship among variables that have been identified as important contributors to the quality of ongoing parental interactions with children.

References

Abidin, R. R. (1992). The determinants of parenting behavior. *Journal of Clinical Child Psychology, 21,* 407–412.

Ahrons, C. R. (1981). The continuing coparental relationship between divorced parents. *American Journal of Orthopsychiatry, 51,* 415–428.

Amato, P. (2005). The impact of family formation change on the cognitive, social, and emotional well-being of the next generation. *The Future of Children, 15*(2), 75–96.

Arditti, J. A., & Kelly, M. (1994). Fathers' perspectives of their co-parental relationships postdivorce: Implications for family practice and legal reform. *Family Relations, 43,* 61–67.

Arendell, T. (1996). *Co-parenting: A review of the literature.* Philadelphia, PA: National Center on Fathers and Families.

Belsky, J. (1984). The determinants of parenting: A process model. *Child Development, 55,* 83–96.

Bernard, J. (1972). *The future of marriage.* New Haven, CT: Yale University Press.

Bonach, K. (2005). Factors contributing to quality coparenting. *Journal of Divorce and Remarriage, 43,* 79–103.

Bonach, K. (2007). Forgiveness intervention model: Application to coparenting post-divorce. *Journal of Divorce and Remarriage, 48,* 105–123.

Bonasch, K., Sales, E., & Koeske, G. (2005). Gender differences in perceptions of coparenting quality among expartners. *Journal of Divorce and Remarriage, 43,* 1–28.

Bronte-Tinkew, J., Horowitz, A., & Carrano, J. (2010). Aggravation and stress in parenting: Associations with coparenting and father engagement among resident fathers. *Journal of Family Issues, 31,* 525–555.

Brown, G. L., Schoppe-Sullivan, S. J., Mangelsdorf, S. C., & Neff, C. (2010). Observed and reported coparenting as predictors of infant-mother and infant-father attachment security. *Early Child Development and Care, 180,* 121–137.

Cabrera, N. J., Shannon, J. D., & La Taillade, J. J. (2009). Predictors of coparenting among Mexican American families and links to parent and child social emotional development. *Infant Mental Health Journal, 30,* 523–545.

Cabrera, N. J., Tamis-LeMonda, C. S., Bradley, R. H., Hofferth, S., & Lamb, M. E. (2000). Fatherhood in the twenty-first century. *Child Development, 71,* 127–136.

Caldera, Y. M., Fitzpatrick, J., & Wampler, K. S. (2002). Coparenting in intact Mexican American families: Mothers' and fathers' perceptions. In J. M. Contreras, K. A. Kerns, & A. M. Neal-Barnett (Eds.), *Latino children and families in the United States: Current research and future directions. Praeger series in applied psychology* (pp. 107–131). Westport, CT: Praeger.

Carlson, M., McLanahan, S., & Brooks-Gunn, J. (2008). Coparenting and nonresident fathers' involvement with young children after a non-marital birth. *Demography, 45*(2), 461-488.

Cohen, R. S., & Weissman, S. H. (1984). The parenting alliance. In R. S. Cohen, B. J. Cohler, & S. H. Weissman (Eds.), *Parenthood: A psychodynamic perspective* (pp. 33–49). New York: Guilford.

Cox, M. J., Paley, B., & Harter, K. (2001). Interparental conflict and parent-child relationships. In J. Grych & F. Fincham (Eds.), *Child development and interparental conflict* (pp. 249–272). Cambridge, UK: Cambridge University Press.

Cowan, C. P., Cowan, P. A., Pruett, M. K., & Pruett, K. (2007). An approach to preventing coparenting conflict and divorce in low-income families: Strengthening couple relationships and fostering fathers' involvement. *Family Process, 46,* 109–121.

Elliston, D., McHale, J., Talbot, J., Parmley, M., & Kuersten-Hogan, R. (2008). Withdrawal from coparenting interactions during early infancy. *Family Process, 47,* 481-499.

Fagan, J. (2008). Randomized study of a pre-birth coparenting intervention with adolescent and young fathers. *Family Relations, 57,* 309–323.

Fagan, J., & Palkovitz, R. (2011). Longitudinal associations between coparenting, relationship quality, and fathering: Variations by residence and romance. *Journal of Marriage and Family, 73,* 637–653.

Fagan, J., Palkovitz, R., Roy, K., & Farrie, D. (2009). Pathways to paternal engagement: Longitudinal effects of risk and resilience on non-resident fathers. *Developmental Psychology, 45,* 1389–1405.

Fagan, J., Lee, Y., Palkovitz, R., & Cabrera, N. (2011). Mediators of the relationship between stable non-resident households and toddler outcomes. *Journal of Family Issues, 32,* 1543–1568.

Feinberg, M.E. (2002). Coparenting and the transition to parenthood: A framework for prevention. *Clinical Child and Family Psychology Review, 5,* 173–195.

Feinberg, M.E. (2003). The internal structure and ecological context of coparenting: A framework for research and intervention. *Parenting: Science and Practice, 3,* 95–131.

Feinberg, M. E., Kan, M. L., & Goslin, M. C. (2009). Enhancing coparenting, parenting, and child self-regulation: Effects of Family Foundations 1 year after birth. *Prevention Science, 10,* 276–285.

Feinberg, M. E., Kan, M. L., & Hetherington, E. M. (2007). The longitudinal influence of coparenting conflict on parental negativity and adolescent maladjustment. *Journal of Marriage and Family, 69,* 687–702.

Fish, L., New, R., & Van Cleave, N. (1992). Shared parenting in dual-income families. *American Journal of Orthopsychiatry, 62,* 83–92.

Furstenberg, F. F., Jr., & Harris, K. M. (1993). When fathers matter/why fathers matter. In R. I. Lerman

& T. J. Ooms (Eds.), *Young unwed fathers: Changing roles and emerging policies* (pp. 117–138). Philadelphia, PA: Temple University Press.

Futris, T. G., & Schoppe-Sullivan, S. J. (2007). Mothers' perceptions of barriers, parenting alliance, and adolescent fathers' engagement with their children. *Family Relations, 56,* 258–269.

Garrity, C. B., & Baris, M. A. (1994). *Caught in the middle: Protecting the children of high-conflict divorce.* New York: Lexington Books.

Gordon, I., & Feldman, R. (2008). Synchrony in the triad: A microlevel process model of coparenting and parent-child interactions. *Family Process, 47,* 465–479.

Insabella, G. M., Williams, T., & Pruett, M. K. (2003). Individual and coparenting differences between divorcing and unmarried fathers: Implications for family court services. *Family Court Review, 41*(3), 290–306.

Katz, L. F., & Low, S. M. (2004). Marital violence, co-parenting, and family-level processes in relation to children's adjustment. *Journal of Family Psychology, 18*(2), 372–382.

Lamb, M. E. (2010). How do fathers influence children's development? Let me count the ways. In M. E. Lamb (Ed.), *The Role of the Father in Child Development, 5th edition* (pp. 1–27). Hoboken, NJ: Wiley.

Lamb, M. E., Pleck, J. H., Charnov, E. L., & Levine, J. A. (1987). A biosocial perspective on paternal behavior and involvement. In J. Lancaster, J. Altmann, A. Rossi, & L. Sherrod (Eds.), *Parenting across lifespan: Biosocial dimensions* (pp. 111–142). Hawthorne, NY: Aldine de Gruyter.

Lindsey, E. W., Caldera, Y., & Colwell, M. (2005). Correlates of coparenting during infancy. *Family Relations, 54,* 346–359.

Manning, W. D., Stewart, S. D., & Smock, P. J., (2003). The complexity of fathers' parenting responsibilities and involvement with nonresident children. *Journal of Family Issues, 24,* 645–667.

Margolin, G., Gordis, E. B., & John, S. R. (2001). Coparenting: A link between marital conflict and parenting in two-parent families. *Journal of Family Psychology, 15,* 3–21.

Marsiglio, W. (2004). *Stepdads, stories of love, hope and repair.* New York: Rowman & Littlefield.

Martin, J. A., Hamilton, P. D., Sutton, S. J., Ventura, F., Mencker, F., & Kirmeyer, S. (2006). *Births: Final data for 2004, vol. 55.* Altanta, GA: Department of Health and Human Services, Center for Disease Control and Prevention, National Center for Health Statistics.

McBride, B. A., & Rane, T. R., (1998). Parenting alliance as a predictor of father involvement: An exploratory study. *Family Relations, 47,* 229–236.

McConnell, M. C., & Kerig, P. K. (2002). Assessing coparenting in families of school-age children: Validation of the coparenting and family rating system. *Canadian Journal of Behavioral Science, 34*(1), 44–58.

McHale, J. (2009). *Shared child rearing in nuclear, fragile, and kinship family systems: Evolution, dilemmas, and promise of a coparenting framework. Strengthening couple relationships for optimal child development* (pp. 77–94). Washington, DC: American Psychological Association.

Morrill, M. I., Hines, D. A., Mahmood, S., & Cordova, J. (2010). Pathways between marriage and parenting for wives and husbands: The role of coparenting. *Family Process, 49,* 59–73.

Osborne, C., & McLanahan, S. (2007). Partnership instability and child wellbeing. *Journal of Marriage and Family, 69,* 1065–108.

Palkovitz, R. (1997). Reconstructing "involvement": Expanding conceptualizations of men's caring in contemporary families. In A. Hawkins & D. Dollahite (Eds.), *Generative fathering: Beyond deficit perspectives* (pp. 200–216). Thousand Oaks, CA: Sage.

Palkovitz, R. (2002). *Involved fathering and men's adult development: Provisional Balances.* Mahwah, NJ: Erlbaum.

Palkovitz, R. (2009, November). *Gendered parenting and development: Implications for theory, research and practice interfaces in human development and family studies.* Theory Construction and Research Methodology Workshop. National Council on Family Relations, San Francisco, CA.

Quinlivan, J. A., & Condon, J. (2005). Anxiety and depression in fathers in teenage pregnancy. *Australian and New Zealand Journal of Psychiatry, 39,* 915–920.

Schoppe-Sullivan, S. J., Brown, G. L., Cannon, E. A., Mangelsdorf, S. C., & Sokolowski, M. S. (2008). Maternal gatekeeping, coparenting quality, and fathering behavior in families with infants. *Journal of Family Psychology, 22*, 389–398.

Schoppe-Sullivan, S. J., Mangelsdorf, S. C., Brown, G. L., & Sokolowski. M. S. (2007).Goodness-of-fit in family context: Infant temperament, marital quality, and early coparenting behavior. *Infant Behavior and Development, 30*, 82–96.

Sobolewski, J. M., & King, V. (2005). The importance of the coparental relationship for nonresident fathers' ties to children. *Journal of Marriage and Family, 67*, 1196–1212.

U.S. Census. (1996). *Marital status and living arrangement: March 1996. Current population reports.* http://www.census.gov/prod/3/98pubs/p20-496.pdf

Waller, M. R. (2009). Family man in the other America: New opportunities, motivations, and supports for paternal caregiving. *Annals of the American Academy of Political and Social Science, 624*, 156–176.

Westerman, M. A., & Massoff, M. (2001). Triadic coordination: An observational method for examining whether children are "caught in the middle" of interparental discord. *Family Process, 40*, 479–493.

Young, A. Y., & Holcomb, P. A. (2007). *Voices of young fathers: The Partners for Fragile Families Demonstration Projects.* Washington, DC: U.S. Department of Health and Human Services. Retrieved from http://aspe.hhs.gov/hsp/07/PFF/voices/index.htm

Van Egeren, L. A. (2004). The development of the coparenting relationship over the transition to parenthood. *Infant Mental Health Journal, 25*, 453–477.

Van Egeren, L. A., & Hawkins, D. P. (2004). Coming to terms with coparenting: Implications of definition and measurement. *Journal of Adult Development, 11*, 65–178.

Ventura, S., & Bachrach, C. (2000). *Nonmarital childbearing in the United States, 1949–99. National Vital Statistics Report 48(6).* Hyattsville, MD: National Center for Health Statistics.

SECTION IV

Cultural Perspectives

Chapter 13

African American and African Caribbean Fathers

Jaipaul L. Roopnarine

Syracuse University

Ziarat Hossain

University of New Mexico College of Education

Brief Historical Overview and Theoretical Perspectives

As is evident from this and other recent volumes (e.g., Gray & Anderson, 2010; Lamb, 2010; Shwalb, Shwalb, & Lamb, in press), we have made modest strides in detailing cultural pathways to parenting processes and childhood outcomes among fathers in diverse ethnic/cultural groups in the United States and in other regions of the world. Following efforts to further understand the meaning of father investment and involvement with children in non-European heritage cultures, we take a closer look at recent research on parenting practices among African American and African Caribbean fathers and the factors that influence their expression in everyday settings. These two groups of men have common ancestral heritage, history of enslavement and prolonged oppression, and they have strong intergenerational and interdependent family units that have served adaptive functions in combating poverty and discrimination. However, there are important differences in their beliefs, goals, and approaches to childrearing.

It is worth mentioning that significant numbers of African American and African Caribbean families do not conform to the two-parent, married, nuclear family system that has guided much of the conceptual thinking and existing research paradigms on early father-child relationships. For example, marriage and co-residence receive quite a bit of attention in studies on families in North America and Europe as protective factors that may insulate children from the negative consequences of poverty, challenging neighborhoods, and poor schools. Their salience for becoming a father and for parenting in African American and African Caribbean families is a bit more complicated though. Family is not always synonymous with biological parents, and marriage may be secondary to the formation of a household in these two cultural groups. The social and psychological boundaries within these families shift and are renegotiated at critical points in the life cycle. There is also the possibility of conceptual separation in beliefs about dyadic, contractual relationships and parenting responsibilities (Anderson, 2007). Conceivably, men could be good fathers but lousy husbands or partners. Inter-partner relationships do influence access to children and parenting practices (Cabrera, Ryan, Mitchell,

Shannon, & Tamis-LeMonda, 2008), but strong emotional pair-bonds may play a far greater role in father-child relationships in nuclear, married families (see Palkovitz & Fagan and Roggman et al., this volume) than in sociocultural milieus where marital bonds are not emphasized and multiple caregivers assume instrumental roles in childrearing.

A strong feature of research on African American and African Caribbean families is the use of theoretical frameworks and conceptual models from diverse disciplines. For instance, the bio-social perspective, rooted in evolutionary biology, has been used to interpret Trinidadian fathers' care interactions toward biological and non-biological offspring (Flinn, 1992), and the sociologically-based structural-functional theory has been instrumental in analyzing partner relationship, role responsibilities, and the division of household labor in Jamaican fathers (Anderson, 2007; Roopnarine et al., 1995). Yet other researchers of the Caribbean diaspora have introduced the retentionist and creolization frameworks in attempts to untangle the role of socio-historical experiences (e.g., slavery, indentured servitude, persistent harsh economic conditions) in shaping current parenting practices (Deen, 1995). Likewise, studies on African American fathers have employed more resilient-adaptive cultural-ecological frameworks that have their genesis in psychological anthropology and focus on the adaptive strategies (e.g., racial socialization, spirituality) families use during parenting (Ogbu, 1981) and on the opportunities and hazards parents encounter in difficult ecological niches (Super & Harkness, 1997; Whiting & Whiting, 1975). Despite the use of such diverse theories and models in designing studies and framing research questions on African American and African Caribbean fathers, it is necessary to develop theoretical formulations on father-child relationships for outside of marriage or romantic relations by focusing on male parenting in collaboration with other caregivers across multiple unions rather than on co-parenting in mother-father dyads only (see Roy & Burton, 2009).

Because so much of the existing research on African American and African Caribbean fathers has focused on time involvement with children in low-income families, in this chapter we discuss parenting practices and their significance for cognitive and social development in young children (0–8 years) from diverse family living arrangements and socioeconomic backgrounds. More specifically, we provide a brief list of research questions that are currently being explored and the methodological approaches used to gather data in different African American and African Caribbean cultural communities, before proceeding to a more extensive account of empirical findings on the parenting practices of African American and African Caribbean fathers and childhood outcomes. Toward the end of the chapter, we examine possible cross-disciplinary connections in research on African American and African Caribbean fathers, suggest a few policy implications for increasing father involvement with children, and make recommendations for future research on these two groups of men.

Current Research Questions

It is only within the last 15 years that studies have moved beyond establishing whether African American and African Caribbean men in different cultural communities and family living arrangements are involved with children to examining what personal, interpersonal, and socio-demographic characteristics influence fathering and childhood outcomes. Recent emphasis has been on family stability and parenting practices. Thus, some of the more pressing questions are geared toward finding out: (a) What are the qualitative dimensions of parenting practices among African American and African Caribbean fathers, and what are their associations with social and cognitive development in young children in different family living arrangements and socioeconomic backgrounds? (b) Compared to other caregivers, what are the relative contributions of African American and African Caribbean fathers to childhood socialization? (c) Do African Caribbean men extend more care interactions to biological versus non-biological offspring? (d) How does the shifting of paternal figures affect childhood development in African Caribbean families?, and (e) What are some of the more salient sociodemographic, personal, and interpersonal factors that are associated with male involvement and parenting behaviors in African American and African Caribbean families?

Research Measurement and Methodology

As was the case with theoretical frameworks and models, a wide range of measurement techniques have been used to document fathers' levels and quality of involvement with children in African American and African Caribbean families. Methods of data collection include, but are not limited to, detailed observations in field settings that provide frequency counts and durations of individual behaviors or aggregates of behaviors by all individuals who care for and interact with children (Flinn, 1992; Roopnarine, Fouts, Lamb, & Lewis-Elligan, 2005), Likert-type behavioral ratings from video-tapes of paternal and maternal sensitivity to children (Shannon, Tamis-LeMonda, & Margolin, 2005), self-reports of parenting behaviors on questionnaires and scales with Likert-type items that are subjected to exploratory or confirmatory factor analysis (Roopnarine & Krishnakumar, 2011), self-reports of mothers' and fathers' own and each other's time involvement in various caregiving and parent-child activities (Hossain & Roopnarine, 1994), telephone interviews with specific family members who furnish estimates of levels of father involvement in different activities inside and outside of the home (Yeung, Sandberg, Davis-Kean, & Hofferth, 2001), focus groups that are convened to discuss issues tied to fatherhood and fathering (Brown, Anderson, & Chevannes, 1993), and face-to-face interviews with families in their homes about involvement in different caregiving and social activities (Roopnarine et al., 1995). While each technique has been a rich source of data, convergence among them is rarely established. There are speculations that fathers' self-reports of involvement with children may be inflated. Among African Americans, self-report measures of time involvement with children (e.g., Yeung et al., 2001) tend to be higher than those obtained via observations (Roopnarine et al., 2005). Furthermore, a number of parenting scales and questionnaires may lack cultural validity as they have not been used widely with diverse groups of families. As a result, concerns have been raised about the meaning of well-established parenting paradigms and constructs for use in non-European heritage cultures (see Chao, 2001; Sorkhabi, 2005).

Most of the studies on father involvement and parenting practices in African American and African Caribbean families have involved cross-sectional designs. Longitudinal studies are conspicuously absent from the literature. So too are studies that use structural equation models that assess the moderating and mediating effects of particular variables that are known to influence paternal involvement and sensitively-attuned caregiving practices. In this regard, links between parenting practices and childhood social and cognitive skills have been established through simple correlations (e.g., Kelly, Smith, Green, Berndt, & Rogers, 1998; Samms-Vaughan, 2005). The problems with making causal inferences from correlations are well-known to researchers. These issues aside, next we outline findings of contemporary studies on parenting practices and childhood outcomes in African American and African Caribbean families.

Empirical Findings

In our review of empirical findings, we first focus on African American fathers' parenting behaviors and styles and their associations with children's cognitive and social skills. This is followed by accounts of African Caribbean fathers' parenting practices and family stability and their relationships to children's cognitive and social skills.

Male Parenting in African American Families

Like other cultural groups, African Americans represent a range of family structural arrangements, have diverse beliefs about childrearing, and use multiple caregiving and socialization strategies. Several researchers have provided detailed accounts of the economic lives (e.g., McLoyd, Kaplan, Hardaway, & Wood, 2007; Wilson, 1987), the structural diversity of African American families and their effects on economic, social, and psychological well-being (e.g., Hunter, 1997b; Williams, Auslander, Houston, Krebill, & Haire-Joshu, 2000), and the "myths" and "stereotypes" attributed to fathers from low-income backgrounds (Tamis-LeMonda & McFadden, 2010). Because there are extensive reviews of qualitative and quantitative studies on the levels and quality of African American fathers' involvement with children (e.g., Jarrett, 1998; Roopnarine, 2004), we provide only a brief account of those studies here. Our main goal is to examine the parenting practices of African American men (e.g., parental warmth and sensitivity, verbal stimulation) and their importance for cognitive and social skills development in young children.

Fathers' time involvement. Father involvement in African American families varies considerably based on fathers' age, economic circumstances, marital status, and family living arrangements. Starting with studies from the 1990s, in lower- to middle-income African American two-parent families with stable jobs and in which the mother worked full-time, fathers spent 1.13 hours feeding, .89 hours cleaning, and 2.19 hours per day playing with infants, and in families in which the mother worked part-time (less than 25 hours per week) fathers spent 1.39 hours feeding, .96 hours cleaning, and 2.80 hours per day playing with infants (Hossain & Roopnarine, 1994). The number of hours mothers worked outside of the home did not influence fathers' participation in caregiving activities with infants. Among lower- to middle-income, two-parent families with preschool-aged children, mothers and fathers both estimated that fathers spent on average 2.8 hours a day in basic caregiving (Ahmeduzzaman & Roopnarine, 1992), and in low-income African American and Puerto Rican families whose children were enrolled in Head Start (84% biological fathers and all lived with the child's mother), fathers spent 1.38 hours in direct interaction (play, talking, caregiving) including .40 hours playing, and about the same amount of time in going on social outings with children per day (averaged across two weekdays and a weekend day) (Fagan, 1998). These data suggest that African American fathers' time involvement with children is comparable to that of European American fathers (Cabrera et al., 2008; Yeung et al., 2001) and to that of fathers in other cultural groups (Roopnarine et al., 1995). It is not clear whether African American fathers' time investment in childrearing has increased appreciably in the intervening decade.

Data on frequency of social contacts between African American fathers and children are primarily based on families who live in difficult social and economic circumstances. A prevailing theme that surfaces is that low-income African American fathers "want to be there for their children" to fulfill and acquire a sense of responsibility as fathers (Allen & Doherty, 1996; Ray

& Hans, 2001; Summers et al., 1999). It is not unusual for low-income fathers to establish social alliances with kinship and nonkinship members to assist with daily caregiving and to share living arrangements with them (Hamer & Marchioro, 2002; Hunter, 1997a; Perry, 2009). Within different family living arrangements, there are extreme variations in social contacts between fathers and father figures and children. In some cases, as many as 72% of resident fathers see their children regularly, at least 4 days per week (Black, Dubowitz, & Starr, 1999) to no contact at all among significant numbers (49%) of young unwed fathers (Rangarajan & Gleason, 1998). Although intermittent social contacts between nonresident African American fathers and children have been reported by several researchers (Greene & Moore, 2000; Lerman & Sorenson, 2000), nonresident fathers and boyfriends appear to have more frequent social contacts with children than has previously been surmised (Cabrera et al., 2004; Mincy & Oliver, 2003). More specifically, in one study of low-income men, a majority of fathers reported engaging in decision-making regarding children's health, education, and religion (Shannon, Tamis-LeMonda, London, & Cabrera, 2002).

Parenting behaviors and styles. Attachment theorists (Ainsworth, 1989; Ainsworth, Blehar, Waters, & Wall, 1978; Bowlby, 1969) propose that sensitively-attuned parent-child interactions help to facilitate the development of secure bonds to mothers and fathers (see Lamb & Lewis, 2010; Leidy, Schofield, & Parke, this volume) and influence co-parenting relationships (Caldera & Lindsey, 2006). Parental responsiveness is associated with diverse social and cognitive skills in childhood (Tamis-LeMonda, Bornstein, & Baumwell, 2001), whereas restrictive and harsh parental practices adversely affect children's linguistic and social competence (Dix, 1991; Roopnarine, Krishnakumar, Metindogan, & Evans, 2006). Bearing this in mind, some have argued that African American parents are more parent-centered (Taylor, Chatters, Tucker, & Lewis, 1990), are less sensitive to infants during parent-child interactions compared to European Americans (Bakermans-Kranenburg, van Ijzendoorn, & Kroonenberg, 2004), and that stricter parenting practices may be necessary for childrearing in neighborhoods that are marred by persistent poverty and violence (Kelly et al., 1998). The merits of these claims are yet to be determined fully in the changing ethos of African American childhood across socioeconomic groups. What is lacking is a better understanding of the behavioral qualities of African American fathers' interactions with children during routine parenting activities.

A series of investigations by developmental psychologists (Cabrera, Hofferth, & Chae, 2011; Mitchell & Cabrera, 2009; Shannon et al., 2002, 2005; Shannon, Tamis-LeMonda, & Cabrera, 2006; Tamis-LeMonda, Kahana-Kalman, & Yoshikawa, 2009) has provided key insights into the qualitative aspects of paternal involvement among African American men and young children, even though at times behavioral interactions were lumped across ethnic groups. Using short videotaped play segments, Shannon et al. (2005) coded a range of responsive didactic behaviors (e.g., positive affect, positive touch, amount and quality of language, responsive to verbal cues and vocalizations, toy play) and negative-overbearing behaviors (e.g., negative affect, negative touch, negative verbal statements, teasing, intrusiveness) between fathers and infants in a diverse ethnic sample (42% African American) from low-SES backgrounds (most men were single and first-time fathers with more than 50% living with the infant since birth). On a 5-point Likert-type scale, fathers were observed to engage in moderate levels of positive interactions and low levels of negative interactions with infants. Basically similar findings were reported for low-income African American men, most (76%) of whom were in romantic relationships and living with the child's mother. Fathers' self-reports of engagement in socialization, management, didactic interactions, physical play, and caregiving, and observations of responsive-didactic interactions revealed medium levels of responsiveness and low levels of negative behaviors directed at toddlers (Mitchell & Cabrera, 2009). In a national representative sample, African American and Latino fathers engaged in higher levels of care and play stimulation than European American fathers (Cabrera et al., 2011).

Two other studies provide additional data on African American fathers' parenting behaviors. Kelly et al. (1998) observed paternal sensitivity (facial expression, vocal expression, position and body contact, expression of affection, pacing of turns, control, and choice of activity) during a brief unstructured 3-minute play interaction session between low-income, married African American mothers and fathers (83%) and their 1- to 3-year-old children. Fathers showed high levels of sensitivity (Mean score of 10.6; Range = 0–14), but were less sensitive toward boys than girls during the free play session. A possible explanation for the gender discrepancy is that through less sensitive activities fathers are teaching sons skills that may assist them to negotiate difficult social ecologies. The other study that followed Dominican and Mexican immigrants and African American fathers from the prenatal period through the first few years of life indicated that a majority of African American fathers were very involved with the pregnancy and were highly engaged in singing, reading books, playing games with toys, participating in rough-tumble games, and playing with ball with infants at 14-months. Levels of involvement were stable over time (Tamis-LeMonda et al., 2009).

A fair number of the aforementioned studies have concentrated on low-income fathers and used brief observations to assess paternal responsiveness and sensitivity to children. A more detailed observational study of low-, middle-, and upper-socioeconomic status African American families by Roopnarine et al. (2005) recorded the interaction patterns (e.g., verbal stimulation, physical and verbal affect, soothing, etc.) between caregivers and 3- to 4-month-old infants for 12 hours each in and around the home environment on weekdays. As documented elsewhere, middle- and upper-SES families were far more likely to be married and to have resident biological fathers; low-income families were more likely to have non-resident fathers and maternal relatives residing with them. The observations revealed that upper-SES fathers were available to infants 30.4% of the time, middle-SES fathers 13.7% of the time, and low-SES fathers 9.8% of the time observed.

Again African American fathers engaged in modes of sensitive caregiving through diverse behavioral activities with infants. In line with many cultural groups around the world, African American mothers engaged in most of the day-to-day care of infants. When behavioral interactions between mothers and fathers were compared as a function of paternal presence, the caregiving patterns of mothers and fathers were more similar than different. Across SES groups, there was no significant gender-of-parent difference in overall levels of basic care, but mothers did feed infants more than fathers did. The most noteworthy findings involved two behaviors that are at the core of behavioral sensitivity: verbal stimulation and affection. Fathers provided more verbal stimulation and showed more affection to infants than mothers did (Roopnarine et al., 2005). These patterns of paternal interactions are very similar to those obtained for AKA foragers in the Central African Republic, who soothed and provided more affection to infants than mothers did (Hewlett, 1992), and to McAdoo's (1988) findings on paternal warmth extended to preschool-aged African American children.

Though far from definitive, the research reviewed so far marks some preliminary advances in our understanding of African American fathers' parenting practices and indicates that overall African American fathers engaged in positive interactions that are geared toward enhancing social and cognitive skills in children during the early childhood period. A related area of interest to developmental scientists concerns parenting styles as defined by Baumrind

(1967)—the emotional qualities of parenting. Assessments of parenting goals and styles among African American fathers and young children are rare. One study (Letiecq, 2007) explored the role of spirituality, a strong tenet of African American family life, on biological fathers' (67.2%) and social fathers' parenting styles. The objective was to assess whether fathers' parenting styles and practices toward preschool-aged children enrolled in Head Start in violent neighborhoods differed based on degrees of spirituality. Unlike previous assertions (Benson & Haith, 2009), subscale scores indicated that fathers rated themselves toward the higher end of the authoritative style and toward the midrange level on the permissive and authoritarian styles of parenting. Fathers who saw spirituality as highly important in their lives were less likely to use the authoritarian parenting style (non-reasoning/punitive) and were more likely to monitor and teach children about personal safety and neighborhood survival strategies than those who rated spirituality as not very important in their lives. Fathers who were more spiritually inclined were also less likely to use permissive and authoritarian parenting styles and more likely to use the authoritative parenting style with sons than those who saw spirituality as less important in their lives. Quite possibly, less spiritual fathers who used the more authoritarian parenting style may have been responding to pressures to socialize children to cope with the realities of life in violent neighborhoods by being stricter and more demanding of compliance. The more democratic approach by fathers who viewed themselves as more spiritual is congruent with the principles of warmth and reasoning rooted in their faith (Letiecq, 2007).

Having laid out the parenting practices of African American fathers, it is necessary to consider what determines time and quality of involvement with children across socio-economic groups. Not unexpectedly, a stable income appears to increase time involvement with young children. For example, income was associated with time spent feeding and comforting infants (Hossain & Roopnarine, 1994), to the care and socialization of preschoolers in two-parent, middle-income families (Ahmeduzzaman & Roopnarine, 1992), to paternal nurturance during play with resident fathers and father figures in low-income families (Black et al., 1999), and to paternal engagement—caregiving, social, cognitive, and physical activities (Perry, 2009). Educational attainment also contributes to men's level and quality of involvement with children. Fathers with greater educational attainment showed more sensitivity and less intrusiveness toward children in a sample that included European Americans, African Americans (21.7%), and other ethnic groups (Tamis-LeMonda, Shannon, Cabrera, & Lamb, 2004). McLoyd (1990) and others (Duncan, Yeung, Brooks-Gunn, & Smith, 1998; Wilson, 1987) have addressed the pernicious effects of poverty and unemployment on family roles and responsibilities, parenting, and childhood development.

At the intrapersonal level, fathers' functioning style (e.g., commitment to the family, cohesion, communication) (Ahmeduzzaman & Roopnarine, 1992) and childrearing competence were associated with paternal time involvement in overall levels of caregiving in middle- and low-income, two-parent families (Fagan & Barnett, 2003), whereas fathers' spiritual beliefs imparted differential effects on parenting styles and childrearing practices in high-risk neighborhoods (Letiecq, 2007). On the interpersonal front, among nonresident fathers, care by and visits with the child's maternal kin (Perry, 2009), positive father-mother/partner relationship (Cabrera et al., 2008), and men's childhood relationships with their fathers are all associated with greater paternal involvement and quality of parenting with children (Shannon et al., 2005). By contrast, conflict between partners predicted less involvement in caregiving and physical play (Cabrera et al., 2011). Some of these associations may be mediated by the quality of the father-mother relationship (Tamis-LeMonda et al., 2009).

In the face of greater understanding of African American fathers' parenting practices and childhood development, a number of issues still loom large. Several studies are not well grounded in theoretical frameworks and models that incorporate multiple dimensions of the socioeconomic and cultural lives of African American families. Nor are the combined and independent effects of ethnicity (culture, ethnic identity, majority or minority status) (Phinney, 1996) and SES (income, education, wealth status, status of parental occupation, income-to-needs assessments) (Entwisle & Astone, 1994) on father-child relationships adequately disentangled (Cabrera et al., 2011). Given that ethnic groups may experience socioeconomic conditions differently (McLoyd, 1990; Murray, Smith, & Hill, 2001), it could be that certain paternal parenting practices are more evident in particular cultural and ecological niches and SES groups than in others. In the absence of studies involving national representative samples of African American fathers/social fathers and other caregivers (e.g., Cabrera et al., 2011), it should not be assumed that ethnicity defines a cultural community or vice versa. Ethnicity and SES are components of a cultural community but not the sum total of its parts.

Parenting practices and styles and childhood outcomes.   Comparatively speaking, there are far more studies on African American fathers' parenting practices and styles and social and cognitive outcomes in adolescents than in young children (e.g., Cooper, 2009; Jordan & Lewis, 2005). Nevertheless, there are a few findings on the influences of paternal parenting practices on young children's development. On the complexity of language use (e.g., mean length of utterance, mean length of turn), fathers who were more dominating during dyadic conversations with their children influenced their children' language skills negatively (Fagan & Iglesias, 1999), a finding obtained for Caribbean immigrant fathers in the United States as well (Roopnarine et al., 2006). Similarly, fathers' restrictive parenting was negatively related to children's cognitive and motor development (Kelly et al., 1998). However, children whose fathers assumed a supportive role had higher cognitive scores compared to children without a father/father figure in such a role (Dubowitz et al., 2001); greater positive paternal engagement reduced the risk of developmental delays at 24 months as measured by the Bayley (Shannon et al., 2002); fathers' sensitivity, positive regard, and cognitive stimulation were related to higher MDI scores at 24 and 36 months and to higher PPVT (Peabody Picture Vocabulary Test) scores at 36 months (Tamis-LeMonda et al., 2004); and paternal nurturance during play was related to children's receptive vocabulary scores (Black et al., 1999). It should be mentioned that in the Black et al. sample, there were no significant differences in children's Stanford-Binet or PPVT-R scores as a function of father or father figure presence in the home. And, self-reported paternal warmth was not related to toddlers' cognitive development in another study (Kelly et al., 1998).

With respect to social development, paternal parenting satisfaction predicted lower behavioral problems in children (Black et al., 1999), and fathers' responsive-didactic scores correlated with infants' scores on social-communication (Shannon et al., 2006). Strained inter-partner relationship was related to internalizing behaviors in preschool-aged children enrolled in Head Start and residing in violent neighborhoods (Oravecz, Koblinsky, & Randolph, 2008) but unrelated to fathers' interactions with infants (Shannon et al., 2005). Just as with cognitive and language development, restrictive parenting by fathers had a negative effect on children's communication, daily living, and socialization skills as measured by the Vineland Adaptive Behavior Scales (Kelly et al., 1998).

Male Parenting in African Caribbean Families

Acknowledging that there is within- and between-country variability in Caribbean men's economic commitment to and investment and involvement with children, certain family practices seem fairly consistent across countries: progressive mating, multiple caregiving, a combination of warm and harsh parenting styles, and age-inappropriate behavioral expectations of children (Brown, Newland, Anderson, & Chevannes, 1997; Roopnarine, Evans, & Pant, in press). Accordingly, our discussion covers areas of commonalities among families across cultural communities in order to make more concrete statements about fathering in the Caribbean. Emphasis is on fathers in the English-speaking Caribbean Islands (e.g., Jamaica, Barbados, Trinidad and Tobago, and St. Kitts and Nevis) and the continental countries of Guyana and Belize. To remain consistent with the overall focus of this chapter, we review studies on parenting practices and childhood development.

Family configurations.   As with African Americans, men in Caribbean cultural communities become fathers in diverse marital/mating systems. A majority of African Caribbean men become fathers in visiting unions, after which they enter into common-law relationships. Marriage rates tend to increase with age and with church membership and attendance (Anderson, 2007), but is not a legitimizing force behind family formation or for having children. Previous non-marital unions are seen as transitory. In the course of establishing these different relationships or "marital careers" over the life cycle (Rodman, 1971), it is typical for men and women to have several "baby mothers" and "baby fathers." That is, men and women have children with several partners as they move from one union to the next. A survey of 1,142 men in four communities in Jamaica indicates that 25.6% of fathers had two, 11.1% had three, 4.1% had four, and 4.5% had five or more "baby mothers" (Anderson, 2007). Fathers with fewer material resources were more likely to embrace traditional masculine beliefs about male dominance and virility, have more baby mothers and larger numbers of children compared to those with better material resources (Anderson, 2007).

Parenting behaviors and styles.   A few studies that measured frequency and time involvement with children by union status in Caribbean families (Brown et al., 1993; Brown et al., 1997; Chevannes, 2001; Clarke, 1957; Roberts & Sinclair, 1978; Roopnarine et al., 1995) did include measures of paternal sensitivity during general caregiving activities. For instance, a survey study conducted in Georgetown, Guyana, revealed that in a multi-ethnic sample of African- and Indo-Guyanese families, most fathers reported attending to the basic needs of infants at night and cuddled and played with infants in stimulating ways. Fathers in low-income families engaged in higher levels of involvement in these caregiving behaviors than those from more privileged economic backgrounds (Wilson, Wilson, & Berkeley-Caines, 2003). Moderately high levels of soothing and play stimulation were also seen between fathers and infants in low-income, common-law Jamaican families (Roopnarine et al., 1995).

There is growing recognition that in many cultures childhood socialization occurs in the context of multiple caregiving and that social and cognitive investment in children by nonparental caregivers waxes and wanes during early childhood depending on household and family composition, economic resources, and children's developmental level (Fouts et al., in press; Marlowe, 2005; Sharma, 2000). As indicated already, mothers and fathers may use multiple caregiving alliances in creative ways as social and cultural capital to buttress childrearing roles, to garner social support, and to acquire economic benefits (Roy & Burton, 2009). In Caribbean societies, multiple caregiving is pervasive and situated within strong intergenerational ties. Systematic observations of families in northern Trinidad by Flinn (1992) illustrate this phenomenon. Using a "behavioral observation route instantaneous scan sample" technique, he recorded the care interactions of 342 inhabitants. Of a total of 24,577 observations made of the villagers, 5,343 constituted interactions between parents and offspring. During the infancy and early childhood periods, the care of children was distributed across several individuals: mothers assumed 44.2%, fathers 10.3%, siblings 16.3%, grandparents 17.6%, aunts and uncles 4.5%, and distant kin and relatives 7.2%. Genetic parent-offspring interactions accounted for 35.6% of observed care overtures, with mothers assuming more responsibility for care overtures during infancy (average for co-resident mothers = 31.9%, range 14%–67%, average for fathers = 3.3%, range 0%–9%) and early childhood (average for co-resident mothers = 22.9%, Range 8%–36%; average for fathers = 4.2%, range 0%–17%) than fathers did. Diverse socialization agents have been observed in other cultural communities across the Caribbean (e.g., Jamaica, Dominica, and Trinidad and Tobago; Durbrow, 1999; Ramkissoon, 2002; Roopnarine & Krishnakumar, 2011). To date, the influence of these diverse caregivers, relative to fathers, on childhood development has not been discerned. As stated earlier, our research models continue to favor the two-parent norm (see Fouts, Roopnarine, Lamb, & Evans, in press; Marlowe, 2005).

Psychological risks to children associated with paternal instability have led researchers to assess the levels of care distributed by fathers to biological and non-biological offspring. Inclusive fitness theory, rooted in evolutionary biology, suggests that care investment would favor biological over non-biological offspring (Hamilton, 1964). Not surprisingly, in Flinn's (1992) observations in Trinidad, care interactions were more frequent across caregivers in resident-father households than nonresident-father households, with far fewer interactions occurring between non-biological fathers and children than between biological fathers and children. The interactions between non-biological fathers and children were characteristically more agonistic than those between biological fathers and children. In nonresident-father households, mothers tended to live with their parents who were heavily involved in the care of infants. Father-child interactions decreased when men or their ex-partners took on a new mate, suggesting that, because of jealousy and resource allocation, the new partner may act as a hindrance to sustained interactions between fathers and young children (Flinn, 1992). In Jamaican families, "outside children" and children from prior unions receive far less care and support for identical reasons (Brown et al., 1997).

A popular claim among scholars (e.g., Leo-Rhynie, 1997) is that parenting practices in Caribbean families are often expressed as a mixture of warmth and indulgence and punitive control. Ample evidence exists that parents in St. Kitts (Rohner, Kean, & Cournoyer, 1991), Guyana (Pant, Roopnarine, & Krishnakumar, 2008), Dominica (Durbrow, 1999), Barbados (Anderson & Payne, 1994), and Trinidad and Tobago (Roopnarine & Krishnakumar, 2012) endorse and use harsh disciplinary practices in regulating young children's behaviors. Additionally, surveys of family socialization practices reveal that Caribbean parents rarely offer rewards and praise to children (see Leo-Rhynie, 1997; Payne & Furnham, 1992), and that they describe children as troublesome and "hardened" or difficult (Durbrow, 1999; Roopnarine, 2011). Interestingly, the nature and prevalence of Caribbean fathers' warmth toward young children has not been explored sufficiently.

Difficulties with self-reports of parenting practices notwithstanding (see Holden & Edwards, 1989), attempts to examine parenting styles have produced findings that are contrary to previously held conceptions about psychological absence and the lack of paternal warmth among Caribbean fathers stated previously. Payne and Furnham (1992) administered a modified version of the Block Child Rearing Practices Report to assess components of nurturance and restrictiveness in Barbadian parents (N = 628) with a school-age child. Mothers and fathers did not differ on positive parent-child contact, encouragement of intellectual curiosity and reflection, and behavioral control through positive expectation; nor did they differ on different measures of restrictiveness. Mothers, though, were more likely to encourage engagement in emotional expression than fathers. Fathers and mothers in non-manual occupations reported offering more nurturance (physical involvement and intellectual nurturance) and being less restrictive during parenting than those in manual occupations.

An assessment of parenting styles in Jamaican fathers (N = 251), using the well-established Baumrind (1967) typologies, found that across different conjugal arrangements the authoritative parenting style was the most prevalent in families with more material resources: 58.6% of fathers employed an authoritative style of parenting, 12.4% an authoritarian style, and 7.6% a permissive style. About 12% of fathers were judged to be uninvolved (Ramkissoon, 2004). With the exception of companionship and warmth, scores on father control, trust in father, paternal companionship and affection, and psychological presence were generally higher in father-resident families than in nonresident-father families, probably an artifact of low levels of social contact between nonresident fathers and children in Jamaica (Anderson, 2007). Men typically honor their ex-partner's entrance into a new mating relationship and may avoid contact with children because of the potential for interpersonal conflicts and demands for economic support from ex-partners.

Drawing on the tenets of PARTheory on parental love (Rohner & Veneziano, 2001), a more recent analysis conducted on responses provided by low- to middle-income two-parent Trinidadian families on the Parental Acceptance-Rejection Questionnaire (PARQ) (Rohner & Pettengill, 1985) showed that both mothers and fathers in low- to middle-socioeconomic groups reported high levels of warmth and affection and behavioral control and moderate levels of hostility and aggression, indifference and neglect, and undifferentiated rejection toward preschool-aged children (Roopnarine & Krishnakumar, 2010). Mothers reported expressing significantly more warmth toward children than fathers did. Nevertheless, paternal and maternal warmth were significantly related. Mothers also punished children more frequently and more severely than fathers did, but they did not differ on behavioral control, hostility and aggression, indifference and neglect, and undifferentiated rejection. Fathers delayed punishing children for longer periods than mothers did. A follow-up study on the parenting practices (using the Ghent Parental Behavior Scale (GPBS); Van Leeuwen, & Vermulst, 2004) of 1504 families across different socioeconomic groups in Trinidad and Tobago confirmed the use of rule-oriented, harsh and ignoring practices, along with encouragement of autonomy, material rewarding, and positive parenting across male and female caregivers (Roopnarine & Krishnakumar, 2011).

In view of the combination of positive and negative parenting practices and varying levels of dyadic commitment across different mating relationships in Caribbean communities, what is the level of functional stability in families? Samms-Vaughan (2005) measured personal functioning via the Family Adaptability and Cohesion Environment Scale (FACES-II) in Jamaican families, most of whom had limited material resources. About 80% of children lived with biological mothers and 50% with biological fathers; 65% of children had both biological parents in the parenting role regardless of residential living status, and 14.8% had female relatives in the parenting role. Children whose parents had better material resources were more likely to have biological parenting figures than those in households where parents worked in unskilled jobs. Despite the absence of biological fathers in the parenting role in a third of the households, most families reported good cohesion in their functioning with more than half of them connected (44.5%) or very connected (17.8%), with 24.6% separated, and 13.1% disengaged. Furthermore, a majority of families were assessed to be flexible or very flexible (63.5%) on adaptability, indicating that in living arrangements in which biological fathers are not residing with children, there is good cohesion and adaptability.

Collectively, variations in the level of early care and stimulation provided by Caribbean fathers are similar to those of men in other technologically developing societies such as Malaysia (Hossain et al., 2005; Hossain, Roopnarine, Isamel, Menon, Sombuling, 2008), and India (Roopnarine, Krishnakumar, & Vagdama, in press). The early patterns of sensitive caregiving along with play interactions provide opportunities for social engagement that may facilitate the development of attachment bonds between fathers and infants (Paquette, 2004; Tamis-LeMonda, 2004). At the same time, the findings on parenting practices and styles across different island communities seem to indicate moderately high levels of warmth and nurturance by fathers that co-occur with high behavioral control and harshness. This mixture of parenting practices by fathers and mothers is rather perplexing to us. On the one hand, they may reflect the cognitive and social adjustments parents and other caregivers may have to make in their guidance of children in difficult ecological niches that are perceived to demand stricter enforcement of rule-oriented, harsher forms of discipline—a point we made about African American families living in poor neighborhoods. In different Caribbean countries (e.g., Dominica, Guyana, and Jamaica), parents state explicitly that it is very important to transmit cultural values, such as manners, respect for others, honesty and integrity, obedience, "the fear of God", and self-discipline to young children in order for them to be compliant to parental demands (Anderson, 2007; Durbrow, 1999; Wilson et al., 2003). On the other hand, the harsher, restrictive parenting practices raise serious questions about their impact on the behavioral and cognitive development of children. Restrictive parenting practices are associated with internalizing and externalizing behavioral problems in children in other cultural groups (Aunola & Nurmi, 2005).

Of the several factors that have been identified as influencing fathers' parenting behaviors (e.g., parenting skills and competence, marital/couple relationship, mental health, etc.) in different cultures, two hold particular significance for Caribbean fathers' investment in biological and non-biological offspring: economic conditions and spirituality as measured by church membership and attendance. Caribbean researchers (Anderson, 2007; Brown et al., 1993, 1997) have argued that poor economic conditions and spare material resources, above all other factors, undermine men's ability to achieve the full responsibility of fatherhood. Among Jamaican families, the inability to provide economic support (minding children) was the major source of dissatisfaction in men's role as fathers (56.1%). Economic resources were related to church attendance which, then, increased the standing of men in the community. Religiosity, as measured by church membership and church attendance, was linked to a greater likelihood of entering marital relationships and to higher levels of commitment to fathering, both of which seem to offer greater stability to families for childrearing (Anderson, 2007).

Parenting practices and childhood outcomes.   As hinted at above, harsher forms of parent-child interactions place children at risk for behavioral difficulties. Instability in living arrangements due to mate shifting, poor material resources, and lack of availability and access to fathers on a consistent basis could compound the social difficulties Caribbean children experience during early and later childhood. Indeed, there is some evidence that poor father-child relationships and lack of father presence in children's lives are linked to lower nutritional status, developmental delays, and running away from home (Sharpe, 1997), and that unstable living arrangements can contribute to conduct problems and passive dependency in children and young adults (Allen, 1985; Crawford-Brown, 1997). Unfortunately, these associations have not considered the wide range of factors that may be linked to family functioning (e.g., cohesion, adaptability, mental health) and that may be more critical to paternal engagement with children than fathers' residential status or presence alone.

To determine the associations among adult functioning, family stability, and children's cognitive and social functioning, Samms-Vaughan (2005) conducted a broad range of assessments on Jamaican families with preschool-aged children through their transition to gradeschool. As might be reasoned, preschool-aged children who lived in homes that were crowded, that lacked modern facilities, that had fewer material possessions, and in which parents were in unskilled jobs had lower cognitive scores than their peers who lived with better material resources. Child-shifting by either mother or father, age of maternal or paternal parenting figure, and presence of biological parents in the home were not significantly related to children's academic achievement or cognitive scores. There were significant positive associations between family functioning (cohesion and adaptability) and children's receptive vocabulary scores, and between paternal and maternal education and achievement and cognitive scores. Children whose parents were married performed better academically and had better cognitive scores than children in other family arrangements. Arguably, the most compelling findings were those that involved stability in family living arrangements and social difficulties in children. Shifting of father figures was associated with internalizing behaviors in children, and children who had multiple father figures exhibited more withdrawn behaviors. Those children who were in living arrangements with a biological father and a surrogate mother also fared poorly, academically and behaviorally.

A subsequent attempt to determine the associations between Trinidadian mothers' and fathers' parenting practices and teacher ratings of children's social behaviors in preschool produced inconsistent results as well (Roopnarine & Krishnakumar, 2010). Even though a positive association was found between the severity of physical punishment by fathers and teachers' ratings of children's aggressive behaviors in preschool settings, paternal warmth was not related to children's prosocial behaviors with peers. A meta-analysis performed on decades of research indicates that the negative consequences of physical punishment on childhood development extend beyond physical aggression to children's mental health (Gershoff, 2002). Moreover, after controlling for "normativeness," physical punishment still seems to have undesirable effects on childhood behaviors across several cultural communities (Lansford et al., 2005).

All together, these findings from a small group of correlational studies begin to show the importance of family cohesion and adaptability, parental education, and stable living arrangements as protective factors in young Caribbean children's academic and social development. The ambiguity in parental presence and level of responsibility associated with mateshifting and multiple father figures can thwart attempts by young children to form close and enduring relationships with male and female caregivers who move on to other mating unions or living arrangements. More troubling is that shifting of father figures occurs within an admixture of warm and rule-oriented, controlling parenting practices. Risks for behavioral and adjustment problems due to instability in living arrangements may become exacerbated with harsh paternal parenting practices and exposure to high levels of violence in the home, school, and community in Caribbean countries (e.g., Jamaica and Trinidad and Tobago) (Roopnarine & Krishnakumar, 2012).

Bridges to Other Disciplines

Research on African American and African Caribbean fathers has emerged out of diverse disciplines such as anthropology, behavioral pediatrics, sociology, child development and early childhood education, family studies, psychology, history, social work, and demography. Despite the meager attempts at cross-disciplinary collaboration, it has become increasingly obvious, however, that in order to fully understand the role of fathers and their importance for childhood development, particularly in difficult ecological niches, it is necessary to consider the diverse needs and processes within families and children in the larger context of cultural communities. This can be achieved through increasing collaboration among researchers who focus on the physical environment/ neighborhood factors, health status, socialization and parenting, kinship structures, beliefs and rituals, early academic socialization at home, and other processes within individuals and families that bear on fathering. Possible benefits may include increased sophistication in design and data collection (multi-method, multi-trait approaches) and the development of more comprehensive theories on fathering. A prominent example of this phenomenon can be witnessed in the fields of anthropology and cultural psychology where researchers have joined forces to shape cultural models on fathering and childhood development that consider the myriad of factors within families, practices and customs within cultures, and the physical environment. Attempts of this nature in disciplines such as demography, allied health, and child development can provide population-level data on the influence of fathers' qualitative involvement and support on children's physical and mental health.

Policy Implications

Policy recommendations grounded in research on fathers have had greater leverage in technologically developed than technologically developing societies (see Cabrera, 2010; Roopnarine et al., in press). Having said that, the data reviewed herein point to three primary issues that have policy implications for African American and African Caribbean fathers' economic, intellectual, and social investment in children's lives: increasing the economic stability of fathers, improving their parenting skills, and strengthening their interpersonal relationships with biological and nonbiological male and female caregivers. The impact of economic stability on family relationships and parent-child relationships has been demonstrated in Caribbean countries (Roopnarine & Krishnakumar, 2011; Samms-Vaughan, 2005) and in the United States (McLoyd, 1990). To achieve economic stability, the United Sates has implemented "back to work" programs and initiatives to strengthen marriage (Cabrera, 2010), whereas some Caribbean countries have developed community work programs (e.g., Trinidad and Tobago) to assist families to get on better economic footing, independent of attempts to improve parenting skills or discuss "responsible fatherhood."

Taking into consideration the large number of out-of-marriage births and the diverse childrearing alliances that nurture and care for children in low-income African American and African Caribbean families, programs that build on educating fathers about the importance of good interpersonal relationships and parenting partnerships with spouses/partners, ex-spouses/ex-partners, and other caregivers are essential to promoting engaged fathering. Targeting these issues rather than marriage makes more sense. Fathers and mothers in low-income families tap into the various elements of human capital embedded in kinship and non-kinship alliances for support in childrearing (see Roy & Burton, 2009). Often, inter-partner conflict can be a deterrent to paternal involvement, and as discussed earlier, it has negative consequences on childhood development (Cabrera et al., 2008).

Summary and Future Directions

In cultural communities across the world, the importance of father investment and engagement in various aspects of children's lives has caught the attention of researchers, educators, and policy makers. Simultaneously, there is growing recognition of the different life-course patterns and family living arrangements within which fatherhood is realized and father-child relationships evolve. Studies on the two groups of men considered in this chapter have shifted from focusing on levels of involvement to cataloging the quality of parenting practices. Data indicate that African American and African Caribbean fathers engage in responsive care practices that are sensitively attuned to children's needs, with fathers across socio-economic groups showing reasonable levels of warmth to children. The two groups of fathers seem to differ on restrictive parenting practices, with African Caribbean fathers engaging in higher levels of harsh, strict practices that require obedience and compliance from children than African American fathers. These childrearing practices may be necessary to socialize children to acquire the skills necessary to navigate their way through daily life in economically and socially challenging environments.

What is clear from the findings reviewed here is that income plays a central role in men's engagement with children—particularly for African Caribbean men. Other factors, such as inter-partner relationship and spirituality, can be just as influential in steering fathers toward greater commitment to their partners/wives and children. There is also consistency in the relationships between parenting practices and childhood outcomes. As in other cultural groups (see Leidy et al., this volume), responsive caregiving promotes social and cognitive growth, whereas restrictive parenting has negative ramifications for language and social development in young children, though some of the relationships are mediated via family process variables. In African Caribbean families, instability in living arrangements due to mate-shifting can lead to social adjustment problems, with children from households with lean economic resources at greater risk for developing behavioral difficulties (Samms-Vaughan, 2005).

Noting the drawbacks of both time involvement and frequency of contact data, today researchers are paying more attention to the nature and quality of fathers' behavioral interactions with children. Although the newer data are informative, longitudinal studies are needed to determine how men's commitment to their families and the quality of their parenting practices and socialization goals take shape as children experience important developmental transitions through the early childhood years. Future emphasis on the factors that mediate and moderate the relationships between the quality of paternal parenting practices and childhood development in both African American and African Caribbean families from different living arrangements, socioeconomic backgrounds, and caregiving alliances may present a more comprehensive picture of African American and African Caribbean fathers' influence on the physical health and the social and intellectual development of children.

References

Ahmeduzzaman, M., & Roopnarine, J. L. (1992). Sociodemographic factors, functioning style, social support, and fathers' involvement with preschoolers in African-American families. *Journal of Marriage and the Family, 54,* 699–707.

Ainsworth, M. (1989). Attachments beyond infancy. *American Psychologist, 44,* 709–716.

Ainsworth, M. S., Blehar, M. C., Waters, E., & Wall, S. (1978). *Patterns of attachment: A psychological situation of the strange situation.* Oxford, England: Erlbaum.

Allen, A. (1985). Psychological dependency among students in a "cross-roads" culture. *West Indian Medical Journal, 34*, 123–127.

Allen, W. D., & Doherty, W. J. (1996). The responsibilities of fatherhood as perceived by African American teenage fathers. *Families in Society, 73*, 142–155.

Anderson, P. (2007). *The changing roles of fathers in the context of Jamaican family life.* Kingston, Jamaica: Planning Institute of Jamaica and the University of the West Indies.

Anderson, S., & Payne, M. A. (1994). Corporal punishment in elementary education: Views of Barbadian school children. *Child Abuse & Neglect, 18*, 377–386.

Aunola, K., & Nurmi, J. E. (2005). The role of parenting styles in children's problem behavior. *Child Development, 76*, 1144–1159.

Bakermans-Kranenburg, M. J., van Ijzendoorn, M. H., & Kroonenberg, P. M. (2004). Differences in attachment security between African American and white children: Ethnicity or socioeconomic status? *Infant Behavior & Development, 27*, 417–433.

Baumrind, D. (1967). Child care practices anteceding three patterns of preschool behavior. *Genetic Psychology Monographs, 75*, 43–88.

Benson, J. B., & Haith, M. M. (2009). *Social and emotional development in infancy and early childhood.* New York: Academic Press.

Black, M. M., Dubowitz, H., & Starr, R. H., Jr. (1999). African American fathers in low-income, urban families: Development, behavior, and home environment of their three-year-old children. *Child Development, 70*, 967–978.

Bowlby, J. (1969). *Making and breaking of affectional bonds.* London: Routledge.

Brown, J., Anderson, P., & Chevannes, B. (1993). *The contribution of Caribbean men to the family.* Report for the International Development Centre, Canada, Caribbean Child Development Centre, Mona: University of the West Indies.

Brown, J., Newland, A., Anderson, P., & Chevannes, B. (1997). Caribbean fatherhood: Underresearched, misunderstood. In J. L. Roopnarine & J. Brown (Eds.), *Caribbean families: Diversity among ethnic groups* (pp. 85–113). Norwood, NJ: Ablex.

Cabrera, N. J. (2010). Father involvement and public policy. In M. E. Lamb (Ed.), *The role of the father in child development (5th edition)* (pp. 517–550). Hoboken, NJ: Wiley.

Cabrera, N. J., Hofferth, S., & Chae, S. (2011). Patterns and predictors of father-infant engagement across race/ethnic groups. *Early Childhood Research Quarterly, 26*, 365–375.

Cabrera, N. J., Ryan, R., Shannon, J.D., Brooks-Gunn, J., Vogel, C., Raikes, H., et al. (2004). Fathers in the early head start national research and evaluation study: How are they involved with their children? *Fathering: A journal of Theory, Research, and Practice about Men as Fathers, 2*, 5–30.

Cabrera, N. J., Ryan, R. M., Mitchell, S. J., Shannon, J. D., & Tamis-Lemonda, C. S. (2008). Low-income nonresident father involvement with their toddlers: Variation by fathers' race and ethnicity. *Journal of Family Psychology, 22*,643–647.

Caldera, Y. M., & Lindsey, E. W. (2006). Coparenting, mother-infant interaction, and infant-parent attachment relationships in two-parent families. *Journal of Family Psychology, 20*, 275–283.

Chao, R. (2001). Extending research on the consequences of parenting style for Chinese Americans and European Americans. *Child Development 72*, 1832–1843.

Chevannes, B. (2001). *Learning to be a man: culture, socialisation and gender identity in five Caribbean communities.* Kingston, Jamaica: The University of the West Indies Press.

Clarke, E. (1957). *My mother who fathered me: A study of family in three selected communities in Jamaica.* London: George Allen & Unwin.

Cooper, S. M. (2009). Associations between father-daughter relationship quality and the academic engagement of African American adolescent girls: Self-esteem as a mediator? *Journal of Black Psychology, 35*, 495–516.

Crawford-Brown, C. (1997). The impact of parent-child socialization on the development of conduct disorder in Jamaican male adolescents. In J. L. Roopnarine & J. Brown (Eds.), *Caribbean families: Diversity among ethnic groups.* (pp. 205–222). Norwood, NJ: Ablex.

Deen, S. (1995). *Research into Indian family history in Trinidad*. Paper presented at ISER-NCIC Conference on challenge and change. University of the West Indies, St. Augustine, Trinidad.

Dix, T. (1991). The affective organization of parenting: Adaptive and maladaptive processes. *Psychological Bulletin, 110*, 3–25.

Dubowitz, H., Black, M. M., Cox, C. E., Kerr, M. A., Litrownik, A. J., Radharishna, A., et al. (2001). Father involvement and children's functioning at age 6 years: A multisite study. *Child Maltreatment, 6*, 300–309.

Duncan, G. J., Yeung, W. J., Brooks-Gunn, J., & Smith, J. R. (1998). How much does childhood poverty affect the life chances of children? *American Sociological Review, 63*, 406–423.

Durbrow, E. H. (1999). Cultural processes in child competence: How rural Caribbean parents evaluate their children. In A. S. Masten (Ed.), *Cultural processes in child development: The Minnesota symposia on child psychology* (Vol. 29, pp. 97–121). Mahwah, NJ: Erlbaum.

Entwisle, D. R., & Astone, N. M. (1994). Some critical guidelines for measuring youths' race/ethnicity and socioeconomic status. *Child Development, 65*, 1521–1540.

Fagan, J. (1998). Correlates of low-income African American and Puerto Rican fathers' involvement with their children. *Journal of Black Psychology, 24*, 351–367.

Fagan, J. (2000). African-American and Puerto Rican American parenting styles, paternal involvement, and Head Start children's social competence. *Merrill-Palmer Quarterly, 46*, 592–612.

Fagan., J., & Barnett, M. (2003). The relationship between maternal gatekeeping, paternal competence, mothers' attitudes about the father role, and father involvement. *Journal of Family Issues, 24*, 1020–1043.

Fagan, J., & Iglesias, A. (1999). Father involvement program effects on fathers, father figures, and their Head Start children: A quasi-experimental study. *Early Childhood Research Quarterly, 14*, 243–269.

Flinn, M. (1992). Paternal care in a Caribbean village. In B. Hewlett (Ed.), *Father-child relations: Cultural and biosocial contexts* (pp. 57–84). New York: Aldine de Gruyter.

Fouts, H., Roopnarine, J. L., Lamb, M. E., & Evans, M. (in press). Infant social partners and multiple caregivers: The importance of ethnicity and socioeconomic status. *Journal of Cross-Cultural Psychology*.

Gershoff, E. T. (2002). Corporal punishment by parents and associated child behaviors and experiences: A meta-analytic and theoretical review. *Psychological Bulletin, 128*, 539–579.

Gray, P. B., & Anderson, K. G. (2010). *Fatherhood: Evolution and human paternal behavior*. Cambridge, MA: Harvard University Press.

Greene, A. D., & Moore, K. A. (2000). Nonresident father involvement and child well-being among young children in families on welfare. *Marriage and Family Review, 29*, 159–180.

Hamer, J. F., & Marchioro, K. (2002). Becoming custodial dads: Exploring parenting among low-income and working-class African American fathers. *Journal of Marriage and the Family, 64*, 116–129.

Hamilton, M. (1964). The genetical evolution of social behavior I. and II. *Journal of Theoretical Biology, 7*, 1–52.

Hewlett, B. S. (1992). The parent-infant relationship and socio-emotional development among Aka Pygmies. In J. J. Roopnarine & D. B. Carter (Eds.), *Parent-child socialization in diverse cultures* (pp. 121–138). Norwood, NJ: Ablex.

Holden, G. W., & Edwards, L. A. (1989). Parental attitudes toward childrearing: Instruments, issues, and implications. *Psychological Bulletin, 106*, 29–58.

Hossain, Z., Roopnarine, J. L., Isamel, R., Menon, S., & Sombuling, A. (2008). Fathers' and mothers' reports of involvement in caring for infants in Kadazan families in Sabah, Malaysia. *Fathering, 5*, 58–78.

Hossain, Z., Roopnarine, J. L., Masud, J., Muhamed, A. A.,Baharudin, R., Abdullah, R., et al. (2005). Mothers' and fathers' childcare involvement with young children in rural families in Malaysia. *International Journal of Psychology, 40*, 385–394.

Hossain, Z., & Roopnarine, J. L. (1994). African-American fathers' involvement with infants: Relationship to their functioning styles, support, education, and income. *Infant Behavior and Development, 17,* 175–184.

Hunter, A. G. (1997a). Counting on grandmothers: Black mothers' and fathers' reliance on grandmothers for parenting support. *Journal of Family Issues, 18,* 251–269.

Hunter, A.G. (1997b). Living arrangements of African American adults: Variations by age, gender, and family status. In R. J. Taylor, J. Jackson, & L. M. Chatters (Eds.), *Family life in Black America* (pp. 262–276). Thousand Oaks, CA: Sage.

Jarrett, R. L. (1998). African American children, families, and neighborhoods: Qualitative contributions to understanding developmental pathways. *Applied Developmental Science, 2,* 2–16.

Jordan, L. C., & Lewis, M. L. (2005). Paternal relationship quality as a protective factor: Preventing alcohol use among African American adolescents. *Journal of Black Psychology, 31,* 152–171.

Kelly, M. L., Smith, T. S., Green, A. P., Berndt, A. E., & Rogers, M. C. (1998). Importance of fathers' parenting to African-American toddlers' social and cognitive development. *Infant Behavior and Development, 21,* 733–774.

Lamb, M. E. (Ed.). (2010). The role of the father in child development (5th edition). Hoboken, NJ: Wiley.

Lamb, M. E., & Lewis, C. (2010). The development and significance of father-child relationships in two-parent families. In M. E. Lamb (Ed.), *The role of the father in child development* (5th edition) (pp. 94–153). Hoboken, NJ: Wiley.

Lansford, J. E., Chang, L., Dodge, K. A., Malone, P. S., Oburu, P., Palmerus, K., et al. (2005). Physical discipline and children's adjustment: Cultural normativeness as a moderator. Child Development, 76, 1234–1236.

Leo-Rhynie, E. (1997). Class, race, and gender issues in child rearing in the Caribbean. In J. L. Roopnarine & J. Brown (Eds.), *Caribbean families: Diversity among ethnic groups* (pp. 25–55). Norwood, NJ: Ablex.

Lerman, R., & Sorenson, E. (2000). Father involvement with their nonmarital children: Patterns, determinants, and effects on their earnings. *Marriage and Family Review, 29,* 137–158.

Letiecq, B. L. (2007). African American fathering in violent neighborhoods: What role does spirituality play? *Fathering, 5,* 111–128.

Marlowe, F. (2005). Who tensds to Hadza children? In B. Hewlett & M. E. Lamb (Eds.), *Hunter-gather childhoods* (pp. 177–190). New Brunswick, NJ: Transactions.

McAdoo, J. L. (1988). A study of father-child interaction patterns and self-esteem in Black preschool children. *Young Children, 34,* 46–53.

McLoyd, V. C. (1990). The Impact of economic hardship on black families and children: Psychological distress, parenting, and socioemotional development. *Child Development, 61,* 311–346

McLoyd, V. C., Kaplan, R., Hardaway, C. R., & Wood, D. (2007). Does endorsement of physical punishment matter? Assessing moderating influences on the maternal and child psychological correlates of physical discipline in African American families. *Journal of Family Psychology, 21,* 165–175.

Mincy, R., & Oliver, H. (2003). Age, race, and children's living arrangements: Implications for TANF reauthorization (policy Brief B-53). Washington, DC: Urban Institute Publications.

Mitchell, S. J., & Cabrera, N. (2009). An exploratory study of fathers' parenting stress and toddlers' social development in low-income African American families. *Fathering, 7,* 201–225.

Murray, V. M., Smith, E. P., & Hill, N. E. (2001). Introduction to the special section: Race, ethnicity, and culture in studies of families in context. *Journal of Marriage and Family, 63,* 911–914.

Ogbu, J. (1981). Origins of human competence: A cultural ecological perspective. *Child Development, 52,* 413–429.

Oravecz, L. M., Koblinsky, S. A., & Randolph, S. M. (2008). Community violence, interpartner conflict, parenting, and social support as predictors of the social competence of African American preschool children. *Journal of Black Psychology, 34,* 192–216.

Pant, P., Roopnarine, J. L., & Krishnakumar, A. (2008, February). *Parenting styles among Indo–Guyanese Fathers: Links to early cognitive and social development.* Paper presented at the Society for Cross-Cultural Research, New Orleans.

Paquette, D. (2004). Theorizing the father-child relationship: Mechanisms and developmental outcomes. *Human Development, 47,* 193–219.

Payne, M. A., & Furnham, A. (1992). Parental self-reports of child rearing practices in the Caribbean. *Journal of Black Psychology, 18,* 19–36.

Perry, A. R. (2009). *The role of the extended family in facilitating African American, non-residential fathers' involvement.* Unpublished dissertation, University of Alabama, Alabama.

Phinney, J. S. (1996). When we talk about American ethnic groups, what do we mean? *American Psychologist, 51,* 918–927.

Ramkissoon, M. W. (2002). *The psychology of fathering in the Caribbean: An investigation of the physical and psychological presence of the Jamaican father.* Unpublished Masters Thesis, University of West Indies, Mona, Jamaica.

Rangarajan, A., & Gleason, P. (1998). Young unwed fathers of AFDC children: DO they provide support? *Demography, 35,* 175–186.

Ray, A., & Hans, S. (2001). *"Being there for my child": Inner city African American fathers' perspective on fathering and sources of stress.* Paper presented at the Biennial meetings of the Society for Research in Child Development, Minneapolis, MN.

Roberts, G., & Sinclair, S. (1978). *Women in Jamaica.* New York: KTO Press.

Rodman, H. (1971). *Lower-class families: The culture of poverty in Negro Trinidad.* New York: Oxford University Press.

Rohner, R. P., Kean, K, J., & Cournoyer, D. E. (1991). Effects of corporal punishment, perceived caretaker warmth, and cultural beliefs on the psychological adjustment of children in St. Kitts, West Indies. *Journal of Marriage and the Family, 53,* 681–693.

Rohner, R. P. & Pettengill, S. M. (1985). Perceived parental acceptance-rejection and parental control among Korean adolescents. *Child Development, 56,* 524–528.

Rohner, R. P., & Veneziano, R. A. (2001). The importance of father love: History and contemporary evidence. *Review of General Psychology, 5,* 382–405.

Roopnarine, J. L. (2004). African American and African Caribbean fathers: Levels, quality, and meaning of involvement. In M. E. Lamb (Ed.), *The role of the father in child development.* New York: Wiley.

Roopnarine, J. L. (2011). Fathers in Caribbean cultural communities. In D. Shwalb, B. Shwalb, & M. E. Lamb (Eds.), *The father's role in cross-cultural perspective.* New York: Routledge

Roopnarine, J., L., Brown, J., Snell-White, P., Riegraf, N. B., Crossley, D., Hossain, Z., et al. (1995). Father involvement in child care and household work in common-law dual-earner and single-earner families. *Journal of Applied Developmental Psychology, 16,* 35–52.

Roopnarine, J. L., Evans, M., & Pant, P. (in press). Parenting and socialization practices among Caribbean families: A focus on fathers. In D. Chadee & J. Young (Eds.), *Current themes in social psychology.* Mona, Jamaica: University of the West Indies Press.

Roopnarine, J. L., Evans, M., & Pant, P. (in press). Parent-child relationships in African and Indo Caribbean families: A social-psychological assessment. In D. Chadee & A. Kostic, (Eds.), *Social psychological dynamics.* Mona, Jamaica: University of the West Indies Press.

Roopnarine, J. L., Fouts, H. N., Lamb, M. E., & Lewis-Elligan, T. Y. (2005). Mothers' and fathers' behaviors toward their 3-4 month-old infants in low-, middle-, and upper-socioeconomic African American families. *Developmental Psychology, 41,* 723–732.

Roopnarine, J. L., & Krishnakumar, A. (2010). Parenting styles and childhood outcomes in Trinidadian and Guyanese families. Unpublished manuscript, Syracuse University, Syracuse, New York.

Roopnarine, J. L., Krishnakumar, A. (2011). The Trinidad parenting and beliefs and practices study. Unpublished manuscript, Syracuse University, Syracuse, New York.

Roopnarine, J. L., & Krishnakumar, A. (2012). Parenting practices and adult functioning and childhood outcomes in families in Trinidad and Tobago. Unpublished manuscript. Syracuse University, Syracuse, New York.

Roopnarine, J. L., Krishnakumar, A., Metindogan, A., & Evans, M. (2006). Links between parenting styles, parent-child academic interaction, parent-school interaction, and early academic skills and social behaviors in young children of English-speaking Caribbean immigrants. *Early Childhood Research Quarterly, 21,* 238–252.

Roopnarine, J. L., Krishnakumar, A., & Vagdama, D. (in press). Kakar's Psychoanalytic interpretation of Indian childhood: A contemporary view on the role of the father. In D. Sharma (Ed.), *Indian fathers.* New Delhi, India: Oxford University Press.

Roy, K., & Burton, L. M. (2009). Mothering through recruitment: Kinscript of nonresidential fathers and father figures in low-income families. *Family Relations, 56,* 24–39.

Samms-Vaughan, M. (2005). *The Jamaican pre-school child: The status of early childhood development in Jamaica.* Kingston, Jamaica: Planning Institute of Jamaica.

Shannon, J. D., Tamis-LeMonda, C. S., & Cabrera, N. J. (2006). Fathering in infancy: Mutuality and stability between 8 and 16 months. *Parenting: Science and Practice, 6,* 167–188.

Shannon, J. D., Tamis-LeMonda, C. S., London, K., & Cabrera, N. (2002). Beyond rough and tumble: Low-income fathers' interactions and children's cognitive development at 24 months. *Parenting: Sciences and Practice, 2,* 77–104.

Shannon, J. D., Tamis-LeMonda, C. S., & Margolin, A. (2005). Father involvement in infancy: Influences of past and current relationships. *Infancy, 8,* 21–41.

Sharma, D. (2000). Children's sociocultural and familial worlds: Pathways and risks through the demographic transition. In A. L. Comunian & U. P. Gielen (Eds.), *International perspectives on human development* (pp. 195–210). Lengerich, Germany: Pabst Science Publishers.

Sharpe, P. (1997). Teaching and learning at home: Features of parental support for the bilingual competence of pre-schoolers. *Early Child Development and Care, 130,* 75–83.

Shwalb, D. W., Shwalb, B. J., & Lamb, M. E. (Eds.). (in press). *The fathers' role in cross-cultural perspectives.* London: Routledge.

Sorkhabi, N. (2005). Applicability of Baumrind's parent typology to collective cultures: Analysis of cultural explanations of parent socialization effects. *International Journal of Behavioral Development, 29,* 552–563.

Summers, J., Raikes, H., Butler, J., Spicer, P., Pan, B., Shaw, S., et al. (1999). Low-income fathers' and mothers' perceptions of the father role: A qualitative study in four early head start communities. *Infant Mental Health Journal, 20,* 291–304.

Super, C., & Harkness, S. (1997). The cultural structuring of child development. In J. Berry, P. Dasen, & T. Saraswathi (Eds.), *Handbook of cross-cultural psychology: Basic processes and human development* (pp. 1–39). Needham, MA: Allyn & Bacon.

Tamis-Lemonda, C. S. (2004). Conceptaulizing fathers' role: Playmates and more. *Human Development, 47,* 220–227.

Tamis-LeMonda, C. S., Bornstein, M. H., & Baumwell, L. (2001). Maternal responsiveness and children's achievement of language milestones. *Child Development, 72,* 748–767.

Tamis-LeMonda, C. S., Kahana-Kalman, R., & Yoshikawa, H. (2009). Father involvement in immigrant and ethnically diverse families from the prenatal period to the send year: Prediction and mediating mechanisms. *Sex Roles, 60,* 496–509.

Tamis-LeMonda, C. S., & McFadden, K. E. (2010). Fathers from low-income backgrounds: Myths and evidence. In M. E. Lamb (Ed.), *The role of the father in child development (5th edition)* (pp. 296–318). Hoboken, NJ: Wiley.

Tamis-LeMonda, C. S., Shannon, J. D., Cabrera, N., & Lamb, M. E. (2004). Fathers and mothers at play with their 2-and3- year olds: Contributions to language and cognitive development. *Child Development, 75,* 1806–1820.

Taylor, R., Chatters, L., Tucker, M., & Lewis, E. (1990). Developments in research on Black families: A decade review. *Journal of Marriage and the Family, 52,* 993–1014.

Van Leeuwen, K., & Vermulst, A. A. (2004). Some psychometric properties of the Ghent Parental Behavior Scale. *European Journal of Psychological Assessment, 20,* 283–298.

Whiting, B. B., & Whiting, J. W. (1975). *Children of six cultures: A psycho-cultural analysis.* Cambridge, MA: Harvard University Press.

Williams, J. H., Auslander, W. F., Houston, C. A., Krebill, H., & Haire-Joshu, D. (2000). African American family structure: Are there differences in social, psychological, and economic well-being? *Journal of Family Issues, 21,* 838–857.

Wilson, L. C., Wilson, C. M., & Berkeley-Caines, L. (2003). Age, gender and socioeconomic differences in parental socialization preferences in Guyana. *Journal of Comparative Family Studies, 34,* 213–227.

Wilson, W. J. (1987). *The truly disadvantaged: The inner city, the underclass, and public policy.* Chicago: University of Chicago Press.

Yeung, W. J., Sandberg, J. F., Davis-Kean, P. E., & Hofferth, S. L. (2001). Children's time with fathers in intact families. *Journal of Marriage and Family, 63,* 136–154.

Chapter 14

Latino Fathers

Natasha J. Cabrera and Daniela Aldoney

University of Maryland

Catherine S. Tamis-LeMonda

New York University

Historical Overview and Theoretical Perspectives

Unlike research on the influence of mothers on children that has been dominated by attachment theory, research on fathers' influence on children has been driven by a variety of content specific micro-theories (Cabrera, Fitzgerald, Bradley, & Roggman, 2007). Research on Latino fathers, in particular, has been conducted within the framework of sociocultural theories that individuals' models of parenting behaviors change or become modified as a consequence of the immigration experience (McAdoo, 1993). Culture, composed of the ways in which people process and make sense of their experiences, influences a wide array of family processes including parenting roles, decision-making patterns, and cognitions and practices around child rearing and child development (Rogoff, 2003). For Latino fathers, the cultural context in which they rear their children might be composed of a combination of the practices and customs of their country of origin as well as of the practices and norms of the United States. This process of adopting new parenting goals and practices due to exposure to the host society, or acculturation, is gradual and occurs over time (Berry & Sam, 1997; Portes & Rumbaut, 1996). Studies have shown that Latino parenting behaviors reflect a conscious change in core values and goals during the acculturative process, resulting in adopting some values or behaviors while rejecting or partially adopting others (García Coll & Pachter, 2002; Harkness, Super, & Keefer, 1992; Marín, Van Oss Marín, Otero-Sabogal, Sabogal, & Pérez-Stable, 1989).

This cultural framework has not always included other aspects of the ecological context influence parenting. Parenting fundamentally reflects a relationship between a parent and his/her developing child. Although parent-child interactions unfold in a dynamic and cultural context, they also follow developmental timetables dictated by children's biological maturity and developing skills (Rogoff, 2003). Thus, fathering behaviors are also dependent on children's characteristics including age.

The notion that parenting practices and behaviors rooted in culture influence children's developmental trajectories is also at the core of sociocultural theories. For example, the ecocultural niche framework, in the tradition of Vygotsky's sociocultural theory, has been used to examine families' efforts to include children in meaningfully structured daily routines and to sustain them over time (Weisner, 1996). This theoretical approach highlights the role of family routines (e.g., cultural scripts, motivations, cultural goals and beliefs) of daily life as the process by which parents transmit culture and socialize their children (Harkness, Hughes, Muller, & Super, 2004). Parents, then, aim to shape sustainable and meaningful daily routines that are reflective of cultural practices and beliefs. Parents also make choices about the social networks in which children grow up, including parents' employment, peers, child care and school staff, and the type of neighborhood they live in. Collectively, these set of proximal and social experiences make up the developmental niche of the child (Super & Harkness, 1997). That is, parents structure the physical and social setting of the child's daily life, transmit culturally regulated customs and norms of childcare and rearing, and apply their "ethnotheories" (beliefs and views that promote development) to the rearing of their children. This view is entirely compatible with developmental theories that suggest that specific cultural messages and family routines should be adapted to meet changes in children's cognitive, social, and physical skills. Thus Latino fathering must be examined using a combination of sociocultural and developmental theories.

Another theoretical approach used to study fathers is family systems theory (Cox & Paley, 1997; McGoldrick, 1989). A family system view suggests that family members (e.g., fathers, mothers, children) are interdependent and influence each other in such a way that one individual can never be fully understood independent of the larger family system (Cox & Paley, 1997). Individuals (e.g., mothers, fathers, and children) affect one another through the quality of their relationships with other subsystems (e.g., parent-child). Thus, the quality of the father-child relationship (father-child subsystem) influences children's development through his parenting behaviors as well as through effects he has on other subsystems such as the mother-child relationship (mother-child subsystem), and vice versa. Family system theories also place great importance on parents' characteristics, including education, income, ethnicity, and culture as factors in a family's beliefs, practices, and values that influence their interactions with others in the system. Parents' income level, for example, is likely to influence many aspects of their decisions and behaviors.

Other theoretical approaches to the study of fathers include identity theory that focuses on the socially and constructed roles that fathers are expected to play in the family (Stryker, 1968; Stryker & Burke, 2000), family stress theory (White, Roosa, Weaver, & Nair, 2009), and capital theories (Coleman, 1990). Other researchers have used models of father involvement to understand how fathers spend time with their children, including examining constructs such as accessibility, engagement, and responsibility (Lamb, Pleck, Charnov, & Levine, 1987; see also Lamb & Lewis, this volume); discipline, praise, and show affection for their children; and, are involved in school activities (Hawkins et al., 2002; Palkovitz,1997). These theoretical ideas are integrated into a heuristic model that includes multiple predictors of father involvement and mediational pathways to context and child development (Cabrera, Fitzgerald, et al., 2007).

Current Research Questions on Latino Fathers

Given that Latinos are the largest ethnic group in the United States, and that the majority of Latino children live in two-parent households with their biological fathers, it is imperative to understand how Latino fathers are engaged with their children and promote their development. To this end, in this section we focus on fathers' influence on children's development during early childhood, a time of rapid growth in children's foundational skills that sets the stage for children's development over more extended periods. Our research questions derive from the Heuristic Model of the Dynamics of Paternal Influences on Children over the Life Course (aka Heuristic model) (Cabrera, Fitzgerald, et al., 2007). This model is based on current theoretical thinking that conceptualizes fathers as individuals with personal histories and distinct personalities embedded in family systems (Cabrera, Fitzgerald, et al., 2007). The model includes multiple determinants of father involvement and proposes direct or "causal" and indirect pathways between father involvement and children's outcomes.

Early research portrayed Latino fathers as harsh disciplinarians who endorsed values of machismo, focused only on the provider role, and did not examine fathers' role in child development (Cabrera & García Coll, 2004). It is therefore important that research on fathers provide data that either support or challenge these stereotypes by examining how Latino fathers spend time with and are invested in their children. Consequently, the first set of research questions is descriptive: *How are Latino fathers engaged with and involved in their children lives? How do they socialize their children?* For example, how are Latino fathers engaged with their infants and toddlers?

A second set of research questions target the determinants of fathering: How do culture, fathers' personal characteristics, and immigration experiences influence fathers' engagement with their children? That is, do individual, family, and contextual characteristics relate to variations in father involvement? Which of these factors is most important in determining how fathers engage with their children? Situating Latino fatherhood in the context of family, examples of such questions include: what are Latino fathers' roles in the family? What parenting styles, values, beliefs, and goals and expectations do they have for their children?

Finally, a third set of questions focuses on fathers' influences on children: How do Latino fathers influence their children directly and indirectly? What are the pathways of father influence? Do fathers influence their children directly through the quality of the interactions and amount of time spent with them or indirectly through the influence that they have on the quality of the home environment and the mother-child and father-child relationships? Examples of these questions include: How do fathers transmit values to their children through language and communication? How do fathers socialize their children?

Research Measurement and Methodology in the Study of Latino Fathers

The influence that fathers have on children's development has generally been studied using a variety of methodological approaches and measures. Challenges endemic to research on fathers, in particular minority fathers, include the *identification of fathers* (who is the father of the focal child), recruitment of fathers as participants, and retention of participants (Mitchell et al., 2007). A related challenge is a lack of consensus regarding *how fathers should be involved with their children* to foster their development, which is often based on what constitutes a "good father." Moreover, the different definitions and ideologies surrounding the definition of an involved father (e.g., fathers main role is to provide for their children) has resulted in a variety of survey instruments, which makes comparison of findings across studies difficult and arduous.

Researchers have applied both quantitative (survey) and qualitative (e.g., focus groups, semi-structured interviews) methodologies to the study of fathers. Early studies relied on mothers as proxy respondents from fathers, with more recent studies using fathers themselves to tell their stories (Cabrera, Fitzgerald, et al., 2007). This methodological shift has been the single most important innovation on how researchers collect data on fathers. Maternal perceptions of father involvement are important and provide information about mothers' views of fathers but do not tell the full story. Given family structure, and patterns of partnering, it is important that fathers' voices and views are included in studies of fathers and parenting, more broadly. If this is not possible, it behooves researchers to clearly use in their studies the title "parenting" only when both parents are included and "maternal reports" or "maternal parenting" when only mothers are included.

Survey methodology is the most common way to collect data from fathers or about them. In general, these questionnaires include questions on sociodemographic (e.g., race, ethnicity, education, income level, number of children) and psychological characteristics (mental health, stress), family processes (quality of marital relationships, father-child engagement, co-parenting), and other contextual characteristics (e.g., immigration status, social support, employment). Fathers also report on their level, type, and frequency of engagement with their children, including discipline, use of psychological and behavioral control, and warmth all of which can vary with, for example, children's age, and gender.

While surveys are expeditious and easy to administer, they can be limited in their reliability and validity. An alternative methodology is to use a naturalistic design that includes videotaping father-child interactions. Observational methods are especially suitable to the study of young children (Lamb, 2010), although they are expensive, time consuming, and may present only a snapshot of an interaction. Another tool often used in survey research is time diaries (Hofferth, 2006). The time diary is an open-ended chronological report by a child or the child's primary caretaker about the child's activities for one randomly selected weekday and/or one weekend day for each child in a family (Hofferth, 2006). The time diary asks questions about children's flow of activities, including what they were doing at that time, when the activity began and ended, who was engaged in the activity with the children, and what else they were doing. Although it accurately represents the daily activities of a sample of children, it represents only a small sample of children's days, limiting its reliability (Hofferth, 2006).

Overall, Latino fathers have been studied using small-scale studies, which are generally based on samples of convenience that may overrepresent low-income Latinos and emphasize the immigration experience. More recently, Latino fathers have been included in large nationally representative studies, which are valuable in studies of father involvement because they enable researchers to make generalizations to the larger population. These studies are especially helpful to policymakers interested in promoting father involvement in a way that is beneficial for children. Although there is some overlap, large-scale studies in the United States can be categorized according to two foci, those that focus on *becoming a dad* and those that focus on *being a dad* (Cabrera et al., 2004). The *becoming a dad* surveys include the National Longitudinal Survey of Youth 1997 (NLSY-97), the National Survey of Family Growth (NSFG), and National Longitudinal Study of Adolescent Health (Add Health). These surveys collect data on fertility decisions, number of partners, timing of relationships, parity, demographic characteristics, and some non-child specific father involvement questions. Surveys that focus on *being a dad* include the Early Head Start National Research and Evaluation Project Father Studies (EHS), the Fragile Families and Child Well-Being Study (FF), and the Early Childhood Longitudinal Study–Birth Cohort (ECLS–B) (see Cabrera, Brooks-Gunn, Moore, West, & Boller, 2002). These surveys collect data on mothers' and fathers' parenting, child characteristics, direct assessment of children. Some collect videotape data of father-child interactions (e.g., EHS), which makes them especially valuable to studying the father-child relationship.

The fathering survey questions in the *being a dad* surveys are often organized according to Lamb, Pleck, Charnov, and Levine's (1987) model of father involvement (e.g., accessibility, engagement, and responsibility) and Palkovitz's (1997) extended definition of involvement (e.g., motivations, and cognitions about being a dad).

Empirical Findings

In this section, we review findings of the association between Latino fathers and children's development, and structure our report on the three sets of research questions outlined above.

Latino fathers' Involvement in their Children's Lives

A common misconception of Latino fathers is that although they may provide financially for their children, they are traditional patriarchs, authoritarian and emotionally uninvolved with their children, controlling, harsh disciplinarians, and not very engaged in the daily care of their children (Mirandé, 1991). However, new empirical findings tell a different story. As a start, the large majority of Latino children lives in two-parent families, and therefore do not have the stress of living in single-headed households. In this two-parent context, Latino fathers have been found to be very involved with their young children, starting at the prenatal period. A study based on a nationally representative sample of Latinos found that Latino fathers were highly involved prenatally with their partners (e.g., buy things for mother during, discussed pregnancy) and baby (e.g., see sonogram, feel baby move, hear heartbeat) (Cabrera, Shannon, Mitchell, & West, 2009). Another study of 204 low income Mexican and Dominican immigrants, and African American fathers found that Mexican immigrant fathers as well as fathers who were resident were reported by their partners to be highly involved during the prenatal period (hospital visitation) and to more frequently eat meals with their 14-month-olds than African American and Dominican fathers (Tamis-LeMonda, Kahana-Kalman, & Yoshikawa, 2009).

Not only are Latino fathers highly involved from the beginning of their children's lives, but there's evidence that they are also, on average, warm and nurturing, and spend more time with their young children in shared and caregiving activities than White fathers (Mirandé, 1991, 1997; Roopnarine & Ahmeduzzaman, 1993; Toth & Xu, 1999). One study of 3- to 12-year-olds and their parents found that Latino fathers spent more time in caregiving activities than fathers from other ethnic groups (Hofferth, 2003). A recent study using a nationally represen-tative sample found that, after including control variables, Latino fathers (as well as African American fathers) had higher levels of engagement in caregiving and physical play activities than White fathers (Cabrera, Hofferth, & Schae, 2011). There were no differences in verbal stimulation activities across race/ethnicity. Fathers' education (college level) predicted more verbally stimulating activities whereas fathers' report of couple conflict predicted less caregiv-ing and physical play (Cabrera, Hofferth, et al., forthcoming). In another longitudinal study of fathers in the Early Head Start National Evaluation study, fathers were interviewed when their children were 2 years, 3 years, and in PreKindergarten. Latino and Black fathers of sons (but not daughters) reported engaging in more physical play (e.g., run and chase games, ball play) and social activities (e.g., taking children out with friends, to visit relatives, etc.) than White fathers (Leavell, Tamis-LeMonda, Ruble, Zosuls, & Cabrera, 2012).

A qualitative study showed that Latino fathers described their parenting experiences as more egalitarian, had similar expectations for both sons and daughters, and were similar to American parents' experiences in terms of parenting styles (Taylor & Behnke, 2005). Other studies found that Mexican American fathers used parenting strategies associated with authoritative parenting and were observed to be supportive and responsive to their children (Gamble, Ramakumar, & Diaz, 2007) and valued their role as a teacher (Raikes, Summers, & Roggman, 2005). In another study, Mexican fathers from both sides of the border reported that the main values they hoped to pass on to their children were the importance of education, a strong work ethic, and having respect for themselves and others (Taylor & Behnke, 2005).

Correlates of Father Involvement

According to the heuristic model, father involvement is multiply determined. In this section, we briefly describe findings on the associations between father involvement and cultural views and practices, the quality of the mother-father relationship (including co-parenting), the immigration experience, fathers' beliefs about the fathering role, and fathers' human capital.

Cultural models of parenting and socialization practices suggest that Latino values of familism (e.g., family obligations, family reciprocity) are linked to behaviors that encourage the fulfillment of family roles, such as taking care of children, and are thus related to high levels of father engagement (Buriel, 1993; Cauce & Domenech-Rodríguez, 2002; Grau, Azmitia, & Quattlebaum, 2009; Landale & Oropesa, 2001). A study of 67 Latino fathers of mostly Mexican and Puerto Rican descent of diverse socioeconomic status found that fathers' level of acculturation and macho attitudes were significantly associated with paternal involvement, whereas ethnic identity and *caballerismo* (chivalrous) attitudes were not (Glass & Owen, 2010). Latino fathers with lower machismo scores and those who were more acculturated rated themselves as being more involved with their children than their counterparts.

Other studies have shown how the immigration experience itself has an enduring influence on fathers' conceptualize their parenting roles. Qualitative data show that many immigrant fathers decide to immigrate to the United States so that their children have a better future (Perreira, Chapman, & Stein, 2006), and that fathers' adaptive strategies to rear their children in the United States are shaped by both risk and protective factors (García Coll et al., 1996; Perreira, et al., 2006). This adaptive process entails *overcoming new challenges* (e.g., coping with loss, discrimination, fear of the new environment, and structural and personal barriers) and *finding new strengths* (e.g., increasing communication with and respect of children, seeking help and fostering support, and developing bicultural coping skills) (Perreira et al., 2006).

Based on a family system perspective, fathers' commitment and sense of responsibility for their children (parent subsystem) as well as the quality of the couple relationship (couple subsystem) are also strong correlates of father involvement. Fathers who are involved prenatally (e.g., attending doctor visits) during pregnancy are also more likely to be involved with their children later on (Cabrera, Fagan, & Farrie, 2008; Shannon, Cabrera, Tamis-LeMonda, & Lamb, 2009; Tamis-LeMonda et al., 2009). Pregnancy intentions also matter. A study of Mexican American mothers and fathers revealed that when mothers wanted the pregnancy, fathers engaged in more caregiving and literacy activities with their nine-month olds than when mothers did not want the pregnancy. Moreover, when couples disagreed about wanting the pregnancy, fathers were more engaged in literacy activities only when they reported being happy with their partners (Cabrera, Shannon, Mitchell, et al., 2009).

Another important correlate of father involvement is the quality of the mother-father relationship. Being in a happy relationship can have spillover effects to other subsystems such as parenting; it explains why fathers who are prenatally involved are also more likely to be involved later in their children's lives than those father who were not (Cabrera et al., 2008; Tamis-LeMonda et al., 2009) as well as why Latino nonresident fathers are more likely than White fathers to be involved with their children (Cabrera et al., 2008).

Moreover, the quality of the couple relationship is related to other aspects of family functioning such as coparenting. A study of Mexican American fathers and mothers found that couples who reported marital conflict also reported conflict over child rearing responsibilities (coparenting conflict), which had a significant and negative effect on mother-infant interaction and father engagement (Cabrera, Shannon, & La Taillade, 2009). That is, when Mexican American couples disagree over child rearing , fathers and mothers are more likely to withdraw from their children than when they agree (Cabrera, Shannon, & La Taillade, 2009; Cabrera, Shannon, Mitchell, et al., 2009; Formoso, Gonzales, Barrera, & Dumka, 2007). Coparenting conflict appears to relate to negative fathering mostly for families where mothers are unemployed; coparenting support, on the other hand, is positively related to parenting regardless of maternal employment (Formoso et al., 2007).

In addition to the added economic stress that a single-earner family might place on the ways parents work together, acculturation might also have a negative effect on coparenting, although findings are inconsistent. Acrimonious parental interactions and disagreements about child rearing (co-parenting conflict) have been shown to undermine the cognitive development of toddlers and to be detrimental to the formation of a secure bond between parents and children in the early years (Cabrera, Scott, & Fagan, in press). This association, however, seems to be moderated by fathers' level of acculturation. In one study, when coparenting conflict was high, more acculturated Latino fathers engaged in more caregiving than less acculturated fathers (Cabrera, Shannon, & La Taillade, 2009). It is possible that acculturation serves as a protective factor when family relationships are hostile, but further research is needed to understand this process.

Self-efficacy theory stipulates that parents who lack certain competencies (e.g., language skills) have few institutional, social, or community supports, or face social or structural barriers would not have feelings of efficacy and thus not act to achieve desirable outcomes for their children (e.g., be an involved parent) (Bandura, 1997). Although most of the research on parents' sense of efficacy and positive behavior toward others has been studied in nonminority mothers, some studies have reported links between fathers' beliefs of self-efficacy and father involvement (Holmes & Huston, 2010; Lindsey & Mize, 2001). One study of minority fathers, including Latinos, found that fathers who felt efficacious were more involved with their children in physical and didactic play, and fathers who believed in their role as fathers were more likely to be involved in socialization (Freeman, Newland, & Coyl, 2008). Moreover, fathers' beliefs (i.e., self-efficacy and role construction) mediated the association between family context and father involvement.

From a capital theory perspective, parents with high levels of resources (or various forms of capital) invest more in their children than those with fewer resources (Coleman, 1990). Financial capital can be used to obtain many types of material benefits for children; human capital can facilitate cognitive and stimulating interactions with children; and, social capital derives from families' skills and from their connections to social networks that can foster children's growth and development (Coleman, 1990). Evidence suggests that Latino fathers who are more educated, have higher income, and are employed are more likely to be involved in their children's lives than those who are not (Cabrera et al., 2008). However, the magnitude and extent to which various forms of fathers' capital influence children's outcomes in a cultural context of beliefs and expectation is not well understood. We know that differences in father involvement are not explained just by differences in fathers' human capital, but rather by other family processes (Cabrera, Fitzgerald, et al., 2007; Hofferth, 2003). For example, differences in father involvement among racial and ethnic groups have been found to be partially attributable to mother-father relationship status (Cabrera, Fitzgerald, et al., 2007).

Fathers' Influence on Children's Development

The most central question regarding fathering concerns the ways in which fathers contribute to their children's development (Lamb, 2010). Although this appears to be an obvious question, researchers have long assumed that mothers, as primary caregivers, have more direct influence on children than fathers. Fathers' influence is often assumed to be largely indirect—through the resources they bring to the household or the support they provide mothers—rather than through their direct interactions with children. However, findings over the last 30 years have provided increasing evidence that fathers have both *direct* and *indirect* effects on their children's development. Specific to Latino fathers, research remains limited for various reasons (Cabrera & García Coll, 2004). We therefore also draw on studies of fathering more broadly as they can provide valuable insights to our understanding of Latino fathers (Cabrera & García Coll, 2004).

In terms of *direct effects*, fathers can influence children's development through interactions with children (e.g., responsiveness during everyday engagements) or by providing children with educational materials that enhance their learning and development; this pathway aligns with human capital theories (Coleman, 1990). Studies of low-income fathers, including Latinos, indicate that fathers' education and income are uniquely associated with measures of children's cognitive and language development (Cabrera, Fitzgerald, et al., 2007; Tamis-LeMonda, Shannon, Cabrera, & Lamb, 2004).

The importance of the quality of father-child interactions for children's development has been documented for cognitive and social emotional outcomes. In a study of low-income fathers (including Latinos) and their toddlers, researchers assessed the quality of father-child interactions along 14 dimensions (e.g., responsiveness, language quality, and intrusiveness) in fathers and 12 dimensions (e.g., play, participation, emotional regulation, and communication) in children (Shannon, Tamis-LeMonda, London, & Cabrera, 2002). They found that fathers who were responsive to their children during play were nearly five times more likely to have children within the normal range on a cognitive measure than were fathers who were low on responsiveness. A longitudinal study of observed father-child and mother-child engagements in a sample of toddlers enrolled in the Early Head Start National Evaluation Study also found that fathers' and mothers' supportive parenting independently predicted children's language and cognitive outcomes after co- varying significant demographic variables (Tamis-LeMonda et al., 2004).

Fathers can also directly influence their children's development through the language they use with children (Tamis-LeMonda, Baumwell, & Cabrera, this volume). A study of Latino fathers' narratives with boys and girls found that fathers communicated gender roles to their children through their narrative constructions about past experiences (Cristofaro &

Tamis-LeMonda, 2008). For example, when talking about the past with their preschoolers, Latino fathers of boys were more likely to talk about "action" events (going to amusement parks, ball games) than fathers of daughters who were more likely to talk about socially shared experiences and quiet time (e.g., family birthday parties, book reading). A study based on a large sample of rural low-income families, including Latinos, found that father education and father vocabulary during a picture book task predicted more advanced language development at both fifteen and thirty-six months of age (Pancsofar, Vernon-Feagans, & The Family Life Project Investigators, 2010). In contrast, only mother education, but not mother vocabulary during book readings, was related to children's later language abilities (Pancsofar et al., 2010).

Other studies have focused on the influence of father-child interactions on children's social development. Findings based on nationally representative samples found that paternal and maternal involvement were independently and significantly associated with children's behavior problems (negatively) and educational attainment (positively) (Amato & Rivera, 1999; Flouri & Buchanan, 2004). These findings have been replicated with low-income samples. For example, a study found that fathers' restrictive attitude was negatively related to social and cognitive development, whereas paternal sensitivity was positively related to aspects of social development that are less dependent on language skills (e.g., motor and daily living skills) (Kelley, Smith, Green, Berndt, & Rogers, 1998). In another study of low-income fathers, including Latinos, after controlling for parents' educational level, when fathers showed more child-directed parenting (i.e., allowed their children to explore, provided positive interactions, and did not overly dictated the child's activities), children had fewer behavioral problems and higher cognitive scores than when they did not (Shears & Robinson, 2005).

Similarly, a study of low-income fathers and their middle school age children, including Latinos, found that adolescents who perceived their fathers to be close to them had fewer behavioral problems and reported having more positive peer relationships than their counterparts (Cabrera, Cook, McFadden, & Bradley, 2011). In one of the few studies that focused exclusively on Latino fathers, researchers used a sample of first-generation Spanish-speaking Latino parents with children (aged 4–9) in a Western rural community and found that fathers' parenting practices (e.g., positive involvement, encouragement, monitoring, effective discipline, and problem solving) predicted fathers' reports of their children's externalizing and internalizing scores on the Child Behavior Checklist (CBCL); this was not the case for mothers (Domenech Rodriguez, Davis, Rodriguez, & Bates, 2006).

In a recent study of Latino youth and their fathers and mothers, level of conflict with either mother or father was consistently related to higher levels of both boys' and girls' internalizing and externalizing symptoms. More specifically, youth-father conflict was significantly linked to boy's internalizing symptoms and girls' internalizing and externalizing symptomatology (Crean, 2008). These findings are similar to those with White middle-class samples that show that the most socially competent children were those whose fathers were sensitive and supportive of their children's autonomy (National Institute of Child Health and Human Development Early Child Care Research Network, 2004).

In terms of peer relationships, fathers who exhibited high levels of positive physical play, allowed for mutual exchanges and followed partners' suggestions, displayed patience, and used less directive or coercive tactics during play had children who were rated as popular and less aggressive, more competent, and better liked by their peers (Leidy, Schofield, & Parke, this volume; McDowell & Parke, 2009). In a study of children and their fathers, a positive father-child relationship at age 3 was associated with less negative friendships at age 5, whereas more negative father-child relationships forecast less satisfactory friendships (Youngblade & Belsky, 1992). Studies with older children have shown that fathers influence children's peer relationships through the lessons children learn in the context of the father-child relationship, fathers' direct advice concerning peer relationships, and father's regulation of access to peers and peer-related activities (McDowell & Parke, 2009).

A study of Mexican American working- and middle-class parents found that although there were no differences in the amount of time mothers versus fathers spent with adolescents and their friends and both parents were aware of their children's daily peer experiences, mothers reported more involvement in and were more knowledgeable about adolescents' peer interactions than were fathers. Moreover, fathers spent significantly more time with adolescents and their peers when they had sons than when they had daughters. In addition, fathers', but not mothers', direct involvement contributed to boys' friendship intimacy and negativity (Davidson, Updegraff, & McHale, 2011). The researchers suggest that fathers providing boys with same-sex role models may be especially important to enabling boys to develop close relationships with other boys. It may also be that fathers are more likely to join in when their sons have developed positive relationships with other boys (Davidson et al., 2011)

In terms of the *indirect* influences, findings suggest multiple pathways. First, fathers influence their children through an influence on the *mother-father relationship*. Studies have shown that compared to fathers who are not prenatally involved, fathers who are prenatally involved have children with higher cognitive and social scores *because* they report having a more positive relationship with their partners (Tamis-LeMonda et al., 2009) and are more likely to move into more stable family structures (e.g., from cohabiting to marriage) and which, in turn, is related to increased father involvement and children's cognition skills (Cabrera, Shannon, & Tamis-LeMonda., 2007; Cabrera et al., 2008). Second, fathers might influence their children through the *mother-child interaction*. Studies of Latinos have found that fathers' education and father sensitivity during infancy as well as engagement in cognitive stimulating activities such as reading and singing songs influence toddlers' cognitive and social skills through its influence on maternal sensitivity (Cabrera, 2011; Cabrera, Fagan, Wight, & Schadler, in press).

Finally, father's influence might be indirect through *fathers' mental health*. A study of Mexican American two-parent families from a southwestern U.S. metropolitan area found that for both mothers and fathers, work pressures were related to fathers' depressive symptoms, which were, in turn, related to lower levels of warmth and disclosure and higher levels of conflict between parents and adolescents (Wheeler, Updegraff, & Crouter, 2011). They also found that fathers with highly demanding and hazardous jobs were more likely to feel overwhelmed, which, in turn, resulted in adolescents reporting lower levels of warmth from their fathers (Wheeler et al., 2011).

Bridges to Other Disciplines

The study of Latino fathers' influence on children is relevant to researchers from a wide range of academic disciplines, including sociology, economics, cultural psychology/anthropology, and education.

Sociologists and demographers tend to focus on research questions permitted by the national datasets, which do not always reflect the nuances of father involvement as uncovered by other disciplines. For example, developmental research suggests that the *quality* of the father-child relationship is more important than unidimensional measures of father presence/absence. Other issues related to the quality of co-parenting and mother-father relationships, core foci of both developmental psychologists and scholars in family studies, are not always included in national surveys. Thus, future research on fathers in general needs to acknowledge this limitation both in design and empirical findings, but also look to other disciplines for interdisciplinary collaborations. On the other hand, sociological research should also focus on how low-income Latino fathers can link with social institutions or create social capital for their children in a context that might preclude them access to such institutions. For example, undocumented Latino families might be excluded from being part of many social institutions or gaining access to specific social services (schools, social service agencies), which may have negative consequences for their children, most of whom are native born (Yoshikawa, 2011). Thus issues of balancing work and family and the effects of maternal employment on family functioning, which are important areas of sociological scholarship, may also look different for this group of individuals.

Similarly, theoretical and methodological approaches in the ways that economists study father involvement (see Bishai, this volume) would suggest that economists and developmental psychologists should need to consider the strengths and limitations of both approaches, which can then inform more collaborative models. For example, economists find that models that can generate predictions without appealing to heterogeneity (or individual differences) are more useful than those that do not. In other words, economic models assume that everybody in a group behaves the same way and still produce useful explanations of outcomes of interest. A theoretical foundation of economic theory is that individuals are rational actors who do the best they can, given their constraints. In economic models, physical and social constraints rather than individuals' preferences are central determinants of choice (Bishai, this volume). This approach might be useful in understanding the physical and social constraints that limit choices available to Latino men living in the United States, but might be enhanced by including psychological constraints in models. For example, fathers' attachment to their own parents poses significant difficulties for parents' attachment to their children, which, in turn, may influence the rationality of their parenting behaviors. Because many immigrant fathers were left behind by their own parents who left for the United States to seek a better future for themselves and their children, they may experience feelings of abandonment and low self-esteem that prevents them from investing optimally on their children.

From cultural and anthropological perspectives, fathers function within an embedded network of social relationships. Although parent-child interactions are influenced by beliefs and values of cultural communities, most of the extant research in these traditions does not consider the role of parents' human capital. Thus the conclusion that parents' beliefs contribute importantly to differences observed in children's outcomes might be premature, at best. Studies of middle-class minority families are almost nonexistent, thus it is unclear how the beliefs and values of middle-class minority families support their children's learning. Moreover, few studies of acculturation examine how beliefs and values change over time as parents adapt to the values and norms of the host society. This process of adaptation in beliefs and values that reflect both acculturation and developmental change is not well understood.

Overall, there are great opportunities for developmental psychologists to design the next generation of research on Latino families in collaboration with scholars from other disciplines. These lines of future research need to also include qualitative research that can elucidate the meaning of parents' beliefs and values as well as composition of families—who are the members of a family? For example, researchers interested in the ecology of Latino children might also include other adults involved in child rearing process, for example, grandmothers, *comadres/compadres*, and siblings. For Latino families, the care of children might be the realm of a wider network of people who are invested in the child's well-being to varying degrees.

Policy Implications

There is mounting and convincing evidence that fathers, in general, contribute to their children's development. In fact, fathers' investment on children is an important source of the variability we see in the adjustment of children from low-income minority households. Children who grow up in poverty with involved and invested fathers tend to have better outcomes than those who do not (Cabrera, Shannon, & Tamis-LeMonda, 2007). Because Latino children live in two-parent families and fathers have been shown to make unique and significant contribution to their children's well-being, fathers are an untapped resource of variation in children's outcomes and should be included in any study of parenting. Programs and policies should include fathers in their parenting programs.

Policies and programs focused on improving the overall psychological well-being of Latino children and their families should also focus on fathers' and mothers' mental health (i.e., depressive symptoms). Immigrant parents might be particularly vulnerable to stresses, including acculturative stress, and stresses related to poor physical health. Another important focus for policies and programs is the quality of fathers' relationships with their partners. The quality of the parent-child and couple relationships is central to the functioning of the entire family. Programs should focus on improving ways that couples relate to one another in the context of stress and challenges. Encouraging constructive conflict resolution skills should also be a central theme of programs aimed at helping families.

Future Directions

We conclude this chapter with a call for researchers to continue to include Latino fathers and their families into rigorous studies. In this regard, we have several recommendations; while some of these are not new, we think it is important to reiterate them in this specific context: (a) Future research should try to disentangle ethnicity from SES and other confounding variables. One way to do this is by conducting more studies with middle-class minority families. Another way is to conduct more within-group analysis and avoid using White middle-class families as controls, which furthers a deficit model and adds very little to our understanding of fathering processes; (b) there is a need to focus more on processes or mechanisms over time, rather than limiting studies to cross-sectional, correlational research. Cross-sectional research has provided important insights about Latino fathering, but they do not speak to issues of causality. Longitudinal studies that can track change over time are needed to understand the development and adaptation of Latino fathers and their children; (c) there is also a need for more culturally sensitive measures. Many studies of Latino fathers have begged the question about the influence of paternal involvement when using measures of behavior designed originally for mothers or members of other socio-demographic groups (Knight, Roosa, & Umaña-Taylor, 2009). This is a complex issue because measures of father involvement must consider the culture-specific ways in which Latino fathers rear their children as well as how these practices and beliefs change as function of acculturation. A dynamic contextual approach that incorporates changes due to children's maturation as well as acculturation must be part of any effort to capture the complexity of Latino fathers in the United States; and, (d) there is also an urgent need for more interdisciplinary and mixed-methods research that can help researchers and others understand how the dynamic context in which Latino men become fathers interacts with individual, family, and community factors to influence their own developmental trajectories as well as those of their children's.

References

Amato, P. R., & Rivera, F. (1999). Paternal involvement and children's behavior problems. *Journal of Marriage and Family, 61*(2), 375–384.

Bandura, A. (1997). *Self-efficacy: The exercise of control.* New York, NY: Freeman.

Berry, J. W., & Sam, D. (1997). Acculturation and adaptation. In J. W. Berry (Ed.), *Handbook of cross-cultural psychology* (Vol. 3, pp. 291–326). Boston, MA: Allyn & Bacon.

Buriel, R. (1993). Childrearing orientation in Mexican American families: The influence of generation and sociocultural factors. *Journal of Marriage and the Family, 55,* 987–1000.

Cabrera, N. J. (2011, August). *Contributions of parenting, socioeconomic status, and nativity to Latino children's school readiness.* Paper presented at the 119th Annual Convention of the American Psychological Association, Washington, DC.

Cabrera, N. J., Brooks-Gunn, J., Moore, K. A., West, J., & Boller, K. (2002). Bridging research and policy: Including fathers of young children in national studies. In C. Tamis-LeMonda & N. J. Cabrera (Eds.), *Handbook of father involvement: Multidisciplinary perspectives* (pp. 489–524). Mahwah, NJ: Erlbaum.

Cabrera, N. J., Cook, G., McFadden, K. E., & Bradley, R. H. (2011). Father residence and young adolescents' perceptions of their relationship with their fathers: Peer relationships and externalizing behavioral problems. *Journal of Family Science, 2*(1), 109–119.

Cabrera, N. J., Fagan, J., & Farrie, D. (2008). Explaining the long reach of fathers' prenatal involvement on later paternal engagement with children. *Journal of Marriage and the Family, 70*(5), 1094–1107.

Cabrera, N. J., Fagan, J., Wight, V., & Schadler, C. (in press). The influence of mother, father, and child risk on parenting and children's cognitive and social behaviors. *Child Development.*

Cabrera, N. J., Fitzgerald, H. E., Bradley, R. H., & Roggman, L. (2007). Modeling the dynamics of paternal influences on children over the life course. *Applied Developmental Science, 11*(4), 185–190.

Cabrera, N. J., & García Coll, C. (2004). Latino fathers: Uncharted territory in need of much exploration. In M. E. Lamb (Ed.), *The role of fathers in child development* (4th ed., pp. 98–120). New York, NY: Wiley.

Cabrera, N. J., Hofferth, S., & Schae, S. (2011). Patterns and predictors of father-infant engagement: Variation by race and ethnicity. *Early Childhood Research Quarterly, 26,* 365–375.

Cabrera, N. J., Moore, K. A., West, J., Brooks-Gunn, J., Reichman, N., Ellingsen, K., … Boller, K. (2004). The DADS initiative: Measuring father involvement in large scale surveys. In R. Day & M. E. Lamb (Eds.), *Measuring father involvement* (pp. 417–452). Mahwah, NJ: Erlbaum.

Cabrera, N. J., Ryan, R. M., Mitchell, S. J., Shannon, J. D., & Tamis-LeMonda, C. S. (2008). Low-income, nonresident father involvement with their toddlers: Variation by fathers' race and ethnicity. *Journal of Family Psychology, 22*(3), 643–647

Cabrera, N. J., Scott, M., & Fagan, J. (in press). Direct and indirect effects of the association between coparenting conflict on children's cognitive and social skills. *Special Issue of Family Process on Coparenting in Fragile Families.*

Cabrera, N. J., Shannon, J. D., & La Taillade, J. J. (2009). Predictors of coparenting in Mexican American families and links to parenting and child social emotional development. *Infant Mental Health Journal Special Issue: Development of Infants and Toddlers in Ethnoracial Families, 30*(5), 523–548.

Cabrera, N. J., Shannon, J. D., Mitchell, S. J., & West, J. (2009). Mexican American mothers and fathers' prenatal attitudes and father prenatal involvement: Links to mother-infant interaction and father engagement. *Sex Roles, 60*(7-8), 510–526.

Cabrera, N. J., Shannon, J. D., & Tamis-LeMonda, C. S. (2007). Fathers influence on their children's cognitive and emotional development: From toddlers to pre-k. *Applied Developmental Science, 11*(4), 208–213.

Cauce, A. M., & Domenech-Rodríguez, M. (2002). Latino families: Myths and realities. In J. M. Contreras, K. A. Kerns, & A. M. Neal-Barnett (Eds.), *Latino children and families in the United States: Current research and future directions* (pp. 3–25). Westport, CT: Praeger.

Coleman, J. (1990). *Foundations of social theory*. Cambridge, MA: Harvard University Press.

Cox, M. J., & Paley, B. (1997). Families as systems. *Annual Review of Psychology, 48*, 243–267.

Crean, H. F. (2008). Conflict in the Latino parent-youth dyad: The role of emotional support from the opposite parent. *Journal of Family Psychology, 22*(3), 484–493.

Cristofaro, T. N., & Tamis-LeMonda, C. S. (2008). Mother-child and father-child personal narratives in Latino families. In A. McCabe, A. L. Bailey, & G. Melzi (Eds.), *Spanish-language narration and literacy* (pp. 54–91). New York, NY: Cambridge University Press.

Davidson, A. J., Updegraff, K. A., & McHale, S. M. (2011). Parent/peer relationship patterns among Mexican-origin adolescents. *International Journal of Behavioral Development, 35*(3), 260–270

Domenech Rodriguez, M., Davis, M. R., Rodriguez, J., & Bates, S. C. (2006). Observed parenting practices of first-generation Latino families. *Journal of Community Psychology, 34*(2), 133–148.

Flouri, E., & Buchanan, A. (2004). Early father's and mother's involvement and child's later educational outcomes. *British Journal of Educational Psychology, 74*(2), 141–153.

Formoso, D., Gonzales, N. A., Barrera, M., & Dumka, L. E. (2007). Interparental relations, maternal employment, and fathering in Mexican American families. *Journal of Marriage and Family, 69*(1), 26–39.

Freeman, H., Newland, L. A., & Coyl, D. D. (2008). Father beliefs as a mediator between contextual barriers and father involvement. *Early Child Development and Care, 178*(7), 803–819.

Gamble, W. C., Ramakumar, S., & Diaz, A. (2007). Maternal and paternal similarities and differences in parenting: An examination of Mexican-American parents of young children. *Early Childhood Research Quarterly, 22*(1), 72–88.

García Coll, C., Crnic, K., Wasik, B. H., Jenkins, R., Vásquez García, H. V., & McAdoo, H. P. (1996). An integrative model for the study of developmental competeneies in minority children. *Child Development, 67*, 1891–1914.

García Coll, C., & Pachter, L. M. (2002). Ethnic and minority parenting. In M. H. Bornstein (Ed.), *Handbook of parenting: Vol. 4. Social conditions and applied parenting* (2nd ed., pp. 1–20). Mahwah, NJ: Erlbaum.

Glass, J., & Owen, J. (2010). Latino fathers: The relationship among machismo, acculturation, ethnic identity, and paternal involvement. *Psychology of Men and Masculinity, 11*(4), 251–261.

Grau, J., Azmitia, M., & Quattlebaum, J. (2009). Latino families: Parenting, relational, and developmental process. In F. Villaruel, G. Carlo, J. Grau, M. Azmitia, N. J. Cabrera, & J. Chahin (Eds.), *Handbook of U.S. Latino psychology: Developmental and community-based perspectives* (pp. 153–170). Thousand Oaks: CA: Sage.

Harkness, S., Hughes, M., Muller, B., & Super, C. M. (2004). Entering the developmental niche: Mixed methods in an intervention program for inner city children. In T. S. Weisner (Ed.), *Discovering successful pathways in children's development: New methods in the study of childhood and family life* (pp. 329–358). Chicago, IL: University of Chicago Press.

Harkness, S., Super, C. M., & Keefer, C. H. (1992). Learning to be an American parent: How cultural models gain directive force. In R. G. D'Andrade & C. Strauss (Eds.), *Human motives and cultural models* (pp. 163–178). New York, NY: Cambridge University Press.

Hawkins, A. J., Bradford, K. P., Palkovitz, R., Christiansen, S. L., Day, R. D., & Call, V. R. A. (2002). The Inventory of Father Involvement: A pilot study of a new measure of father involvement. *The Journal of Men's Studies, 10*(2), 183–196.

Hofferth, S. (2003). Race/ethnic differences in father involvement in two-parent families: Culture, context, or economy? *Journal of Family Issues, 24*(2), 185–216.

Hofferth, S. (2006). Response bias in a popular indicator of reading to children. *Sociological Methodology, 36*(1), 301–315.

Holmes, E. K., & Huston, A. C. (2010). Understanding positive father-child interaction: Children's, fathers', and mothers' contributions. *Fathering, 8*(2), 203–225.

Kelley, M. L., Smith, T. S., Green, A. P., Berndt, A. E., & Rogers, M. C. (1998). Importance of fathers' parenting to African-American toddlers' social and cognitive development. *Infant Behavior and Development, 21*, 733–744.

Knight, G., Roosa, M., & Umaña-Taylor, A. J. (2009). *Studying minority and economically disadvantaged populations: Methodological challenges and best practices.* Washington, DC: American Psychological Association.

Lamb, M. E. (Ed.). (2010). *The role of the father in child development* (5th ed.). Hoboken, NJ: Wiley.

Lamb, M. E., Pleck, J. H., Charnov, E. L., & Levine, J. A. (1987). A biosocial perspective on paternal behavior and involvement. In J. B. Lancaster, J. Altmann, A. S. Rossi, & L. R. Sherrod (Eds.), *Parenting across the lifespan: Biosocial dimensions* (pp. 111–142). Hawthorne, NY: Aldine.

Landale, N., & Oropesa, R. S. (2001). Father involvement in the lives of mainland Puerto Rican children: Contributions of nonresident, cohabiting and married fathers. *Social Forces, 79*, 945–968.

Leavell, A., Tamis-LeMonda, C., Ruble, D., Zosuls, K., & Cabrera, N. J. (2012). African American, White and Latino fathers' activities with their son and daughters in early childhood. *Sex Roles, 66*(1–2), 53–65.

Lindsey, E. W., & Mize, J. (2001). Interparental agreement, parent-child responsiveness, and children's peer competence. *Family Relations, 50*, 348–354.

Marín, G., Van Oss Marín, B., Otero-Sabogal, F., Sabogal, F., & Pérez-Stable, E. J. (1989). The role of acculturation in the attitudes, norms, and expectancies of Hispanic smokers. *Journal of Cross-Cultural Psychology, 20*, 399–415.

McAdoo, H. P. (1993). Ethnic families: Strengths that are found in diversity. In H. P. McAdoo (Ed.), *Family ethnicity: Strength in diversity* (pp. 3–14). Thousand Oaks, CA: Sage.

McDowell, D. J., & Parke, R. D. (2009). Parental correlates of children's peer relations: An empirical test of a tripartite model. *Developmental Psychology, 45*(1), 224–235.

McGoldrick, M. (1989). Ethnicity and the family life cycle. In B. Carter & M. McGoldrick (Eds.), *The changing family life cycle* (2nd ed.). Needham Heights, MA: Allyn and Bacon.

Mirandé, A. (1991). Ethnicity and fatherhood. In F. W. Bozett & S. M. H. Hanson (Eds.), *Fatherhood and families in cultural context* (pp. 53–82). New York, NY: Springer.

Mirandé, A. (1997). *Hombres y machos: Masculinity and Latino culture.* Boulder, CO: Westview.

Mitchell, S. J., See, H. M., Tarkow, A. K. H., Cabrera, N. J., McFadden, K. E., & Shannon, J. D. (2007). Conducting studies with fathers: Challenges and opportunities. *Applied Developmental Science, 11*(4), 239–244.

National Institute of Child Health and Human Development Early Child Care Research Network. (2004). Fathers' and mothers' parenting behavior and beliefs as predictors of children's social adjustment in the transition to school. *Journal of Family Psychology, 18*(4), 628–638.

Palkovitz, R. (1997). Reconstructing "involvement": Expanding conceptualizations of men's caring in contemporary families. In A. J. Hawkins & D. C. Dollahite (Eds.), *Generative fathering: Beyond deficit perspectives* (pp. 200–216). Thousand Oaks, CA: Sage.

Pancsofar, N., Vernon-Feagans, L., & The Family Life Project Investigators. (2010). Fathers' early contributions to children's language development in families from low-income rural communities. *Early Childhood Research Quarterly, 25*, 450–463.

Parke, R. D., Coltrane, S., Duffy, S., Buriel, R., Dennis, J., Powers, J., ... Widaman, K. F. (2004). Economic stress, parenting, and child adjustment in Mexican-American and European American families. *Child Development, 75*, 1613–1631.

Perreira, K. M., Chapman, M. V., & Stein, G. L. (2006). Becoming and American parent. *Journal of Family Issues, 27*(10), 1383–1414.

Portes, A., & Rumbaut, R. (1996). *Immigrant America: A portrait* (2nd ed.). Berkeley, CA: University of California Press.

Raikes, H., Summers, J. A., & Roggman, L. (2005). Father involvement in Early Head Start programs. *Fathering, 3,* 29–58.

Rogoff, B. (2003). *The cultural nature of human development.* New York, NY: Oxford University Press.

Roopnarine, J. L., & Ahmeduzzaman, M. (1993). Puerto Rican fathers' involvement with their preschool-age children. *Hispanic Journal of Behavioral Sciences, 15*(1), 96–107.

Shannon, J. D., Cabrera, N. J., Tamis-LeMonda, C. S., & Lamb, M. E. (2009). Who stays and who leaves? Father accessibility across children's first 5 years. *Parenting: Science and Practice, 9*(1–2), 78–100.

Shannon, J. D., Tamis-LeMonda, C. S., London, K., & Cabrera, N. J. (2002). Beyond rough and tumble: Low-income fathers' interactions and children's cognitive development at 24 months. *Parenting: Science and Practice, 2*(2), 77–104.

Shears, J., & Robinson, J. (2005). Fathering attitudes and practices: Influences on children's development. *Child Care in Practice, 11*(1), 63–79.

Stryker, S. (1968). Identity salience and role performance: The importance of symbolic interaction theory for family research. *Journal of Marriage and the Family, 30,* 558–564.

Stryker, S., & Burke, P. J. (2000). The past, present and future of identity theory. *Social Psychology Quarterly, 63,* 284–297.

Suarez-Orozco, C., Bang, H. J., & Kim, H. Y. (2010). I felt like my heart was staying behind: Psychological implications of family separations & reunifications for immigrant youth. *Journal of Adolescent Research, 26*(2), 222–257.

Suarez-Orozco, C., Todorova, I. L. G., & Louie, J. (2002). Making up for the lost time: The experiences of separation and reunification among immigrant families. *Family Process, 41*(4), 625–643.

Super, C. M., & Harkness, S. (1997). The cultural structuring of child development. In J. Berry, P. Dasen, & T. S. Saraswathi (Eds.), *Handbook of cross-cultural psychology* (2nd ed., Vol. 2:, pp. 1–39). Boston, MA: Allyn and Bacon.

Tamis-LeMonda, C. S., Kahana-Kalman, R., & Yoshikawa, H. (2009). Father involvement in immigrant and ethnically diverse families from the prenatal period to the second year: Prediction and mediating mechanisms. *Sex Roles, 60,* 496–509.

Tamis-LeMonda, C. S., Shannon, J. D., Cabrera, N. J., & Lamb, M. E. (2004). Fathers and mothers at play with their 2- and 3-year-olds: Contributions to language and cognitive development. *Child Development, 75*(6), 1806–1820.

Taylor, B., & Behnke, A. (2005). Fathering across the border: Latino fathers in Mexico and the U.S. *Fathering, 3*(2), 99–120.

Toth, J. F., & Xu, X. (1999). Ethnic and cultural diversity in fathers' involvement: A racial/ethnic comparison of African American, Hispanic, and White fathers. *Youth and Society, 31*(1), 76–99.

Weisner, T. S. (1996). Why ethnography should be the most important method in the study of human development. In R. Jessor, A. Colby & R. A. Shweder (Eds.), *Ethnography and human development: Context and meaning in social inquiry* (pp. 305–324). Chicago, IL: University of Chicago Press.

Wheeler, L. A., Updegraff, K. A., & Crouter, A. C. (2011). Work and Mexican American parent-adolescent relationships: The mediating role of parent well-being. *Journal of Family Psychology, 25*(1), 107–116.

White, R. M. B., Roosa, M. W., Weaver, S. R., & Nair, R. L. (2009). Cultural and contextual influences on parenting in Mexican American families. *Journal of Marriage and Family, 71*(1), 61–79.

Yoshikawa, H. (2011). *Immigrants raising citizens: Undocumented parents and their young children.* New York, NY: Russell Sage Foundation.

Youngblade, L. M., & Belsky, J. (1992). Parent-child antecedents of 5-year-olds' close friendships: A longitudinal analysis. *Developmental Psychology, 28,* 700–713.

Chapter 15

Asian American Fathers

Desiree Baolian Qin and Tzu-Fen Chang

Michigan State University

Brief Historical Overview and Theoretical Perspectives

On January 8, 2011, the *Wall Street Journal* published an excerpt of Yale Law School professor Amy Chua's new book *Battle Hymn of the Tiger Mother* with a provocative subtitle, *Why Chinese Mothers Are Superior*? The short article quickly caught the attention of the general public, and Asian American mothers were suddenly thrust into the limelight, their parenting debated and contested throughout the media and on social network sites. Curiously missing from this heated discussion is the role of fathers. In this chapter, we review scholarly research on Asian American father involvement.

Our chapter primarily relies on two theoretic frameworks that offer explanations for father involvement in contemporary Asian and Asian American families: gender-ideology theory and family systems theory. Gender-ideology theory proposes that gender norms affect how people define the appropriate roles played by men and women (Coltrane, 1996). Traditional Asian society is mainly dominated by patriarchy, which defines a clear gender norm directing disparity of roles between the father and the mother within a family (Chao & Tseng, 2002; Ho, 1987). According to this norm, the father is the master of the family and the primary breadwinner, who possesses the highest authority among family members and takes on the central responsibility of providing financial resources for the family. He is expected to keep his distance from the realm of domestic chores and childrearing responsibilities. The role of the mother is quite different. She is seen as the primary person taking on household tasks and child care activities. The gender-ideology theory posits that men's ideology has stronger influence on the division of family roles than that of women given that women are in a lower status in the gender hierarchy. Thus, mothers will continue to be involved in household and childrearing tasks due to their lack of power. In addition, this theory contends that gendered beliefs override the comparative resources of men and women (e.g., time availability).

Family systems theory includes a number of key concepts: (a) interdependent components: all members of a family system being interconnected and influenced by changes in any one member; (b) equifinality: family systems being able to achieve a goal through diverse options;

(c) change: family systems readjusting themselves in response to changes within the family or in the outside environment; and (d) variety: some family systems being flexible to adapt to change while others remaining rigid (Chibucos & Leite, 2005; White & Klein, 2008). Most contemporary Asian societies are shifting from agrarian to more urbanized/industrialized societies, leading to blurred boundaries of gender roles and women's increased participation in the labor force (Chao & Tseng, 2002; Ishii-Kuntz, 2000). When family systems are flexible, fathers and mothers will readjust their traditional family roles (men as breadwinners and women as caregivers) to meet this social restructuring while still achieving economic needs and childrearing functions. The readjustment of family roles for men and women influences each other. For instance, if the mother chooses full-time employment, the father will contribute more time to domestic and childrearing tasks in order to maintain family goals. In contrast, rigid family systems will continue to follow traditional norms on division of gender roles.

Family systems theory can also be applied to father involvement in Asian American families. After migration, Asian families in North America are often faced with two main challenges—cultural adjustment and changes of economic situation/employment status (Chao & Tseng, 2002). In response to these challenges, flexible family systems will reorganize the previous pattern (before migration) of division of family roles for men and women yet also strive to attain both economic and childrearing needs. For example, Asian families are likely to shift from single-wage (husband mainly) to double-wage (husband and wife jointly) after migration for economic needs (Qin, 2009). Given that women's accessibility to domestic and child-care tasks decreases, their husbands are likely to increasingly share these responsibilities. On the other hand, rigid family systems will follow the same pattern of division of family roles for men and women both before and after migration.

Current Research Questions

In this chapter, we integrate previous research work and address the following two research questions: How do fathers' family roles shift in contemporary Asian families? How are fathers' family roles defined in contemporary Asian immigrant families in North America (primarily the U.S.)? We address some parallel themes in both sections including (a) father involvement and paternal childrearing styles in today's Asian and Asian American families; (b) variations of fathers' involvement and childrearing styles in relation to factors such as family restructuring, socioeconomic status (SES) and occupation types (white-collar vs. blue-collar); and (c) father involvement and child development. Due to the process of migration, many Asian immigrant families undergo cultural adjustment and transitions of economic situation and employment status (Chao & Tseng, 2002). Thus, we address variations of fathers' family role in relation to changes of economic situation/employment status (e.g., from single-wage to double-wage families and extended working hour) and acculturation in Asian American families.

Research Measurement and Methodology

Research on contemporary Asian families.   In this section, a total of 25 empirical studies were reviewed regarding fathers' involvement and childrearing styles in contemporary Asian families. We also cited findings from two national statistics that demonstrate ideology of men and women toward gender roles in families in contemporary Chinese and Filipino societies (National Bureau of Statistics of China, 2001; National Statistic Office, Philippines, 2008).

Among the empirical studies, nine studies examined families with young children below the age of 6, three studies with elementary-school age children, nine studies with adolescents, and three studies with children at early adulthood or older. The majority of these studies collected small to middle sample size (below 500), five studies collected larger sample size (over 1,000; Berndt, Cheung, Lau, Hau, & Lew, 1993; Kim & Rohner, 2003; Shek, 2005, 2008; Shwalb, Kawai, Shoji, & Tsunetsugu, 1997), while only one study used national dataset (Song, 2004). About two-thirds of these studies were conducted in Chinese communities (including China, Hong Kong, and Taiwan), others were conducted in Japan (Ishii-Kuntz, Makino, Kato, & Tsuchiya, 2004; Shwalb et al., 1997), Asian India (Suppal & Roopnarine, 1999; Roopnarine, Talukder, Jain, Joshi, & Srivastav, 1990, 1992), South Korea (Jung & Hoing, 2000; Kim & Rohner, 2003; Kim, 2008; Rohner & Pettengill, 1985), and the Philippines (Esteban, 2006; Harper, 2010). With respect to recruitment area, all studies collected sample from urban areas except that Song (2004) focused on families from both urban and rural areas. In terms of familial SES background, the majority (68%) of the studies examined families from middle-class or beyond.

Studies on families with adolescents and adults were all based on a quantitative approach that uses surveys to assess primarily the following domains: (a) parenting styles including authoritative and authoritarian style (Chinese version of Child Rearing Practices Report-CRPR, Block, 1981; combination of Parental Warmth Scale, Zaslow, Dion, & Morrison, 1997; and Limiting Setting Scale, Alwin, 1997), responsiveness and demand (Parenting Style Scale, Lamborn, Mounts, Steinberg, & Dornbusch, 1991), and acceptance versus rejection (Children's Report of Parental Acceptance-Rejection Questionnaire-PARQ, Rohner, 1991; Children's Report of Parent Behavior Inventory-CRPBI, Schaefer, 1965); (b) parent-child conflict (Father-Child and Mother-Child Conflict Scale, Robin & Foster, 1989; the Asian American Family Conflict Scale, Lee, Choe, Kim, & Ngo, 2000); (c) parental control (the control subscale drawn from Schludermann and Schludermann's 1970 revision of Schaefer's 1965 Children's Report of Parental Behavior Inventory-CRPBI; Psychological Control Scale, Barber, 1996, 2002; Chinese revision of Barber's 1996 Psychological Control Scale, Shek, 2005); (d) parental monitoring (Paternal and Maternal Monitoring Scale, Shek, 2005); (e) parental discipline (Paternal and Maternal Discipline Scale, Shek, 2005); and (f) parent-child communication in both quality domain (Readiness to Communicate with the Father and the Mother Scale, Shek, 2005) and frequency domain (assessed by adolescent report of the number of hours per day and per week). Most of these studies relied on children's self-reports, while only a few studies assessed parent reports (based on fathers only: Abbott, Ming, & Meredith, 1992 and Harper, 2010; based on both fathers and mothers: Yang, 1999).

Studies on young children and children in elementary-school utilized diverse research methods in assessing fathers' childrearing behaviors and styles, e.g., time diary recall (Chuang & Su, 2008), observations (Roopnarine et al., 1990; 1992), interviews (Jung & Hoing, 2000; Bowes, San, Chen, & Yuan, 2004), mixed methods integrating findings from interviews and national dataset (Song, 2004; Sun & Roopnarine, 1996), and quantitative surveys. Eight of these studies aimed to assess father involvement that primarily includes: (a) time accessibility (measured by paternal report of the number of work hours per day excluding weekend); (b) engagement behaviors, e.g., caregiving, affection displaying, playing, disciplining, and decision-making in childrearing (assessed through observation method and surveys, i.e., Paternal Involvement in Child Care Index-PICCI, Radin, 1982 and Parental Involvement in Child-care Scale, Hossain & Roopnarine, 1994); and (c) ideology toward parental role (assessed by simple questions such as "I feel strongly about being 'masculine' as opposed to 'feminine'").

Among the remaining studies, three (Lin & Fu 1990; Bowes et al., 2004) focused on assessing (a) parenting styles, i.e., encouragement of independence, warmth, and acceptance (assessed by Child Rearing Practices Report-CRPR, Block, 1986); (b) parental control (the control subscale of CRPR, Block, 1981, 1986); (c) parental monitoring (assessed by interviews), and (4) parental involvement in education, i.e., emphasis on achievement (one subscale of CRPR, Block, 1986); and one study (Jung & Hoing, 2000) focused on intergenerational similarities and differences in childrearing practices and attitudes in pairs of grandfathers and fathers.

Research on contemporary Asian American families.   This chapter integrated findings of 22 empirical studies and our findings based on The Longitudinal Immigrant Student Adaptation (LISA) study, which portrays fathers' involvement and childrearing styles in contemporary Asian American families. Among the empirical studies, five studies examined families with young children below the age of 6 and fourteen studies with adolescents, including our study based on the LISA data. With respect to recruitment country, only four studies were conducted in Canada (Chuang & Su, 2008, 2009; Costigan & Dokis, 2006; Costigan & Su, 2008), while the remaining studies (including our LISA study) examined families in the United States. With respect to sample size, the majority of these studies collected small to middle-sized samples (below 500), while only one study collected a larger-size sample (over 1,000; Kanatsu & Chao, 2008). Our study was based on a small sample size (n = 72). In terms of sampled immigrant families' ethnic origin, 14 studies recruited families with Chinese origin (including China, Hong Kong, and Taiwan), others included families from Asian India (Jain & Belsky, 1997), Vietnam (Cooper, Baker, Polochar, & Welsh, 1993; Nguyen, 2008; Nguyen & Cheung, 2009), and the Philippines (Cooper et al., 1993; Fuligni, 1998; Fuligni, Tseng, & Lam, 1999). Our study focused on families with Chinese origins. With respect to familial SES background, half of the studies (11 studies) included families from middle-class background or beyond (i.e., moderate income and white-collar positions); three studies had sample primarily from lower to middle class (i.e., low income and working class) (Qin, 2009; Tamis-LeMonda, Niwa, KAhana-KAlman, & Yoshikawa, 2008; Yeh, Kim, Pituc, & Atkins, 2008). Our study included families primarily from lower to middle class.

The majority of studies on families with adolescents and young adults were based on a quantitative approach to assess primarily the following domains: (a) parenting styles including authoritative, authoritarian, and permissive style (assessed by Buri's Parenting Scale 1991, and the Parental Authority Questionnaire-PAQ, Reitman, Rhode, Hupp, & Altobello, 2004); (b) parental control (Psychological Control Scale, Barber, 1996); (c) parental discipline (the Role Disposition Questionnaire, Segal, 1985); (d) quality of parent-child relationship including intensity of conflict (assessed by Issues Checklist developed by Prinz, Foster, Kent, & O'Leary, 1979 and Robin & Foster, 1984, 1989), and closeness (a subset of the Family Adaptation and Cohesion Evaluation Scales II inventory separately for each parent, Olson, Sprenkle, & Russell, 1979); (e) parent-child communication including autonomy-supporting versus connectedness-oriented (Expectations for Behavioral Autonomy Scale, Feldman & Quatman, 1988 and Feldman & Rosenthal, 1990; Interdependent childrearing goals Scale adapted by Kim et al., 1996), the extent of openness (Mother-and Father-Adolescent Communication, Olson et al., 1985; the Communication Scale, Barnes & Olsen, 1985), and appropriateness of openly disagreeing (developed by Fuligni, 1998); (f) parental involvement in education, i.e., school engagement and expectation on academic (assessed by Steinberg, Dornbusch, & Brown's, 1992, Parental Involvement Scale); and (g) children's endorsement of parental authority (Smetana's 1989 scale of adolescents' reasoning about parent-child relationships). Most (12) of the survey-based studies relied on children's self-report, while only two studies assessed parent reports (Chao & Kim, 2000; Costigan & Su, 2008) or reports from fathers, mothers and children (Benner & Kim, 2009; Costigan & Dokis, 2006; Kim et al., 2009). These survey-based studies aimed to compare whether fathers and mothers are different in parenting styles and multiple parenting practices, as well as the ways in which they build parent-child relationship and communication. Only three studies and our present findings based on LISA study relied on a qualitative approach to assess parental involvement in education and childrearing, parenting styles, parent-child relationship and communication (Qin, 2008, 2009; Yeh et al., 2008). Qin (2008, 2009) and our present findings all were drawn from LISA study, directed by Marcelo and Carola Suarez-Orozco and designed to understand immigrant children's academic engagement, psychosocial adaptation, and family relations over time during a 5-year period from school year 1997–1998 to 2001–2002. Data for this study came from the first-, second-, and final-year student interviews and first- and final-year parent interviews. In these interviews, parents and children were asked questions regarding family immigration history, socioeconomic background, parental adaptation after migration, and family relations (e.g., changes in parent-child relations after immigration, communication between parents and children, and time parents and children spend together).

Studies on young children and children in elementary-school utilized diverse research methods in assessing fathers' childrearing behaviors and styles including quantitative surveys (Lin & Fu, 1990), time diary recall method (Chuang & Su, 2008), quantitative data obtained from interviews (Chuang & Su, 2009), and both observation of family interaction and survey methods (Jain & Belsky, 1997). Tamis-LeMonda et al. (2008) utilized multiple methods including surveys, ethnographies, videotaped observation, and semi-structured interviews. Four of these studies aimed to assess father involvement that primarily includes time accessibility (paternal report of time allocation per day), engagement behaviors, e.g., caregiving, affection displaying, playing, disciplining, and decision-making in childrearing (assessed through observation method and interviews), and ideology toward parental role (assessed by questions regarding traditional beliefs on gender role, Jain & Belsky, 1997). Only the study of Lin and Fu (1990) focused on assessing parenting styles including encouragement of independence and expression of affection, parental control, and parental involvement in education (i.e., emphasis on achievement) (the all were measured by CRPR, Block, 1986).

Empirical Findings

In this next section, we review findings on contemporary families in Asia, followed by findings on contemporary Asian-American families.

Father Involvement in Contemporary Families in Asia

Vast economic transitions in most Asian societies bring social and cultural changes that affect family systems, including the roles of men and women (Chao & Tseng, 2002; Ishii-Kuntz, 2000). In the past decade the proportion of women (over 15 years old) participating in the labor force has approached 50% in many Asian societies, e.g. China (44.4%; United Nation Statistic archive, 2006), Japan (49.3%; Foundation of Women's Rights Promotion and Development, 2004), South Korea (48.3%; Foundation of Women's Rights Promotion and Development, 2004), Vietnam (48.2%; United Nations Statistic archive, 2006), and Hong Kong (50.7%;

Hong Kong Government, 2002). Women's high participation in labor force produces drastic challenges to the traditional definition of gender roles in family systems-fathers as a breadwinner and mothers as childcare-providers. Growing evidence demonstrates that Asian women no longer adhere to traditional family roles and are likely to continue working even after marriage. For example, among the married population in China, men and women are similar in the rate of labor force participation (men: 75.8%; women: 79.7%; National Bureau of Statistics of China, 2001). In the Philippines, 60% of married women (in the age range between 15 and 49) are still employed (National Statistic Office, Philippines, 2008). Given that women's social and familial roles are changing in contemporary Asian society, how do fathers' family roles shift in contemporary Asian families?

Change and Continuity of Father Involvement and Paternal Childrearing Styles

Father involvement.   Corresponding to family restructuring in contemporary Asia society, the patterns of father involvement in their children's development are shifting away from the traditional role of being less involved in childrearing, which were recognized in national statistics and empirical studies focusing on two-parent families in China, Japan, and Korea (e.g., Abbott et al., 1992; Chuang & Su, 2008, 2009; Ishii-Kuntz et al., 2004; Song, 2004). Contemporary Asian fathers no longer assume the role of sole breadwinner and authoritarian figure over family members. Quite the contrary, fathers are more willing to engage in child care activities and respect their wives' opinions. According to National Bureau of Statistics of China (2001), 77.2 % of the men agreed that men should share domestic and childrearing work with their wives. Moreover, half of the men and women surveyed disagreed that men and women should follow the traditional differentiation of sex-roles in the family. A national survey in the Philippines (National Statistic Office, Philippines, 2008) demonstrated that women's voices are clearly heard in making major household decisions (40% and 49% of families adopted a mainly wife and wife-and-husband joint decision-making style, respectively). With respect to empirical findings, small-scale studies examining East Asian families found that fathers shared equal responsibility of child care with their wives, e.g. helping children with school work and participating in social activities (Abbott et al., 1992; Lin & Fu, 1990), actively took the role of a playmate with their infants or young children (Chuang & Su, 2008), and were more likely to involve themselves in childcare activities, especially when their wives had full-time employment or the family had multiple children (Ishii-Kuntz et al., 2004). In a large-scale study using national databases in both Chinese and Korean (Song, 2004), fathers reported a strong desire to perform the role of care-provider for their children and perceived themselves as being more involved in child-care compared to their own fathers.

Albeit with plentiful evidence that suggests a change in the parenting behaviors of Asian fathers, a body of research suggests that the way contemporary Asian fathers are involved in children's development is still largely dictated by traditional definitions of the fathers' role. In both small- and large-scale studies on East Asian families with infants in urban and rural areas (Sun & Roopnarine, 1996) and preschoolers in urban areas (Shwalb et al., 1997), the amount of time fathers engage in child-caring duties remains relatively small compared to mothers. Furthermore, the behaviors of child-caring involvement were quite gendered: mothers were generally responsible for feeding, smiling at, talking to, and engaging in object play with their infants, while fathers' involvement was largely limited to rough play. In Song's (2004) qualitative data, findings on Chinese and Korean families with older children (between 8 and 10) showed that the domains of father involvement were more confined to education-related matters in both urban and rural areas. Put together, these findings suggest that there are both changes and continuities in fathers' involvement in childcare and household responsibilities in contemporary Asian societies.

Paternal childrearing styles.   Unlike traditional fathers, contemporary Asian fathers strive to avoid the image of authority figure or aloof disciplinarian for their children. On the contrary, they desire closer and more affectionate relations with their children, especially in interacting with young children. Albeit with exception in some Asian societies, e.g. Asian India (Roopnarine et al., 1992; Suppal & Roopnarine, 1999), research findings suggest that fathers and mothers no longer report drastic differences in their efforts to sooth or be affectionate to infants (Sun & Roopnarine, 1996). Indeed, today's fathers display more affection and warmth toward their younger children relative to their own fathers (Jung & Hoing, 2000), and they prefer not to appear as the stern disciplinarian in front of their children (Chuang & Su, 2008). However, these findings need to be interpreted with caution as researchers examined families with infants or younger children instead of older children. A body of research (of both small- and large-scale) on families with middle- and high-school age children, and early and older adults (between 20 and 40 years of age) found that both children and adults view their fathers as being more strict or authoritarian than their mothers in many Asian societies, including China (Berndt et al., 1993) and Korea (Kim & Rohner, 2003; Rohner & Pettengill, 1985). Further, the stern image of fathers is especially strong for boys more than for girls in contemporary Asian cultures, e.g. the Chinese (Shek, 2005, 2008), Korean (Kim, 2008; Rohner & Pettengill, 1985), and Filipino cultures (Harper, 2010). Most of the abovementioned studies recruited participants from middle-class families and in urban areas, except that Kim and Rohner (2003) recruited participants from working-class families, and that 40% of Harper's sample (2010) was below the poverty line (which was somewhat representative of the whole Filipino population). The overall findings suggest that contemporary Asian men, at least in middle-class families, still follow certain traditional roles that fathers should exert authority toward school-aged children, especially sons.

Variations of Fathers' Involvement and Childrearing Styles

Family restructuring.   Given that women are likely to continue working even after marriage in contemporary Asian societies, how does wives' participation in the labor force affect husbands' involvement in household and childrearing work? According to our review, very few empirical studies examined whether there is any difference between double-wage (husbands and wives jointly) and single-wage (husbands primarily) families in the extent to which fathers are involved in household and child-care tasks. In a study randomly recruiting participants from daycare centers and kindergartens in urban areas of Japan (Ishii-Kuntz et al., 2004), fathers reported willingness to share household and childrearing responsibilities when their wives were employed full-time. In contrast, studies on Asian Indian families indicate that fathers are likely to keep their distance from household and child-care work even when their wives participate in the labor force (Roopnarine et al., 1992; Suppal & Roopnarine, 1999). These findings suggest that while family restructuring influences fathers' involvement in childcare and household responsibilities in some Asian societies, a patriarchal-centered value system remains the norm in other societies despite the shift of women's familial and social roles.

SES and occupation types.   In today's Asia, the quality, interaction patterns, and amount of father involvement tend to differ by fathers' educational level and income. In terms of the quality of involvement and interaction patterns, consistent findings show that middle- or upper-class fathers display more emotional support toward, and have more intimate interactions with their children relative to their working-class counterparts in many Asian countries, for example in China (Chuang & Su, 2008), Korea (Yang, 1999), the Philippines (Tan, 1997), and India (Roopnarine, Talukder, Jain, Joshi, & Srivastav, 1990). Wong, Lam, and Lai Kwok (2003) explained that middle- or upper-class fathers are usually more knowledgeable and more likely to learn contemporary parenting skills (e.g., building closer relationship with children) and favor these over traditional ones, and are thus more flexible in adjusting their parental roles.

In terms of the amount of father involvement, findings show differences across Asian societies. In Filipino (Tan, 1997) or Asian India families (Roopnarine et al., 1990), for example, fathers of higher SES tend to share more duties and invest more time in childrearing compared to those of lower SES. However, a study conducted in Korea showed that middle-class fathers reported less frequency and fewer hours in child-caring duties than working-class fathers (Yang, 1999). Such mixed findings across Asian societies might be related to fathers' perceptions of the paternal role. For example, in a study conducted in another East Asian society, China, Chuang and Su (2008) found that highly educated fathers, who generally had higher income jobs, were more likely to identify themselves as financial providers rather than child caregivers.

Residential region.   With rapid urbanization across Asian countries, differences in father involvement between urban and rural regions start to emerge. Although significant distinctions were not found in some Asian societies, e.g., Korea (Song, 2004), a body of research on Chinese families indicates that relative to rural fathers, urban fathers have stronger desires to share responsibility of child care and household work and are less oriented toward traditional paternal roles (e.g., Bowes et al., 2004; Chen, Liu, & Li, 2000; Song, 2004). Furthermore, urban fathers, generally more well off than their rural counterparts, tend to have closer interactions with and display more warmth and affection toward their children. According to Jankowiak (1992), the disparity between urban and rural regions may be attributed to factors related to the urban infrastructure characterized by the following: (a) most employed women work outside home in urban areas; (b) fathers and children live in a smaller domestic space which facilitates closer contact in urban areas; and (c) new notions of paternal role are more easily propagated through mass media than in rural areas.

Father Involvement and Child Development

Although to a certain extent contemporary Asian fathers still maintain a traditional role in their involvement in their children's lives, i.e. being authoritarian or stern, the studies conducted in urban areas recognize that a father's warmth can benefit their children's development, and the positive effects are distinctive from those brought by maternal warmth. In a longitudinal study conducted in an urban area in China (Chen et al., 2000), paternal warmth was beneficial for children's education and social adjustment, e.g., high academic achievement, great social competences and leadership skills. Maternal warmth, on the other hand, did not predict these outcomes, but were found to have significant influence on children's emotional management, e.g., less depression and loneliness. Similarly, studies on the influence of parenting style showed that children's social development is more negatively affected by the authoritarian style of fathers than of mothers among the population of young children and early adults living in urban areas (Chen, Dong, & Zhou, 1997; Esteban, 2006). Esteban (2006) also found that children with authoritarian fathers were more likely to report feeling frustrated, stressful, angry, and out of control compared to those without an authoritarian father. In contrast, children with authoritarian mothers reported more internalized problems, e.g., feeling sad, helpless, and discouraged, compared to those with less authoritarian mothers.

To summarize, the father role has undergone significant changes in many contemporary Asian societies, especially among urban fathers. However, the traditional aloof and disciplinarian father image remains strong in certain segments of some societies. In the next section, we turn to Asian American families and examine further adjustments of fathers' role in these families.

Contemporary Asian American Families

Since the passage of the 1965 Immigration Reform Act, the United States has witnessed a drastic increase of immigrants from Asia. On average, the United States annually admits more than 220,000 Asian immigrants, accounting for 35% of total immigrants to the country (Min, 2006). After migration, Asian families in North America are often faced with two main challenges—cultural adjustment and changes of economic situation/employment status (Chao & Tseng, 2002). These transitions often call for family restructuring and the redefinition of the roles of fathers and mothers.

Father Involvement and Paternal Childrearing Styles

The United States is a developed industrialized nation that stresses gender equality and diminished gender roles in family systems (Cabrera, Tamis-LeMonda, Bradley, Hofferth, & Lamb, 2000; McFadden & Tamis-LeMonda, in press; Tamis-LeMonda & McFadden, 2010). According to the report of U.S. Bureau of Labor Statistics (1997, 2009), about two-thirds of married women participate in the labor force. Compared to women from Asian countries such as Japan, South Korea, Taiwan, and Singapore, U.S. women tend to report stronger intentions of being employed after marriage (Executive Bureau of Directorate-General of Budget, Accounting and Statistics, Taiwan, 2004). With respect to gender roles in families, the gender gap of parental involvement is also narrowed. Yeung, Sandberg, Davis-Kean, & Hofferth (2001) found that U.S. fathers of today spend two-thirds to four-fifths as much time as mothers caring of children, while formerly husbands only spent about a third as much time as did their spouse. In a cross-country survey (German Social Science Intrastructure Services – International Social Survey Programme, 2002), a higher percentage of U.S. men and women (52.5%) disagreed with the traditional ideology that "the husband is a breadwinner and the wife is a care-provider" than those from Asian countries, e.g., Japan (48.5%), Taiwan (38.5%), and Philippines (14.6%).

Because the U.S. society generally stresses gender equality more than Asian societies, Asian immigrants often have to readjust their family structure and roles in the process of adaptation. Among East Asian immigrant families, it was found that fathers tend to shoulder child care responsibilities as much as their wives do (Chuang & Su, 2009), and display similar levels of warmth and closeness toward their children as their spouses (Chao & Kim, 2000; Hardway & Fuligni, 2006). Studies comparing immigrant and native Chinese families found that immigrant Chinese fathers contribute more time to child care giving and household chores as well as exert less control over younger children (Chuang & Su, 2008; Lin & Fu, 1990). Nevertheless, another body of findings indicated that Asian traditional values remain strong in defining parenting roles of Asian immigrant fathers. In a study comparing college students from multiple ethnic groups with somewhat comparable SES backgrounds, Asian Americans, including Chinese, Filipino, and Vietnamese Americans, perceived less power in the process of making decisions with fathers when compared to their European counterparts (Cooper et al., 1993). Similarly, recent studies on middle-class adolescents indicate that Asian Americans perceived less closeness and had less freedom to assert own opinions with fathers in contrast to their European counterparts (Rhee, Chang, & Rhee, 2003; Hardway & Fuligni, 2006). In a study on first-generation Vietnamese families (Nguyen & Cheung, 2009), findings based on adolescents' self-report demonstrate that their fathers' parenting style is more punishment-oriented rather than authoritativeness-oriented.

In addition to parenting style, our findings, based on LISA study, suggest that the domains of childrearing that Asian American fathers involve in is very confined to academic achievement and value transmission in both low- and middle-class families. This pattern of father involvement confirms the traditional family role defined in Asian society that fathers take on the role of educators or trainers for their children. Along this line, Dundes, Cho, and Kwak (2009) found that Asian American fathers place more emphasis on academic achievement (e.g., entering into a prestigious college) than European American counterparts. Overall, these findings suggest that there are both continuities and readjustments in Asian American fathers' involvement and childrearing styles. However, caution needs to be taken in interpreting the abovementioned findings since these findings are primarily based on middle-class-dominated sample or group-level comparison (Asian vs. European Americans). These findings did not consider variation of father involvement and fathers' parenting styles in relation to SES and occupation types, acculturation, and changes of economic situation/employment status.

Variations of Fathers' Involvement and Childrearing Styles

SES and occupation types.   In terms of general accessibility, fathers from higher SES are more likely to contribute comparable time to childrearing as their wives when compared to fathers from lower SES. Our analyses drawn from LISA study demonstrate that in the majority of the middle-class families, fathers were quite involved in children's education both before and after migration. In contrast to their working-class counterparts, middle-class fathers expressed more concern over their children's education and were more involved and engaged in children's education after migration. Furthermore, while working-class fathers emphasized a single focus on scores and grades, middle-class fathers often articulated clear, coherent philosophies of education that emphasized educating the whole child, including paying attention to the development of morality and character. Our findings highlight that there are SES differences in the extent to which fathers are involved in childrearing in both quantity and quality.

With respect to parenting styles, previous findings suggest that Asian American fathers from middle-class families are more likely to use authoritative parenting style rather than authoritarian style in contrast to their working-class counterparts. Drawing data from a LISA study, Qin (2008) found that Chinese immigrant children from working-class families were more likely to perceive authoritarian parenting styles from both fathers and mothers when compared to those from middle-class families. In a study on Vietnamese Americans (Nguyen, 2008), findings also highlighted that adolescents from working-class families were more likely to have authoritarian fathers than authoritative fathers in contrast to those from middle-class families.

Changes of economic situation/employment status and father involvement.   In addition to cultural adjustment, many Asian immigrant families undergo transitions of economic situation and employment status (Chao & Tseng, 2002). In the process of migration, a substantial portion of Asian families experience downward mobility due to language barriers or unfamiliarity with the new culture (Qin, 2009). In response to such changes, Asian families often restructure their family employment status from single-wage (husband mainly) to double-wage earner (husband and wife jointly). In families already with dual incomes, work hours may be extended after migration to cope with the new economic pressure. Interestingly, these transitions can bring both positive and negative effects on the quality of father involvement among Asian American families (also see Bishai & Scott, this volume and Hofferth, 2003, for a discussion on results from non-Chinese samples). In a study on Chinese, Korean, and Filipino American families, Kanatsu and Chao (2008) suggested that when both mothers and fathers were employed, fathers were more likely to share childcare responsibilities and therefore children were more likely to identify fathers as an important care-provider. In contrast, our LISA study and some studies found that economic/employment transition can be a threat to Asian American fathers' involvement given that they over commit themselves to the breadwinner role to compensate for the downward economic mobility accompanying migration (Tamis-LeMonda et al., 2008; Yeh et al., 2008). For example, Tamis-LeMonda et al. (2008) found that immigrant Chinese fathers spent very long hours (over 50 hours per week) working, which resulted in them being often absent in infant care. Yeh et al. (2008) also found that after migration fathers contributed less time to talk with children because they need to work overtime in order to overcome economic disadvantages. Similarly, our findings based on LISA study indicate that while women's participation in the labor market rate has increased after migration, our data did not show any evidence of corresponding increase of men's involvement in household or childcare activities. The inconsistent findings on the quality of father involvement might be due to different economic situations in the families. Relative to the sample in the study of Kanatsu and Chao (2008), the sample of our study and the studies of Tamis-LeMonda et al. (2008) and Yeh et al. (2008) mainly consisted of working-class families. Therefore, fathers in the latter studies might feel more economic pressure, which negatively affected their quality of their involvement.

Acculturation.   Fathers' acculturation orientation is another critical factor accounting for why some fathers shift gender roles at home but some maintain traditional roles. In a study on Asian Indian families (Jain & Belsky, 1997), compared to those in less acculturated families (measured by attitudes, feelings, behaviors, and home artifacts), fathers in the more acculturated families reported higher levels of parental involvement (including playing, caring, and disciplining) and stressed paternal warmth more. In another study focusing on generational difference, Fuligni (1998) found that third-generation Chinese adolescents were more willing to challenge fathers' authority in contrast to their first-generation counterparts. In a study on Chinese Canadian families (Costigan & Su, 2008), fathers highly oriented toward Chinese culture were more likely to endorse the beliefs of traditional parenting style, e.g., stressing authority and interdependence for their children. One exception is Nguyen's (2008) finding that parenting style is not associated with fathers' acculturation (measured by values and behaviors) in Vietnamese American families. Interestingly, Nguyen's study assessed fathers' acculturation based on adolescents' self-report rather than fathers' own report, which might decrease the reliability of measuring fathers' acculturation. Even though these studies did not necessarily investigate paternal familial roles prior to immigration, emerging findings suggest that acculturation exerts an important influence on fathers' involvement and childrearing styles among Asian American families.

Acculturation's effects on fathers' family roles can vary with familial SES backgrounds. Based on our findings on LISA study, in middle-class families after migration, fathers and mothers generally were more willing to incorporate Western parenting styles into childrearing. For example, they tended to respect children's opinions and adopt democratic communication. In contrast, fathers and mothers in working-class families tended to adopt a more traditional parenting style, i.e., stressing authority and obedience from their children. In addition, fathers in working-class families were faced with more barriers in providing their children effective and substantial assistance in education as a result of their limited English ability when compared to fathers in middle-class families.

Father Involvement and Child Development

Similar to the findings on Asian families, the findings on Asian American families indicate that children's development is influenced by the quality of father involvement. The quality of father involvement is linked to an acculturation gap in the father-child dyad. In the study of Kim et al. (2009), for example, incongruence between Chinese and American cultural orientations in the father-child dyad predicted fathers' lower levels of reported warmth toward their children, which is further related to children's depressive symptoms. Similarly, another study on immigrant Chinese families in Canada found that father-child discrepancy in Chinese values is associated with children's increased levels of depression (Costigan, & Dokis, 2006). However, this pattern was not found for the mother-child dyad in both studies. This parental gender difference in the involvement quality suggests that fathers in Asian American families play an important role in their children's emotional development.

Although immigrant Asian fathers start to stress their role of emotional caregiver for their children, they still play the primary educator or value conveyer role in their children's life as traditional Asian fathers do. According to Benner and Kim (2009), Asian American fathers' acculturation experiences and attitudes determine whether their role as educator/value conveyer has positive or negative effects on children's development. They found that fathers who experienced discrimination tend to pass along foreigner stress and the anticipation of racial bias to their children. They also found that fathers' foreigner stress predicted children's cultural misfit and paternal anticipation of racial bias predicted children's negative views toward school. In contrast, fathers who experienced less discrimination were more likely to emphasize the positive aspects of American society, which in turn benefited their children's social and cultural adjustment in the new land.

Bridges to Other Disciplines

In this chapter, we reviewed research on father involvement in contemporary Asian and Asian American families, drawing primarily from the fields of development psychology, gender, and family studies. Our review of research produced in these fields draw on quantitative and qualities data to document both the pattern and process of shifting father involvement in these families and the influence of father involvement on child developmental outcomes. Our review of research in these domains compliments findings from studies in other disciplines, such as demography, sociology and economics that examined macro-level patterns of father economic contribution, decision making, and influences on father involvement in the household. Further, the studies we have reviewed include mostly studies with small to medium sample sizes. Research from other domains such as demography or economics can provide clearer overall patterns in some of these issues we have discussed in the review based on analyses of national samples that are likely to be more representative, and therefore less threatened by selection bias.

Policy Implications and Future Directions

Our review shows that Asian American fathers play very important and distinct roles in child education and development. In particular, paternal warmth and support have significant positive influence on children's developmental outcomes and authoritarian fathers are associated with various negative outcomes in children and adolescents. Our review also shows that economic pressure after migration is a serious threat to the quality and quantity of paternal involvement in children's lives (Tamis-Lemonda et al., 2008). This has significant negative influence on father roles and the development of children, especially those from working-class immigrant families. The lack of presence and involvement of working-class fathers significantly disadvantages their children's education and development. This provides important implications for policies and practices relevant to Asian immigrant families in this country.

Finally, we would like to recommend a number of directions for future research. First, the majority of the research studies we reviewed relied on quantitative methods. It is important for future research to draw on rigorous qualitative or mixed method design to explore the nuanced, lived experiences of fathers and their involvement in Asian American families. Second, future studies are needed to examine father involvement both prior to and after migration in order to determine how fathers' familial roles might be adjusted due to the exposure to the new culture. Third, it is important for future research to examine the interaction between acculturation and SES on father involvement across different Asian subgroups. Lastly, more research is needed to examine how we can design effective intervention programs to improve father involvement which may have long lasting influence on Asian American child development.

References

Abbott, D. A., Ming, Z. F., & Meredith, W. H. (1992). An evolving redefinition of the fatherhood role in the People's Republic of China. *International Journal of Sociology of the Family, 22*, 45–54.

Alwin, D. (1997). Detroit Area Study, 1997: Social change in religion and child rearing (ICPSR04120-v1). Ann Arbor, MI: Detroit Area Studies.

Barber, B. K. (1996). Parental psychological control: Revisiting a neglected construct. *Child Development, 67*, 3296–3319.

Barber, B. K. (Ed.). (2002). *Intrusive parenting: How psychological control affects children and adolescents.* Washington, DC: American Psychological Association.

Barnes, H. L., & Olsen, D. H. (1985). Parent-adolescent communication and the circumplex model. *Child Development, 56*(2), 438–447.

Benner, A. D., & Kim, S. Y. (2009). Intergenerational experiences of discrimination in Chinese American families: Influences of socialization and stress. *Journal of Marriage and Family, 71,* 862–877.

Berndt, T. J., Cheung, P. C., Lau, S., Hau, K., & Lew, W. J. (1993). Perceptions of parenting in Mainland China, Taiwan, and Hong Kong: Sex differences and societal differences. *Psychology, 29*(1), 156–164.

Block, J.H. (1981). The Child-Rearing Practices Report (CRPR): A set of Q items for the description of parental socialization attitudes and values. Berkeley: University of California, Institute of Human Development.

Block, J. (1986). *The child-rearing practices report (CRPR): A set of Q items for the description of parental socialization attitudes and values.* Berkeley: University of California.

Bowes, J. M., San, L. Q., Chen, M-J., & Yuan, L. (2004). Reasoning and negotiation about child responsibility in urban Chinese families: Reports from mothers, fathers and children. *International Journal of Behavioral Development, 28*(1), 48–58.

Buri, J. (1991). Parental authority questionnaire. *Journal of Personality Assessment, 57,* 110–119.

Cabrera, N. J., Tamis-LeMonda, C. S., Bradley, R. H., Hofferth, S., & Lamb, M. E. (2000). Fatherhood in the twenty-first century. *Child Development, 71*(1), 127–136.

Chao, R. K., & Kim, K. (2000). Parenting differences among immigrant Chinese fathers and mothers in the United States. *Journal of Psychology in Chinese societies, 1,* 71–91.

Chao, R. K., & Tseng, V. (2002). Parenting of Asians. In M. H. Bornstein (Ed.), *Handbook of Parenting,* Vol. 4 (2nd ed., pp. 59–93). Mahwah, NJ: Erlbaum.

Chen, X., Dong, Q., & Zhou, H. (1997). Authoritative and authoritarian parenting practices and social and school performance in Chinese children. *International Journal of Behavioral Development, 21,* 855–873.

Chen, X., Liu, M., & Li, D. (2000). Parental warmth, control, and indulgence and their relations to adjustment in Chinese children: A longitudinal study. *Journal of Family Psychology, 14*(3), 401–419.

Chibucos, T. R., & Leite, R. W. (2005). *Readings in family theory.* Thousand Oaks, CA: Sage.

Chuang, S. S., & Su, Y. (2008). Transcending Confucian teachings on fathering. In S.S. Chuang and R. P. Moreno (Eds.), *On new shores: Understanding immigrant fathers in North America* (pp. 129–150). Lanham, MD: Lexington Books.

Chuang, S. S., & Su, Y. (2009). Says who?: Decision-making and conflicts among Chinese-Canadian and Mainland Chinese parents of young children. *Sex Roles, 60,* 527–536.

Coltrane, S. (1996). *Family man: Fatherhood, house-work, and gender equity.* New York: Oxford University Press.

Cooper, C. R., Baker, H., Polochar, D., & Welsh, M. (1993). Values and communication of Chinese, European, Filipino, Mexican, and Vietnamese American adolescents with their families and friends. In S. Shulman & W. A. Collins (Eds.), *Father-adolescent relationships* (Vol. 62, pp. 73–89). San Francisco: Jossey-Bass.

Costigan, C. L., & Dokis, D. P. (2006). Relations between parent-child acculturation differences and adjustment within immigrant Chinese families. *Child Development, 77*(5), 1252–1267.

Costigan, C., & Su, T. F. (2008). Cultural predictors of the parenting cognitions of immigrant Chinese mothers and fathers in Canada. *International Journal of Behavioral Development, 32*(5), 432–442.

Dundes, L., Cho, E., & Kwak, S. (2009). The duty to succeed: honor versus happiness in college and career choice of East Asian. *Pastoral Care in Education, 27*(2), 135–156.

Esteban, E. J. (2006). Parental verbal abuse: Culture-specific coping behavior of college students in the Philippines. *Child Psychiatry & Human Development, 36*(3), 243–259.

Executive Bureau of Directorate-General of Budget, Accounting and Statistics, Taiwan. (2004). Employment and marriage of women. *2005 Annual report on social indexes.* Retrieved from http://www.dgbas.gov.tw/public/Data/6121512261271.pdf

Feldman, S. S., & Rosenthal, D. A. (1990). The acculturation of autonomy expectations in Chinese high schoolers residing in two Western nations. *International Journal of Psychology, 25,* 259–281.

Feldman, S. S., & Quatman, T. (1988). Factors influencing age expectations for adolescent autonomy. *Journal of Early Adolescence, 8,* 325–343.

Foundation of Women's Rights Promotion and Development. (2004). *Report on women's rights in Taiwan.* Taipei, Taiwan: Author.

Fuligni, A. J. (1998). Authority, autonomy, and parent-adolescent conflict and cohesion: A study of adolescents from Mexican, Chinese, Filipino, and European backgrounds. *Developmental Psychology, 34,* 782–792.

Fuligni, A. J., Tseng, V., & Lam, M. (1999). Attitudes toward family obligations among American adolescents with Asian, Latin American, and European Backgrounds. *Child Development, 70,* 1030–1044.

German Social Science Intrastructure Services, International Social Survey Programme (2002). *Family and Changing Gender Roles III.* Retrieved from http://www.za.uni-koeln.de/data/en/issp/codebooks/ZA3880cdb.pdf

Hardway, C., & Fuligni, A. J. (2006). Dimensions of family connectedness among adolescents with Mexican, Chinese, and European backgrounds. *Developmental psychology, 42*(6), 1246–1258.

Harper, S. E. (2010). Exploring the role of Filipino fathers: Paternal behaviors and child outcomes. *Journal of Family Issues, 31,* 66–89.

Ho, D. Y. F. (1987). Fatherhood in Chinese culture. In M. H. Lamb (Ed.), *The father's role: Cross-cultural perspectives.* (pp. 227–245). Hillsdale, NJ: Erlbaum.

Hofferth, S. L. (2003). Race/ethnic differences in father involvement in two-parent families culture, context, or economy? *Journal of Family Issues, 24*(2), 185–216.

Hong Kong Government. (2002). *Women and men in Hong Kong: Key statistics.* Hong Kong: Census and Statistics Department.

Hossain, Z., & Roopnarine, J. L. (1994). African-American fathers' involvement with infants: Relationship to their functioning style, support, education, and income. *Infant Behavior and Development, 17,* 175–184.

Ishii-Kuntz, M. (2000). Diversity within Asian American families. In D. H. Demo, K. Allen, & M. A. Fine (Eds.), *Handbook of family diversity* (pp. 274–292). New York: Oxford University Press.

Ishii-Kuntz, M., Makino, K., Kato, K., & Tsuchiya, M. (2004). Japanese fathers of preschoolers and their involvement in child care. *Journal of Marriage and Family, 66*(3), 779–791.

Jankowiak, W. (1992). Father–child relations in urban China. In B. S. Hewlett (Ed.), *Father–child relations (pp. 345–363).* New York: Aldine.

Jain, A., & Belsky, J. (1997). Fathering and acculturation : Immigrant Indian families with young children. *Journal of Marriage and Family, 59,* 873–883.

Jung, K., & Hoing, A. S. (2000). Intergenerational comparisons of paternal Korean child rearing practices and attitudes. *Early Child Development and Care, 165*(1), 59–84.

Kanatsu, A., & Chao, R. K. (2008). Asian immigrant fathers as primary caregivers of adolescents. In S.S. Chuang & R. P. Moreno (Eds.), *On new shores: Understanding immigrant fathers in North America* (pp. 151–173). Lanham, MD: Lexington Books.

Kim, A-H. (2008). Korean parents' and adolescents' reports of parenting styles: A developmental study (Doctoral dissertation). Retrieved from Dissertations & Theses http://search.proquest.com.proxy2.cl.msu.edu/dissertations/docview/194003173/fulltextPDF/13603F3AB6D41543237/1?accountid=12598

Kim, M., Hunter, J. E., Miyahara, A., Horwath, A., Bresnahan, M., & Yoon, H. (1996). Individual- vs. culture-level dimensions of individualism and collectivism: Effects on preferred conversational styles. *Communication Monographs, 63,* 29–49.

Kim, S-I., & Rohner, R. P. (2003). Perceived parental acceptance and emotional empathy among university students in Korea. *Journal of Cross-Cultural Psychology, 34,* 723–735.

Kim, S. Y., Chen, Q., Li, J., Huang, X., & Moon, U. J. (2009). Parent-child acculturation, parenting , and adolescent sepressive symptoms in Chinese immigrant families. *Journal of Family Psychology, 23,* 426–437.

Lamborn, S. D., Mounts, N. S., Steinberg, L., & Dornbusch, S. M. (1991). Patterns of com petence and adjustment among adolescents from authoritative, authoritarian, indulgent, and neglectful families. *Child Development, 62,* 1049–1065.

Lee, R., Choe, J., Kim, V., & Ngo, G. (2000). Construction of the Asian American family conflicts scale. *Journal of Counseling Psychology, 47,* 211–222.

Lin, C. Y. C., & Fu, V. R. (1990). A Comparison of child-rearing practices among Chinese, immigrant Chinese, and Caucasian-American parents. *Child Development, 61,* 429–433.

McFadden, K., & Tamis-LeMonda, C. S. (in press). Fathers in the U.S. To appear in D. Shwalb, B. Shwalb, & M.Lamb (Eds.), *The father's role: International perspectives.* New York: Routledge.

Medina, B. (2001). *The Filipino family.* Quezon City, Philippines: University of the Philippines Press.

Min, P. G. (2006). *Asian Americans: Contemporary trends and issues* (2nd ed.). Thousand Oaks, CA: Pine Forge Press.

National Bureau of Statistics of China. (2001). *Women and men in China.* Retrieved August 29, 2010, from http://www.stats.gov.cn/tjsj/qtsj/men&women/men&women.pdf

National Statistic Office, Philippines. (2008). *2008 National Demographic and health survey (NDHS).* Manila, Philippines: Author.

Nguyen, P. V. (2008). Perceptions of Vietnamese fathers' acculturation levels, parenting styles, and mental health outcomes in Vietnamese American adolescent immigrants. *Social work, 53*(4), 337–346.

Nguyen, P. V., & Cheung, M. (2009). Parenting styles as perceived by Vietnamese American adolescents. *Child and Adolescent Social Work Journal, 26,* 505–518.

Olson, D. H., McCubbin, H. I., Barnes, H., Larsen, A., Muxen, M., & Wilson, M. (1985). *Family inventories.* St. Paul: Family Social Science, University of Minnesota.

Olson, D. H., Sprenkle, D. H., & Russell, C. S. (1979). Circumplex model of marital and family systems: I. Cohesion and adaptability dimensions, family types, and clinical applications. *Family Process, 18,* 3–28.

Prinz, R. J., Foster, S., Kent, R. N., & O'Leary, D. (1979). Multivariate assessment of conflict in distressed and nondistressed mother-adolescent dyads. *Journal of Applied Behavior Analysis, 12,* 691–700.

Qin, D. B. (2008). Doing well vs. feeling well: Understanding family dynamics and the psychological adjustment of Chinese immigrant adolescents. *Journal of Youth and Adolescence, 37,* 22–35.

Qin, D. B. (2009). Gendered processes of adaptation: Understanding parent-child relations in Chinese immigrant familes. *Sex Roles, 60,* 467–481.

Radin, N. (1982). *Paternal involvement in Child Care Index.* Ann Arbor: University of Michigan School of Social Work.

Reitman, D., Rhode, P. C., Hupp, S. D. A., & Altobello, C. (2004). Development and validation of the parental authority questionnaire-revised. *Journal of Psychopathology and Behavioral Assessment, 24,* 119–127.

Rhee, S., Chang, J., & Rhee, J. (2003). Acculturation, communication patterns, and self-esteem among Asian and Caucasian American adolescents. *Adolescence, 38,* 749–768.

Robin, A. L., & Foster, S. L. (1984). Problem-solving communication training: A behavioral-family systems approach to parent-adolescent conflict. In P. Karoly & J. Steffen (Eds.), *Adolescent behavior disorders.* Lexington, MA: Heath.

Robin, A. L., & Foster, S. L. (1989). *Negotiating parent-adolescent conflict.* New York: Guilford.

Rohner, R. P. (1991). *Handbook for the study of parental acceptance and rejection.* Stoors, CT: Center for the Study of Parental Acceptance and Rejection, University of Connecticut at Storrs.

Rohner, R. P., & Pettengill, S. M. (1985). Perceived parental acceptance-rejection and parental control among Korean adolescents. *Child Development, 56,* 524–528.

Roopnarine, J., Talukder, E., Jain, D., Joshi, P., & Srivastav, P. (1990). Characteristics of holding, patterns of play, and social behaviors between parents and infants in New Delhi, India. *Developmental Psychology, 26,* 667–673.

Roopnarine, J. L., Talukder, E., Jain, D., Joshi, P., & Srivastav, P. (1992). Personal well-being, kinship tie, and mother-infant and father-infant interactions in single-wage and dual-wage families in New Delhi, India. *Journal of Marriage and the Family, 54,* 293–301.

Schaefer, E. S. (1965). Children's reports of parental behavior: An inventory. *Child Development, 36,* 413–424.

Schludermann, E., & Schludermann, S. (1970). Replicability of factors in Children's Report of Parental Behavior Inventory (CRPBI). *Journal of Psychology, 76,* 239–249.

Segal, M. (1985). A study of maternal beliefs and values within the context of an intervention program. In I. Sigel (Ed.), *Parental belief systems: The psychological consequences for children* (pp. 227–245). Hillsdale, NJ: Erlbaum.

Shek, D. T. (2005). Perceived parental control processes, parent-child relational qualities, and psychological well-being in Chinese adolescents with and without economic disadvantage. *The Journal of Genetic Psychology, 166,* 171–188.

Shek, D. T. (2008). Perceived parental control and parent-child relational qualities in early adolescents in Hong Kong. *Sex Roles, 58,* 666–681.

Shwalb, D. W., Kawai, H., Shoji, J., & Tsunetsugu, K. (1997). The middle class Japanese father. *Journal of Applied Developmental Psychology, 18,* 497–511.

Smetana, J. (1989). Toddlers' social interactions in the context of moral and conventional transgressions in the home. *Developmental Psychology, 25,* 499–508.

Song, Y-J. (2004). *Fatherhood and childcare: A comparative analysis of Chinese and Korean families* (Doctoral dissertation). Retrieved from Dissertations & Theses http://search.proquest.com.proxy2.cl.msu.edu/dissertations/docview/305228456/fulltextPDF/13603F50E15745C35F6/1?accountid=12598

Steinberg, L., Dornbusch, S., & Brown, B. (1992). Ethnic differences in adolescent achievement: An ecological perspective. *American Psychologist, 47,* 723–729.

Sun, L-C, & Roopnarine, J. L. (1996). Mother-infant, father-infant interaction and involvement in child-care and household labor among Taiwanese families. *Infant Behavior and Development, 19*(1), 121–129.

Suppal, P., & Roopnarine, J. L. (1999). Paternal involvement in child care as a function of maternal employment in nuclear and extended families in India. *Sex roles, 40,*731–744.

Tamis-LeMonda, C. S., & McFadden, K. E. (2010). Development in the United States of America. In M. H. Bornstein (Ed.), *Handbook of cultural developmental science* (pp. 299–322). Mahwah, NJ: Erlbaum.

Tamis-LeMonda, C. S., Niwa, E. Y., KAhana-KAlman, R., & Yoshikawa, H. (2008). Breaking new ground: Dominican, Mexican, and Chinese fathers and families. In S.S. Chuang and R. P. Moreno (Eds.), *On new shores: understanding immigrant fathers in North America* (pp. 231–255). Lanham, MD: Lexington Books.

Tan, E. A. (1997). Economic development and well-being of women. *Philippines Human Development Report.* Manilla, Philippines: United Nations Development Program.

United Nation Statistic Archive. (2006). *Women's share of labour force.* Retrieved August 29, 2010, from http://data.un.org/Explorer.aspx?d=GenderStat.

U.S. Department of Labor, Bureau of Labor Statistics. (1997). *Employment characteristics of families 1997.* Retrieved from http://www.bls.gov/news.release/history/famee_052198.txt

U.S. Department of Labor, Bureau of Labor Statistics. (2009). *Employment characteristics of families 2009.* Retrieved from http://www.bls.gov/news.release/archives/famee_05272010.pdf

White, J. M., & Klein, D. M. (2008). *Family Theories* (3rd ed.). Thousand Oaks, CA: Sage.

Wong, D. F. K., Lam, D. O. B., & Lai Kwok, S. Y. C. (2003). Stresses and mental health of fathers with younger children in Hong Kong: Implications for social work practices. *International Social Work, 46,* 103–119.

Yang, J. (1999). An exploratory study of Korean fathering of adolescent children. *The Journal of Genetic Psychology, 160*(1), 55–68.

Yeh, C. J., Kim, A. B., Pituc, S. T., & Atkins, M. (2008). Poverty, loss, and resilience: The story of Chinese immigrant youth. *Journal of Counseling Psychology, 55*(1), 34–48.

Yeung, W. J., Sandberg, J. F., Davis-Kean, P., & Hofferth, S. L. (2001). *Children's time with fathers in intact families. Journal of Marriage and Family, 63*, 136–154.

Zaslow, M. J., Dion, M. R., & Morrison, D. R. (1997, April). Effects of the JOBS program on mother-child relations during the early months of program participation. Paper presented at the biannual meetings of the Society for Research in Child Development as part of the symposium "Mother-Child Relations in the Context of Contrasting Programs for Welfare Families," Washington, DC.

SECTION V

Sociological Perspectives

Chapter 16
Cohabiting Fathers

Wendy D. Manning and Susan L. Brown

Bowling Green State University

Historical Overview and Theoretical Perspectives

Cohabiting families are increasingly common in the United States. Over 40% of children will experience parental cohabitation by the age of 12, and children are spending longer stretches of their childhood in cohabiting families (Kennedy & Bumpass, 2011). Roughly half of these cohabiting families include a biological father and half involve a stepfather (Kreider, 2008). Thus, when considering residential fathers, researchers must expand their focus beyond married fathers to include cohabiting fathers. Restricting the focus to just married resident fathers is no longer appropriate given cohabitation is now a common family context (Stewart, 2007; Yeung, Sandburg, Davis-Kean, & Hofferth, 2001).

Expectations for fathering behaviors in cohabiting parent families depend, in part, on whether the father is a biological or stepparent. Although the term "stepfather" suggests a man who is not biologically related to a child but is married to the child's mother. we expand this term to encompass men in cohabiting families. Cohabiting stepfathers are men who share a residence with a child's biological mother, but are not married to them. It is also possible that in some cohabiting families the father is biologically related to some children and a cohabiting stepfather to others in the same household. To our knowledge, this "hybrid" father role has not been examined among cohabiting families. The high levels of unmarried childbearing and divorce, as well as continuing high prevalence of remarriage means that among families with residential fathers, it is important to distinguish between biological and stepfathers (Smock & Greenland, 2010; Stewart, 2007; Sweeney, 2010). Thus, we review the research findings on how fathering in cohabiting families is similar to or different from fathering in married families and discuss results according to the biological relationships between fathers and children. Then, using nationally representative data from the 2006–2008 National Survey of Family Growth (NSFG, 2011), we provide a new, descriptive portrait of today's cohabiting and married resident fathers to assess how the groups compare in terms of types of resident children (biological vs. step vs. hybrid) and fathering behaviors.

Biological Fathers

The parenting behaviors (e.g., time spent with children, activities, warmth) of married and cohabiting biological fathers appear quite similar, indicating that fathering does not differ much according to union type. For example, cohabiting and married biological fathers of children under age 13 display similar levels of father involvement (weekly hours engaged, number of activities), warmth, and fathering motivation (importance of fatherhood role) (Hofferth & Anderson, 2003), although father involvement (weekly hours) is marginally lower in cohabiting than married biological parent families with children ages 3–13 (Hofferth, 2006). Nonetheless, a comprehensive assessment of fathering using five national data sources indicates that cohabiting biological fathers appear remarkably similar across a range of outcomes, including time spent with the child, activities engaged in with child, responsibility (e.g., managing the child's welfare), and warmth (Hofferth et al., 2007). The few differences that exist are not uniform across data sources. For instance, in the Child Development Supplement to the Panel Study of Income Dynamics (PSID, n.d.), a nationally representative longitudinal sample of U.S. families, mothers with children under age 13 reported that married fathers spent more time with their child than did cohabiting fathers Similarly, in the Three Cities Study (Angel, Burton, Lindsay Chase-Lansdale, Cherlin, & Moffitt, 2009) based on a sample of urban low-income mothers, 10- to 14-year-old teens reported greater accessibility and warmth to married than cohabiting fathers. Also, in married families, mothers reported that fathers took more responsibility for the child's behavior and they reported greater parental agreement than in cohabiting parent families. Overall, it is notable there were more similarities than differences in married and cohabiting fathers' behavior. The differences observed in the Three Cities Sample may be due in part to the economically disadvantaged (less than 200% of poverty) nature of the study families.

A challenge to comparing cohabiting and married biological fathers is that the instability of cohabiting unions (which persist for roughly two years, on average [Bumpass & Lu, 2000]) means cohabiting biological fathers tend to be parenting very young children. By middle childhood and adolescence, nearly all children in two biological parent families live with married parents. Hence, birth cohort studies such as the Fragile Families and Child Well-Being Study (Fragile Families, n.d.) provide unique insights on how biological fathering in cohabiting and married parent families compares. The Fragile Families study follows a birth cohort of nearly 5,000 children born in large U.S. cities between 1998 and 2000. About three-quarters of the children were born to unmarried parents and the study includes interviews with both mothers and fathers of the children.

For the most part, these studies yield findings that are consistent with those described above for children up to age 13. For example, data from the Fragile Families study of unmarried mothers and their 15 and 36 months old children indicate cohabiting biological fathers (father or mother reports) share similar levels of aggravation, instrumental support, and positive engagement as married fathers. Initially higher levels of spanking reported by cohabiting fathers are explained by sociodemographic differences (Gibson-Davis, 2008). Using mother's reports of children 5 years old in the same data set, Berger, Carlson, Bzostek, and Osborne (2008) find that father engagement (e.g., number of days per week participates in eight activities with the child) is actually lower among married biological fathers than cohabiting biological fathers, whereas cooperative parenting is more common in married than cohabiting biological father families. They also find that shared responsibility and maternal trust are similar in the two types of biological families. A recent analysis of the Early Childhood Longitudinal

Study-Birth Cohort (ECLS-B), a nationally representative sample of births that occurred in 2001 mirrors some of the findings from the Fragile Families data (1998–2000 birth cohort). According to Cabrera, Hofferth, and Cha (2011), cohabiting fathers of infants report greater levels of caregiving and physical play than married fathers and cohabiting and married fathers of infants report similar levels of verbally stimulating activities. Finally, a study of Puerto Rican children reveals that mothers' report of cohabiting and married biological fathers are similar in terms of financial support at the time of the birth (Landale & Oropesa, 2001).

Stepfathers

As noted, about half of cohabiting parent families includes stepfathers (Kreider, 2008). Research explicitly comparing fathering (activities, responsibility, monitoring) among various types of stepfathers is quite limited and mixed. It has been argued parenting behaviors that require stronger relationship quality with mothers (e.g., cooperation and trust) may more often be observed among married than cohabiting stepfathers because of the father's legal relationship to the mother (Berger et al., 2008). Qualitative evidence based on a sample of families whose children varied in age reveals that some cohabiting stepparents face more challenges in their parenting roles, in part, because they lack the institutional support provided to married couples as well as the fact faced by all stepparents, they do not possess biological ties to the children (Manning, Smock, & Bergstrom-Lynch, 2009). Moreover, cohabiting stepparents report more advantages (e.g., solidify family roles, gain parenting authority) to marriage than cohabiting biological parents. Thus, it is not cohabitation itself, but the stepparent role, that makes marriage desirable and a route to more effective parenting.

The empirical evidence is mixed. Among stepfathers of children ages 5 and younger (Fragile Families data children born between 1998 and 2000), the levels of engagement with children, maternal trust, shared responsibility, and parental cooperation are higher, on average, in married than cohabiting families (Berger et al., 2008). Research on older children suggests that cohabiting and married stepparents report similar levels of father involvement. Analyses of fathers' reports of parenting children ages 5–18 in the National Survey of Families and Households (NSFH) indicate that cohabiting and married stepfathers spend similar amounts of time together eating meals (breakfast and dinner), engaged in home activities, and outings (Thomson, McLanahan, & Curtin, 1992). Cohabiting stepfathers spend less time in youth activities than married stepfathers (Thomson, McLanahan, & Curtin, 1992). Further, cohabiting stepfathers report similar levels of positive (praise and hug) and negative (yell and spank) parenting. In terms of supervision the authors find that cohabiting stepparents report lower levels of monitoring and fewer rules than married stepparents. Analyses of mother's reports of father involvement with 0- to 12-year-old children in the Child Development Supplement to the PSID suggest that cohabiting stepfathers spend fewer houses in activities than married stepparents, but married and cohabiting stepfathers share similar levels of warmth, fathering motivation, number of activities, and availability (Hofferth & Anderson, 2003). Research focusing on adolescents in the National Longitudinal Study of Adolescent Health (Harris, 2009) suggest that the levels of parental monitoring (not specifically father's monitoring) is similar in married and cohabiting stepfather families (Manning & Lamb, 2003; Sweeney, Wang, & Videon, 2009).

The empirical literature is quite limited on how cohabiting step and cohabiting biological fathers compare. Given the majority of cohabiting biological families consist of young children, there are few comparisons available of teenagers. Based on theoretical arguments and the marital literature cohabiting biological fathers are expected to be more involved than cohabiting stepfathers. Statistical contrasts between biological and step cohabiting parents are not available in the analysis of mother's reports of children ages 0–12 in the PSID, but similarities appear to exist in terms of time available, warmth, number of activities, and fathering motivation as well as differences in hours spent in activities (Hofferth & Anderson, 2003). Research using the Fragile Families data (children under age 5) suggests stepfathers in cohabiting and married families demonstrate more positive engagement, instrumental support, and generally higher quality parenting than biological resident fathers, on average (Berger et al., 2008; Bzostek, 2008; Gibson-Davis, 2008). These differences are consistent with other evidence based on the same dataset suggesting that mothers often trade up (from their biological partners to cohabiting) when forming new relationships with stepfathers. That is, single mothers of very young children (under age 3) tend to form relationships with new partners who have higher levels of education and lower levels of addiction and incarceration than the mother's original partner (biological father of the child) (Bzostek, Carlson, & McLanahan, 2010). It is then possible that as a result of mothers' union formation stepfathers may be as involved and exhibit positive parenting as biological fathers.

Hybrid Fathers

A complicating factor in assessments of cohabiting and married fathers is the complexity of their family lives, namely, the presence of biological and stepchildren in the same household. Much work does not address the complex family configurations in their assessments of father involvement and to date no work directly assesses differences among cohabiting and married fathers. About 1 in 7 (15.2%) of children who live with a sibling and two parents live in blended families (or with hybrid fathers) (Kreider & Ellis, 2011). To some extent this type of family configuration can be evaluated indirectly from research on multiple partner fertility. Analysis of mothers with more than one child participating in the Fragile Families study indicate that only 22% of married fathers had children from prior relationships while 64% of unmarried fathers did so (Carlson & McLanahan, 2010). Yet, multiple partner fertility does not capture residence with children and stepfathering. In terms of resident fathers, 40% of children living with two biological cohabiting parents lived with half- or stepsiblings, while 8% of children in two biological stepfamilies did so (Balistreri, Manning, & Brown, 2009).

In some cases family complexity is related to fathering. For example, in the PSID stepfathers who have no other children view themselves as warmer than biological fathers with no resident stepchildren (Hofferth & Anderson, 2003). Stepchildren in hybrid families (both biological and stepchildren) have been found to experience similar levels of father involvement (e.g., activities, time spent, time available) as children residing in two-biological parent families (Hofferth & Anderson, 2003). This level of involvement by fathers in hybrid families is believed to have important ramifications for the well-being of children in hybrid families (Hofferth, 2006), but there are mixed findings on the well-being of children in blended families (e.g., Ginther & Pollak, 2004; Halpern-Meekin & Tach, 2008; Tillman, 2008). Thus, we consider how family complexity (i.e., biological relationship of children) is related to fathering in cohabiting versus married parent families.

Theoretical Perspectives

There are three primary perspectives applied to the analysis of father involvement in cohabiting families: sociological, evolutionary or sociobiological, and family systems along with attention to a life course perspective. From a sociological perspective, the social institution of marriage is characterized by legal and social protections not available in cohabiting unions (Cherlin, 2004; Nock, 1995). Children raised by cohabiting parents arguably do not benefit, on average, from the legal protections, and possibly either the economic security or attachment that typically results from living with two married parents (Manning, 2002; Nock, 1995). Given the weaker social and legal recognition of cohabiting families, cohabiting biological and stepparents must actively negotiate their obligations and rights, especially in step cohabiting parent families, which could generate greater stress and conflict that may undermine effective parenting. At the same time the ambiguity in cohabiting families could allow for more involved fatherhood with less traditional gender roles. The social norms that support high levels of father involvement in marriages may not be as strong in cohabiting relationships (Nock, 1995). Still, it is possible that the social norms are shifting as increasing number of children live in with cohabiting parents.

The emphasis on biological and stepfatherhood underlines the importance of considering evolutionary or sociobiology orientations. According to an evolutionary perspective, men invest in their biological offspring to ensure the continuance of their genetic line (Trivers, 1972; see Waynforth as well as Stacey and Walsh, in this volume). Marriage may enter the equation among humans because it ensures a stronger bond resulting in greater investments in biological children. At the same time, men may invest in stepchildren to showcase fathering skills in hopes of fathering children with their partners in the future (mating effort) (Anderson, Kaplan, & Lancaster, 1999; Daly & Wilson, 1987). However, the underlying argument is that biology, and not marriage, is the driving motivation for fathers' investments in children.

Variants of family systems theory have been introduced into some work on fathering in cohabiting families (Cabrera et al., 2011) and a family systems approach also has been applied to research on family complexity, such as stepfamily, cohabitation, and divorce (e.g., Stewart, 2007). Cox and Paley (1997) argue that assessments of parenting require viewing the family as an integrated whole and not simply an analysis of just marriage or biology. Consistent with this approach we would expect differential types of parenting in various family configurations, such as the hybrid families described above.

Furthermore, although studies examining father involvement in cohabiting families do not directly refer to a life course perspective, it often undergirds such research. The historical context is key as we have witnessed growth in father involvement and expectations of men's roles in families have moved away from an exclusive breadwinner role leading to new models of fatherhood. Indeed, Parke (2002) argues for integrating the life course of children, fathers, and families in assessments of father involvement. Cohabitation is certainly becoming an important part of the life course with marriage no longer the sole accepted pathway to residential fatherhood. Consistent with life course theory, cohabitation thus contributes to the complexity of developmental trajectories with implications for the timing of fatherhood and family formation and dissolution.

Current Research Questions

The literature on fatherhood typically differentiates among fathers according to either residential or biological status. But studies to date largely have ignored an additional layer of complexity in residential father families: union type. Despite the rapid growth in cohabitation as a living arrangement for children, relatively little attention has been paid to cohabiting fathers. Using data from the 2006–2008 (NSFG), we compare the individual and family characteristics of cohabiting versus married fathers. Specifically, we are able to gauge the complexity of fathers' family configurations in terms of biological versus stepchildren. We also examine how fathers' involvement (measured by activities they engage with their children) and assessments of their fathering roles vary according to their union type (cohabiting and married) and family configuration (biological, step, or hybrid). We are not arguing that union type (cohabitation or marriage) or the type of resident children cause better or worse fathering. We recognize that selection processes may be operating such that men with greater socioeconomic resources are more likely to marry and that the women they marry are more likely to be without children from prior relationships (Goldscheider & Sassler, 2006; Stewart, Manning, & Smock, 2004). The prior literature on cohabiting fathers has considered an extensive array of indicators of fathering. These studies have not always considered the father's own reports of his involvement and family configuration, in part because there are few national studies that collect data from men themselves. Further, much of the research has focused on relatively young children, which results in a limited understanding of cohabiting stepfathers across the lifespan. Our goal is to integrate the theoretical perspectives and provide an update and extension of the literature on cohabiting fathers.

Research Measurement and Methodology

Drawing on data from the 2006–2008 NSFG, we draw on a family systems and life course approach to provide a descriptive profile of resident fathers and to provide a starting point to better understand cohabiting fatherhood. The NSFG includes a nationally representative sample of men ages 15–44 as well as detailed questions about parenthood and family life (Lepowski, Mosher, Davis, Groves, & Van Hoewyk, 2010). A key advantage of the NSFG is that it contains a large, recently collected, national sample of men. The NSFG affords us the opportunity to document contemporary family patterns and to gain this perspective from men themselves. In addition, the NSFG includes a wide range of father involvement measures assessed across a broad age range of children's (0–17) with separate indicators for young children (under age 5) and school age children (age 5 and older). These items are asked about all children within the specified age range and not a focal child. The NSFG permits more refined definitions of family context by including questions about men's biological *and* stepchildren. Our analytic sample is based on 312 cohabiting and 1,271 married resident fathers living with step and/or biological children. Cohabitation (or living together) in the NSFG is defined as "having a sexual relationship while sharing the same usual residence."

Findings reported in this chapter are based on a general measure of father involvement four indicators for father involvement with young children (under age 5), six indicators for father involvement with school age children (age 5 and older), and an overall assessment of fatherhood roles. These indicators improve upon prior studies that are limited to just one or two questions about father involvement, but certainly do not include an exhaustive list of parenting indicators. While the 5–8 age range is broad, it improves on prior studies that are limited to only young children or do not specify the age range. As noted above, the questions asked of fathers are not directed toward a specific child but all children within the specified age range.

The general indicator of father involvement is based on the question, "In the last 12 months how often would you say you spent time on an outing away from home to places such as museums, zoos, movies, sports, parks, playgrounds, etc.?" with responses ranging from 0 (not at all) to 6 (every day). Fathers of young children were asked questions about caregiving: in the last four weeks how often did you "feed or eat or meals with," "Bathe, diaper, or dress or help to bathe, dress, or use the toilet," "play with," or "read to" with responses ranging from 1 (not at all) to 6 (every day; at least once a day). Fathers with resident children ages 5 to 18 were asked in the last four weeks how often did you "help with homework or check their homework," "talk about things that happened during the day," "take to or from activities," and "eat meals with __" and responses ranged from 1 (not at all) to 6 (every day; at least once a day). Fathers of children ages 5 through 18 were asked in the "last 12 months how often did you go to religious services with" and responses ranged from 0 (not at all) to 6 (every day). Fathers were also asked in "the last 12 months did you go to a parent-teacher conference or PTA meeting?" and responses include 0 (no) or 1 (yes). Finally, we include an assessment of the fatherhood role based on the question to resident fathers, "how good a job do you think you do as a father to [this child/these children]?" The reference children for this item were all the resident children. The response categories ranged from 1 (a very good job) to 5 (a bad job).

Empirical Findings

Resident Fathers: Cohabiting and Married Fathers

We found that most resident fathers participating in the NSFG are married, 83.6%, while 16.4% are living in cohabiting unions. The distributions of the socioeconomic characteristics of cohabiting and married fathers are presented in Table 16.1. Fathers in cohabiting relationships have more complex families than do married fathers, on average. In terms of relationships with children in their household, Table 16.1 indicates that about half (52%) of cohabiting fathers have only biological children present in their household in contrast to 81% of married fathers. Cohabiting fathers more often are parenting just stepchildren than are married fathers (29% vs. 7%), and overall nearly half of cohabiting fathers are parenting at least one stepchild (48%) versus 19% of married fathers. As a result, biological children in cohabiting parent families are much more likely to be living with a stepsibling (17%) than are biological children in married parent families (10%) (results not shown). We also found that married fathers have more biological children (not just resident children) than cohabiting fathers (2.6 and 2.2, respectively). These complex family configurations may create more parenting challenges.

Cohabiting and married fathers differ in terms of relationship and sociodemographic characteristics. Married fathers typically have been in their relationships for longer time periods with a mean duration of the current relationship of 9.6 years compared to cohabiting fathers who have been in their current relationship on average 4.6 years. Cohabiting fathers are on average younger (31 years old) than their married counterparts (36 years old), and they enter fatherhood at a slightly younger age (24 vs. 26). About one-fifth (22%) of cohabiting fathers enter their relationships with prior marital experience, while 14% of married fathers have been previously married. The racial and ethnic distribution of cohabiting fathers differs from married fathers. Two-fifths (40%) of cohabiting fathers are White, 16% are Black, 13% are native-born Hispanic, and 24% foreign-born Hispanic. In contrast, about 63% of married fathers are White, 10% are Black, 7.5% are native-born Hispanic, and 11.5% foreign-born Hispanic. Cohabiting fathers report similar average levels of religiosity as married fathers. Similar percentages of cohabiting and married fathers were raised in two biological parent families.

In terms of socioeconomic status, cohabiting fathers report lower average levels of education, income, and employment than married fathers. About half of cohabiting fathers have not graduated from high school and only one-quarter pursued some education after high school. Only about one-fifth of married fathers had less than a high school education and over half (57%) had post-high school education. The income of cohabiting fathers is lower than married fathers. Table 16.1 reflects the mean income category value, which represents income ranges,

Table 16.1   Socioeconomic Characteristics of Married and Cohabiting Fathers

	Married			Cohabiting	
	%/Mean	S.E.		%/Mean	S.E.
Family Configuration			°		
Only Biological	81.2			52.5	
Only Step	6.7			28.5	
Both Biological and Step	12.1			19.0	
Number of Biological Children	2.6	0.06	°	2.2	0.15
Relationship Duration	9.6	0.26	°	4.6	0.40
Age	36.0	0.24	°	30.7	0.57
Prior Marriage	14.0		°	21.9	
Race/Ethnicity			°		
White	63.4			40.3	
Black	9.6			16.2	
Latino Native Born	7.5			12.6	
Latina Foreign Born	11.4			23.9	
Other	7.9			7.0	
Religiosity	2.2	0.05		2.1	0.08
Raised Two Bio Parents	69.6			62.7	
Education					
< 12 years	16.3			47.1	
12 years	26.9			28.1	
Some College	27.1			20.4	
College Graduate	29.8			4.6	
Income	11.4	0.17	°	4.6	0.41
Employed Full-Time	85.8		°	68.2	
N	1,271			312	

Source: NSFG 2006–08 Weighted %s and Unweighted Ns
° p < .05
S.E. = Standard error

on average. Among cohabitors the income range is $30,000–34,999 and among married fathers the income range is $40,000–49,999. Cohabiting fathers are less likely to be working full-time (68%) than married fathers (86%). Income in the data is measured in a categorical manner with values ranging from 1 to 14. The income range associated with 11 is $40,000-$49,999 and the income range indicated by a value of 9 is $30,000-$39,999.

Father Involvement and Family Configurations

Table 16.2 showcases a variety of indicators of father involvement, including a general indicator of number of outings and age-specific activities. Fathers in cohabiting relationships report going on similar numbers of outings (about once a week) with their children as married fathers. Father involvement appears to differ only slightly according to whether there are only biological children present, only stepchildren, or both biological and stepchildren. The number of reported outings is greatest when only biological children are present and appear to be lowest when only stepchildren are living in the household. Married and cohabiting fathers regardless of family configuration report a statistically similar numbers of outings.

Father involvement with young children (ages 5 or under) is generally similar among men in cohabiting and married families. About 62% of cohabiting and 52% of married fathers have younger children. Overall cohabiting and married fathers score similarly in terms of caregiving activities such as feeding, bathing, and playing with their child under age five. Married fathers reported more time spent reading to their young child than cohabiting fathers. This gap in time spent reading according to relationship status differs only among fathers living with only their biological children. Cohabiting fathers parenting stepchildren read as often to children under 5 as married fathers in families with stepchildren.

Cohabiting fathers are less likely than married fathers to be living with older children (61% vs. 75%). Analysis of father involvement with older children ages 5 to 18 indicates that cohabiting fathers reported lower attendance of religious services with children and talking about their child's day than married fathers. Cohabiting and married fathers report similar levels of involvement in helping with homework, taking to activities, eating meals together, and participating in the PTA. Further analyses contrasting father involvement according to family configuration indicate that differences in religious involvement exist across most of the family configurations, except families with only stepchildren. Cohabiting fathers with both biological and stepchildren less often participated in parent teacher conferences or PTA meetings than married fathers. Cohabiting and married fathers who are living with just their own biological children are similar in terms of all of the indicators except attending religious services (Table 16.2). There appears to be no difference in father involvement according to relationship status among fathers who are parenting only stepchildren. Finally, cohabiting and married fathers who are parenting both step and biological children share similar levels of involvement except for parent-teacher meetings and religious involvement.

Fatherhood Assessments and Family Configurations

We examine whether and how union status and family configurations are associated with fathers' assessments of their role (Table 16.3). Overall, cohabiting and married fathers rank their role as fathers to their coresidential children similarly with mean scores slightly above the midpoint of very good to good. Cohabiting and married fathers who only have biological

Table 16.2   Father Involvement among Married and Cohabiting Fathers

	TOTAL		Only Biological		Only Step		Both Bio and Step	
	Mean	S.E.	Mean	S.E.	Mean	S.E.	Mean	S.E.
Time Spent Outings (0–6)								
Married	3.77	0.07	3.83	0.07	3.34	0.22	3.60	0.15
Cohabiting	3.83	0.13	3.89	0.18	3.80	0.28	3.69	0.21
AGE 5 or under								
Feed (1–5)								
Married	4.65	0.03	4.64	0.04	4.91	0.09	4.67	0.10
Cohabiting	4.53	0.13	4.41	0.19	4.78	0.12	4.74	0.11
Bath (1–5)					°			
Married	4.32	0.06	4.37	0.05	1.98	0.66	4.30	0.11
Cohabiting	4.22	0.16	4.17	0.21	4.05	0.38	4.56	0.13
Play (1–5)								
Married	4.79	0.02	4.78	0.02	4.93	0.06	4.79	0.07
Cohabiting	4.68	0.12	4.67	0.18	4.56	0.20	4.81	0.09
Read (1–5)	°		°					
Married	3.63	0.07	3.69	0.08	3.21	0.63	3.22	0.18
Cohabiting	2.93	0.16	2.83	0.20	3.06	0.41	3.16	0.33
AGES 5–18								
Religious (0–6)	°		°				°	
Married	2.22	0.12	2.31	0.12	2.02	0.27	1.87	0.22
Cohabiting	1.57	0.23	1.53	0.25	1.91	0.45	1.14	0.24
Help Homework (1–5)								
Married	3.48	0.08	3.53	0.09	3.22	0.28	3.41	0.19
Cohabiting	3.57	0.17	3.57	0.20	3.70	0.34	3.38	0.32
Talk (1–5)	°							
Married	4.57	0.04	4.58	0.05	4.30	0.13	4.68	0.07
Cohabiting	4.27	0.12	4.38	0.13	4.11	0.28	4.31	0.14
Take (1–5)								
Married	3.33	0.07	3.42	0.07	3.17	0.23	2.99	0.15
Cohabiting	3.24	0.16	3.32	0.18	2.99	0.28	3.47	0.21
Meals (1–5)								
Married	4.57	0.04	4.62	0.04	4.35	0.16	4.43	0.13
Cohabiting	5.00	0.10	4.55	0.08	4.46	0.24	4.48	0.18
Parent-Teacher (0–1)								
Married	0.71	0.02	0.71	0.03	0.69	0.09	0.74	0.06
Cohabiting	0.67	0.04	0.74	0.06	0.73	0.09	0.48	0.09

Source: NSFG 2006–08 Weighted %'s and Unweighted N's
° p < .05
Note: Higher values indicate more involvement the range is provided in parentheses.
N = 1,271 Married, N = 312 Cohabiting

children present share similar average fatherhood assessment scores (1.65). Married fathers who are raising only stepchildren have significantly worse fatherhood assessments (2.0) than cohabiting fathers raising only stepchildren (1.5). Cohabiting and married fathers who are raising stepchildren and biological children share similar fatherhood assessment scores (1.9 and 1.8, respectively).

Among married fathers, those with only biological children have more favorable assessments of their fatherhood role than married fathers with only stepchildren or fathers with both biological and stepchildren (denoted by superscript *a* in the table). Among cohabiting fathers there are no statistically significant differences in fatherhood assessments according to the configuration of children in the family.

Summary

The findings presented in this chapter extended prior research on resident fathering by focusing explicitly on cohabiting fathers and how they compare to married fathers. Furthermore, we demonstrated the importance of distinguishing between biological and stepfathers, and argued for greater attention to hybrid fathers, or those with both resident biological and stepchildren. Using recent data from the NSFG, we documented the disparate family configurations of cohabiting and married fathers. Whereas more than three-quarters of married fathers have only biological children in their household, just one-half of cohabiting fathers do. Nearly 50% of cohabiting fathers have either only stepchildren or both biological and stepchildren. Thus, union type and men's relationship to their children are confounded. As the share of fathers that are cohabiting rises, we can expect these families to be more complex in terms of the men's relationships to the children.

The existing literature on fathering in cohabiting families is rather limited and tends to be restricted to younger children. Consistent with prior research, we found that cohabiting and married fathers of young children tend to exhibit similar fathering behaviors, although there are a few differences. One reason for the similarity may be that young children have the same needs and fathering roles may not differ much in terms of meeting the basic needs of children (Cabrera et al., 2011). A key contribution of our study is its examination of fathering of children ranging in age from 0–18 years. We find that even among children ages 5–18, fathers in cohabiting and married parent families are similarly involved with their children. Additional

Table 16.3 Mean Father Assessments in Married and Cohabiting Fathers

	Married			Cohabiting	
	Mean	S.E.		Mean	S.E.
Only Biological Children	1.65	0.03	a	1.65	0.07
Only Stepchildren	2.01	0.12	°	1.53	0.13
Both Biological and Step	1.86	0.09		1.80	0.15
Total	1.70	0.03		1.64	0.07
N	1,271			312	

Source: NSFG 2006–08 Weighted %'s and Unweighted N's
° p < .05 (married vs. cohabiting fathers)
a p < .05 (biological vs. step children, biological vs. both biological and step)
Note: How good of a job do you do as a father? 1= Very good job 5= Bad Job

research that examines more refined age categories may provide a more nuanced understanding of fathering.

Fathers' overall assessments of their parenting tend to be fairly positive, Although married fathers' assessments are sensitive to the type of children present, cohabiting fathers' assessments are not. Married men with only biological children are especially positive about their fathering ability. It appears that the ways that men father their children is not dependent upon their marital status or their family configuration. Among men, marriage and involvement in fatherhood activities do not seem to be a package deal; in this study, cohabiting fathers are as involved as married fathers. Furthermore, men appear to parent their biological and stepchildren in a similar manner.

Bridges to Other Disciplines

By elucidating the importance of distinguishing between married and cohabiting fathers in research on resident fathering, this sociodemographic study informs work in a range of social science disciplines, including developmental psychology and economics. Developmental psychologists distinguish different periods of a child's life and focus on the developmental tasks to be accomplished in each period (Kalil, 2002, see chapters by Lamb and Lewis as well as Leidy, Schofield, and Parke, this volume). The findings here capture two broad periods of a child's life and the measurement is specific to these periods. Further, developmental psychology highlights the importance of considering multiple indicators of father-child relationship quality, such as language to child, emotional warmth, or responsiveness, and not just a focus on parenting activities. Developmental psychology could further build on our findings by examining not only father involvement but the family processes that are related to parenting in different types of unions.

Economic perspectives on father involvement focus on the costs and benefits of investing in children (see Bishai in this volume). Married fathers may invest more because they possess an enforceable contract with potentially high costs to dissolution and differential bargaining positions (England & Folbre, 2002). As differences between cohabitation and marriage have diminished in the United States (i.e. no-fault divorce, see Applegate, Schwartz, & Holtzworth-Munroe, in this volume), the bargaining dynamics in marriage and cohabitation may have become more similar. Yet the economics literature often overlooks cohabitation as a family form which may include key investments in children. Given the traditional role of men in most families as a breadwinner or critical financial contributor, it may be important to consider how economic circumstances shape father involvement across types of family configurations and types of unions.

Policy Implications

Children benefit from involved fathers. Prior research demonstrates that resident fathers are integral to child development and engage with children in a manner distinctive from mothers (Marsiglio, Amato, Day, & Lamb, 2000; see Lamb & Lewis Chapter, this volume). From a policy perspective, encouraging positive father involvement is critical. Our research informs policy by calling attention to the growing diversity among resident fathers: roughly 1 in 6 (16%) of resident fathers are cohabiting, not married, to the children's mother. Importantly, cohabiting fathers reside in more complex households that often include stepchildren. This complexity can potentially pose challenges to effective family functioning and thus may inhibit father involvement for resident fathers. Our results though are encouraging in this regard as we uncover few differences in the fathering behaviors of men in cohabiting versus married families. Nonetheless, our study demonstrates policies designed to promote resident father involvement must be responsive to the varied environments in which fathers raise children: cohabitation and marriage (see Benkeh and Coltrane as well as Holmes, Cowan, Cowan, and Hawkins, this volume). More specifically, the growing share of fathers who are cohabiting coincides with rising shares of fathers parenting stepchildren, which can present unique challenges.

Future Directions

This chapter provides an important update and extension of prior work, but there are many key questions about fathering in cohabiting families to be pursued. This chapter focuses on family configurations and could be expanded to include additional indicators of family complexity, such as nonresident children, relationship histories, and family instability.

Prior research has documented differentials in the well-being of children in married and cohabiting parent families (e.g., Brown, 2010), but often cannot explain the reasons for the union status gap in child well-being. Our findings suggest that differentials in father involvement with children may not be the reason why children raised in cohabiting families fare worse than children in married families. The NSFG is limited to indicators of involvement, and future research should be extended to include a broader array of fathering measures, such as hours of contact, support, caring, or discipline, ,and quality of father-child interactions. Additionally, the behaviors of fathers may affect or be affected by mothering behaviors and thus future research should consider the joint effects of fathering and mothering behaviors along with the quality of parental interactions. Longitudinal data could permit a focus on how attitudes about fathering roles influence involvement and relationships with mothers.

These findings are based on a cross-sectional assessment and provide only a static view of father involvement. Certainly, father involvement is dynamic and responsive to changes in family circumstances as well as economic and psychological factors. More directly, levels of father involvement may depend on the nature of the parent-child relationship, especially after age 5. Further investigation of the connections between father involvement and child well-being are warranted.

Attention to selection issues is an important next step to better understand why cohabiting and married fathers are similar or different in their fathering behaviors. Research that addresses the circumstances under which cohabiting versus married fathers produce biological children and determines how stepchildren influence fertility in cohabiting and married unions will help address selection issues. Further attention to how childbearing influences transitions in cohabitation and marriage will aid in understanding sources of selection.

Our analyses draw on father's reports of involvement with children. While a focus on father's own reports provides an important contribution, it would be informative to draw on reports from children as well as mothers. Data collections from multiple family members would be consistent with a broader family systems orientation. Furthermore, reports from multiple family members could allow assessments of how child-adult and couple relationships are tied to father involvement and child well-being.

We present a descriptive profile that indicates further attention should be paid to factors predicting father involvement and the implications of father involvement among children in cohabiting and married father families. Our work is an important first step, but as an overall portrait it may obscure variation in cohabiting and married fathers according to race and ethnicity or social class. Attention to demographic subgroups would provide a more complete understanding of father involvement, particularly since cohabiting fathers tend to be more racially diverse and economically disadvantaged than their married counterparts (Manning & Brown, 2006). The lack of differences we report on average among married and cohabiting fathers may mask key distinctions among subgroups of men and calls for further attention to fathering in cohabiting unions. Overall, men who share a residence with a child share similar levels of father involvement regardless of their biological relationship to the child or legal relationship to the mother.

References

Anderson, K., Kaplan, H., & Lancaster, J. (1999). Paternal care by genetic fathers and stepfathers I: Reports from Albuquerque men. *Evolution and Human Behavior, 20*, 405–431.

Angel, R., Burton, L., Lindsay Chase-Lansdale, P., Cherlin, A., & Moffitt, R. (2009). *Welfare, children, and families: A three-city study.* ICPSR04701-v7. Ann Arbor, MI: Inter-university Consortium for Political and Social Research [distributor], 2009-02-10. doi:10.3886/ICPSR04701.v7

Balistreri, K., Manning, W., & Brown, S. (2009, April). *New family measures: An examination of direct measures of cohabitation and parent pointers.* Presented at the annual meeting of the Population Association of America, Detroit, MI.

Berger, L. M., Carlson, M. J., Bzostek, S. H., & Osborne, C. (2008). Parenting practices of resident fathers: The role of marital and biological ties. *Journal of Marriage and Family, 70*(3), 625–639.

Brown, S. (2010). Marriage and child well-being: Research and policy perspectives. *Journal of Marriage and Family, 72*(5), 1059–1077.

Bumpass, L., & Lu, H. (2000). Trends in cohabitation and implications for children's family contexts in the United States. *Population Studies, 54*(1), 29–41.

Bzostek, S. (2008). Social fathers and child well-being. *Journal of Marriage and Family, 70*, 950–961.

Bzostek, S., Carlson, M. J., & McLanahan, S. (2010). *Mothers' repartnering after a nonmarital birth. Fragile Families Working Paper, 6-27.* Princeton, NJ: Princeton University.

Cabrera, N., Hofferth, S., & Cha, S. (2011). Patterns and predictors of father–infant engagement across race/ethnic groups. *Early Childhood Research Quarterly, 26*, 365–375.

Carlson, M., & McLanahan. S. (2010). Fathers in fragile families. In M. Lamb (Ed.), *The role of the father in child development* (pp. 241–269). New York, NY: Wiley.

Cherlin, A. (2004). The deinstitutionalization of American marriage. *Journal of Marriage and Family, 66*, 848–861.

Child Development Supplement to the Panel Study of Income Dynamics (PSID). (n.d.). Panel Study of Income Dynamics, Produced and distributed by the Institute for Social Research, Survey Research Center, University of Michigan, Ann Arbor, MI. Retrieved from http://simba.isr.umich.edu/data/data.aspx

Cox, M., & Paley, B. (1997). Families as systems. *Annual Review of Psychology, 48*, 243–267.

Daly, M., & Wilson, M. (1987). The Darwinian psychology of discriminative parental solicitude. *Nebraska Symposium on Motivation, 35*, 91–144.

England, P., & Folbre, N. (2002). Involving dads: Parental bargaining and family well-being. In C. S. Tamis-LeMonda & N. Cabrera (Eds.), *Handbook of father involvement: Multidisciplinary perspectives* (pp. 387–408). Mahwah, NJ: Erlbaum.

Fragile Families and Child Well-Being Study. (n.d.). Retrieved from http://www.fragilefamilies.princeton.edu/index.asp

Gibson-Davis, C. (2008). Family structure effects on maternal and paternal parenting in low-income families. *Journal of Marriage and Family, 70*(2), 452–465.

Ginther, D., & Pollak, R. (2004). Family structure and children's educational outcomes: Blended families, stylized facts, and descriptive regressions. *Demography, 41*, 671–696.

Goldscheider, F., & Sassler, S. (2006). Creating stepfamilies: Integrating children into the study of union formation. *Journal of Marriage and Family, 68,* 275–291.

Halpern-Meekin, S., & Tach, L. (2008). Heterogenity in two-parent families and adolescent well-being. *Journal of Marriage and Family, 70,* 435–451.

Harris, K. M. (2009). The National Longitudinal Study of Adolescent Health (Add Health), Waves I & II, 1994–1996; Wave III, 2001–2002; Wave IV, 2007-2009 [machine-readable data file and documentation]. Chapel Hil: Carolina Population Center, University of North Carolina at Chapel Hill.

Hofferth, S. (2006). Residential father family type and child well-being: Investment versus selection. *Demography, 43*(1), 53–77.

Hofferth, S., & Anderson, K. (2003). Are all dads equal? Biology versus marriage as a basis for paternal investment. *Journal of Marriage and Family, 65,* 213–232.

Hofferth, S., Cabrera, N., Carlson, M., Coley, R. L., Day, R., & Schindler, H. (2007). Resident father involvement and social fathering. In S. Hofferth & L. Casper (Eds.), *Handbook of measurement issues in family research* (pp. 335–374). Mahwah, NJ: Erlbaum.

Kalil, A. (2002). Cohabitation and child development. In A. Booth & A. C. Crouter (Eds.), *Just living together: Implications of cohabitation for children, families, and social policy* (pp. 153–159). Mahwah, NJ: Erlbaum.

Kennedy, S., & Bumpass, L. (2011, April). *Cohabitation and trends in the structure and stability of children's family lives.* Paper presented at the annual meeting of the Population Association of America, Washington, DC.

Kreider, R. (2008). Improvements to demographic household data in the current population survey. *Housing and Household Economic Statistics Division Working Paper.* http://www.census.gov/population/www/documentation/twps08/twps08.pdf

Kreider, R. M., & Ellis, R. (2011). *Number, timing, and duration of marriages and divorces: 2009* (Current Population Reports, P70-125). Washington, DC: U.S. Census Bureau.

Landale, N., & Oropesa, R. S. (2001). Father involvement in the lives of mainland Puerto Rican children: Contributions of nonresident, cohabiting, and married fathers. *Social Forces, 79*(3), 945–968.

Lepkowski, J., Mosher, W., Davis, K., Groves, R., & Van Hoewyk, J. (2010). The 2006–2010 NSFG: Sample design and analysis of a continuous survey. National Center for Health Statistics. *Vital Health Statistics, 2*(150). Retrieved from http://www.cdc.gov/nchs/data/series/sr_02/sr02_150.pdf

Manning, W. D. (2002). The implications of cohabitation for children's well-being. In A. Booth & A. C. Crouter (Eds.), *Just living together: Implications of cohabitation for children, families, and social policy* (pp. 121–152). Mahwah, NJ: Erlbaum.

Manning, W. D., & Brown, S. L. (2006). Children's economic well-being in married and cohabiting parent families. *Journal of Marriage and Family, 68,* 345–362.

Manning, W. D., & Lamb, K. A. (2003). Adolescent well-being in cohabiting, married, and single-parent families. *Journal of Marriage and Family, 65,* 876–893.

Manning, W. D., Smock, P., & Bergstrom-Lynch, C. (2009). Cohabitation and parenthood: Lessons from focus groups and in-depth interviews. In H. E. Peters & C. K. Dush (Eds.), *Marriage and family perspectives and complexities* (pp. 115–142). New York: Columbia University Press.

Marsiglio, W., Amato, P., Day, R. D., & Lamb, M. E. (2000). Scholarship on fatherhood in the 1990s and beyond. *Journal of Marriage and the Family, 62,* 1173–1191.

Nock, S. (1995). A comparison of marital and nonmarital households. *Journal of Family Issues, 16,* 53–76.

Parke, R. (2002). Father involvement: A developmental psychologist perspective. *Marriage and Family Review, 2,* 43–58.

Smock, P., & Greenland, F. (2010). Diversity in pathways to parenthood: Patterns, implications and emerging research directions. *Journal of Marriage and Family, 72,* 576–593.

Stewart, S. (2007). *Brave new stepfamilies: Diverse paths toward stepfamily living.* New York, NY: Sage.

Stewart, S., Manning, W., & Smock, P. (2004). Union formation among men in the U.S.: Does having prior children matter? *Journal of Marriage and Family, 65,* 90–104.

Sweeney, M. (2010) Remarriage and Stepfamilies: Strategic sites for family scholarship in the 21st century. *Journal of Marriage and Family,* 72(3), 667–684.

Sweeney, M. M., Wang, H., & Videon, T. M. (2009). Reconsidering the association between stepfather families and adolescent well-being. In H. E. Peters & C. M. K. Dush (Eds.), *Marriage and family: Multiple complexities and perspectives* (pp. 177–226). New York, NY: Columbia University Press.

Thomson, E., McLanahan, S., & Curtin, R. (1992). Family structure, gender, and parental socialization. *Journal of Marriage and Family,* 54, 25–37.

Tillman, K. (2008). "Non-traditional" siblings and the academic outcomes of adolescents. *Social Science Research,* 37, 88–108.

Trivers, R. (1972). Parental investment and sexual selection. In B. G. Campbell (Ed.), *Sexual selection and the descent of man 1871–1971* (pp. 136–179). Chicago, IL: Aldine.

United States Department of Health and Human Services. National Center for Health Statistics. (2011). *National Survey of Family Growth, 2006–2010.* Ann Arbor, MI: Institute for Social Research.

Yeung, J., Sandburg, J., Davis-Kean, P., & Hofferth, S. (2001). Children's time with fathers in intact families. *Journal of Marriage and the Family,* 63(1), 136–154.

Chapter 17
Gender Roles and Fathering

Andrea Doucet

Brock University

Introduction

Fathering—as a research field and as a set of practices and identities—is inextricably tied up with mothering as well as with gender roles and relations. As this book demonstrates, much of the interest in fatherhood initially arose out of concerns about father absence and the need to attend to father-child relationships as an important part of men's lives and men's identities. Yet, the now burgeoning scholarly and popular attention given to fathering is also rooted in rapidly changing gender roles and relationships at home and in the workplace over the past few decades, particularly within North America, Scandinavia, Australia, New Zealand, and much of Europe.

In a chapter that focuses on gender roles, we need to be clear, in the first instance, about what we mean by gender and how this lens has been useful for understanding fathering. Given that the literature on gender has become nothing less than "a growth industry in the academy" (Risman, 2004, p. 429), only a basic overview of the concept of "gender" can be provided here.

Although there are now ample theoretical treatments of gender (Ferree, Lorber, & Hess, 2000; Martin, 2003; Risman, 2004), Connell's theoretical approach to gender is a useful guide to the study of gender roles and relationships. While Connell did not develop nor specifically apply her model to fathering, this approach can still illuminate men's and fathers' experiences and the wider social relations within which fathering is enacted. Specifically, Connell's approach seeks to "understand the different dimensions of structures of gender, the relations between bodies and society and the patterning or configuration of gender" (Connell, 2000, pp. 24–25). It is also a four-fold model of gender relations—incorporating relations of power between women and men, production (e.g., gender divisions of labor), emotional relations, and gender symbolism (e.g., images of masculinity and femininity in language, culture, media and social norms) (Connell, 1987, 2000, 2005).

Connell's approach focuses on gender as *structure* and *agency*, thus recognizing local and global structures within which fathering and mothering practices are located while also noting the potential for change by individuals. Put differently, her work, along with many other leading gender scholars, points to how gender exists at both the *macro* and *micro* levels. At the macro level, a range of words and theories have been used to describe factors which create and sustain gender differences; some examples include "the gender regime" or the "gender order" (Connell, 1987), the "relations of ruling" (Smith, 1987) or the "gender structure" (Risman, 2004). Others have noted that fathering and mothering are shaped by social institutions (e.g., workplaces, state policies, schools, health institutions) and can also be viewed as social institutions themselves (e.g., Rich, 1986). At the micro-level, theorists have explored concepts such as "doing gender" or "displaying gender," both of which are explored later in this chapter.

Throughout this chapter, I intersperse the terms *gender roles, gender relations,* and *gender divisions* in order to explore how scholars have studied fathering in relation to an expansive field of gender studies. There is, indeed, a wide array of terms associated with the concept of gender, each with their own history and with many critiques and debates as to which one is the most useful.[1] I purposely steer clear of debating this historical and contemporary field; instead, what guides the chapter is a sense of how a theoretical and applied concept of 'gender' has intersected with fathering. My own view is that gender is a relational concept and that femininities and masculinities as well as mothering and fathering are relational sets of practices and identities. As we shall see below, the field of *'gender divisions of labour'* has been one of the most prominent areas of study in research on mothers, fathers and gender roles; yet although 'divisions' is the guiding word, I have also argued that this field is about both gender divisions *and* relations (see Doucet, 2006, 2009a,b).

This chapter on fathering and gender roles is organized into six sections:

1. Brief Historical and Theoretical Overview of Fathering and Gender Roles; Current Research Questions: Gender Divisions of Domestic Labor (Measurement and Methodology; Attention to diversity)
2. Empirical Findings
3. Policy Implications
4. Bridges to Other Disciplines (mainly Feminist studies and Masculinity studies)
5. Future Directions

Throughout the chapter, attention is given to varied theoretical and methodological approaches and to the diversity of fathering experiences (e.g., differences of class, ethnicity and race, cultural background, as well as different family forms).

Brief Historical and Theoretical Overview of Fathering and Gender Roles

Early examinations of fathering and gender roles focused almost exclusively on fathers' roles as family breadwinners (for a good overview, see Griswold, 1993; Lamb, 2000). Looking back over 50 years, a well-known advocate of this family model of breadwinning fathers and caregiving mothers was one of the American fathers of sociology, Talcott Parsons. He famously promoted the notion of complementary spheres of home and work and corresponding distinct gender divisions of labor with women taking on unpaid work in the private sphere and men taking on paid work in the public sphere (Parsons, 1967; Parsons & Bales, 1955; but see Bishais, this volume for an alternative theory of the economics of fatherhood).

It could be argued that Parson's model of separate and complementary gender roles characterized to some extent the early stages of industrial capitalism where the re-organization of work and capitalist production physically separated the home from the workplace. Yet although there was some evidence of distinct gender roles (spatially, ideologically, and in practice), these spheres were in fact not as separate as they appeared. Cross-cultural research, for example, has clearly demonstrated that many working class households have always required more than the male wage; that is, women and mothers have contributed to the domestic coffers by intensifying domestic self-provisioning work inside the home (e.g., taking in boarders, caring for others' children, informal selling of homemade clothes or baked goods), by earning money through the informal economy, or by earning a part-time or full-time wage themselves (e.g., Bradbury, 1984, 1993; Tilly & Scott, 1987). Moreover, research on agricultural families and family businesses has demonstrated how both women and men have played more fluid roles in paid and unpaid work (Bradley, 1989). In short, gender roles, although normative and ideologically prescribed, were never completely distinct for fathers and mothers.

Although a model and ideology of male breadwinner and female caregiver was, thus, never an all-encompassing one, its effects have nevertheless remained in scholarship, in national policies regarding paid work and care work, and in popular discourses. There was, for example, a noticeable divide throughout the 1970s and 1980s between scholarly work on mothers and fathers. On the one hand, research on women tended to focus mainly on their roles as caregivers; research on men, on the other hand, tended to focus predominantly on their roles as workers and as breadwinners.

In the late 1970s and early 1980s, however, two theoretical developments occurred that shifted research on mothering and fathering and gender roles. First, the view that domestic labor and care work were indeed work entered the scholarly and activist agenda. Instigated mainly by the work of feminist scholars working on mothering as well as particular strands of feminism (e.g., radical feminism and socialist feminism), scholars began to study the meanings and practices of the daily work that women did, both as a form of work and as a subject that required scholarly attention (Lopata, 1981; Luxton, 1980; Oakley, 1974). Second, in the early 1980s, as women's employment increased, there was a surge of attention given to the women's indivisible experiences of paid and unpaid work. Even more specifically, many books were published with a preponderance of the words "women, work, and family" in the titles or as central themes (Lamphere, 1987; J. Lewis, Porter, & Shrimpton, 1988; Zavella, 1987).

These early studies, and many more that followed, concluded that even when women worked full-time, they still did most of the unpaid domestic work. At the same time, one of the criticisms of early studies on housework and childcare was that they did not fully investigate men's roles in domestic work. That is, women's lives were viewed through theoretical lenses that linked work and family while men's lives were still being looked at only in terms of paid work (Siltanen & Stanworth, 1984).

Others pointed to how this state of affairs, especially the fact that women were taking on most of the household work, affected women and men in detrimental ways. On the one hand, many feminist scholars highlighted, and continue to do so, that there are high costs to women, economically, socially, and politically of different and unequal gender roles (e.g., Crittenden 2001; Folbre, 1994).

On the other hand, it was argued that distinct gender roles for men and women, fathers and mothers, would also lead to adverse effects for *men*. Since the mid-1970s, feminist scholars were pointing to the deep social and personal problems that ensued when mothers and fathers filled largely separate gender roles. This focus on the social costs of constrictive gender roles was well expressed in the work of leading feminist psychoanalytic scholars writing in the late

1970s. This was well captured in the classic works of Dorothy Dinnerstein's *The Mermaid and the Minotaur* (1977) and Nancy Chodorow's *The Reproduction of Mothering* (1978). Dinnerstein, for example, drew together the fundamental imbalances that occur in a society when *one* gender does most of the metaphoric rocking of the cradle while the *other* gender rules the world. Referring to "sexual arrangements" as the "division of responsibility, opportunity, and privilege that prevails between male and female humans, and the patterns of psychological interdependence that are implicit in this division," she argued that a central "human malaise" thus "stems from a core fact that has so far been universal: the fact of primary female responsibility for the care of infants and young children" (Dinnerstein, 1977, p. 4; see also Bales, Waynforth, & Storey, this volume).

Meanwhile Chodorow's oft-cited work on mothering also referred to the losses for men and for society more generally that female dominated parenting engenders. She wrote that "the very fact of being mothered by a women generates in men conflicts over masculinity, a psychology of male dominance, and a need to be superior to women" (1978, p. 214).

Fathering scholars also picked up on this issue of the effects of constrictive gender roles and the need to study and understand men's lives not only as breadwinning fathers, but also as caregivers of children (e.g., Coltrane, 1996; Lamb, 1981). Thus, as women's and men's lives and gendered roles continued to change, so did the scholarship on fathering. Specifically, socio-economic and demographic changes such as men's declining wages, increasing male unemployment, sustained growth in women's labor force participation and changing ideologies associated with men and women's roles and identities all led to an increased focus on understanding men's lives as fathers and shifting gender roles and relations around paid and unpaid work (see also Cabrera, Tamis-LeMonda, Bradley, Hofferth, & Lamb, 2000).

By the late 1980s and early 1990s, it became clear that the issue of unpaid work and childcare were not simply issues that mattered to women; it was also apparent that leaving men out would further solidify the binary distinction between paid and unpaid work that it was seeking to dissolve. While there were a few scholars who picked up on the importance of examining men, work, and family in the early 1980s (C. Lewis, 1986; O'Brien, 1987), this crucial focus only became part of mainstream sociological work on work and family in the 1990s and into the new millennium.

Since that time, many studies have sought to challenge the idea that it is only housewives who do housework. Indeed, the past five decades have produced an astonishing number of case studies on gender divisions of labor, that is on *who* does *what* in relation to unpaid work and paid work. Indeed, research on men as fathers, as domestic partners, and as care givers has become a burgeoning literature (Coltrane, 1996; Coltrane & Adams, 2001; Dermott, 2008; Dienhart, 1998; Doucet, 2006; Dowd, 2000; Hobson, 2002; Lamb & Day, 2004; Miller, 2011; Unger 2010). These studies constitute a minor academic industry in family studies, gender studies, and in mothering and fathering scholarship. They generally fall under the rubric of gender divisions of labor and they hold several key questions which guide current research on gender roles and fathering.

Current Research Questions

Some of the most pressing questions about fathering and gender roles have fallen under this umbrella theme of gender divisions of labor. Key questions have focused especially on questions of what, how, and why changes and continuities have occurred in the gender division of labor between mothers and fathers. Furthermore, multiple variations on the intersections of equality and differences abound when we examine mothers and fathers and gender roles in parenting. Intriguing questions include: Are women and men *different* in parenting? If so, how so? Can they be *equal*? If so, what does this mean and how do we define, measure, and evaluate this?

These questions, and the larger field of gender divisions of labor, are rooted in broad areas of scholarship, including feminist work on gender equalities as well as multidisciplinary work on families, households, mothering, fathering, work-family policies, and the identities and practices that constitute housework and caring labor. It has been nothing short of a massive area of attention for many scholars. It has also been methodologically and theoretically diverse and has produced a mixed set of findings.

Measurement and Methodology

Beginning in the 1970s, academic studies of gender and domestic divisions of labor began collecting basically three major types of data on gender and domestic labor: time, tasks, and responsibilities. Each of these is reviewed briefly below. Some of the earliest studies time budget studies were carried out in the 1970s in Canada, the United States, and the United Kingdom (e.g., Meissner, Meis, Scheu, & Scheu, 1975; Walker & Woods, 1976). Since that time, they have grown successively through the refining of measurement techniques such as time diaries (Sullivan, 1996, 1997, 2000) and through large-scale cross-national comparisons (e.g., Gershuny, 2000; Hook, 2006; Robinson & Godbey, 1997; Sullivan, 2011).

The results from time use studies have been mixed, depending on measures used, but there is also an overall consensus that we are slowly reaching a point of gender convergence (see also Palkovitz & Fagan, this volume).Three points can be emphasized here. First, as Kan, Sullivan, and Gershuny (2011, p. 235) noted, there has been a "slow and incomplete convergence of women's and men's work patterns" (see also Marshall, 2006).

Second, while convergence is slowly occurring, there are still differences in what women and men do; that is time use data shows that gender segregation in domestic work is quite persistent over time. More specifically, women continue to take on most routine housework (e.g., cooking and cleaning and laundry) while men have increased their contribution to non-routine housework (e.g. shopping, gardening, and household repairs). One of the most comprehensive reviews of the Multinational Time Use Study (MTUS), a harmonized database of large nationally-representative time-use diary surveys collected from 16 countries (from 1960s to 2000s) arrived at the following conclusion about changes in unpaid work:

> … men and women tend to undertake different types of domestic work. Women have been responsible for the bulk of routine housework and caring for others, while men tend to spend their domestic work time on non-routine domestic work. There is evidence to show that the gender gap in routine housework is narrowing gradually. Nevertheless, this narrowing is achieved mainly through a large reduction in women's routine housework time, as well as through a less substantial increase in men's. (Kan et al., 2011, p. 238)

A third point about time use studies is the critical importance of the indicators for measuring change. It is now a well-known fact that the highly publicized estimations, as revealed in *The Second Shift* (Hochschild & Machung, 1989) were based on rather narrow indicators of men's time use. That is the oft-repeated statistic that women took on *an extra month* of housework per year, in comparison to their male partners, was based on the exclusion of weekend activities as well as driving children to activities, shopping and non-routine household tasks, some of which can be fairly time intensive (e.g., household repair, car maintenance and repairs) (see Coltrane, 1996; Pleck, 1985).

Finally, there is some diversity in these patterns of gender and paid and unpaid work. For example, variations exist according to ethnic diversity (e.g., Sayer & Fine, 2011), social class (e.g., Hamermesh & Lee, 2007), family structure (e.g., Kalenkoski, Ribar, & Stratton, 2007), whether leisure time is also included (Bittman & Wajcman, 2000), as well as according to how tasks are defined and how overlapping time use for tasks are dealt with (e.g., Folbre & Yoon, 2007; Floro & Miles, 2003).

Complementing quantitative time use studies, there has also been considerable attention given to collecting both qualitative and quantitative data on the gender division of labor according to who-does-what household *tasks*. These studies also began to take off in the 1970s and 1980s (e.g., Hoffman & Nye, 1974; Pahl, 1984; Ross, 1987).

As with the surge in time use studies over the past three decades, the literature on the gender division of tasks and gender roles associated with those tasks has been nothing short of overwhelming. Studies have focused on a multitude of countries, differences in family structure, and differences according to ethnicity, class, sexuality, and generation. Again, while findings vary depending on all of these factors as well as the methodologies and theoretical lenses used, the overall picture is one where there has been substantial change in the overall gender division of tasks, along with some stability in the gender division of specific tasks.

In addition to time and tasks, a key focus for scholarly studies on the gender division of domestic labor has been a focus on the *responsibilities* of fathers and mothers. These responsibilities for parenting work involve a wide range of tasks and an overall orientation that includes organization, managing, and remembering (see, for example, Berk, 1985; Cabrera, Shannon, & Tamis-LeMonda, 2007; Cowan & Cowan, 1987; Doucet, 2006; Lamb et al., 1987).

Two complementary approaches to the issue of fathering, gender roles and the responsibility for childcare are those of Michael Lamb and colleagues (1987) and my own approach (Doucet, 2006). Lamb, Charnov, and Levine (1987), on the one hand, argue that childcare includes a broad range of fathering practices, including meeting children's needs through *interaction* (direct engagement), *accessibility* (physical and psychological presence and availability), and *responsibility* (indirect childrearing tasks such as planning and scheduling).

My own work builds on, and widens, this conceptualization of fathering involvement (Lamb et al., 1987) into three childcare responsibilities; it does so by recognizing that the first two tasks denoted by Lamb and colleagues also have dimensions of responsibility woven into them, partly because they also require cognition and commitment (see Palkovitz, 1997). These three childrearing responsibilities, which can be taken up by fathers and/or mothers are: *emotional responsibility*,[2] *community responsibility*,[3] and the *moral responsibilities*[4] of parenting (see Doucet, 2004, 2006, 2009b).

Overall, the extensive literature on gender divisions of domestic time, tasks, and responsibilities has spanned more than 50 years and includes a massive cross-cultural body of research. While informed by multiple theoretical perspectives and divergent methods of investigation, the overwhelming consensus is that men's participation in housework and childcare have increased gradually. Longitudinal perspectives indicate that that today's fathers are more involved in their children's lives than fathers of previous generations. This is the case, whether the measurements are based on time (Gershuny, 2000; Gershuny & Sullivan, 2003; Hook, 2006; Kan et al., 2011; Robinson & Godbey, 1997; Sullivan, 1996, 1997, 2000) or tasks (Bianchi, Robinson, & Milkie, 2006; Coltrane, 2000; O'Brien & Shemilt, 2003; Pleck & Masciadrelli, 2004; Pleck & Pleck, 1997). Nevertheless, there is also some consensus that the *responsibility* for childcare and domestic life has remained overwhelmingly in women's hands (Crittenden, 2001; Doucet, 2006, 2009a; Fox, 2009).

While there has been great attention to substantive issues of *how much* change has actually occurred, there has also been extensive attention to theoretical and methodological issues. That is, researchers have also attended to how the lenses we use to view, define, collect, and measure data on fathering and mothering and gendered roles and contributions to domestic life can matter greatly. A small sample of recent developments include: a focus on how care work should also include work that occurs in community settings (such as volunteer work, the forming of connections with other households (see Doucet, 2006; Marsiglio, 2008, 2009; Marsiglio & Roy, 2012); the view that we must constantly scrutinize the alignment between theories and every day domestic life and labor (Daly, 2001, 2003; Lynch, 2007); and the issue of how to define and measure equality in domestic life and labor (Doucet, 2001, 2006, 2009b).

A recurring issue within this field of gender divisions of labor is how to best collect data that reflect what is actually occurring in men and women's lives. Methods and measurements matter in both quantitative and qualitative research. In time use studies, for example, many have pointed out that time-use diaries are more reliable than retrospective recall questions posed in questionnaires (see Bianchi et al., 2006; Juster & Stafford, 1985; Sullivan, 2011). In qualitative studies focused on the division of domestic tasks for couples, the issue of the advantages or disadvantages of couple interviews or individual interviews is a topic that has been debated over several decades (see Komarovsky & Phillips, 1987; Mansfield & Collard, 1982; Pahl, 1989).

Researchers have also developed ways of gleaning evidence that move beyond individual and couple interviews, focusing for example on 'networks of care' which includes other people directly involved in the care of children (see Hansen, 2005). Others have experimented with participatory and visual methods such as the Household Portrait technique for facilitating discussion of the division of domestic labor (Doucet, 1996, 2001, 2006), the use of creative family mapping (Gabb, 2008), and family diaries to study gender shifts in intimacy in family life (Haldar & Waerdahl, 2009).

Issues of Diversity

Attention to diversity was a slow but gradual process within research on gender divisions of domestic labor. Throughout the 1980s and early 1990s, most of the research on gender divisions of labor, as well as on role-reversed couples, was on varied combinations of white, middle class and heterosexual couples (Deutsch, 1999; Kimball, 1988; Russell, 1983, 1987). Yet since then, there has been significant attention to father involvement for diverse groups of fathers across, for example, class, race and ethnicity (e.g., Ball & Daly, in press; Chuang & Moreno, 2008; Meteyer & Perry-Jenkins, 2010; Miller & Maiter, 2008; Roy & Cabrera, 2010). There has also been increasing attention to divisions of labor in gay and lesbian individuals and couples (i.e., Berkowitz & Marsiglio, 2007; Carrington, 1999; Dunne, 2001). Most of these studies on gay fathers have noted that that the removal of gender as a marker of difference leads to the removal of gender roles and expectations and ultimately greater flexibility in how and why care work and domestic labor gets done (see Benson, Silverstein, & Auerbach, 2005: Biblarz & Stacey, 2010).

Issues of income and class have also been noted in studies on gender roles and domestic work. From extensive Canadian time use studies, Katherine Marshall from Statics Canada has noted that "When wives have an income of $100,000 or more, the division of paid labour and housework between partners is more likely to be split equally" (2006, p. 13). Similarly, studies from the United States and the United Kingdom have indicated that "women with higher earning power do less housework than those with lower earning power" (Sullivan, 2011, p. 5; see also Crompton & Lyonette, 2010; Gupta, 2007). As speculated by Sullivan (2011) and confirmed by Canadian data (Palameta, 2003), this is partly due to how the decision to hire housework help is dictated more by women's earning power than by that of men.

Attention to diversity in fathering further underscores a critical point in this discussion. The diversity of fathering forms (married, common law, divorced, widower, sole-custody, joint-custody, re-married with new children, re-married with stepchildren, parenting across different households, fathering of one or several children, number of hours in paid employment, eligibility for parental leave or not) means that it is very difficult to paint one clear picture of fathering and changing gender roles in relation to both childcare and domestic work.

Empirical Findings

There has been an incredibly large array of explanations developed over the last four decades to explain the change, and lack of change, in gender divisions of labor, in gender roles in mothering and fathering, and in gender relations. These key findings and explanations span a wide array of macro and micro level factors. Seven are highlighted here.

Cross-generational Transmission

First, researchers have focused on cross-generational transmission of gender roles for fathers (e.g., Brannen & Nilsen, 2006) and a complicated mix of cross-generational ideals combined with policies and mothers' preferences (Bjørnholt, 2010). Issues of race and ethnicity also feature as part of this conversation and debate. Canadian research on Aboriginal fathers, for example, has highlighted how fathering involvement is related both to the "disrupted inter-generational transmission of fathering" and to the long-term negative influences of residential school abuse (Ball, 2009).

"Doing Gender" or "Displaying Gender"

A second set of explanations as to how and why gender divisions of labor continue include theoretical explanations around "doing gender or "displaying gender" (Berk, 1985; Coltrane, 1989, 1996; Risman, 1998; West & Zimmerman, 1987). Rooted in ethnomethodological analyses of gender relations (e.g., Garfinkel, 1967), the "doing gender" approach is a theoretical approach that examines the routine performance of housework and childcare and how gender is viewed as something that is actively accomplished and negotiated in interaction within a heterosexual relationship. That is, when women and men "do gender," they partake in activities and expression that befit their gender. As stated by Thompson and Walker (1989): "Women and men participate together to construct the meaning of gender and distinguish themselves from each other *as* women or *as* men" (p. 865).

The "doing gender" approach appears in a wide array of studies that examine women and men's roles in varied social settings, including in employment settings (Bruni, Gherardi, & Poggio, 2004; Martin, 2003; Priola, 2007). This theoretical lens has also been used by scholars investigating gender roles in domestic life where they have explored how mothers and fathers together create and co-create gender (Deutsch, 1999; Cranny-Francis, Kirby, Stavropoulos, & Waring, 2003). Others have also explored how mothers and fathers actively work at "undoing gender" in care work and in mothering and fathering (Crompton & Lyonette, 2010; Deutsch, 2007; Risman, 2009).

There is a performance element in "doing gender" and thus a further variation on this theme is the "displaying gender," which can be seen in both quantitative and qualitative literature on gender roles and fathering (see Sullivan, 2011). This concept was first introduced into the quantitative literature on the domestic division of labor by Judith Brines (1994). Furthermore, it has recently received renewed attention with veteran qualitative researcher Janet Finch (2007) reworking the concept to look at how families display many kinds of performances, including gender. A recent edited volume (Dermott & Seymour, 2011) builds on Finch's research to examine a wide range of displays in families, including the display of gender by fathers in community settings (Doucet, 2011).

Gender Ideologies and Discourses

A third foci for understanding changing gender roles and fathering is that of gender ideologies, which has been a key source of exploration and explanation for several decades (e.g., Brannen & Moss, 1991; Deutsch, 1999; Greenstein, 1996; Hochschild & Machung, 1989). A related issue has been that of stable and changing discourses of fatherhood and motherhood (Dermott, 2008; Dienhart, 1998; Henwood & Proctor, 2003; Lupton & Barclay, 1997; Mandell, 2002).

Social Networks and Community Responsibilities

While most research on gender divisions of labor focuses on how gender roles play out within households, there is a growing body of work that also examine how community connections reinforce or support traditional gender roles. Some of this work dates back to the 1950s when America anthropologist Elizabeth Bott (1957) argued that gender role differentiation would be particularly marked when couples were most deeply embedded in close-knit social networks which reinforced traditional gender roles. These ideas were, in turn, further developed by UK sociologist Lydia Morris (1985, 1990) in her South Wales research. She suggested that men with highly developed local social networks were most likely to maintain a rigid attitudes about traditional gender divisions of domestic labor; she also argued, in a parallel manner, how women's social networks could be a source of social pressure reinforcing their traditional roles as wives and mothers.

In the past 20 years, a wide range of multidisciplinary studies have explored the complex links between social networks, domestic labor, paid labor, and gender roles and identities (e.g., Bell & Ribbens, 1994; Brannen & Moss, 1991; Doucet, 2001, 2006; Gregson & Lowe, 1993; Hansen, 2005; Marsiglio, 2008; Wearing, 1984). My own work, for example, has focused on how community networks, especially parenting groups for infant and toddlers, can reinforce distinct gender roles in parenting, mainly through the community exclusion and surveillance of men (Doucet, 2001, 2006, 2009a,b). On the other hand, Karen V. Hansen's (2005) research moves from a nuclear family focus to one based on community networks of care; her extensive fieldwork highlights how class differences are also critical to the how families draw on networks of friends, paid caregivers, and extended kin collectively close the care gap for their school-aged children.

Masculinities and Breadwinning

The issue of paid work and fathering and the link between work and masculinities and the breadwinner ideology has been a dominant theme in discussions of gender roles and fathering (Deutsch, 1999; Dowd, 2000; Pleck, 1985; J. Lewis, 2001).

Early studies on male unemployment from the United Kingdom provided initial insights into the links between breadwinning and gender identities. While high unemployment rates in the recession of the mid-1980s were heralded by some commentators as a factor that could lead to gender role sharing or even role reversal within households, most studies conducted at that time demonstrated how sudden male unemployment could create "involuntary home centeredness" (Wheelock, 1990, p. 43). That is, studies pointed to how men actually exhibited low self-esteem, isolation, and multiple hardships and indeed, an enhanced sense of polarized gender roles (Morris, 1985, 1990; Russell, 1983, 1987; Wheelock, 1990). As one well-known study noted, both men and women believed that a man's authority and his masculinities were threatened by male unemployment; as stated by a female respondent in a study of male unemployment: "He likes to be the breadwinner and that's hard on a man" (McKee & Bell, 1986, p. 142).

Over the past 30 years, there have been some dramatic changes in fathering, mothering, gender identities, and gender roles; there has also been a sense of continuity. Ethnographic work on fathers as primary caregivers and men who are actively involved in caregiving points to how the breadwinner ideology is still in play (see J. Lewis, 2001). For example, Nicholas Townsend has noted how the "contributing cultural primacy of providing for children means that men's time and energy are devoted to, and consumed by, their paid work" (2002, p. 78). For Townsend and for other 21st-century observers of changing fatherhood (see Cabrera et al., this volume), there is a resulting tension between the breadwinner ideology and new father ideals that emphasize how fathers should be emotionally present for their children. Much of the work on involved fathers indicates that even when men are primary caregivers and where they have rescinded a strong or full-time attachment to the labor market, fathers still feel judged as primary breadwinners (Doucet, 2005, 2006; Miller, 2010, 2011).

Gender ideologies in relation to breadwinning and caregiving are also important considerations in research focused on fathers of varied ethnic backgrounds. For example, in recent research on Russian immigrant and Sudanese refugee fathers living in Canada, the disruption to the provider role was viewed as detrimental to their identities and roles and fathers (Este & Tachble, 2009). Meanwhile, research on low-income teen dads in Canada also demonstrates the vital role that breadwinning role plays in their motivation to be good fathers (DeVault et al., 2008).

Policy Implications

Over the past two decades, considerable attention has been given to the role of policies and how these matter, or not, in engendering gender role change in relation to parenting. One policy issue that has been increasingly examined over the past decade is that of paternal leave policies.

Parental leave has been a critical focus for research on fathering and gender roles because the first year of parenting is one where gender roles are especially pronounced (see Doucet, 2009a). Parental leave policies are thus one means of encouraging fathers of infants and young children to take time off to care for their children. The Nordic countries notably Sweden, Norway, and Iceland, have come up with innovative ways of encouraging leave by fathers. Most notable are "daddy days" (leave reserved exclusively for fathers (e.g., Sweden and Norway) or the equal division of the parental leave periods between mother, father and both parents (Iceland) (for an overview see O'Brien, 2009; Kamerman & Moss, 2009; see also Sigle-Rushton et al., this volume).

In spite of policy measures directed specifically towards men, it is worth noting, however, that parental leave is still taken up mainly by women, both in terms of numbers of women in comparison to men and the amount of time taken by mothers. This has raised the question of how to achieve equality within parenting, and whether gender roles remain distinct and resistant to change particularly during periods such as the early months of childcare. It has also led to discussions of how to define and measure equality in parenting in both short-term and long-term ways (see Doucet, 2009a,b).

While, in all countries, mothers continue to take more leave than fathers, it is still the case that leave entitlement set specifically for fathers can lead to an increase in fathers' take-up of at least some leave from work to be with their infants. In this regard it is worth noting that in Sweden, over 90% of fathers now took parental leave, mainly when their children were 13 to 15 months of age (Chronholm, 2009). In countries such as Sweden, Norway, and Canada (in one province, Quebec) the proportion of fathers taking some leave time increased significantly after the introduction of "daddy weeks" or a use-it-or lose it quote reserved for fathers only. In the Canadian province of Quebec, 86% of fathers take an average of 7 weeks off (McKay & Doucet, 2010); in Norway 89% of fathers take time off (Brandth & Kvande, 2009). At the same time, even when fathers have access to parental leave, they may take this leave via sick leave or vacation days rather than through their legal entitlement to parental leave (see Cabrera & Peters, 2000; Coltrane & Behnke, this volume).

In the case of parental leave, traditional gender norms about the importance of male wages intersect with new gender norms about men as highly involved caregivers. That is, the highest paternal participation rates occur in countries where there are non-transferable leave programs combined with high wage replacement rates; these include mainly the Nordic countries of Sweden (90% participation rate), Norway (89%), Iceland (84%), and the province of Quebec (Marshall, 2008; O'Brien, 2009). Conversely, countries with low replacement wage rates have lower uptake by fathers (for example, Belgium with under 7%, Austria, 2%, and France, 1%).

However, even within these countries, the take-up of leave is uneven. For example, recent research from Sweden and demonstrates some variations in leave patterns between rural and urban areas (Almqvist, Sandberg, & Dahlgren, 2011) while Canadian research points to the different take-up rates between provinces that have non-transferable leave for fathers (such as Quebec) and those that do not (e.g., the rest of Canada) (see McKay & Doucet, 2010).

It is thus critical to note that policies do make a difference in the slow shift and transformation of gender roles. At the same time, policies cannot work alone; they are part of a larger configuration of ideological and institutional change across work places, communities, education, and the overall package of work-family policies in each country.

Bridges to Other Disciplines

The study of fathering and gender roles has been located mainly within the disciplines of family studies as well as sociology, psychology, and, to some degree, political studies or political economy. This continually evolving and expanding field of research has also been informed by, and is linked to, feminist studies and masculinity studies. Fathering and gender roles are also joined with multi-disciplinary conversations with feminist studies and masculinities studies.

Feminist Studies and Gender Studies

Feminist studies and gender studies have existed in a close relationship with research on fathering and gender roles and the study of gender divisions of labor. Two important points can be drawn from this connection. First, feminist work in the 1970s and early 1980's, such as the work by Dinnerstein (1977) and Chodorow (1978) cited above, as well as the work of Sara Ruddick (1995) and feminist scholars focused on shared caregiving mothers and fathers (Ehrensaft, 1984; Kimball, 1988; Radin, 1982; Russell, 1987) all pointed to what Ruddick called the "revolutionary" outcomes that would flow from men's greater involvement in care work.

Yet, this initial enthusiasm over the radical potential of men's involvement in care work was followed by more sobering analyses of the challenges to achieving this. That is, throughout the 1980s and 1990s, many commentators pointed out that the greater participation of men in care work and in domestic work could only be regarded as one small step towards transformative social change. As Iris Marion Young astutely saw it: "It has not taken feminists long, however, to see that matter is not simple" since the "(g)ender division of parenting is only one of the many institutional structures that produce and maintain the oppression of women" (1984, pp. 142–143). In other words, feminists began to notice that you could not just "add men and stir" (Doucet, 1995).

While recognizing the larger institutional changes that need addressing in order for women and men's lives to change, there is now a very large body of feminist and gender studies scholarship generated over the past three decades on this wide topic of encouraging and achieving men's inclusion in care. This voluminous attention partly emerged because, in spite of the enormity of work required to bring about social change, the issue of men's involvement is still considered critically important one with personal, political, social and economic implications for women, men, and children.

A second point that emerges in the bridging of scholarship on fathering with feminist and gender studies relates to the issue of attending to the wide array of differences within the categories of man and women or, what feminist scholars point to as intersectionality theory.

Briefly put, throughout the 1980s' feminists and gender scholars began to give increasing attention to differences between women. This focus emerged from within second wave feminism as well as critiques around inclusion and exclusion from women of color, women from Third World settings, pro-feminist men, the GBLT (Gay, Bisexual, Lesbian, and Transgendered) community, and from postmodern and poststructuralist theory (e.g.. Collins, 2000; hooks, 1981; Spelman, 1988). The general line of thinking is that any analysis of the lives of women and men must not only include a focus on gender, but one that focused on intersecting categories of both structural and experiential dimensions of differences in class, race and ethnicity, sexuality, age, culture, and ability/disability.

Studies on gender and household labor were slowly influenced by intersectional theory. While the initial focus of many of these studies on parenting and gender roles were predominantly on middle-class, white heterosexual couples, there has gradually been greater attention accorded to working-class or low income households (Bolak, 1997; Luxton & Corman, 2001; Segura, 1994; Waller, 2002); ethnic diversity (Hofferth, 2003; Jain & Belsky, 1997; Mirande, 1988); and non-heterosexual couples (Bozett, 1988; Carrington, 1999; Doucet & Dunne, 2000; Dunne, 1999).

Men's Studies and Masculinities

A further impetus for understanding gender roles and gender relations in relation to men's lives as fathers came from the interdisciplinary field of masculinity studies which began to burgeon in the 1990s.

While there has certainly been tensions within feminism as to how to theorize mothering and its place within feminist politics, the issue of fathering has actually been much less central within masculinity studies and has tended to be located within the field of family studies and much less centrally within the field of men's studies and masculinities (Connell, 1995; Gardiner, 2002; Kimmel, Hearn, & Connell, 2005). Indeed, much of the early work on men and masculinities surprisingly left out the issue of men and family. For example, the earliest versions of the well-known text used in masculinity studies, men and masculinities paid very little attention to the role of men in families (see Kimmel &Messner, 2003).

What has emerged from this initial lack of attention to fathering within masculinity studies is the sense that compared to the study of mothering within feminist studies, fathering studies has taken much longer to find its theoretical footing. Since the 1990s, however, fatherhood studies has been a growing multi-disciplinary and international subfield within masculinity studies (for a review, see Doucet, 2006).

Other Disciplinary Bridges

Fatherhood scholarship has also grown into sub-fields of scholarly investigation within several other academic disciplines. These include, for example: sociology (e.g., Coltrane, 1996; Doucet, 2005, 2006; Marsiglio, 1995); history (e.g., Griswold, 1993; Johansen, 2001; LaRossa, 1997), psychology (e.g., Henwood & Proctor, 2003), literary studies (e.g., Wahlstrom, 2010), demography (e.g., Eggebeen, 2002), and social work (Featherstone, 2009).

Future Directions

There are several key questions that still need exploring in relation to the topic of fathering and gender roles. Two key issues are explored below.

Fathering and Policies

First, there is the question of the relationship between family policies, on the one hand, and changing gender roles in paid work as well as in unpaid work and parenting, on the other hand. Another way of putting this is to ask: What policies have the most direct effect on parenting and gender roles? Is it policies aimed at increasing and enhancing women's labor market participation as well as policies aimed at assisting men with work-family balance issues? Or are the most effective policies those that directly target the division of domestic labor. This remains an open question. As recently pointed out by Kan et al. (2011, p. 245):

> In general the policy literature on the relationship between domestic work and policy has tended to focus on care as the aspect of domestic work primarily affected by the *direct* consequences of policy aimed at supporting employed parents through the provision of early childhood education and care (ECEC). Much research effort has been directed at

trying to show an effect of such policies in large-scale data. We can reasonably assume that state policies are likely to have less *direct* influence on the performance of routine housework than on the taking of parental leave in order to care for small children. However, the results shown here imply that the direct effects of ECEC policies may not be as significant as, for example, the effect of policies aimed at supporting female engagement in the primary labour market (and leading indirectly to a decline in the proportion of routine housework undertaken by women).

These authors and many others point to how changes in gender roles may be best achieved through public and social policies which promote gender equality in the workplace and the home as well as more subtle national-level and cultural shifts in gender ideologies around work and care.

Fathering, Gender Roles, and Changing Masculinities

Many multidisciplinary and international scholars have highlighted how there is an intersection between 'new' or active fatherhood and changing conceptions of masculinities (Brandth & Kvande, 1998; Connell & Messerschmidt, 2005; Dermott, 2008; Doucet, 2006; Dowd, 2000; Plantin, Sven-Axel, & Kearney, 2003). Furthermore, there is also a related and overlapping psychological and psychoanalytic literature on male identity and active caregiving (see Edley & Wetherell, 1999; Henwood & Proctor, 2003; Hollway, 2006). Overall, it has been argued that the study of fathers who take on caregiving raises the interesting question of what happens to masculinities when men engage in female-dominated and feminine-defined activities such as caring. As detailed above, it remains the case that the issue of fatherhood has been dealt with somewhat sparsely in key works on masculinities (e.g., Connell, 1987, 2000).

Most of the attention to masculinities and fatherhood has been given to how hegemonic masculinity is present as fathers push their boys to concentrate on sports (Connell, 2000, p. 167) or to the links between fathering, breadwinning, and hegemonic masculinity. As mentioned in the Introduction to this chapter, fatherhood is not explicitly touched in a leading account of masculinities, which is Connell's theory of gender relations (Connell, 1987, 2000); nevertheless, her recent work does mention fathering in a more direct way (e.g., Connell, 2005).

The link between masculinities and caring is an important one, since hegemonic masculinity is largely associated with the devaluation of the feminine while caring is often equated with feminine practice, thus raising the question of the relationship between hegemonic masculinity and care. British sociologist David Morgan's compelling claim is worth repeating here: "one strategy of studying men and masculinities would be to study those situations where masculinity is, as it were, *on the line*" (1992, p. 99).

A few authors have investigated these connections and have argued that the fathering can become incorporated into hegemonic masculinity (Brandth & Kvande, 1998; Dryden, 1999) or, alternatively, exist in a *complicit* relationship so that fathers express support for equal parenting while also maintaining more traditional patterns of gender divisions of labor (see Plantin et al., 2003). Still others have argued that involved fathering neither reproduces nor challenges hegemonic masculinity, but creates new forms of masculinity. That is, while enacted against a weighty backdrop of hegemonic masculinity, involved fathering also incorporates varied aspects of femininities. In my own work, I have argued that men's practices and identities of caregiving combine shifting conceptions of masculinities and femininities; they may also reflect philosophical and political concepts of self, identity and subjectivity which embrace varied degrees of dependence, independence and interdependence (see Doucet 2005, 2006). As argued recently by Wahlstrom (2010, p. 20): "like masculinity, fatherhood is also relationally constructed and hence must be understood as varied and depending on encounters and juxtapositions with other identities and practices, notably motherhood, childhood, and childlessness, as well as other masculinities."

Conclusions

As detailed in this chapter, the study of fathering and gender roles is a wide and robust area of scholarly work. Multidisciplinary, multi-method, and rich in its diversity of empirical findings and theoretical directions, it will continue to occupy a central place within fathering studies. It will also continue to hold the attention of many researchers within sociology, psychology, feminist and gender studies, masculinity studies, demography, social work, literary studies, and history.

It is important to underscore that fatherhood continues to be diverse, multilayered, and multidimensional. Even where it occurs without the possible active participation of mothers, it continues to exist relationally with mothering scholarship as well as with the identities and practices of mothering and the social institution of motherhood.

Changes in gender roles for fathers have not been a linear nor uniform process from uninvolved to involved father. The type and scale of involvement has always varied and has also been analyzed, measured, and understood differently depending on the specificity of particular fathering experiences, as well as the theoretical lenses and methodological tools employed. What is clear is that for men who do have children, there are evolving set of relations between their fathering practices and identities, their wide sets of social relationships, issues of masculinities, and gendered identities, ideologies and roles.

Notes

1. While this chapter centers on roles, for example, it is important to note that throughout the 1970s and early 1980s these questions of gender identity were explored largely through "sex role theory," which was one of the most popular accounts of the construction of gender identities in sociology (Connell, 1987). The concept of "role" was centered around a distinction between people and the social positions they occupy. That is, society provides different gender roles or scripts which men and women learn and follow (see Siltanen & Doucet, 2008).
2. Emotional responsibility is defined as the daily care, attentiveness, and nurturing of children (see Doucet, 2006).
3. Community responsibility is defined as the community-based dimensions of parenting and care work.
4. The concept of "moral responsibilities" is rooted in a symbolic interactionist conception of the interactional relational sense (Daly, 2002, 1996; Finch & Mason, 1993; McMahon 1995) relates to people's identities as "moral" beings and how they feel they ought to and should act in society as parents.

References

Almqvist, A.-L., Sandberg, A., & Dahlgren, L. (2011). Parental leave in Sweden: Motives, experiences and gender equality among parents. *Fathering: A Journal of Theory, Research, and Practice about Men as Fathers,* 9(2), 189–209.

Ball, J., & Daly, K. (Eds.). (in press, 2012). *Father involvement in Canada: Contested terain* Vancouver, BC: UBC Press.

Ball, J. (2009). Fathering in the shadows: Indigenous fathers and Canada's colonial legacies. *The ANNALS of the American Academy of Political and Social Science, 642,* 29–48.

Bell, L., & Ribbens, J. (1994). Isolated housewives and complex maternal worlds: The significance of social contacts between women with young children in industrial societies. *The Sociological Review, 42*(2), 227–262.

Benson, A. L., Silverstein, L. B., & Auerbach, C. F. (2005). From the margins to the center: Gay fathers reconstruct the fathering role *Journal of GLBT Family Studies 1*(3), 1–29.

Berk, S. F. (1985). *The gender factory: The apportionment of work in American households.* New York: Plenum.

Berkowitz, D., & Marsiglio, W. (2007). Gay men: Negotiating procreative, father, and family identities. *Journal of Marriage and Family, 69,* 366–381

Bianchi, S. M., Robinson, J. P., & Milkie, M. A. (2006). *Changing rhythms of American family life.* New York: Russell Sage Foundation

Biblarz, T. J., & Stacey, J. (2010). How does the gender of parents matter? *Journal of Marriage and Family, 72,* 3–22.

Bittman, M., & Wajcman, J. (2000). The rush hour: the character of leisure time and gender equity. *Social Forces, 79*(1), 165–189.

Bjørnholt, M. (2010). Like father, like son? The transmission of values, family practices, and work-family adaptations to sons of work-sharing men. *Fathering: A Journal of Theory, Research, and Practice about Men as Fathers, 8*(3), 276–299.

Bolak, H. C. (1997). When wives are major providers: Culture, gender, and family work. *Gender & Society, 11*(4), 409–433.

Bott, E. (1957). *Family and social networks.* London: Tavistock.

Bozett, F. W. (1988). Gay fatherhood. In P. Bronstein & C. P. Cowan (Eds.), *Fatherhood today: men's changing role in the family* (pp. 214–235). New York: Wiley.

Bradbury, B. (1984). Pigs, cows and boarders. Non-wage forms of survival among Montreal families, 1861–1881. *Labour/Le Travail, 14*(Autumn), 9–46.

Bradbury, B. (1993). *Working families: Age, gender and daily survival in industrializing Montreal.* Toronto: McClelland and Stewart.

Bradley, H. (1989). *Women's work, men's work.* Cambridge, UK: Polity

Brandth, B., & Kvande, E. (1998). Masculinity and child Care: The reconstruction of fathering. *The Sociological Review, 46*(2), 293–313.

Brandth, B., & Kvande, E. (2009). Gendered or gender-neutral care politics for fathers? *The ANNALS of the American Academy of Political and Social Science, 624,* 177–189.

Brannen, J., & Moss, P. (1991). *Managing mothers: Dual earner households after maternity Leave.* London: Unwin Hyman.

Brannen, J., & Nilsen, A. (2006). From fatherhood to fathering: Transmission and change among British fathers in four-generation families. *Sociology 40*(2), 335–352.

Brines, J. (1994). Economic dependency, gender, and the division of labor at home. *American Journal of Sociology, 100,* 652–688.

Bruni, A., Gherardi, S., & Poggio, B. (2004). Doing gender, doing entrepreneurship: An ethnographic account of intertwined practices. *Gender, Work & Organization 11*(4), 406–429.

Cabrera, N., & Peters, H. E. (2000). Public policies and father involvement. *Marriage & Family Review, 29*(4), 295–314.

Cabrera, N., Tamis-LeMonda, C. S., Bradley, B., Hofferth, S., & Lamb, M. (2000). Fatherhood in the 21st century. *Child Development, 71*(1), 127–136.

Cabrera, N. J., Shannon, J. D., & Tamis-LeMonda, C. (2007). Fathers' influence on their children's cognitive and emotional development: From toddlers to pre-k. *Applied Developmental Science, 11*(4), 208–213.

Carrington, C. (1999). *No place like home: Relationships and family life among lesbians and gay men.* Chicago: University of Chicago Press.

Chodorow, N. (1978). *The reproduction of mothering: Psychoanalysis and the sociology of gender.* Berkeley: University of California Press.

Chronholm, A. (2009). Sweden: Individualization or free choice in parental leave. In S. B. Kamerman & P. Moss (Eds.), *The politics of parental ;eave policies: Children, parenting, gender, and the labour market* (pp. 227–242). Bristol, UK The Policy Press.

Chuang, S. S., & Moreno, R. (2008). *On new shores: Understanding immigrant fathers in North America.* New York: Lexington Books.

Collins, P. H. (2000). *Black feminist thought: Knowledge, consciousness, and the politics of empowerment* (2nd ed.). London: Routledge.

Coltrane, S. (1989). Household labor and the routine production of gender. *Social Problems, 36*(5), 473–490.

Coltrane, S. (1996). *Family man: Fatherhood, housework, and gender equity.* New York: Oxford University Press.

Coltrane, S. (2000). Research on household labor. *Journal of Marriage and Family, 62*, 1209–1233.

Coltrane, S., & Adams, M. (2001). Men's family work: Child-centered fathering and the sharing of domestic labor. In R. Hertz & N. L. Marshall (Eds.), *Working families: The ran of the American home* (pp. 72–99). Berkeley: University of California Press.

Connell, R. W. (1987). *Gender and power.* Cambridge, UK: Polity Press.

Connell, R. W. (1995). *Masculinities.* Berkeley: University of California Press.

Connell, R. W. (2000). *The men and the boys.* Berkeley: University of California Press.

Connell, R. W. (2005). *Masculinities.* London: Polity Press.

Connell, R. W., & Messerschmidt, J. (2005). Hegemonic masculinity: Rethinking the concept. *Gender & Society, 19*(6), 829–859.

Cowan, C. P., & Cowan, P. A. (Eds.). (1987). *Men's involvement in parenthood: Identifying the antecedents and understanding the barriers.* Hillsdale, NJ: Erlbaum.

Cranny-Francis, A., Kirby, J., Stavropoulos, P., & Waring, W. (Eds.). (2003). *Gender studies: Terms and debates.* London: Macmillan.

Crittenden, A. (2001). *The price of motherhood: Why the most important job in the world is still the least valued.* New York: Henry Holt and Company.

Crompton, R., & Lyonette, C. (2010). Family, class and gender 'strategies' in mothers' employment and childcare. In J. Scott, R. Crompton, & C. Lyonette (Eds.), *Gender inequalities in the 21st century: new barriers and continuing constraints* (pp. 174–192). Cheltenham, UK: Edward Elgar.

Daly, K. (1996). *Families and time: Keeping pace in a hurried culture.* Thousand Oaks, CA: Sage.

Daly, K. (2001). Deconstructing family time: From ideology to lived experience. *Journal of Marriage and Family, 63*, 283–294.

Daly, K. (2002). Time, gender, and the negotiation of Family Schedules. *Symbolic Interaction, 25*(3), 323–342.

Daly, K. (2003). Family theory versus the theory families live by. *Journal of Marriage and Family,* (63), 283–294.

Dermott, E. (2008). *Intimate fatherhood: A sociological analysis.* London: Routledge.

Dermott, E., & Seymour, J. (Eds.). (2011). *Displaying families: A new concept for the sociology of family life.* London: Palgrave Macmillan.

Deutsch, F. M. (2007). Undoing gender. *Gender and Society, 21*(1), 106–127.

Deutsch, F. M. (1999). *Halving it all: How equally shared parenting works.* Cambridge, MA: Harvard University Press.

DeVault, A., Milcent, M. P., Ouellette, F., Lauren, I., Jargon, M., & Anchorite, C. (2008). Life stories of young fathers in contexts of vulnerability. *Fathering: A Journal of Theory, Research, and Practice about Men as Fathers, 6*, 226–248.

Dienhart, A. (1998). *Reshaping fatherhood: The social construction of shared parenting.* London: Sage.

Dinnerstein, D. (1977). *The mermaid and the minotaur: Sexual arrangements and human malaise.* New York: Harper Colophon Books.

Doucet, A. (1995). Gender equality and gender differences in household work and parenting. *Women's Studies International Forum, 18*(3), 271–284.

Doucet, A. (1996). Encouraging voices: Towards more creative methods for collecting data on gender and household labor. In L. Morris & S. Lyon (Eds.), *Gender relations in the public and the private* (pp. 156–173). London: Macmillan.

Doucet, A. (2001). "You see the need perhaps more clearly than I have": Exploring gendered processes of domestic desponsibility. *Journal of Family Issues, 22*(3), 328.

Doucet, A. (2004). Fathers and the responsibility for children: A puzzle and a tension. *Atlantis: A Women's Studies Journal, 28*(2), 103–114.

Doucet, A. (2005). 'It's slmost like I have a job but I don't get paid': Fathers at home reconfiguring work, care and masculinity. *Fathering: A Journal of Theory, Research, and Practice about Men as Fathers, 2*(3), 277–304.

Doucet, A. (2006). *Do men mother? Fathering, care, and domestic responsibility.* Toronto: University of Toronto Press.

Doucet, A. (2009a). Dad and baby in the first year: Gendered embodiment. *The ANNALS of the American Academy of Political and Social Science, 624,* 78–98.

Doucet, A. (2009b). Gender equality and gender differences: Parenting, habitus and embodiment. *Canadian Review of Sociology, 48*(2), 99–117.

Doucet, A. (2011). 'It's not good for a man to be interested in other people's children': Fathers and public displays of care. In E. Dermott & J. Seymour (Eds.), *Displaying family: New theoretical directions in family and intimate life* (pp. 81–101).London: Palgrave Macmillan.

Doucet, A., & Dunne, G. A. (2000). Heterosexual and lesbian mothers challenging 'feminine' and 'male' conceptions of mothering. In A. O'Reilly & S. Abbey (Eds.), *Mothers and daughters: Connection, empowerment and transformation* (pp. 103–120). Savage, MD: Rowman and Littlefield.

Dowd, N. E. (2000). *Redefining fatherhood.* New York: New York University Press.

Dryden, C. (Ed.). (1999). *Being married, doing gender: A clinical analysis of gender relationships in marriage.* London: Routledge.

Dunne, G. A. (1999). *The different dimensions of gay fatherhood.* London: Report to the Economic and Social Research Council. Retrieved from http://www2.lse.ac.uk/genderinstitute/pdf/gayfatherhood.pdf

Dunne, G. (2001). 'The lady vanishes?' Reflections on the experiences of married and divorced gay fathers *Sociological Research Online, 6,* 1–17.

Edley, N., & Wetherell, M. (1999). Imagined futures: Young men's talk about fatherhood and domestic life. *British Journal of Social Psychology, 38*(2), 181–194.

Eggebeen, D. J. (2002). The changing course of fatherhood: Men's experiences with children in demographic perspective. *Journal of Family Issues, 23*(4), 486–506.

Ehrensaft, D. (1984). When women and men mother. In J. Trebilcot (Ed.), *Mothering: Essays in feminist theory* (pp. 41–61). Totowa, NJ: Rowman and Allanheld.

Este, D. C., & Tachble, A. A. (2009). The perceptions and experiences of Russian immigrant and Sudanese refugee men as fathers in an urban center in Canada. *The ANNALS of the American Academy of Political and Social Science, 624,* 139–155.

Featherstone, B. (2009). *Contemporary fathering: Theory, policy and practice.* Bristol, UK: The Policy Press.

Ferree, M. M., Lorber, J., & Hess, B. B. (2000). *Revisioning gender.* Lantham MD: Rowman and Littlefield.

Finch, J. (2007). Displaying families. *Sociology, 41*(1), 65–81.

Finch, J., & Mason, J. (1993). *Negotiating family responsibilities.* London: Routledge.

Floro, M. S., & Miles, M. (2003). Time use, work and overlapping activities – Evidence from Australia. *Cambridge Journal of Economics, 27*(6), 881–904.

Folbre, N. (1994). *Who pays for the kids? Gender and the dtructures of constraint.* London: Routledge, Chapman and Hall.

Folbre, N., & Yoon, J. (2007). What is child care? Lessons from time-use surveys of major English-speaking countries. *Review of Economics of the Household, 5*(3), 223–248.

Fox, B. (2009). *When couples become parents: The creation of gender in the transition to parenthood.* Toronto: University of Toronto Press.

Gabb, J. (2008). *Researching intimacy in families.* Basingstoke, UK: Palgrave Macmillan.

Gardiner, J. K. (Ed.). (2002). *Masculinity studies and feminist theory.* New York Columbia University

Garfinkel, H. (1967). *Studies in ethnomethodology.* Englewood Cliffs, NJ: Prentice-Hall.

Gershuny, J. (2000). *Changing times: Work and leisure in postindustrial society.* Oxford, UK: Oxford University Press.

Gershuny, J., & Sullivan, O. (2003). Time use, gender, and public policy regimes. *Social Politics, 10,* 205–288.

Greenstein, T. N. (1996). Gender ideology and perceptions of the fairness of the division of labor: Effects on marital quality. *Social Forces, 74*(3), 1029–1042.

Gregson, N., & Lowe, M. (1993). Renegotiating the domestic division of labour: A study of dual career households in North East and Southeast England. *The Sociological Review, 41*(3), 475–505.

Griswold, R. L. (1993). *Fatherhood in America: A history.* New York: Basic Books.

Gupta, S. (2007). Autonomy, dependence, or display? The relationship between married women's earnings and housework. *Journal of Marriage and Family, 63,* 399–417.

Haldar, M., & Waerdahl, R. (2009). Teddy diaries: A method for studying the display of family life. *Sociology, 43,* 1141–1150.

Hamermesh, D. S., & Lee, J. (2007). Stressed out on four continents: Time crunch or yuppie kvetch? *The Review of Economics and Statistic, 89*(2), 374–383.

Hansen, K. V. (2005). *Not-so-nuclear families: Class, gender, and networks of care.* Piscataway, NJ: Rutgers University Press.

Henwood, K. L., & Proctor, J. (2003). "The 'good father': Reading men's accounts of paternal involvement during the transition to first time fatherhood". *British Journal of Social Psychology, 42,* 337–355.

Hobson, B. (2002). *Making men into fathers: Men, masculinities and the social politics of fatherhood.* Cambridge, UK: Cambridge University Press.

Hochschild, A. R., & Machung, A. (1989). *The second shift.* New York: Avon Books.

Hofferth, S. L. (2003). Race/ethnic differences in father involvement in two-parent families: Culture, context, or economy. *Journal of Family Issues, 24*(2), 185–216.

Hoffman, L. W., & Nye, F. I. (1974). *Working mothers* Ann Arbor: University of Michigan.

Hollway, W. (2006). *The capacity to care: Gender and ethical subjectivity.* London: Routledge.

Hook, J. L. (2006). Care in context: Men's unpaid work in 20 countries, 1965–2003. *American Sociological Review, 71*(4), 639–660.

hooks, b. (1981). *Ain't I a woman? Black women and feminism.* Boston: South End Press.

Jain, A., & Belsky, J. (1997). Fathering and Acculturation: Immigrant Indian families with young children. *Journal of Marriage and the Family, 59,* 873–883.

Johansen, S. (2001). *Family man: Middle class fatherhood in early industrializing America.* New York: Routledge.

Juster, F. T., & Stafford, F. P. (1985). *Time, goods, and well-being.* Ann Arbor, MI: Institute for Social Research.

Kalenkoski, C. M., Ribar, D. C., & Stratton, L. S. (2007). The effect of family structure on parents' child care time in the United States and the United Kingdom. *Review of Economics in the Household, 5*(4), 353–384.

Kamerman, S., & Moss, P. (Eds.). (2009). *The politics of parental leave policies.* Bristol, UK: Policy Press.

Kan, M. Y., Sullivan, O., & Gershuny, J. I. (2011). Gender convergence in domestic work: Discerning the effects of interactional and institutional barriers from large-scale data. *Sociology, 45*(2), 234–251.

Kaufman, G., Lyonette, C., & Crompton, R. (2010). Post-birth employment leave among fathers in Britain and the United States. *Fathering: A Journal of Theory, Research, and Practice about Men as Fathers, 8*(3), 321–340.

Kimball, G. (1988). *50-50 parenting: Sharing family rewards and responsibilities.* Lexington, MA: Lexington Books.

Kimmel, M., Hearn, J., & Connell, R. W. (2005). *Handbook of studies on men & masculinities.* London: Sage.

Kimmel, M., & Messner, M. (2003). *Men's sives (sixth edition).* New York: Allyn and Bacon

Komarovsky, M., Phillips, J. H. (1987). *Blue collar marriage* (2nd ed.). New Haven, CT: Yale University Press.

Lamb, M. E. (Ed.). (1981). *The role of the father in child development.* New York: Wiley.

Lamb, M. E. (2000). The history of research on father involvement: An overview. *Marriage and Family Review, 29*(2/3), 23–42

Lamb, M. E., Charnov, E., & Levine, J. A. (1987). A biosocial perspective on parental behavior and involvement. In J. B. Lancaster, J. Altman, & A. Rossi (Eds.), *Parenting across the life span* (pp. 11–42). New York: Academic Press.

Lamb, M. E., & Day, R. D. (Eds.). (2004). *Reconceptualising and measuring father involvement.* Mahwah, NJ: Erlbaum.

Lamphere, L. (1987). *From working daughters to working mothers: Immigrant women in a New England community.* London: Cornell University Press.

LaRossa, R. (1997). *The modernization of fatherhood.* Chicago: University of Chicago Press.

Lewis, C. (1986). *Becoming a father.* Milton Keynes, UK: Open University Press.

Lewis, J. (2001). The decline of the male breadwinner model: implications for work and care. *Social politics, 8*(2), 152–169.

Lewis, J., Porter, M., & Shrimpton, M. (Eds.). (1988). *Women, work and the family in the British, Canadian and Norwegian offshore oil fields.* London: MacMillan.

Lopata, H. (1981). *Occupation: Housewife.* New York: Oxford University Press.

Lupton, D., & Barclay, L. (1997). *Constructing fatherhood: Discourses and experiences.* London: Sage.

Luxton, M. (1980). *More than a labor of love: Three generations of women's work in the home.* Toronto: Women's Press.

Luxton, M., & Corman, J. (2001). *Getting by in hard times: Gendered labor at home and on the job.* Toronto: University of Toronto Press.

Lynch, K. (2007). Love labour as a distinct and non-commodifiable form of care labour. *The Sociological Review, 53*(3), 550–568.

Mandell, D. (2002). *Deadbeat dads: Subjectivity and social construction.* Toronto: University of Toronto Press.

Mansfield, P., & Collard, J. (1982). *The beginning of the rest of your life.* Bassingstock, UK: Macmillan.

Marshall, K. (2006). Converging gender roles. *Perspectives on Labour and Income, 18*(3), 7–19.

Marshall, K. (2008). Fathers' use of paid parental leave. *Perspectives on Labour and Income, 20*(3), 5–14.

Marsiglio, W. (Ed.). (1995). *Fatherhood: Contemporary theory, research, and social policy* Oaks, CA: Sage.

Marsiglio, W. (2008). *Men on a mission: Valuing youth work in our communities* Baltimore, MD: Johns Hopkins University Press.

Marsiglio, W. (2009). Men's relations with kids: Exploring and promoting the mosaic of youth eork and fathering. *The ANNALS of the American Academy of Political and Social Science, 624*, 118–138.

Marsiglio, W., & Roy, K. (2012). *Nurturing dads: Fatherhood initiatives beyond the wallet.* New York: Russell Sage Foundation.

Martin, P. Y. (2003). 'Said and done: Versus 'saying and doing': Gendering practices, practicing gender at work. *Gender and Society, 17*(3), 342–366

McKay, L., & Doucet, A. (2010). 'Without taking away her leave': A Canadian case study of couples' decisions on fathers' use of paid parental leave. *Fathering: A Journal of Theory, Research, and Practice about Men as Fathers, 8*(3), 300–320.

McKee, L., & Bell, C. (1986). His unemployment, her problem In S. Allen, A. Waton, K. Purcell, & S. Wood (Eds.), *The experience of unemployment* (pp. 20–34). London: Macmillian

McMahon, M. (1995). *Engendering motherhood: Identity and self-transformation in women's lives*. New York: Guilford.

Meissner, M., Meis, S., Scheu, M., & Scheu, W. J. (1975). No exit for wives: Sexual division of labour and the culmination of household demands. *Canadian Review of Sociology and Anthropology, 12*(4), 424–439.

Meteyer, K., & Perry-Jenkins, M. (2010). Father involvement among working-class, dual-earner couples. *Fathering: A Journal of Theory, Research, and Practice about Men as Fathers, 8*(3), 379–403.

Miller, W., & Maiter, S. (2008). Fatherhood and culture: Moving beyond stereotypical understandings. *Journal of Ethnic & Cultural Diversity in Social Work, 17*, 279–300.

Miller, T. (2010). "It's a triangle that's difficult to square": Men's intentions and practices around caring, work and first-time fatherhood. *Fathering: A Journal of Theory, Research, and Practice about Men as Fathers, 3*(3), 362–378.

Miller, T. (2011). *Making sense of fatherhood: Gender, caring and work*. New York: Cambridge University Press.

Mirande, A. (1988). Chicano fathers: Traditional perceptions and current realities. In P. Bronstein & C. P. Cowan (Eds.), *Fatherhood today: Men's changing role in the family* (pp. 113–128). New York: Wiley.

Morgan, D. H. J. (1992). *Discovering men*. London: Routledge.

Morris, L. (1985). Local social networks and domestic organisations: A study of redundant steelworkers and their wives. *The Sociological Review, 33*(2), 327–342.

Morris, L. (1990). *The workings of the household: A US-UK comparison*. Cambridge, UK: Polity Press.

O'Brien, M. (1987). Patterns of kinship and friendship among lone fathers. In C. Lewis & M. O'Brien (Eds.), *Reassessing fatherhood: New observations on fathers and the modern family* (pp. 225–245). London: Sage.

O'Brien, M. (2009). Fathers, parental leave policies, and infant quality of life: International perspectives and policy ompact. *The ANNALS of the American Academy of Political and Social Science, 624*, 190–214.

O'Brien, M., & Shemilt, I. (2003). *Working fathers: Earning and caring*. Manchester, UK: Equal Opportunities Commission.

Oakley, A. (1974). *Housewife*. London: Allen Lane.

Pahl, R. E. (1984). *Divisions of labour*. Oxford, UK: Basil Blackwell.

Pahl, J. (1989). *Money and marriage*. Basingstoke, UK: Macmillan.

Palameta, B. (2003). Who pays for domestic help. *Perspectives on Labour and Income, 15*(3), 12–15

Palkovitz, R. (1997). Reconstructing "involvement": Expanding conceptualizations of men's caring in contemporary families. In A. J. Hawkins & T. Dollahite (Eds.), *Generative fathering: Beyond deficit perspectives* (pp. 200–216). Thousand Oaks, CA: Sage

Parke, R. D. (1996). *Fatherhood*. Cambridge, MA: Harvard University Press.

Parsons, T. (1967). *Sociological theory and modern dociety*. New York: Free Press.

Parsons, T., & Bales, R. F. (1955). *Family socialization and interaction process*. New York: Free Press.

Plantin, L., Sven-Axel, M., & Kearney, J. (2003). Talking and doing fatherhood: On fatherhood and masculinity in Sweden and England. *Fathering, 1*(1), 3–26

Pleck, J. H. (1985). *Working wives, working husbands*. London: Sage.

Pleck, J. H., & Masciadrelli, B. P. (2004). Parental involvement: Levels, sources and consequences. In M. E. Lamb (Ed.), *The role of the father in child development* (4th ed., pp. 222–271). Hoboken, NJ: Wiley.

Pleck, E. H., & Pleck, J. H. (1997). Fatherhood ideals in the United States: Historical dimensions. In M. E. Lamb (Ed.), *The role of the father in child development* (pp. 33–48). New York: Wiley.

Priola, V. (2007). Being female doing gender: Narratives of women in education management. *Gender and Education, 19*(1), 21–40.

Radin, N. (1982). Primary care-giving and role sharing fathers. In M. E. Lamb (Ed.), *Non-traditional families: Parenting and child development* (pp. 173–204). Hillsdale, NJ: Erlbaum.

Rich, A. (1986). *Of woman born: Motherhood as experience and institution* (2nd ed.). New York: W.W. Norton.

Risman, B. J. (1998). *Gender vertigo: American families in transition.* New Haven, CT: Yale University Press.

Risman, B. (2004). Gender as a social structure: theory wrestling with activism. *Gender & Society, 18*(4), 429–450.

Risman, B. J. (2009). From doing to undoing: Gender as we know it. *Gender and Society, 23*(1), 81–84.

Robinson, J. P., & Godbey, G. (1997). *Time for life: The surprising ways Americans use their time.* University Park: The Pennsylvania State University Press.

Ross, C. E. (1987). The division of labor at home. *Social Forces, 65*(3), 816–833.

Roy, K., & Cabrera, N. (2010). Not just provide and reside: Engaged fathers in low-income families. In B. J. Risman (Ed.), *Families as they really are* (pp. 301–306). New York: W.W. Norton.

Ruddick, S. (1995). *Maternal thinking: Towards a politics of peace* (2nd ed.). Boston, MA: Beacon.

Russell, G. (1983). *The changing role of fathers.* St. Lucia, Australia: University of Queensland Press.

Russell, G. (1987). Problems in role-reversed families. In C. Lewis & M. O'Brien (Eds.), *Reassessing fatherhood: New observations on fathers and the modern family* (pp. 161–182). London: Sage.

Sayer, L. C., & Fine, L. (2011). Racial-ethnic differences in U.S. married women's and men's housework. *Social Indicators Research, 101,* 259–265.

Segura, D. A. (1994). Working at motherhood: Chicana and Mexican immigrant mothers and employment. In E. N. Glenn, G. Chang, & L. R. Forcey (Eds.), *Mothering: Ideology, experience and agency* (pp. 211–233). London: Routledge.

Siltanen, J., & Stanworth, M. (1984). *Women and the public sphere: A critique of sociology and politics.* London: Huthinson & Co.

Siltanen, J., & Doucet, A. (2008). *Gender relations in Canada: Intersectionality and beyond.* Peterborough, Ontario: Oxford.

Smith, D. (1987). *The everyday world as problematic: A feminist sociology.* Milton Keynes, UK: Open University Press.

Spelman, E. V. (1988). *Inessential Women: Problems of exclusion in feminist thought.* Boston MA: Beacon Press.

Sullivan, O. (1996). Time co-ordination, the domestic division of labour and affective relations: Time use and the enjoyment of activities within couples. *Sociology, 30*(1), 79–100.

Sullivan, O. (1997). Time waits for no (wo)man: an investigation of the gendered experience of domestic time. *Sociology, 31*(2), 221–239.

Sullivan, O. (2000). The division of domestic labour: Twenty years of change? *Sociology, 34,* 437–456.

Sullivan, O. (2006). *Changing gender relations, changing families: Tracing the pace of change.* New York: Rowman and Littlefield.

Sullivan, O. (2011). An end to gender display through the performance of housework? A review and reassessment of the quantitative literature using insights from the qualitative literature. *Journal of Family Theory & Review, 3,* 1–13.

Thompson, L., & Walker, A. (1989). Gender in families: Women and men in marriage, work and parenthood. *Journal of Marriage and the Family, 51*(4), 845–871.

Tilly, L. A., & Scott, J. W. (1987). *Women, work and family.* New York: Holt, Rinehart and Winston.

Townsend, N. W. (2002). *The package deal: Marriage, work, and fatherhood in men's lives.* Philadelphia: Temple University Press.

Unger, D. (2010). *Men can: The changing image and reality of fatherhood in America.* Philadelphia: Temple University Press.

Wahlstrom, H. (2010). *New fathers; Contemporary American stories of masculnity, domesticity, and kinship.* Newcastle Upon Tyne, UK: Cambridge Scholars Press.

Walker, K., & Woods, M. E. (1976). *Time use: A measurement of household production of goods and services.* Washington, DC : American Home Economics Association.

Waller, M. M. (2002). *My baby's father: Unmarried parents and paternal responsibility.* Ithaca, NY: Cornell University Press.

Wearing, B. (1984). *The ideology of motherhood: A study of Sidney suburban mothers.* Sydney, Australia: Allen and Unwin.

West, C., & Zimmerman, R. (1987). Doing gender. *Gender & Society, 1*, 30–37.

Wheelock, J. (1990). *Husbands at home: The domestic economy in a post industrial society.* London: Routledge.

Young, I. M. (1984). Is male gender identity the cause of male domination? In J. Trebilcot (Ed.), *Mothering: Essays in feminist theory* (pp. 129–146). Totowa, NJ: Rowman and Allenheld.

Zavella, P. (1987). *Women's work and Chicano families: Cannery workers of the Santa Clara Valley.* Ithaca, NY: Cornell University Press.

Chapter 18

Nonresident Fathers, Kin, and Intergenerational Parenting

Kevin Roy and Jocelyn Smith

University of Maryland

In this chapter, we review the literature on fathering in intergenerational kin networks, with particular emphasis on studies of the last 20 years on the experiences of low-income, young nonresident fathers. We apply concepts from a life course framework to clarify how nonresident fathers navigate and negotiate their parental roles through family relationships. We use our own life history interview data from 146 such fathers to describe the processes of men's kin work as it unfolds in the context of shifting residence and poverty. Together, our data and the review of the literature suggest a need for understanding processes and contexts of kin networks that shape nonresidential fathering, including socialization to parenting, negotiation of kin work responsibilities, and creation of family legacies for intergenerational parenting. We conclude the chapter with consideration of bridges to other disciplines, policy implications, and a range of compelling questions that may lead to development of methodological techniques, data sets, and theoretical orientations to inform understanding of nonresident fathers' experiences in deep, rich family networks.

Historical Overview and Theoretical Perspectives

Demographic and socioeconomic shifts in recent decades, such as decline of the sole breadwinner role, the stagnation of men's wages, the shrinking job prospects of young men with limited educational attainment and records of incarceration, and the flow of mothers into the paid labor force, have transformed family life for generations of fathers. In general, residential fathers are more involved in family life than ever before (Bianchi, Robinson, & Milkie, 2006). And although larger numbers of fathers do not reside with their children (26% of all fathers; see U.S. Census, 2010), nonresident fathers also are more involved with their children than their nonresidential counterparts from twenty to thirty years ago (Amato, Meyers, & Emery, 2009).

Outside of committed relationships and often with limited resources, nonresident fathers struggle to achieve the self-sufficiency and accomplishments reflective of responsible parents who care and provide for their children. For example, during the recent economic recession in 2008–2010, young adult men find themselves increasingly without stable jobs and with few prospects as marriageable partners. They exhibit the lowest rate of marriage on record (just 44% for ages 25–34), and compared with young women, they are twice as likely to live with their own parents (20%; Yen, 2011). Expectations for their participation in the lives of children are often unclear for nonresident fathers, and men may turn to other family members for support and guidance. Their participation in a network of maternal and paternal kin, as well as close friends, help them to secure support for their involvement in children's lives (Madhavan & Roy, 2012; Roy, Dyson, & Jackson, 2010).

There are a range of theories that offer tools to help us understand and even explain nonresident fathers' interaction in kin systems. A bioecological framework (Bronfenbrenner, 2005) situates men in various household and community settings in which they collaborate with family members to nurture their children. The processes of dyadic and complex interaction can be mapped out through a systems approach that models nonresident fathers' involvement as a factor in shifting family feedback and boundary maintenance issues (Whitchurch & Constantine, 1993). Neither of these frameworks identifies the nature of family roles as they change over time, or accounts for individual experience in the face of larger structural forces, such as class, race, or gender.

Life course theorists consider ways in which individual lives both shape and are shaped by social structure over time (Bengtson & Allen, 1993). A life course perspective offers four concepts that can provide insight into nonresidential fathering processes in context (Roy, 2006, 2008). First, men demonstrate *personal agency* to make critical decisions to act as fathers and to navigate family relationships, through direct interaction, responsibility as providers or caregivers, or indirect access through communication. Most contemporary fathers also give meaning to their parenting, motivated to become the "ideal" man as someone who is a successful financial provider as well as an involved father, partner, and son (Aumann, Galinsky, & Matos, 2011). With the need to negotiate even basic guidelines for contact and interaction, nonresident fathers have to be more proactive in securing their role as do-it-all fathers than men who reside and interact with their children on a daily basis. Racial and ethnic differences also emerge in active nonresidential parenting, with African American and Latino men more engaged outside of shared residence than White men (Cabrera, Ryan, Mitchell, Shannon, & Tamis-LeMonda, 2008; King, Harris, & Heard, 2004).

Most studies attempt to describe how nonresident father involvement is related to child outcomes (Amato & Gilbreth, 1999) or adolescent outcomes (Coley & Medeiros, 2007; Hawkins, Amato, & King, 2007). However, fathering is not an individual enterprise. Fathering rests on a web of social arrangements, of *linked lives*—a second life course concept (Marsiglio & Roy, 2012; in press). Negotiation with mothers is a key process by which nonresidential fathers can become involved and influence their children's well-being (Roy & Burton, 2007; Sobolewksi & King, 2005). A key factor in nonresident father involvement in low-income families is not simply the interaction between mothers and fathers, but the entry of mothers into new intimate relationships (Tach, Mincy, & Edin, 2010).

Father and child relationships are embedded in an extensive network of linked kin relationships as well. Such networks are created and maintained primarily through the work of women, through household labor, care, emotion work, financial obligations, and tailoring connections between children and significant family kinworkers, such as grandmothers, sisters, aunts, and friends (DiLeonardo, 1987; Gerstel & Gallagher, 1993). Kin work can be broadly defined as family members' ongoing actions to "regenerate families, maintain lifetime continuities, sustain intergenerational responsibilities, and reinforce shared values" (Stack & Burton, 1993, p. 160). Family members may feel that men drain valuable resources that help sustain family systems, and they hold tight to time-proven mental representations of low-income fathers as "renegade relatives" (Stack & Burton, 1993, p. 164). Although inclusion of fathers could enhance children's lives, many nonresident fathers encounter complex challenges with financial contributions to children from multiple partners and across multiple households (Manning, Stewart, & Smock, 2003). In effect, men's kin work maintains trust and confidence in these linked lives, despite men's shortcoming as providers or partners in failed relationships.

Third, the life course framework emphasizes the *multiple notions of time* that undergird family life. Fathers' individual paths of development are wrapped in movement through historical time. They are also linked across generations to children, parents, and grandparents. A snapshot of family structure cannot adequately encapsulate men's experiences as nonresident fathers. The residential status of one-third of nonresident fathers changes over time (Cheadle, Amato, & King, 2010). For example, family members tailor commitments from kin systems to developmental needs of both children and fathers. Fathers may take on multiple roles that accumulate and diversify over time, adapting to the realities of resource-seeking activities and environmental constraints. This more dynamic approach envisions families as networks that stretch into future years as well as back into past decades.

A fourth concept that guides a life course approach is the appreciation of *context and place* of fathering (Marsiglio, Roy, & Fox, 2005). Fathers, mothers, and siblings of many generations confront the difficulties of incarceration, unemployment or underemployment, attendance at resource-strapped schools, immigration to the United States during harsh battles over immigrant rights, or the intervention of child support or paternity establishment through courts. For disadvantaged fathers, the ecological constraints of local neighborhoods can directly shape relationships in kin systems (Roy, 2004), and they may also affect multiple family members, not simply fathers. Each of these contextual challenges may appear as individual problems, but they also affect the ability of kin systems to function over time.

Current Research Questions

Despite these findings, we know relatively little about the processes and contexts of kin networks that shape nonresident fathering. In communities with few resources, management of kin care for children is critical. Family well-being relies on the commitment of multiple family households work together to nurture children. Boys raised in these families take part in kin work, assuming responsibility for younger siblings and cousins. Their nascent parenting skills may be utilized once they become fathers (Jarrett, Roy, & Burton, 2002). A life course perspective sensitizes us to notice how lives are linked in kin systems, and how the timing of *socialization to fathering* matters to the development of young men's commitment to parenting.

When men become fathers themselves, a second research question emerges. The processes of men's *negotiation of kin work and social capital* are often dismissed or unexplored, especially for nonresident fathers who many assume are not involved in their children's lives, because they are not married and do not reside with their children. Not all fathers are active with their family members to secure their place as engaged parents, but we know little about contexts that might support men's motivation to "be there" with their children. A life course perspective can sensitize us to look carefully at family interactions that carry the potential of social capital to secure a positive father presence, even for nonresident fathers.

Finally, a life course perspective emphasizes the "long view" on lives, and how families continue over time through persistence of patterns of parenting. The limited availability of longitudinal data, and the few studies that examine parenting across multiple generations, point to a third remaining question, regarding how patterns of nonresident fathering emerge as *intergenerational parenting and potential family legacies*. This question flips the focus from exploration of how kin systems shape nonresident fathering, recast as a focus on how nonresident fathers forge social capital that can improve children's well-being over time.

Research Measurement and Methodology

Research on intergenerational parenting and men in kin networks has been limited to a large extent by the capacities of existing data sets. Researchers have relied on mothers' reports to measure nonresident father involvement (Coley & Morris, 2002; Mikelson, 2008). This reliance limited father involvement to what could be observed within a couple relationship, and usually within a single family household. Data sets typically link a focal father to one of his biological children. Until the past decade, it was difficult to find longitudinal data that would capture multiple time points, to show changes in men's involvement over time or to measure differential involvement across generations (Hofferth et al., in press). The Fragile Families study (n.d.) has given researchers data to examine nonresident fathers' involvement over time, and the continued support of the National Longitudinal Survey of Youth (NLSY) has given researchers multiple generations of parents and children to examine patterns of intergenerational parenting.

Qualitative and ethnographic approaches may help to identify these broader network processes and contexts. Stack (1974) and Furstenberg (1995) utilized ethnographic designs to explore African American nonresident fathers' engagement with extended kin. Stack and Burton (1993) developed a conceptual framework for kin work from ethnographic research with low-income families, and Roy and Burton (2007) utilized ethnographic data to examine mothers' kinscription of nonresident fathers to be involved with their children. Interview data has been collected and analyzed to articulate the intergenerational dynamics between fathers and sons, as they struggle to define how the contours of fathering unfold over the life course (Snarey, 1993).

With the Life History Studies, we addressed the three current research questions for nonresident fathers' engagement in kin systems (Marsiglio & Roy, 2012; Roy, Buckmiller, & McDowell, 2008). We recruited 146 low-income fathers in four different projects, linking eligibility to children's receipt of public assistance or attendance in Head Start programs. Retrospective life history interviews were conducted with 40 African American men in a community-based fathering program on the South Side of Chicago, 40 incarcerated men in a work release correctional facility in Indiana, 35 young African American men in a community-based fathering program in Indianapolis, and another 35 low-income Latino and African American men from West Side communities in Chicago.

The sample was diverse in terms of race/ethnicity (66% African American (n = 96); 20% European American (n = 29); 13% Latino (n = 19)) as well as age (35%, 18–24 yrs (n = 51); 36%, 25–35 yrs (n = 52); 29%, 36 yrs and older (n = 43)). About 45% (n = 66) of the fathers had used alcohol or drugs consistently. Just under half of the men (49%, n = 72) were employed for 20 hours per week or more at the time of the interview. Men who chose to be interviewed tended to participate more actively in the programs than other fathers, which suggested that they placed greater emphasis on their involvement as parents.

In these projects, we used qualitative methods to examine the processes, contexts, and constructed meanings of low-income fathers' participation in broad kin networks, including families of origin and families of procreation. Ethnographic field methods allowed us to study multi-level processes and patterns that are missed by less intensive methods. Interview data provided insight into how men negotiated roles as kin workers in families, and garnered both support and burdens from their participation in family relationships.

Over the course of many months in community-based programs, research team members served as case managers or classroom facilitators for life skills curricula. During two-hour life history interviews, we adapted a semi-structured retrospective protocol based on the life history calendar methodology. We developed life history grids to mark dates of transitions in five key domains: relationship trajectories with partners and children; residential change; involvement with family of origin; work in mainstream and underground economies; and education. We also developed genograms for about half of the fathers, to systematically capture the wide range of family relationships that proved influential in men's fathering efforts. Interviews were transcribed and imported into qualitative analysis software for data management and retrieval.

We drew upon basic elements of grounded theory method, including the technique of constant comparison (Strauss & Corbin, 1998). In the first wave of open coding, we identified common and important relationship themes. We used sensitizing concepts from prior research to orient our consideration of the data and developed new codes that emerged from our reading of the interviews. In the second wave of axial coding, we compared and contrasted men's reports of kinscription. For example, we explored contexts in which some fathers clearly relied on their own mothers, or the mothers of their children, to define a set of obligations as fathers. Other fathers, in contrast, were pro-active in working with family members to organize care. Finally, during the final phase of coding, we developed the core trajectory of kin worker status.

We also used a range of methods to enhance the trustworthiness of the data (Lincoln & Guba, 1985). Credibility and dependability of the data were enhanced by the use of multiple sources of data and multiple methods of data collection, as well as many months of interaction in field settings. In many cases, we used in-person discussions with some fathers weeks after their interviews (i.e., member checks) to validate our initial understanding of how they maintained their own kin work to nurture their children.

Empirical Findings

Socialization to Fathering

Across race, class, and ethnicity boundaries, young men's lessons about how to care emerge through the enactment of relationships as sons to their parents, as siblings, or as junior family members with aunts and uncles, cousins, or grandparents. In circumstances of divorce, parental depression, or economic downturn, children may take on adult responsibilities at a young age (Elder, 1999; Newman, 1999). During family crises, young men minimize losses and focus on their fathers' capacity to find a job quickly. As they adapt to changes in residence (moving from home to apartment), clothing, and ultimately social status, adolescents begin to assume more financial responsibility and offer more emotional support to their parents.

Exploratory qualitative work that uncovers the mechanisms and meanings of kin work shows that taking on adult roles can result in both assets and liabilities for young adults, relative to timing, social and parental capital, and family culture (Burton, 2007). As we have found in our own qualitative research, boys may be obligated to care for younger siblings, when extra hands are needed in economically-disadvantaged households (Roy & Vesely, 2009). These first steps toward learning to parent may lead to a new sense of self confidence, empathy, or leadership (Roy et al., 2010). At a young age, boys may also feel increased anxiety, forego education or personal growth, limit peer relationships, and even practice risky behavior. Burton (2007) identifies four successive levels of adultification: precocious knowledge, mentored adultification, peerification or spousification, and parentification.

In recent analyses, we have found that fathers who have experienced involvement of their fathers and mothers may benefit from explicit lessons on how to be a parent. Longitudinal data from a nationally-representative dataset shows that involvement of parents during adolescence guards sons from being at-risk for disconnection from work and school due to early fatherhood (Roy, Vesely, Fitzgerald, & Buckmiller Jones, 2010). Young unmarried fathers often live with their parents and may rely on them to help maintain course toward successful adult achievements. For young fathers with jobs, involvement with their own fathers was not associated with full-time employment.

In other circumstances, however, family support is related to young men's employment and wages. In the same study, we found that father-son relationships were dramatically different for young fathers who were underemployed (20–34 hours per week). Young fathers turn to their own fathers in need of emotional support, as they confront the frustrations of not being able to contribute as a full-time provider. Parents may buffer their sons during this risky transitional period—especially if they are parents in need of support for the next generation. In part, these findings may be due to perceptions of closeness, as young fathers begin to see how closely their own lives parallel their own fathers' pathways into work and family life.

When men discuss who taught them to be fathers, their answers reflect a range of interactions with significant adults. In the Life History Studies (Roy et al, 2008), about a half of the 146 men reported that their own fathers taught them how to be father. Life course theory draws attention to the contextual challenges of economically-disadvantaged families, such as when fathers struggle to become successful financial providers for their children. In turn, their sons may witness fewer models of care and nurturance from these men. Joe, a 40-year-old nonresident father of three children, reflected on the lessons that his father taught him about life. "He didn't teach me about relationships, but I learned patience and understanding from him. My dad showed me how to persevere with my child by the way he was patient with me. He bought a brand new pickup and I dented it. I felt bad, but he never really felt that bad."

Likewise, Malcolm thought about how he absorbed lessons from his fathers' tough life experiences, often without any words from his father to him directly. He witnessed his father's life, and he learned how to structure his own life in response.

> I learned from my father's life experience. He worked every day, come home on time every day. When I was 12, he lost his job at Ford Motors and turned away … Moved on to selling narcotics. He was never really at home, moving from one state to another. He got locked up twice, and the second time was found strangled in his cell. He was always there to say, "I know you can do it, son, you can get that."

At 35, Malcolm was married with three preschool-age children, although he moved in and out of his household. He tried repeatedly to secure a position as a manager at restaurants in Chicago, driven by his father's pride in the face of failure.

The value of linked lives, as a concept from the life course framework, suggests that close relationships between mothers and sons are influential as well. When these nonresident fathers shifted to talk about how they learned to nurture their children, increasingly they indicated that their mothers had taught them these skills, which made them involved and effective fathers. Tremaine was a young 22-year-old unmarried father who saw little of his infant daughter, due to conflict with his former girlfriend. He was wary of relationships with potential partners, and began to realize how strongly he had bonded with his mother.

> The only person in this world who really knows me is my mother. Knows me like a book that she's read five thousand times. My mom taught me how to take care of a household. If you were down and out, you had to come up with an idea to pay the bills and feed your family. Even though a mother can't teach you how to be a man, she can teach you some good qualities in what she would like in a man.

Other fathers reported learning how to cook, to sew, or to find food for the family from their mothers. A young veteran returning from deployment in Somalia noted that "I had no father figure around. I made a lot of mistakes, but they weren't mistakes, because I learned parenting skills from my moms and my sister" (Roy et al., 2010). Miles, a 30-year-old member of a work release program, returned to his community after 18 months of incarceration. He was anxious about resuming contact with his six children, with two former partners. His mother became the guiding voice in his head as he contemplated life changes.

> My mother taught me to be a good father. She was always there. Things that I did wrong, she would always tell me. She told me I have to think about everything, about girls, about money, and girls getting pregnant. She drilled it into me, she had me thinking. It's just that I didn't want to listen.

The actual shape and health of family networks may be overstated. We cannot assume that all fathers emerged from supportive kin networks, into a full understanding of how to be a parent. In a subsample of the Life History Studies participants, about half (46%) of young African American fathers in an Indianapolis sample had strong supportive ties with multiple family members (Roy & Vesely, 2009). However, 37% had only one or two family members who they could count on, and 17% lacked a family member who could support them as young adults and parents. Some studies suggest that cultural values and economic deprivation clearly predict men's participation in social support networks, but it may be that proximity of family members and availability of resources (housing, jobs, social capital) is more important (Roschelle, 1997). Increasing social isolation and economic deprivation may have reduced the participation of men in minority family networks over the past three decades.

Men often become dependent on female-headed households and networks (Roy et al., 2010), and they generally engage in fewer intergenerational exchange relationships than women. Some of these patterns can be traced to the effects of early family structure. The experience of an unstable family is associated with an early transition to parenthood and nonresident fatherhood status, and multiple transitions during childhood is associated with a reduced likelihood that men father their first child within marriage, and an increased likelihood that they become fathers while they cohabit (Hofferth & Goldscheider, 2010). Economic disadvantage, behaviors during adolescence, and parenting of one's own parents can shift the effects of family structure (Goldscheider, Hofferth, Spearin, & Curtin, 2009).

Even if fathers had few family members to socialize them into responsible parenting behavior, often men found motivation in learning to father on their own terms. This was reflective of their sense of personal agency as fathers. The necessity of supervising younger family members in the absence of a parent was a formative experience, and even without explicit teaching, nonresident fathers referred confidently to their own emergent skills as parents. Delmon was a 27-year-old father of a young son, and the maternal family members doubted his ability to care responsibly for the infant. He reflected back on these early interactions, and he found confidence in how he resolved the doubt and distrust.

> How did I first become involved with my son? I asked to get involved. I made myself involved … nobody asked me. When he was born, he was little, and [her family] didn't really want him to come out because they didn't think I could care for him. And I was like, "No, no, I can care for my son. I done dealt with babies before." I think his mother got the wrong idea when I said that. She said, "He got other kids." But I meant that [I cared for] my brothers and sisters.

Negotiation of Kin Work and Social Capital

Studies have identified a growing capacity for kin networks in middle-class as well as working-class communities to include a range of non-traditional social arrangements in which fathers are trusted caregivers (Hansen, 2005). Resident and nonresident fathers share care arrangements for transportation to and from sports practice, make meals for neighborhood friends, provide advice on schooling or dating to other parents, or coordinate care schedules during snow days or school holidays. As we see changes over time in men's involvement after divorce with multiple households and former partners, life course theory highlights men's alliances with nonbiological or social fathers, including residential stepfathers (Marsiglio, 2004).

In unmarried couples in low-income communities, mothers may take initiative as kin keepers to recruit them into greater involvement (Roy & Burton, 2007). This process of kinscription allows economically-disadvantaged mothers to tailor a set of obligations to men's capacities as parents. Women aspire to find "good fathers" for their children, who can offer legitimacy to families. Their efforts to monitor and assess nonresident fathers' involvement can draw on all available resources from kin networks.

The process of how family roles change over biological, family, and historical time is at the heart of a life course perspective. Nonresident fathers seek meaning in their role as parents by turning to kin members who demand clear expectations and who secure their place as valued, trusted adults. Both Hamer's (2001) and Waller's (2002) use of qualitative methods with small samples of low-income fathers indicate that kin members support fathers who are at risk for separation from their children, if they are poor and cannot provide financially; if they are unprepared for commitment to the mothers of their children; or if they do not interact on a consistent basis with their children. A review of research in these fragile family contexts indicates that fathers are encouraged to play a role as an involved and experienced parent, even if paternal grandmothers or young mothers are the primary caregivers (Coley, 2001).

In our own research, we found as well that kin members negotiated norms of reciprocity with fathers, including what men were responsible for regarding care, and how they were expected to participate with children who were not their own biological children (Madhavan & Roy, 2012; Roy & Vesely, 2009). In the Life History Studies, family members shared a special bond with one another when they were in the same network, primarily because each individual understood the value of the investments made in him or her. It was clear to many of the young fathers whom to go to for financial assistance, emotional support, or life advice. As Jared said:

> If you're going to go to the family, you know ... who you can depend on, who you can run to, talk to. You got that support and you feel more comfortable too when your around nothing but family. Everybody is out to take care of you. (Roy & Vesely, 2009, p. 221)

Obligations in supportive kin networks offered more explicit expectations about nurturance of "the family child." Kinkeepers made certain that young fathers understood the group's fundamental beliefs before they engaged them in activities. Many fathers indicated that their family members shared common beliefs about appropriate child care behavior, and that these beliefs were taken seriously. Ben spoke about the willingness of his family members to do whatever they could for children born into their network:

> [In] my family, everybody looks out for everybody. It's not just the mother father and the child it's the family child. I had a cousin that was, my aunt she was on drugs; the kids were in the worst state. Nobody has been able to adopt anybody in our family. Nobody outside of our family. If we had a problem, someone in the family steps up and takes them in. That's one thing with my grandma she refused to let any child born into our family go. If their father or mother are no good, somehow they are going to make it so the child stays with the family. That's how it was taught to us. (Roy & Vesely, 2009, pp. 221–222)

However, fathers were also assessed on their abilities to live up to these responsibilities of care for children. Men embedded in kin networks perceived clear messages on responsibility and the sanctions for irresponsibility. A father's failure to understand and comply with maternal kin's desires and needs could result in a mother granting him limited time with his child. For some men, then, responsible fathering began early. Brian discussed his attempts to gain acceptance into the network of his child's mother while she was pregnant:

> I visited her at the hospital trying to make good relationships with her family, trying to vouch for the fact that I am presently in school, I am educated, I do have ambitions, I'm not out here trying to make babies all over the place. It's just, I'm going to do the right thing, I'm going to be responsible, I'm going to handle what I can, I'm going to build the relationship I need to. (Roy & Vesely, 2009, p. 232)

Families continue to shape young men's participation in kin networks. Young men learned to utilize networks to build shared understanding about their own roles as fathers. Moreover, family members confirm and legitimize men's paternity status. They may facilitate men's involvement with a child, or potentially with multiple children, when fathers attempt to bring together children in different households. In return, these family members helped to ensure fulfillment of a certain level of responsible behavior as fathers, which often involved renegotiation of mainstream ideals of providing.

Kin systems also require shared control over construction of fathering roles and men's involvement (Roy & Vesely, 2009). Although loss of control may threaten some fathers, the decisions of central kin workers in families (paternal grandmothers in particular) are deemed necessary to protect the viability of close reciprocal relationships around child care. They may also pace age-appropriate blueprints for responsible fathering behavior for young fathers who seek guidance in very basic questions about parenting. Otis, a 23-year-old father, felt that his obligations to his sister—and her expectations that he would be a caregiver for children in the family—held him back from improving his own life by finding a job or going back to school.

> My sister, on the other hand, we not so cool. She has this idea that she's been taking care of me for 5 years or so, like they don't want to give me no credit on nothing I do. The arrangement is that if they have to work or something, I'll watch the kids. Then it got to a point where it was like I was always watching kids. I'm not bettering myself. And then when something goes wrong in the house, they're not paying me. I'm not producing nothing, so there's not income in the house. So if a bill gets super high or something, I get all kinds of heat on me.

Support from kin ultimately had consequences for control over resources and relationships within growing families. Extensive support for paternal involvement often translated into a tradeoff: young men gave up control over the terms of their involvement to family members who managed men's interaction with their children. This was especially important as it related to the men's mothers, who frequently controlled when, where, and how their sons became involved in reciprocal exchanges. Taquan talked about how the relationship between his mother and his girlfriend influenced his own interactions with his son. Through coresidence with his own mother, he allowed her to supervise his interactions, to make sure he was fulfilling his fatherly obligations, and to dictate the terms of his relationships.

> I'm [living] here, at my mom's, again … so it's really their [mother and girlfriend] arrangement and I just happen to be living here. So that's what allows me to see him [son] like that. It's not like I got my own place and that's the arrangement. So actually, I'm on someone else's time with him. I'm on my mama's time—his grandma's time—with him. (Marsiglio & Roy, 2012; Roy & Vesely, 2009, p. 134)

Nonresident fathers face unique challenges with consistency of involvement over time. Once they were able to visit and play and care for their children, only the first job was completed. Living with a child provides a sense of momentum and routine, both of which had to be recreated every week for nonresident fathers. For Carlos, a 31-year-old Mexican father in Chicago, the mother of his girlfriend was always "on him" to visit his son. He said, "My mother-in-law kept me more involved with my son. When there are special events, like the circus coming she says you should take your son, you know things like that or Disney on Ice is coming you should take your son. She gives me ways to get more involved." Consistent involvement was also a way to reassert a long-sought-after identity as a mature adult, a "real man." For Bryan, it was a way to prove that he could be part of a traditional family household.

> By being there for my son, teaching him all the manly things in life, then I could get in good with my baby's mama and we could all just be one big family. Even though she can be a pain cause she listens to her mama, I want to prove both of them wrong.

Many unmarried nonresident fathers like Brian and Carlos have to negotiate involvement with multiple partners (such as former spouses or current girlfriends; see Marsiglio & Roy, 2012; Roy et al., 2008). The building of trust in these networks seems paramount, and likely requires daily emotion work on the part of fathers to move toward agreement on their involvement as coparents of multiple children.

Intergenerational Parenting and Potential Legacies

Discerning patterns of similarities and differences in parenting behavior and motivations across generations obliges researchers to take a life course perspective on how lives change over time. Kin networks shift year to year, and men pass in and out of core positions. By examining nonresident fathers' nurturance within broad intergenerational networks of kin, we can trace patterns of transmission: how fathers withhold or share intimate expressions, which influences subsequent generations to also value men's involvement with children.

Research on modeling behavior for all fathers distinguishes among types of behavior. Harsh parenting practices, such as anger, aggression, or excessive punishment, are modeled across generations (Conger, Neppl, Kim, & Scaramella, 2003; Thornberry, Freeman-Gallant, Lizotte, Krohn, & Smith, 2003). Similarly, more constructive parenting, reflecting authoritative practices that combine warmth and support with structure, is also transmitted from fathers (and mothers) to their sons, who utilize similar practices (Belsky, Jaffee, Sligo, Woodward, & Silva, 2005; Chen & Kaplan, 2004; Hofferth et al., in press). Harsh and constructive behavior can have both direct effects, but also indirect effects, as children's own behavior can mediate how parents respond in kind (Neppl, Jaffee, Sligo, Woodward, & Silva, 2009). However, a careful examination of multiple generations requires multiple reports of behavior, which is lacking in most studies.

To further complicate our understanding of intergenerational parenting, all fathers regardless of their background give their own meaning to how they were parented, and may opt to compensate for poor fathering behavior. A reinterpretation of their experience with their own fathers leads to the belief that they will "take the good, leave the bad" examples set by their own fathers. Careful attention to fathers' meaning making process prioritizes men's agency to reflect on what is best for their own children, which may be best captured with a narrative methodology For example, Daly (1995) interviews middle-class White fathers, who clearly note how disappointed they were with many of their fathers' decisions (such as prioritization of work over family life). In turn, these men purposively chose to be different fathers, who were attentive to the needs and emotional support of their children.

The evolving stories that low income African American fathers tell of their own parents also reflect their choices to compensate for paternal absence (Roy, 2006). In research with low-income fathers who did not live with their children, and may have been completely absent from their early lives, we find evidence that some men loop back into active engagement when their children become adults themselves (Roy & Lucas, 2006). The reclamation of opportunities for involvement demands extensive kin work to overcome anger, resentment, and misunderstanding that can come in the wake of disrupted partnerships with mothers of children. Men need to enter into complicated negotiations with these mothers, as well as various kin members, in becoming an involved father with a young adult son or daughter, who may have children of their own (Snarey, 1993). We know little about how these relationships evolve across all social contexts.

Careful attention to multigenerational kin work also uncovers an important insight about fathering: it does not end when children become adults. With the support of kin networks, nonresident fathers adapt their involvement across different children and grandchildren, alongside in-laws, ex-partners, step relatives, and fictive kin who are significant adults in children's lives. As men's life expectancy has increased in recent decades, a new field of research on grandfatherhood has emerged (Bates, 2009; Bullock, 2005). Family members collaborate to integrate older fathers into the lives of their grandchildren, based on trust and appreciation for life experiences that these older men may bring to care. In turn, kin networks create a space for care and support of these older men as they develop in later life.

However, networks may also be closed to men's involvement in later life, if relationships have become strained or have dissolved (Calasanti, 2004). With dwindling institutional resources, contemporary cohorts of older nonresident fathers may be isolated from family members. We can expect that even in the best circumstances, kin work and communication with older men may tend towards ambivalence and conflict. As Thompson argues (1994), the new roles for engaged grandfathers can be a place to craft creative and meaningful relationships.

The reciprocity that can mark relationships between fathers and other kin members also emerges among multiple generations in an extended family network. This level of kin work requires a father to tap into the social capital that his parents, or other family members, can provide for his children. Brian, a 19-year-old father in Indianapolis, spoke with a sense of security and planfulness for the future of his extended family network. He conveyed that the legacy of his family would be shared parenting by all available adults.

> Everybody—because it's taken all of us, all of our raising has been done by a combination of everyone. And so not of that's going to be different for the child I have now, or children to come. They're always going to want to be open if able, or care for them, do things like that. Uhh, that's how we do it. It's something, you know I have more female cousins and family than I do males and they have a lot of children, at least 2 or 3 also, and we just all do our fair share covering for one another.

A different example might be the care for aging generations of grandparents. After decades of support and sacrifice of mothers for their growing sons in low-income African American families, middle-age fathers may reciprocate through direct care for their aging mothers (Roy et al., 2010). The demands of interdependence of family lives meant that men had to play an important part in constructing new kin scripts when their parents became inactive in kin work. Sudden illnesses prompted some men to move in with their mothers, effectively ending their relationships with other women.

At 37, Rodney has spent his whole life in Chicago, growing up in the projects and moving out after graduating high school. A turning point in Rodney's life was a bad accident 15 years ago while working for a shipping company, in which he injured his back. Rodney married and left that relationship when his son was only 2 years old. He has served as a father for his step-daughter from that relationship, as well as for two other children with his current fiancé. As an active kin worker, he arranged shared custody of his son with his ex-wife. She receives child support and public aid, which upsets him, given that he has custody of the boy. Rodney went further to create an intergenerational support system, urging his teenage son to live with his incapacitated mother as a caretaker and protector.

Nonresident fathers also learned not to take intergenerational commitments for granted. Older adults had "put in their time" as caregivers, and they needed to be cared for in return. They might provide life advice, or a sense of history for younger children, but many men were reluctant to assume that they could hand over their responsibilities to their own parents without violating the fragile agreements in kin networks. Ignacio, a 27-year-old Mexican American father in Chicago, saw his decision to sparingly rely on his mother as a related issue of the proof of his own adequacy as a responsible parent and, one might suggest, a capable kin worker.

That is one thing my parents always said, you have a kid you support it even if it don't work out with your girl. The way I look at it my brother's kids are always there and I don't want to bother them by bring my kids and running around. My parents already raised us so it's my turn to raise my kids. That is the way I do it. I do take them to see my mom but once I see her get frustrated it's time to go. My mom is one of a kind and used to put up with a lot. I guess it's my turn to help them out as much as I can.

If the consequences of productive kin work can attest to anything, it is the existence of a thriving family culture and well-being over time. The transition to fathering usually offers men their first chance at generativity, of working beyond their own well-being and dyadic relationships, in order to secure a continuity of care for coming generations over time. Fathers contribute to and often orchestrate the sense of belonging to a network of family members, and the passing on of unique family knowledge or routines. These family legacies are the result of the continuity of commitment of fathers with their children, their partners, and the extended kin to care for each other. By supporting their own and each other's generative urges, fathers and kin share responsibility for caring for future generations, by cooperatively saving for college, building vacation homes or planning family reunions, or exchanging family pictures, videos, letters, or stories (Marsiglio & Roy, 2012).

In summary, concepts from the life course perspective sensitize researchers to how kin systems provide ground rules for the engagement of nonresident fathers with their children. Men's personal motivation and decisions prompt them to learn about care as a young person and to participate in negotiation with kin members when they are fathers themselves. The ever-changing relationships with family members, across households and generations, can provide opportunities as well as foreclose on options for positive fathering. Perhaps most importantly, a life course approach emphasizes that nonresident fathers also shape kin systems, as men opt to recommit and adapt to the challenges that parenting outside of residence and marriage may present.

Bridge to Other Disciplines

The study of nonresident fathers' engagement with kin work in family networks serves to extend many of the discussions of scholars in this volume. Some of the most relevant linkages are with sociological perspectives on construction of men's roles in a gendered division of household labor (see Doucet, this volume). As we explore men's efforts to care for their children, we also acknowledge that these efforts are shaped by conflict over control, trust, and authority between mothers and nonresident fathers. Our study encourages researchers to ask whether such conflicts are similar in different social contexts. How can we characterize a gendered division of labor that emerges among a complex constellation of extended family members, across generations and across households? Hansen's (2005) notion of networks of care in middle-class White families is particularly insightful, in light of our emphasis on nonresident fathering as a social arrangement with kin members.

Nonresident fathers actively craft a place for themselves as parents outside of marriage or residence, in processes that reflect findings from research on coparenting (see Palkovitz & Fagan, this volume). As these authors note, coparenting processes shift with subtle contextual nuances, which may include a consideration of how kin members guide or even aggravate negotiation between mothers and fathers. It would be a challenge to the emerging economics of fathering (see Bishai, this volume) to include both mothers and a wider range of influential kin members (such as paternal grandmothers) in the examination of how fathers decide to invest time and resources in their children. Do fathers invest time and resources in kin networks in order to support their place as parents, and if so, how? This look at nonresident fathers' activities as kin workers also complicates studies of epigenetics and children's phenotypes that emerge due to father absence (Waynforth, this volume). Our data suggest that fathers who do not reside with their children are not necessarily absent or uninvolved. Their ambiguous relationships may encourage greater kin involvement, thereby introducing more changes in care arrangements and physical environments for children.

Policy Implications

Social policy is often developed and implemented without regard to what happens informally in family networks. Our studies suggest that some nonresident fathers need to do more kin work, in coordinating obligations of adults for children's well-being. There is an opportunity to investigate—perhaps with a wide range of qualitative and quantitative methodology—how, why, and in which contexts do kin systems play a prominent role in men's fathering. But management of conflicting and reciprocal roles is not easy. Policy makers and local programs seem less concerned with supporting kin members in children's lives than in investing in fathers' human capital or the possibility of coparenting relationships (Marsiglio & Roy, 2012). Kin networks are usually treated as informal arrangements that families are free to build—or not—depending on their needs, preferences, and circumstances. In themselves, however, social networks can help men to build the human capital necessary to be successful providers and caregivers for their children.

A different perspective is to frame policies for nonresidential fathering in a manner that incorporates intergenerational family strengths. This move shifts away from prioritizing only married couples and men's personal potential as providers (through an emphasis on jobs and training for fathers) towards a recognition of the importance of relational resources, or social capital that can secure and even hold men accountable to committed parenting. Reconnecting nonresident fathers who are no longer intimately involved with mothers of children, these men can link their children to an even broader network of concerned and motivated paternal kin and friends. Fathers and family members may replenish overly-burdened kin networks, provide additional role models for children, and enhance a range of informal social supports for children.

Policy makers and courts have increasingly acknowledged the place of maternal and paternal kin in relation to men's roles as fathers (Marsiglio & Roy, 2012). Decisions about custody in child welfare cases often take into account extended family involvement, as officials seek to place children with fathers or related kin. Courtroom judges often turn to the mothers of young men to ensure the stability of an established household to steady men's first steps as providers and caregivers. Fathers, irrespective of age, class, and race/ethnicity, grow accustomed to a much more nuanced position in family networks over time. As their own relationships evolve with the mothers of their children, and with kin from both sides, fathers' responsibilities to help their children manage connections to groups and individuals outside the family are transformed as well (Roy et al., 2010; Roy & Burton, 2007; Roy & Vesely, 2009).

Future Directions

The state of research on nonresident fathers in kin networks leaves social scientists with more questions than answers. Consequences of dramatic shifts in men's fathering and in family demographics in recent decades are not well understood, and researchers are faced with the paramount challenge of finding new methods to capture family life as it unfolds in daily routines.

True to a life course framework, researchers should also expect that nonresident fathers in low-income families do not engage in kin network activities in the same way over time. Has kin work become more relevant or more effective as a way to secure a role as an involved nonresident parent? For example, literature on emerging adulthood suggests that the very nature of parent/adult child relations is being transformed. Both parties may see continuing interaction as elective, even in the midst of substantial numbers of young adults (even nonresident fathers) moving back into their parents' households for support through hard economic times.

Family scientists have also challenged researchers to adequately measure and theorize about how and why kin networks emerge and change. Most current data collection efforts are limited in their use of multiple methods, or how a range of methods could inform further data collection or theory development. The use of multiple methods to understand frequency and quantity as well as quantity, cause as well as meaning, explanation as well as discovery, would prove beneficial. A social network analysis is increasingly promising, with its capacity to tap into multiple interactions between multiple members, at the same time discerning more active and central kin work players. Network analyses would enhance an understanding of the degree of reciprocity among mothers, grandmothers, children, and related kin such as uncles and brothers alongside a range of residential and nonresident fathers (McHale et al., 1995; Oliver, 1988).

Theory development may be the most daunting goal of new directions for fathers in whole family networks. How can research step beyond the driving assumptions of fathering defined by men's relationships with mothers of their children, or by direct interaction with children, regardless of social context or time? We would need to think in new ways about common factors like residence. A shared household may mean more than proximity to children that leads to expectable daily interaction. Nonresident fathers may, by necessity, have to cultivate trust among kin, to create a set of obligations to their children, which they can take part in and supervise. These theoretical advances could lead research into a broader and more accurate understanding of men's participation as kin workers in dynamic, conflictual, and complex family arrangements.

References

Amato, P., & Gilbreth, J. (1999). Nonresident fathers and children's well-being: A meta-analysis. *Journal of Marriage and Family, 61,* 557–563.

Amato, P., Meyers, C., & Emery, R. (2009). Changes in nonresident father-child contact from 1976 to 2002. *Family Relations, 58*(1), 41–53.

Aumann, K., Galinsky, E., & Matos, K. (2011). *The new male mystique.* Families and Work Institute. www.familiesandwork.org.

Bates, J. (2009). Generative grandfathering: A conceptual framework for nurturing grandchildren. *Marriage and Family Review, 45,* 331–352.

Belsky, J., Jaffee, S., Sligo, J., Woodward, L., & Silva, P. (2005). Intergenerational transmission of warm-sensitive-stimulating parenting: A prospective study of mothers and fathers of 3-year-olds. *Child Development, 76,* 384–396.

Bengtson, V., & Allen, K. (1993). The life course perspective applied to families over time. In P. Boss, W. Doherty, R. LaRossa, W. Schumm, & S. Steinmetz (Eds.), *Sourcebook of family theories and methods: A contextual approach* (pp. 469–499). New York: Plenum.

Bianchi, S., Robinson, J., & Milkie, M. (2006). *Changing rhythms of American family life.* New York: Russell Sage.

Bronfenbrenner, U. (2005). *Making human beings human: Bioecological perspectives on human development.* Thousand Oaks, CA: Sage.

Bullock, K. (2005). Grandfathers and the impact of raising grandchildren. *Journal of Sociology and Social Welfare, 32,* 43–59.

Burton, L. (2007). Childhood adultification in economically disadvantaged families: A conceptual model. *Family Relations, 56,* 329–345.

Cabrera, N., Ryan, R., Mitchell, S., Shannon, J., & Tamis-LeMonda, C. (2008). Low-income, nonresident father involvement with their toddlers: Variation by fathers' race and ethnicity. *Journal of Family Psychology, 22*(4), 643–647.

Calasanti, T. (2004). Feminist gerontology and older men. *The Journals of Gerontology, Series B, 59,* S305–S314.

Cheadle, J., Amato, P., & King, V. (2010). Patterns of nonresident father contact. *Demography, 47*(1), 205–225.

Chen, G., & Kaplan, H. (2004). Intergenerational transmission of constructive parenting. *Journal of Marriage and Family, 63,* 17–31.

Coley, R. L. (2001). (In)visible men: Emerging research on low-income, unmarried, and minority fathers. *American Psychologist, 56,* 743–75

Coley, R., & Medeiros, B. (2007). Reciprocal longitudinal relations between nonresident father involvement and adolescent delinquency. *Child Development, 78*(1), 132–147.

Coley, R. L., & Morris, J. E. (2002). Comparing father and mother reports of father involvement among low-income minority families. *Journal of Marriage and Family, 64,* 982–997.

Conger, R. D., Neppl, T., Kim, K. J., & Scaramella, L. (2003). Angry and aggressive behavior across three generations: A prospective, longitudinal study of parents and children. *Journal of Abnormal Child Psychology, 31,* 143–160.

Daly, K. (1995). Reshaping fatherhood: Finding the models. In W. Marsiglio (Ed.), *Fatherhood: Contemporary theory, research, and social policy* (pp. 21–40). Thousand Oaks, CA: Sage.

DiLeonardo, M. (1987). The female world of cards and holidays: Women, families, and the work of kinship. *Signs: Journal of Women in Culture and Society, 12,* 440–453.

Elder, G. H., Jr. (1999). *Children of the Great Depression: Social change in life experience* (25th anniversary ed.). Boulder, CO: Westview Press.

Furstenberg, F.F. Jr. (1995). Fathering in the inner city: Paternal participation and public policy. In W. Marsiglio (Ed.), *Fatherhood: Contemporary theory, research, and social policy.* Research on men and masculinities series, 7 (pp. 119–147). Thousand Oaks, CA: Sage.

Fragile Families study. (n.d.). Retrieved from http://www.fragilefamilies.princeton.edu

Gerstel, N., & Gallagher, S. (1993). Kinkeeping and distress: Gender, recipients of care, and work-family conflict. *Journal of Marriage and the Family, 55,* 598–607.

Goldscheider, F., Hofferth, S., Spearin, C., & Curtin, S. (2009). Fatherhood across two generations: Factors affecting early family roles. *Journal of Family Issues, 30,* 586–604.

Hamer, J. (2001). *What it means to be daddy: Fatherhood for black men living away from their children.* New York: Columbia University Press.

Hansen, K. (2005). *Not-so-nuclear families: Class, gender, and networks of care.* New Brunswick, NJ: Rutgers University Press.

Hawkins, D., Amato, P., & King, V. (2007). Nonresident father involvement and adolescent well-being: father effects or child effects? *American Sociological Review, 72*(6), 990–1010.

Hofferth, S., & Goldscheider, F. (2010). Family structure and the transition to early parenthood. *Demography, 47,* 415–437.

Hofferth, S., Pleck, J., & Vesely, C., (in press). The transmission of parenting from fathers and mothers to sons. *Parenting: Science & Research.*

Jarrett, R., Roy, K., & Burton, L. (2002). Fathers in the 'hood: Qualitative research on African American men. In C. Tamis-LeMonda & N. Cabrera (Eds.), *Handbook of father involvement: Multidisciplinary perspectives* (pp. 211–248). Hillsdale, NJ: Erlbaum.

King, V., Harris, K., & Heard, H. (2004). Racial and ethnic diversity in nonresident father involvement. *Journal of Marriage and Family, 66*, 1–21.

Lincoln, Y., & Guba, E. (1985). *Naturalistic inquiry.* Thousand Oaks, CA: Sage.

Madhavan, S., & Roy, K. (2012). Securing fatherhood through kin work: A comparison of Black low income fathers and families in South Africa and the U.S. *Journal of Family Issues.* doiI: 10.1177/0192513x11426699

Manning, W., Stewart, S., & Smock, P. (2003). The complexity of fathers' parenting responsibilities and involvement with nonresident children. *Journal of Family Issues, 24*, 5, 645–667.

Marsiglio, W. (2004). *Stepdads: Stories of love, hope, and repair.* Lanham, MD: Rowman & Littlefield.

Marsiglio, W., & Roy, K. (2012). *Nurturing dads: Social initiatives for contemporary fatherhood.* ASA Rose Series. New York: Russell Sage Foundation.

Marsiglio, W., & Roy, K. (in press) Fathers' nurturance of children over the life course. In G. Petersen & K. Bush (Eds.), *Handbook of marriage and the family* (3rd ed). New York: Springer.

Marsiglio, W., Roy, K., & Fox, G. L. (2005). Father involvement as a situated experience: Conceptualizing spatial issues. In W. Marsiglio, K. Roy, & G. L. Fox (Eds.), *Situated fathering: A focus on physical and social spaces* (pp. 3–26). Boulder, CO: Rowman & Littlefield.

McHale, J., Khazan, I., Erera, P., Rotman, T., DeCourcey, W., & McConnell, M. (1995). Coparenting in diverse family systems. In M. Bornstein (Ed.), *Handbook on parenting, vol. 3: Being and becoming a parent* (pp. 75–107). Mahwah, NJ: Erlbaum.

Mikelson, K. (2008). He said, she said: Comparing mother and father reports of father involvement. *Journal of Marriage and Family, 70*(3), 613–624.

Newman, K. (1999). *Falling from grace: Downward mobility in the age of affluence.* Berkeley: University of California Press.

Neppl, T. K., Conger, R. D., Scaramella, L. V., & Ontai, L. L. (2009). Intergenerational continuity in parenting behavior: Mediating pathways and child effects. *Developmental Psychology, 45*, 1241–1256.

Oliver, M. (1988). The urban Black community as network: Toward a social network perspective. *Sociological Quarterly, 29.* 623–645.

Roschelle, A. (1997). *No more kin: Exploring race, class and gender in family networks.* Thousand Oaks, CA: Sage.

Roy, K. (2004). Three-block fathers: Spatial perceptions and kin-work in low-income neighborhoods. *Social Problems, 51*, 528–548.

Roy, K. (2006). Father stories: A life course examination of paternal identity among low-income African American men. *Journal of Family Issues, 27*, 31–54.

Roy, K. (2008). A life course perspective on fatherhood and family policies in the United States and South Africa. *Fathering: A Journal of Theory, Research, and Practice about Men as Fathers, 6*, 92–112.

Roy, K., Buckmiller, N., & McDowell, A. (2008). Together but not "together:" Trajectories of relationship suspension for low-income unmarried parents. *Family Relations, 57*, 197–209.

Roy, K., & Burton, L. (2007). Mothering through recruitment: Kinscription of non-residential fathers and father figures in low-income families. *Family Relations, 56*, 24–39.

Roy, K., Dyson, O., & Jackson, J. (2010). Intergenerational support and reciprocity between low-income African American fathers and their aging mothers. In W. Johnson & E. Johnson (Eds.), *Social work with African American males* (pp. 42–60). New York: Oxford University Press.

Roy, K., & Lucas, K. (2006). Generativity as second chance: Low-income fathers and transformation of the difficult past. *Research on Human Development, 3*, 139–159.

Roy, K., & Vesely, C. (2009). Caring for "the family's child": Social capital and kin networks of young low-income African American fathers. In R. Coles & C. Green (Eds.), *The myth of the missing Black father* (pp. 215–240). New York: Columbia University Press.

Roy, K., Vesely, C., Fitzgerald, M., & Buckmiller Jones, N. (2010). Young fathers at work: The influence of parental closeness and contact on employment. *Research on Human Development, 7*, 123–139.

Sobolewski, J., & King, V. (2005). The importance of the coparental relationship for nonresident fathers' ties to children. *Journal of Marriage and Family, 67*(5), 1196–1212.

Snarey, J. (1993). *How fathers care for the next generation: A four-decade study*. Cambridge, MA: Harvard University Press.

Stack, C. (1974). *All our kin: Strategies for survival in a black community*. New York: Random House.

Stack, C., & Burton, L. (1993). Kinscripts. *Journal of Comparative Family Studies, 24*, 157–170.

Strauss, A., & Corbin, J. (1998). *Basics of qualitative research: Techniques and procedures for developing grounded theory* (2nd ed.). Thousand Oaks, CA: Sage.

Tach, L., Mincy, R., & Edin, K. (2010). Parenting as a "package deal": Relationships, fertility, and nonresident father involvement among unmarried parents. *Demography, 47*, 1, 181–204.

Thompson, E. (1994). *Older men's lives*. Sage Series on Men and Masculinity. Thousand Oaks, CA: Sage.

Thornberry, T. P., Freeman-Gallant, A., Lizotte, A. J., Krohn, M. D., & Smith, C. A. (2003). Linked lives: The Intergenerational transmission of antisocial behavior. *Journal of Abnormal Child Psychology, 31*, 171–184.

U.S. Census Bureau. (2010). America's families and living arrangements: 2009. Table C3:Living arrangements of children under 18 years and marital status of parents by age,sex, race, and Hispanic origin, and selected characteristics of the child. Retrieved from http://www.census.gov/population/www/socdemo/hh-fam/cps2009.html

Waller, M. (2002). *My baby's father: Unmarried parents and paternal responsibility*. Ithaca, NY: Cornell University Press.

Whitchurch, G., & Constantine, L. (1993). Systems theory. In P. Boss, W. Doherty, R. LaRossa, W. Schumm, & S. Steinmetz (Eds.), *Sourcebook of family theories and methods: A contextual approach* (pp. 325–352). New York: Plenum.

Yen, H. (2011, September 21). *Census: Recession takes big toll on young adults*. Associated Press. Retrieved from www.guardian.co.uk/world/feedarticle/9880674

Chapter 19

The Implications of Fatherhood for Men

David J. Eggebeen

The Pennsylvania State University

Chris Knoester

The Ohio State University

Brandon McDaniel

The Pennsylvania State University

Historical Overview and Theoretical Perspectives

Every year approximately 4 million children are born. For many of the parents this will be their introduction to parenthood, arguably one of the most significant life transitions they will make as adults. What makes parenthood unique among the many choices and changes in life? Parenthood is for life. One never grows out of motherhood or fatherhood. Surprisingly, our attention to this remarkable transition for adults has been selective.

We know a considerable amount about how children change the lives of women. There is also a substantial literature on the consequences of the transition to parenthood for marital relationships. The impact of fatherhood for the lives of men has commanded comparatively little attention. This is changing. Today, there is a growing body of research on the consequences of becoming a father that spans across psychology, sociology, demography, and economics. This review will attempt to make sense of this literature.

Before beginning our review, we need to address two questions: (a) Who is a father? (b) What is fatherhood? The simple answer to the first question is that fathers are men who have obtained children. Usually, this happens through biologically fathering a child. Data from the 2002 National Survey of Family Growth show that 47% of men fathered a child (Martinez, Chandra, Abma, Jones, & Mosher, 2006). Therefore, approximately 55,312,420 men aged 15 and older are fathers. If we limit ourselves to men aged 40–44, nearly 78% of men are fathers. This is probably an underestimate. Studies show that men under report the number of children they fathered. In addition, this estimate leaves out men who have become fathers via adoption or remarriage. Thus, becoming a father is nearly universal for men.

Moving beyond this demographic snapshot, the forces that shape the experience and practice of fathers have made the answer to the second question much more complex. There was a time when becoming a father, the practice of fatherhood, and the life course of fathers were easy to identify and describe. Overwhelmingly, men who were fathers were biologically related to their children and they were living with them (Eggebeen, 2002). The path of men who became fathers was assumed to follow a sequence of completing schooling, obtaining a job, getting married, becoming a father and raising these children until they were launched from the home. It was assumed there was a behavioral consistency to fathering rendered by the fact that it was done in the context of a marriage, and this marriage was characterized by a stay-at-home wife whose main responsibility was the care of children (Mintz & Kellogg, 1988). This behavioral consistency was also maintained by normative uniformity in expectations for fathers. Fathers were expected first and foremost to be "good providers" for their children by making work a priority. Good fathers were the heads of their families, the court-of-last-resort when it came to discipline, and limited to the playful aspects of childrearing (Griswold, 1993).

Of course, even in the 1950s and early 1960s when these expectations predominated, there were significant numbers of men who departed from these ideals. The diversity in the context of fatherhood was unacknowledged or hidden. For many men, fatherhood was conducted in the context of poverty, low-paying, harsh, degrading jobs, difficult or stressful marriages, divorce or remarriage, in times of extended absences because of military commitments or with the experience of racial or ethnic oppression (Nelson, 2004). Some men did not see fatherhood as a call to solely focus on breadwinning, but as an opportunity to become actively involved in the lives of their children as well (LaRossa, 1997).

Today, there is more sensitivity to the diversity of fathers and the conduct of fathering. This sensitivity is driven by three trends that are reshaping family life: (a) the changing demography of family life, (b) the changing social and cultural context, and (c) the changing economy. The dramatic changes in partnering and childbearing are well known and are covered in more detail in the chapter in this volume by Manning and Brown, so this will be brief. The most obvious change since mid-century has been the growing number of fathers who live apart from their children. Divorce and non-marital childbearing often present formidable challenges to father involvement (Townsend, 2002). Approximately 41% of children are born outside of marriage, including a growing proportion of births to cohabiting couples. Over half of currently cohabiting men, about 55% in 2002, are fathers (Hamilton, Martin, & Ventura, 2010; Martinez et al., 2006). The growth of stepfamilies, both marriage-based and cohabitation-based, means that many men negotiate the role of father with non-biological children. Finally, when men have children by different partners, the negotiation of involvement with children becomes even more complicated (Tach & Edin, 2010).

The social and cultural contexts of family life have also changed. The rise in female labor participation and the changing cultural norms surrounding gender relationships have led to a redefining of what is expected of fathers. Today, the expectation is that fathers are to be emotionally connected to their children, be involved in their lives, more egalitarian in their gender role expectations, and more willing to be the principal provider of care for their children. Nevertheless, breadwinning remains an essential component of "good" fathering (Doherty, Kouneski, & Erickson, 1998).

There is also increasing diversity in the racial-ethnic backgrounds and sexual orientations of fathers. The United States is increasingly a multi-racial and multi-ethnic society and this is clearly the case for fathers. Approximately 75% of Latino men and 71% of African American men aged 25–44 are fathers. They represent nearly 23% of all American fathers (Martinez et al., 2006). The growing visibility and acceptance of gays and lesbians as well as the debate over the legalization of same-sex marriages has sparked interest in the number of children being raised by gay and lesbian parents. Studies of gay fathers remain sparse, in part because it is comparatively rare. Reliable estimates remain hard to come by, but recent analysis of survey data from California suggest that between 1% and 11% of gay men live in households with a child (Carpenter & Gates, 2008). These proportions probably are an underestimate, given that it misses gay men who are non-resident fathers.

Through the work of Glenn Elder, Rand Conger and their many collaborators over the past few decades, much has been learned about the connections between financial stresses for couples and parent-child relationships (Conger & Elder, 1994). This work is especially germane given the recent changes in the economic context within which families, and fathers, are embedded. For example, since the mid-1970s there has been a significant drop in the wages of men who have no post-high school education. This has resulted in a widening gap in wages by level of education, accelerating income inequality (Levy, 1998). As a result, poorly educated fathers are at great risk today of bouts of unemployment, financial pressure from high debt or an inability to pay bills, and work related stresses. In addition, since 2008 the United States has experienced one of the worse economic recessions in recent history. Although the current recession was broad based, there is some evidence that working class families were especially devastated (Bureau of Labor Statistics, 2011).

In conclusion, the incredible changes in the context and the practice of fatherhood cannot be easily summarized in a few pithy statements. Should we not expect the same complexity and diversity in the consequences of fatherhood for men? Further complicating matters is the extent to which the demographic, cultural, and economic contexts of family life are intertwined (McLanahan, 2004; Townsend, 2002). As we shall see in this review, some headway has been made in understanding the variable nature of the consequences of fatherhood for men.

A number of theoretical explanations have been deployed in empirical studies of the consequences of fatherhood for men. A classic sociological explanation for patterned behavior is role theory (Biddle, 1986). A role explanation would posit that the reasons why fatherhood should affect men is that fatherhood is first and foremost a status with associated expectations. When men become fathers their behavior changes because they understand that fathers are supposed to behave in certain ways. That is, there is a code of conduct for fathers that is widely known and accepted by both the new father and those around him (Doherty et al., 1998; Eggebeen & Knoester, 2001). If they don't behave as expected, they may experience sanctions. Small deviations from these expectations may result in a gentle reminder from those in close proximity to fathers such as spouses or friends, to "shape up". Severe deviations such as systematic or extreme failure to own up to their responsibilities may spur more serious or even public sanctions, such as being labeled a "dead-beat dad" or running afoul with the law for not paying child support.

Developmentally oriented scholars have long viewed parenthood as a transition that facilitates adult development (Bronfenbrenner, 1979). In this view, parenthood provides an opportunity for personal reorganization and growth. This transition can lead to changes in family and social relationships, work experiences, moral values or life priorities, etc. These developmental changes are not only initiated by the birth event, but evolve as men continuously adjust their fathering, family life, and work life to the changing needs and capabilities of growing children (Palkovitz, 2002; Palkovitz & Palm, 2009).

Fatherhood can also affect men by initiating a change in identity. Identity theory begins with the premise that the self is a structure of identities organized in hierarchical fashion (Rane

& McBride, 2000). For example, a man can occupy a variety of social roles such as employee, weekend athlete, spouse, or brother. However one's identity is shaped by the importance or salience of these roles for an individual. Becoming a father, then, can initiate a reordering of the importance of the many roles that form the basis for a man's identity. Townsend (2002) builds on these ideas by arguing that the good-provider role is part of a "package deal" along with marriage, holding a steady job, and owning a home that form the basis of men's identity. When fathering roles become central to one's identity, behavior begins to fall in line with the expectations that surround the fathering roles (Rane & McBride, 2000). In other words, a man may begin to reexamine his behavior, attitudes, relationships and priorities because "now I am a father…".

A fourth theoretical perspective that is used to frame research on the consequences of fatherhood is life course theory. One of the central tenets of a life course perspective is that of linked lives; the events, transitions, values and behavior of both parents and children remain intertwined through the life course (Knoester, 2003). Indeed a number of studies show that children continue to exert an influence on the psychological well-being of parents well after they have become adults (Knoester, 2003; Umberson, Pudrovska, & Reczek, 2010). When this perspective is used with rich longitudinal data, it has the potential to integrate aspects of socio-logical, developmental and psychological perspectives.

These theoretical perspectives offer different approaches to understanding how fatherhood might influence the lives of men. In some cases these theories are complementary, such as generativity and identity theories, or integrative, such as life course theory. However, role theory and developmental theory offer differing predictions about the stability or permanence of the changes wrought by fatherhood. Role theory suggests that a number of the outcomes associated with fatherhood dissipate once men "lose" fatherhood roles, either through divorce or when children age into adulthood. In contrast, a developmental theoretical perspective that posits that fatherhood is a transformative event anticipates that the social and psycho-logical changes associated with fatherhood have "staying power" even after men's fathering experiences become distal. At this point, there have been few systematic tests of competing hypotheses drawn from these explanations (cf. Eggebeen & Knoester, 2001; Eggebeen, Dew, & Knoester, 2010, for exceptions).

Current Research Questions

As will be evident from our review of the literature, scholars from a variety of disciplines and theoretical perspectives have been investigating the consequences of fatherhood across a broad array of domains of men's well-being. In general, early studies tended to assess the effects of fatherhood per se by controlling for a host of other characteristics such as marital status, race-ethnicity, education, and age of child (Eggebeen & Knoester, 2001). In addition, these studies typically compared fathers with childless men (cf. Eggebeen & Knoester, 2001; Snarey, 1993; Umberson, 1987). Recent studies have extended this work in two important ways. First, researchers have begun to pay more attention to how the con-sequences of fatherhood may vary by such contexts as marital status, and characteristics of children. Second, many studies have moved beyond comparing fathers with childless men to also examine how the consequences of fatherhood change over the life courses of both children and fathers.

Research Measurement and Methodology

The empirical evidence that is scrutinized in our review relies on a variety of different, yet often complementary analytical methods. These include a focus on men's self-reports of their behaviors and feelings, but also an increased use of other sources of information (e.g., co-parents, hormone measurements). Cross-sectional and longitudinal data are both utilized. The majority of research looks at survey components from large national samples, but in-depth qualitative inquiries are common as well. Statistical sophistication has led to an increasing emphasis on modeling change over time while attempting to account for unobserved heterogeneity. Primary methodological challenges include identifying more detailed and consistent evidence of the processes that are theorized to operate, envisioning appropriate ways to model the increasing complexities of family structures, recognizing and measuring reciprocal effects, and disentangling selection effects.

Qualitative research tends to elicit rich descriptions from individuals about how fatherhood has affected them. Although useful patterns of processes are often identified, questions frequently remain about the robustness and generalizability of the findings—largely as a result of the use of small, selective samples with little variance across different fatherhood contexts. In contrast, quantitative research in the field tends to identify broad and statistically significant patterns of differences in the effects of fatherhood across different contexts. Yet, this approach tends to be largely limited in detailing and measuring exactly how the processes that are envisioned actually occur. Theoretical perspectives like those presented earlier tend to be described, but linking these broad theoretical orientations to specific hypotheses are often left to one's imagination. Clearly, the strengths and weaknesses of each approach make them complementary methods. Yet, the challenge is for each approach to continue to improve at addressing its weaknesses and for an increased application of mixed methods within individual studies.

The increasing complexities of family life, described in Chapter 5 of this volume, also present methodological challenges. How can one accurately describe the effects of fatherhood when men may have multiple children, at different ages and developmental stages, across different households, with multiple partners? These complexities are exacerbated when one begins to consider the influence of the nature of the father-child relationships, the entries and exits of a father's presence in each child's life, and whether a father has biological, adoptive, foster, or social ties to the children. There are enormous methodological challenges embedded in trying to categorize the different fatherhood contexts that occur and identifying appropriate comparison groups. The frequency and implications of experiences such as multi-partner fertility have just begun to receive widespread attention (e.g., Tach & Edin, 2010).

The traditional approach when studying fatherhood has been to consider how fathers affect children's lives. Yet, consideration of reciprocal influences in tracing the mechanisms of how fatherhood affects men's lives is rare. For example, it is reasonable to expect that relationship quality with the birth mother not only affects father involvement, but is largely shaped by how a father interacts with his children. Similarly, not only may men's lives be altered because they interact in different ways and with varying frequencies with their children, but these interactions may largely be influenced by the children's behaviors as well. Methodological challenges remain in both recognizing and modeling reciprocity. Recent work has begun to take these paths of mutual influence more seriously and has utilized techniques such as cross-lagged structural equation models to better understand directions of causality (e.g., Carlson, McLanahan, & Brooks-Gunn, 2006; Hawkins, Amato, & King, 2007).

Finally, concerns about the implications of selection effects pose substantial method-ological challenges. Variations in the experience of fatherhood and fathering behaviors are largely connected to a web of factors such as family background, educational attainment, age at the transition to fatherhood, marital status, (non)resident status, relationship quality with the birth mother, gender ideologies, commitments to fathering, mental health, job prospects, and expected earnings growth. It is becoming increasingly clear that not only children, but also parents, experience diverging destinies. Middle-class, well-educated, and White men are especially likely to marry, experience the transition to fatherhood at a later age, live with their children, maintain a stable relationship with the birth mother, and have promising career opportunities (Edin & Kafalas, 2005; McLanahan, Garfinkel, Mincy, & Donahue, 2010). Especially because these characteristics tend to cluster together, the relevance of any one of them is difficult to isolate. One interpretation of the trends is that two major fatherhood tra-jectories occur: one for privileged men and the other for disadvantaged men. In other words, there is positive selection into married, coresident fatherhood experiences at later ages.

Scholars have attempted to address concerns about selection into different fatherhood expe-riences by using sophisticated statistical analyses with longitudinal data and by increasingly fine-tuning comparison groups. Methods such as fixed effects, random effects and growth curves seek to identify unique starting points in outcomes of interest and to consider the influ-ence of factors that induce change in the dependent variable over time while attempting to eliminate the effects of unobserved heterogeneity. Reconsiderations of appropriate comparison groups and experimental designs are other approaches that may be used to disentangle selec-tion effects. For example, most studies tend to compare fathers to nonfathers or to compare different fatherhood contexts to married, coresident fatherhood. However, considering how fatherhood changes men's lives over time among a sample of only men who become fathers at similar ages and in the same family structure arrangement is a novel approach (Astone, Dari-otis, Sonenstein, Pleck, & Hynes, 2010). Similarly, experimental designs that trace the impacts of changes in economic resources, improvements in parents' relationship quality and fathers' commitments to parenting may provide better understandings of causality. There is experi-mental evidence that indicates that income subsidies, relationship enhancement programs, and parenting counseling can increase parental cooperation, relationship quality, and father-ing commitments (McLanahan & Beck, 2010; McLanahan & Percheski, 2008). Future work is well-advised to continue these points of emphasis.

Empirical Findings

Psychological consequences of fatherhood.   It might seem obvious that fatherhood would have psychological consequences. After all, as was noted in the introduction to this chapter, parenthood is permanent. As such the act of becoming a parent is likely to be a major transi-tion, a turning point, in the life course (Palkovitz, 2002). It is also a common experience for men to report that the birth of their child was a profoundly emotional event. Some of these emotions are positive, with new fathers reporting joy, excitement, and positive anticipation for being a father (Palkovitz, 2002). However, as the abundant literature on the consequences of the transition to parent demonstrates, parenthood comes with significant changes, not all of which are psychologically positive (Palkovtiz, 2002; Umberson et al., 2010). New parents often report increased stress, anxiety, frustration, depression, and marital conflict. Rob Palko-vitz reports that while the 40 fathers in his qualitative study talked about both positive and negative emotions associated with fathering, on balance the reported emotions were mostly positive.

Generally, parenthood is thought to have negative consequences for the psychological well-being of adults (Evenson & Simon, 2005). Yet, Umberson and colleagues' (2010) review concluded that parenthood per se does not predict the psychological well-being of parents. Social contexts can significantly moderate the consequences of being a parent. Studies that have specifically examined the implications of becoming a father for men have generally have found this to be the case as well. For example, the effects of becoming a father have been found to be contingent on marital status (Nomaguchi & Milke, 2003). For married men, becoming a father was unrelated to self-efficacy, depressive symptoms, or self-esteem; fatherhood was linked with negative effects of unmarried fathers. It is unclear from this work why marriage may offset the negative effects of fatherhood. Is the advantage because of the availability of another adult in the home, or because marriage has unique advantages attached to it such as social legitimacy, access to support networks, etc.? One the few studies that addressed this found that single fathers have the highest levels of depression, but the relationship between fatherhood and depressive symptoms is similar for married and cohabiting men (Woo & Raley, 2005). Other work finds that being a stepparent is associated with higher levels of stress and lower levels of life satisfaction for fathers (Eggebeen & Knoester, 2001; Kohler, Behrman, & Skytthe, 2005). However this effect appears to dissipate with union duration (Umberson et al., 2010). Work by Pudrovska (2009) is consistent with this conclusion, finding that middle-aged stepfathers are no more likely than either stepmothers or biological fathers to suffer decreased psychological well-being.

A number of studies show that becoming a young father is negatively related to men's well-being. This is because young fathers are less likely to be living with their children, have higher rates of multi-partner fertility, are likely to be high school dropouts, have erratic work histories, and low-paying jobs (Hofferth & Goldscheider, 2010). Also, there is evidence that young men's transition to fatherhood negatively affects the quality of their romantic relationships, although this effect was weaker for young fathers who were living with their child and partner (Taillade, Hofferth, & Wight, 2010). Late timing of entry into fatherhood has not received much attention, probably because older fathers tend to have more economic, emotional, and family resources to bring to their fathering. However, older fathers are likely to have the challenges of complex family relationships brought on by divorce and remarriage (Settersten & Cancel-Tirado, 2010).

Relative to White fathers, African American fathers of 2-year olds tended to report more depressive symptoms (Gross, Shaw, Dishion, Moilanen, & Wilson, 2008). This finding is consistent with at least one other study that found that Black fathers tend to exhibit more depressive symptoms than White fathers (Bronte-Tinkew, Moore, Matthews, & Carrano, 2007). It is unclear why Black fathers experience more negative effects. One possibility is that the greater involvement on the part of Black fathers, at least among those who are non-resident (Cabrera, Ryan, Mitchell, Shannon, & Tamis-LeMonda, 2008), may make them more susceptible to the stresses of parenting.

When relationships between fathers and their children are positive or healthy, both potentially benefit. However when children have problems, under certain circumstances, fathers have problems. A longitudinal study that followed children (Gross et al., 2008) found that depression in mothers tended to decline as children aged from two to four, while father's depressive symptoms remained unchanged. They also found that for both parents, initial high levels of depression were related to increased levels of internalizing behaviors in children.

Fathers were less negatively affected than mothers by children who exhibited conduct problems. Similarly, the stress of raising a difficult adolescent had negative health outcomes for mothers, but not fathers in a sample of rural parents (Wickrama et al., 2001).

When adult children experience challenges such as job loss or divorce, evidence suggests that both parents are vulnerable to stress, depression, or declines in their well-being. One source of psychological distress for middle age fathers is a poor relationship with one or more of their adult children. When adult children experience a negative event such as divorce, illness, or money problems, both fathers and mothers experience an increase in depressive symptoms (Milke, Bierman, & Schieman, 2008; Pudrovska, 2009).

The ties between adult children and parents change as parents enter old age and the need for care grows. Yet, one constant in this dramatic shift in the linked lives of parents and children is that parents remain emotionally invested in their children. Elderly parents continue to express concern for their middle-aged children's health, family life, and career success, and these concerns are associated with their well-being (Ryff, Lee, Essex, & Schmutte, 1994).

Fatherhood and physical health.   Fatherhood can be a turning point in the health behaviors and overall health of men. This change can be both positive and negative; for example, fathers may become more mindful of their behaviors, but, on the other hand, there is less time to tend to one's health (Settersten & Cancel-Tirado, 2010). Three main ways that fatherhood may affect men's health have been proposed: (a) children's mere presence may affect men's health; (b) children may produce a strain on the couple relationship; and (c) children's own health may indirectly affect men's health (Garfield, Clark-Kauffman, & Davis, 2006). It is important to note that the effects of fatherhood on men's physical health will depend on such things as stage of life, residential status, and household income.

Expectant fathers may experience physiological changes that can influence physical health. During pregnancy, some studies detect increased cortisol levels (Wynne-Edwards & Reburn, 2000), a hormone associated with stress and worse physical health over time, as well as changes in other hormone levels (Storey, this volume). Married men and married fathers also tend to show lower levels of testosterone than unmarried men (Gray, Kahlenberg, Barrett, Lipson, & Ellison, 2002). Research on couvades syndrome, in which fathers' symptoms mimic their partners', has shown that expectant fathers may be more likely to experience nausea, loss of appetite, weight gain, sleep disturbance, and colds (Condon, 1987).

Fatherhood may have the potential to not only influence men to become "good" citizens, but also to discourage men from "bad" behavior. Settersten (2010) frames this in terms of risk. Fathers may more carefully assess risky behaviors or choices because of their potential consequences for children. In general, the research literature supports this. For example, the majority of fathers—even low-income fathers—try to quit smoking at some point or indicate an intention to quit in the near future (Blackburn et al., 2005; Everett et al., 2005). Some studies show that fatherhood is associated with decreases in alcohol use. For example, in a qualitative study of urban U.S. fathers, over 75% made positive changes in their health behaviors, including decreased alcohol use (Garfield, Isacco, & Bartlo, 2010), and many of these fathers identified the transition to fatherhood as a turning point in their perspective on life. However, at least one study finds that becoming a father does not reduce the frequency of drinking for men (Christie-Mizell & Peralta, 2009) and can increase it (Halme, Tarkka, Nummi, & Astedt-Kurki, 2006). Other work suggests that declines in alcohol use occur when fatherhood is combined with other roles such as paid labor and partnership (Kuntsche, Knibbe, & Gmel, 2009). Yet, fathers have also been found to drink more after interacting with a difficult child (Pelham

& Lang, 1999). One possible explanation for these findings is that there are pressures in our society for parents to be models for their children (Dykstra & Hagestad, 2007). In support of this, Palkovitz (2002) found in his interviews with fathers that many felt inclined to be better role models and to settle down. Of course, the variable findings of the effect of fatherhood on alcohol use suggest that under some circumstances, the social pressures to be role models may overwhelmed.

The transition to fatherhood may affect men's health differently according to their stage of life and socioeconomic status. There is some evidence that men who become fathers early in life, which occurs disproportionately among men of lower social and economic status and among delinquent teenagers, may continue or increase previous patterns of drug and substance abuse or risky behavior (Little, Handley, Leuthe, & Chassin, 2009; Stouthamer-Loeber & Wei, 1998).

Becoming a father at a young age may indirectly affect men's physical health. Teenage and young parenthood is likely to be highly stressful and have long-term, irreversible consequences across the entire lifespan (Pearlin, Schieman, Fazio, & Meersman, 2005). Consistent with this hypothesis, stress is associated with the limitations early fatherhood imposes on schooling, stable employment, and good paying jobs (Nock, 1998). The constraints these limitations pose increase the likelihood of being in poverty, which leads to further health risks (Williams, 2003).

Fathers of very young children tend to experience a decline in their general health status with an increase in stress, sleep disruption, and psychological distress (Condon, Boyce, & Corkindale, 2004; Schytt & Hildingsson, 2011). In addition, the decline in marital and relationship functioning following the birth of a child may offset the potential health benefits of that partnership (Garfield et al., 2006).

Divorced fathers are especially likely to engage in health-compromising behaviors such as drug and substance use and drinking and driving, and be depressed (Umberson, 1987; Umberson & Williams, 1993). Yet, even when controlling for other factors such as negative life events and antisociality, the salience of the fathering role in divorced fathers' lives predicts a decrease in health-related problems and marijuana use. Also, extensive involvement with their children is associated with reduced drinking and marijuana use. Smoking, however, appears to be less affected by raising children (DeGarmo, Reid, Leve, Chamberlain, & Knutson, 2010).

There is some evidence that parenthood influences eating habits. Parents with children under 17 years of age in the home consume significantly more fat and saturated fat than adults without children. Parents took in more calories than nonparents and frequently ate many high-fat foods, such as salty snacks, pizza, cheese, beef, ice cream, cake/cookies, processed meats, and peanuts—perhaps because parents are more pressed for time and thus choose more convenient meals (Laroche, Hofer, & Davis, 2007). An additional explanation is that children tend to prefer high fat, high sugar foods, which may influence parents' meal decisions.

Fatherhood, especially in the context of marriage, is associated with lower mortality, perhaps due to the deterrent effect that parenthood has on negative health behaviors (Umberson, 1987). Reduced mortality may also be a consequence of children providing structure and meaning for fathers' lives (Palkovitz, 2002). However, this effect may be contingent on age and number of children. Men with two children have the lowest risk of heart disease, but for every child after two the risk increases (Lawlor et al., 2003). Other studies find no effect on mortality (Kotler & Wingard, 1989) or a progressive decrease in mortality as the number of children increases (Smith & Zick, 1994).

There is only fragmentary research on the link between health and fatherhood at midlife. One study in the United Kingdom found that fathers who had ever experienced being a caregiver, parent, and worker at the same time reported lower functional ability in daily activities at midlife (Glaser, Evandrou, & Tomassini, 2005). Living with a mentally ill child or having to care for a child with problems at midlife has not only been associated with increased distress (Pillemer & Suitor, 1991), but also lower self-reported health (Gallagher & Mechanic, 1996). Finally, single fathers at midlife report worse health and more chronic illness than married fathers (Popay & Jones, 1990), and those who have custody of their children report better health than those without custody (for a review, see Bartlett, 2004). Clearly, research has only begun to examine the effects of fatherhood on men's health at midlife.

Research on the health consequences of parenthood for older men is also limited. In one study based on data from the Netherlands, fathers were less likely to smoke or drink alcohol and more likely to exercise in old age than childless men (Kendig, Dykstra, van Gaalen, & Melkas, 2007). They also found that the loss of a spouse was more detrimental on the health and health behaviors of elderly men without children than of fathers. Finally, older individuals with adult children report positive influences on their physical activity, social activity, and healthy eating (Kendig, 1996). However, fathers of adult children with problems report experiencing more negative health outcomes (Pillemer & Suitor, 1991; Milkie, Bierman, & Schieman, 2008). Children, then, may evoke both positive and negative health outcomes. Fathers may be motivated to engage in healthy behaviors in order to responsibly raise their children or to meet social and familial expectations. Children may also provide meaning and purpose to life that helps fathers cope with widowhood. On the other hand, as noted above, problematic relationships with children may undermine health.

The consequences of fatherhood for social connections.   Fatherhood not only can transform men's "inner selves," but also can potentially have consequences for men's "outer selves"—their behavior. With the onset of fatherhood, the pressures of children's needs, the expectations of others, as well as the transformation in one's identity all suggest that men reorganize their time and reconsider their life priorities. These changes in the allocation of their leisure time, the importance of family and community ties, investment in service organizations, and involvement in church are likely to continue beyond the transition to parenthood as children move from toddlerhood to school age to adolescence. Studies to date have found consistent evidence in support of these expectations.

Children strengthen men's intergenerational ties (Eggebeen et al., 2010). Fathers report more visiting, letter writing, and phone calls with relatives, especially parents, than men who are not fathers. Fathers are also significantly more likely to be involved in instrumental exchange relationships. They are more likely to give and receive money, tangible help, and caregiving with extended family members than non-fathers. This tightening of cross-generation family ties probably happens for two reasons: aging parents are motivated to spend time with their grandchildren and parents raising children occasionally need help. Consistent with these ideas is the finding that one of the most significant predictors of intergenerational support is the presence of young children (Eggebeen, 1992). Settersten (2010) notes, however, that the positive effects of fatherhood for men's family relationships may be tempered when these relationships are negative, risky or have few resources to offer. In some cases becoming a father may involve separation from those extended family members who may present risks for their child.

Parenthood also is related to participation in service organizations such as parent-teacher associations or school boards, community action organizations, and youth-oriented activities such as Little League coaching or leading Boy or Girl Scout groups (Wilson, 2000). While this relationship varies by the age of the child, marital status and gender, show fathers are significantly more likely to be involved in service organizations than men who don't have children (Eggebeen & Knoester, 2001; Snarey, 1993). The civic engagement of men does vary by type of fathering. Non-resident fathers and fathers of adult children are less likely than resident fathers of dependent children to be engaged in service organizations, especially ones that are child or youth-oriented (Eggebeen & Knoester, 2001; Knoester & Eggebeen, 2006). Furthermore, fathers do not limit their involvement just to organizations that serve their children. There is also evidence that fathers are more involved in a broad spectrum of community groups such as labor unions, professional societies, political groups or nationality organizations (Eggebeen & Knoester, 2001). It does not appear that fathers are more civic minded because they are less likely to be socially isolated than men who are not fathers. Rather, when men become fathers they change how they spend their leisure time. Relative to men who do not have children, fathers spend more time volunteering and less time going out to bars or playing recreational sports such as golf or bowling (Eggebeen & Knoester, 2001). Finally, there is some evidence that the reach of fatherhood extends into middle age, even after children have left the home. The defining aspect of the effect of fatherhood is their level of engagement with children while the children are growing up (Eggebeen et al., 2010).

Men may become more religious and more involved in religious institutions when they become fathers. This may happen for several reasons. Parenthood may prompt men to evaluate the importance of religion, especially when they are faced with teaching their children what to value (King, 2003). Fathers may find that religious teachings and becoming involved in a church reinforces the meaning and purpose of parenthood and children (Palkovitz, 2002; Sherkat & Ellison, 1999). Finally, fathers may increasingly attend churches because churches provide a ready-made social support network of other families and fathers in similar situations as their own (Edgell, 2006). The evidence is consistent with these hypotheses, especially among stably married fathers (Eggebeen & Knoester, 2001; Knoester, Petts, & Eggebeen, 2007; Stolzenberg, Blair-Loy, & Waite, 1995). Yet, the effects of children on church attendance are sensitive to the age of the child, with parents of children between the ages of 5 and 10 having the highest attendance rates and with church attendance declining with older children (Stolzenberg et al., 1995).

There are important qualifications to these empirical findings about the consequences of fatherhood for men's social lives. Most of the above mentioned studies show that unmarried fathers are no different than childless men in their involvement with kin, civic engagement, risky or aberrant behavior, or church attendance. This pattern is not necessarily because fathers are not living with their children. Cohabiting fathers, for example, are also less likely than married fathers to be involved with kin or attend religious services (Eggebeen, 2005; Stozenberg et al., 1995). Second, many of the consequences of fatherhood for men are contingent on their level of commitment to being a father or their level of engagement with their child. Fathers who resist adhering to the role expectations of fatherhood, fail to assume the identity of father, show less commitment to being a father, or are less involved with their children are significantly less likely to change in response to the transition to fatherhood (Eggebeen et al., 2010; Knoester et al., 2007). Third, with few exceptions, most of the studies have not paid attention to the life course patterns of the consequences. Attention has mostly concentrated on the transition to fatherhood or more generally on comparing fathers and non-fathers. Finally, there has been little examination of race-ethnic variations in the consequences of fatherhood. As will be argued below, attention to African American fathers is especially needed given the large differences relative to white fathers in family contexts and conceptions of the meaning of fatherhood.

Fatherhood and the work lives of men.   Commitment to paid employment has long been seen as a hallmark of responsible fathering (Doherty et al., 1998; Townsend, 2002). Yet, the implications of fatherhood for men's work lives have never been more in doubt. The "new" expectations for involved fathering urge men to spend more time with their children and to share more equally in domestic labor responsibilities. High rates of women's labor force participation and joint custody mean that it is relatively rare for fathers to be the sole economic providers for families. Parents increasingly negotiate how to fulfill domestic and paid labor responsibilities—the division of labor is less clear than in the past. Work-family conflict has increased substantially for men in recent decades (Winslow, 2005).

Within this context, it is especially important to understand how fatherhood may affect men's work behaviors. Role theories, perspectives that emphasize developmental transformations, and identity theory are commonly applied to analyses of the associations between fatherhood and men's work behaviors. Fatherhood can act as motivation or a source of social pressure to either increase commitments to paid labor or to seek a reduced emphasis on breadwinning in favor of a greater emphasis on domestic responsibilities (Palkovitz, 2002). On the one hand, one might expect fathers to become more committed to paid labor and motivated to increase their earnings. Providing for children is expensive. Parents often specialize in paid or domestic labor—and fathers rarely specialize in domestic labor (Bianchi, Robinson, & Milkie, 2006). On the other hand, one might expect fathers to cut back on their commitments to work. Time is a finite resource and children bring both opportunities for engagement as well as greater demands for domestic labor. Hours devoted to paid labor might restrict father involvement and contributions to domestic labor. Indeed, time spent with children is negatively correlated with hours at work among men who reside with their biological children (Eggebeen & Knoester, 2001; Knoester et al. 2007).

The links between fatherhood and men's work behaviors are a complex function of many factors including: human capital, marital status, (non)resident status with children, age at the transition to fatherhood, race-ethnicity, desires and abilities to embrace "new" father ideals, and selection effects. Overall, fathers are more likely to be employed, work longer hours, earn higher wages, report higher earnings, and accumulate more assets than men who are not fathers (Eggebeen et al., 2010; Glauber, 2008; Hodges & Budig, 2010).

For example, one study, drawing on data from the Panel Study of Income Dynamics, finds that both the transition to parenthood and a second child, but not a third child, are each associated with increases in men's wages and in hours of paid employment (Lundberg & Rose, 2002). Other studies extend this by showing that these effects may be contingent on race and marriage. For example, a recent study found evidence that the fatherhood wage premium exists only within marriage and that the premium is disproportionately lower for Black fathers (Glauber, 2008). Hodges and Budig (2010) found evidence that marriage explains a substantial portion of a fatherhood effect, and that well-educated, White, professionals are especially likely to obtain an increase in earnings after becoming fathers. This is consistent with a recent study which finds that fatherhood is associated with an increase in asset accumulation (Eggebeen et al., 2010). However, this study also shows that married fathers accumulate assets at significantly higher rates than unmarried fathers and that younger and African American men exhibited larger increases in their asset levels after becoming fathers.

Some studies challenge these findings. Percheski and Wildeman (2008) examine the employment trajectories of first-time fathers from the Fragile Families and Child Well-being Study. Although baseline models indicate that the transition to fatherhood is associated with increases in men's weekly hours in paid labor over the next 5 years, the results identify substantial differences in the work behaviors of married, cohabiting, and nonresident fathers. Prior to the birth of the child, married fathers worked more hours per year than cohabiting and nonresident fathers. Yet, cohabiting and nonresident fathers display marked increases in their commitments to the labor force, whereas married fathers generally maintain consistently high levels of commitment to paid labor. However, after accounting for human capital and demographic differences, Percheski and Wildeman (2008) find that married fathers are not significantly different than other fathers in terms of the average number of hours per week or the number of weeks per year that they work both before and after the transition to fatherhood. Astone and colleagues report similar findings (Astone et al., 2010). They find that fatherhood is associated with an increased likelihood of working and an increase in hours worked among young unmarried men. However, among married men who became fathers at similar ages, the transition to fatherhood is not associated with an increase in the probability of working or the number of hours worked. In fact, there is evidence that—among married men who become fathers in their late 20s—the transition to fatherhood leads to a decline in the probability of working and in the number of hours worked. This finding may reflect the greater likelihood of married fathers in their late 20s planning for the birth and coordinating more equal domestic and paid labor responsibilities with full-time working wives. Yet, the finding may also be driven by ceiling effects since married childless men are already working at very high levels, on average (Astone et al., 2010; Glauber, 2008). Finally, Loughran and Zissimopoulos (2009) found that there is no significant fatherhood effect on wages in their analysis of the two cohorts of men in the National Longitudinal Survey (NLSY). They suggest that childbearing (and marital) decisions are potentially made on the basis of earning potential.

How can these seemingly contradictory findings be synthesized? Sample restrictions, methodology, decisions about independent and control variables, choices about comparison groups, and consideration of fathers' ages appear to make a substantial difference. First, there appears to be more consistency in fatherhood encouraging increases in work hours and income when samples include greater proportions of older, White, professional, and married men who are or become fathers. It is likely that markers of disadvantage become much more salient among men who become fathers because human capital, race-ethnicity, marital decisions, the likelihood of residing with one's children, the timing of births, and the extent of preparation for births are interrelated and can reasonably be expected to be associated with job prospects, commitments to paid labor, and expected wage growth. Second, the traditional patterns of fatherhood effects are most pronounced when fixed-effects methods are used. There is reason to be cautious about having confidence in these results (Loughran & Zissimopoulos, 2009). Third, accounting for a positive association between hours worked and income seems to increase the likelihood that fatherhood encourages more disadvantaged men to increase hours in paid labor, but that fatherhood disproportionately rewards more privileged men with higher earnings. More privileged and salaried men may be better able to maintain a target income without markedly adjusting their work hours. Yet, married men appear especially likely to have a partner specialize in domestic work while they specialize in paid work after the birth of a child. In addition, there is evidence that institutionalized discrimination functions to disproportionately reward married, professional, and White fathers with higher earnings. Workplaces are gendered and racialized organizations that reward White men, in part, by maintaining a culture that interprets Caucasian and masculine traits as signals of heightened work commitments and productivity (Correll, Stephen, & Paik, 2007; Hodges & Budig, 2010). Finally, when comparisons are made that highlight the salience of a man's age and marital status during the transition to fatherhood, there is stronger evidence that young, unmarried, and African American fathers are more likely to experience a "jolt" from the transition to fatherhood and increase their hours in paid labor and asset accumulation (Astone et al., 2010; Settersten & Cancel-Tirado, 2010).

Further complicating the relationship between fatherhood and work-related outcomes is the extent to which fathers desire to be, and are, involved in the lives of their children. Breadwinning can be viewed as an integral component of father involvement and fathers who adhere to more traditional gender ideologies and divisions of labor are more likely to increase their hours in paid labor and focus on earnings (Glauber, 2008; Kaufman & Uhlenberg, 2000). In contrast, there is some evidence that fathers who hold more egalitarian gender ideologies, become more frequently engaged in activities with their children, have full-time working wives, and contribute more effort to domestic labor are less likely to increase—and may even cut back--their hours in paid labor (Eggebeen & Knoester, 2001; Glauber, 2008; Kaufman & Uhlenberg, 2000; Knoester et al., 2007). A negative relationship between father engagement and hours in paid labor appears more likely to occur among fathers who reside with their children (Eggebeen & Knoester, 2001; Knoester & Eggebeen, 2006), and father engagement appears likely to be positively associated with hours in paid labor and earnings for nonresident fathers (Guzzo, 2009).

Overall, the relationships that emerge from studying fatherhood and men's work behaviors suggest a number of patterns. First, married men typically seem to have planned births that they have prepared for, in part, by securing stable, well-paying jobs. They seem to experience fatherhood while maintaining high levels of commitment to the labor force and relatively high wages. They are also more likely to engage in gender specialization, whereby they become more committed to the labor force, while a spouse exhibits greater commitment to domestic labor. White, married, professional men appear especially likely to benefit from a fatherhood premium in earnings and asset accumulation—in part, because of institutionalized discrimination (Correll et al., 2007; Eggebeen et al., 2010; Hodges & Budig, 2010). Second, unmarried men appear to have births at younger ages and seem more likely to have unplanned births. Subsequently, they appear more likely to experience fatherhood as a "jolt" that requires greater commitment to the labor force and to asset accumulation (Astone et al., 2010; Eggebeen et al., 2010; Settersten & Cancel-Tirado, 2010). There is also evidence that African American fathers are especially likely to experience fatherhood as a turning point and to subsequently increase their hours in paid labor and asset accumulations (Eggebeen et al., 2010; Percheski & Wildeman, 2008). Third, father engagement and fulfillment of domestic work responsibilities appear to be negatively correlated with men's work hours, especially among fathers who live with their children (Eggebeen & Knoester, 2001; Knoester et al., 2007). There is some evidence that father engagement is positively associated with nonresident men's work hours (Guzzo, 2009).

Bridges to Other Disciplines

With the possible exception of the work that focuses the consequences of psychological and physical health, the extant research literature of the 1980s and 1990s largely proceeded along disciplinary lines with minimal attention paid to findings in other areas. In part this was symptomatic of the absence of a widely utilized theoretical frame that promoted cross-disciplinary investigations, data sets that contained rich measures of interest to scholars from the full range of behavioral and psychological sciences, and incentives to form cross-disciplinary collaborative research teams. Today, the potential to address these limitations has never been better. Integrative, dynamic theories that emphasize the importance of multiple contexts, from social structures to biological systems, are increasingly being honed and deployed. Longitudinal data sets that contain measures developed by biologists, psychologists, demographers, sociologists, and economists, as well as the statistical techniques to analyze these data are now readily available. Finally, institutional mechanisms such as cross-disciplinary research centers and funding sources that encourage inter-disciplinary research teams are breaking down the traditional barriers that encourage parallel research literatures.

Policy Implications

Quite reasonably, the predominate focus of policies that involve fathers and fatherhood described in other chapters of this volume is on enhancing the well-being of children. However, the implications of the accumulating body of research described above strongly suggest that when men become actively involved in the lives of their children there can be marked improvements in their health, work lives, and well-being. In addition, the transforming effects of fatherhood on men potentially have the benefit of strengthening their family ties and enriching their communities. The questions that remain unanswered are what interventions and policies might strengthen the link between becoming a father and positive changes in men.

Future Directions

The literature reviewed in this chapter demonstrates a growing interest in the extent to which fatherhood shapes the lives of men. This interest is driven by dual, almost contradictory trends of increasing "good" dads and "bad" dads (Furstenburg, 1988). The rise of "good" dads comes from the changing cultural expectations of father behavior, primarily among the middle class, that pushed fathers beyond a narrow focus on bread-winning to being actively involved in the rearing of their children. At the same time, high rates of divorce and non-marital childbearing, increasingly common among the disadvantaged, has meant a growing fraction of fathers have comparatively limited contact or engagement in the lives of their children. The intensification of fatherhood for some men and rejection of fatherhood by other men leads to questions about how fatherhood affects men's lives differently in different contexts. Overall, research demonstrates that being a father has a substantial influence on men. However, there remain important gaps in the literature that must be addressed.

Our understanding of how fatherhood affects men is largely built on analyses that have ignored race and ethnic differences. It is important for the next round of studies to move from controlling for race-ethnicity to explicitly testing theoretically driven hypotheses about racial differences or similarities. For example, how might the cultural notions of machismo shape the changes children bring to the lives of Latino men? There is evidence of distinct patterns of father involvement among African American men (Demo & Cox, 2000). How might the all-too-common experiences of poverty, joblessness, or social marginality affect their identity as fathers?

Fathers practice their trade in a wide range of settings. Some attention has been given to the effects of fatherhood for men who are stepfathers or who do not live with their children because of divorce or non-marital childbearing. However there is growing recognition that men are embedded in other contexts that are likely to profoundly affect their fathering experiences. For example, incarceration has become a part of the life course of a significant fraction of African American men (Wildeman, 2009). Questions that have yet to be addressed include: Does fatherhood reduce the risk of criminal behavior? Or is recidivism reduced by fatherhood? There is also growing recognition that some children place special demands on fathers, yet, with the few exceptions described above, there has been little exploration of how fathering children with special needs challenges and changes men's lives. Finally, the current debate over whether same-sex couples should be allowed to marry has raised the visibility of children raised by gay or lesbian parents. While the focus of research has been on the consequences for children, there has been little or no attention to impact of fatherhood on the lives of gay men.

It is clear from this review, as well as from others, that most of the attention on the consequences of fatherhood has been on the initial transition (Settersten, 2010; Umberson et al., 2010). The fragmentary evidence thus far suggests that fatherhood continues to have an influence on the lives of men throughout their life course. However most of this work focuses on psychological outcomes, and often this work only indirectly addresses consequences for men. In addition, much of what we know about these findings has come from cross-sectional studies or relatively short spans of longitudinal data. The potential of such long-running longitudinal data sets such as the Wisconsin Longitudinal Study or the National Longitudinal Survey for following men from young adulthood into middle age remains to be exploited. Despite the profound changes in family life over the past five decades, fatherhood remains a central feature of the life course of men. Much work remains understanding the implications of this defining role for men's lives.

References

Astone, N. M., Dariotis, J. K., Sonenstein, F. L., Pleck, J. H., & Hynes, K. (2010). Men's Work Efforts and the Transition to Fatherhood. *Journal of Family and Economic Issues, 31*, 3–13.

Bartlett, E. E. (2004). The effects of fatherhood on the health of men: A review of the literature. *Journal of Men's Health, 1*, 159–169.

Bianchi, S. M., Robinson, J. P., & Milkie, M. A. (2006). *Changing rhythms of American family life.* New York: Russell Sage.

Biddle, B. J. (1986). Recent developments in role theory. *Annual Review of Sociology, 12*, 67–92.

Blackburn, C., Bonas, S., Spencer, N., Dolan, A., Coe, C., & Moy, R. (2005). Smoking behaviour change among fathers of new infants. *Social Science & Medicine, 61*, 517–526.

Bronfenbrenner, E. (1979). *The ecology of human development: Experiments by design and nature.* Cambridge, MA: Harvard University Press.

Bronte-Tinkew, J., Moore, K. A., Mathews, G., & Carrano, J. (2007). Symptoms of major depression in a sample of fathers of infants: Sociodemographic correlates and links to father involvement. *Journal of Family Issues, 28*, 61–99.

Bureau of Labor Statistics. (2011). The employment situation-January 2011. Retrieved February 7, 2011. http://www.bls.gov/news.release/pdf/empsit.pdf

Cabrera, N. J., Ryan, R. M., Mitchell, S. J., Shannon, J. D., & Tamis-LeMonda, C. S. (2008). Low-income, nonresident father involvement with their toddlers: Variation by fathers' race and ethnicity. *Journal of Family Psychology, 22*, 643–647.

Carlson, M. J., McLanahan, S. S., & Brooks-Gunn, J. (2006). Coparenting and nonresident fathers' involvement with young children after a nonmarital birth. *Demography, 45*, 461–488.

Carpenter, C., & Gates, G. J. (2008). Gay and lesbian partnership: Evidence from California. *Demography, 45*, 573–590.

Christie-Mizell, C. A., & Peralta, R. L. (2009). The gender gap in alcohol consumption during late adolescence and young adulthood: Gendered attitudes and adult roles. *Journal of Health and Social Behavior, 50,* 410–426.

Condon, J. T. (1987). Psychological and physical symptoms during pregnancy: A comparison of male and female expectant parents. *Journal of Reproductive and Infant Psychology, 5,* 207–219.

Condon, J. T., Boyce, P., & Corkindale, C. J. (2004). The first-time fathers study: A prospective study of the mental health and wellbeing of men during the transition to parenthood. *Australian and New Zeeland Journal of Psychiatry, 38,* 56–64.

Conger, R. D., & Elder, G. H. (1994). *Families in troubled times: Adapting to change in rural America.* New York: Aldine De Gruyter.

Correll, S. J., Stephen, B., & Paik, I. (2007). Getting a job: Is there a motherhood penalty? *American Journal of Sociology, 112,* 1297–1338.

DeGarmo, D. S., Reid, J. B., Leve, L. D., Chamberlain, P., & Knutson, J. F. (2010). Patterns and predictors of growth in divorced fathers' health status and substance abuse. *American Journal of Men's Health, 4,* 60–70.

Demo, D. H., & Cox, M. J. (2000). Families with young children: A review of research in the 1990's. *Journal of Marriage and Family, 62,* 876–895.

Doherty, W. J., Kouneski, E. F., & Erickson, M. F. (1998). Responsible fathering: An overview and conceptual framework. *Journal of Marriage and the Family, 60,* 277–292.

Dykstra, P. A., & Hagestad, G. O. (2007). Roads less taken: Developing a nuanced view of older adults without children. *Journal of Family Issues, 28,* 1275–1310.

Edgell, P. (2006). *Religion and family in a changing society.* Princeton, NJ: Princeton University Press.

Edin, K., & Kafalas, M. (2005). *Promises I can keep: How poor women put motherhood before marriage.* Berkeley: University of California Press.

Eggebeen, D. J. (1992). Family structure and intergenerational exchanges. *Research on Aging, 14,* 427–447.

Eggebeen, D. J. (2002). The changing course of fatherhood: Men's experience with children in demographic perspective. *Journal of Family Issues, 23,* 486–506.

Eggebeen, D. J., & Knoester, C. (2001). Does fatherhood matter for men? *Journal of Marriage and the Family, 63,* 381–393.

Eggebeen, D.J., Dew, J., & Knoester, C. (2010). Fatherhood and men's lives at middle age. *Journal of Family Issues, 31,* 113–130.

Evenson,R. J., & Simon, R. W. (2005). Clarifying the relationship between parenthood and depression. *Journal of Health and Social Behavior, 46,* 341–358.

Everett, K. D., Gage, J., Bullock, L., Longo, D. R., Geden, E., & Madsen, R. W. (2005). A pilot study of smoking and associated behaviors of low-income expectant fathers. *Nicotine & Tobacco Research, 7,* 269–276.

Furstenburg, F.F., Jr. (1988). Good dads-bad dads: Two faces of fatherhood. In A. J. Cherlin, (Ed.). *The changing American family and public policy* (pp. 193–218). Washington, DC: The Urban Institute.

Gallagher, S. K., & Mechanic, D. (1996). Living with the mentally ill: Effects on the health and functioning of household members. *Social Science and Medicine, 42,* 1691–1701.

Garfield, C. F., Clark-Kauffman, E., & Davis, M. M. (2006). Fatherhood as a component of men's health. *Journal of the American Medical Association, 296,* 2365–2368.

Garfield, C. F., Isacco, A., & Bartlo, W. D. (2010). Men's health and fatherhood in the urban Midwestern United States. *International Journal of Men's Health, 9,* 161–174.

Glaser, K., Evandrou, M., & Tomassini, C. (2005). The health consequences of multiple roles at older ages in the UK. *Health & Social Care, 13,* 470–477.

Glauber, R. (2008). Race and gender in families at work. *Gender and Society, 22,* 8–30.

Gray, P. B., Kahlenberg, S. M., Barrett, E. S., Lipson, S. F., & Ellison, P. T. (2002). Marriage and fatherhood are associated with lower testosterone in males. *Evolution and Human Behavior, 23,* 193–201.

Griswold, R. L. (1993). *Fatherhood in American: A history.* New York: Basic Books.

Gross, H .E., Shaw, D. S., Dishion, T. J., Moilanen, K. L., & Wilson, M. N. (2008). Reciprocal models of child behavior and depressive symptoms in mothers and fathers in a sample of children at risk for early conduct problems. *Journal of Family Psychology, 22,* 742–751.

Guzzo, K. B. (2009). Men's visitation with nonresident children. *Journal of Family Issues, 30,* 921–944.

Halme, N., Tarkka, M.-T., Nummi, T., & Astedt-Kurki, P. (2006).The effect of parenting stress on fathers' availability and engagement. *Child Care in Practice, 12,* 13–26.

Hamilton, B. E., Martin, J. A., & Ventura, S. J. (2010). Births: Preliminary data for 2009. National Vital Statistics Reports web release; Vol. 59, no. 3. Hyattsville, MD: National Center for Health Statistics. Retrieved February 2, 2011. http://www.cdc.gov/nchs/data/nvsr/nvsr59/nvsr59_03.pdf

Hawkins, D. N., Amato, P. R., & King, V. (2007). Nonresident father involvement and adolescent well-being: Father effects or child effects? *American Sociological Review, 72,* 990–1010.

Hodges, M. J., & Budig, M. J. (2010). Who gets the daddy bonus? *Gender and Society, 24,* 717–745.

Hofferth, S. L., & Goldscheider, F. G. (2010). Family structure and the transition to early parenthood. *Demography, 47,* 415–437.

Kaufman, G., & Uhlenberg, P. (2000). The influence of parenthood on the work effort of men and women. *Social Forces, 78,* 931–949.

Kendig, H. (1996). Understanding health promotion for older people: Sociological contributions. In V. Minichiello, N. Chappell, H. Kendig, & A. Walker (Eds.), Sociology of aging: International perspectives (pp. 360–375). Melbourne, Australia: International Sociological Association, Research Committee on Aging.

Kendig, H., Dykstra, P. A., van Gaalen, R. I., & Melkas, T. (2007). Health of aging parents and childless individuals. *Journal of Family Issues, 28,* 1457–1486.

King, V. (2003). The influence of religion on fathers' relationships with their children. *Journal of Marriage and the Family, 65,* 382–395.

Knoester, C. (2003). Transitions in young adulthood and the relationship between parent and offspring well-being. *Social Forces, 81,* 1431–1457.

Knoester, C., & Eggebeen, D.J. (2006). The effects of the transition to parenthood and subsequent children on men's well-being and social participation. *Journal of Family Issues, 27,* 1532–1560.

Knoester, C., Petts, R. J., & Eggebeen, D. J. (2007). Commitments to fathering and the well-being and social participation of new, disadvantaged fathers. *Journal of Marriage and Family, 69,* 991–1004.

Kohler, H.-P., Behrman, J. R., & Skytthe, A. (2005). Partner + children=happiness? The effects of partnenships and fertility on well-being. *Population and Development Review, 31,* 407–445.

Kotler, P., & Wingard, D. L. (1989). The effect of occupational, marital, and parental roles on mortality: The Alameda County Study. *American Journal of Public Health, 79,* 607–612.

Kuntsche, S., Knibbe, R. A., & Gmel, G. (2009). Social roles and alcohol consumption: A study of 10 industrialized countries. *Social Science & Medicine, 68,* 1263–1270.

Laroche, H. H., Hofer, T. P., & Davis, M. M. (2007). Adult fat intake associated with the presence of children in households: Findings from NHANES III. *The Journal of the American Board of Family Medicine, 20,* 9–15.

LaRossa, R. (1997). *The modernization of fatherhood: A social and political history.* Chicago: University of Chicago Press.

Lawlor, D. A., Emberson, J. R., Ebrahim, S., Whincup, P. H., Wannamethee, S. G., Walker, M., et al. (2003). Is the association between parity and coronary heart disease due to biological effects of pregnancy or adverse lifestyle risk factors associated with childrearing? Findings from the British Women's Heart and Health Study and the British Regional Heart Study. *Circulation, 107,* 1260–1264.

Levy, F. (1998). The New Dollars and Dreams: American Incomes and Economic Change. New York: Russell Sage.

Little, M., Handley, E., Leuthe, E., & Chassin, L. (2009). The impact of parenthood on alcohol consumption trajectories: Variations as a function of timing of parenthood, familial alcoholism, and gender. *Development and Psychopathology, 21,* 661–682.

Loughran, D., & Zissimopoulos, J. (2009). Why wait? The effect of marriage and childbearing on the wages of men and women. *Journal of Human Resources, 44*, 326–349.

Lundberg, S., & Rose, E. (2002). The effects of sons and daughters on men's labor supply and wages. *Review of Economics and Statistics, 84*, 251–268.

Martinez, G. M., Chandra, A., Abma, J. C., Jones, J., & Mosher, W. D. (2006). Fertility, Contraception, and Fatherhood: Data on Men and Women from Cycle 6 (2002) of the National Survey of Family Growth: National Center for Health Statistics. Vital Health Stat 23(26). Retrieved February 3, 2011, from http://www.cdc.gov/nchs/data/series/sr_23/sr23_026.pdf

McLanahan, S. S. (2004). Diverging destinies: How children are faring under the second demographic transition. *Demography, 41*, 607–627.

McLanahan, S., & Beck, A. N. (2010). Parental relationships in fragile families. *The Future of Children, 20*, 17–37.

McLanahan, S., & Percheski, C. (2008). Family structure and the reproduction of inequalities. *Annual Review of Sociology, 34*, 257–276.

McLanahan, S. S, Garfinkel, I., Mincy, R., & Donahue, E. (2010). Introducing the issue. *The Future of Children, 20*, 3–16.

Milke, M. A., Bierman, A., & Schieman, S. (2008). How older adult children influence older parents' mental health: Integrating stress-process and life-course perspectives. *Social Psychology Quarterly, 71*, 86–105.

Mintz, S., & Kellogg, S. (1988). *Domestic revolutions: A social history of American family life.* New York: The Free Press.

Nelson, T. J. (2004). Low-income fathers. *Annual Review of Sociology, 30*, 427–451.

Nock, S. (1998). The consequences of premarital fatherhood. American Sociological Review, 63, 250–263.

Nomaguchi, K. M., & Milke, M. A. (2003). Costs and rewards of children: The effects of becoming a parent on adult's lives. *Journal of Marriage and Family, 65*, 356–374.

Palkovitz, R. (2002). *Involved fathering and men's adult development: Provisional balances.* Mahwah, NJ: Erlbaum.

Palkovtiz, R., & Palm, G. (2009). Transitions within fathering. *Fathering, 7*, 3–22.

Pearlin, L. I., Schieman, S., Fazio, E. M., & Meersman, S. C. (2005). Stress, health, and the life course: Some conceptual perspectives. *Journal of Health and Social Behavior, 46*, 205–219.

Pelham, W. E., & Lang, A. R. (1999) Can your children drive you to drink? Stress and parenting in adults interacting with children with ADHD. *Alcohol Research and Health, 23*, 292–298.

Percheski, C., & Wildeman, C. (2008). Becoming a dad: Employment trajectories of married, cohabiting, and nonresident fathers. *Social Science Quarterly, 89*, 482–501.

Pillemer, K., & Suitor, J. J. (1991). "Will I ever escape my child's problems?" Effects of adult children's problems on elderly parents. *Journal of Marriage and Family, 53*, 585–594.

Popay, J., & Jones, G. (1990). Patterns of health and illness amongst lone parents. *Journal of Social Policy, 19*, 499–534.

Pudrovska, T. (2009). Parenthood, stress, & psychological well-being in late middle life and early old age. *International Journal of Aging and Human Development, 68*, 127–147.

Rane, T. R., & McBride, B. A. (2000). Identity theory as a guide to understanding fathers' involvement with their children. *Journal of Family Issues, 21*, 347–366.

Ryff, C. D., Lee, Y. H., Essex, M. J., & Schmutte, P. S. (1994). My children and me: Midlife evaluations of grown children and self. *Psychology and Aging, 9*, 195–205.

Schytt, E., & Hildingsson, I. (2011). Physical and emotional self-rated health among Swedish women and men during pregnancy and the first year of parenthood. Sexual & *Reproductive Healthcare.* doi:10.1016/j.srhc.2010.12.003

Settersten, R. A. (2010). The consequences of fatherhood for men's lives. *Research in Human Development, 7*, 70–82.

Settersten, R. A., Jr., & Cancel-Tirado, D. (2010). Fatherhood as a hidden variable in men's development and life courses. *Research in Human Development, 7,* 83–102.

Sherkat, D .E., & Ellison, C. G. (1999). Recent developments and current controversies in the sociology of religion. *Annual Review of Sociology, 25,* 363–394.

Smith, K. R., & Zick, C. D. (1994). Linked lives, dependent demise? Survival analysis of husbands and wives. *Demography, 31,* 81–93.

Snarey, J. 1993. *How fathers care for the next generation: A four decade study.* Cambridge, MA: Harvard University Press.

Stolzenberg, R. M., Blair-Loy, M., & Waite, L .J. (1995). Religious participation in early adulthood: Age and the family life cycle effects on church membership. *American Sociological Review, 60,* 84–103.

Stouthamer-Loeber, M., & Wei, E. H. (1998). The precursors of young fatherhood and its effects on delinquency of teenage males. *Journal of Adolescent Health, 22,* 56–65.

Tach, L., & Edin, K. (2010) Parenting as a "package deal": Relationships, fertility, and non-resident father involvement among unmarried parents. *Demography, 47,* 181–204.

Taillade, J. J., Hofferth, S., & Wight, V. R. (2010). Consequences of fatherhood for young men's relationships with partners and parents. *Research on Human Development, 7,* 103–122.

Townsend, N. (2002). *The package deal: Marriage, work, and fatherhood in men's lives.* Philadelphia: Temple University Press.

Umberson, D. (1987). Family status and health behaviors: Social control as a dimension of social integration. *Journal of Health and Social Behavior, 28,* 306–319.

Umberson, D., Pudrovska, T., & Reczek. (2010). Parenthood, childlessness, and well-being: A life course perspective. *Journal of Marriage and Family, 72,* 612–629.

Umberson, D., & Williams, C. L. (1993). Divorced fathers: Parental role strain and psychological distress. *Journal of Family Issues, 14,* 378–400.

Wickrama, K. A. S., Lorenz, F. O., Wallace, L. E., Peiris, L., Conger, R. D., & Elder, G. H. Jr. (2001). Family influence on physical health during the middle years: The case of onset of hypertension. *Journal of Marriage and Family, 63,* 527–539.

Wildeman, C. (2009). Parental imprisonment, the prison boom and the concentration of childhood disadvantage. *Demography, 46,* 265–280.

Williams, D. R. (2003). The health of men: Structured inequalities and opportunities. *American Journal of Public Health, 93,* 724–731.

Wilson, J. (2000). Volunteering. *Annual Review of Sociology, 26,* 215–240.

Winslow, S. (2005). Work-family conflict, gender, and parenthood, 1977–1997. *Journal of Family Issues, 26,* 727–755.

Woo, H., & Raley, R. K. (2005). A small extension to "Costs and rewards of children: the effects of becoming a parent on adults' lives." *Journal of Marriage and Family, 67,* 216–221.

Wynne-Edwards, K. E., & Reburn, C. J. (2000). Behavioral endocrinology of mammalian fatherhood. *Trends in Ecology & Evolution, 15,* 464–468.

SECTION VI

Economic and Legal Perspectives

Chapter 20

Economics of Fatherhood

David Bishai

Johns Hopkins University

Introduction

Few mammalian species exhibit any social contact between fathers and offspring. Humans are notable but not exceptional for having involved fathers. However, humans are unparalleled in the variety of ways they express fatherhood. A taxonomy of fathering would include: step-fathers, never married, divorced, polygynous, polyandrous, married, co-fathers, and various gradations of involvement for resident and non-resident fathers. The list is growing. One of the critical tasks in the economics of fatherhood is to explain this variety of social forms as human adaptations to resource scarcity, technology, and information. Economists share the general concern that the forms of fatherhood can critically determine the forms and magnitude of parental investments of time and money that determine a child's success in life.

The policy relevance of the economic approach to families stems from a public concern in the welfare of children. Fathers have the potential to affect child well-being, and understanding the causal connections between what fathers do and how their children fare can form the basis of sound policy decisions. The current obsession with father's child support payments needs to be broadened if a father's parenting behavior (aside from spending behavior) is indeed relevant to child well-being. Furthermore, in an aging society fathers reap what they sow, and the welfare of legions of "lonely old men" is emerging as the flip side of changes in the role of fathers. Understanding economic antecedents of the multiple forms of fatherhood makes one more mindful of potential unintended consequences of well-meaning attempts to circuit the expression of fatherhood into one or more socially sanctioned forms.

This chapter will first cover the foundations of economic theories about fathers. Economists have struggled to explain how gendered patterns in behavior of agents can emerge without stipulating that an agent has intrinsic gendered properties. The mind of *Homo economicus* is neither a man's mind nor a woman's mind, so the reasons that mothers and fathers differ ought to be extrinsic to the cognitive process of rational choice. The chapter will show how empirical findings have actually set limits on just how intrinsically similar men and women can be and still square economic predictions with theory. After covering key theories of fatherhood, the chapter will offer an overview of current research questions and critical elements of research measurement and methodology in the economic tradition. Several connections between approaches to fatherhood in economics and evolutionary biology and psychology are drawn out in a section entitled "Bridges to Other Disciplines." Finally the chapter will discuss policy implications and future directions for research.

Theoretical Perspectives and Empirical Findings

The economic approach starts with the premise that well-meaning rational actors are doing the best they can given their constraints. In economic models, the critical determinants of choice are the physical and social constraints-not the preferences of the individual. This stands in contrast to approaches centered on individuals for whom all lifestyles are seen as equally viable options. Equal viability might imply that individuals whose life choices diverge from normatively defined "pro-child" lifestyles have weaker commitment to child welfare. Economic models start from the optimistic premise that everyone is trying to do the best they can with their circumstances.

The general approach to economic theories of family behavior is to view agents as maximizing their well-being under the constraints set by resources and the reactions of fellow agents. The two pieces of an economic explanation are (a) the agent's preferences; and (b) the constraints. While both elements matter, the focus of most economists lies in tracing the implications of alterations in the constraints rather than the preferences. An insightful economic model finds interesting behavior emerging from agents with mundane preferences who have to do their best under complex social and physical conditions. From this perspective the best economic theories of fathers will start with the assumption that men and women are symmetrical in their interest in children's well-being. Behavioral differences between fathers and mothers are not assumed, they are derived as stemming from asymmetries in the physical and social circumstances that fall to men and women. The history of the economics of fatherhood has been a succession of studies of asymmetric circumstances for men and women in their drive to cooperate for reproductive success. Gary Becker's seminal contributions focused on asymmetrical wages for men and women in the labor market. Later contributions by Willis focused on asymmetric information about how much resident caregivers would invest in children. Other economists have focused on paternity uncertainty and the current policies that surround biological paternity testing in child support enforcement agencies.

Becker's Theories of Fatherhood

There is simply no way to do justice to all of Gary Becker's contributions to the economics of fatherhood. This chapter will present two of his most important contributions: his theory of the gendered division of household labor and his theory of polygamy (Becker, 1981). A more general discussion of Becker's contributions to the theory of time allocation can be found elsewhere (Grossbard-Schechtman, 1988).

Becker is credited with enriching the study of families with his classical theories of comparative advantage and the returns to trade to derive an explanation for the division of labor in households. Essentially, Becker's theory explains why fathers should be expected to perform different tasks than mothers. There are no obstacles to applying Becker's theories of task specialization to same sex couples as long as one realizes that there can be just as much heterogeneity in skills and talents in same sex couples as mixed sex couples. If skills and talents vary in any couple, then the theory predicts task-specialization in couples raising children.

In Becker's model the household "produces" high quality children using two inputs: domestic work and market work. Domestic work involves the cooking, cleaning, diaper changing, and cognitive stimulation, etc., that is required to keep children healthy and to help them prosper in the future. Market work involves remunerative activities to generate or finance the food, shelter, clothing, books, and PCs that are ancillary to domestic work. Becker's model is populated by multiple non-identical adults and multiple identical children. It is important that the adults are non-identical, because if they were identical and if there was no way to get better at either domestic or market work by doing more of it, then there would be no reason to specialize. But, if the adults are heterogeneous or if they could potentially become heterogeneous by specializing then they and their children would all be better off if every adult in the household specialized in either 100% market work or 100% adult work. The simple version of the theory makes an extreme prediction that there will be 100% specialization. (No wage worker will ever do laundry and no domestic worker will ever go out to draw a paycheck.)

The simple theory is thus difficult to square with empirical facts of time allocation. Gendered patterns of time allocation among couples have been eroding for over 30 years. Nowadays, U.S. households almost never contain members who allocate either 0% or 100% of their discretionary time to domestic work. Men's share of parenting time continues to rise from 1975 when they supplied one-quarter as much time as mothers in activities with children to 2003 when they supplied one-half as much (Bianchi, Wight, & Raley, 2005; Sayer, Bianchi, & Robinson, 2004). To reconcile the theory to the data one needs to either modify the household member's objective function or modify the constraints they face. If objectives included not just child outcomes but also participatory utility from enjoying diverse activities, then these patterns would make sense. The market worker would dabble in recreational domestic work as an indulgence. Dabbling might lower household income, but the foregone earnings would be worth the extra enjoyment. The irony of this theoretical patch is that the child would still be financially better off if the dabbling parent suppressed their self-indulgence. More starkly, if parent A earned $10 per hour and parent B earned $20 per hour, the child would have a larger college fund if the couple allocated 40 hours of parent B to wage labor than if the choice was 39 hours for parent B and 1 hour for parent A.

Another way to shore up Becker's theory so it squares with data would be to explore whether the process of producing quality children could be optimized by a diversity of caregivers. What if children actually thrived from direct exposure to a variety of committed caregivers? In this case parental specialization would be sub-optimal. Testing these patches to Becker's model would require measuring a capacity for the household to derive either participatory utility or improved child outcomes from "dabbling" whose value exceeded the foregone product from spending the same time specializing. The potential recreational value of time with children is hardly controversial. On the other hand, the causal impact of diverse stable caregivers on child well-being has been elusive to demonstrate and its under recognition may be driving both policy and personal choices about intra-household time allocation. Substantial adverse selection contaminates estimates of the impact of fathers' child care time on child development. Decisions to divorce or have non-marital children are correlated with unmeasured background factors that could confound the inference that the inferior outcomes of children in these settings were caused by the time allocation of the father. We discuss empirical evidence on whether children benefit from dual parent time in caregiving later in the chapter.

The general form of the theory of the allocation of time does not identify market work with men and domestic work with women. There is nothing overtly gendered in Becker's theory of time allocation. For Becker, it is a historical happenstance that the last 10 millennia have been characterized by higher returns to households for men participating in market work than in domestic work. During humanity's traditional agrarian phase, there were male advantages in using violence to defend property boundaries and in plowing and forceful aspects of animal husbandry or large game hunting. These extrahousehold factors would have determined that fathers are more heavily engaged in work outside of child care and less in domestic work, but these historical contingencies are changing.

With accumulating machinery and capital the biological advantage of muscle strength becomes less determinative (Galor & Weil, 1996). In modern knowledge and service economies, both pregnancy and breastfeeding are becoming increasingly irrelevant to a worker's productivity. Wages for men and women in the United States have converged dramatically in the last 50 years (Mulligan & Rubinstein, 2008). This has reduced the comparative advantage for fathers to allocate time preferentially to work. Becker's theory predicts that reductions in gendered wage differentials would be associated with more men allocating time to child care. Wage equality may explain part of the rise in fathers' time spent with children in the American Time Use Survey (Table 20.1). The closing of the female-male wage gap has also been statistically linked to the rise in female headed households (Moffitt, 2000). One of the explanations for the association between wage equality and a decline in marriage rates is that a couple no longer can expect economic gains from specializing their time allocation in home or workforce. It should strike readers as paradoxical that wage equality between men and women should both increase the amount of time fathers spend with children in biparental households and at the same time lower the prevalence of biparental households. This paradox is the motivating force for Willis's theories of fatherhood which will be discussed later in the chapter.

The major changes in time allocation to child care seen in Table 20.1 are all attributed to changes in the remunerative productivity of women's time spent at work. There is no reason to believe that fathers have become more productive in their role in child care. Indeed there is no reason to believe there ever were productivity differentials between men and women in the parental role. Aside from sentimentality or sexism, there is no empirical basis for a belief in women's comparative advantage in domestic work and child care. One study of time allocation by mothers and fathers in Bangladesh found no statistically significant difference in the productivity of an hour of a father's or a mother's time in reducing stunting or wasting in children under 5 (Bishai, 1996).

Table 20.1 Hours per Week Spent in Child Care

Year	Mothers	Fathers
1965	10.2	2.5
1975	8.6	2.6
1985	8.4	2.6
1995	9.6	4.2
2000	12.6	6.8
2003	14.1	7

Source: ATUS data cited in (Bianchi, et al., 2005)

Polygyny, Fatherhood, and Children

Becker's theory of polygyny is an extension of his theory of time allocation (Becker, 1991). Far from having limited applicability to non-Western societies, the theory remains very relevant to explain fatherhood under multi-partner fertility and the patterns of serial monogamy that are familiar in the west. The theory is founded on a basic biological asymmetry: men's fertility is virtually unlimited while women's fertility has a double digit maximum (Suchindran & Lachenbruch, 1975).

The economic theory of polygyny assumes that all women are identical, but that men are heterogeneous. With male heterogeneity comes the presence of some men with 2×, 3×, … N× multiples of the income of the average man. Suppose, the average income, x, supports the production of 5 average children. Monogamy creates a dilemma for a rich man making 10 times more than the average income. The 10× man's high income could potentially finance 50 children, but one wife could biologically only produce a maximum of around 15 (Suchindran & Lachenbruch, 1975). The rich man's remaining resources could be used to buy extra material goods or even hire extra nannies for the 15 children if he remained monogamous. This strategy would produce children with too much quality and not enough quantity and both quantity and quality are assumed to be valuable. Wealthy men constrained to monogamy would be forced to have a ratio of resources per child that was wastefully indulgent. It would be an inefficient way to maximize the number of high quality children. A rich man would be better off spreading his wealth among more children than one wife can bear, so he needs additional wives to achieve this goal. Polygyny allows the rich man to optimize the ratio of market goods to children to produce offspring with both higher quality and quantity.

The theory of polygyny assumes that there are neither negative nor positive externalities from having multiple co-mothers raising children. Positive externalities might ensue from having multiple stable caregivers for children. Negative externalities might ensue if there is rivalry among co-mothers set up by winner-take-all inheritance norms or simple jealousy. The theory also assumes that father's own time in child care can be perfectly substituted for by inputs from the co-mothers. Hence the 50 children of the 10× wealthy polygynist suffer no disadvantage relative to the 5 children of the 1× monogamist because co-mothers' time investments compensate for the 10 to 1 disparity in access to the undivided time with father faced by the polygynist's child.

Becker's theory of polygyny predicts that a system of polygyny leaves women no worse off than monogamy. "No worse off" is measured relative to a biological fitness criterion in which fitness is the ability to produce high quality children. The model presumes that all men and women are able to make non-coerced decisions to marry and leaves out 21st-century policy concerns related to the exploitation of teenage brides. The model also does not include other factors, such as jealousy and harmony. One expert on this matter would be noted polygynist, King Solomon, who wrote: Prov. 21:9 "[It is] better to dwell in a corner of the housetop, than with brawling women in a wide house."

Polygyny makes some men better off, but unequivocally makes the full population of men worse off. Not only does polygyny create a wife-shortage that denies reproductive opportunities to men with low income, but it accentuates competitive forces between men that compel every man to strive harder to acquire wealth to compete for extra wives. A monogamist equilibrium is characterized by higher equality among males and more fathers' time spent with children. As the average number of wives per husband increases, the level of equality between men will fall and children become less exposed to fathers (Becker, 1991). The relevance to

Western societies with a rising prevalence of serial monogamy and blended families is the implied prediction of a rising prevalence of male inequality and an increase in children's lifetime exposure to fatherlessness.

Post-Becker: Theories of Fatherhood—Bergstrom, Weiss, Willis

Theories of non-marital fatherhood bridged a chasm between the phenomenon of non-resident fathers paying little child support and Becker's theories, which explained intact households where co-resident fathers specialized in bringing in money to support their children. A facile (non-economic) explanation would have been that some men care about their children and others don't. Economists don't deny that people are indeed different, but, the goal of economics is to see how much of human behavior can be explained without appealing to variance in human preferences and motivation. Economists want to avoid using explanations that boil down to "They did this because that was what they preferred," and instead indicate how the circumstances around homogeneous actors could lead to variety in their behaviors. How could a single theory explain the emerging co-existence of deadbeat dads and Bill Cosby's character Cliff Huxtable?

Weiss and Willis's (1985) initial insight was literally as simple as pie If mother, father, and baby make three, the problem for the household was how to split a pie three ways. Bargaining over a pie between a pair of selfish adults (without a baby) is a zero sum affair—more for her is less for him. Bargaining with a baby's welfare at stake is far more intriguing. Weiss and Willis tabled Becker's concern about where the household's income came from and focused on how to divide up household income. Suspend gendered concepts of which parent "cares" more about baby. Weiss and Willis assume that basking in pride about their baby's accomplishments is a public good that both the man and the woman might value similarly. A parent's own consumption is something they value privately and differently. Using the concept of a utility function one can write for the father:

$$U_{Father}(Q_C, X_{Father}) = f_{Father}(\rho_f Q_C) + g(X_{Father}) \qquad [1]$$

where Q_C is an indicator of child's quality, and X_{Father} is the father's private consumption. Parameter ρ_f is the father's marginal utility of child quality. It measures how much happiness he gets from an incremental unit of the child's well-being. The equation says that a man's utility or "satisfaction with a state of affairs" depends on two things: the quality of his children and his own share of personal goods to consume. The function "f_{Father}" gets bigger as child quality increases and the function "g" gets bigger as the father has more goods to consume.
Mothers' utility would be:

$$U_{Mother}(Q_C, X_{Mother}) = f_{Mother}(\rho_m Q_C) + g(X_{Mother}) \qquad [2]$$

The maternal utility function is analogous to [1] except that ρ_m is not equal to ρ_f. These ρ factors are simple constants to determine how much satisfaction a parent gets from a unit of improvement of child quality. To keep things simple, we assume that child quality is just an increasing function of the child's share of resources:

$$Q_c = f_{child}(X_{Child}) \qquad [3]$$

This simple model allows ample insight into fatherhood. Note that the partners are both selfish with respect to each other—the model makes no provision for them to derive utility from each other. The fact that real partners actually do care about each other doesn't invalidate the model. That element of realism would distract from a distillation of the critical choices that selfish agents would make about child care. For now, equations [1] and [2] imply that they are willing to give up their own consumption for the baby, but not for each other. They "grudgingly" concede shares of the household income for their partner's consumption because they are forced to bargain over the fixed stock of resources.

Inherent in these three equations is an explanation for why fathers have co-resided and why societies have invested in cooperatively stabilizing unions through investing marriage with social rewards. Being in the household allows each parent to monitor the other's allocation to the child. Suppose the pie is divided as one-third for each parent and one-third for the child. This occurs after each has been satisfied that any other division could not make the parents better off. Both parents have sacrificed the other two-thirds of the pie. Co-residing helps each ensure that the baby gets the fair share that was agreed to. If the father was happy to concede two-thirds of the pie on condition that the baby receive one-third, he cannot be certain that the mother was content with actually allocating this entire third to the baby. What if she sneaks a little extra for herself? By being in the household, he can better monitor the other parent, and vice versa. The theory is completely symmetrical around gender—it equally explains why mothers co-reside. Part of being a non-custodial mother or father is suspicion that the child support payments that are being made are being consumed more by the custodial parent than the child. Without oversight, the custodial parent trades between allocating resources to themselves and their child according to their own personal willingness to make these tradeoffs. The non-custodial parent has few options for enforcing their own wishes on how these tradeoffs should play out.

If the non-custodial parent showers the custodial parent with resources hoping that their happiness will spill over into resources for the child, it does not alter that internal willingness to trade and can be much less effective than being inside the household to directly affect the consumption of the child. A self-centered parent receiving child support payments of $40 per month may be just as self-centered with $400 per month.

We will explore three extensions to this basic structure that will show its flexibility as a point of departure for exploring aspects of the economics of fatherhood: (a) Bergstrom Cornes Theorem; (b) the theory of out of wedlock child bearing; (c) the inefficiency of the child support system.

Bergstrom-Cornes Theorem

The basic assumption that child well-being is a public good can be a platform to analyze policies. There are a number of social policies to transfer financial assistance to low income mothers preferentially over fathers, with the reasoning that money in the hands of mothers will do more for children than money in the hands of fathers. Is there a theoretical justification for this?

If we take linear versions of equations [1] and [2], they would become:

$$U_{Father} = A(Q_c)X_{Father} + B_{Father}(Q_c) \qquad [1']$$

$$U_{Mother} = A(Q_c)X_{Mother} + B_{Mother}(Q_c) \qquad [2']$$

Here $A(Q_C)$ and $B(Q_C)$ are increasing functions of child quality. The linear version of the theory has a special property. The parents may disagree on how much direct satisfaction they get from child quality (because $B_{Father} \neq B_{Mother}$) but they agree on the extent to which child quality affects the satisfaction they obtain from all other aspects of life because $A(Q_c)$ is exactly the same for both parents. Someone who believes that mothers get more utility from their children's success than fathers would assume that $B_{Mother}(Q_c) > B_{Father}(Q_c)$ for all values of Q_c.

Bergstrom and Cornes theorem demonstrates that even if $B_{Mother} > B_{Father}$, that whether the father receives a windfall or the mother receives a windfall, the resultant child quality will be the same (Bergstrom & Cornes, 1983). The result only holds for these linearized versions of the parental utility function, but the reason it holds is crucial to the economics of fatherhood.

Let us suppose we are flies on the wall of a house where $B_{Father}(Q_c) = 0$ and $B_{Mother}(Q_c) > 0$. This implies that the child's welfare is of direct importance to the mother, but the father gets no direct happiness from improvements in their child's well-being. Each parent had been earning $2,000 a month and contributing $1,000 to their child's consumption and $1000 for themselves (Column A in the table below). Suppose the mother has qualified for a social program where she will receive a monthly $1,000 check made out specifically to her.

She tells her husband that because $B_{Mother}(Q_C) > 0$ that she will devote $700 from the check to improve Q_C. So she proposes the allocations shown in column B in Table 20.2. This makes the husband happier than before because $A(Q_C)$ will be bigger and according to equation [1'] he will derive more utility from his consumption of X_{Father}. But the father would be even better off if he took this opportunity to reduce his child contribution down to $300. He can be confident that the mother will make up the difference to keep the child no worse off at $2,000 as shown in column C. The bargaining may continue for several more rounds, but every time the mother tries to devote any of her new earnings to the child, the father will reduce his share accordingly, she finds that she cannot lift X_{Child} above $2,000.

Bergstrom-Cornes theorem has been tested. Thomas (1990) notes that income in the hands of mothers has 20 times the impact on child survival compared to fathers in developing country settings. Another study from the UK found that a child welfare allowance that was paid to wives led to additional spending on children's clothing (Lundberg, Pollak, & Wales, 1997).

Table 20.2   Bargaining between Father and Mother over Allocating a Windfall Experienced by the Mother.

	A	B	C
	Before the Social Program	After the Social Program: Mother Proposes	Father Counter Proposes
Income			
Father earns	$2,000	$2,000	$2,000
Mother earns	$2,000	$3,000	$3,000
Allocation			
X_{Father}	$1,000	$1,000	$1,700
X_{Mother}	$1,000	$1,300	$1,300
X_{Child}	$2,000 = ($1,000 from each parent)	$2,700 (= $1,700 from mother and $1,000 from father)	$2,000 (= $1,700 from mother and $300 from father)

Findings like this strongly suggests that $A(Q_C)$ cannot be the same for both parents. This is a stronger claim than simply claiming that mothers have a generally higher preference for child well-being. Bergstrom-Cornes theory predicted that children's consumption would not be increased by windfalls to either parent even if mothers had a higher concern for child consumption, $B_{Mother}(Q_C)$. The empirical findings suggest that mothers and fathers must differ in $A(Q_C)$ which reflects the *interaction* of child quality and their own consumption. In English, mothers take less joy in all other aspects of life than do fathers when their children are suffering. The empirical findings thus place limits on the intrinsic similarity of mothers and fathers. Mathematically, it is not simply that $B_{Mother}(Q_C) > B_{Father}(Q_C)$. The data requires that $A_{mom}(Q_c) > A_{dad}(Q_c)$ as well. This deeper insight is only available through the lens of an economic theory of parenting. The theory was symmetrical across gender and did not impose assumptions about which parent cared more about children, but the data showed that mothers and fathers are not symmetrical in how much their children's well-being matters. Gender differences in behavior cannot all be explained as deriving from the social environment.

Willis's Theory of Out of Wedlock Parenting

Willis's theory of out of wedlock childbearing offers a compelling model that explains why mothers who care deeply about having the best possible outcomes for their child, might nevertheless choose to have a non-marital birth (Willis, 1999). In Willis's model, there is a critical income, y^*, above which it is just barely possible to conceive and raise a child as a single parent. A heterogeneous distribution of earning ability distributes female incomes above and below this critical point. If there are factors that lead to a shortage of suitable men (e.g. poor male performance in the labor market; Wilson, 1987), marital sorting will lead the most well-off women to marry the most well-off men, leading to a male shortage that is most acutely experienced by low income women. Those whose incomes are higher than y^*, but not high enough to compete against other women for one of the scarce suitable men, will have sufficient resources to have a child outside of marriage, and they will do so.

In the absence of effective child support enforcement, women seeking to have children outside marriage need not fear that male offers of semen without paternal commitment will be scarce. Here, the theory is explicitly gendered. The biology of reproduction allows men to offer their gametes unencumbered by the immediate costs of a pregnancy. Men whose utility function depends heavily on the quality of their children would opt out of this system, but there would be some men who still volunteered for out of wedlock fatherhood. (It really only takes one man.) Out of wedlock child bearing may also be second best for women. Outcomes could be better for children receiving biparental care, primarily because two parents can devote their income, knowledge, and oversight to the process. (It may also be the case that being raised by multiple stable care-givers offers advantages in the range and repertoire of socializing encounters.) If outcomes are better under biparental care, then women who intentionally bear non-marital children must either have been denied access to adequate partners or perhaps they are prioritizing other life goals besides child quality (e.g., independence and autonomy).

Willis's model thus predicts that there will be adverse selection into non-marital childbearing for both men and women, and it suggests that at least part of the explanation for poorer child outcomes (e.g., school completion, test scores, birthweight, etc.) in single parent families may be due to unobservable factors that correlate both with child outcomes and the decision to have a non-marital birth despite controlling for the standard measures of race and socioeconomic status (SES). Willis's model also predicts that better child support enforcement would decrease the fertility of unmarried males by increasing their expectation of financial obligation if they do father a child (Aizer & McLanahan, 2005; Case, 1998).

Current Research Questions

The growth in non-resident fatherhood and the availability of datasets such as Fragile Families (McLanahan, Garfinkel, & Carlson, 2000) and The Three City Study (Angel et al., 2002) have enabled new analysis of the behavior of non-resident fathers and their responses to policy initiatives related to child support. The leading policy approach to non-resident fathers is to establish and enforce child support orders. Evaluating this policy has become an econometric challenge because the incidence of child support orders may be confounded with adverse selection. Not every mother seeks a child support order from the non-custodial parent—some may maintain a system of informal payments. Furthermore, men who comply with child-support orders are not a random sample of all men who receive the orders. One study finds that when one uses extensive covariates and lagged measures of child support to control for current payments, that current formal payments are not associated with father-child contact (Nepomnyaschy, 2007). This finding does not hold for informal payments.

An additional upcoming concern in current research efforts is an analysis of paternity establishment. Prior scholarship on fatherhood has focused on asymmetry between men and women in their wage offers and their control of resources. Paternity establishment research is based on asymmetrical biology between men and women. Child support agencies use genetic testing to establish paternity for men who do not voluntarily acknowledge paternity. Over the last 10 years, the use of lab-based paternity determination has increased to over 340,000 per year (American Association of Blood Banks, 2002). These tests cost about $90 per case and are capable of establishing a paternal relationship between a man and a child with 99.99+% certainty. State governments subsidize these tests for unmarried women receiving Temporary Assistance for Needy Families (TANF) in order to recoup funds and on the premise that paternity establishment and child support orders will improve child well-being. The rationale is that a man whose paternity is proven will be more likely to invest money and time in supporting a child, especially when compelled to make child support payments. Although few now doubt that child support payments are more likely when paternity is established (Argys, Peters, & Waldman, 2001; Freeman & Waldfogel, 2001; Miller & Garfinkel, 1999), there has been no systematic study of the effect of paternity testing on child outcomes or the effect on the father and mother's parental behavior. The tests have the potential for harm, in that there are substantial rates of contact between the men and the children tested, but roughly 25% of these involved men will learn that they are not the father and could sever their relationship with a child as a result of the test (Bishai, Astone, Argys, Gutendorf, & Filidoro, 2006).

Extending notions of child support beyond just financial support would appeal to the availability, interaction, and responsibility theory of fatherhood (Lamb, Pleck, Charnov, & Levine, 1985). To cast this approach in an economic framework one would start with a new version of equation [3] as follows:

$$Q_c = Q(\theta L_{Father}, L_{Mother}, X_{Child}) \qquad\qquad [4]$$

where θ is the fraction of a father's free time spent with children and L_{Father} is father's daily hours outside of wage labor and L_{Mother} is mother's daily hours. This model indicates that child quality depends on inputs of time from each parent, L_{Parent}, and resources X_{Child}. That time spent with children improves their quality is uncontroversial. What remains unknown is whether father's time has independent and qualitatively different effects on children's outcomes from mother's time. This remains among the most important questions in studies of fatherhood.

If mother's time is just as productive as father's time then parenting time should be allocated by the labor market as described by Becker and the outcome won't change. Family policy across the United States and Europe has essentially assumed that father's time is as productive as mother's time. Child support enforcement is directed to ensure that men stick with their responsibilities to supply money to children they have fathered. Father's time with the child is viewed to be an indulgence to be enjoyed at the discretion of the father. It is not viewed as a critical input into child quality. In theory, time spent with fathers can help children understand the world of adult men and offer connections to male culture that would be valuable for the successful socialization of sons or daughters.

The American Academy of Pediatrics (Coleman, Garfield, & Committee on Psychosocial Aspects of Child and Family Health, 2004) and several independent groups (Allen & Daly, 2003; Magill-Evans, Harrison, Rempel, & Slater, 2006; McLanahan & Sandefur, 1994; Sarkadi, Kristiansson, Oberklaid, & Bremberg, 2008) have reviewed the literature on this topic. The quality of the studies in this literature is variable—as discussed in the next section existing literature suffers from endogeneity bias. That means that the "independent" variable of father involvement could be correlated with unmeasured or omitted confounders that are related to the "dependent" variables of maternal and child health and well-being. For instance, Levy-Shiff found in a study of 50 preterm infants that the number of paternal visits was positively correlated with later weight gain and improved social personal development (Gesell Scores) at 8 and 18 months (Levy-Shiff, Hoffman, Mogilner, Levinger, & Mogilner, 1990). A similar analysis in Finland found similar outcomes (Latva, Lehtonen, Salmelin, & Tamminen, 2004). Tamis-LeMonda, Shannon, Cabrera, and Lamb (2004) videotaped fathers' engagement styles and found correlations between engaged father behavior and later measures of child development. However, if unobservable salutary household factors or even fortuitous child personality traits predicted which fathers behaved better, it would account for these findings and it would be inappropriate to attribute causal impact to the fathers' behavior rather than the other factors. Fathers may practice "adverse" selection, choosing only to become more involved when they observe that their child needs extra attention, or "positive" selection, becoming more involved with healthier more engaging children. Ethnicity and language have also been shown to alter father's level of engagement (Cabrera, Shannon, West, & Brooks-Gunn, 2006).

Research Measurement and Methodology

Applied economics focuses on obtaining causal inferences about the statistical connections between the socioeconomic environment of families and family outcomes. Economists often use the term "endogeneity" to describe their concern that an independent variable with a putative causal effect on the independent outcome variable is actually linked to the outcome through either reverse causation or through a simultaneous process that is not depicted by the model.

The best example would be an attempt to test the hypothesis that a father's presence in the household causes better child outcomes. With panel data on father's presence and child outcomes, the statistical model of equation [4] would be:

$$\text{Child Outcome}_{it} = C + \beta_1 \text{FatherExposure}_{it\text{-}1} + \beta_2 X_{it} + \mu_i + \varepsilon_{it} \qquad [5]$$

Father Exposure is a variable that is chosen "endogenously" by the household and can be modeled as:

$$\text{Father Exposure}_{it} = \gamma_0 + \gamma_1 X_{it} + \gamma_2 \text{Child Outcome}_{it} + \mu_i + \varepsilon_{it} \qquad [6]$$

The μ_i term that appears in both equation [5] and [6] represents unobserved features of the household that determine both how much father exposure is occurring and child outcomes. For example μ_i might reflect substance use, mental illness, employment patterns, intelligence, or relationship quality. Efforts to just measure more variables cannot possibly account for all the possible features of life in the household that might matter. Because [6] says that Father Exposure is correlated with μ_i it implies that in equation [5] that the β_1 is measured with bias because Father Exposure is correlated with the error term—violating a critical assumption for regression analysis.

Panel data techniques like using fixed effects or random effects models are not adequate to solve the problem because as indicated by equation [6] father's exposure is simultaneously caused by child outcomes. Men may be more or less likely to be involved depending on how successful/unsuccessful their child is. The methodological solution in simultaneous systems like this is difficult. Economists search for natural experiments that might alter father exposure but have no effect on child outcome except for their effect on father exposure. An example would be a paternity leave act with differences in date or place of implementation. Instrumental variable approaches are based essentially on stipulating that sets of variables have the same function as natural experiments: they predict father exposure but have no other direct effect on children.

To date, economists have found methodological fault with virtually all attempts to show a link between father exposure and child outcomes. Extensive studies in the literature (Cherlin, Chase-Lansdale, & McRae, 1998; McLanahan & Sandefur, 1994) have either limited their methodological correction to fixed effects corrections or not bothered to correct for endogeneity. No work to date has successfully invoked a natural experiment or unimpeachable instrument that would predict father involvement in order to identify its causal effects on child outcomes. This very compelling hypothesis still requires a proper test.

Bridges to Other Disciplines

Paternity uncertainty lies at the foundation of many evolutionary perspectives on fathers discussed by Waynforth (this volume). This uncertainty may lie at the heart of the asymmetry between men and women in the way child outcomes matter. When a model stipulates that a father's utility function depends on child well-being, it implies that the child belongs to that father. Paternity uncertainty for animals implies that a father's fitness calculations must multiply the utility of each putative child times the probability that they are the father. This great biological insight has been formalized as Hamilton's rule (Hamilton, 1964). In non-human species where much of parenting behavior is instinctual a father's instinctual propensity to care for offspring will evolve to be proportional to the average level of paternity certainty in that species. Human fathers' solicitousness is diagnostic of millennia of high levels of paternity certainty. Observing that human fathers might not be as solicitous as human mothers suggests that paternity certainty, though high, has not been 100% as high as that of mothers.

For individual humans it is unclear exactly why biological non-paternity should matter so much—however socially created norms seem to reinforce this custom. Television shows have made it a cliché to observe angry cuckolded fathers receiving the DNA test results that make them think that an emotional bond they have formed with a child is now illegitimate because of a biological test result. The experience of adoptive parents proves that humans can learn to love and care for any child over time and get satisfaction regardless of a genetic relationship.

Game theory has become a shared tool that bridges economics to evolutionary biology. Game theoretic perspectives have been able to show the conditions where biparental care can become an evolutionarily stable alternative to male-only or female-only care patterns (Yaniv & Motro, 2004).

Given human diversity in the expression of fatherhood—cooperation between economists and biologists can be fruitful in explaining fatherhood in a species like humans where there are so many various parenting patterns. Part of the solution to this riddle lies in explaining why there are any differences between males and females. The question of sexual differences is not the question of why there is sexual reproduction? Many answers to the question, "Why is there sex?" leave unanswered, "Why are the sexes so different?" If males and females were identical except for their gametes, there would be little point to studying fathers.

So why are fathers different from mothers? Biologists have parsed flora and fauna into k-strategists and r-strategists to stress how "k" species emphasize offspring quality and "r" species emphasize offspring quantity (Rushton, 1988; see Storey & Walsh, this volume). Ecologists then explain these different categories as emerging from environments where some niches favor "r" strategists and some favor "k" strategists. One can view the r vs. k dichotomy as operating even within the same species. In general, high male sperm counts make males the relative "r" strategists within a species while females are the species specialists in "k" strategies. If the sexes diverge in their focus on quantity and quality, sexual reproduction insists that each offspring inherit traits from a successful "k" strategist and from a successful "r" strategist. In game theory these offspring can be said to have played a game in mixed strategies (Gibbons, 1997). The "game" is the organism's strategic choice of genetic alleles and social memes to yield maximal fitness against the shifting selective forces of nature.

In many games the "best" move can often be a statistical superposition of two different moves. Suppose programmers of a chess playing robot like "Deep Blue" found a situation where moving bishop to the left was the best move with 70% probability and moving bishop to the right was the best move with 30% probability. The programmers would then instruct the machine to actually play "left" 70% of the times it faced that situation and "right" the other 30% of times. That would actually be better than telling Deep Blue to always play "left". The genetic and phenotypical differences between fathers and mothers pass along a broader repertoire to offspring of both sexes. This allows each individual of any gender to play elements of "r" or "k" reproductive strategies with non-zero probability. Male and female phenotypes determine gamete size and number giving men a relative advantage at r strategies and women an advantage at k, when needed. But sex offers individuals a flexible repertoire. Social and economic circumstances can shift the emphasis from r to k and vice versa.

Viewed in this light, sexual reproduction combining sexually dimorphic parents forces newborns to successfully combine a genetic draw that is 50% k strategist and 50% r strategist. Each generation is forced to have parents who have *both* succeeded at the respective strategies. When economists observe games where winners are playing mixed strategies they interpret this as a way to hedge against incomplete information about what the opponent's next move will be (Gibbons, 1997). In the game between the organism and nature—nature's next move is uncertain and the organism, regardless of gender, will need to be able to draw on both r- and k-related traits. Gendered differences in reproductive strategies, may often be exaggerated through a process of sexual selection. But gender differences also have the potential to add versatility to an organism's survival repertoire that can be used to weather climatic changes or new threats to survival from predation or social forces. Greater parental dimorphism offers the organism a wider library of traits that have proven their worth in each parent's respective struggle to reproduce. *"Vive la difference"* indeed!

Policy Implications

Child support enforcement plays a very positive role in improving child well-being, but it remains focused on money and not time allocation. As per Willis's theory, enforcing paternity obligations is predicted to lower male willingness to participate in out of wedlock childbearing and to select partners more carefully. This prediction has received empirical support in a study of both the Fragile Families data and in fixed effects analysis of state natality files. States with stricter child support enforcement have lower fertility and higher rates of prenatal care (Aizer, 2006). Women in the Fragile Families study who anticipated future child support from their non-marital partners were more likely to seek prenatal care earlier. Child support enforcement can also improve cognitive outcomes for children (Argys, Peters, Brooks-Gunn, & Smith, 1998) and it clearly does improve the financial situation of children in non-marital unions (Argys & Peters, 2001). Argys's papers achieved causal inference because they used an instrumental variables approach whereby the probability that a man would pay child support was predicted by his state's success level in child support enforcement. Child support enforcement can have ambiguous effects on time spent with children. One analysis indicated higher rates of father-child contact resulting from child support enforcement (Argys et al., 1998). The studies by Argys and Peters focused on how exogenous policy changes affecting payment had an impact on fathers' time use so it does not suffer from pitfalls of reverse causality where fathers who actually spend time with children would be more likely to pay child support. However, there are theoretical reasons that child-visitation could diminish if custodial mothers "sell" child visitation to achieve child support payment compliance (Del Boca & Ribero, 2001).

Figure 20.1 illustrates the father's dilemma. With child support enforcement, a man is obligated to pay money to Temporary Assistance for Needy Families (TANF). He unambiguously must spend time in the labor force to make these payments and this reduces his time available for other uses including child visitation. There would be reasons for the non-custodial father to increase time with children after a child support order, if the child support was supplying new resources to the mother that he would like to ensure reached the child. However as shown in Figure 20.1, U.S. child support payments for women on TANF do not go to the mother. Typically, only $50 of the man's payment passes through to the mother (Vinson & Turetsky, 2009). The state retains the balance and allocates TANF payments to the mother according to her eligibility.

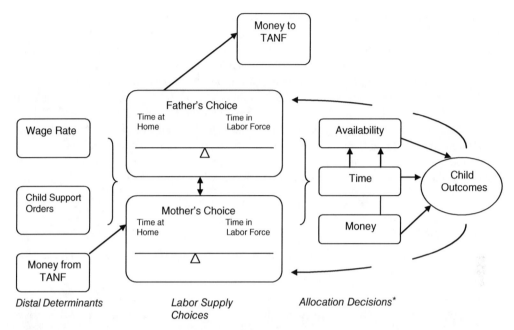

FIGURE 20.1 Conceptual model relating allocation of parental time and money to child outcomes.

If it were discovered that time spent with fathers had independent salutary effects on child outcomes, state policies would need to be altered to enable and encourage non-custodial fathers to spend more time with their child in lieu of or in addition to monetary payments. For instance, non-custodial fathers might receive child support credits if their child care time contributions become dependable enough to enable a mother to participate in the labor market. The recognition of independent effects of time with fathers would change the calculus of all parents in their daily time allocation.

Future Directions

This chapter has shown how the starting point of the economics of fatherhood remains the foundation laid by Becker in his theory of the allocation of time. Child outcomes are "produced" by fathers and mothers out of their allocations of time and resources. Parents must jointly decide on the scope of these allocations. Even though the economics of the family begins with the allocation of time to children, we know surprisingly little about how productivity of fathers' time differs from that of mothers' time. Natural experiments that alter men's contact with children may some day offer a platform on which to derive causal estimates of the differential impact of father's time with children from mother's time with children. There are interventions that could be experimentally allocated to fathers to alter their subsequent engagement with children (Fagan, 2008; Melnyk et al., 2006), and these interventions could be used to identify causal effects. Identifying conclusively what children gain from engagement with their fathers remains of utmost impact for the field.

The future of scholarship in the economics of fatherhood must continue to adapt with the modern variety of family forms and expressions of fatherhood. There has been a refreshing wave of studies looking at the impact of fatherhood on fathers (Bianchi, Subaiya, & Kahn, 1999; see chapter by Eggebeen, Knoester, & McDaniels, this volume). With an aging population, contact between fathers and their adult children will echo the profound shifts in families. There is emerging evidence of a growing number of "lonely old men." Many non-marital fathers or divorced fathers have become estranged from their children and suffer deficits in intergenerational transfers of money, not to mention child visitation time (Pezzin & Schone, 1999). Data are emerging that a flip side of diminished connections between fathers and their children occurs in old age. Men who spent more time divorced show health effects with more chronic conditions and mobility limitations (Hughes & Waite, 2009). Economic theories of the fatherhood are destined to mature.

References

Aizer, A. (2006). The impact of child support enforcement on fertility, parental investment, and child well-being. *Journal of Human Resources, 41*(1), 28–45.

Aizer, A., & McLanahan, S. (2005). *The impact of child support enforcement on fertility, parental investment and child well-being.* Cambridge, MA: National Bureau of Economic Research.

Allen, S. M., & Daly, K. (2003). The effects of father invovlement: A summary of the research evidence. U. O. Guelph (Ed.). Retrieved from http://www.cfii.ca/fiion/fiionconvincers.pdf

American Association of Blood Banks. (2002). *Annual report summary for testing in 2001* Bethesda, MD.

Angel, R., Burton, L., Chase-Lansdale, L., Cherlin, A., Moffitt, R., & Julius Wilson, W. (2002). Welfare Children and Families, A Three City Study. Retrieved April 9, 2012, from http://web.jhu.edu/three-citystudy/index.html

Argys, L. M., & Peters, H. E. (2001). Interactions between unmarried fathers and their children: The role of paternity establishment and child-support policies. *American Economic Review, 91*(2), 125–129.

Argys, L. M., Peters, H. E., Brooks-Gunn, J., & Smith, J. R. (1998). The impact of child support on cognitive outcomes of young children. *Demography, 35*(2), 159–173.

Argys, L. M., Peters, H. E., & Waldman, D. M. (2001). Can the Family Support Act put some life back into deadbeat dads. *Journal of Human Resources, 36*(2), 226–252.

Becker, G. (1991). *Families in non human species: A treatise on the family.* Cambridge, MA: Harvard Press.

Becker, G. S. (1981). *A treatise on the family* (2nd ed.). Cambridge, MA: Harvard University Press.

Bergstrom, T., & Cornes, R. (1983). Independence of allocative efficiency from distribution in the theory of public goods. *Econometrica, 51*, 1753–1765.

Bianchi, S., Subaiya, L., & Kahn, J. R. (1999). The gender gap in the economic well-being of non-resident fathers and custodial mothers. *Demography, 36*(2), 195–203.

Bianchi, S., Wight, V., & Raley, S. (2005). *Maternal employment and family caregiving: Rethinking time with children in the ATUS.* College Park, MD: University of Maryland.

Bishai, D. (1996). Quality time: How parents' schooling affects child health through its interaction with childcare time in Bangladesh. *Health Economics, 5*, 383–407.

Bishai, D., Astone, N., Argys, L., Gutendorf, R., & Filidoro, C. (2006). A national sample of US paternity tests: do demographics predict test outcomes? *Transfusion, 46*(5), 849–853.

Cabrera, N. J., Shannon, J. D., West, J., & Brooks-Gunn, J. (2006). Parental interactions with Latino infants: variation by country of origin and English proficiency. *Child Development, 77*(5), 1190–1207. doi:CDEV928 [pii] 10.1111/j.1467-8624.2006.00928.x

Case, A. (1998). The effect of stronger child support enforcement on nonmarital fertility. In I. Garfinkel, S. McLanahan, D. Meyer, & J. A. Seltzer (Eds.), *Fathers under fire* (pp. 191–215). New York: Russell Sage.

Cherlin, A. J., Chase-Lansdale, P. L., & McRae, C. (1998). Effects of parental divorce on mental health throughout the life course. *American Sociological Review, 63*(2), 239–249.

Coleman, W. L., Garfield, C., & Committee on Psychosocial Aspects of Child and Family Health. (2004). Fathers and pediatricians: Enhancing men's roles in the care and development of their children. *Pediatrics, 113*(5), 1406–1411.

Del Boca, D., & Ribero, R. (2001). The effect of child-support policies on visitations and transfers. *American Economic Review, 91*(2), 130–134.

Fagan, J. (2008). Randomized study of a prebirth coparenting intervention with adolescent and young fathers. *Family Relations, 57*, 309–323.

Freeman, R. B., & Waldfogel, J. (2001). Dunning delinquent dads: The effects of child support enforcement policy on child support receipt by never married women. *Journal of Human Resources, 36*(2), 207–225.

Galor, O., & Weil, D. (1996). The gender gap, fertility and growth. *American Economic Review, 86*(3), 374–387.

Gibbons, R. (1997). An introduction to applicable game theory. *Journal of Economic Perspectives, 11*(1), 127–150.

Grossbard-Schechtman, S. (1988). Women's labor supply and marital choice. *Journal of Political Economy, 96*(6), 1294–1302.

Hamilton, W. D. (1964). The genetical theory of docial behaviour. *Journal of Theoretical Biology, 7*(1), 1–16.

Hughes, M. E., & Waite, L. (2009). Marital biography and health at mid-life. *Journal of Health and Social Behavior, 50*(3), 344–358.

Lamb, D., Pleck, J., Charnov, E. L., & Levine, J. A. (1985). Paternal behavior in humans. *American Zoologist, 25*, 883–894.

Latva, R., Lehtonen, L., Salmelin, R. K., & Tamminen, T. (2004). Visiting less than every day: a marker for later behavioral problems in Finnish preterm infants. *Archives of Pediatrics and Adolescent Medicine, 158*(12), 1153–1157.

Levy-Shiff, R., Hoffman, M. A., Mogilner, S., Levinger, S., & Mogilner, M. B. (1990). Fathers' hospital visits to their preterm infants as a predictor of father-infant relationship and infant development. *Pediatrics, 86*(2), 289–293.

Lundberg, S., Pollak, R. A., & Wales, T. (1997). Do Husbands and Wives Pool Their Resources? Evidence from the United Kingdon Child Benefit. *Journal of Human Resources, 32*(3), 463.

Magill-Evans, J., Harrison, M. J., Rempel, G., & Slater, L. (2006). Interventions with fathers of young children: systematic literature review. Journal of Advanced Nursing, 55(2), 248–264.

McLanahan, S., Garfinkel, I., Reichman, N., Teitler, J., Carlson, M., & Norland Audigier, C. (2003). *The Fragile Families and Child Wellbeing Study: Baseline National Report (Revised March 2003)*. Princeton, NJ: Bendheim-Thoman Center for Research on Child Wellbeing.

McLanahan, S., & Sandefur, G. (1994). *Growing up with a single parent*. Cambridge, MA: Harvard University Press.

Melnyk, B. M., Feinstein, N. F., Alpert-Gillis, L., Fairbanks, E., Crean, H. F., Sinkin, R. A., … Gross, S. J. (2006). Reducing premature infants' length of stay and improving parents' mental health outcomes with the Creating Opportunities for Parent Empowerment (COPE) neonatal intensive care unit program: a randomized, controlled trial. *Pediatrics, 118*(5) e1414–27

Miller, C., & Garfinkel, I. (1999). The determinants of paternity establishment and child support award rates among unmarried women. *Population Research and Policy Review, 18*, 237–260.

Moffitt, R. A. (2000). Welfare benefits and female headship in U.S. Time Series. *American Economic Review, 90*(2), 373–377.

Mulligan, C., & Rubinstein, Y. (2008). Selection, investment, and women's relative wages over time. *Quarterly Journal of Economics, 123*(3), 1061–1110.

Nepomnyaschy, L. (2007). Child support and father-child contact. *Demography, 44*(1), 93–112.

Pezzin, L., & Schone, B. (1999). Parental marital disruption and intergenerational transfers: An analysis of lone elderly parents and their children. *Demography, 36*(3), 287–297.

Rushton, J. P. (1988). Do r/K reproductive strategies apply to human differences? *Social Biology, 35*(3–4), 337–340.

Sarkadi, A., Kristiansson, R., Oberklaid, F., & Bremberg, S. (2008). Fathers' involvement and children's developmental outcomes: a systematic review of longitudinal studies. *Acta Paediatr, 97*(2), 153–158.

Sayer, L., Bianchi, S., & Robinson, J. P. (2004). Are parents investing less in children? Trends in mothers' and fathers' time with children. *American Journal of Sociology, 110*(1), 1–43.

Suchindran, C. M., & Lachenbruch, P. A. (1975). Estimates of fecundability from a truncated distribution of conception times. *Demography, 12*(2), 291–301.

Tamis-LeMonda, C. S., Shannon, J. D., Cabrera, N. J., & Lamb, M. E. (2004). Fathers and mothers at play with their 2- and 3-year-olds: contributions to language and cognitive development. *Child Development, 75*(6), 1806–1820.

Thomas, D. (1990). Intra-household resource allocation: An inferential approach. *The Journal of Human Resources, 25*(4), 635–664.

Vinson, M., & Turetsky, V. (2009). State shild support pass-through policies. Washington, DC: Center for Law and Social Policy (CLASP).

Weiss, Y., & Willis, R. J. (1985). Children as collective goods and divorce settlements. *Journal of Labor Economics, 3*(3), 268–292.

Willis, R. J. (1999). A theory of out of wedlock childbearing. *Journal of Political Economy, 107*(6), S33–S64.

Wilson, W. J. (1987). *The Truly Disadvantaged*. Chicago: University of Chicago Press.

Yaniv, O., & Motro, U. (2004). The parental investment conflict in continuous time: St. Peter's fish as an example. *Journal of Theoretical Biology, 228*(3), 377–388.

Chapter 21

Fathers, Divorce, and Child Custody

Matthew M. Stevenson, Sanford L. Braver,
Ira M. Ellman, and Ashley M. Votruba

Arizona State University

Historical Overview and Theoretical Perspectives

Introduction

A great many fathers will have their fathering eliminated, disrupted, or vastly changed because they become divorced from the child's mother. In fact, between 40% and 50% of marriages end in divorce (Cherlin, 2010). Although the divorce rate (measured as divorces per 1,000 people) is high by the standards prior to the late 1960s, it has actually fallen more than 30% since its peak in 1980. The decline in divorce rates in recent years has, however, been concentrated among the college-educated portion of the population; divorce rates among the less-well educated may have even increased (Cherlin, 2010). But for both groups, divorce remains the most prevalent reason for changes in paternal parenting opportunities. For almost all divorced fathers (as well as for most mothers and children), divorce is a life-defining event, around which all other experiences are organized: before the divorce versus after the divorce. Although mothers' parenting is generally changed by divorce, the revision to the parent-child interaction patterns is generally not as far-reaching as it is to fathers' (Braver & Lamb, in press; Braver, Shapiro, & Goodman, 2005; Fabricius, Braver, Diaz, & Velez, 2010). The reason, of course, is the radical difference between the two parents' custodial arrangements that typically occurs. As will be documented more precisely below, mothers generally become chief custodians of children, with fathers having visiting rights only. Although that situation has changed in recent years, due in large part to the fact that research has accumulated that illuminates the unintended negative consequences of that practice on fathers and children, it remains normative. Thus, no review of fathers and divorce can be complete or enlightening unless it also considers custody matters, as we do here.

Child Custody Distinctions

A number of distinctions concerning child custody are important to understand. *Legal custody* refers to the right to make decisions regarding medical care, education, religion, etc., of the child, whereas *physical custody* refers to the living arrangements, and rights and responsibilities for the daily care of the child. With respect to legal custody, *joint legal custody* allows a continuation of decision making authority the parents had before the divorce: either parent may make these parental decisions. In practice, this arrangement requires some degree of coordination and agreement between the parents. *Sole legal custody,* in contrast, grants major decision making rights exclusively to one parent, the "custodial" parent, who is solely authorized to make decisions regarding the child without regard to the views of the other parent. With respect to physical custody, in *joint physical custody,* the child spends substantial time living with each parent. Time splits in the latter are often not 50%–50%; time distributions as unequal as 30%–70% are often deemed joint physical custody (Kelly, 2007; Venohr & Griffith, 2005). With *sole physical custody,* the child lives primarily with one parent, with the other (noncustodial or nonresidential) parent typically having visitation rights, such as on weekends, holidays, and vacations. There is a natural association between the two divisions of custody: Joint *physical* custody parents almost always share joint *legal* custody, as well; but parents with joint *legal* custody may or may not also have joint *physical* custody.

History of Child Custody Standards

Child custody policies have changed greatly over the course of history, generally following the prevailing gender roles of the time (Braver & O'Connell, 1998; Mason, 1994). English law originally followed Roman practice and applied a broad preference for paternal custody (but English law at this time did not allow divorce except by Act of Parliament, which means occasions on which to apply the rule were limited). By the early 19th century, however, American courts were applying the "tender years doctrine," under which it was presumed best to place young children with their mothers (sometimes combined with a preference for placing older children with their fathers), and this became the dominant rule for much of the 20th century. However, reform beginning in the 1960s eventually led all states to adopt the Best Interest of the Child standard (BIS), in which what should prevail was whatever arrangement was deemed best for the child (Ellman et al., 2010). While there is some variation among the states, the version of BIS set out in 1970 by the Uniform Marriage and Divorce Act is broadly representative. It specifies that in determining the child's best interests, a court should consider: (a) the wishes of the child's parents as to custody; (b) the wishes of the child as to custody; (c) the interaction and relationship of the child with his parents, his siblings, and any person who may significantly affect the child's best interest; (d) the child's adjustment to his home, school, and community; and (e) the mental and physical health of all individuals involved. The BIS also has been adopted internationally by the United Nations under article 9.1 of the United Nations Convention of the Rights of the Child (1989).

The BIS has generally been viewed as an improvement over past standards because it focuses on the needs and interests of children as the impetus for custody decisions rather than on justice for the parents, the gender or parental rights of the parents, or other standards (Schepard, 2004). In addition, the BIS has been praised for being flexible, simple, and egalitarian, and for allowing individualized decision making (Chambers, 1984; Warshak, 2007). However, considerable criticism has also been leveled at the BIS because its definition of children's best interests is so vague (Emery, Otto, & O'Donohue, 2005; Tippins & Wittman, 2005). Some have argued that the ambiguity of that standard enables judges to rely on idiosyncratic biases and subjective value judgments (Chambers, 1984); allows judges to favor one gender (mothers: Warshak, 2007; fathers: Polikoff, 1982); and that the unpredictability of judicial outcomes due to BIS promotes custody litigation (O'Connell, 2007). Several hotly debated alternative child custody standards have been proposed to address various perceived drawbacks of the BIS and are discussed at length in a recent book chapter (Fabricius et al., 2010), but are beyond the scope of the present chapter.

Theoretical Perspectives

Attachment theory is important with respect to child custody, in that custody standards have continually sought to maintain close relationships between one or both parents with their children following divorce. Implicit in custody decisions is the importance of high quality parenting to enable strong, positive relationships to form between parents and their children. Although early theories of attachment focused on mother-child attachment (interestingly child custody statistics also favored mothers), more recently theorists have begun to consider the unique role played by the father in the exploration system (Paquette, 1994). In this sense, the father is thought to open children up to the world and promote exploration, particularly in arousing play contexts that improve children's ability to assess and take risks, improve social skills, and reduce inappropriate aggression in social contexts. This perspective of the father as an agent to further exploration places the father in a complimentary role to the mother, considered more apt to provide comfort, soothing, and a secure base in times of distress. Thus, recent theoretical advances argue that children receive complimentary benefits from both mothers and fathers, provided both parents are fit to parent.

Family systems theory (Cox & Paley, 1997) holds that the functioning of any relationship in a family is influenced by the characteristics of relationships in other family subsystems, through the principle of interdependence. For example, parents engaging in conflict, whether before or after divorce, negatively affect the quality of parent-child relationships. Family systems theory is near-ubiquitous in guiding research on divorce, parent conflict, and child outcomes, and has some influence in custody law. For example, some states have a "friendly parent" provision in custody statutes, which favors the parent who is more likely to encourage continuing child contact with the other parent.

Current Research Questions

We believe that the most important issue confronting custody research concerns the BIS and its application in current practice and policy. After a brief overview of measurement issues in child custody research, we next examine, under the heading "Empirical Findings," the following issues about which research has provided rather firm answers: (a) What are the rates of various child custody arrangements? (b) What is the process of obtaining a custody arrangement? (c) What factors impact children's adjustment postdivorce? (d) What measures are currently used in custody evaluations under the BIS? (e) Do other measures exist in psychological research that can be used to improve custody evaluations? (f) Are there empirically-based intervention programs in existence that improve parenting and children's outcomes? Finally, we conclude with sections on "Bridges to Other Disciplines," "Policy Implications," and "Future Directions."

Research Measurement and Methodology

We should begin by noting one limitation in our discussion of measurement in custody decision making. Custody decisions necessarily involve value judgments as well as factual assessments. For example, courts must consider values about which parents may differ: whether parents want their children to be religious or freethinking, spirited or compliant, aggressive or modest, creative or conventional. Parents of different religious faiths may have conflicting views on what their children should be taught to believe. Some parents want their children to appreciate and accept diversity in sexual orientation, but others want them to view heterosexuality as morally superior to homosexuality. Courts have often struggled when required to resolve *value* conflicts of this kind, and with good reason (Ellman, 1999a, 2003; Ellman et al., 2010). Such conflicts over values are beyond the scope of this chapter to the extent they do not have an impact on child outcome variables that existing research findings can measure with accepted indicators of child maladjustment (such as mental health problems), or developmental competence (Masten & Coatsworth, 1998) (such as indicators of success in developmental tasks like school or employment). Our operational definition of *the child's best interests* is therefore positive outcomes on measures of child adjustment, mental health, and developmental competence.

In a later section, we also review and critique measures that are common in child custody evaluations by professional psychologists, and suggest other factors that could and should be measured.

Empirical Findings

Child Custody Statistics

Several studies have examined jurisdiction, state, and national-level data on physical and legal custody rates in the United States, and found that custody arrangements differ drastically between mothers and fathers, as noted in the introduction. Joint physical custody of children was specified in only 2%–6% of cases, fathers received primary physical custody in 8%–14% of cases, while in fully 68%–88% of cases, mothers received primary physical custody (Argys et al., 2007; Braver & O'Connell, 1998; Maccoby & Mnookin, 1992; Seltzer, 1990). However, research suggests that the amount of time specified with nonresident parents has generally increased in recent decades. Before the 1980s, most decrees specified the traditional pattern: that children should spend every other weekend with the nonresident parent, which is about 14% of children's time (Kelly, 2007). Two methodologically identical studies on randomly selected case files in Arizona the late-80s and late-90s, respectively (Braver & O'Connell, 1998; DeLusé, 1999) found the decade was marked by increases in the parenting time ordered, such as added visitation during the week, and uninterrupted weeks with the nonresidential parent during the summer. The present century registered even further increases. A review of randomly selected cases in Arizona for divorces filed in 2001–2002, indicated that about half of the decrees specified 24%–32% of the days of the year for noncustodial parenting time, and another fifth specified 33%–50% of the days of the year (Venohr & Griffith, 2003). Fewer than one fifth of the cases specified as little as the formerly traditional every-other-weekend. By 2008, 29% of decrees specified more than 35% of time with the nonresident parent and parenting time was essentially equally divided in about 22% of those cases (Venohr & Kaunelis, 2008). The recent increase in Arizona nonresidential parenting time appears to be matched in other states: 24% of divorcing parents in Wisconsin had equal parenting time according to 2003 data (Brown & Cancian, 2007), and 46% of fathers in Washington state received at least 35% parenting time in 2007–2008 (George, 2008).

With respect to joint legal custody, rates appear to be more variable from state to state, ranging from as low as 21% (Seltzer, 1990) to as high as 76% (Maccoby & Mnookin, 1992) and 93% (Douglas, 2003). However, joint legal custody rates also seem to be generally increasing over time, despite their increased variability (Braver et al., 2005). Interestingly, changes in rates of legal and physical custody appear to be informal and unofficial rather than resulting from a formal rule change (Fabricius et al., 2010).

Process of Obtaining a Divorce and a Custody Arrangement

Every state has statutes that provide its courts with authority to determine the custody of children when their parents separate. Custody law makes no distinction between divorcing parents and unmarried parents, once the identity of the legal father is established, and about one-third of custody decrees issued by family courts involve unmarried parents. Although a judicial decree setting forth the custody arrangement is the final result of any case, the standard procedure for reaching that result varies among states. The dominant trend is away from the traditional adversarial system employed in normal civil litigation. Contested custody contests in which a judge must decide between competing parental claims are relatively rare; for example, a California study found 25 years ago that more than 78% of divorcing parents agreed on their custody arrangement from the very beginning of their case (Maccoby & Mnookin, 1992). Most of the rest come to an agreement before a judge was asked to decide; studies find judicial resolution of a contested custody dispute occurs in only 2%–10% of divorces (Braver & O'Connell, 1998; Maccoby & Mnookin, 1992).

A variety of forces push parents to agree. In many states, the courts themselves adopt a variety of measures to encourage them to do so—and to discourage them from asking for judicial resolution. Semple (2011) notes that this "settlement mission" (the effort to bring about a voluntary resolution between the adult parties) has largely replaced the courts' former "analytical mission" (the effort to determine what parenting arrangement would be in the best interests of the child or children involved; i.e., to determine the "right answer"). Mediation, in which a neutral professional facilitates the resolution of custody, parenting time, and other child-related disputes, is often required of the parents before they may have access to judicial resolution (Braver & O'Connell, 1998). Judges may meet with parties before the mediation to impress upon them the importance of coming to agreement to their children. (For more on mediation and dispute resolution see Applegate, Schwartz, & Holtzworth-Munroe, this volume). There is general agreement among professionals that a negotiated or mediated settlement is better for children than the judicial resolution of custody contests, which many believe can promote long-lasting and deleterious parental conflict (Pruett & Jackson, 1999). Some studies have found that no attorney at all was involved in about 30% of divorces, and only one attorney in an additional 30% (Braver & O'Connell, 1998); thus the proportion of two-attorney cases appears to be decreasing, although this differs by state. In recent years, parent education classes have become more commonplace in an attempt to help facilitate negotiations, improve parental agreements, and prevent parents from litigating; yet there is little evidence that they are achieving the intended effect (Goodman, Bonds, Sandler, & Braver, 2004; Sigal, Sandler, Wolchik, & Braver, 2011).

In 5%–10% of cases, an expert (usually a psychologist) is hired by the parents to evaluate the family and make non-binding custody recommendations, often first to the parents and later to the court if settlement is not reached (Gould & Martindale, 2007). However, the legal and ethical propriety, and scientific basis of custody evaluations remains hotly debated (Bow & Quinell, 2004; Emery et al., 2005; Kelly & Ramsey, 2009; Tippins & Wittman, 2005). More discussion of custody evaluations follow later.

The fact that most custody arrangements result from parental agreement does not mean the legal rules are unimportant, because they may influence the terms of the parents' agreement. Parents may also be influenced by what they are told by the professionals (i.e., attorneys, mediators, custody evaluators, parent educators) they encounter along the way. Accordingly, alterations in the professional standards regarding custody, such as we recommend, may still have an important impact on custody arrangements.

Research on Child Outcomes after Divorce

Children of divorced parents have about 20%–35% rate of evidencing adjustment problems, compared to 12% (some studies suggest as much as 15%) in married families (Braver & Lamb, in press). Thus, the majority of children from divorced families evidence no psychopathology or behavioral symptoms, although they are likely to experience psychic pain for at least some time (Laumann-Billings & Emery, 2000). There is a very high degree of variability found in responses of children and families to divorce. These dramatic individual differences in outcomes have prompted a close examination of the primary factors that research finds mediates child adjustment postdivorce. These factors consistently identified by research (Braver, Hipke, Ellman, & Sandler, 2004; Amato, 2001; Braver & Lamb, in press) are (roughly in order of importance): (1) the nature of the relationship between the two parents; (2) the custodial parent's functioning and parenting of the child; (3) the quality of the noncustodial parent's relationship to the child; (4) the characteristics of the child, in terms of coping, resilience, and temperament; and (5) the level—and change in level—of economic circumstances of the custodial parent. Although the child's characteristics are important, for any given family, they are a constant whatever the custody decision. Hence, we don't consider this factor further here. Similarly, we don't consider economic circumstances further, but for a different reason. Although the child's economic level after divorce is important, courts tend to prefer to disallow this factor as a consideration in awarding custody (for example, by awarding custody to the more economically well-off parent) and prefer attempts to alter these circumstances through child support orders (Ellman et al., 2010). Instead, our further focus is on the first three factors, which can profitably be used by courts and evaluators to choose a custody arrangement.

Nature of the interparental relationship postdivorce.   Interparental conflict in divorced families is generally thought to be the most detrimental mediator of child outcome (e.g., Grych & Fincham, 1990). Parental conflict is associated with a number of negative child outcomes including externalizing problems such as conduct disorder, aggression, delinquency, and antisocial behavior, as well as internalizing problems such as depression and anxiety (Grych & Fincham, 1990). Although interparental conflict is certainly not unique to divorce, Hetherington and Stanley-Hagan (1999) suggest that high levels of conflict are even more detrimental to children of divorced parents than high levels of conflict in still married couples because there are fewer resources available to the children during a time of increased life stressors.

Postdivorce conflict can be especially harmful to children because it is frequently centered on the child-related issues, including disagreements over child custody, child support, and visitation (Hetherington & Stanley-Hagan, 1999). Research shows that high hostility and discord among parents who have low cooperative communication results in children feeling caught between their parents, which is related to poor adjustment outcomes (Buchanan, Maccoby, & Dornbusch, 1991). Given the potential influence of interparental conflict on children's adjustment, custody arrangements and resolution processes that shield the children from conflict, and those that work against encouraging hostile alliances against the other parent, and focus on not pulling the children into the conflict are very desirable (Grych & Fincham, 1990; Hetherington & Stanley-Hagan, 1999).

On the reverse side, children also appear to greatly benefit from cooperative parenting. Cooperative parenting, or coparenting, is more than the absence of conflict. It is cooperative, mutually supportive, and non-confrontational parenting (Hetherington, Bridges, & Insabella, 1998). Successful coparenting involves showing respect for the other parent, maintaining open and useful dialog about the children, and sharing child-rearing tasks (Whiteside, 1998). Studies have linked successful coparenting with improved psychological functioning, academic performance, social competence, and lower levels of externalizing and internalizing symptoms in children of divorced parents (e.g., Buchanan et al., 1991). Unfortunately, cooperative parenting can be difficult for many parents to achieve postdivorce. A little more than 50% of parents postdivorce report an excellent or cooperative coparenting relations, but the rest of divorced parents report a relationship that includes inadequate support and some tension or intense difficulties and conflict (Whiteside, 1998).

Custodial parent's functioning and parenting of the child. Various studies support the finding that parenting issues are likely a cause of child maladjustment and behavior problems postdivorce (Forgatch & DeGarmo, 1999). Since the primary custodial parent has the largest parenting role, the level of both emotional support and parental authority s/he provides as the family transitions through the stressful divorce process is crucial. Postdivorce children need parents who are authoritative: supportive, responsive, and communicative, and yet exerting firm and consistent control and discipline as well as close monitoring (Hetherington & Stanley-Hagan, 1999). Authoritative parenting is linked with high social competence and fewer behavior problems (Hetherington et al., 1998). In addition, studies have shown that children of custodial parents with positive parenting qualities have higher self-esteem and better academic performance (Wyman, Sandler, Wolchik, & Nelson, 2000).

Unfortunately, postdivorce parents themselves often suffer from an increased risk of psychological problems such as depression, anxiety, irritability, and impulsive behaviors, which limits their ability to be responsive and sensitive parents during a time when children can be especially demanding and difficult (Hetherington & Stanley-Hagan, 1999). However, research suggests that many of these problems diminish by two years after the divorce as the parent's emotional state improves and as the family restabilizes, which improves the overall quality of parenting (Hetherington & Stanley-Hagan, 1999).

Quality of the noncustodial parent's relationship to the child. Noncustodial parents continue to play a vital role in their children's lives and well-being. According to Amato and Gilbreth's meta-analysis (1999), it is not only contact with fathers, but feelings of closeness between fathers and children and authoritative parenting that are positively associated with child wellbeing such as higher academic achievement and decreased internalizing and externalizing problems. It is the quality, not the quantity, of contact with the noncustodial father that is vital. Children do best with noncustodial parents who are actively involved in their children's lives beyond providing "treats" and fun activities when they visit. It is important that they be involved in their children's daily lives and participate in extracurricular activities, and enforcement of responsibilities including homework and chores, discipline, etc. (Braver & Lamb, in press; Warshak, 2000). This involvement will increase the quality of the noncustodial parent-child relationship (Amato & Gilbreth, 1999). Research also shows beneficial secondary effects from increased involvement, including increased child support payments, which reduces economic complications for custodial parents and children, improving their relationships (Warshak, 2000). Studies have also shown that increased child support payments are positively associated with children's academic success and inversely with externalizing problems (Amato & Gilbreth, 1999).

Assessment Instruments Currently Used In Custody Evaluations

We next consider the current state of assessment tools commonly used in child custody evaluations, with special attention to their scientific validity. These tools include various types of family observations, structured interviews, and psychological testing instruments (Keilin & Bloom, 1986). With respect to the first, observations of family interaction lack standardization and uniformity across professionals and no studies exist to determine if they are reliable or valid. Concerning structured interviews, no validated protocols for custody evaluation based on empirical research currently exist (Gould & Stahl, 2000). Finally, no psychological tests currently in widespread use have been found to have adequate levels of reliability or validity for purposes of deciding on a suitable custody arrangement.

By far the most common tests used in custody evaluations are IQ tests and the MMPI (Ackerman & Ackerman, 1997). Although both have excellent psychometric qualities generally, neither assesses the qualities most at stake in custody evaluations, and hence have no demonstrated validity in that context. General projective tests, such as the Rorschach Inkblot Technique, Thematic Apperception Test, and Sentence Completion Test, are the next most often used (Ackerman & Ackerman, 1997). These instruments have been sharply criticized in the scientific literature, and have shown little, if any, empirical support for their validity (Erickson, Lilienfeld, & Vitacco, 2007). Despite lack of scientific validity, current assessments remain infrequently challenged for use in court (Shuman, 2002). The Bricklin Scales (Bricklin, 1984) were developed specifically for child custody, yet remain criticized for a near-complete absence of data supporting their reliability and validity (Emery et al., 2005). In general, both the attributes measured and the instruments employed have elicited a legion of critics skeptical of the scientific basis of custody evaluations (Bow & Quinell, 2004; Emery et al., 2005; Kelly & Ramsey, 2009; Tippins & Wittman, 2005).

What Should and Could Be Assessed In Custody Evaluations

Note, however, that conspicuously lacking in the list above is the attempt to measure the qualities that are demonstrably linked to child outcomes. As mentioned earlier, the focus should be instead on constructs associated with positive child outcome variables identified by existing research findings: indicators of both child maladjustment (such as mental health problems), and developmental competence (Masten & Coatsworth, 1998) (such as indicators of success in developmental tasks like school or employment). There is a large, consistent and impressive literature (reviewed above) that has linked the interparental relationship, custodial and non-custodial parenting to both short- and long-term child well-being. To arrive at these scientific conclusions (and pass peer-review), the empirical research had to reliably and validly measure the constructs found to have desirable effects on child well-being. In other words, the research not only points to the factors implicated, it perforce must have assessed these factors with psychometrically sound instruments; or else it couldn't have reached the strong conclusions it did (Shadish, Cook, & Campbell, 2002). To put it otherwise, all the results finding significant relationships with child well-being outcomes simultaneously identified and verified the relationship, as well as provided construct validity evidence for the instruments that measured these variables.

What are these validated measures? What scales do we assert *should* be used in custody evaluations, in place of the at-best questionable instruments typically employed? The first construct, parental conflict, has been repeatedly and validly assessed by the O'Leary Porter Scale (Porter & O'Leary, 1980), the Conflict Tactics Scales (CTS; Straus, 1979) the Revised Conflict Tactics Scales (CTS2; Straus, Hamby, Boney-McCoy, & Sugarman, 1996), the Divorce Conflict Measure (DCM; Nicholas, Slater, Forehand, & Fauber, 1988), the Marital Problems Questionnaire (MPQ; Douglass & Douglass, 1995), and the Conflicts and Problem-Solving Scales (CPS; Kerig, 1996). The child's view of parental conflict has been assessed with the Children's Perception of Interparental Conflict Scale (CPIC; Grych, Seid, & Fincham, 1992), and the Post-Divorce Parental Conflict Scale (PPCS; Morris & West, 2001), while others have used questionnaires to assess frequency of conflict, both overt and covert, by creating some new items and combining or adapting items from Ahrons (1981) and Grych et al. (1992). The Berkley Puppet Interview (Ablow, Measelle, Cowan, & Cowan, 2009), designed to investigate young children's perceptions of the family environment, has also shown that it is valid for capturing marital conflict. Others, such as the Couple Communication Questionnaire (CCQ; Cowan & Cowan, 1990a) include subscales on conflict, but also ask about broader issues such as problem-solving and intimacy. The Interparental Conflict Scale (ICS; Black & Pedro-Carroll, 1993) asks young adults retrospectively about parental conflict when growing up and includes 4 items from Ahrons' (1981) Coparent Communication Scale.

Coparenting refers to the ways in which parents coordinate their parenting, manage conflict regarding child rearing, and mutually support versus undermine each other (McHale, Kuersten-Hogan, Lauretti, & Rasmussen, 2000), and has been strongly related to child outcomes (Abidin & Brunner, 1995). (For a more detailed discussion of coparenting see Palkovitz & Fagan, this volume.) Coparenting has been well-measured via parent report on the Parenting Alliance Inventory (PAI; Abidin & Brunner, 1995), Perceptions of Coparenting Partners Questionnaire (Stright & Bales, 2003), the Coparenting Questionnaire (Margolin, Gordis, & John, 2001), and the Coparent Communication Scale (Ahrons, 1981). Co-parental involvement and division of labor has been measured by the Who Does What? questionnaire (WDW; Cowan & Cowan, 1990b). Parents also have conflict over coparenting, which has been assessed via the Child Rearing Issues: Self and Spouse Scale (Hetherington & Clingempeel, 1992), and The Acrimony Scale (AS; Shaw & Emery, 1987). Coparenting can be observationally coded as well (Belsky, Crnic, & Gable, 1992).

An apparent difficulty with the constructs of interparental conflict and coparenting is that conflict is typically measured at the dyadic level, and thought of as a couple-level construct ("it takes two to tango"). As such, it might be thought useless in choosing between the parents. In fact, experienced divorce professionals are beginning to recognize that postdivorce conflict isn't always, or even commonly, mutual. For example, Kelly and Emery (2003) argue that

> although high conflict postdivorce is generally assumed to be a shared interaction between two angry, culpable parents, our clinical, mediation, and arbitration experience in high conflict postdivorce cases indicates that it is not uncommon to find one enraged or defiant parent and a second parent who no longer harbors anger, has emotionally disengaged, and attempts to avoid or mute conflict that involves the child. (p. 353)

Thus, attention should turn to identifying which of the parents is contentious and fomenting conflict. Efforts with parental report measures to identify which of two divorcing parents is most to blame for conflict haven't been promising thus far (Cookston, Griffin, Braver, & Williams, 2004; each largely accuses the other). However, observational measures, such as the Marital Daily Record coding system (MDR; Cummings, Goeke-Morey, Papp, & Dukewich, 2002), and semi-structured interviews of children and parents (Crockenberg & Langrock, 2001) have proved more successful. Child report has yielded some promising results as well (Braver, Coatsworth, & Peralta, 2006). In any event, the quote above suggests that experienced professionals can readily detect whether the conflict is most commonly instigated be the mother, the father, or both. An inter-rater reliability study of this assertion should certainly be high on the research agenda.

Parenting has been measured well in numerous studies. Parenting encompasses a variety of constructs and the distinction is often made between parenting style and parenting practices. Parenting style is viewed as a parent's attitude towards parenting, expressed across situations, that provides an emotional climate for the parent-child relationship, whereas parenting practices refers to specific behaviors (often goal-directed) that parents exhibit towards their child, and may be situation-specific (Darling & Steinberg, 1993). Parenting styles have long been derived from Baumrind (1971) and Maccoby and Martin (1983) by grouping parents into four categories based on levels of parental demandingness and responsiveness: Authoritative, Authoritarian, Indulgent (Permissive), and Uninvolved (Indifferent). Of these, authoritative parents have by far the children with the best outcomes on a variety of arenas. Validated measures of self-reported style of parenting include the Parenting Styles and Dimensions Questionnaire (PSDQ; Robinson, Mandelco, Olsen, & Hart, 2001), the Parental Authority Questionnaire - Revised (Reitman, Rhode, Hupp, & Altobello, 2002), and by combining measures of parenting with respect to demandingness and responsiveness. Broad measures of parenting include the Parenting Scale (Arnold, O'Leary, Wolff, & Acker, 1992), the Parenting Knowledge Test (Gordon, 1994), Child Rearing Practices Report (CRPR; Roberts, Block, & Block, 1984), Parenting Behaviour Checklist (PBC; Fox, 1994), Parenting Behavior Questionnaire (Hart, Nelson, Robinson, Olsen, & McNeilly-Choque, 1998), the Child Report of Parent Behavior Inventory (CRPBI; Schaefer, 1965), the Parent Child Relationship Inventory (PCRI; Gerard, 1994), and the Family Environment Scales (FES; Moos & Moos, 1994). Parental monitoring of their children is also strongly related to child outcomes and has been measured with the Assessment of Child Monitoring Scale (Hetherington & Clingempeel, 1992) and the Parental Monitoring Scale (PMS; Small & Kerns, 1993). Others have developed similar items that capture child disclosure, parental knowledge and parental solicitation as important constructs to monitoring (Stattin & Kerr, 2000). Numerous studies have used observational measures of parenting behavior, such as the Iowa Family Interaction Rating Scales (Melby et al., 1990) and the HOME Inventory (Bradley, & Caldwell, 1984), however home observations require time consuming coding, typically of videotaped observations, and time-consuming training of coders to achieve reliability for live and videotaped interaction. (See Holden & Miller, 1999, for a more complete discussion of parenting constructs.)

Importantly, tests that reliably and validly assess a construct, such as parenting, in a general research context may not be so in a forensic custody evaluation context. Careful attention needs to be paid to validating research instruments for use in custody decisions with respect to response style and validity as well as documenting the appropriate norms for a forensic population.

Custody Assessments Are a Snapshot in Time of Changing or Changeable Characteristics

Careful readers following our arguments might conclude that we strongly recommend that courts and divorce professionals such as custody evaluators seek to assess, in contrast to current practice, the level of and initiator of interparental conflict, as well as the two parents' parenting skills, and that rigorous instruments exist to do so. This is not entirely correct; although we concur that the constructs in the sentence above are the correct ones to investigate in order to further the child's best interests, we also note that any assessment provides only a *snapshot* of parenting ability at a given point in time. The problem remains that even with good measures of parenting characteristics, mothers and fathers are under a great deal of stress (and distress) at the time of divorce, and thus this is likely not a representative point in time to provide information on their "true" parenting. In addition to distraught parents, the custody arrangements are soon to change through a divorce agreement, mediation, or court-ordered custody arrangement. Moreover, a parent with given characteristics, who is best able to parent the child now may not be the best parent 1, 5, or 10 years later, given that parenting practices show variation across time (Holden & Miller, 1999). Indeed, changes in the appropriateness of parenting were similarly noted by Baumrind (1989, as cited in Holden & Miller, 1999, p. 246):

> … parents who are highly effective at one stage in the child's life are not necessarily as effective at another; … similar practices do not necessarily produce the same effects at successive stages in a child's life.

Moreover, the court system is not simply a measuring rod, attempting to impartially choose among competing alternatives. Like the Heisenberg principle, the very act of "assessing" within a court-room adversarial model has clear and generally negative impact on the characteristics assessed (Pruett & Jackson, 1999). Parental conflict, the single best predictor of child outcomes (Lamb, in press; Kelly, in press) can be exacerbated when a contentious parent uses the legal system as an instrument of attack. That is an unavoidable possibility, even when courts attempt to discourage it, because courts have no choice, when parents refuse to settle their differences, but to allow them each to present the evidence and the arguments they believe will show that the other would be a poor choice of custodian. This conflict, as well as the stress that accompanies prolonged and circuitous negotiation and uncertainty, also has been shown to diminish the parenting capabilities of both parents (Emery et al., 2005). This implies that courts should devise and reform procedures to minimize these undesirable unintended consequences and instead to maximize the parents' resources and cooperative parenting. Many such programs are documented in Applegate (this volume).

Interventions to Improve Child Outcomes after Divorce

Parenting is a skill that is mutable and a number of parent training programs have proven astonishingly successful at improving parenting in divorcing families. For example, Parent Management Training (PMT) improved effective parenting, which in turn led to positive changes in child behavior (Patterson, DeGarmo, & Forgatch, 2004), including child internalizing, externalizing, better school adjustment and less delinquency, and reduced child ratings of depression (Forgatch & DeGarmo, 1999). Another program, the New Beginnings Program (NBP), has shown program-induced reductions in child behavior problems (internalizing, externalizing, drug use, number of sexual partners), improved mother-child relationship quality, effective parenting and discipline, and increased GPA (Zhou, Sandler, Millsap, Wolchik, & Dawson-McClure, 2008). Most impressively, children whose parents underwent this program retained their substantial well-being advantage over children in the control condition six-years later (McClain, Wolchik, Winslow, Tein, Sandler, & Millsap, 2010; Wolchik, Schenck, & Sandler, 2009). The NBP is currently undergoing a redesign to include sessions for fathers as well as planned for a large-scale effectiveness trial in collaboration with the family courts (Wolchik et al., 2009). A third program, the Collaborative Divorce Project, has shown promise in decreased mothers' gatekeeping, reduced interparental conflict, increased positive father involvement, reduced child problems, increased interparental cooperation as reported by attorneys, and an increased likelihood of paying child support (Pruett, Insabella, & Gustafson, 2005). Finally, the Dads for Life program, designed expressly for noncustodial fathers, has shown remarkable success in improving children's outcomes (Braver, Griffin, & Cookston, 2005; Cookston, Braver, Griffin, DeLuse, & Miles, 2007).

Bridges to Other Disciplines

Divorce and child custody, by their very nature, necessitate interdisciplinary participation from the court system, legal policy and research, social work, custody evaluators, and psychological research from a wide range of areas. We hope it is evident from our review that a great deal of collaboration already exists across multiple disciplines, with the overarching goal of promoting the best possible outcomes for children and families. Particularly fruitful has been the ongoing relationship between courts and programmatic interventions for families undergoing divorce. However, developmental psychology and family studies have much to offer the development of custody evaluation methods, particularly in terms of assessment of constructs known to relate to children's' well-being following divorce.

Policy Implications

Courts and custody evaluators will better evaluate the child's best interest if the use of instruments of questionable value is eliminated and the use of empirically validated instruments that measure interparental conflict, parenting by the mother and parenting by the father is increased. We do not suggest statutory revisions that would lock in a preference for some measures over others, but our discussion of the relation of these three factors to child well-being suggests that it would be appropriate for courts to give these measures more weight than others in custody determinations. The number of validated instruments already available suggests that a transition among professionals to more empirically validated measures of interparental conflict and parenting abilities would be relatively straightforward.

Indeed the benefits of incorporating empirical measures on conflict and parenting into divorce proceedings are many. Increased use of objective measurements (with careful attention to reporter bias) would strengthen courts and evaluators against criticism of partiality in making child custody determinations (although the accumulated clinical expertise and observations of a custody evaluator remains crucial to any determination of custody), and may decrease the number of couples who choose to extend their custody battles. In addition, the use of empirically valid measures of interparental conflict and parenting would greatly improve researchers' abilities to investigate determinants of child custody decisions, enable meaningful comparison across custody evaluations, and more reliably document the effects of custody plans and intervention programs on parental conflict and parenting practices.

Future Directions

A clear priority for professionals wishing to follow the recommendations in this chapter is to validate research measures in a forensic setting. We also contend it would be short sighted to stop with simply substituting rigorous measures for the faulty ones currently in use. For example, even if one could validly identify a single conflict-instigating parent, one cannot assume that awarding more custodial time to the other parent will alone stop parental behavior that is harmful to the child. Courts need not limit themselves to choosing between alternative arrangements, but can also improve the available alternatives by requiring parents' participation in programs that improve parenting and children's outcomes. The child's interests favor extending the judicial role from adjudicator between contending parties to include facilitating such participation in programs of established validity. Many family courts are already willing to assume this "therapeutic jurisprudence" role (Cookston, Sandler, Braver, & Genalo, 2007). Indeed, custody evaluations could include recommendations for specific therapeutic programs depending on the issues present in a given separating family. More and more, courts are partnering with behavioral science researchers to develop systems and procedures that cannot merely choose among litigants but improve outcomes for children of divorcing families (Hita, Braver, Sandler, Knox, & Strehle, 2009). As a result of these developments, we believe the future looks brighter for divorcing fathers and children (and mothers).

References

Abidin, R. R., & Brunner, J. F. (1995). Development of a parenting alliance inventory. *Journal of Clinical Child Psychology*, *24*, 31–40.

Ablow, J. C., Measelle, J. R., Cowan, P. A., & Cowan, C. P. (2009). Linking marital conflict and children's adjustment: The role of young children's perceptions. *Journal of Family Psychology*, *23*(4), 485–499. DOI: 10.1037/a0015894.

Ackerman, M. J., & Ackerman, M. C. (1997). Child custody evaluation practices: A survey of experienced professionals (revisited). *Professional Psychology: Research & Practice*, *28*(2), 137–145.

Ahrons, C. R. (1981). The continuing coparental relationship between divorced spouses. *American Journal of Orthopsychiatry*, *5*, 415–428.

Amato, P. R. (2001). Children of divorce in the 1990s: An update of the Amato and Keith (1991) meta-analysis. *Journal of Family Psychology*, *15*(3), 355–370.

Amato, P. R., & Gilbreth, J. G. (1999). Nonresident fathers and children's well-being: A meta-analysis. *Journal of Marriage and the Family*, *61*(3), 557–573. doi: 10.2307/353560

Arbuthnot, J. (2002). A call unheeded: Courts' perceived obstacles to establishing divorce education programs. *Family Court Review*, *40*, 371–382.

Argys, L. H., Peters, E. Cook, S. Garasky, S., Nepomnyaschy, L., & Sorensen, E. (2007). Measuring contact between children and nonresident fathers. In S. Hofferth & L. Casper (Eds.), *Handbook of measurement issues in family research*. Mahwah, NJ: Erlbaum.

Arnold, D. S., O'Leary, S. G., Wolff, L. S., & Acker, M. M. (1992). The parenting scale: A measure of dysfunctional parenting in discipline situations. *Psychological Assessment, 4,* 66–83.

Baumrind, D. (1971). Current patterns of parental authority. *Developmental Psychology Monograph, 4,* 1–103.

Baumrind, D. (1989). The permanence of change and the impermanence of stability. *Human Development, 32,* 187–195.

Belsky, J., Crnic, K., & Gable, S. (1992). *Manual for coding coparenting*. Pennsylvania State Child and Family Development Project, University Park, Pennsylvania State University.

Black, A. E., & Pedro-Carroll, J. (1993). Role of parent-child relationships in mediating the effects of marital disruption. *Journal of the American Academy of Child and Adolescent Psychiatry, 32*(5), 1019–1027.

Bow, J. M., & Quinell, F. A. (2004). Critique of child custody evaluations by the legal profession. *Family Court Review, 42*(1), 115–127.

Bradley, R. H., & Caldwell, B. M. (1984). The HOME inventory and family demographics. *Developmental Psychology, 20,* 315–320.

Braver, S. L., Coatsworth, D., & Peralta, K. (2006). *Alienating behavior within divorced and intact families: Matched parents' and now-young adult children's reports.* Presented at International Conference on Children and Divorce (ICCD), Norwich, UK.

Braver, S. L., Griffin, W. A., & Cookston, J. T. (2005). Prevention programs for divorced nonresident fathers. *Family Court Review, 43*(1), 81–96. doi:10.1111/j.1744-1617.2005.00009.x

Braver, S. L., Hipke, K. N., Ellman, I. M., & Sandler, I. N. (2004). In K. I. Maton, C. J. Schellenbach, B. J. Leadbeater, & A. L. Solarz (Eds.), *Strength-building public policy for children of divorce* (pp. 53–72). Washington, DC: American Psychological Association.

Braver, S. L., & Lamb, M. E. (in press). Marital dissolution. In G. W. Peterson & K. R. Bush (Eds.), *Handbook of marriage and the family* (2nd ed.). New York: Springer.

Braver, S. L., & O'Connell, D. (1998). *Divorced dads: Shattering the myths*. New York: Tarcher/Putnam.

Braver, S. L., Shapiro, J. R., & Goodman, M. R. (2005). The consequences of divorce for parents. In M. A. Fine & J.H. Harvey (Eds.), *Handbook of divorce and relationship dissolution* (pp. 313–337). Mahwah, NJ: Erlbaum.

Bricklin, B. (1984). *Bricklin perceptual scales*. Furlong, PA: Village.

Brown, P., & Cancian, M. (2007). *Wisconsin's 2004 shared-physical-placement guidelines: Their use and implications in divorce cases.* University of Wisconsin-Madison: Institute for Research on Poverty.

Buchanan, C. M., Maccoby, E. E., & Dornbusch, S. M. (1991). Caught between parents: Adolescents' experience in divorced homes. *Child Development, 62,* 1008–1029.

Chambers, D. L. (1984). Rethinking the substantive rules for custody disputes in divorce. *Michigan Law Review, 83,* 477–569.

Cherlin, A. (2010). Demographic trends in the United States: A review of research in the 2000s, *Journal of Marriage and the Family, 72,* 403–419.

Cookston, J. T., Braver, S. L., Griffin, W. A., DeLuse, S. R., & Miles, J. C. (2007). Effects of the Dads For Life intervention on coparenting in the two years after divorce. *Family Process, 46*(1), 123–137.

Cookston, J. T., Griffin, W. A., Braver, S. L., & Williams, J. (2004). *Predicting interparent conflict and child outcomes following divorce: The role of parent argument behaviors.* Unpublished manuscript.

Cookston, J. T., Sandler, I. N., Braver, S. L., & Genalo, M. T. (2007). Predicting readiness to adopt evidence-based programs for divorcing families: Champions, attitudes, and access to funding. *American Journal of Orthopsychiatry, 77*(4), 573–581.

Cowan, C. P., & Cowan, P. A. (1990a). *Couple communication questionnaire*. Berkeley: Institute of Human Development, University of California.

Cowan, P. A., & Cowan, C. P. (1990b). Who does what? In J. F. Touliatos, B. F. Perlmutter, & M. A. Straus (Eds.), *Handbook of family measurement techniques* (pp. 447–448). Thousand Oaks, CA: Sage.

Cox, M., & Paley, B. (1997). Families as systems. *Annual Review of Psychology, 48*, 243–267.

Crockenberg, S., & Langrock, A. (2001). The role of specific emotions in children's responses to interparental conflict: A test of the model. *Journal of Family Psychology, 15*, 163–182.

Cummings, E. M., Goeke-Morey, M. C., Papp, L. M., & Dukewich, T. L. (2002). Children's responses to mothers' and fathers' emotionality and tactics in marital conflict in the home. *Journal of Family Psychology, 16*, 478–492.

Darling, N., & Steinberg, L. (1993). Parenting style as context: An integrative model. *Psychological Bulletin, 113*(3), 487–496. doi:10.1037/0033-2909.113.3.487

DeLusé, S. R. (1999). Mandatory divorce education: A program evaluation using a "quasi-random" regression discontinuity design. Doctoral dissertation, Arizona State University. *Dissertation Abstracts International, 60*, 13–49.

Douglas, E. M. (2003). The effect of a presumption for joint legal custody on father involvement in divorced families. *Journal of Divorce and Remarriage, 40*(3/4), 1–10.

Douglass, F. M., & Douglass, R. (1995). The marital problems questionnaire (MPQ): A short screening instrument for marital therapy. *Family Relations, 44*, 238–244.

Ellman, I. M. (1999a). The maturing law of divorce finances: Toward rules and guidelines. *Family Law Quarterly, 33*(3), 801–814.

Ellman, I. M. (1999b). Brigitte M. Bodenheimer memorial lecture on the family: Inventing family law, *University of California Davis Law Review, (32)*, 855–886.

Ellman, I. M. (2003). Why making family law is hard. *Arizona State Law Journal, (35)*, 699–714.

Ellman, I. M., Kurtz, P .M., Weithorn, L. A., Bix, B. H., Czapanskiy, K., & Eichner, M. (2010). *Family law: Cases, text, problems (5th ed.)*. New Providence, NJ: LexisNexis.

Emery, R. E., Otto, R. K., & O'Donohue, W. T. (2005). A critical assessment of child custody evaluations: Limited science and a flawed system. *Psychological Science in the Public Interest, 6*(1), 1–29.

Erickson, S. K., Lilienfeld, S. O., & Vitacco, M. J. (2007). Failing the burden of proof: The science and ethics of projective tests in custody evaluations. *Family Court Review, 45*(2), 185–192.

Fabricius, W. V., Braver, S. L., Diaz, P., & Velez, C. E. (2010). Custody and parenting time: Links to family relationships and well-being after divorce. In M. E. Lamb (Ed.), *The Role of the Father in Child Development* (5th ed., pp. 201–240. New York: Wiley.

Forgatch, M. S., & DeGarmo, D. S. (1999). Parenting through change: An effective prevention program for single mothers. *Journal of Consulting and Clinical Psychology, 67*, 711–724.

Fox, R. (1994). *Parent behaviour checklist*. Brandon, VT: Clinical Psychology Publishing Co.

George, T. (2008). *Residential time summary reports filed in Washington from July 2007– March 2008*. Olympia: Administrative Office of the Courts: Washington State Center for Court Research.

Gerard, A. B. (1994). *The parent–child relationship inventory*. Los Angeles: Western Psychological Services.

Goodman, M., Bonds, D., Sandler, I. N., & Braver, S. L. (2004). Parent psychoeducational programs and reducing the negative effects of interparental conflict following divorce. *Family Court Review, 42*(2), 263–279.

Gordon, T. (1994). *Parenting knowledge test*. Unpublished measure. Ohio University, Athens.

Gould, J. W., & Martindale, D. A. (2007). *The art and science of child custody evaluations*. New York: Guilford Press.

Gould, J. W., & Stahl, P. M. (2000). The art and science of child custody evaluations: Integrating clinical and forensic mental health models [Special issue: Child Custody Evaluations]. *Family & Conciliation Courts Review, 38*(3), 392–414.

Grych, J. H., & Fincham, F. D. (1990). Marital conflict and children's adjustment: A cognitive-contextual framework. *Psychological Bulletin, 108*(2), 267–290. doi:10.1037/0033-2909.108.2.267

Grych, J. H., Seid, M., & Fincham, F. D. (1992). Assessing marital conflict from the child's perspective: The children's perception of interparental conflict scale. *Child Development, 63*, 558–572.

Hart, C. H., Nelson, D. A., Robinson, C. C., Olsen, S. F., & McNeilly-Choque, M. K. (1998). Overt and relational aggression in Russian nursery school-age children: Parenting style and marital linkages. *Developmental Psychology, 34*(4), 687–697.

Hetherington, E. M., Bridges, M., & Insabella, G. M. (1998). What matters? What does Not?: Five perspectives on the association between marital transitions and children's adjustment. *American Psychologist, 53*(2), 167–184. doi:10.1037/0003-6X.53.2.167

Hetherington, E. M., & Clingempeel, G. (1992). Coping with marital transitions: A family systems perspective. *Monographs of the Society for Research in Child Development, 57*(2–3).

Hetherington, E. M., & Stanley-Hagan, M. (1999). The adjustment of children with divorced parents: A risk and resiliency perspective. *Journal of Child Psychology and Psychiatry and Allied Disciplines, 40*(1), 129–140. doi:10.1111/1469-7610.00427

Hita, L. C., Braver, S. L., Sandler, I. N., Knox, P., & Strehle, M. (2009). Family court-university partnership to benefit divorcing families: The experience of Maricopa County (Arizona) Family Court Department and Arizona State University's Prevention Research Center. *Family Court Review, 47*(3), 436–450.

Holden, G. W., & Miller, P. C. (1999). Enduring and different: A meta-analysis of the similarity in parents' child rearing. *Psychological Bulletin, 125*(2), 223–254.

Keilin, W. G., & Bloom, L. J. (1986). Child custody evaluation practices: A survey of experienced professionals. *Professional Psychology: Research and Practice, 17*, 338–346.

Kelly, J. B. (2007). Children's living arrangements following separation and divorce: Insights from empirical and clinical research. *Family Process, 46*, 35–52.

Kelly, J. B. (in press). Risk and protective factors associated with child and adolescent adjustment following separation and divorce: Social science applications. In K. Kuehnle & L. Drozd (Eds.), *Parenting plan evaluations: Applied research for the family court.* New York: Oxford University Press.

Kelly, J. B., & Emery, R. E. (2003). Children's adjustment following divorce: Risk and resilience perspectives. *Family Relations, 52*, 352–362.

Kelly, R. F., & Ramsey, S. H. (2009). Child custody evaluations: The need for systems-level outcome assessments. *Family Court Review, 47*(2), 286–303. doi:10.1111/j.1744-1617.2009.01255.x

Kerig, P. K. (1996). Assessing the links between interparental conflict and child adjustment: The conflicts and problem-solving scales. *Journal of Family Psychology, 10*(4), 454–473.

Lamb, M. E. (in press) Critical analysis of research on parenting plans and children's well-being In K. Kuehnle & L. Drozd (Eds.), *Parenting plan evaluations: Applied research for the family court.* New York: Oxford University Press.

Laumann-Billings, L., & Emery, R. E. (2000). Distress among young adults from divorced families. *Journal of Family Psychology, 14*, 671–687.

Maccoby, E. E., & Martin, J. A. (1983). Socialization in the context of the family: Parent-child interaction. In P. Mussen (Ed.), *Handbook of Child Psychology* (pp. 1–101). New York: Wiley.

Maccoby, E. E., & Mnookin, R. H. (1992). *Dividing the child: Social and legal dilemmas of custody.* Cambridge, MA: Harvard University Press.

Margolin, G., Gordis, E. B., & John, R. S. (2001). Coparenting: A link between marital conflict and parenting in two-parent families. *Journal of Family Psychology, 15*, 3–21.

Mason, M. A. (1994). *From father's property to children's rights: The history of child custody in the United States.* New York: Columbia University Press.

Masten, A. S., & Coatsworth, J. D. (1998). The development of competence in favorable and unfavorable environments: Lessons from research on successful children. *American Psychologist, 53*(2), 205–220. doi:10.1037/0003-066X.53.2.205

McClain, D. B., Wolchik, S. A., Winslow, E., Tein, J., Sandler, I. N., & Millsap, R. E. (2010). Developmental cascade effects of the New Beginnings Program on adolescent adaptation outcomes. *Development and Psychopathology, 22*, 771–784. doi:10.1017/S0954579410000453

McHale, J. P., Kuersten-Hogan, R., Lauretti, A., & Rasmussen, J. L. (2000). Parental reports of coparenting and observed coparenting behavior during the toddler period. *Journal of Family Psychology, 14*(2), 220–236. doi:10.1037/0893-3200.14.2.220

Melby, J., Conger, R., Book, R., Rueter, M., Lucy, L., Repinski, D., et al. (1990). *The Iowa family interaction coding manual.* Ames, IA: Iowa Youth and Families Project.

Moos, R., & Moos, B. (1994). *Family environment scale manual* (2nd ed.). Palo Alto, CA: Consulting Psychologists Press.

Morris, M. H., & West, C. (2001). Post-Divorce conflict and avoidance of intimacy. *Journal of Divorce & Remarriage, 35*(3/4), 93–105.

Nicholas, L., Slater, E., Forehand, R., & Fauber, R. (1988). Continued high or reduced interparental conflict following divorce: Relation to young adolescent adjustment. *Journal of Consulting and Clinical Psychology, 56*(3), 467–469. doi:10.1037/0022-006X.56.3.467

O'Connell, M. E. (2007). When noble aspirations fail: Why we need the Approximation Rule. *Child Development Perspectives, 1*, 129–131.

Paquette, D. (1994) Theorizing the father-child relationship: Mechanisms and developmental outcomes. *Human Development, 47*(4), 193–219. doi:10.1159/000078723

Patterson, G. R., DeGarmo, D., & Forgatch, M. S. (2004). Systematic changes in families following prevention trials. *Journal of Abnormal Child Psychology, 32*(6), 621–633.

Polikoff, N. D. (1982). Why are mothers losing: A brief analysis of criteria used in child custody determinations. *Women's Rights Law Reporter, 14*, 175–184.

Porter, B., & O'Leary, D. (1980). Marital discord and childhood behavior problems. *Journal of Abnormal Psychology, 8*, 287–295.

Pruett, M. K., Insabella, G. M., & Gustafson, K. (2005). The collaborative divorce project: A court-based intervention for separating parenting with young children. *Family Court Review, 43*, 38–51.

Pruett, M. K., & Jackson, T. (1999). The lawyer's role during the divorce process. Perceptions of parents, their young children, and their attorneys. *Family Law Quarterly, 33*, 283–310.

Reitman, D., Rhode, P. C., Hupp, S. D. A., & Altobello, C. (2002). Development and validation of the parental authority questionnaire – revised. *Journal of Psychopathology and Behavior Assessment, 24*, 119–127.

Roberts, G. C., Block, H., & Block, J. (1984). Continuity and change in parents' child-rearing practices. *Child Development, 55*, 586–597.

Robinson, C. C., Mandelco, B., Olsen, S. F., & Hart, C. H. (2001). Parenting styles and dimensions questionnaire. In B. F. Perlmutter, J. Touliatos & G. W. Holdem (Eds.), *Handbook of family measurement techniques: Instruments and index* (pp. 319–321). Thousand Oaks, CA: Sage.

Schaefer, E. S. (1965). Children's report of parental behavior: An inventory. *Child Development, 36*, 413–424.

Schepard, A. I. (2004). *Children, courts, and custody: Interdisciplinary models for divorcing families.* New York: Cambridge University Press.

Seltzer, J. A. (1990). Legal and physical custody arrangements in recent divorces. *Social Science Quarterly, 71*, 250–266.

Semple, N. (2011, June). *The settlement mission in custody and access cases.* Presented at Association of Family and Conciliation Courts, Orlando, Florida.

Shadish, W. R., Cook, T. D., & Campbell, D. T. (2002). *Experimental and quasi-experimental designs for generalized causal inference.* Boston: Houghton-Mifflin.

Shaw, D., & Emery, R. E. (1987). Parental conflict and the adjustment of school-aged children whose parents have separated. *Journal of Abnormal Child Psychology, 15*, 269–281.

Shuman, D. W. (2002). The role of mental health experts in custody decisions: Science, psychological tests, and clinical judgment. *Family Law Quarterly, 36*(1), 135–162.

Sigal, A., Sandler, I., Wolchik, S., & Braver, S. L. (2011). Do parent education programs promote healthy post-divorce parenting? Critical distinctions and a review of the evidence. *Family Court Review, 49*(1), 120–139.

Small, S. A., & Kerns, D. (1993). Unwanted sexual activity among peers during early and middle adolescence: Incidence and risk factors. *Journal of Marriage and the Family, 55*, 941–952.

Stattin, H., & Kerr, M. (2000). Parental monitoring: A reinterpretation. *Child Development, 71*(4), 1072–1085.

Straus, M. A. (1979). Measuring intrafamily conflict and violence: The conflict tactics (CT) scales. *Journal of Marriage and Family, 41*(1), 75–88.

Straus, M. A., Hamby, S. L., Boney-McCoy, S., & Sugarman, D. B. (1996). The revised conflict tactics scales (CTS2). *Journal of Family Issues, 17*(3), 283–316.

Stright, A. D., & Bales, S. S. (2003). Coparenting quality: Contributions of child and parent characteristics. *Family Relations, 52*(3), 232–240.

Tippins, T. M., & Wittman, J. P. (2005). Empirical and ethical problems with custody recommendations: A call for clinical humility and judicial vigilance. *Family Court Review, 43*(2), 193–222.

United Nations. (1989). Convention on the rights of the child. Retrieved November 26, 2008, from http://www.unhchr.ch/html/menu3/b/k2crc.htm

Venohr, J. C., & Griffith, T. E. (2003). Arizona child support guidelines: Findings from a case file review. Denver, CO: Policy Studies.

Venohr, J. C., & Griffith, T. E. (2005) Child support guidelines: Issues and reviews. *Family Court Review, 43*, 415–428.

Venohr, J. C., & Kaunelis, R. (2008). *Arizona child support guidelines review: Analysis of case file data.* Denver, CO: Center for Policy Research.

Warshak, R. A. (2000). Social science and children's best interests in relocation cases: *Burgess* revisited. *Law Quarterly, 34*(1), 83–113.

Warshak, R. A. (2007). Punching the parenting time clock: The Approximation Rule, social science, and the baseball bat kids. *Family Court Review, 45*(4), 600–619.

Whiteside, M. F. (1998). The parental alliance following divorce: An overview. *Journal of Marital and Family Therapy, 24*(1), 3–24. doi:10.1111/j.1752-0606.1998.tb01060.x

Wolchik, S. A., Sandler, I. N., Jones, S., Gonzales, N., Doyle, K, Winslow, E., et al. (2009). The New Beginnings Program for divorcing and separating families: Moving from efficacy to effectiveness. *Family Court Review, 47*(3), 416–435.

Wolchik, S. A., Schenck, C. E., & Sandler, I. N. (2009). Promoting resilience in youth from divorced families: Lessons learned from experimental trials of the New Beginnings Program. *Journal of Personality, 77*(6), 1833–1868. doi: 10.1111/j.1467-6494.2009.00602.x

Wyman, P. A., Sandler, I. N., Wolchik, S. A., & Nelson, K. A. (2000). Resilience as cumulative competence promotion and stress protection: Theory and intervention. In D. Cicchetti, J. Rappaport, I. N. Sandler, & R. P. Weissberg (Eds.), *The promotion of wellness in children and adolescents* (pp. 133–184). Thousand Oaks, CA: Sage.

Zhou, Q., Sandler, I. N., Millsap, R. E., Wolchik, S. A., & Dawson-McClure, S. R. (2008). Mother-child relationship quality and effective discipline as mediators of the 6-year effects of the new beginnings program for children from divorced families. *Journal of Consulting and Clinical Psychology, 76*(4), 579–594. doi: 10.1037/0022-006X.76.4.579

Chapter 22

Fathers and Family Dispute Resolution

Amy G. Applegate

Indiana University Maurer School of Law

Katherine Schwartz and Amy Holtzworth-Munroe

Indiana University-Bloomington[1]

Introduction

Parents seeking dissolution of marriage or establishment of paternity soon learn that the court has the ultimate authority for making decisions about their children. When the parents do not agree in a family law case involving parental separation (i.e., a dissolution (divorce) case or paternity action (where the parents were never married)), the judge, frequently a stranger to the family, weighs the often competing interests of each parent, while determining what is in the best interests of the children involved. However, parents are, or should be, the experts about their children, and most want to make the decisions about what is best for their children. Many family law cases will never reach the courtroom (Maccoby & Mnookin, 1992), preserving the chance for parental autonomy in child-rearing after parental separation. More specifically, the development of family court reforms, use of attorney-driven settlement negotiations, and the emergence of alternative dispute resolution (ADR) processes provide parents with opportunities to assert their decision-making power in matters related to their children.

This chapter will review the ADR processes that can be helpful to fathers and other family members, with a special focus on domestic relations mediation (family mediation) for resolving cases involving children. We will discuss the effects of parental separation (in cases in which the parents have dissolved their marriage or were never married) on children and their relationships with their fathers and mothers; the potential benefits of ADR processes for families; and two special issues related to family mediation: (a) modifying mediation to focus on the best interests of the children and (b) dealing with high-conflict families in mediation.

Brief Historical Overview and Theoretical Perspectives

Family systems theory (e.g., Cox & Payley, 1997) presents a framework for the current focus on ADR processes generally, and family mediation more specifically.[2] Family systems theory stresses the ways in which relationships between specific family members (e.g., mother-father) have spillover effects for other family relationships (e.g., father-child; mother-child). For example, children are adversely affected by conflict between their parents, and the dissolution of a marriage or other parental separation can impose stresses on children in the developmental context.

Effects of Parental Separation on Children

The sheer number of children affected by parental separation begs scrutiny of the official processes through which parents dissolve their marriage or intimate relationship with each other while attempting to preserve relationships with their children. It is difficult to obtain actual divorce and separation rates,[3] but the commonly cited statistic that nearly half of all marriages end in divorce is considered a reasonable estimate among researchers (Amato, 2000, 2010; Cherlin, 2010; U.S. Census Bureau, 2005). In addition, over one third of children are born to unmarried parents (U.S. National Center for Health Statistics, 2009), with such relationships being even less durable than marriage (Cherlin, 2010). It is estimated that up to half of the children in the United States will experience parental separation (Cherlin, 2010; Lansford, 2009).

Though court proceedings for some parental separations are short-lived, other families return to court many times, litigating and re-litigating issues about their children. The costs of parental separation to individuals, families, and society appear high. From a purely financial standpoint, Henry, Fieldstone, and Bohac (2009) estimate that a typical divorce can cost individual parties between $30,000 and $35,000 (citing Fried, 2005, and SmartMoney.com, 2008). In addition, a single divorce case "costs the state and federal governments an estimated $30,000 in assistance for factors such as increased food stamp use, public housing, bankruptcies, and juvenile delinquency" (Henry et al., citing Popenoe & Whitehead, 2004, p. 683). This is to say nothing of the costs associated with overcrowded court dockets. The longer a case remains in the system, the higher the cost to parents, children, and the community.

From the social science perspective, researchers have studied the effects of parental separation on individual family members and their future relationships; again, the stakes for families, especially for children, are high. Children of divorced parents are at nearly double the risk to experience social, behavioral, internalizing, and academic problems when compared to children from continuously married parents (Amato, 2001; Kelly & Emery, 2003). Further, researchers have found that the risks for children of divorce persist beyond genetic and selection factors (Amato, 2010; D'Onofrio et al., 2007; Lansford, 2009). At a minimum, parental separation introduces a host of life changes for parents and children (e.g., financial, residential, emotional) which create opportunities for negative reactions, even if the changes do not directly cause negative outcomes (Amato, 2010; Potter, 2010; Wade & Pevalin, 2004). Finally, relative to children whose parents remain married to each other, and even if children of divorce are not more likely to suffer clinical levels of psychological problems, researchers have found that they are more likely to report psychological distress and emotional pain even a decade after the separation (Laumann-Billings & Emery, 2001). The risks associated with parental separation are most pronounced for children when they are exposed to continued parental conflict post-divorce, when the separation is followed by lower levels of positive parenting, and when children are unable to maintain a positive relationship with the nonresidential parent (Amato & Afifi, 2006; Emery, Sbarra, & Grover, 2005; Hetherington, Bridges, & Insabella, 1998; Kelly & Emery, 2003; Lansford, 2009).

The adversarial nature of traditional litigation may exacerbate or even create conflict between separating parents (Emery & Emery, 2008; Emery et al., 2005; Firestone & Weinstein, 2004; Schepard, 2004). In addition, judicial discretion and primacy in decision-making often limit direct parental input into child-rearing arrangements after a litigated separation, which may further hinder the ability of parents to adopt positive parenting techniques and improve child outcomes (Emery & Emery, 2008). Accordingly, well-designed and well-executed processes are needed to help reduce post-separation parental conflict and support the use of adaptive and positive parenting practices by both parents. In fact, many jurisdictions have worked to improve traditional family court procedures and have facilitated the use of ADR processes for separating parents with children.

Improving Parental Separation Processes and Outcomes for Children

Family court reforms began with the 1920's concept of a "unified family court" and regained momentum in the 1970s. This movement advanced the principle that a family court should be a resource for both legal services and additional social support for families facing difficult transitions, resulting in related training for family court judges and an increase in the number of services delivered by the courts (Boyan & Termini, 2005). Still, the unified family court model fails to address the adversarial tenor of court proceedings. In addition, while lawyers representing parents are charged with advocating for their clients' rights and interests as parents, legal codes of ethics do not require attorneys to protect, or even to consider separately, the best interests of children involved (Toofanian, 2007).

The American Academy of Matrimonial Lawyers (AAML) recognized the tension between the requirement for lawyers to zealously advocate for their clients and the importance of protecting the best interests of the clients' children. AAML has supplemented the American Bar Association's (ABA) Model Rules of Professional Conduct (2010) with the AAML Bounds of Advocacy (2000). The AAML guidelines provide that matrimonial attorneys "should consider the welfare of, and seek to minimize the adverse impact of the divorce on, the minor children";[4] "should not permit a client to contest child custody, contact, or access for either financial leverage or vindictiveness"[5]; and "should advise the client of the potential effect of the client's conduct on a child custody dispute."[6]

ADR processes have allowed families to resolve disputes outside of the court system, theoretically increasing the chance that parents and children will better weather separation and experience more positive long-term outcomes. The use of ADR processes for family disputes has become increasingly popular in the United States and internationally (Astor, 2008), and some jurisdictions require parties to attempt ADR prior to proceeding with litigation.

Benefits of Alternative Dispute Resolution Processes in Cases of Parental Separation

From the courts' perspective, facilitating the use of ADR processes in parental separation cases communicates discouragement of litigation for matters that could otherwise be resolved outside the court system and reallocates valuable resources (e.g., courtrooms, court staff, and judges) for use in other types of cases more likely to require that parties have their day in court (see Emery & Emery, 2008, for further discussion).

From the participating families' perspective, ADR processes provide more informal and flexible ways to resolve parental separation, which could result in improved long-term outcomes. For example, in contrast to judicial reliance on rules of evidence, ADR processes allow for more detailed and less rigid presentation of facts and more opportunities for open discussion of issues involved. Perhaps more importantly, ADR processes are typically less adversarial in nature, reducing opportunities for the mud-slinging so often associated with highly contested child custody battles in court. The goal of well-implemented ADR processes is to produce more longstanding agreements and court orders, resulting in fewer instances of re-litigation; because parents are allowed more input into resolutions resulting from ADR processes, it is hoped that they will be more likely to follow agreements that become court orders. Finally, successful use of ADR processes can result in less time and energy spent by parents resolving their separation, potentially shortening the time family members remain under the stress of an ongoing dispute. These key characteristics of ADR processes ultimately may result in strengthened ongoing relationships between family members, bolstering the chance that separated parents, their children, and even members of the extended families, will experience the fewest possible disruptions after parental separation.

Research Foci

We describe the current status of knowledge regarding ADR processes and their effects on family and child well-being. Three main questions/foci frame the chapter: (a) What are the various ADR processes, including family mediation, available to families? (b) What efforts have been made to modify family mediation to address the best interests of children? (c) What are some of the challenges to family mediation when working with high-conflict families?

Methods and Measurement

Empirical research on ADR processes is very limited, and extant studies are plagued by various methodological weaknesses (Beck, Sales, & Emery, 2004). Existing studies, which focus mostly on mediation, usually rely on convenience sampling, small sample sizes, and qualitative methods. Indicators of "success" include agreement rates and client satisfaction, rather than measures of long-term effects on parents and children (Beck & Sales, 2000). Even fewer studies compare mediation to litigation or compare various types or styles of mediation (Beck & Sales, 2000; Beck et al., 2004), or explore the efficacy of other related ADR processes for dissolving families (Emery et al., 2005; Kelly & Emery, 2003). In only one study to date was random assignment used to assign parents to mediation or litigation; this study also advanced the field by testing the effects of mediation over time and assessing multiple outcomes (Emery et al., 2005).

Empirical Findings

Types of ADR Processes for Families Beyond Mediation

Currently, there are a number of different ADR processes available to help families with children. This chapter reports primarily on family mediation; a comprehensive review of mediation follows brief descriptions of other often-utilized ADR processes in family law cases: arbitration, collaborative and cooperative law, and parenting coordination.

Arbitration.   In arbitration, the arbitrator (an impartial decision-maker), or arbitration panel (a panel of impartial decision-makers), chosen or agreed to by the parties, considers the facts and arguments as presented by each party and renders a decision. The decision may be binding (enforceable without any court review) or nonbinding (in which case, the court must review and approve the decision). An arbitrator functions much like a judge, and parties are often, though not always, represented by legal counsel. The process, however, is more informal than traditional court proceedings; unlike litigation, the formal rules of evidence do not apply. In addition, an arbitrator's involvement in a case is usually short-term. This type of ADR process may be most attractive to parents who want a less formal and more efficient process, but still want someone else to make the decisions.

Collaborative and cooperative law.   Collaborative law is an ADR process in which both parents' attorneys work together to find and support their clients' shared values through honest, civil discussions and negotiation (Tesler, 2008). Collaborative law gives divorcing spouses the chance to resolve the dissolution of their marriage in an atmosphere of attorney-supported cooperation, considering the family's legal and non-legal concerns (Daicoff, 2009). Collaborative law attorneys freely share information and work with each other and their clients to reach an agreement that is in the family's best interests. Some collaborative law practitioners choose to work with collaborative teams, utilizing accountants, financial advisors, parenting coaches, family therapists, and other professionals in planning for the family's future (Hoffman, 2008; Tesler, 2008).

One risk of collaborative law is that if an agreement cannot be reached through the collaborative law process, the parties' attorneys are typically disqualified from handling any litigation and the parties must retain new attorneys. The collaborative attorneys may not represent either client for any future dispute between the parties (Hoffman, 2008; Tesler, 2008). Accordingly, failure to reach agreement can result in serious delay and loss of resources. Cooperative law is similar to collaborative law, except that there is no attorney disqualification agreement in the event the parties are unable to resolve their disagreements outside of court. Collative and cooperative law may be most attractive to divorcing parents who are not experiencing high conflict.

Parenting coordination.   Parenting coordination is a relatively new, hybrid, quasi-legal and mental health intervention for high-conflict parents. Typically, though not always, parenting coordination follows the dissolution of a marriage. As an intervention, parenting coordination provides families with assessment, education, and case management. As an ADR process, parenting coordination is intended to manage family conflict, as parenting coordinators typically decide how to resolve disputes when their clients reach stalemates (Coates, Deutsch, Starnes, Sullivan, & Sydlik, 2004; Kirkland & Sullivan, 2008).

The Association of Family and Conciliation Courts (AFCC) Task Force on Parenting Coordination developed Guidelines for Parenting Coordination in 2005, but state courts vary in how and when they employ parenting coordinators. In some states, parenting coordinators become involved with the parents after an initial parenting plan[7] has been created through mediation, arbitration, or litigation (Kirkland, 2008). In other states, the services of a parenting coordinator are ordered by the judge if parents meet the legal requirements for such an order, e.g., the parents have engaged in continuing conflict. Parents may also voluntarily agree to use a parenting coordinator during or after separation (Coates et al., 2004; Kirkland, 2008). In some states, when parents choose to enlist the help of a parenting coordinator and agree that his/her decisions will be binding, only decisions that impact existing court orders must be submitted for court review. In some states, every decision of the parenting coordinator is subject to appeal and review by the court. Some judges are inclined to refer high-conflict families to parenting coordinators in the hopes of diverting conflicts away from the court. However, the possibility remains that these families will continue to experience high conflict, and one or both parties may grow dissatisfied with the parenting coordinator. There is almost no empirical research on the effectiveness of parenting coordination even though parenting coordination is now being conducted in many places throughout the United States (Beck, Putterman, Sbarra, & Mehl, 2008).

Family Mediation

Mediation is an ADR process in which a neutral and impartial facilitator (the mediator) helps parents create their own agreements to resolve all or some of the issues related to their separation and/or child custody and parenting time arrangements. The mediation process is party-driven, meaning that the mediator does little or no independent investigation of the facts and refrains from making any decisions (American Arbitration Association, American Bar Association, & Association for Conflict Resolution, 2005).[8] Like arbitrators, mediators typically have a short-term relationship with the parties. They meet with parents for one or a limited number of sessions. If there is an existing court case, the court typically reviews and approves any written agreement reached through the mediation process.

Key Characteristics of Mediation

Though there are differing styles of mediation, several characteristics of mediation are viewed as essential to the process: (a) *party self-determination*, that the participant has a right, once in mediation, to decide whether to continue in mediation and on what terms, if any, to settle (even if ordered to mediation); (b) *mediator impartiality*, that the mediator does not favor one party over another party in the mediation; (c) *mediator neutrality*, that the mediator has no personal preference that the dispute be resolved in one way rather than another; and (d) *confidentiality* of the process, that the participants should be able to talk freely and explore settlement possibilities without fear that what they say will be used against them in court (Frenkel & Stark, 2008).[9]

The practice of family mediation varies from jurisdiction to jurisdiction. Some, but not all, jurisdictions require specific mediator education (e.g., a 40-hour course or some other form of intensive mediator training). In some jurisdictions, only attorneys may mediate; in other jurisdictions, other professionals (especially mental health professionals) or individuals with a bachelor's degree may mediate. Certain jurisdictions encourage or require attorney participation in mediation; in some jurisdictions, attorneys are excluded from the mediation process (though typically not from reviewing agreements reached in mediation). Though mediation is typically treated as a confidential settlement process, jurisdictions vary on whether the confidentiality may be waived by the parties. Some jurisdictions restrict or regulate what mediators may do with self-represented mediation parties (i.e., parties without lawyers). This last area has been particularly controversial in recent years, due to concerns by some in the legal community that mediators are engaging in the practice of law when they discuss the law with parties or draft documents for the parties for review by the court.

Mediation Styles

How mediation is conducted will vary from mediator to mediator. During the mediation process, mediators are expected to establish a climate in which creative problem solving by the parties can occur (Frenkel & Stark, 2008), but mediators can and do employ a variety of styles to further that basic goal.

In "facilitative" mediation, the focus typically is to identify the interests of the parties that underlie their stated positions, and then generate and evaluate possible solutions to resolve the parties' disputes, considering how the solutions meet the parties' interests. By revealing the values and concerns of the parties, a facilitative mediator helps parties move away from using distributive or competitive, position-oriented bargaining tactics (Alexander, 2008; Levin, 2001). A facilitative mediation style may be particularly useful in family law cases involving children since the parties expect to have future dealings with each other and thus may benefit from better understanding the other parent's point of view (Alexander, 2008). Some, but not all, facilitative mediators, prefer to mediate with the parties in the same room, so that the parties learn better methods of communication.

In "evaluative" or "directive" mediation, the focus typically is to solve problems by assisting the parties to propose and consider possible offers or counter-proposals. Evaluative mediators may evaluate the strengths and weaknesses of each party's case and may offer predictions about what might happen in court; some evaluative mediators also explore party interests and concerns to assist in creating solutions acceptable to both parties. Some, but not all, directive mediators prefer to mediate with the parties in separate rooms (also called caucus or shuttle mediation) in order to test reality with the parties on the weaknesses of their case and control the flow of information between the parties. Some mediators believe that keeping the parties separate is more efficient (time-wise), because the mediator is able to keep better control over the process and how messages are delivered between the parties. Other mediators, however, find that going back and forth between the parties is less efficient because the parties are not talking directly to each other.

Finally, in "transformative" mediation, the focus is to permanently affect how parties relate to each other and ultimately heal dysfunctional relationships (Alexander, 2008; Bush & Pope, 2003). The mediator is charged with creating an environment that empowers each party to define his or her own issues while simultaneously recognizing the other party's point of view on the issues. Effective recognition requires that each party both acknowledge and empathize with the other party's perspective. Immediate problem solving is not the focus of a transformative mediation; rather, settlement is a by-product of the parties' growth toward understanding each other.

Some mediators use multiple styles of mediation, even during the same mediation. What might start as facilitative mediation may end with the mediator becoming directive if the parties resolve all issues but one (e.g., the location for the exchange of the children). Additionally, facilitative mediators are often directive about the process, even if they are not directive about the outcome. Some facilitative mediators attempt to ensure that the parties acknowledge and empathize with one another (a key element of transformative mediation). Each style of mediation has its proponents who tout its advantages and the disadvantages of the other styles of mediation (Alexander, 2008).

Core Components of the Mediation Process

Whatever the mediator's approach, there are several identifiable components of mediation that parties may expect in any mediation: (a) an opening during which the mediator explains the process and the rules of the process; (b) gathering information and identifying the issues to be mediated; (c) framing the issues; (d) considering and negotiating options; (e) reaching agreement (if agreement is reached); (f) preparation of the written agreement (again, assuming that agreement is reached); and (g) closing. Though mediation styles may differ, an effective mediator should have these four basic skills: (a) good communication skills; (b) good diagnosis skills (i.e., of the parties' issues, interests, and concerns); (c) the ability to establish a climate in which creative problem solving and negotiation can occur; and (d) good persuasion skills (Frenkel & Stark, 2008). During mediation, the parties should expect to have the mediator engage in active listening, ask many questions, focus on parties' interests and priorities, and test reality about the practicality of, and the likelihood of the court ordering, suggested resolutions.

Benefits of Mediation

Supporters of mediation for resolving family disputes list many potential benefits for participants in these processes. Theoretically, like other ADR processes, mediation should reduce time and fees associated with courts, attorneys, and re-litigation and offer individuals a less adversarial and less acrimonious way to resolve the issue involved in their disputes (Beck & Sales, 2000; Beck et al., 2004; Frenkel & Stark, 2008). Further, in family mediation, parents may explore options for settlement with an honest and open exchange of information in a confidential process designed to protect the parties from embarrassment in court. By focusing on interests and concerns rather than adversarial positions, family mediation should empower parents to make decisions that are reasonable for them and good for their children. Importantly, family mediators are not only encouraged, but in some jurisdictions, ethically required to assist the parties in focusing on promoting the best interests of their children.[10]

Unfortunately, there is limited empirical research on the effectiveness of family mediation. Nevertheless, there is some promising evidence that family mediation participation results in beneficial outcomes when compared with litigation. Emery et al. (2005) randomly assigned separating parents to mediation or litigation, and found multiple benefits of mediation for participants initially and at a 12-year follow-up. Participation in mediation resulted in higher rates of agreement, decreased litigation following divorce, *greater satisfaction with the agreement among fathers, and more father involvement with their children.* Despite these encouraging initial findings, it is important to realize that this study examined one type of mediation, at one site, with one sample. Additionally, there were no effects found relating to positive child adjustment or the parental relationship between the parents. Thus, the need to continue developing and evaluating mediation programs persists, particularly with a view to improving outcomes for children at risk after their parents' separation.

Modifications to Mediation to Focus on the Best Interests of the Children

Clinical psychologist Jennifer McIntosh, in Australia, hypothesized that family mediation could help reduce family conflict and improve outcomes for children if the process provided parents with an improved opportunity and better resources to focus on the best interests of their children. McIntosh and her colleagues developed two forms of child-informed mediation: Child-Focused Mediation (CF) and Child-Inclusive Mediation (CI) (McIntosh, 2000). In CI, parents and the mediator meet with a child consultant, i.e., a trained mental health professional. The child consultant meets with both parents and their children to gain an understanding of their experience, needs, and concerns related to the parents' separation. The child consultant then provides individualized feedback to the parents based on the interview with the children. In CF, there is no feedback session between the child consultant and the parents. Instead, the mediator offers parents general developmental information about children and education about the impact of parental conflict and separation on children, while trying to individualize the message to fit the possible concerns and needs of the parents' children (McIntosh, Wells, Smyth, & Long, 2008).

McIntosh designed both CI and CF to allow the child's needs to be voiced in mediation while also addressing concerns raised about that process, e.g., the potential harm of burdening children with the sense that they are responsible for adult decision making (Kelly & Emery, 2003). Specifically, child consultants were trained to communicate to participating children that only the parents would make decisions in mediation and that child consultants would not make promises about the outcome of mediation (McIntosh, 2000); child consultants also helped children to understand issues of confidentiality and obtained the children's permission to pass along certain messages to the parents.

McIntosh et al. (2008) compared CI and CF in a study of 150 families who received either CF or CI. One year after the interventions, results showed that both forms of mediation lowered parental conflict and child distress about parental discord, and both improved child mental health. Relative to CF, the CI group had better outcomes on several measures including less litigation following divorce, *increased father satisfaction with parenting arrangements, and greater father involvement in their children's lives.* However, McIntosh et al. did not use random assignment, instead studying CF for 6 months and then CI for the following 6 months, thus making it difficult to be sure that the CI process was more effective than the CF process (instead of some other cause). Further, McIntosh did not compare CI and CF to traditional family mediation, making it difficult to know whether CF and/or CI would result in better outcomes than traditional mediation.

Currently, we are expanding on Emery and McIntosh's research at Indiana University (IU), through our Child Informed Mediation Study (CIMS; Holtzworth-Munroe, Applegate, D'Onofrio, & Bates, 2010). Parents seeking mediation at the IU law school's mediation clinic, if they consent to participate in our study, are randomly assigned to one of three mediation conditions: (a) CI; (b) CF; or (c) the clinic's traditional family mediation (no systematic, standardized assessment of the children or feedback to parents about their children). In contrast to McIntosh et al.'s 2008 study, the IU child consultants provide feedback to parents in both CI and CF, though interviews of the children are only done in CI. Given both the nature of the clinic (a university training clinic) and an interest in minimizing costs of the intervention, law students or faculty serve as the mediators and clinical psychology graduate students or faculty serve as the child consultants; law students are supervised by the attorney (law professor) director of the mediation clinic and child consultants are supervised by clinical psychology professors. The CIMS pilot study is underway and will last through 1-year follow-up assessments of intervention outcomes.

Intimate Partner Violence and Abuse (IPV/A) in Mediation Cases

Working with high-conflict families presents practical and ethical challenges to both the practice and study of mediation. These challenges may be greatest when the conflict is severe enough to be defined as intimate partner violence or abuse (IPV/A), meaning that the conflict involves physical or sexual violence, threats of violence, or coercive control.[11] IPV/A, like parental separation, has serious implications for child well-being; children exposed to IPV/A are more likely to exhibit both internalizing and behavioral problems later in life (Evans, Davies, & DiLillo, 2008; Kitzmann, Gaylord, Holt, & Kenny, 2003). Thus, it is important to discuss IPV/A issues related to family mediation.

Though the definition and detected rates of IPV/A among mediated cases of divorce or separation vary among researchers, it is common to find physical violence reported in more than 50% of mediation cases (e.g., Ballard, Holtzworth-Munroe, Applegate, & Beck, 2011; Beck, Menke, Brewster, & Figueredo, 2009; Beck, Walsh, Mechanic, & Taylor, 2009; Beck, Walsh, & Weston, 2009). When the definition of IPV/A is expanded beyond physical violence to include coercive control, Beck and Raghavan (2010) found that only 10% of cases in their study reported no IPV/A by either party. The number of mediation cases involving IPV/A perhaps is not surprising; research has shown that IPV/A is an important predictor of family dissolution (Anderson, 2010, citing Demaris, 2000, 2001) and is often cited as a reason for family dissolution by separating couples (e.g., Amato & Previti, 2003; Ayoub, Deutsch, & Maraganore, 1999; see also Anderson, 2010). Ostensibly, many cases referred to family mediation present with issues related to IPV/A.

IPV/A Screening for Mediation Cases

In order to appropriately safeguard the mediation process and facilitate suitable agreements for families experiencing IPV/A, mediators must be able to detect whether violence has occurred between the parties (Holtzworth-Munroe, Beck, & Applegate, 2010). This requires sensitive screening measures and protocols that detect a full picture of IPV/A-related issues that might affect whether and how to conduct negotiations, and that should be considered in reaching agreements in mediation. Many professionals support the use of IPV/A screening measures for participants in mediation, citing both an ethical responsibility for doing such screening and disproportionate risk to unscreened versus screened mediation participants (Beck & Sales, 2000; Ellis, 2008; Holtzworth-Munroe et al., 2010; Kelly & Johnson, 2008; Mathis & Tanner, 1998; Salem & Dunford-Jackson, 2008). However, some family mediators question whether IPV/A screening is necessary or appropriate in the mediation setting,[12] and IPV/A screening is not a universal practice among family mediators.

Without systematic screening for IPV/A, mediators may underestimate the prevalence of IPV/A among their clients and may not recognize risks present in particular cases. In two studies of mediation programs, approximately 70% reported that mediators received IPV/A training and 60-80% reported screening for IPV/A in some way (Clemants & Gross, 2007; Thoennes, Salem, & Pearson, 1995). However, screening protocols varied widely among the programs, with many failing to use formal, standardized screening tools (questionnaires or interviews) in ways that would obtain complete information about IPV/A from their mediation clients. Specifically, research in other areas has shown that the common practice of screening couples together, which could be intimidating for IPV/A victims, results in under-reporting of

IPV/A. The same is true when practitioners ask general questions about assault or victimization rather than behaviorally specific questions (Ehrensaft & Vivian, 1996; Langhinrichsen-
Rohling, 2005). In an early study of IPV/A screening at the IU law school mediation clinic, we
found that despite some screening for IPV/A (including searching civil and criminal records for
the parties attending mediation, reading court records, asking the parties privately about their
history of conflict and whether they were comfortable sitting with each other in mediation),
mediators did not identify the presence of physical violence in over 50% of mediation cases
in which at least one of the mediation parties reported physical violence by the other party
to researchers on a behaviorally specific IPV/A screening questionnaire (Ballard et al., 2011).

Few IPV/A screening measures have been specifically designed for use in mediation. One
is the Relationships Behavior Rating Scale (RBRS; Beck, Menke, et al., 2009), but this is a
copyrighted measure and mediators must pay to use it. Another is the Domestic Violence
Evaluation (DOVE; Ellis & Stuckless, 2006), but this screen requires time-intensive specialized training to administer. Holtzworth-Munroe et al. (2010) worked to combine and improve
elements in previously validated IPV/A screening instruments to create the Mediator's Assessment of Safety Issues and Concerns (MASIC). The MASIC asks both parents (privately) about
IPV/A victimization ever during the parents' relationship and during the last 12 months to
capture changing patterns of IPV/A. To maximize the amount of IPV/A captured, the MASIC
incorporates a wide range of behaviorally specific items, including items related to emotional
abuse, coercive control, threats of severe violence, physical violence and severe physical violence, sexual violence, stalking, and fear.

At the IU law mediation clinic the MASIC is administered during a confidential intake
process, where the parties are kept separate. The intake is conducted on a day prior to the
scheduled negotiations between the parties (to provide the mediators and the parties with an
opportunity to consider the information obtained through the screening process). Due to a risk
that mediation parties' self-incriminating statements made in mediation might be admissible
in a criminal proceeding,[13] the MASIC only asks mediation parties about IPV/A experienced
as victims. Finally, the MASIC is not copyrighted, is available at no charge, and can be widely
disseminated. Validation and reliability checks on the MASIC are in progress.

Mediation Procedure Accommodations for Cases Involving IPV/A

Regardless of whether mediators agree about when and how to screen for IPV/A, practical and
ethical questions arise when mediation clients report that there has been IPV/A. At that point,
mediators must decide whether to mediate, and if so, whether and how IPV/A issues will dictate the structure of the mediation process and/or affect the outcome of mediation (see, e.g.,
Holtzworth-Munroe, 2011). In the United States, mediation guidelines and requirements vary
in how and whether they address IPV/A issues.[14] It follows that mediation cases with IPV/A
are handled differently among mediators in different jurisdictions, and even among mediators
in the same jurisdictions (Clemants & Gross, 2007; Thoennes et al., 1995; Salem, Kulak &
Deutsch, 2007).[15]

Some experts have raised serious concerns about the appropriateness of mediation for parents who have experienced IPV/A. Mediation assumes that parents are capable of negotiating for themselves and reaching an agreement that is safe and in the best interests of their
children, and that mediators can provide safe environments that facilitate non-coercive

negotiations. However, some researchers express concern that many mediators do not understand the dynamics of families with a history of IPV/A, and that victims will suffer as a result (Grillo, 1991; Hart, 2007).[16] There is also a risk of physical harm to victims following separation (Beck & Sales, 2000; Campbell et al., 2003). In addition, an abused partner's fears of the batterer could lead the victim to give in to demands in mediation, potentially even increasing the partner's and children's exposure to continued unsafe contact with the abuser (Beck & Sales, 2000; Tishler, Bartholomae, Katz, & Landry-Meyer, 2004). It has been suggested that some IPV/A victims may not even meet the legal standard of competence to mediate, due to impaired decision-making related to self-interested outcomes (Beck & Frost, 2006). Finally, if IPV/A is bidirectional, meaning that the separating couple is enmeshed in conflict initiated and perpetuated by both parties, mediation may only work to intensify and prolong the conflict by providing an opportunity for couples to continue to air past wrongs (Beck & Sales, 2000).

Proponents of mediation counter that mediation offers unique, individually-tailored safeguards to promote safety and consideration of children's needs in agreements. Edwards, Baron, and Ferrick (2008) contend that automatically excluding victims of violence from mediation falsely assumes that all victims are not capable of promoting their interests and those of their children. Moreover, proponents are concerned about the loss of mediation's benefits over adversarial litigation for families and question the appropriateness of screening out cases with IPV/A. It is arguably disempowering to a party victimized by IPV/A to be refused mediation services, particularly if the victim prefers to mediate (assuming this can be done in a safe and well-designed mediation process sensitive to the IPV/A issues) rather than face the abuser in court. Indeed, there is no research demonstrating that courts resolve family disputes better than parents in mediation (Beck et al., 2004).

Of particular relevance to fathers, Dutton and his colleagues have argued that the field of family law focuses too much on male-to-female violence, while ignoring female-to-male violence (e.g., Dutton, 2005; Dutton, Hamel, & Aaronson, 2010). They also argue that mediators may address all levels of violence, even the more commonly occurring less severe violence, as if it were the type of severe IPV/A experienced by clinical samples. They propose, among other things, more careful assessment of IPV/A (e.g., of the perpetration of violence by both partners and of the levels of IPV/A) and unbiased training in IPV/A family law professionals.

After considering the results of the IPV/A screen, if a party reports being victimized by the other party and does not want to mediate because of that history, fear, or safety concerns, the mediator should decline to mediate and return the case to court without prejudicing either party. If one or both parties report IPV/A, both parties want to mediate, and the mediator believes that both parties are competent to mediate and that the mediation can be conducted safely, the mediator should consider keeping the parties in separate rooms during the mediation, staggering arrival and departure times, arranging for a party to attend by telephone, moving the mediation to a secure facility, and/or any other accommodations appropriate or necessary to protect the parties' safety and ability to make voluntary decisions.[17]

In some cases, one or both of the parties should be accompanied in mediation.[18] Some parties may need to be represented by an attorney during the mediation. Other parties may be well served by the presence of an advocate from a domestic violence shelter during the mediation. Other parties may simply need the encouragement of a family member or friend as a support person during the process. The mediator may suggest that one or both parties be accompanied, but the mediator typically does not decide who must attend mediation with a particular party. Nevertheless, the mediator should make appropriate suggestions and referrals to parties, or decline to mediate (or continue mediating) when an unaccompanied party appears to be in physical danger or appears unable to make decisions in the party's (and/or children's) interests.

Mediation Agreements in Cases with IPV/A

Although mediators should be neutral, meaning that the mediator does not dictate the terms of agreements, some researchers have made recommendations about what should be included in mediation agreements of families who report IPV/A. In the most detailed proposal to date, Jaffe, Johnston, Crooks, and Bala (2008) advocate that the content of mediation agreements reflect the family's level of IPV/A; they make specific content recommendations based on each family's level of IPV/A. In cases with no IPV/A, Jaffe et al. promote co-parenting, in which parents share decision making, communicate and jointly solve problems, and display flexibility in parenting time. Their most restrictive proposal, for families with high violence and ongoing threats, is a suspended contact model, with sole decision making authority and physical custody given to the less violent parent, suspension of all parenting time with the violent parent, and stipulation of goals for the violent parent to acquire supervised parenting time in the future.

Only a few studies have compared the mediation agreements of violent and nonviolent parents to determine if these kinds of suggestions are implemented by families. The findings so far demonstrate that these kinds of recommendations are not typically followed. Specifically, the agreements reached by families reporting IPV/A versus families not reporting IPV/A have not consistently differed in terms of parents' legal or physical custody arrangements, even when mediators were aware of the presence of IPV/A (Beck, Walsh, et al., 2009; Holtzworth-Munroe, 2011; Mathis & Tanner, 1998; Putz, Ballard, Arany, Applegate, & Holtzworth-Munroe, 2011).

The argument that the mediation agreements of families who report IPV/A should include certain provisions is problematic to many mediators as it conflicts with what most mediators would agree are three of the key characteristics of mediation described above: party self-determination, mediator impartiality, and mediator neutrality (Frenkel & Stark, 2008).[19] Though a mediator might hesitate or refuse to require that parties reach specific agreements, the mediator instead might be required to withdraw from mediation when a proposed resolution is unconscionable, e.g., it does not protect the physical safety and psychological well-being of themselves and/or their children.[20]

Bridges to Other Disciplines

As noted above, empirical research into the benefits of different ADR processes is limited. Effective evaluation of such processes should rely on valid and reliable measurement of adjustment and functioning in both parents and children. In this regard, researchers in Developmental Psychology, Family Studies, and other related areas could provide useful resources and collaboration. Additionally, economists could assist by estimating the long-term costs and benefits to various interventions, including effects on children's academic achievement and well-being.

Policy Implications

In the last few years, advocates and mediators have begun to work together to discuss how to appropriately handle high-conflict families and cases of IPV/A in mediation (Salem & Dunford-Jackson, 2008). For example, the Wingspread Conference on Domestic Violence and Family Courts (co-sponsored by the Association for Family and Conciliation Courts and the

National Council of Juvenile and Family Court Judges) brought advocates, family court professionals, mediators and researchers together to specifically address this topic. As noted in Ver Steegh and Dalton (2008), the Wingspread Conference attendees generated a list of consensus points that included recognizing the necessity of screening for violence, the importance of differentiating varying forms and types of IPV/A, and a call for practitioners to continue to work collaboratively. Such a consensus may help bridge the gaps among the various perspectives on handling mediation cases where IPV/A issues are present (Kelly & Johnson, 2008).

Future Directions

Though mediation may be the most studied ADR process for separating parents, parents may consider a variety of ADR options outside of the traditional court system. Different ADR processes provide parents with varied levels of autonomy in decision-making regarding their children and offer families settings and procedures that foster cooperation and discourage continued conflict, ultimately benefiting the children involved. Though the empirical evidence supporting the benefits of ADR processes in cases of parental separation is increasing, future research is needed to explore the long-term of effects of participation in ADR. In particular, researchers should expand their work to explore the potential positive effect of ADR processes on father-child relationships. Finally, researchers should recognize that each type of ADR process may present practical and ethical challenges for practitioners, especially in cases where parents experience high levels of ongoing conflict; more research is needed to determine the best ways to overcome these challenges.

Notes

1. The authors would like to thank Rebecca Billick, J.D., M.A. and Renee Skeete, J.D. for their assistance with this chapter. The authors would also like to acknowledge their colleagues in the Department of Psychological and Brain Sciences, with whom they frequently collaborate: Brian M. D'Onofrio, Ph.D., John E. Bates. Ph.D., and Robin H. Ballard. The authors would further like to acknowledge Connie J. A. Beck, Ph.D. from the University of Arizona, and Jennifer McIntosh, Ph.D. from LaTrobe University, Australia, for their collaboration and support of our work. Finally, the authors would like to thank Professor D'Onofrio for funding Katherine Schwartz while she worked on this chapter.
2. In cases with intimate partner violence or abuse, however, the family systems model has been called into question (see, e.g., Grillo, 1991).
3. There is no national, uniform standard for reporting marriage and divorce rates. In fact, several states do not report these and related vital statistics (see U.S. Census Bureau, 2002).
4. AAML (2000) §6.1.
5. AAML (2000) §6.2.
6. AAML (2000) §5.2.
7. A parenting plan is a plan created either by the court or through mutual party agreement that defines how the parents will exercise legal custody, physical custody, parenting time, and other relevant topics.
8. Hereafter: ABA Model Standards of Conduct for Mediators.
9. As an exception to the confidentiality of the process, mediators are typically mandated reporters of child abuse or neglect that has not previously been reported.
10. See, for example, the Model Standards of Practice for Family and Divorce Mediation (AFCC Symposium on Standards of Practice, 2000), at Standard VIII; Ind. A.D.R Rule 2.7(A) (2) requiring that the mediator shall "in child related matters, ensure that the parties consider fully the best interests of the children and that the parties understand the consequences of any decision they reach concerning the children."
11. Coercive control, according to Beck and Raghavan (2010), includes behaviors like stalking, withholding money and other resources, and emotional abuse.
12. Resistance to IPV/A screening may stem from various beliefs held by mediators about the perceived risks of

screening. For example, mediators may not want to distress IPV/A victims before mediation by reminding them of past conflict or violence; they may be concerned that mediation participants asked to recount traumatic events may experience anger or sadness over past wrongs or fear about the consequences of reporting abuse. Further, mediators may have concerns about whether IPV/A victims, after being screened, are able to switch gears from their heightened emotional state to be able to compromise and negotiate (Beck & Frost, 2006; Grillo, 1991; Hart, 2007). Mediators also may feel uncomfortable asking sensitive questions. Alternatively, they may worry that their own reaction to IPV/A reports would challenge their ability to mediate; mediators' neutrality and/or impartiality (or the parties' perception thereof) might be affected if they learned through screening that one party was the perpetrator of violence against the other or that there was an obvious power imbalance between parties. Finally, mediators may be concerned about the possibility that parents may make false allegations of IPV/A, which could impact the outcome of mediated disputes about their children, without evidence that corroborates the parents' reports (Dutton, 2005).

13. In Indiana, there is precedent that discussions in mediation, though protected from disclosure in the underlying case, may be admissible in a separate criminal proceeding. See *In re March, 1994 Special Grand Jury, 897 F. Supp. 1170* (S.D. Ind. 1995) in which the mediator was compelled to testify in a federal grand jury proceeding about discussions in mediation.

14. The ABA Model Standards of Conduct for Mediators (2005) provide minimally that, "If a mediator is made aware of domestic abuse or violence among the parties, the mediator shall take appropriate steps including, if necessary, postponing, withdrawing from or terminating the mediation" (Standard VI.B.). In addition, the Model Standards of Practice for Family and Divorce Mediation (AFCC Symposium on Standards of Practice, 2000; Standard X) suggest that mediators make efforts to assess IPV/A throughout the mediation process and possibly adjust mediation procedures. These adjustments include encouraging participants to bring a support person or legal counsel to mediation, holding separate mediation sessions, procuring appropriate security, or suspending or terminating mediation sessions to protect the safety of the participants (Standard X). Other possible procedural modifications include shuttle mediation, separate waiting rooms, staggered arrival and departure times, and security personnel (Beck et al., 2004).

15. In Indiana, for example, "The mediator shall terminate mediation whenever the mediator believes that continuation of the process would harm or prejudice one or more of the parties or the children or whenever the ability or willingness of any party to participate meaningfully in mediation is so lacking that a reasonable agreement is unlikely." Ind. A.D.R Rule 2.7(D).

16. The majority of researchers cited here as expressing concern about the possible dangers of conducting mediation in cases involving IPV/A have focused on male perpetrated violence and female survivors. However, the occurrence of any IPV/A is potentially of concern, and the effect on both partners, as well as their children, should be considered.

17. The mediator should also consider any other imbalances of power that may affect the mediation process. When the parties are equally matched in cognitive ability (Beck & Frost, 2006) or legal representation (Petterson, Ballard, Putz, & Holtzworth-Munroe, 2010) there is less concern that one party is unknowingly waiving his or her rights during the course of negotiating an agreement. However, when courts order unrepresented parties to mediation without any pre-screening process to determine sufficient understanding and ability to participate in mediation, the agreements are at risk of being unjust to a less competent party (Beck & Frost, 2006). A mediator may not assist a less competent party during the negotiations without threatening the tenets of impartiality and neutrality. Thus, when a mediator has reason to believe that there may be a cognitive or emotional imbalance between the parties that will disproportionately affect the rights of one party, the mediator may need to consider declining to mediate the case or implementing procedures so that the less competent party is able to participate appropriately in the process.

18. It is recognized that a mediator "cannot personally ensure that each party has made free and informed choices to reach particular decisions, but, where appropriate, a mediator should make the parties aware of the importance of consulting other professionals to help them make informed choices" (ABA Model Standards of Conduct for Mediators, 2005).

19. These concepts are routinely found in rules relating to mediation. See, for example, AFCC Symposium on Standards of Practice, 2000; the ABA Model Standards of Conduct for Mediators, 2005; and Indiana Rules for Alternative Dispute Resolution, including amendments through January 1, 2011. Putz et al. (2011); Holtzworth-Munroe (2011).

20. Id. Ind. A.D.R. Rule 7.5(B), for example, provides that, "A neutral shall withdraw whenever a proposed resolution is unconscionable." The Model Standards of Practice for Family and Divorce Mediation (AFCC Symposium on Standards of Practice; Standard X (E) provides that, "The mediator should facilitate the participants'

formulation of parenting plans that protect the physical safety and psychological well-being of themselves and their children."

References

Alexander, N. (2008). The mediation metamodel: Understanding practice. *Conflict Resolution Quarterly, 26*(1), 97–123.

Amato, P. R. (2000). The consequences of divorce for adults and children. *Journal of Marriage and Family, 62,* 1269–1287.

Amato, P. R. (2001). Children of divorce in the 1990s: An update of the Amato and Keith (1991) meta-analysis. *Journal of Family Psychology, 15*(3), 355–370.

Amato, P. R. (2010). Research on divorce: Continuing trends and new developments. *Journal of Marriage and Family, 72,* 650–666.

Amato, P. R., & Afifi, T. D. (2006). Feeling caught between parents: Adult children's relations with parents and subjective well-being. *Journal of Marriage and Family, 68*(1), 222–235.

Amato, P. R., & Previti, D. (2003). People's reasons for divorcing: Gender, social class, the life course adjustment. *Journal of Family Issues, 24,* 602–626.

American Academy of Matrimonial Lawyers. (2000). *The bounds of advocacy.* Retrieved from http://www.aaml.org/library/publications/19/bounds-advocacy

American Arbitration Association, American Bar Association, & Association for Conflict Resolution. (2005). *The model standards of conduct for mediators.* Retrieved from http://www.americanbar.org/content/dam/aba/migrated/2011_build/dispute_resolution/model_standards_conduct_april2007.authcheckdam.pdf

American Bar Association. (2010). *Model rules of professional conduct.* Retrieved from http://www.americanbar.org/groups/professional_responsibility/publications/model_rules_of_professional_conduct/model_rules_of_professional_conduct_table_of_contents.html.

Anderson, K. L. (2010). Conflict, power, and violence in families. *Journal of Marriage and Family, 72,* 726–742.

Association of Family and Conciliation Courts Task Force on Parenting Coordination. (2005). *The guidelines for parenting coordination.* Retrieved from http://www.afccnet.org/pdfs/AFCC2GuidelinesforParentingcoordination2.pdf

Association of Family and Conciliation Courts Symposium on Standards of Practice. (2000). *Model standards of practice for family and divorce mediation.* Retrieved from http://www.afccnet.org/resources/resources_model_mediation.asp

Astor, H. (2008). Making a genuine effort in family mediation: What does it mean? *Australian Journal of Family Law, 22,* 102.

Ayoub, C. C., Deutsch, R. M., & Maraganore, A. (1999). Emotional distress in children of high-conflict divorce: The impact of marital conflict and violence. *Family and Conciliation Courts Review, 37*(3), 297–314.

Ballard, R. H., Holtzworth-Munroe, A., Applegate, A. G., & Beck, C. J. A. (2011). Detecting intimate partner violence in family and divorce mediation: A randomized trial of intimate partner violence screening. *Psychology, Public Policy, and Law, 17*(2), 241–263.

Beck, C. J. A., & Frost, L. E. (2006). Defining a threshold for client competence to participate in divorce mediation. *Psychology, Public Policy, and Law, 12*(1), 1–35.

Beck, C. J. A., Menke, J. M., Brewster, K. O., & Figueredo, A. J. (2009). Validation of a measure of intimate partner abuse with couples participating in divorce mediation. *Journal of Divorce & Remarriage, 50*(5), 295–308.

Beck, C. J. A., Putterman (Levenson), M. D., Sbarra, D. A., & Mehl, M. R. (2008). Parenting coordinator roles, program goals and services provided: Insights from the Pima County, Arizona program. *Journal Child Custody, Special Issue on Parenting Coordination, 5*(1/2), 122–139.

Beck, C. J. A., & Raghavan, C. (2010). Intimate partner abuse screening in custody mediation: The importance of assessing coercive control. *Family Court Review, 48*(3), 555–565.

Beck, C. J. A., & Sales, B. D. (2000). A critical reappraisal of divorce mediation research and policy. *Psychology, Public Policy, and Law, 6*(4), 989–1056.

Beck, C. J. A., Sales, B. D., & Emery, R. E. (2004). Research on the impact of family mediation. In J. Folberg, A. L. Milne, & P. Salem (Eds.), *Divorce and family mediation* (pp. 447–482). New York: Guilford.

Beck, C. J. A., Walsh, M. E., Mechanic, M., & Taylor, C. (2009). Mediator assessment, documentation, and disposition of child custody cases involving intimate partner abuse: A naturalistic evaluation of one county's practices. *Law and Human Behavior, 39*(3), 227–240.

Beck, C. J. A., Walsh, M. E., & Weston, R. (2009). Analysis of mediation agreements of families reporting specific types of intimate partner abuse. *Family Court Review, 47*(3), 401–415.

Boyan, S. M., & Termini, A. (2005). *The psychotherapist as parent coordinator in high-conflict divorce: Strategies and techniques*. Binghamton, NY: Haworth Clinical Practice Press.

Bush, R. A. B., & Pope, S. G. (2003). Changing the quality of conflict interaction: The principles and practice of transformative mediation. *Pepperdine Dispute Resolution Law Journal, 3*(1), 67–80.

Campbell, J. C., Webster, D., Koziol-McLain, J., Block, C., Campbell, D., Curry, M. A., ... & Laughon, K. (2003). Risk factors for femicide in abusive relationships: Results from a multisite case control trial. *American Journal of Public Health, 93*(7), 1089–1097.

Cherlin, A. J. (2010). Demographic trends in the United States: A review of the research in the 2000s. *Journal of Marriage and Family, 72*, 403–419.

Clemants, E., & Gross, A. (2007). "Why aren't we screening?" A survey examining domestic violence screening procedures and training protocol in community mediation centers. *Conflict Resolution Quarterly, 24*(4), 413–431.

Coates, C.A ., Deutsch, R., Starnes, H., Sullivan, M. J., & Sydlik, B. (2004). Parenting coordination for high conflict families. *Family Court Review, 42*, 246–262.

Cox, M. J., & Paley, B. (1997). Families as systems. *Annual Review of Psychology, 48*, 243–267.

Daicoff, S. (2009). Collaborative law: A new tool for the lawyer's toolkit. *University of Florida Law Journal and Public Policy, 20*, 113–146.

D'Onofrio, B. M., Turkheimer, E., Emery, R. E., Harden, K. P., Slutske, W. S., Heath, A. C., ... Martin, N. G. (2007). A genetically informed study of the intergenerational transmission of marital instability. *Journal of Marriage and Family, 69*, 793–809.

Dutton, D. G. (2005). Domestic abuse assessment in child custody disputes: Beware the domestic violence research paradigm. *Journal of Child Custody, 2*, 23–42.

Dutton, D. G., Hamel, J., & Aaronson, J. (2010). The gender paradigm in family court processes: Rebalancing the scales of justice from biased social science. *Journal of Child Custody, 7*, 1–31.

Edwards, L., Baron, S., & Ferrick, G. (2008). A comment on William J. Howe and Hugh McIsaac's article "Finding the Balance" published in the January 2008 issue of Family Court Review. *Family Court Review, 46*(4), 586–591.

Ehrensaft, M. K., & Vivian, D. (1996). Spouses' reasons for not reporting existing marital aggression as a marital problem. *Journal of Family Psychology, 10*(4), 443–453.

Ellis, D. (2008). Divorce and the family court: What can be done about domestic violence? *Family Court Review, 46*(3), 531–536.

Ellis, D., & Stuckless, N. (2006). Separation, domestic violence, and divorce mediation. *Conflict Resolution Quarterly, 23*(4), 461–485.

Emery, R. E., & Emery, K. C. (2008). Should courts or parents make child-rearing decisions?: Married parents as a paradigm for parents who live apart. *Wake Forest Law Review, 43*, 365–389.

Emery, R. E., Sbarra, D., & Grover, T. (2005). Divorce mediation: Research and reflections. *Family Court Review, 43*(1), 22–37.

Evans, S. E., Davies, C., & DiLillo, D. (2008). Exposure to domestic violence: A meta-analysis of child and adolescent outcomes. *Aggression and Violent Behavior, 13*(2), 131–140.

Firestone, G., & Weinstein, J. (2004). In the best interests of children: A proposal to transform the adversarial system. *Family Court Review, 42*, 203–212.

Frenkel, D. N., & Stark, J. H. (2008). *The practice of mediation*. New York, NY: Aspen.

Grillo, T. (1991). The mediation alternative: Process dangers for women. *The Yale Law Journal, 100*(6), 1545–1610.

Hart, B. J. (2007). Gentle jeopardy: The further endangerment of battered women and children in custody mediation. *Conflict Resolution Quarterly, 7*(4), 317–330.

Henry, W. J., Fieldstone, L., & Bohac, K. (2009). Parenting coordination and court relitigation: A case study. *Family Court Review, 47*, 682–696.

Hetherington, E. M., Bridges, M., & Insabella, G. M. (1998). What matters? What does not? Five perspectives on the association between marital transitions and children's adjustment. *American Psychologist, 53*(2), 167–184.

Hoffman, D. (2008). Colliding worlds of dispute resolution: Towards a unified field theory of ADR. *Journal of Dispute Resolution, 2008*, 11–44.

Holtzworth-Munroe, A. (2011). Controversies in divorce mediation and intimate partner violence: A focus on the children. *Aggression and Violent Behavior, 16*, 319–324.

Holtzworth-Munroe, A., Applegate, A. G., D'Onofrio, B., & Bates, J. (2010). Child Informed Mediation Study (CIMS): Incorporating the children's perspective into divorce mediation. *Journal of Family Studies, 16*, 116–129.

Holtzworth-Munroe, A., Beck, C. J. A., & Applegate, A. G. (2010). The Mediator's Assessment of Safety Issues and Concerns (MASIC): A screening interview for intimate partner violence and abuse available in the public domain. *Family Court Review, 48*(4), 646–652.

Jaffe, P. G., Johnston, J. R., Crooks, C. V., & Bala, N. (2008). Custody disputes involving allegations of domestic violence: Toward a differentiated approach to parenting plans. *Family Court Review, 46*(3), 500–522.

Kelly, J. B., & Emery, R. E. (2003). Children's adjustment following divorce: Risk and resilience perspectives. *Family Relations, 52*(4), 352–362.

Kelly, J. B., & Johnson, M. P. (2008). Differentiation among types of intimate partner violence: Research update and implications for interventions. *Family Court Review, 46*(3), 476–499.

Kirkland, K. (2008). Parenting coordination (PC) laws, rules, and regulations: A jurisdictional comparison. *Journal of Child Custody, 5*(1), 22–52.

Kirkland, K., & Sullivan, M. (2008). Parenting coordination (PC) practice: A survey of experienced professionals. *Family Court Review, 46*, 622–636.

Kitzmann, K. M., Gaylord, N. K., Holt, A. R., & Kenny, E. D. (2003). Child witnesses to domestic violence: A meta-analytic review. *Journal of Consulting and Clinical Psychology, 71*(2), 339–352.

Langhinrichsen-Rohling, J. (2005). Top 10 greatest "hits": Important findings and future directions for intimate partner violence research. *Journal of Interpersonal Violence, 20*, 108–118.

Lansford, J. E. (2009). Parental divorce and children's adjustment. *Perspectives on Psychological Science, 4*(2), 140–152.

Lauman-Billings, L., & Emery, R. E. (2001). Distress among young adults from divorced families. *Journal of Family Psychology, 14*(4), 671–687.

Levin, M. S. (2001). The propriety of evaluative mediation: Concerns about the nature and quality of an evaluative opinion. *Ohio State Journal on Dispute Resolution, 16*(2), 267–296.

Maccoby, E. E., & Mnookin, R. H. (1992). *Dividing the child: Social and legal dilemmas of custody*. Cambridge, MA: Harvard University Press.

Mathis, R. D., & Tanner, Z. (1998). Effects of unscreened spouse violence on mediated agreements. *American Journal of Family Therapy, 26*, 251–260.

McIntosh, J. E. (2000). Child inclusive divorce mediation: Report on a qualitative research study. *Mediation Quarterly, 18*(1), 55–61.

McIntosh, J. E., Wells, Y. D., Smyth, B. M., & Long, C. M. (2008). Child-focused and child-inclusive divorce mediation: Comparative outcomes from a prospective study of post-separation adjustment. *Family Court Review, 46,* 105–124.

Petterson, M. M., Ballard, R. H., Putz, J. W., & Holtzworth-Munroe, A. (2010). Representation dispari-ties and impartiality: An empirical analysis of party perception of fear, preparation, and satisfaction in divorce mediation when only one party has counsel. *Family Court Review, 48*(4), 663–671.

Potter, D. (2010). Psychosocial well-being and the relationship between divorce and children's academic achievement. *Journal of Marriage and Family, 72,* 933–946.

Putz, J. W., Ballard, R. H., Arany, J. G., Applegate, A. G., & Holtzworth-Munroe, A. (2011). *Compar-ing the mediation agreements of families with and without a history of intimate partner violence.* Manuscript submitted for publication.

Salem, P., & Dunford-Jackson, B. L. (2008). Beyond politics and positions: A call for collaboration between family court and domestic violence professionals. *Family Court Review, 46*(3), 437–453.

Salem, P., Kulak, D., & Deutsch, R. M. (2007). Triaging family court services: The Connecticut judicial branch's family civil intake screen. *Pace Law Review, 27*(4), 101–146.

Schepard, A. I. (2004). *Children, courts, and custody: Interdisciplinary models for divorcing families.* Cambridge, UK: Cambridge University Press.

Tesler, P. H. (2008). Collaborative family law, the new lawyer, and deep resolution of divorce-related conflicts. *Journal of Dispute Resolution, 11,* 83–130.

Thoennes, N., Salem, P., & Pearson, J. (1995). Mediation and domestic violence: Current policies and practices. *Family and Conciliation Courts Review, 33*(1), 6–29.

Tishler, C. L., Bartholomae, S., Katz, B. L., & Landry-Meyer, L. (2004). Is domestic violence relevant? An exploratory analysis of couples referred for mediation in family court. *Journal of Interpersonal Violence, 19*(9), 1042–1062.

Toofanian, P. (2007). Ethical obligations to children in marital dissolutions. *Journal of Contemporary Legal Issues, 16,* 197–202.

U.S. Census Bureau. (2002). *Number, timing, and duration of marriages and divorces: 1996.* Retrieved from http://www.census.gov/prod/2002pubs/p70-80.pdf

U.S. Census Bureau. (2005). *Number, timing, and duration of marriages and divorces: 2001.* Retrieved from http://www.census.gov/prod/2005pubs/p70-90.pdf

U.S. National Center for Health Statistics. (2009). Changing patterns of nonmarital childrearing in the United States. Data Brief No. 19. Retrieved from http://www.dc.gov/nchs/data/databriefs/db18.pdf

Ver Steegh, N., & Dalton, C. (2008). Report from the Wingspread Conference on domestic violence and family courts. *Family Court Review, 46*(3), 454–475.

Wade, T. J., & Pevalin, D. J. (2004). Marital transitions and mental health. *Journal of Health and Social Behavior, 45*(2), 155–170.

SECTION VII

Policies and Program

Chapter 23

Fatherhood and Family Policies

Scott Coltrane

University of Oregon

Andrew Behnke

North Carolina State University

Introduction

Although all modern industrialized nations have policies and programs designed to fulfill specific family-related goals, most legislation affecting families in the United States does not explicitly spell out its goals for fathers or families (Bogenschneider, 2000; Kamerman & Kahn, 2001). Just two decades ago, researchers were arguing that family policy does not really exist in the United States, because there is no set of laws or administrative orders labeled *family policy* and because there are no high level offices in federal or state governments that are responsible for directly overseeing policies that affect families (Bane & Jargowsky, 1989). Although most concede that things have changed, a recent decade review (Bogenschneider & Corbett, 2010b, p. 783) begins by stating "*family policy* is still not a term that is widely used by knowledge consumers, such as policymakers, journalists, or the public. It has not yet achieved the status of economic or environmental policy, nor is it even recognized in its own right as a subfield of social policy."

Nevertheless, a huge range of government policies and programs at the federal, state, and local levels have had dramatic impacts on family well-being and have shaped the roles of men and women as partners and as parents (Coltrane & Adams, 2008; Gornick & Meyers, 2003; Moen & Coltrane, 2004). In this chapter, we define family policy as the state's deliberate shaping of laws and programs intended to help families and children. Such a definition limits family policy to programs consciously undertaken to affect families in a positive way, making it easier to study recent policy initiatives, especially those aimed at fathers, though it leaves unexamined other important effects on families of less targeted programs and policies. As Cabrera (2010) points out, the mid-1990s was a turning point because the Clinton administration established the Fatherhood Research Initiative aimed at promoting research and policy development relating to fathers' involvement with their children, followed by the Bush administration's Healthy Marriage Initiative which focused on keeping low-income men connected to the mothers of their children (see also Cabrera, Brooks-Gunn, Moore, West, & Boller, 2002;

419

Coltrane, 2001; Mincy, Garfinkel, & Nepomnyaschy, 2005). In this chapter we build on this earlier scholarship by discussing federal and state level policies, bridges to other disciplines, and future directions for research on father-related policy.

Brief Historical and Theoretical Overview

Many social scientists and child advocates have defined family policies in terms of the well-being of children (Hernandez, 1993). For example, Marian Wright Edelman (2003), founder of the Children's Defense Fund, suggested that instead of formulating something called family policy, we should fund health, nutrition, education, and housing programs aimed at directly benefiting children (virtually all of whom live in some sort of family), and others have suggested we should focus on job training or poverty reduction to benefit at-risk youth (Lerman, 2010). A large number of researchers and policy makers have focused on the plight of children living in single parent families, most of whom live at or near the poverty level, with special attention to African American and Latino children, whose life chances have been declining. When compared to White children, African American children are much more likely to be poor, lack health insurance, and live with one or no parents in the household (Edelman, 2003; Haskins, 2009). Similar declining life chances are evident for Latino youth (Eamon, 2005; Lieb & Thistle, 2005).

Studies comparing child poverty in the United States to other industrialized countries show that things may be getting worse for American children (Adamson, 2010). Children living in single-mother homes worldwide are at particular risk for being poor, although, in most nations, government assistance is more effective than in the United States at lifting poor families and children out of poverty (Barrientos & DeJong, 2006; Rainwater & Smeeding, 2003). The tendency to spend so little on children and to avoid creating explicit family policies in the United States stems from the common assumption that families are private and separate from the government (or the church, schools, economy, or any other social institution), a conclusion that is challenged by most recent social science research (Coltrane & Adams, 2008).

Sometimes child or family policies can influence family form, such as with the American Aid to Families with Dependent Children (AFDC) program, the federal welfare effort phased out in 1996 to become TANF (Temporary Assistance to Needy Families). One of the problems with AFDC, designed to help single mothers with children, was that it actually discouraged fathers from living with their children. Early-on in the AFDC program, mothers and children were denied benefits if a social worker visited the home and found a man's clothes or other belongings in the house. Following historical patterns and in conjunction with low wages and systemic patterns of job discrimination, this discouraged low-income African American fathers from marrying the mother and living in the child's home. By the late 1990s, less than half of African American children were living with two parents, compared to over three-fourths of White children (Haskins, 2009; McLanahan, 2009). An unintended consequence of AFDC, this provision was changed when AFDC was replaced by TANF in conjunction with the 1996 overhaul of welfare known as PRWORA (Personal Responsibility and Work Opportunity Reconciliation Act) as discussed below. Unlike AFDC, which provided cash payments to single-parent families, TANF gives block grants to states. The states are then guided by the federal government to use the funds primarily to provide basic assistance with food (Supplemental Nutrition Assistance Program [SNAP]), child care, and transportation with the stated aim of aiding families in producing healthy and productive citizens.

Today, some government programs aimed at low-income children are designed to bring men (and their limited incomes) back into the family by encouraging them to sign paternity declarations at the child's birth, by performing blood tests to determine paternity, and by directly withholding child support payments from their pay checks (Sorensen, 2010). For example, the Paternity Opportunity Program (POP) in many states works through hospitals, prenatal clinics, county welfare offices, local vital records offices, and courts to increase paternity declarations and conduct paternity blood tests. Additionally, programs like Support Has A Rewarding Effect (SHARE) helped some noncustodial parents to work more, earn more, and pay more child support after their involvement in the program (Perez-Johnson, Kauff, & Hershey, 2003). Head Start and Early Head Start have encouraged increased father involvement through the Male and Father-Involvement Initiative. As discussed below, recent initiatives changed focus from encouraging poor men to pay up or to marry the mother of their children, to instead focus on helping provide fathers with education, job training, and access to jobs so they can be the dads they want to be (Haskins, 2009; Lerman, 2010; Sorensen, 2010; Waller, 2009).

During most of the 20th century, both researchers and policy makers assumed that pre-school children's well-being was largely determined by mothers' contributions to parenting and fathers financial contributions to families, with state level contributions focused on serving populations with special needs (poor families, single-parent families, orphans and foster children, children with health problems or developmental disabilities). With men's and women's patterns of labor force participation converging in the late 20th century, governments in developed countries have focused on ways to aid both mothers and fathers with parenting, as well as providing child care, educational and health services directly to children.

Several decades of accumulated social and behavioral science research affirms that investments in the early years of children's lives can "pay off" in terms of the reduction of future social costs associated with criminality, employability, and mental and physical health (Featherstone, 2010; Wagmiller & Adelman, 2010). Recent research (Leidy, Schofield, & Parke, this volume) finds that enhancing father involvement can also have beneficial influence on child development and social efficacy in middle childhood. Across the globe, governments are investing in paternal involvement schemes to support the healthy development of infants and children. Scandinavian countries first offered innovative leave programs for employed fathers as well as employed mothers in the 1970s, with the pace of adoption in other nations accelerating in the mid-1990s (Liera, 2002; Moss & Deven, 2006; O'Brien, 2009). By 2007, 66 nations had enacted policies that included fathers' entitlement to paid parental leave, typically adopted in the context of more general work-family reconciliation frameworks geared toward both women and men (Gornick & Meyers, 2003; Heyman, Earle, & Hayes, 2007). Most of these father-friendly policies now exist in European Union countries, though many new initiatives also came from Australia and Canada (Lero, Ashbourne, & Whitehead, 2006; O'Brien, 2009; Sullivan, Coltrane, McAnnally, & Altintas, 2009). Although the United States lags behind many nations in promoting child well-being and father involvement, U.S. efforts have increased recently, as researchers and policy makers have focused on fathers.

In this chapter we briefly review such efforts drawing on a multidisciplinary life course perspective (Elder, 1998). We explore how such policies are seen as influencing the lives of fathers and children over time depending on their circumstances and stages in life. This framework helps us to understand how policies influence the linked lives of fathers and their children, and how policies can impact the life course trajectories on which these men and their children embark (Coltrane & Galt, 2000; Doherty, Kouneski, & Erickson, 1998).

Current Research Questions

Several overarching sets of research questions are crucial to exploring how policies and father involvement are related, including (a) What are the implicit and explicit goals of specific policies? (b) What are the conditions under which different policies are developed, adopted, and implemented? (c) What influence do these policies have on women, men, children, families, and society? As discussed below, the first question is typically seen as self-evident, although some research does focus on specifying more directly why we should worry about promoting father involvement. The second set of research questions is most often addressed in comparative perspective with historical data. Such studies often focus on the importance of differing political cultures and processes, as well as social structural conditions, with theoretical emphasis on nation states and differences among policy regimes. In contrast, the more plentiful research on the third set of questions about the consequences of various policies takes many forms and ranges from assessing individual psychological outcomes to studies focused on how various policies are associated with different demographic and economic indicators. Assessing the specific consequences of individual policies, or of clusters of policies, is not an easy matter, even when a specific target population is identified. Researchers must always consider the possibility of endogeneity and spurious associations, as well as facing the difficult task of determining causal order. As Kelly (2008) notes and as we discuss below, the best research uses sophisticated methodologies to address these challenges, but also acknowledges the limitations of any chosen method.

Finally, it is important to note that despite our best efforts, there seems to be a tenuous relationship between academic research and social policy. Not only is there often a weak and indirect relationship between societal needs and the passage of policies designed to address those needs, but the influence of academic research on the creation and implementation of policy is typically much less than assumed. For example, in a chapter titled "Exploring the Disconnect between Research and Policy," two prominent distinguished professors from one of the leading American research universities comment,

> It is hard to shake the impression that we may be functioning in a policy environment that operates, ironically enough, according to an inverse relationship between science and politics the more and better research we produce, the less effect it has on the policymaking process. With increasing amounts of data and analysis emerging from our universities and research/evaluation firms, the likelihood that even the most studious of public officials can sort through and make sense of the science available to them is not very high. (Bogenschneider & Corbett, 2010a, p. 3)

As these scholars point out, the relationship between social science and public policy is complex, ambiguous, and very contextual. Sometimes social science research influences policy making and sometimes it does not. Even when research does inform a specific policy or influence a specific piece of legislation, the researchers themselves typically admit that their work carried far less weight than they wanted and was viewed with far more skepticism than they expected (Danzinger, 2001). And in those instances when policy based on social science evidence is implemented, the results are so hard to attribute to individual programs that the true cause of the trend or outcome remains unclear. Most policies are the result of many years of work by diverse coalitions of advocates and policymakers, and resulting programs often reflect competing understandings from lengthy processes of legislative drafting, executive rulemaking, judicial interpretation, and legislative modification (Feldblum & Appleberry, 2008). Finally, given the cyclical nature of influence in American politics, policies, and programs are often abandoned before they have a chance to accomplish their goals.

Coupled with an academic environment at most top U.S. research universities that is assumed to give only bland support and no real encouragement to policy-related research (Bogenschneider & Corbett, 2010a), why should researchers even care about conducting research on fatherhood policy? In our view, this is a question with a simple answer. As fathers and sons we know on a personal level that fathers matter to their children, and as the chapters in this volume attest, the social and behavioral science evidence from the last several decades is helping us to understand how and why father involvement influences child development and family well-being. Despite the complexity of the task, we advocate for parallel research into how and why policies might help men become better partners and parents.

Research Measurement and Methodology

Among the many approaches taken to the study of family and fatherhood policies, some research focuses on the purposes of specific policies or the political processes that produce them, whereas other researchers evaluate the impact of policies and programs on the lives of fathers and their families. First, policy researchers often assess the explicit goals of specific policies by studying their written narratives and background materials, and then attempt to understand the reasoning and underlying goals of these policies by interviewing and surveying policy makers and those that influence their decisions. Second, large-scale national studies (e.g., ECLS-K) and census data are often used to understand and contextualize how and why these policies are developed, adopted, and implemented in the lives of fathers and their families. Third, these same large-scale studies, as well as numerous qualitative and mixed method studies (e.g., Fragile Families, FCI) provide considerable important descriptive information to assess the influence of these policies on women, men, children, families, and society. These studies can take years to be adequately assessed and interpreted, causing some lag between implementation and outcomes. However, these studies can influence conversations about the effectiveness of public and private policies and programs. A detailed methodological critique is beyond the scope of this review, but we provide some basic information on research methods related to various family and fatherhood policies of the last decade.

Empirical Findings

Exploring Implicit and Explicit Goals of Fatherhood Policies

Before reviewing how policies related to fathers are framed or adopted and before evaluating how effective they are at accomplishing their objectives, it is important to ask more fundamental questions. Why should we target special policies and programs toward fathers? On what basis do researchers claim that promoting father involvement will be beneficial for men, women, and children? These are the sorts of questions that are left implicit in most research, but they are important for scholars to explore in more depth than has been done in the past.

Although research on fatherhood is becoming more prevalent, it still represents only a tiny fraction of research on families and child development (Goldberg, Tan, & Thorson, 2009). For most of the 20th century, practitioners and academics either focused on fathers as symbolic heads of families and/or assumed that fathers were relatively unimportant figures in terms of child development outcomes (Coltrane, 1996; Parke, 1996). Although many have been concerned that father absence might have deleterious effects on children and mothers, most studies did not collect information on what fathers actually did with and for children and families (Coltrane & Galt, 2000; Griswold, 1993; Pleck & Pleck, 1997). Not only did most family and child development studies in the twentieth century ignore fathers, but family-related policies focused almost exclusively on mothers and children.

With the rise of female labor force participation in the late twentieth century, a critique of stereotyped separate public and private spheres for men and women emerged, and the cultural contradictions of motherhood and fatherhood became a topic for scholarly exploration (e.g., Bernard, 1981; Hays, 1996). Part of this dialog concerned the extent to which public policies were designed to protect men's privileged position in the family, including a "family wage" and the rights and opportunities to enjoy the domestic services of wives and mothers (Coltrane & Adams, 2008; Thorne, 1992). In the late twentieth century, these debates highlighted the well-being of mothers and children versus the rights and obligations of fathers, sometimes framed in the context of campaigns to limit divorce, promote marriage, or defend paternal custody rights (e.g., Adams, 2006; Coltrane, 2001; Doherty, 1991; Hays, 2003).

A new father ideal gained prominence in American popular culture during the 1980s (Coltrane, 1996; Griswold, 1993; Pruett, 1987). According to Furstenberg (1988), "[T]elevision, magazines, and movies herald the coming of the modern father—the nurturant, caring, and emotionally attuned parent.... Today's father is at least as adept at changing diapers as changing tires" (p. 193). No longer limited to being protectors and providers, at least some fathers came to be seen as intimately involved in family life. Fatherhood proponents focused on the potential of the new ideals and practices (Biller, 1976), but many researchers reported that fathers resisted assuming responsibility for daily housework or child care (Thompson & Walker, 1989). Some researchers claimed that popular images far exceeded men's actual behaviors (LaRossa, 1988), and others suggested that men were less committed to families than they had been in the past (Ehrenreich, 1984). In contrast, some claimed that the sensitive or androgynous parenting styles of new fathers might lead to gender identity confusion in sons (Blankenhorn, 1995; Popenoe, 1996) and others questioned whether the symbolic importance granted to fathers was supported by available empirical evidence (Stacey, 1996; Silverstein & Auerbach, 1999). The debates of the 1980s and 1990s thus seemed to focus on a contrast between old-style breadwinner fathers and new-style nurturing fathers, though in reality most of the empirical evidence showed that the two were intimately linked in the everyday lives of average Americans (e.g., Coltrane, 1996; Pleck & Masciadrelli, 2004; Townsend, 2002).

In contrast to earlier eras, there now seems to be an emerging consensus that fathers matter to the well-being of children and families, and this view has made its way into policy formulations and political rhetoric. It is difficult to attribute priority to a specific cause, but whether propelled by women's increasing ability to command economic, political and personal resources, or the recognition of the intrinsic importance of men to family life and child development, the late twentieth century witnessed a remarkable transformation in family policy justifications. The Department of Health and Human Services' policies on fathers are now shaped by five principles (see Cabrera, 2010, p. 530): (a) All fathers can be important contributors to the well-being of their children; (b) Parents are partners in raising their children, even when they do not live in the same household; (c) The role fathers play in families is diverse and related to cultural and community norms; (d) Men should receive the education and support necessary to prepare them for the responsibility of parenthood; (e) Government can encourage and promote father involvement through its programs and through its workforce policies.

Despite these principles, most public policies in America are still primarily shaped by a focus on fathers' provision of financial support to mothers and children. On the one hand, we have cultural and legal traditions that treat fathers as financial providers and family heads, but on the other, we have an emerging view that treats fathers as equal partners to their wives and equal parents to their children. Not surprisingly, the dilemmas and contradictions inherent in the tensions between these views of fatherhood underlie most policy efforts to promote men's involvement in families (Coltrane & Adams, 2008; Hays, 2003).

Although typically taken for granted, we believe that research is still needed to address the first question of why we would want to promote father involvement in marriages and families, and further, what types and what level of involvement we should expect from men. Studies designed to address these questions typically lack sophisticated empirical data, but usually raise provocative issues about ethics, family values and gender equity (Coltrane, 2001; Nock, 1998; Stacey, 1996; Wilcox, 2004). For example, research on domestic violence (e.g., Johnson, 2006; Stark, 2007) tends to take a different view of the influence of masculinity on family dynamics than that offered by fatherhood advocates who champion male family headship and masculine role models (Blankenhorn, 1995) or men's rights advocates who argue for paternal custody on the basis of parental alienation syndrome (Adams, 2006). We need more studies that delineate the specific objectives of various constituencies related to men and fathers, and research methods that can trace their impact on the legislative initiatives that garner support.

The promotion of father involvement policies and the funding of fatherhood research efforts have been the product of very different political constituencies. For example, Democratic Vice President Al Gore was one of the first top-ranking officials to promote the study of fathers and to advocate for policies designed to encourage father involvement, especially among disadvantaged groups (Marsiglio et al., 1998). Republican George W. Bush defeated Gore in his 2000 presidential bid. President Bush, through appointment of fatherhood advocates such as Wade Horn, maintained an emphasis on the importance of fathers, but changed the policy focus to family values and marriage-related media campaigns, provision of faith-based counseling and services, and promotion of (heterosexual) couple relationship education (Coltrane, 2001). The passage of new policy initiatives frequently depends on forging coalitions among ideologically competing constituencies, and fatherhood and marriage policies are a prime example of this, though few would have predicted this based on the history of policy development around issues of child support, child custody, and divorce reform in the previous decade (Coltrane & Adams, 2008). Research in this area should highlight which aspects of father involvement the policies are trying to advance and which family and social goals are being promoted (e.g. compare Hays, 2003 or Stacey, 1996 with Popenoe, 1996 or Wilcox, 2004).

What Predicts How Different Policies Are Developed, Adopted, and Implemented?

Studies designed to address how and why specific policies arise and are implemented in different contexts exemplify the second set of research questions noted above. Over the past several decades, scholars have provided many theories and empirical studies to illuminate how changes in state policies and programs are related to the organization of paid labor and family life, with related implications for fatherhood and gender relations (Fraser, 1994; Gornick

& Meyers, 2003; Hobson & Morgan, 2002; O'Brien, 2009). Gornick and Meyers (2007) suggest that researchers and policy makers have been engaged in at least three overlapping but nonintersecting conversations about work and family life focused on child well-being, work-family conflict, and gender equality (see Coltrane, 2009). The *Child Well-Being* conversation focuses on maternal care during the child's first months and on the quality of care throughout childhood. A major concern in this conversation is the lack of availability of parents to their children and a secondary concern is the quality of both parental and substitute child care provision. The *Work-Family* conversation focuses on the problems of working parents (especially mothers) whose conflicting responsibilities leave them penalized at work and overburdened at home. This conversation, motivated by women's rapid entry into the paid labor force, tends to focus on how to "balance" work and family obligations. The *Gender Equality* conversation uses feminist insights to highlight gender equity issues in the workplace and in the home, including historically lower wages and a disproportionate expectation that women will do the domestic work associated with raising children and maintaining homes.

Gornick and Meyers (2007) suggest that these conversations produce very different policy proposals. A *Child Well-Being* approach suggests the need for policies like child tax credits and maternity leaves so that mothers can drop out of the labor market, at least temporarily. A *Work-Family* approach also tends to locate the major conflict in the lives of mothers, suggesting policies such as part-time work, job sharing, telecommuting and flextime that allow for individual women (and sometimes men) to balance their work and family commitments. A *Gender Equality* perspective views inequities as stemming from women's weak and intermittent connection to employment and the assumption that they should perform the unpaid family work. Policies suggested by this approach focus on reducing employment barriers, raising women's wages, and providing alternatives to maternal care through the provision of child care centers or subsidies.

As Gornick and Meyers point out (2007, p. 15), although they differ in naming the problem and in the solutions they propose, the conversations they identify have two things in common (see Coltrane, 2009). They all focus on women and do little to question assumptions about the organization of men's employment and caregiving activities. These conversations also suggest that the interests of men, women, and children are essentially in conflict. Children can have more time with their parents only if women reduce their employment commitments and career prospects; women and men can achieve greater equality in their employment only by reducing their time and commitment to caring for their children. In contrast to these approaches, Gornick and Meyers (2003, 2007) assume that the interests of women, men, and children are only "apparently" competing. They suggest that the real culprit, and the cause of the putative competition between interests, is the failure of social, market, and policy institutions to adequately address the care of children in high-employment societies. They propose (following others such as Crompton, 1999; Fraser, 1994; Hobson & Morgan, 2002; Knijn & Kremer, 1997) that the solution must involve men as well as women, and the state as well as the family. They envision a dual-earner/dual-caregiver society, one that supports equal opportunities for men and women in employment, equal contributions from mothers and fathers at home, and high quality care for children provided both by parents and by well-qualified and well-paid non-parental caregivers.

Just as the state facilitated and even encouraged women to become workers, it is reasonable to expect that states, through different political processes and social policies, can also facilitate and encourage fathers to become caregivers. However, as Hobson and Morgan (2002) demonstrate, there is no neat fit between the welfare regimes of industrialized countries and their fatherhood policy regimes (defined as fatherhood obligations and fatherhood rights). Because of wide variation in political, economic, social, and cultural context, and because historical events and institutional forces have shaped many different, sometimes conflicting, policies related to fathers and families, it has often proved difficult to categorize countries using such typologies. In the area of parental leave, for example, O'Brien (2009) presents a typology of national policy contexts specifically focused on what she terms "father-care sensi-tive" policies, in which the major classifying dimensions are (a) the length of paternal leave and men's access to parental leave and (b) the level of income replacement available during such leave. This kind of typology, explicitly designed to address children's access to men's parental resources, provides a framework sensitive to differences in policies affecting men's caregiving. There have been some recent studies focused on such complexities with promising results (Folbre, 2008; Fuwa & Cohen, 2007; Gornick & Meyers, 2003; Hook, 2006; Smith & Wil-liams, 2007). We need more research on such questions incorporating the local complexity of multiple policies and their adoption in specific national contexts.

What Influence Do Fatherhood Policies Have on Women, Men, Children, Families, and Society?

Research questions focused on the consequences of policies promoting father involvement are likely to have great influence on scholarship and legislation in the coming decade. As noted above, the social and policy contexts in which fathers parent has changed dramatically over the past several decades. Because research on the Healthy Marriages Initiative is only now making its way into the published literature in sufficient volume to assess it, we can begin to identify a new set of questions about the consequences of these specific policies on fathers and families. For example, Cabrera (2010, p. 525) reminds us that issues of poverty, non-marital fertility, cohabitation, and nonresidential parenting pose a challenge for fathers who want to support their children and for policies designed to protect child welfare: "The Healthy Marriage Initia-tive created a policy context that may be untenable for some families and may be inconsistent with how families are organized and do not offer the help these families need to provide a healthy and stimulating environment for their children. The question is under what conditions and for whom is marriage good?" And the situation is complicated by the fact that the Obama administration is promoting only some aspects of the previous emphasis on healthy marriages. If we hope to fulfill the promise of evidence-based policy making, we need to document how different policies and programs have affected the lives of men, women, and children who have been touched by them (Bogenschneider & Corbett, 2010a).

Some emerging questions that come out of our own and others' recent research agendas include identifying the conditions under which it is best to (a) involve nonresidential fathers in the lives of their children; (b) value fathers for their contribution to families outside of the provider role; and (c) encourage healthy relationships regardless of marital status or living situation. These questions are not independent from the political situations that give rise to specific policy agendas, but we have faith that scientific inquiry can indeed shed light on when and how we should invest in the well-being of future generations through family programs. We are confident that research will begin to address these sorts of questions in the coming decade, along with continuing to address the ones that came out of the last 20 years of scholarship dur-ing which attention to fathers increased dramatically (Goldberg et al., 2009).

Bridges to Other Disciplines

Policy oriented research is necessarily multi-disciplinary and typically spans several social science fields, including sociology, psychology, political science, history, anthropology, and economics as exemplified by the studies noted above. In this section we further highlight potential bridges to other disciplines by investigating one realm of fatherhood policy; father provisioning, which has a relatively long and contentious history in sociology, economics, law enforcement, political science, and legal circles. Fathers are often seen by policy makers as primarily, if not solely, providers for their families. Commentators have observed that policy in the United States focuses primarily on a father's financial support role, as compared to the nurturing and care aspects of fathering (Vann, 2007). Indeed research continues to show that fathers agree that they are the providers, or at least that they should be (Bianchi & Milkie, 2010; Townsend, 2002). Providing monetary support might facilitate more nurturing aspects of fathering, and Bianchi and Milkie (2010) note that fathers who are earning more income are more likely to live with their children, and non-resident fathers are more likely to have closer ties to active parenting when they contribute monetarily as in child support. The impact of non-resident fathers' monetary contribution on engagement with children depends on other factors such as relationship with mother, which differ by race and ethnicity (e.g., Cabrera, Ryan, Jolley, Shannon, & Tamis-Lemonda, 2008; Tach, Mincy, & Edin, 2010).

Though the emphasis of fatherhood policy may be changing somewhat, most government programs aimed at fathers continue to be seen by many as punitive in nature, because they are focused primarily on child support enforcement. Child support is essential for many single-parents raising families with limited incomes. In fact, some of these families receive support that amounts to more than one-quarter of their typical yearly salaries (Sorensen & Zibman, 2001). Each state designs its own child support enforcement program, typically enforcing punishments for those in arrears without regard for ability to pay, including garnishing wages, seizing of bank accounts or other assets, and suspension of driving or professional licenses.

Studies show that state initiated child support enforcement policies for low-income parents have discouraged payments and led fathers to participate in the underground economy, have fewer contacts with children, and develop less healthy coparenting arrangements (e.g., Jarrett, Roy, & Burton, 2002). Low-income non-resident fathers often face significant barriers to acquiring employment such as criminal histories, limited schooling or job experience, few employable skills, lack of transportation, and limited social skills (Tach, Mincy, & Edin, 2010). Ethnographic studies show how this situation is often exacerbated by mounting child support payments that spiral out of control, with fathers becoming less able and willing to pay.

Indeed, single mothers play a role in a resulting situation that has been termed "low-disregards." This refers to the phenomenon where women on government assistance choose not to cooperate in filing for child support because they realize the risk of losing some or all of their benefits (Jarrett et al., 2002). Mothers recognize that complying with state laws and filing for child support will likely reduce their assistance benefits, because child support is inconsistent and the state takes a percentage off the top to recoup its costs. In this system, fathers often feel that it would be easier to pay the mothers of their children outside of the welfare system even if it means they face potential future legal action. Sometimes parents get caught playing both sides, leading to negative repercussions for the father-child relationship and the mother-father relationship (Furstenberg & Featherstone, 2010; Roy, 1999, 2006).

Policy Implications

In this section we briefly review five major policies of the last decade designed—at least in part—to influence how fathers connect with their children. The recession of 2007–10 has been one of the most significant influences on families during this period. Effects felt by many families include increased difficulty in finding employment, heightened unemployment, plummeting real estate values, increasing foreclosure rates, as well as diminished retirement resources. One of the most salient repercussions of the recession is the nearly doubled rate of unemployment and its impact on families. Children in these families are hit hard in the short-term (e.g., nutrition, housing, school changes), but also face negative long-term effects (e.g., health, future education and employment opportunities, risky behaviors, substance abuse; Conger & Elder, 1994; Holzer, Schanzenbach, Duncan, & Ludwig, 2008). As with studies of the depression of the 1930s, it will take considerable time before researchers can document the multiple effects of the recent economic recession on children and families (Elder, 1998).

Early Childhood Education

Enacted in 2009, the American Recovery and Reinvestment Act (ARRA) included increased federal funding of programs that benefit children with an infusion of more than $2.1 billion to enhance Head Start and Early Head Start to provide child care, education, and parent classes for low-income families. Research on early childhood education (ECE; e.g., Head Start, Early Head Start, Smart Start) and measurement of the impacts on early learning in children has expanded and grown in the past 15 years. For example, Head Start programming has increased the availability of, and access to, quality child care centers and school readiness programming for low-income families and their children, success for children is both mediated and moderated by several factors, ranging from parental involvement, to level of parent education, to the relationship between both parents (Fagan, Newash, & Schloesser, 2000; Palm & Fagan, 2008).

In their overview, Palm and Fagan (2008) examined factors influencing fatherhood involvement in ECE. Overall, there is relatively low father involvement at Head Start centers, fathers tend to be more involved with their child's education when more educated and less depressed, and fathers are more likely to engage in the learning process with their children when they have more social support at large or by the mothers and teachers (Palm & Fagan, 2008). Research shows that while mothers *and* fathers may express interest in their children's early learning experiences and practice this in the home, fathers may not opt to become involved with Head Start or other ECE type programming due to work-family conflict, feeling discouraged by mothers, and lack of encouragement from child care teachers (Fagan et al., 2000). Fathers are less likely to engage with teachers, visit children in school settings, and co-parent regarding school issues due to their feelings about paternal role expectations, gatekeeping experiences with mothers, and discouragement from teachers.

Making Work Pay

In 2009, the ARRA legislated various provisions to help "make work pay" for low-income families. It included the creation of the Child Care Development Fund (CCDF) to help low-income parents find work and participate in programs which provide them with the necessary skills to retool for new employment. Laws making work pay have historically been largely focused on low-income women and their families; when in fact men also need incentives or supports to encourage employment. However this current legislation takes a different approach supporting any and all low-income parents.

For example, provisions within the Act expand the child tax credit for low-income working families. These tax incentives "make work pay" by providing a $400–$800 tax credit for lower and mid-income families. Other such financial benefits include the Child Tax Credit, the Child Care Credit, and the Earned Income Tax Credit. The credits are not linked to gender; single fathers as well as single mothers can obtain tax breaks. Research has shown that these incentives are promising in terms of their economic and social impact (e.g., Immervoll & Pearson, 2009). Families that participate in these programs appear to have more stable employment, improved financial standing, and reduced reliance on social services. However, only a few impact studies have measured the long-term influence of such programs (for one exception see Holt, 2006). And there are downsides to these policies; for example, some individuals have learned to "play the system," claiming to have custody of children in order to receive unlawful tax breaks. Some parents justify their actions by declaring that parenting is much more than claiming one's children on court documents, and that if they care for a child physically, emotionally, and financially, they should be eligible to claim such tax incentives.

Heatlh Care Supports

In 2009 President Obama signed a reauthorization of State Children's Health Insurance Program (SCHIP) which expanded its reach across the nation to help families and single parents who did not meet requirements for Medicaid to access public health insurance at very low costs. The SCHIP program has been widely successful insofar as it is an effective means for poor and low-income families' children to access routine and urgent care, prevent serious illnesses, and reduce hospitalizations (Johnson, Rimsza, & Johnson, 2006). However, as the economy has worsened, more and more families have become eligible for Medicaid, while states' tax revenues have decreased. The resulting financial burden has forced most states to make changes to their SCHIP programming in order to decrease enrollment, such as: raising premiums, adding co-payments, and even reducing benefits (Johnson et al., 2006). In 2010 President Obama signed into law sweeping healthcare reform legislation which is projected to provide health care to more than 11 million children, which will have implications for eligible fathers as they attempt to care for the health of their children.

TANF and Welfare Programs

The welfare reform legislation of 1996 was intended to reduce single motherhood, increase family self-sufficiency, and increase monetary support for children by their non-resident fathers (Bronte-Tinkew et al., 2007). However, since TANF was aimed at encouraging employment for mothers, it did little to help fathers stay in the lives of their children, nor did it improve father's employability (Cabrera, 2010). Some argue that both past and present welfare systems lack support and programming for poor fathers of children (other than SNAP—previously food stamps, and in some cases Medicaid). Because of the focus on employment at any cost, and lack of focus on education and skills, welfare today appears to favor work over family well-being in the first years of children's lives (Hays, 2003). TANF still has rigid requirements such as the maximum benefit clock of 60 months, strict guidelines on documentation and proof of job searches and employment, and requiring employment within a year of a child's birth. The latter requirement is noteworthy; this means a mother and/or father must work and obtain child care, even in a home with two parents. Following the birth of a child, poor fathers and mothers who lack education or work skills often find themselves working minimum wage jobs, taking unpredictable work shifts, and trying to arrange child care (much less survive down-turns, health problems, or other family issues) just to complete this requirement of TANF. In addition, job loss plagues many of these families due to schedule changes, child illness, or loss of hours and lay-offs; approximately 20% of those who leave welfare return within one to two years (Brodkin, 2003).

Family Medical Leave

Prior to the Family and Medical Leave Act of 1993 (FMLA) mothers and fathers' jobs were not protected if they took new parent leave, had a long-term illness, or ill family members. The FMLA allows for *parents* (including fathers) of biologically related newborns or adopted children to take unpaid leave of up to 12 weeks without penalty (Wisensale, 2003). There has been legislative movement to strengthen unpaid leave under the FMLA in recent years. More than 10 states have improved and expanded the unpaid FMLA policies, including more time off, flexibility regarding the minimum size of employer requirement, and permitting intermit-tent leave (Appelbaum & Milkman, 2011). Unfortunately, there remain some drawbacks to the FMLA that prevent it from being utilized by the poor yet employed, and by under-employed workers. First, part-time employees are not eligible to receive it; second, companies with less than 50 employees are not required to provide it unless mandated in certain states; and, third, workers must be employed for at least a year before taking the leave. FMLA guidelines and implementation details will continue to be adjusted providing a good example of the complex and sometimes contradictory legislative, implementation, and legal processes producing fam-ily policy (see Feldblum & Appleberry, 2008). California pioneered the first *paid* family leave expansion program for employers and four other states have followed suit and approved paid leave (Appelbaum & Milkman, 2011).

Future Directions

There are many opportunities for improved policy and programming for fathers and children, and we briefly review a few key areas below.

Early Child Education

In the realm of Early Childhood Education programming such as Head Start and subsidized quality daycare, there is great need to better engage both parents (fathers and mothers) in chil-dren's early learning experiences. First, ECEC center/school policies and staff should reflect an expectation of—and support of—fathers' involvement in their child's education, such as classroom volunteering, meetings with teachers, and special school programming just for fathers. Often times, fathers are an afterthought, encouraged to come to father nights once a year, or seen as lacking competence in the realm of child education. Second, more research is needed to document the impact that fathers do have on children when involved at this level. From a legislative perspective, policies should stress that father involvement in early children's development is more than financial support. Third, policy makers and program developers are encouraged to explore what specific types of programming will help fathers to engage with children and stay engaged when they encounter hardship. To accomplish this, a multi-pronged approach is warranted, whereby providers and relevant communities are educated about the impact fathers can have on child development, along with program offerings that are easily accessible, salient, and interesting to non-resident and resident fathers alike.

Non-Resident Fatherhood

Support for non-resident fathers is a ripe area for policy enhancements. Although research shows most non-resident fathers have high interest levels in coparenting and supporting their children, poor non-resident fathers are in need of additional programmatic supports in order to fulfill their roles and responsibilities (Raikes & Belloti, 2007; Roy, 1999, 2006). In response to this need, programs have emerged in various regions of the country that focus on providing poor fathers job training and parenting advice. Responsible Fatherhood initiatives have made grants available to public and private groups, including religious organizations, to promote healthy couple relationships, educate men about good parenting practices, and build career skills. It appears that policy makers are beginning to realize that fatherhood is more than contributing dollars each month to support a family. The hypothesis is that fathers who are encouraged through programmatic efforts and incentives to be committed partners and parents will be more likely to remain involved in their children's lives and to have positive influence on their development. We lack systematic studies to support the validity of such policies and practices, however, and future research is needed to evaluate their merits.

Moreover, non-resident fathers report difficulties staying close to their children due to issues with finding employment, criminal backgrounds, and troubled relationships with the mothers of their children (Tach, Mincy, & Edin, 2010). It is not difficult to imagine a father's apprehension and frustration when he is informed by a case worker that he must obtain employment, perhaps seek some vocational training, and pay child support, yet be offered few incentives or support to succeed. Some call attention to the negative effects of a pervasive assumption in the welfare system that a non-resident father will *not* want to work or be involved with his children (Roy, 1999). Indeed, a shift in thinking and behavior can be supported by policy, program adjustments, and research into the relationships among them, as demonstrated by changes in Headstart, where federal regulations required programmatic activities specifically for fathers (Cabrera, 2010; Raikes, Summers, & Roggman, 2005).

Researchers point to the importance of broad policy change impacting fathers because the current welfare-to-work programming is not wholly effective. We suggest evaluation of policies and legislation that attempt to provide fathers with employment programs similar to those for single mothers, increase fatherhood/parenting programming, and continue to provide support for fathers involved with programs such as Head Start or other forms of child development/parenting programming (Raikes & Belloti, 2007). We envision a time when non-resident fathers would receive "credit" from welfare programs for visiting with, providing in-kind support, coparenting, and nurturing their children (Roy, 2006). However significant questions remain: How would this work in practice and what unintended consequences might result? Under this type of programming, non-resident fathers might be allowed to receive some financial benefits such as Medicaid and potentially a portion of TANF type programming if they complied with the program and provided proof of their efforts. With such a programmatic shift, fathers might be more responsible as caregivers, yet would still receive support to obtain work, increase education opportunities, and make earnest efforts in supporting themselves and their children.

According to Ron Haskins (2009), a former White House and congressional advisor on welfare issues, in order to make such programs work for men, an enticing incentive must be created. Such an incentive may entail utilizing the child support system. For example, upon gaining employment fathers' back-pay/pay toward child support might be suspended or a tax credit could be introduced. Other ideas include mandatory work programs to promote job-skills and relationship/parenting skills. Such programs would help provide individuals with not only the skills to obtain or keep jobs but the actual incentives to continue because they could receive a tax credit, or their child support payments could be reduced/ suspended.

One example of this approach is the multi-site Fathers to Work program launched in 2001 which attempted to bridge the gap between public and private programming for fathers. Studies of such programs have shown consistently positive results for fathers and their children (Spaulding, Grossman, & Wallace, 2009). By offering fathers a unique combination of services, training, access to resources, and support, the programs promote significant increases in fathers' employment rates and wages, level of engagement and involvement with their children, and increased child support payments. More research is needed to examine the impact of job training combined with paid work for fathers (and for mothers). In addition, further research is needed to understand how to help fathers retain employment, and how to increase actual financial support received by children (Spaulding et al., 2009).

Fatherhood Programming

Across the nation fatherhood programs are targeting areas where social services have historically provided little support to fathers: supports for financial stability, coparenting, and effective communication (Bronte-Tinkew et al., 2007; Roy & Dyson, 2010). The Administration for Children and Families (ACF) has actively supported efforts to integrate fathers into other funded services through grants, policies, and promotion of best practices, however, impact evaluation reports show that they have had limited measurable benefits for participants (Bronte-Tinkew et al., 2007). Further research is needed.

Because fatherhood and family policies have received so little attention in the academic literature, we have limited our review to introducing a few key questions in this chapter and highlighting the need for more focused research. We hope that with more research on why various constituencies advocate for specific policies; the circumstances under which various policies are adopted, implemented, and changed through legal challenges; and a more thorough assessment of the impacts such policies have on fathers, mothers, children, and society; researchers will be in a better position to make valid contributions to the policy process. If we can answer these questions, researchers will be better able to work with advocates and legislators to produce real and lasting impact on the laws and policies that shape the everyday lives of American fathers, mothers, and children.

References

Adams, M. (2006). Framing contests in child custody disputes: Parental alienation syndrome, child abuse, gender, and fathers' rights. *Family Law Quarterly, 40*, 315–338.

Adamson, P. (2010). *The children left behind.* Florence, Italy: Innocenti Research Center. Retrieved January 15, 2011, from http://www.unicef-irc.org/publications/619

Appelbaum, E., & Milkman, R. (2011). *Leaves that Pay.* Report by the Center for Economic and Policy Research. Retrieved May 20, 2011, from http://www.cepr.net/documents/publications/paid-family-leave-1-2011.pdf

Bane, M. J., & Jargowsky, P. (1989). The links between government policy and family structure: What matters and what doesn't. In A. J. Cherlin (Ed.), *The changing American family and public policy* (pp. 219–262). Washington, DC: Urban Institute.

Barrientos, A., & DeJong, J. (2006). Reducing child poverty with cash transfers: A sure thing? *Development Policy Review, 24,* 537–552.

Bernard, J. (1981). The good provider role: Its rise and fall. *American Psychologist, 36,* 1–12.

Bianchi, S., & Milkie, M. (2010). Work and family research in the first decade of the 21st Century. *Journal of Marriage and Family, 72,* 705–725.

Biller, H. B. (1976). The father and personality development. In M. E. Lamb (Ed.), *The role of the father in child development.* New York: Wiley.

Blankenhorn, D. (1995). *Fatherless America.* New York: Basic Books.

Bogenschneider, K. (2000). Has family policy come of age? A decade review of the state of U.S. family policy in the 1990s. *Journal of Marriage and the Family, 62,* 1136–1159.

Bogenschneider, K., & Corbett, T. J. (2010a). *Evidence-based policymaking.* New York: Taylor & Francis.

Bogenschneider, K., & Corbett, T. (2010b). Family policy: Becoming a field of inquiry and subfield of social policy. *Journal of Marriage and the Family, 72,* 783–803.

Brodkin, E. Z. (2003). Requiem for Welfare. *Dissent, 50*(1), 29–36.

Bronte-Tinkew, J., Carrano, J., Allen, T., Bowie, L., Mbwana, K., & Matthews, G. (2007). *Elements of promising practice for fatherhood programs.* Washington, DC: Child Trends.

Cabrera, N. (2010). Father Involvement and Public Policies. In M. E. Lamb (Ed.), *The role of the father in child development* (pp. 517–550). Hoboken, NJ: Wiley.

Cabrera, N., Brooks-Gunn, J., Moore, K., West, J., & Boller, K. (2002). Bridging research and policy. In C. S. Tamis-LeMonda & N. J. Cabrera (Eds.), *Handbook of father involvement* (pp. 489–523). Mahwah, NJ: Erlbaum.

Cabrera, N., Ryan, R., Jolley, S., Shannon, J., & Tamis-Lemonda, C. (2008). Nonresident father engagement with and responsibility to their toddlers. *Journal of Family Psychology, 22,* 643–647.

Coltrane, S. (1996). *Family man.* New York: Oxford University Press.

Coltrane, S. (2001). Marketing the marriage 'solution'. *Sociological Perspectives, 44,* 387–418.

Coltrane, S. (2009). Fatherhood, Gender and Work-Family Policies. In J. C. Gornick, M. K. Meyers, & E. O. Wright (Eds.), *Gender Equality* (pp. 385–409), New York: Verso.

Coltrane, S. & Adams, M. (2008). *Gender and families.* Lanham, MD: Rowman & Littlefield.

Coltrane, S., & Galt, J. (2000). The history of men's caring. In M. H. Meyer (Ed.), *Care work: Gender, labor, and welfare states* (pp. 15 36). New York: Routledge.

Conger, R. D., & Elder, G. H., Jr. (1994). *Families in troubled times.* New York: DeGruyter.

Crompton, R. (1999). *Restructuring gender relations and employment.* Oxford, UK: Oxford University Press.

Danzinger, S. (2001). Welfare reform policy from Nixon to Clinton. In D. Featherman & M. Vinovskis (Eds.), *Social science and policy making* (pp. 137–164). Ann Arbor: University of Michigan Press.

Doherty, W. J. (1991). Beyond reactivity and the deficit model of manhood. *Journal of Marital and Family Therapy, 17,* 29–32.

Doherty, W. J., Kouneski, E. F., & Erickson, M. F. (1998). Responsible fathering: An overview and conceptual framework. *Journal of Marriage and the Family, 6,* 227–292.

Eamon, M. K. (2005). Social-demographic, school, neighborhood, and parenting influences on the academic achievement of Latino young adolescents. *Journal of Youth and Adolescence, 34,* 163–174.

Edelman, M. W. (2003). Why don't we have the will to end child poverty. *Georgetown Journal on Poverty Law & Policy, 10,* 273–277.

Ehrenreich, B. (1984). *The hearts of men.* Garden City, NY: Anchor Press/Doubleday.

Elder, G. H. (1998). The life course and human development. In R. Lerner (Ed.), *Handbook of child psychology, vol 1* (pp. 939–991). New York: Wiley.

Fagan, J., Newash, N., & Schloesser, A. (2000). Female caregivers' perceptions of fathers' and significant adult males' involvement with their Head Start children. *Families in Society, 81,* 186–196.

Featherstone, B. (2010). Writing fathers in but mothers out. *Critical Social Policy, 30,* 208–224.

Feldblum, C., & Appleberry, R. (2008). Legislatures, agencies, courts, and advocates: How laws are made, interpreted, and modified. In M. Pitt-Catsouphes, E. E. Kossek, & S. Sweet (Eds.), *The work and family handbook* (pp. 627–650). New York: Psychology Press.

Furstenberg, F. F., Jr., & Featherstone, B. (2010). Writing fathers in but mothers out! *Critical Social Policy, 30,* 208–224.

Folbre, N. (2008). *Valuing children.* Cambridge, MA: Harvard University Press.

Fraser, N. (1994). After the family wage. *Political Theory, 22,* 591–618.

Furstenberg, F. F. (1988). Good dads—bad dads. In A. Cherlin (Ed.), *The changing American* family and public policy (pp. 193 218). Washington, DC: Urban Institute Press.

Fuwa, M., & Cohen, P. (2007). Housework and social policy. *Social Science Research, 36,* 512–530.

Goldberg, W. A., Tan, E. T., & Thorsnn, K. L. (2009). Trends in academic attention to fathers, 1930–2006. *Fathering, 7,* 159–179.

Gornick, J., & Meyers, M. (2003). *Families that work.* New York: Russell Sage Foundation.

Gornick, J., & Meyers, M. (2007). Institutions for gender egalitarianism. New York: Verso.

Griswold, R. L. (1993). *Fatherhood in America: A history.* New York: Basic Books.

Haskins, R. (2009). Moynihan was right: Now what? *The Annals of the American Academy of Political and Social Science, 621,* 281–314.

Hays, S. (1996). *The cultural contradictions of motherhood.* New Haven, CT: Yale University Press.

Hays, S. (2003). *Flat broke with children.* New York: Oxford University Press.

Hernandez, D. J. (1993). *America's children.* New York: Russell Sage Foundation.

Heyman, J., Earle, A., & Hayes, J. (2007). *The work, family and equity index: How does the United States measure up?* Montreal, Quebec: Institute for Health and Social Policy.

Hobson, B., & Morgan, D. (2002). *Making men into fathers.* UK: Cambridge University Press.

Holt, S. (2006). *The earned income tax credit at age 30: What we know.* Washington, DC: The Brookings Institution.

Holzer, H., J., Schanzenbach, D. W., Duncan, G. J., & Ludwig, J. (2008). The economic costs of childhood poverty in the United States. *Journal of Children and Poverty, 14,* 41–61.

Hook, J. (2006). Care in context. *American Sociological Review, 71,* 639–660.

Immervoll, H., & Pearson, M. (2009). *A dood time for making work pay?* OECD Social, Employment, and Migration Working Paper No. 81. Retrieved on March 12, 2011, from www.iza.org/en/webcontent/publications/policypapers

Jarrett, R., Roy, K., & Burton, L. (2002). Fathers in the 'hood: Qualitative research on African American men. In C. Tamis-LeMonda & N. Cabrera (Eds.), *Handbook of father involvement: Multidisciplinary perspectives* (pp. 211–248). Hillsdale, NJ: Erlbaum.

Johnson, M. P. (2006). Conflict and control gender symmetry and asymmetry in domestic violence. *Violence Against Women, 12,* 1003–1018.

Johnson, T., Rimsza, M., Johnson, W. (2006). The effects of cost-shifting in the state children's heath insurance program. *American Journal of Public Health, 96,* 709–715.

Kamerman, S. B., & Kahn, A. J. (2001). Child and family policies in an era of social policy retrenchment and restructuring. In K. Vleminckx & T. M. Smeeding (Eds.), *Child well-being, child poverty and child policy in modern nations: What do we know?* (pp. 501–525). Bristol, UK: Policy Press.

Kelly, E. L. (2008). Work-family policies: The United States in international perspective. In M. Pitt-Catsouphes, E. Kossek, & S. Sweet (Eds.), *The work and family handbook* (pp. 99–123). New York: Psychology Press.

Knijn, T., & Kremer, M. (1997). Gender and the caring dimension of welfare states: Toward inclusive citizenship. *Social Politics, 4,* 328–361.

LaRossa, R. (1988). Fatherhood and social change. *Family Relations, 37,* 451–458.

Lerman, R. I. (2010). Capabilities and contributions of unwed fathers. *The Future of Children, 20,* 63–85.

Lero, D., Ashbourne, L., & Whitehead, D. (2006). *Inventory of policies and policy areas influencing father involvement.* Guelph, Canada: Father Involvement Research Alliance.

Lieb, H., & Thistle, S. (2005). The changing impact of marriage, motherhood and work on women's poverty. *Journal of Women, Politics & Policy, 27,* 5–22.

Liera, A. (2002). *Working parents and the welfare state.* Cambridge, UK: Cambridge University Press.

Marsiglio, W. R., Day, J., Evans, M., Lamb, M., Braver, S., & Peters, E. (1998). Report of the Working Group on Conceptualizing Male Parenting. In *Nurturing fatherhood.* Washington DC: Federal Interagency Forum on Child and Family Statistics.

McLanahan, S. (2009). Fragile families and the reproduction of poverty. *The Annals of the American Academy of Political and Social Science, 621,* 111–131.

Mincy, R. B., Garfinkel, I., & Nepomnyaschy, L. (2005). In-hospital paternity establishment and father involvement in fragile families. *Journal of Marriage and Family, 67,* 611–626.

Moen, P., & Coltrane, S. (2004). Families, theories, and social policy. In V. Bengtson, D. Klein, A. Acock, K. Allen, & P. Dilworth-Anderson (Eds.), *Sourcebook of family theory and research* (pp. 534–556). Thousand Oaks, CA: Sage.

Moss, P., & Deven, F. (2006). Leave policies and research: A cross-national perspective. *Marriage and Family Review, 39,* 255–285.

Nock, S. L. (1998). *Marriage in men's lives.* New York: Oxford University Press.

O'Brien, M. (2009). Fathers, parental leave policies, and infant quality of life. *The Annals of the American Academy of Political and Social Science, 624,* 190–212.

Palm, G., & Fagan, J. (2008). Father involvement in early childhood programs: Review of the literature. *Early Child Development and Care, 178,* 745–759.

Parke, R. D. (1996). *Fatherhood.* Cambridge, MA: Harvard University Press.

Perez-Johnson, I., Kauff, J., & Hershey, A. (2003). *Giving Noncustodial Parents Options.* Washington, DC: Mathematica Policy Research, Inc.

Pleck, J. H., & Masciadrelli, B. P. (2004). Paternal involvement. In M. E. Lamb (Ed.), *The role of the father in child development* (4th ed., pp. 222–271). New York: Wiley.

Pleck, E. H., & Pleck, J. H. (1997). Fatherhood ideals in the United States. In M. E. Lamb (Ed.), *The role of the father in child development* (3rd ed., pp. 33 48). New York: Wiley.

Popenoe, D. (1996). *Life without father.* New York: Free Press.

Pruett, K. D. (1987). *The nurturing father.* New York: Warner Books.

Raikes, H., & Belloti, J. (2007). Policies and programmatic efforts pertaining to fatherhood: Commentary. *Applied Development Science, 11*(4), 271–272.

Raikes, H., Summers, J. A., & Roggman, L. A., (2005). Father involvement in EHS programs. *Fathering 3,* 29–58.

Rainwater, L., & Smeeding, T. M. (2003). *Poor kids in a rich country.* New York: Russell Sage.

Roy, K. (1999). Low-income single fathers in an African American community and the requirements of welfare reform. *Journal of Family Issues, 20,* 432–457.

Roy, K. (2006). Father stories: A life course examination of paternal identity among low-income African American men. *Journal of Family Issues, 27,* 31–54.

Roy, K., & Dyson, O. (2010). Making daddies into fathers. *American Journal of Community Psychology, 45,* 139–154.

Silverstein, L. B., & Auerbach, C. F. (1999). Deconstructing the essential father. *American Psychologist, 54,* 397–407.

Smith, A., & Williams, D. R. (2007). Father-friendly legislation and paternal time across Western Europe. *Journal of Comparative Policy Analysis, 9,* 175–192.

Sorensen, E. (2010). Rethinking public policy toward low-income fathers in the child support program. *Journal of Policy Analysis and Management, 29,* 604–610.

Sorensen, E., & Zibman, C. (2001). *Poor dads who don't pay child support: Deadbeats or disadvantaged?* Research Report B-30. Washington, DC: Urban Institute.

Spaulding, S., Grossman, J., & Wallace, D. (2009). *Working dads.* Retrieved March 12, 2011, from http://www.ppv.org/ppv/publications/assets/310_publication.pdf

Stacey, J. (1996). *In the name of the family.* Boston: Beacon.

Stark, E. (2007). *Coercive control.* New York: Oxford University Press.

Sullivan, O., Coltrane, S., McAnnally, L., & Altintas, E. (2009). Father-friendly policies and time use data in a cross-national context: Potential and prospects for future research. *The Annals of the American Academy of Political and Social Science, 624,* 234–257.

Tach, L., Mincy, R. B., & Edin, K. (2010). Parenting as a "package deal". *Demography, 47,* 181–204.

Thompson, L., & Walker, A. (1989). Gender in families: Women and men in marriage, work, and parenthood. *Journal of Marriage and the Family, 51,* 845–871.

Thorne, B. (Ed.). (1992). *Rethinking the family.* Boston: Northeastern University Press.

Townsend, N. W. (2002). *The package deal.* Philadelphia, PA: Temple University Press.

Vann, N. (2007). Reflections on the development of fatherhood work. *Applied Developmental Science, 11*(4), 266–268.

Wagmiller, R. L., & Adelman, R. M. (2010). Childhood and intergenerational poverty. National Center for Children in Poverty, Columbia University, Mailman School of Public Health. Retrieved January 15, 2011, from http://www.nccp.org/publications/pub_909.html

Waller, M. (2009). Viewing low-income fathers' ties to families through a cultural lens. *The Annals of the American Academy of Political and Social Science, 629,* 102–124.

Wilcox, W. B. (2004). *Soft patriarchs, new men.* Chicago, IL: University of Chicago Press

Wisensale, S. (2003). Two steps forward, one step back: The Family and Medical Leave Act as retrenchment policy. *Review of Policy Research, 20*(1), 135.

Chapter 24

Marriage, Fatherhood, and Parenting Programming

Erin Kramer Holmes

Brigham Young University

Phillip A. Cowan and Carolyn Pape Cowan

University of California, Berkeley

Alan J. Hawkins

Brigham Young University

Brief Historical Overview and Theoretical Perspectives

In this chapter we answer questions about the ways in which federal and state initiatives, including marriage and relationship education programs, may connect fathering to positive outcomes for children, fathers, and mothers. Following a brief historical overview of correlational research and policy initiatives, we raise current research questions relevant to identifying and evaluating "best practices" in our intervention and evaluation efforts. We explore methodological issues relevant to evaluation and discuss current empirical findings regarding the types of federal and state programs that seem to effectively promote healthy father and family outcomes. We integrate knowledge from three independent but related intervention strategies: parenting education interventions, fatherhood initiatives, and couple relationship interventions. Although each strategy is focused on the goal of strengthening family relationships, each has developed relatively independent of the others. Thus, we argue that without efforts to bridge gaps among these intervention strategies, scholars from each camp may miss the important efforts of other individuals focused on the same goal. Finally, we close with bridges to other disciplines, policy implications, and directions for future research.

Links Between Positive Father Involvement and Healthy Family Outcomes

The issue of whether fathers become positively involved in their children's lives has traditionally been treated as either an issue of men's motivation or their family circumstances (married, cohabiting, separated, divorced, remarried, e.g., Blankenhorn, 1995). More recent formulations tend to understand father involvement as a product of multiple systemic factors that interact to affect whether and how fathers establish relationships with their children: fathers' level of adjustment to the transition; the quality of the relationship with the mother of the child; intergenerational patterns of family relationships; characteristics of the child; and stresses that interfere or social supports that enhance each man's behavior toward his child (Cowan, Powell, & Cowan, 1998; Doherty, Kouneski, & Erickson, 1998; Holmes & Huston, 2010). The systemic view implies that there are bidirectional interaction effects. For example, if parents have high unresolved conflict, fathers may be less involved, but fathers' low level of involvement may also become a source of conflict in the co-parenting relationship, and both of these might have negative effects on the quality of the parent-child relationship and on the developing child. We would expect, then, to find indirect as well as direct effects when we try to trace the links between fathers' involvement and children's development.

How does the positive presence of a father in his child's life yield healthy family outcomes? Correlational evidence suggests that father involvement supports children's social, cognitive, and physical development across the lifespan (see, for example, Amato, 1987; Davidov & Grusec, 2006; Flouri, 2005; Ryan, Martin, & Brooks-Gunn, 2006; Tamis-LeMonda, Shannon, Cabrera, & Bradley, 2004). Fathers also benefit from being positively involved with their children (Palkovitz, 2002). For example, men engaged with their children gain a stronger sense of purpose in life (Palkovitz, Copes, & Woolfolk, 2001), increased intergenerational and extended family interaction (Knoester & Eggebeen, 2006), and increased job performance (Graves, Ohlott, & Ruderman, 2007). Further, fathers who share responsibility for childrearing before and after the birth of their children are more likely to directly and indirectly support mothers in their parenting efforts, regardless of marital status (Cabrera, Fagan, & Farrie, 2008; Hawkins, Bradford, Palkovitz, Christiansen, Day, & Call, 2002), although positive co-resident father involvement and marital satisfaction have also been associated (see Cummings, Merrilees, & George, 2010). In short, the impact of fathers' involvement on their children is determined not simply by what fathers do with their children, but by the ways in which family and outside-the-family forces influence, and are influenced by, the quality of the father-child relationship (Cabrera, Fitzgerald, Bradley, & Roggman, 2007).

Governments and communities are invested in father involvement not only because it promotes healthy child development, healthy adult development, and is associated with support of mothering, but also because it minimizes delinquency (Coley & Medeiros, 2007), externalizing and internalizing behaviors (Day & Padilla-Walker, 2009), alcohol and substance use (Nash, McQueen, & Bray, 2005), and early sexual activity and teen pregnancy in the next generation (Ellis et al., 2003). These correlational studies provide a weight of evidence supporting the hypothesis that men's involvement plays a positive causal role in children's, fathers', and mothers' healthy development. If intervention studies can demonstrate that increased father involvement is followed by increased child, father, and/or mother well-being, scholars can more persuasively argue for a causal link between father involvement and healthy development. Unfortunately, as we will establish below, few intervention-based studies exist on this point (yet).

Fatherhood Policy Initiatives

Research suggesting that positive father involvement can promote healthy family outcomes supports policymakers' investment in quality parent-child relationships as protective factors which buffer individuals from risk (Coie et al., 1993; Holmes, Galovan, Yoshida, & Hawkins,

2010). Lamb and Tamis-Lemonda (2004) have indicated that "the research-to-policy link on fathers is bidirectional," noting that "political emphasis on the importance of fathers fosters the research agenda" and that research also "influences social policies and program initiatives" (p. 15). Thus, better research will promote better policy and vice versa (see also Bronte-Tinkew, Bowie, & Moore, 2007).

Three decades of research promoting the idea that fathers were important figures in families ultimately led to formal recognition of fatherhood in policy. In 1995 President Clinton issued an executive order which directed "federal agencies to support fathers' positive involvement in their families" and ensured "that federally funded research on children and families incorporated fathers" (Marsiglio, Amato, Day, & Lamb, 2000, p. 1174). Clinton issued his executive order in the wake of other organizations stressing the importance of fatherhood in the broader culture. For example, in 1994, the National Fatherhood Initiative was organized following a meeting of fathering scholars in which attendees agreed that there was a need for "an organization that would stimulate a broad-based social movement to combat father absence and promote responsible fatherhood" (National Fatherhood Initiative History, n.d.).

The Bush administration continued to support responsible fatherhood. In 2001, President Bush indicated that he was "determined to make committed, responsible fatherhood a national priority," allocating $60 million to fund efforts "that promote responsible fatherhood" (Executive Office of the President of the United States, 2001, p. 75). Since then, policy support has continued. As part of the Healthy Marriage and Responsible Fatherhood Initiative, up to $50 million per year (2006–2011) has been allocated to promote responsible fatherhood (Administration for Children and Families, 2008; U.S. Department of Health and Human Services, 2007), and calls from both the Clinton and Bush administrations launched efforts in multiple states to set aside money for fathering programs (Cabrera, 2010). Fatherhood holds a place in current policy agendas.

Marriage and Co-parenting as Contexts for Fatherhood: A Family Systems Perspective

At the same time federal and state support for fatherhood emerged, so did federal and state policies to help couples form and sustain healthy relationships (Hawkins, Blanchard, Baldwin, & Fawcett, 2008). Some view healthy relationship education as an additional resource to bolster co-resident fathers' involvement with their children. These programs generally involve voluntary parent and couple educational programming. Some evidence suggests that such programs can directly and indirectly impact father involvement through groups that focus on parenting, co-parenting, and other domains of family functioning (Cowan, Cowan, Pruett, Pruett, & Wong, 2009). Such programs exist based on a current research hypothesis that interactions between mothers and fathers have a direct and indirect impact on parenting behavior and child outcomes (for review see Fincham & Hall, 2005).

Early research on interactions between mothers and fathers highlighted correlations between marital satisfaction and fathers' participation in childcare. McBride and Rane (1998) discovered, however, that the co-parenting relationship affects men's parenting practices more strongly than global measures of marital satisfaction. Co-parenting refers to the quality of the coordination (undermining or encouraging) between partners in their parenting roles (Schoppe-Sullivan, Mangelsdorf, Brown, & Sokolowski, 2006) and incorporates the degree of support and solidarity a couple shares, the way roles within the household are shared, the affirmation (or lack thereof) of the partner's parenting, and the way spouses work together to manage their daily life as parents (Feinberg, 2003; McHale, Kuersten-Hogan, & Rao, 2004). McHale and colleagues (2004) report results similar to those of McBride and Rane. Although co-parenting is clearly a part of the couple relationship, it constitutes an important domain of family functioning in itself; it is quite possible for two parents to function well in one realm and not in the other. Although relationship processes such as problem solving, conflict management, and affection that are present in marriage before the birth of a baby predicted some aspects of parenting quality after, the mismatch between co-parents' expectations about issues such as fairness in the division of childcare labor predicted less effective parenting practices and poorer marital quality, particularly across the transition to parenthood (McHale et al., 2004). Thus it would appear that co-parenting processes serve as a less-studied link between marriage and parenting practices. Those in favor of incorporating co-parenting skills into other fatherhood initiatives suggest that targeting specific co-parenting practices may indirectly and directly affect positive father involvement and improve family outcomes (for a full review, see Palkovitz, Fagan, & Hull, this volume).

Family systems theory postulates that times of family transition imply instability and disequilibrium, which can stimulate more complex integration and differentiation, or exacerbate ongoing dysfunctional family relationships (Cowan, 1991). Theorists also recognize that family interactions can swiftly stabilize to promote family equilibrium (Minuchin, 1985), although this family equilibrium is just as likely to reflect positive functionality as it is to reflect some measure of unhealthy dysfunction. More than 30 studies over the past three decades in a number of industrialized countries suggest that, on average, marital satisfaction declines after the birth of a first child and keeps on declining throughout the childrearing years (Twenge, Campbell, & Foster, 2003). The negative consequences of unresolved marital distress for children include increased risk of both academic and behavior problems in childhood and adolescence (Cummings, Goeke-Morey, & Raymond, 2004). These findings suggest that co-parenting interventions prior to and immediately following the birth of a new baby will come at a critical time in which family life educators could help new parent partners co-create positive shared parenting patterns. In one of the few empirical tests of critical periods for family life education, Fivaz-Depeursinge and Corboz-Warnery (1999) demonstrated that couples begin to solidify their newly established co-parenting behaviors within the first 3 to 4 months after the birth of a first child. Thus family systems theory suggests that prevention during transition periods, such as the transition to parenthood, may promote positive family processes that can be solidified early in the couples' parenting experiences, with potentially long-lasting positive effects for the couple's co-parenting and romantic partnerships.

Current Research Questions

What sorts of programs will most effectively promote the types of positive developmental and relational outcomes that theory and correlational research imply for fathers, children, and mothers? Could federal and state attention to healthy relationship education, including a focus on co-parenting, be a viable approach to promote positive father involvement? If so, is it still best to pursue healthy relationships and father involvement intervention separately or together? When might couple interventions be contra-indicated? What methods will be the best ways to evaluate our state and federal efforts? These questions lie at the heart of current debate related to fatherhood and couple relationship education policy and intervention strategies. We spend the remainder of our chapter addressing these questions.

Research Measurement and Methodology

To answer current research questions regarding the best policy and intervention strategies for fathers and families, there needs to be a long-term commitment to a substantial, sustained, and sophisticated research agenda. First, while correlational research can suggest possibilities for increasing father involvement, investments in rigorous experimental research of programmatic interventions are needed. The gold standard for evaluation research is classical experimental design (Orr, 1999), which requires randomized assignment to a control group and at least one comparison treatment group. This gold standard is challenging and expensive to achieve, but to get answers strong enough to push policy along we need to invest in randomized control trials.

Second, these evaluations need to be designed with multiple treatment groups to compare different approaches to fathering interventions. Specifically, we argue for studies that compare programming directed at fathers (alone) vs. programming directed at couples (fathers and mothers together). Systems theory leads us to expect that increased father involvement is more likely to occur and to be maintained when both parents are involved in an intervention (Cowan & Cowan, 2002). This hypothesis has received some empirical support (Cowan et al., 2009; Rienks, Wadsworth, Markman, Einhorn, & Etter, 2011) but needs more empirical testing.

Third, a significant task for researchers will be to explore programming sensitive to different family contexts and circumstances rather than assume that a universal approach will suffice. Specifically, programs may need to be tailored to father-resident and non-resident families (Fagan & Stevenson, 2002; Holmes et al., 2010). Moreover, fathers experiencing multi-partner fertility will have challenges not experienced by fathers with a child only from a current partner (Monte, 2007). Also, we need empirical examinations of whether programming works well for both cohabiting and married fathers. Other family, child, and social address dimensions such as socioeconomic status, race/ethnicity, child age, and timing (pre-natal vs. post-natal) may affect programming effectiveness (Cabrera et al., 2007).

Fourth, programming to strengthen father involvement should be expected to affect a wide range of outcomes, many of which are not commonly evaluated in fathering programming. In addition to various aspects of father involvement, evaluation researchers should assess co-parenting behavior and attitudes, effective problem-solving skills, and couple violence. Further, evaluators should test whether changes in father involvement are mediated by couple processes. And, ultimately, we hope the primary benefit of increased father involvement will be increased child well-being. Measuring change in child well-being will likely require research designs that follow children and their families over several years.

Finally, even when researchers have good answers to the "best-practices" questions raised here, there will need to be continued research support for effective implementation of programming. How can practitioners best recruit and maintain fathers for programs? What are the best means for disseminating programs widely in communities? What settings are most attractive to fathers? These and many other implementation issues will need empirical attention if we are to affect a significant proportion of fathers and their families.

Empirical Findings: Fatherhood, Couple, and Combined Interventions

The brief summary of research, policy, and methods above points to what seems like an obvious conclusion: if fathers' positive involvement with their children, and fathers' collaborative co-parenting with the child's mother, are associated with positive outcomes for children and families, then interventions designed to increase that involvement ought to have high payoff for child and adult development. This argument in support of preventive intervention early in the period of family formation was strengthened by recent research on fragile families—low-income unmarried parents having a child (McLanahan & Carlson, 2001). Earlier research on the transition to parenthood, although extensive, was focused almost entirely on middle- and upper-income families. The Fragile Families studies found that, contrary to popular belief, most unmarried women are in a romantic relationship with the father of the child, and about half the couples are living together at the time of the baby's birth (McLanahan & Beck, 2010). Further, Cabrera et al. (2008) found that fathers who are engaged prenatally are more likely to move into stable relationships with the mother of their children than fathers who do not stay engaged with their infants prenatally. However, in addition to the general vicissitudes accompanying the transition to parenthood in middle-class families, poverty and non-marital status lead to an increased risk that the couple relationship will not last, and that fathers will not remain actively involved with their children. Taken together, findings from studies of both middle-income and low-income families suggest that preventive interventions to enhance father involvement and maintain or increase the quality of the partners' relationship as a couple or as co-parents are needed all along the economic spectrum, and that interventions focused early in the transitions to parenthood, even prenatally, may be most effective.

Responsible Fatherhood Programs

It seems reasonable to develop programs to increase fathers' involvement by recruiting men to individual and group meetings with other men. A recent review of father involvement interventions (Knox, Cowan, Cowan, & Bildner, 2011) points out that early efforts (1980–2000) to help men become more actively involved with their children recruited men who had long since given up contact with the child and the mother, and focused largely on helping the men develop skills that would result in child support payments ("responsible fatherhood"). The program staff did not work with mothers (who were often in new relationships) to increase the chance that they would allow the fathers access to their children. Nor did the programs work with men to help them negotiate with the mothers. It is not surprising then to find that, with rare exceptions (Knox & Redcross, 2000), the programs with systematic evaluations did not show positive increases in men's direct connection with their children (see also Mincy & Pouncy, 2002).

Marriage and Relationship Education Programs

Whereas responsible fatherhood programs were receiving mixed to negative research reviews, the picture was decidedly brighter for marriage and relationship education programs (MRE). A number of recent meta-analytic studies provide support for the ability of MRE to strengthen relationship quality and/or communication skills (Blanchard, Hawkins, Baldwin, & Fawcett, 2009; Fawcett, Hawkins, Blanchard, & Carroll, 2010; Hawkins et al., 2008; Hawkins, Stanley, Blanchard, & Albright, 2012). While most research in this field has focused on middle-class, well-educated couples, research is now beginning to document the effectiveness of MRE for lower-income couples as well (Cowan, Cowan, & Knox, 2010; Hawkins & Fackrell, 2010; Hawkins & Fellows, 2011; Stanley, Allen, Markman, Rhoades, & Prentice, 2010). These

couple-focused interventions were not conceptualized within the framework of father involvement interventions, but, in fact, the active involvement of men in the discussion of family issues
turned out to be one way of encouraging fathers' engagement in family life. For instance, one
study of a *self-guided* couple intervention for middle-class couples transitioning to parenthood
did not find significant effects on the couple relationship but did find significant effects on
father involvement in daily child care tasks (Hawkins, Lovejoy, Holmes, Blanchard, & Fawcett,
2008).

A Combined Couple and Father Involvement Approach

A recent program to engage low-income fathers more directly in the lives of their children
involves components for both fathers and couples. The Supporting Father Involvement Study
(Cowan et al., 2009), sponsored by the California Office of Child Abuse Prevention, has published findings on a randomized clinical trial of two parallel intervention strategies. There
were 279 participants, primarily low-income, two-thirds of them Mexican American, living in
four California counties. Couples were eligible if their youngest child was from birth to 7, and
if they had not been referred for child abuse/neglect or domestic violence in the past year, and
were not involved with mental health or drug abuse problems that compromised the management of their daily lives.

Participants agreed to be randomly assigned to (a) a single 3-hour meeting with a curriculum focused on the importance of fathers (a low dose comparison condition), or (b) a 16-week
fathers group, led by a male-female team of trained mental health professionals, that met for
2 hours each week, or (c) a 16-week couples group with the same leaders, meeting over the
same period of time and using an almost identical curriculum. The intervention approach and
its curriculum were based on a model validated for middle- class couples having a first child
(Cowan & Cowan, 2000), and for couples with a first child making the transition to elementary school (Cowan, Cowan, & Heming, 2005). After an open-ended check-in period in which
participants were invited to bring their personal experiences of the past week to the group,
the leaders presented curriculum topics concerning each participant's individual well-being
or distress, changes each partner wanted to make from his/her family of origin, parenting
issues, couple relationship issues (including co-parenting disagreements), and outside the family sources of stress and support. The approach did not involve skills training, but rather used
short presentations, games, role-playing, and homework to encourage participants to become
the kind of parents and partners they were hoping to be. In addition to having regular input
from the group leaders, each participant, including those in the comparison condition, were
offered the services of a case manager to refer the family for help from outside sources for
financial, housing, or mental health problems.

Results published so far (Cowan et al., 2009) show that the participants in the low-dose
comparison condition either remained stable (e.g., no change in father involvement) or experienced more stress and distress on measures of couple relationship satisfaction, parenting
stress, and children's behavior problems. Men in the fathers-only groups (which did include 2
sessions for mothers to encourage their support of the men's participation in the project), were
significantly more involved in the daily tasks of childcare according to both parents, and their
children did not increase in problem behaviors over 18 months. Unfortunately, their satisfaction with the couple relationship declined. Participants in the couples groups—in addition
to the benefits of fathers' increased involvement and no increases in the children's behavior
problems—showed reductions in parenting stress and stable couple relationship satisfaction.

Unpublished results include a successful replication with another 280 families (including 40 African American families, and a new random assignment trial (ongoing) in which half the participating families had been referred for child abuse or neglect during the past year). It is clear to us that while a fathers-only group was able to increase fathers' involvement in their children's care, a couples group did the same, but had added benefits for the couple in terms of reducing parenting stress and preventing the decline in relationship satisfaction, both of which function as risk factors for children's development.

Reinks and colleagues (Rienks et al., 2011), using a randomized clinical trial design, recently reported a new couples-focused father involvement program called FRAME, based on an adaptation of the Prevention and Relationship Enhancement Program (Markman, Stanley, & Blumberg, 2010). A 14-hour MRE program attended by couples was compared with the same program attended by only one of the partners, and with a no-treatment control condition. In the control condition, father involvement did not change over time. When only one partner attended, father involvement actually declined, even though the attending partner was asked to teach the communication skills to the non-attending partner at home. But when fathers and mothers participated together, there was a significant increase in parents' reports of fathers spending time, encouraging cognitive skills, and providing emotional warmth to the children. No outcomes for the children were reported.

In one additional study, early results were recently released for a rigorous, large-scale, multi-site, randomized control trial of the Building Strong Families programs designed to help unmarried, low-income couples strengthen their relationships and increase father involvement. Overall, this study found few significant effects approximately one year after the intervention, perhaps because rates of full participation in the program were very low. However, African American couples in this study reported positive effects. Specifically, treatment-group couples reported significantly greater relationship support and affection, and less use of destructive conflict behaviors. Moreover, one study site—the one with the largest recruitment of participants and most successful efforts at retaining couples for a strong dosage of the intervention—found significant program effects on both couple relationships and father involvement, including improved co-parenting relationships, higher paternal co-residence with the child, and more financial support for the child (Wood, McConnell, Moore, Clarkwest, & Hsueh, 2010).

In summary, interventions that target fathers and deal primarily with men's issues have not achieved much success when the men are long-separated from the mothers and their children. By contrast, interventions that focus on family relationships have the power to increase fathers' involvement with the children while improving those relationships, or at least preventing the slide in relationship quality that tends to occur over time. Couples groups have also been effective in preventing declines in marital quality in both middle- and low-income families. In one study, at least, couples groups with clinically trained leaders have shown a value-added impact on parenting stress, on the couples' relationship, and on parents' descriptions of their children's behavior problems. Of course, recruitment, retention, and dosage of the intervention also affect the success of the program.

Bridges to Other Disciplines

Our call to integrate historically independent perspectives of parenting programs, fatherhood initiatives, and couple relationship programs is inherently interdisciplinary. It calls for developmental scholars, social psychologists, family scholars, clinicians, sociologists, policy analysts, and others to combine efforts toward the common goal of strengthening families. We further recognize that bridging the gap between these bodies of work and already existing initiatives will take time. We hope our brief attempt here will begin to facilitate this.

We have much to learn from other disciplines. We note the importance of cost-benefit analyses to more accurately assess the true "costs" of intervention efforts, and recognize that economists and policy analysts may be key collaborative partners in this endeavor. Such cost benefit analyses can help us better utilize limited state and federal funds, while still promoting our common goal of supporting and strengthening individuals and families. By combining efforts and investing in collaborative, interdisciplinary, integrative work we hope those invested in strengthening father involvement and positive family outcomes can all benefit.

Policy Implications

As we attempt to build bridges among disciplines, we need to acknowledge that achieving our interdisciplinary goals will require public policy shifts to encourage service delivery changes that may prove challenging to put into practice. Two of us have noted elsewhere (Cowan et al., 2010), that each approach is managed by different public and private funding and service structures, in which the proponents of each approach view each other as competitors for limited funding streams (see Ooms et al., 2006, for a vivid analysis). It will take very strong directives from funders, who themselves may be advocates of one of the three alternatives, to encourage parent education, marriage education, and father involvement programs to collaborate in creating the kind of integrated approaches we have called for.

Another policy issue for funders and service providers is the question of where such integrated services should be located. One quick answer is that it will not work simply to announce the availability of these services and hope that people will use them. That is, it is not the case that if we build it, families will necessarily come. Staff must be ready either to locate the institutions where people are used to going for services (e.g., hospitals, schools, family service agencies), or provide extensive outreach skills to staff who can help to facilitate the likelihood of potential participants coming into an existing family service or mental health agency (Hawkins & Ooms, 2010).

Here too, we suggest needed policy changes to remove or minimize institutional barriers that discourage men from coming to service institutions. Despite shifts toward a more egalitarian ideology in which men's role as active parents has been increasing in importance, service institutions have not kept pace. As we, the authors, have visited family resource centers in many states, we note the presence of a feminine aesthetic in decorations (wall colors, pictures of mothers and babies), materials in waiting rooms (no men's magazines or brochures addressed to men or fathers), staffing (primarily female), and attitudes (often a prevailing message that women need to be protected from violent, shiftless partners). We are not talking here about legitimate concerns that female clients must feel safe in their relationships, but rather about pervasive cultural and organizational myths that men are dangerous or not important to their children's well-being and development. We cannot simply urge, then, that a particular setting become more "father friendly"; it will likely take some ongoing work with the staff, including organizational evaluation, before this can be accomplished (Fagan, Newash, & Schloesser, 2000; McBride, Rane, & Bae, 2001; McFarland, 2000; White, Brotherson, Galovan, Holmes, & Kampmann, 2011).

A final policy issue that concerns us could equally have been raised in the section on directions for future research. Those of us engaged in the business of designing and evaluating MRE and fatherhood interventions are inevitably asked: How much does your intervention cost? And, Could you conduct your intervention with fewer meetings, using less highly trained staff? Whatever the answers, what is missing from these conversations is the question about how much public and private money could be saved by preventive interventions that integrate the goals of increasing couple relationship and parenting quality, fathers' involvement, and children's developmental outcomes. As yet, there have been no cost-benefit analyses to show that when couples resolve their conflict and disagreements more effectively, or when fathers become more engaged and more positively connected with their children, there are subsequent large savings to public funding for domestic violence, divorce, child abuse, and/or the incidence of depression or aggressive behavior problems in the parents or the children. The need for this kind of integrative research—the kind that public policy and economics scholars are well-trained to help us do—is clear. The policy issue is to encourage government funders and private foundations to solicit and support research that identifies the most cost effective approaches to meeting the needs of all members of the family.

At this point in our discussion of policy implications, we think it is important to acknowledge that couple and family relationships exist in a social and economic ecology that both supports and constrains enactment of positive behaviors. Family systems are embedded in economic and employment systems that affect couple behaviors and may be particularly crucial to supporting positive father involvement. In addition, it is becoming clear now that lack of educational attainment is a risk factor for positive parenting behavior and healthy, stable couple relationships (Cherlin, 2009). Similarly, the struggle to balance work and family demands is associated with lower couple relationship quality (Allen, Herst, Bruck, & Sutton, 2000). The implication of these observations is that while there is merit in publically supported programs to improve couple relationships and positive father involvement, we cannot neglect the need for public policy to strengthen the economic and social ecologies that support family life. Thus, our call is to add these relatively new policy forays into strengthening couple relationships and father involvement to a broader set of coterminous economic and social policies that can support healthy families, not replace them.

Future Directions

Research on interventions to promote couple relationship quality and increase father involvement represents the beginning of the research-to-policy process. A number of important questions remain unanswered. We offer the following admittedly incomplete list of unresolved questions to identify next steps in the creation and evaluation of programs to enhance fathers' involvement with their children, to strengthen family relationships, and to foster children's development.

First, an argument for integrating marriage and fatherhood programs would be strengthened if we can show that marital quality is not simply correlated with father involvement, but that improving marital quality results in increased father involvement and other positive effects on relationships between fathers and children. Fragmentary findings suggest that this might be the case, but more evidence is needed. The Schoolchildren and their Families project (Cowan et al., 2005) found that in comparison with couples groups emphasizing parenting issues, couples groups emphasizing couple relationship issues improved marital quality, and this change was followed by increases in observed parenting effectiveness for mothers *and* fathers. The systemic view implies that increased father involvement should also have a positive influence on the couple. The Supporting Father Involvement study for low-income families described above found that while fathers groups were able to increase father involvement, this benefit did not carry over to couple relationship quality, whereas couples groups led to greater father involvement and stemmed the decline in couple relationship satisfaction found in fathers group and control group parents. In a similar vein, a non-intervention study by Cabrera and colleagues (2008) showed that increases in father involvement during the prenatal period were associated with increased couple relationship quality after the birth. Clearly, we need more research to create a picture of the direction of effects in the links between couple relationship quality and father engagement. In addition, future intervention studies should directly test whether any effects on couple relationships mediate change in quantity and quality of father involvement. Evaluation research is fraught with difficulties, but if we want to make stronger assertions about causation, we will need to go beyond correlation to carefully designed experimental research.

It is puzzling to us that a second research question remains unanswered. The stated primary rationale for instituting MRE and fatherhood programs is that increasing father involvement and couple relationship quality will provide direct benefits for children. Until recently, very few studies have assessed the impact of interventions with parents on parent-child relationship quality or children's adaptation (for exceptions, Cowan et al., 2009; Dion, Avellar, Zaveri, & Hershey, 2006; Knox & Fein, in press). If marriage and fatherhood programs begin to provide promising results concerning outcomes for children, two important goals will be accomplished. On the level of theory, we will be able to draw stronger conclusions about connections among marital quality, positive father involvement, and how children fare. On the level of practice and policy, the justification for widespread efforts to mount these programs would become more compelling. Accordingly, an important future research agenda item is to assess the effects of couple relationship education on child outcomes. As straightforward as this recommendation sounds, it has rarely been done. Of course, this also suggests that evaluation studies need to follow participants over longer periods of time than the usual 3–6 months, because it will likely take time for any potential child outcomes to respond to changes in the marital and parenting subsystems.

Third, we remind our readers that we have focused on interventions for parents that reduce risks and enhance benefits for children. Within the systemic view we have presented, there is also room to consider interventions that take into account the myriad of factors associated with the child (age, sex, temperament, health, and so on) that can affect fathers, mothers, and the system of relationships in the family. Although some of these factors are not modifiable, they can be considered in the intervention curricula in the programs that parents attend (e.g., special issues of dealing with adolescent children, aggressive children, or disabled children, among many possible topics).

A fourth set of questions is needed to evaluate whether an integration of couple and fatherhood interventions would produce more positive outcomes for children and families than either approach administered alone. We noted that the fields of parent education, marriage education, and father involvement evolved separately. At present each approach has fervent proponents, and significant sums of both private and public money have been devoted to separate programs for parents (primarily mothers), fathers, and couples. Our reading of both basic research on family systems, and evaluations of interventions in parenting, marriage, and father involvement suggests that combinations of approaches might produce more promising results. That is, parenting programs might reach out to fathers more than they do and address the co-parenting aspects of parent-child relationships. Father involvement programs, too, might profitably explore the relationship between the parents, either the intimate relationship between partners, or the co-parenting collaboration regardless of whether the parents are in a romantic relationship. Future research should also consider whether an integration of couple and fatherhood interventions produces more positive outcomes than either approach administered alone in situations of multi-partner fertility.

Finally, marriage and relationship education programs could learn from current research about the importance of helping couples resolve co-parenting dilemmas and provide tools for both partners to coordinate their parenting strategies and become more effective parents. An added potential benefit of this integration is that it may enlarge the recruitment pool for MRE. We find that many parents, both men and women, who are less open to participating in an intervention addressing issues in their couple relationship, are open to participating in services to foster their children's development and well-being.

We are not advocating that all father involvement and family interventions involve couples, or that couples groups be granted pride of place in constructing interventions to benefit families with young children. So far, there are few studies that compare couples groups with other intervention formats; we need more evaluation studies designed to compare different intervention formats to guide future decisions about optimal intervention strategies. For example, we need to know more about how co-parenting and fatherhood programs could be integrated with existing parenting interventions, now attended largely by mothers. Also, some of these approaches need not be considered as mutually exclusive alternatives, but rather as sequenced approaches to strengthening families (e.g., starting with a fathers or mothers group, followed by a group for both parents).

Another reason for caution in considering the couples approach to encouraging father involvement is that for some couples, working together in pairs or couples groups may be contraindicated if there are reports of violence in the couple relationship. It has been argued that when there is violence between partners, it is undesirable, and possibly unsafe to work with partners together. Some have further suggested that there are different types of couple violence (e.g., situational violence and chronic intimate terrorism) (Johnson, 2009). Studies are beginning to document that couples who have experienced situational violence are present in non-trivial numbers for MRE targeted to more disadvantaged couples (Bradford, Skogrand, & Higginbotham, 2011; Halford, Petch, Creedy, & Gamble, 2011; Wilde & Doherty, 2011). While it may not be safe to treat a small minority of chronically violent couples conjointly, we may find that a majority of couples who report situational violence could benefit from help in collaborative parenting in a carefully-structured intervention (Babcock, Green, & Robie, 2004).

The specific issue of domestic violence raises a more general question worthy of future intensive study. It is unlikely that one kind of program fits all. It is time for program evaluators to go beyond the question of whether an MRE or fatherhood intervention "works" by considering issues of matching interventions to specific target populations. In order to do this, we need to know what kinds of intervention are more successful for which kinds of fathers, mothers, and couples. The question of matching is not simply concerned with the choice between targeting fathers or couples. We need more information about which program modifications are necessary to reach fathers who have been separated from their children for a short or long time? What modifications of program recruitment, intervention approach, or curricula will be required for potential participants who differ in income (Hawkins & Ooms, 2010), race/ethnicity (Skogrand, Barrios-Bell, & Higginbotham, 2009) or family structure (Higginbotham & Skogrand, 2010)? The main message here is that it is time to go beyond simple comparisons of control and intervention participants as they change over time, to ask more differentiated questions about the characteristics of both participants and programs that produce the most optimal outcomes for parents and their children. One caveat is that our standard measures of father involvement may not be up to the task of such specific analyses. As we intervene in families of greater complexity, fewer resources, and more diversity, we may need to make sensitive adjustments to how we define and observe "positive father involvement."

In conclusion, we see an exciting opportunity for interdisciplinary collaboration in which family scholars, policy analysts, family life educators, and others integrate the multitude of prevention and intervention efforts in MRE, parenting, and fathering. Throughout this chapter we have tried to orient our readers to current preventive intervention efforts to promote father involvement, including a history of policies focused on fatherhood, methodological issues to strengthen our evaluation efforts, and empirical support for associations between father involvement, couple-focused interventions, and policy efforts. We invite others to join us in efforts to bridge the gaps among the three independently developing efforts to strengthen family relationships: parenting education focused primarily on mothers, parenting education focused primarily on fathers, and couple relationship education efforts that pay scant attention to partners as parents. We further call for increased effort to move beyond simple comparisons of control and intervention participants to more differentiated questions about the characteristics of the participants and programs that can be matched to produce the most optimal outcomes for parents and children. We argue that the results of these evaluative efforts will allow all to revisit, refine, and revise the current curricula to create more effective policies and programs to strengthen fathers, mothers, and children.

References

Administration for Children and Families. (2008). The healthy marriage initiative: General information. Retrieved November 29, 2008 from http://www.acf.hhs.gov/healthymarriage/about/mission.html

Allen, T. D., Herst, D. E. L., Bruck, A. S., & Sutton, M. (2000). Consequences associated with work-to-family conflict: A review and agenda for future research. *Journal of Occupational Health Psychology, 5,* 278–308.

Amato, P. R. (1987). Family processes in intact, one-parent, and step-parent families: The child's point of view. *Journal of Marriage and the Family, 49,* 327–337.

Babcock, J., Green, C., & Robie, C. (2004). Does batterers' treatment work? A meta-analytic review of domestic violence treatment. *Clinical Psychology Review, 23*(8), 1023–1053.

Blanchard, V. L., Hawkins, A. J., Baldwin, S. A., & Fawcett, E. B. (2009). Investigating the effects of marriage and relationship education on couples' communication skills: A meta-analytic study. *Journal of Family Psychology, 24,* 203–214.

Blankenhorn, D. (1995). *Fatherless America: Confronting our most urgent social problem.* New York: BasicBooks.

Bradford, K. P., Skogrand, L., & Higginbotham, B. J. (2011). Risk for intimate partner violence among participants in a statewide relationship education initiative. *Journal of Couple & Relationship Therapy, 10,* 169–184.

Bronte-Tinkew, J. , Bowie, L., & Moore, K. (2007). Fathers and public policy. *Applied Developmental Science, 11*(4), 254–259.

Cabrera, N. (2010). Father involvement and public policies. In M. E. Lamb (Ed.), *The role of the father in child development* (5th ed., pp. 517–550). Hoboken, NJ: Wiley.

Cabrera, N., Fagan, J., & Farrie, D. (2008). Explaining the long reach of fathers' prenatal involvement on later paternal engagement. *Journal of Marriage and Family, 70*(5), 1094–1107.

Cabrera, N., Fitzgerald, H. E., Bradley, R. H., & Roggman, L. (2007). Modeling the dynamics of paternal influences on children over the life course. *Applied Developmental Science, 11*(4), 185–189.

Cherlin, A. J. (2009). *The marriage-go-round.* New York: Knopf.

Coie, J. D., Watt, N. F., West, S. G., Hawkins, J. D., Asarnow, J. R., Markman, H. J., … Long, B. (1993). The science of prevention: A conceptual framework and some directions for a national research program. *American Psychologist, 48,* 1013–1022.

Coley, R. L., & Medeiros, B. L. (2007). Reciprocal longitudinal relations between non-resident father involvement and adolescent delinquency. *Child Development, 78*(1), 132–147.

Cowan, C. P., & Cowan, P. A. (2000). *When partners become parents: The big life change for couples.* Mahwah, NJ: Erlbaum.

Cowan, C. P., Cowan, P. A., & Heming, G. (2005). Two variations of a preventive intervention for couples: Effects on parents and children during the transition to school. In P. A. Cowan, C. P. Cowan, J. C. Ablow, V. K., Johnson, & J. R. Measelle (Eds.), *The family context of parenting in children's adaptation to elementary schoo,* (pp. 277-314). Mahwah, NJ: Erlbaum.

Cowan, P. A. (1991). Individual and family life transitions: A proposal for a new definition. In P. A. Cowan & M. Hetherington (Eds.), *Family transitions* (pp. 3–30). Hillsdale, NJ: Erlbaum.

Cowan, P. A., & Cowan, C. P. (2002). Interventions ans tests of family systems theories: Marital and family relationships in children's development and psychopathology. *Development and Psychopathology, 14,* 731–759.

Cowan, P. A., Cowan, C. P., & Knox, V. (2010). Marriage and fatherhood programs. *Future Child, 20*(2), 205–230.

Cowan, P. A., Cowan, C. P., Pruett, M. K., Pruett, K. D., & Wong, J. (2009). Promoting fathers' engagement with children: Preventive interventions for low-income families. *Journal of Marriage and the Family, 71,* 663–679.

Cowan, P. A., Powell, D., & Cowan, C. P. (1998). Parenting interventions: a family systems perspective. In W. Damon (Ed.), *Handbook of child psychology* (5th ed., Vol. 4, pp. 3–72). New York: Wiley.

Cummings, E. M., Goeke-Morey, M. C., & Raymond, J. (2004). Fathers in family context: Effects of marital quality and marital conflict. In M. E. Lamb (2004). *The role of the father in child development* (4th ed., pp. 196–221). Hoboken, NJ: Wiley.

Cummings, E. M., Merrilees, C. E., & George, M. W. (2010). Fathers, marriages, and families: Revisiting and updating the framework for fathering family context. In M. E. Lamb (Ed.) *The role of the father in child development* (5th ed., pp. 154–177). Hoboken, NJ: Wiley.

Davidov, M., & Grusec, J. E. (2006). Untangling the links of parental responsiveness to distress and warmth to child outcomes. *Child Development, 77,* 44–58.

Day, R. D., & Padilla-Walker, L. M. (2009). Mother and father connectedness and involvement during early adolescence. *Journal of Family Psychology, 23*(6), 900–904.

Dion, M. R., Avellar, S. A., Zaveri, H. H., & Hershey, A. M. (2006). *Implementing healthy marriage programs for unmarried couples with children: Early lessons from the Building Strong Families Project.* Washington, DC: Mathematica.

Doherty, W. J., Kouneski, E. F., & Erickson, M. F. (1998). Responsible fathering: An overview and conceptual framework. *Journal of Marriage and the Family, 60,* 277–292.

Ellis, B. J., Bates, J. E., Dodge, K. A., Fergusson, D. M., Horwood, L. J., Pettit, G. S., & Woodward, L. (2003). Does father absence place daughters at special risk for early sexual activity and teenage pregnancy? *Child Development, 74,* 801–821.

Executive Office of the President of the United States. (2001). A blueprint for new beginnings: A responsible budget for America's priorities. Retrieved November 29, 2008, from http://www.whitehouse.gov/news/usbudget/blueprint/blueprint.pdf

Fagan, J., Newash, N., & Schloesser, A. (2000). Female caregivers' perceptions of fathers' and significant adult males' involvement with their Head Start children. *Families in Society, 81,* 186–196.

Fagan, J., & Stevenson, H. (2002). An experimental study of an empowerment-based intervention for African American Head Start fathers. *Family Relations, 51,* 191–198.

Fawcett, E. B., Hawkins, A. J., Blanchard, V. L., & Carroll, J. S. (2010). Do premarital education programs really work? A meta-analytic study. *Family Relations, 59,* 232–239.

Feinberg, M. E. (2003). The internal structure and ecological context of coparenting: A framework for research and intervention. *Parenting: Science and Practice, 3*, 95–131.

Fincham, F., & Hall, J. (2005). Parenting and the marital relationship. In T. Luster & L. Okagaki (Eds.), *Parenting: An ecological perspective* (pp. 205–234). Mahwah, NJ: Erlbaum.

Fivaz-Depeursinge, E., & Corboz-Warnery, A. (1999). *The Primary triangle. A developmental systems view of fathers, mothers and infants.* New York: Basic Books.

Flouri, E. (2005). Fathering and child outcomes. New York: Wiley.

Graves, L. M., Ohlott, P. J., & Ruderman, M. N. (2007). Commitment to family roles: Effects on managers' attitudes and performance. *Journal of Applied Psychology, 92*(11), 44–56.

Hawkins, A. J., Blanchard, V. L., Baldwin, S. A., & Fawcett, E. B. (2008). Does marriage and relationship education work? A meta-analytic study. *Journal of Consulting and Clinical Psychology, 76,* 723–734.

Hawkins, A. J., Bradford, K. P., Palkovitz, R., Christiansen, S., Day, R., & Call, V. (2002). The inventory of father involvement: A pilot study of a new measure of father involvement. *The Journal of Men's Studies, 10*(2), 183–196.

Hawkins, A. J., & Fackrell, T. A. (2010). Does relationship and marriage education for lower-income couples work? A meta-analysis of emerging research. *Journal of Couple and Relationship Therapy. 9,* 181–191.

Hawkins, A. J., & Fellows, K. J. (2011). *Findings from the field: A meta-analytic study of the effectiveness of healthy marriage and relationship grantee programs.* Washington D.C.: National Healthy Marriage Resource Center. Retrieved from http://www.healthymarriageinfo.org/resource-detail/index.aspx?rid=3928

Hawkins, A. J., Lovejoy, K. R., Holmes, E. K., Blanchard, V. L., & Fawcett, E. B. (2008). Increasing fathers' involvement in childcare with a couple-focused intervention during the transition to parenthood. *Family Relations, 57.* 49–59.

Hawkins, A. J., & Ooms, T. (2010). *What works in relationship and marriage education? A review of lessons learned with a focus on low-income couples.* Oklahoma City: National Healthy Marriage Resource Center Research Report. Retrieved from http://www.healthymarriageinfo.org/docs/WhatWorks.pdf

Hawkins, A. J., Stanley, S. M., Blanchard, V. L., & Albright, M. (2012). Exploring programmatic moderators of the effectiveness of marriage and relationship education: A meta-analytic study. *Behavior Therapy, 43,* 77–87.

Halford, W. K., Petch, J., Creedy, D. K., & Gamble, J. (2011). Intimate partner violence in couples seeking relationship education for the transition to parenthood. *Journal of Couple & Relationship Therapy, 10,* 152–168.

Higginbotham, B. J., & Skogrand, L. (2010). Relationship education with both married and unmarried stepcouples: An exploratory study. *Journal of Couple & Relationship Therapy, 9,* 133–148.

Holmes, E. K., Galovan, A. M., Yoshida, K., & Hawkins, A. J. (2010). Meta-analysis of the effectiveness of resident fathering programs: Are family life educators interested in fathers? *Family Relations, 59*(3), 240–252.

Holmes, E. K., & Huston, A. C. (2010). Understanding positive father-child interaction: Children's, fathers', and mothers' contributions. *Fathering: A Journal of Research, Theory, and Practice About Men As Fathers, 8*(2), 203–225.

Johnson, M. P. (2009). *Differentiating among types of domestic violence: Implications for healthy marriages.* In E. H. Peters, & C. M. Kamp Dush, (Eds.), *Marriage and family: Perspectives and complexities* (pp. 281–297). New York: Columbia University Press.

Knoester, C., & Eggebeen, D. J. (2006). The effects of the transition to parenthood and subsequent children on men's well-being and social participation. *Journal of Family Issues, 27,* 1532–1560.

Knox, V., Cowan, P. A., Cowan, C. P., & Bildner, E. (2011). Policies that strengthen fatherhood and family relationships: What do we know and what do we need to know? *Annals of the American Academy of Political and Social Science, 635,* 216–239.

Knox, V., & Fein, D. (in press). Supporting healthy marriage: Designing a marriage education demonstration and evaluation for low-income married couples. In H. E. Peters & C. M. Kamp Dush (Eds.), *Marriage and family: Complexities and perspectives.* New York: Columbia University Press.

Knox, V., & Redcross, C. (2000). *Parenting and providing: The impact of Parents' Fair Share on paternal involvement.* New York: Manpower Research Development Corporation.

Lamb, M. E., & Tamis-LeMonda, C. S. (2004). In M. E. Lamb (Ed.). *The role of the father in child development* (4th ed., pp.). Hoboken, NJ: Wiley.

Markman, H., Stanley, S., & Blumberg, S. (2010). *Fighting for your marriage.* San Francisco: Jossey-Bass.

Marsiglio, W., Amato, P., Day, R. D., & Lamb, M. E. (2000). Scholarship on fatherhood in the 1990s and beyond. *Journal of Marriage & the Family, 62,* 1173–1191.

McBride, B. A., & Rane, T. R. (1998). Parenting alliance as a predictor of father involvement: An exploratory study. *Family Relations, 47,* 229–236.

McBride, B. A., Rane, T. R., & Bae, J. (2001). Intervening with teachers to encourage father/male involvement in early childhood programs. *Early Childhood Research Quarterly, 16,* 77–93.

McFarland, L. (2000). Involving fathers in the preschool classroom. *Texas Child Care, 24*(2), 2–7.

McHale, J. P., Kazali, C., Rotman, T., Talbot, J., Carleton, M., & Lieberson, R. (2004). The transition to coparenthood: Parents' pre-birth expectations and early coparental adjustment at 3 months postpartum. *Development and Psychopathology, 16,* 711–733.

McHale, J. P., Kuersten-Hogan, R., & Rao, N. (2004). Growing points for coparenting theory and research. *Journal of Adult Development, 11*(3), 221–234.

McLanahan, S., & Beck, A. (2010). Parental relationships in fragile families. *The Future of Children, 20*(2), 17–37.

McLanahan, S. S., & Carlson, M. (2001). Welfare reform, fertility, and father Involvement. *Children and welfare reform: The Future of Children, 12*(1), 147–166.

Mincy, R. B., & Pouncy, H. W. (2002). The responsible fatherhood field: Evolution and goals. In C. Tamis-LeMonda and N. Cabrera (Eds.), *Handbook of father involvement: Multidisciplinary perspectives* (pp. 555–597). Mahwah, NJ: Erlbaum.

Minuchin, P. (1985). Families and individual development: Provocations from the field of family therapy. *Child Development, 56,* 289–302.

Monte, L. M. (2007). Blended but not the Bradys: Navigating unmarried multiple partner fertility. In P. England and K. Edin (Eds.), *Unmarried couples with children* (pp. 183–203). New York: Russell Sage Foundation.

Nash, S. G., McQueen, A., & Bray, J. H. (2005). Pathways to adolescent alcohol use: Family environment, peer influence, and parental expectations. *Journal of Adolescent Health, 37*(1), 19–28.

National Fatherhood Initiative History. (n.d.). Retrieved from http://www.fatherhood.org/about/organization-history

Ooms, T., Boggess, J., Menard, A., Myrick, M., Roberts, P., Tweedie, J., & Wilson, P. (2006). *Building bridges between healthy marriage, responsible fatherhood, and domestic violence programs: A preliminary guide* (pp. 1–19). Washington, DC: Center for Law and Social Policy.

Orr, L. L. (1999). *Social experiments: Evaluating public programs with experimental methods.* Thousand Oaks, CA: Sage.

Palkovitz, R. (2002). *Involved fathering and men's adult development: Provisional balances.* Mahwah, NJ: Erlbaum.

Palkovitz, R., Copes, M. A., & Woolfolk, T. N. (2001). "It's like … You discover a new sense of being": Involved fathering as an evoker of adult development. *Men and Masculinities, 4,* 49–69.

Rienks, S. L., Wadsworth, M. E., Markman, H. J., Einhorn, L., & Etter, E. M. (2011). Father involvement in urban low-income fathers: Baseline associations and changes resulting from preventive intervention. *Family Relations, 60,* 191–204.

Ryan, R. R., Martin, A., & Brooks-Gunn, J. (2006). Is one good parent good enough? Patterns of mother and father parenting and child cognitive outcomes at 24 and 36 months. *Parenting: Science and Practice, 6,* 211–228.

Schoppe-Sullivan, S. J., Mangelsdorf, S. C., Brown, G. L., & Sokolowski, M. S. (2006). Goodness-of-fit in family context: Infant temperament, marital quality, and early coparenting behavior. *Infant Behavior & Development, 30,* 82–96.

Skogrand, L., Barrios-Bell, A., & Higginbotham, B. J. (2009). Stepfamily education for Latino families: Implications for practice. *Journal of Couple & Relationship Therapy, 8,* 113–128.

Stanley, S. M., Allen, E. S., Markman, H. J., Rhoades, G. K., & Prentice, D. L. (2010). Decreasing divorce in U. S. Army couples: Results from a randomized controlled trial using PREP for Strong Bonds. *Journal of Couple & Relationship Therapy, 9,* 149–160.

Tamis-LeMonda, C. S., Shannon, J. D., Cabrera, N., & Bradley, B. (2004). Mothers and fathers at play with their 2- and 3-year olds. *Child Development,* 75, 6, 1806–1820.

Twenge, J. M., Campbell, W. K., & Foster, C. A. (2003). Parenthood and marital satisfaction: A meta-analytic review. *Journal of Marriage and Family,* 65(3), 574–583.

U.S. Department of Health and Human Services. (2007). *Promoting responsible fatherhood.* Retrieved November 29, 2010, from http://fatherhood.hhs.gov/index.shtml

White, J. M., Brotherson, S. E., Galovan, A. M., Holmes, E. K., & Kampmann, J. A. (2011). The Dakota Father Friendly Assessment: Measuring father friendliness in Head Start and similar settings. *Fathering: A Journal of Research, Theory, and Practice About Men As Fathers,* 9(1), 22–43.

Wilde, J., & Doherty, W. J. (2011). Intimate partner violence between unmarried parents before and after participation in a couple education program. *Journal of Couple & Relationship Therapy, 10,* 135–151.

Wood, R. G., McConnell, S., Moore, Q., Clarkwest, A., & Hsueh, J. (2010). *The Building Strong Families project: Strengthening unmarried parents' relationships: The early impacts of Building Strong Families.* Princeton, NJ: Mathematica Policy Research, Inc.

Author Index

Subject Index

accessibility: and conceptualization of father
involvement, 61; responsibility and gender
roles, 302–3
acculturation and Asian American fathers, 271–72
adolescents: and Asian American families, 271–
72; coparenting and father involvement, 209,
211; and father-child relationships, 125–26
affect management, father-child interactions, 156
African American and African Caribbean fathers:
overview, 223–24; current research, 224–25;
future research directions, 237; male parenting
in African American families, 226–30; male
parenting in African Caribbean families,
231–35; policy implications, 236; psychological
consequences of fatherhood, 344; and related
research, 236; research measurement and
methodology, 225. *See also* cohabiting fathers
Aid to Families with Dependent Children
(AFDC) program, 420
alcohol use disorder (AUD), 173–74, 179–80, *180*
alcoholism, Michigan Longitudinal Study (MLS),
168–69, 172, 173–76
alloparenting, 45
alternative dispute resolution (ADR): about, 397,
399; benefits, 399–400; process types, 401–2
altricial young, 4
American Academy of Matrimonial Lawyers
(AAML), 399
antisocial alcoholic (AAL) fathers, 174–76
arbitration and family dispute resolution, 401
arginine vasopresin (AVP), 7, 12
Asian American fathers: overview, 261–62;
and child development in Asian American
families, 272; and child development in Asian

families, 268–69; and contemporary Asian
American families, 269; and contemporary
Asian families, 265–66; current research, 262;
future research directions, 273; and paternal
childrearing styles in Asian American families,
269–72; and paternal childrearing styles in
Asian families, 266–68; policy implications,
273; and related research, 273; research
measurement and methodology, 262–65
assessments and custody evaluations, 386–89
attachment theory: and African American fathers,
227; and child custody, 381; and father-child
relationships, 120–22, 154–55
attention regulation, father-child interactions,
157
autobiographical memory, 179–80
availability, father involvement and family
contexts, 188–89
avpr1a gene, 7

baboons, 4
"baby mothers" and "baby fathers", African
Caribbean families, 231
Bayley Scales of Infant Development (BSID-II),
138, 140
Becker's theories of fatherhood, 362–66, *364*
bed nucleus of stria terminatus (BNST), 8, 14
behavioral data collection, non-human primate
fathering, 42–43
Bergstrom-Cornes theorem, economics of
fatherhood, 367–69, *368*
Best Interest of the Child (BIS) standard, 380–81
biological-evolutionary motivations for father
involvement, 60, 77